TAKING ON
THE WORLD

JOSEPH AND STEWART ALSOP—
Guardians of the American Century

TAKING ON

JOSEPH AND
GUARDIANS OF THE

ROBERT W. MERRY

THE WORLD

STEWART ALSOP—
AMERICAN CENTURY

VIKING

VIKING
Published by the Penguin Group
Penguin Books USA Inc., 375 Hudson Street,
New York, New York 10014, U.S.A.
Penguin Books Ltd, 27 Wrights Lane,
London W8 5TZ, England
Penguin Books Australia Ltd, Ringwood,
Victoria, Australia
Penguin Books Canada Ltd, 10 Alcorn Avenue,
Toronto, Ontario, Canada M4V 3B2
Penguin Books (N.Z.) Ltd, 182–190 Wairau Road,
Auckland 10, New Zealand

Penguin Books Ltd, Registered Offices:
Harmondsworth, Middlesex, England

First published in 1996 by Viking Penguin,
a division of Penguin Books USA Inc.

10 9 8 7 6 5 4 3 2 1

LIBRARY OF CONGRESS CATALOGING IN PUBLICATION DATA
Merry, Robert W.
   Taking on the world : Joseph and Stewart Alsop—guardians of the American
century / by Robert W. Merry.
      p.   cm.
   Includes index.
   ISBN 0-670-83868-3
   1. Alsop, Joseph, 1910–. 2. Alsop, Stewart. 3. Journalists—United States—
Biography.   4. Press and Politics—United States—History—20th century.
5. n-us. I. Title.
PN4874.A43M47   1996
070'.92273—dc20   95-9445

This book is printed on acid-free paper.

Printed in the United States of America
Set in Sabon

To
the Memory of
CAROL B. MERRY
Nurturer, Mentor, Exemplar

ACKNOWLEDGMENTS

A SINGLE NAME normally graces the title page of a book such as this, but a single name is not enough. This is the product of a multitude of avid supporters and gifted critics without whose ministrations it would not now be in your hands.

The list must begin with Al Silverman, senior vice president and editor at large at Viking Penguin, whose investment of toil and sweat reached awesome proportions. If there is a more deft editor—and handler of authors—anywhere on the planet, such a person would be difficult to imagine.

Robert E. Merry, my father, devoted untold hours and his considerable command of the language to the manuscript, at every phase of its development. That vast contribution was in addition to a lifetime of instruction on the grand themes and fine points of history, which provided an underpinning for whatever coherence can be found in this volume.

My agent, Gerard McCauley, in addition to securing the contract for this work and extending encouragement at every crucial juncture, also read the manuscript and provided insights. His friendship helped fuel the project.

Though the faults imbedded in the book are mine, certain merits can be attributed to a group of literate and learned friends who read the manuscript in whole or in part and offered counsel on words and facts: Michael Barone, who provided helpful suggestions on the early chapters; Frank Mankiewicz, whose command of historical detail never ceases to amaze me; Thomas Malone, whose pungent observations proved invaluable; David Shribman, whose quality counsel is reflected in his own elegant prose; and Richard Whalen, whose ability to home in on gaps in the narrative proved a great service to author and reader. Though Dick Whalen didn't know it, he served a dual function: his own biography of Joseph P. Kennedy was one of the models for this effort.

From the beginning I was struck by the generosity of time and encouragement I encountered from members of the Alsop family. Patricia Alsop sat for numerous interviews, received in good spirit innumerable phone calls, provided valuable family papers and bound volumes of the Alsop columns, and turned over heirloom photos, including some still in frames. Her generosity and candor are a gift to history.

Likewise, Susan Mary Alsop offered time in abundance, family photo albums, cherished books, and a willingness to discuss matters that were both private and delicate. Tea time on Twenty-ninth Street is always a highly enjoyable experience. John Alsop readily opened up his home and his memory for long discussions of times past, while his wife, Gussie, added uncommon hospitality. John was a little more hesitant about sharing Joe Alsop's wartime diaries, but eventually relented on that request as well.

And Elizabeth Winthrop, daughter of Stewart and Tish Alsop, brought to our discussions a manifest desire to capture the family in all its particulars, including some that normally are kept behind the curtain of privacy.

Others who consented to multiple interviews were Joseph Wright Alsop VI, Tom Braden, Evangeline Bruce, Mel Elfin, Rowland Evans, Katharine Graham, Dorothy Kidder, Arthur Schlesinger, Jr., and Warren Zimmermann.

I should like to acknowledge those who helped with the research, beginning with Ross Kerber, who delved into the Stewart Alsop Collection at Boston University's Mugar Library with aggressiveness and a level of historical judgment that extended beyond his years. Heather Iarusso and Shannon Henry provided invaluable assistance at the Library of Congress's Documents Room. Dr. Howard Gotlieb and Charles Niles of the Mugar Library gave encouragement and assistance. And I want particularly to thank the team at the Congressional Quarterly Library— Kathleen Walton, Myra Weinberg, and Michael Williams—for unfailingly prompt and friendly assistance in locating important books and articles.

Bonnie Forrest, my assistant, and her predecessor, Jeanne Kislitzin, rendered invaluable service on this project, as on all things they touch.

Then there is the realm of those whose encouragement made the book possible, beginning with those I work for: Andrew Barnes, chairman of Times Publishing Company of St. Petersburg, Florida, who buoyed my efforts with streams of questions about the project and expressions of support; Andrew Corty, vice chairman of Congressional

Quarterly Inc., who lent abundant moral sustenance; and, particularly, Neil Skene, my boss, friend, and mentor, who cheered me on from beginning to end and slipped me increments of time when the pressures built up to ominous levels.

My most deeply felt expressions of gratitude go to Susan Pennington Merry, my wife and pal, who, besides bucking me up with loving understanding at times of frustration and weariness, picked up more household slack than I care to quantify. My thanks also to Rob, Johanna, and Stephanie, whose sacrifices on the altar of this work were offered with unconditional appreciation and love.

Finally, a prayer of peaceful respite for my mother, Carol B. Merry, who, before her death in 1993, spent several months toiling away in the Documents Room of the Library of Congress, gathering material from the vast Alsop Papers. I shall forever cherish the memory of her expression of wonderment as I would drive up to the Madison Building on Independence Avenue to pick her up in the afternoon and she would climb into the car and exclaim: "You simply won't believe what Joe did today!"

McLean, Virginia
May 15, 1995

CONTENTS

INTRODUCTION

JOSEPH AND STEWART ALSOP:

The Pinnacle of the Reporter's Trade

MARCH 15, 1961, dawned with promise in Washington—clear skies, temperatures in the sixties. And a gala dinner-dance that night at 1600 Pennsylvania Avenue would add a special luster for seventy guests of Jack and Jackie Kennedy.

John F. Kennedy had been in the White House less than two months, but already the feeling was taking hold that his presidency would repre sent a kind of American renaissance—a time when style and elegance would reign at the White House and throughout the upper reaches of of- ficial and social Washington. The young president and his beautiful wife were giving Americans a sense that the nation was moving into an era of splendor.

The White House party on this balmy early-spring evening was orig- inally meant to be an intimate gathering to honor Jacqueline Kennedy's sister, Lee Radziwill, and her husband, Prince Stanislas Radziwill, a Polish exile. But the plan had been changed, and the guest list had expanded.

The party would not be an official White House function. There would be no toasts or speeches and no receiving line. This was to be a party for people who were considered friends of the First Family. The guests would enter the mansion via the South Entrance, the family en- trance, and not the North Portico traditionally used for formal White House events. Dinner—French, of course—would be served in the State

Dining Room and would start with saumon mousseline normande, to be followed by poulet à l'estragon, grilled tomatoes, mushrooms aux fines herbes, and casserole Marie-Blanche. The wines: a Pouilly Fuissé 1959, Château Haut-Brion 1955, Bollinger champagne 1953. After dinner there would be dancing in the Blue Room to the music of the trendy New York orchestra of Lester Lanin, the same orchestra that had performed at Jackie's debut into New York society and at the Kennedys' Newport wedding eight years before.

This party was intended as a celebration of youth, of the men and women of the wartime generation who now, in their forties, were taking over the country, ready to confront a turbulent world.

AROUND SEVEN THIRTY in the evening, on Springland Lane in Washington's fashionable Cleveland Park neighborhood, Stewart Alsop, in black tie, descended the stairs of his palatial home and went into his den to pour himself a bourbon, to be savored as his young wife, Patricia, finished dressing upstairs. This was a frequent ritual at the Stewart Alsop residence. Stewart nearly always was dressed for evening social events well before Tish, and he would fix himself a drink and chat with his children as he waited. The older boys, Joe and Ian, were away at Groton School in Massachusetts. But Elizabeth, twelve, known in the family as Fuff, was there; she attended Sacred Heart School and was showing signs of serious writing talent. Little Stewart, nine, attended St. Albans Episcopal School. And Nicky, not yet two, loved to climb aboard his father's lap for the tickling game that often accompanied these late-afternoon interludes. The children savored these moments; they were among the few times when they could break into their father's hectic business and social schedule.

It was close to eight o'clock when Stewart and Tish climbed into his red Saab and began the short drive down Connecticut Avenue to the White House.

"You know," said Stewart, "it's hard to believe it's been sixteen years since we were last at the White House for a social event."

They reminisced about that long-ago time, in the spring of 1945, when they had been asked to have lunch with Franklin and Eleanor Roosevelt—Cousin Franklin and Cousin Eleanor, as the Alsops called them—in the First Family's private quarters. It had been only about three weeks before Roosevelt's death. He had seemed almost totally deaf and looked like an actor trying, without much success, to play the part of Franklin Roosevelt.

AROUND THE SAME TIME, on Georgetown's Dumbarton Avenue, Joseph Alsop, in his tuxedo, emerged from his house and walked briskly down the hill to M Street to hail a cab. He was not imposing physically. He had a large nose; his hair was thinning; but his appearance gave the impression of a man of mark. There was a certain cockiness in his demeanor, as if he were quite aware that he was of a special breed. Getting into the car, he quickly took command. Speaking in a kind of ersatz British accent, he addressed the cabbie as "my good man" and issued precise instructions on what route he wished to follow to the White House.

IT WAS NOT surprising that the brothers Alsop, Joseph and Stewart, would be among the presidential guests on this evening. They were reporters, and Kennedy liked reporters. But they were no ordinary members of the Washington press corps. The Alsops, in fact, were among the capital's most prominent and influential journalists—and often its most controversial. They enjoyed easy access at the highest echelons of government; their prose reached millions of readers throughout the country; and they had attained a level of fame that was equaled by hardly anyone else in the news business.

Joe, at fifty the older of the two, was a syndicated columnist whose work appeared in nearly two hundred newspapers and reached 25 million readers throughout the United States and in foreign lands. He had come to Washington in 1935 as a twenty-five-year-old reporter, and within three years had managed to become a celebrated political pundit. Thus for some twenty-three years (with time out for World War II) he had been edifying and terrorizing official Washington with his in-depth reporting and rapier analysis. He was an odd mixture—an aristocrat with aristocratic tastes and an aristocratic bearing, but also a shoe-leather reporter who scampered through Washington's warrens of power and traversed the world in search of information. This was no Olympian sage who sat in an ivory tower spinning out opinions after reading the newspapers; his stock in trade was the face-to-face interview.

Stewart, forty-six, was contributing editor for national affairs at the *Saturday Evening Post*, a leading general-interest magazine with a weekly circulation of six million and a readership of twenty million. Known for lucid prose and dispassionate analysis, Stewart wrote for the *Post* long, expository pieces designed to lay bare the inner workings of government and the intricacies of major issues facing the country and the world. He spent plenty of time interviewing Washington's high and mighty, but he also was known for his ability to find that obscure expert in some partitioned corner of the bureaucracy who could help him elucidate a complex matter of public policy.

But it wasn't just the brothers' professional standing that had got them invited to this dinner-dance. They also were known for their talents and class, their glittering friends, their ability to amuse. They mingled comfortably with the elite of the capital—with senators, Supreme Court justices, ambassadors, the decision-makers of the country.

When John Kennedy was a senator, Stewart had interviewed him innumerable times, and had encountered the senator and Jackie at social events through the years. He had traveled with them during their arduous political journeys through the presidential primaries the previous winter. And in his prose he had portrayed Kennedy as a clever, charming, even erudite politician with an instinct for the main chance. Yet he did not consider himself truly a friend of the president. He viewed himself as more of a "friendly acquaintance."

Joe, on the other hand, was a close friend of Jack Kennedy, and an even closer friend of Jackie. Both Kennedys enjoyed his biting wit and passion for political gossip, along with the fascinating people he always managed to collect around his big table on Dumbarton Avenue. Jackie loved talking with the highly cultivated Joe Alsop about art and antique furniture, and she appreciated his advice on how to handle the complexities and burdens of the political life. During the campaign, Joe and Jackie had become closer than ever, calling each other frequently and exchanging affectionate letters. When Lee and Stas Radziwill had been in town the previous spring, Joe had organized an intimate champagne lunch for them and Jackie; the future First Lady later described the event as "voluptuous."

Immediately after the Kennedys moved into the White House, they had invited Joe, along with Franklin Roosevelt, Jr., and his wife, to an intimate little Sunday night dinner for five, the first social occasion of the Kennedy presidency. They ate caviar and drank champagne and then toured the family quarters, still in disarray as the Kennedys continued the process of moving in. In the presidential bedroom, Kennedy motioned to a large highboy that the Eisenhowers had pushed up against a door.

"That must be the door to Mamie's room," he said with a wry smile.

During that evening Joe was appalled to hear Franklin Roosevelt address Kennedy as "Jack" instead of "Mr. President." At one point Joe told him to stop; he considered that to be one of the worst gaffes that could be committed in the American democracy. In fact, the day after Kennedy's election Joe had written the senator a "Dear Mr. President" letter, saying he wanted to be the first to address his friend thus. "I do feel," wrote Joe, "that I've lost a friend while gaining a President."

STEWART AND TISH drove through the southwest gate at the White House shortly before eight, arriving around the same time as the Arthur Schlesingers and the Rowland Evanses. Schlesinger was the well-known Harvard professor and Franklin Roosevelt biographer who now was a White House adviser. Evans was a leading Washington reporter for the

New York *Herald Tribune*. Both couples were close friends of the Stewart Alsops, and the six early arrivals chatted amiably as they ascended the winding stairs to the main floor. In the entrance hall they received their place cards, then entered the East Room for cocktails and hors d'oeuvres. The cocktails were mixed very strong, the hors d'oeuvres redolent of caviar.

Near the large windows overlooking the South Lawn stood Jackie and Lee, along with Letitia Baldrige, Jackie's social secretary. The First Lady wore a "dramatic white sheath," as *The Washington Post* would describe it later. The *Evening Star* would call it "divine." The guests mingled among themselves, some making their way to chat briefly with Jackie, others holding back for fear of appearing intrusive.

Then Joe arrived. Never one to hold back, he moved quickly through the crowd to Jackie and Lee, to engage them in animated conversation. Joe loved to be in the company of beautiful and captivating women, and these two were among the most beautiful and captivating he knew— Jackie, wife of the leader of the most powerful nation in the world; and Lee, an international jet-setter who could be seen frequently in the pages of *Vogue* magazine modeling the Givenchy clothes for which she was well known.

Everyone stopped talking briefly when the president entered the room. He was tanned from a recent trip to Palm Beach, Florida, but looked a bit fleshy under the eyes and chin. He seemed in high spirits as he moved through the crowd, displaying the famous Kennedy smile as he shook hands and greeted guests.

As the Alsops mingled in the East Room, Stewart was struck by the beauty and style of the women in their long dresses and white gloves. And he noted that the guests included few members of Congress. Those invited were of the "dining-out" variety who frequented Washington's higher social circuit—senators John Sherman Cooper of Kentucky, Stuart Symington of Missouri, George Smathers of Florida. All these also were frequent or occasional guests of the Alsops. And there was Ben Smith of Massachusetts, known around Washington as "Kennedy's private senator." Besides Attorney General Robert Kennedy, only three administration officials were in attendance—Treasury Secretary Douglas Dillon, Vice President Lyndon Johnson, and White House press secretary Pierre Salinger.

But there was a surprisingly large contingent of newsmen. This was a new development in recent memory; neither Harry Truman nor Dwight Eisenhower had wanted to spend any more time with reporters than was required by the job. But Kennedy had what Stewart called "an eccentric but laudable taste" for the breed. So mingling with the guests on this evening, besides Evans and the Alsops, were columnist Charles Bartlett, an old Kennedy friend; Benjamin Bradlee, the dashing Washington bureau chief for *Newsweek*; Philip Geyelin, diplomatic correspondent for *The Wall Street Journal*; and Edward P. Morgan of CBS. But there was no one from *Time* magazine or *The New York Times*— Kennedy didn't like those publications.

Many Kennedy relatives were there—Jackie's mother, Mrs. Hugh D. Auchincloss; Michel Bouvier, her cousin; Kennedy's sister Jean Smith. And the guest list included a number of social lions, such as Clark Clifford, influential Washington lawyer and former aide to President Truman; Major General Anthony Biddle; His Highness Prince Sadruddin Aga Khan. Franklin Roosevelt, Jr., was there, "somewhat weaseled and acting as though Daddy still owned the place," as Stewart later described him.

Nearly everyone in the East Room that night brought to the cocktail hour a strong reputation as a leading player in Washington's councils of power or its social salons. They were men and women of attainment and style. Most had interesting histories. Some had pedigrees as descendants of the country's lingering aristocracy, the so-called Eastern establishment.

The personas of the Alsop brothers included all those attributes; among discerning Americans they were known not only as influential newsmen but as men of weight with noteworthy backgrounds. They were blue-blood Americans who were born into the country's Anglo-Saxon elite and who pronounced their name with a high-toned inflection: All-*sup*. The brothers' father had been a prominent dairy farmer and insurance executive in Connecticut, a civic leader and personification of the American gentry. Forebears on their father's side had included some of the richest men in America. Their maternal grandmother had been the sister of Theodore Roosevelt, and their mother had been Eleanor Roosevelt's first cousin. So it wasn't surprising that during the Franklin Roosevelt presidency they had visited the White House frequently for social and family gatherings.

Those who took note of such things knew the Alsops had attended Groton School in Massachusetts, the academic foundry where the nation's elite sent its sons to be molded into men of leadership and service in the tradition of the British aristocracy. Joe had gone on to Harvard, where he had been a member of the famous Porcellian Club and had met many of the people he later would socialize with and write about. Stewart had gone to Yale, the family university, which his father and grandfather had attended before him.

The brothers had served with distinction during World War II. Joe, a leading advocate of America's entry into the war, had relinquished a lucrative and high-profile job as Washington columnist to enlist in the navy even before Pearl Harbor. He later made his way to China and joined General Claire Chennault's American Volunteer Group, the famous "Flying Tigers," to help China's Nationalist leader Chiang Kai-shek fight the invading Japanese. He was captured by the Japanese in

Hong Kong after Pearl Harbor, and spent seven months in an enemy internment camp before being placed on a prisoner-exchange list and repatriated. He quickly returned to China to serve Chennault's cause against the Japanese, and also against the general's U.S. adversaries, who disputed his vision of the uses and values of air power.

Stewart was viewed in Washington as something of a war hero. He had joined the British infantry after his own country had rejected him on medical grounds. As a lieutenant, he led a platoon in North Africa and fought in the Italian campaign before transferring to the U.S. Army and becoming an OSS intelligence operative. He parachuted behind enemy lines in France shortly after D-Day to help the French resistance against the Germans. Between missions he fell in love with a beautiful British teenager named Patricia Hankey, daughter of a landed family. She was serving in British intelligence during the war, and met Stewart at a raucous house party at the mansion of Britain's premier baron, the Baron Mowbray and Stourton. She was only eighteen when they were married in London, with buzz bombs screaming overhead; Stewart was then thirty.

Joe, whose life had been one of bachelorhood until just the month before the Kennedys' dinner, harbored a dark personal secret. He was homosexual. Privately, some of his friends speculated about his sexuality, but no one ever asked him about it, and he discussed it with only his very closest friends or with those who knew because of their own connection with the homosexual community. One person he told was Susan Mary Patten, the beautiful widow of one of his closest friends from his Harvard days, Bill Patten. Joe had proposed to Susan Mary a few months after Bill's death, and in February they were married.

Her maiden name was Jay, and she was descended directly from John Jay, first chief justice of the United States, an author of the Federalist Papers, and negotiator of the Jay Treaty ending the Revolutionary War. For fifteen years after World War II, while her husband served the foreign service in France, Susan Mary had been a leading socialite in the diplomatic world of Paris. She was not at the party this evening; she had returned to Paris after the wedding to make preparations for her move to Washington and to be with her children until they finished the school year.

IT WAS AFTER NINE when White House servants signaled that guests were to make their way to the State Dining Room for dinner. There they encountered nine round tables for eight, decorated with gold candelabra and muted pastel flowers. Once the guests were seated, Lanin's strolling musicians weaved in and out among the tables playing soft tunes.

Tish Alsop found herself seated at a table that included Vice President Johnson, the irrepressible Texan and former Senate majority leader who had wanted the Democratic nomination himself—"so bad he can taste it," as Stewart once had observed. He now seemed a bit out of sorts, perhaps envious that all this glitter belonged to the Kennedys and not the Johnsons. Stewart too, in talking with the vice president before dinner, had noticed that he looked "a bit sad."

The president managed, as always, to surround himself with beautiful women at dinner. Seated on either side of him were the lovely "Pinchot sisters," Tony Bradlee and Mary Meyer. Tony was the wife of Ben Bradlee. Mary, a divorcée in her forties, frequently attended White House functions in the company of her sister and brother-in-law. Later she was to become one of the president's lovers, a frequent clandestine visitor to the White House when Jackie was away. Also at the president's table was a divorcée named Helen Chavchavadze, once married to a Russian prince and now one of Washington's most eligible single women.

Rowland Evans, also seated at the president's table, leaned over to Helen and said the evening had the makings of being the best Washington party since Jordan's King Hussein had pursued her at the famous dance at Joe Alsop's. Everyone at the table laughed at the memory of that exciting evening of a couple years before.

Joe had become friendly with Hussein during one of his frequent reporting trips through the Middle East, and in the late 1950s, when the king came to Washington for a state visit, Joe had decided to show him off. So he had called a few friends at the last minute and told them to dress in black tie and arrive at his Dumbarton Avenue house at nine o'clock on the appointed evening. He and the king would arrive shortly thereafter, he said, following an official dinner on the king's—and Joe's—schedule. He instructed the women to remember to curtsy before the royal personage.

The guests mingled at Joe's and made themselves at home in preparation for the king's arrival. But no king, no Joe—they couldn't break away from the scheduled dinner as early as they had planned. Finally, an hour late, they arrived, and everyone began dancing. The king took one look at Helen Chavchavadze and was smitten. He wanted to dance with her all night. Helen was at least a foot taller than the man known behind his back (but affectionately) as "the little king," but she promptly kicked off her shoes and flicked them under a sofa to lessen the disparity. Everyone was having a wonderful time.

Then a problem developed. Joe had instructed his guests that protocol required them to remain until after the king's departure. But the king wouldn't depart. He was having too much fun dancing with Helen. Finally Archibald Roosevelt, son of the first President Roosevelt and an Alsop cousin, decided that protocol was robbing him of his sleep. He slipped out, and soon others took heart in his boldness and slipped out too. It had been a typically memorable evening at Joe Alsop's, the kind guaranteed to draw comment and laughter for years to come.

After dinner at the White House, the guests were escorted toward the Blue Room, where the carpets had been taken up and dancing was to commence. Joe, smoking a large cigar and swirling a brandy snifter in his palm, circulated among the guests, making his way once again to Jackie and Lee. Stewart, on his way through the Red Room, saw John Kennedy holding forth in front of the fireplace and wandered over, joining Franklin Roosevelt, Jr., Rowly Evans, and Charles Bartlett in a semicircle around the president.

The conversation turned to the Wisconsin primary of the previous year. Kennedy called it the low point of his life. He had won the primary, but not by enough votes to draw the support of party bosses, who wanted a winner. The narrowness of his victory had forced him to compete later in West Virginia, where he had blown away Hubert Humphrey and secured his party's nomination. Now he recalled the standoffishness of the stolid Germans of Wisconsin, the endless handshaking, the constant efforts to draw some warmth from Wisconsinites.

"You couldn't get a smile out of lots of those people," said the president. But West Virginia was different. "You could tell they were interested in you."

Then the president turned to Stewart.

"What kind of bird," he asked, "is this fellow Dayal?"

The question was a high compliment. Stewart had recently written a three-part series on Africa for the *Saturday Evening Post*, based on a seven-week tour of seven countries in the continent. In the Congo he had encountered Rajeswar Dayal, an Indian intellectual who headed the UN command in that war torn country. Kennedy's question indicated he had read Stewart's pieces. Stewart hadn't liked Dayal, and he couldn't resist the opportunity to diminish him in the eyes of the Free World leader.

"Dayal," said Stewart, "is aloof, conceited, brazen, dismissive of the Congolese and hence hated by them."

Stewart was a plain-spoken man who looked at the world with the cold eye of a realist. He spoke with deliberation, but often in vivid metaphors and with literary references. He could be eloquent as well as witty, and people listened when he spoke. But he felt no need to thrust himself into conversations or demonstrate his knowledge or wit. He let the conversation come to him, and because people wanted to hear what he had to say, it almost always did. At six feet, Stewart was imposing, clearly a man to be taken seriously. But he was never intimidating. People gravitated to him, and nearly everyone who knew him liked him.

Not everyone felt the same about Joe. He was always entertaining and full of fun, and he was generous with his friends—but he could be outrageous, caustic, and insulting. Invariably he spoke with the air of a man who never had the slightest doubt about anything he said or thought; his likes and dislikes were tossed out unabashedly for all to see.

Joe stood at five feet, nine inches, and his hair was receding markedly from his forehead. He never considered himself particularly good-looking. But he dressed impeccably in Savile Row suits, had his shoes tailor-made by a London bootery, and walked with a bit of a strut. With his British inflection and mannerisms, he seemed to be something of an eccentric, and he played the role to the hilt, addressing women friends as "dahling" and men as "my dear boy." And he had a knack for the devastating putdown. Once, angry about *New York Times* coverage of a subject dear to his heart, he struggled for just the right phrase to wrap his contempt around the paper's reputation as an august institution. "It's a . . . it's a lunatic cathedral over there," he said. To Joe the greatest compliment was to be considered amusing, the greatest insult to be thought boring. He was nearly always amusing, never boring.

As Kennedy conversed with his guests in the Red Room, the butler came up to whisper that Jackie wanted everyone to join the dancing in the Blue Room. They wandered in to see people gyrating in a new dance called the twist. Joe, who didn't dance, found himself sidelined, but there was plenty of opportunity for conversation. People were milling about, talking, resting on the many sofas and chairs placed strategically in the Red Room and along the west side of the Blue Room.

Stewart walked up to see a comical scene involving Lyndon Johnson and Bobby Kennedy. Johnson, wanting to conduct a little business at the party, had urged Kennedy to accept Johnson's recommendation for a particular judgeship. The president's brother wouldn't commit himself, and the vice president was applying what was known as the "Johnson treatment"—he would close in on his prey with his full bulk, place his big face inches away from his victim, grab him by the lapel, rub his knee, place a lanky arm around his shoulder, all the while unfurling an endless string of cajolery. Nobody had been known to resist the famous Johnson tactic. Most people would accede to his wishes just to get him out of their face. But Bobby just sat there with a wolfish grin as guests moved in to witness the spectacle. Occasionally he would toss out a cutting wisecrack and peer around to smile at the onlookers. Finally, it occurred to Johnson that he was making a fool of himself, and he retreated with the new wisdom that his "treatment" didn't work now that he was a mere vice president, with nothing to barter.

Later, while dancing, Johnson slipped and fell to the floor, and the curious gathered around. The angry Texan blamed his dance partner for tripping him. It was not a good night for the vice president.

The party was thinning out, but still proceeding, at two a.m. when Stewart and Tish went by to thank the president for the evening.

"Good night, Mr. President," said Stewart.

Kennedy held him for a moment.

"What did you find out on this lecture tour?" he asked.

"Well, for one thing, you've really plucked some sort of nerve with this Peace Corps thing. Everybody was asking about it."

"What did you tell them?"

"I told them I was a rancid old reactionary and didn't believe in it."

"Neither do I. Good night."

Both men laughed loudly as Stewart and Tish turned to leave. Stewart was still smiling at the president's candor when he and Tish stepped into the refreshing night air. Behind them Joe Alsop continued in revelry. He always was the last to leave any party.

TAKING ON
THE WORLD

JOSEPH AND STEWART ALSOP—

Guardians of the American Century

Part One

FAMILY AND FAMILY HERITAGE

NEW WORLD ROOTS

The Alsops, the Robinsons, and the Roosevelts

TURN-OF-THE-CENTURY America bustled with promise and expectation. The last years of the old century had given the country a pair of stunning naval victories in nearby Cuba and far Asia that had transfigured America into a global power. And now the new century brought marvels of Western technology, many created and developed on American soil, that were reshaping the nation and the lives of her people. Motorcars, paved roads, electricity, telephones, radio, aeroplanes—all were contributing to a sense of impending national greatness. Soon the country would take up its role in a momentous European war, sending its sons into battle under the banner of democracy. The United States was coming of age and meeting its destiny. The country was young, like the century, and full of sap.

But in the white farmhouse off Route 44 in Avon, Connecticut, where Joseph and Corinne Alsop had established themselves among the American gentry, one thing seemed unchangeable. The country's self-definition, its folkways and legends, its outlook and values, its national stewardship, all seemed firmly in the hands of its historic elite, the Anglo-Saxon establishment centered in the populous Northeast. This elite cast its influence across what was still predominantly an Anglo-Saxon land. It dominated the nation's financial centers and corporate boardrooms, its prestigious academic institutions and major newspapers and magazines, its big law firms and foreign-policy apparatus. This leadership class had always served as custodian of the nation's affairs, and the nation in turn looked to it instinctively for governance.

It was into this established American world, in the little front bedroom of the family farmhouse at Avon, that Joseph Wright Alsop V, eldest of four children, and Stewart Johonnet Oliver Alsop were born to Joseph and Corinne—Joe ten years into the new century, Stewart four years later in the fateful year of 1914.

The children grew up amid relics that bespoke their own connection to the establishment—portraits of forebears rendered in oils; pre-Revolutionary objects of silver with the Alsop family crest; framed letters from presidents; a silver sauce boat crafted and signed by Paul Revere. Accompanied by the rich family lore that seasoned conversation at clan gatherings, these heirlooms provided a strong sense of family heritage—and of the heritage of Anglo-Saxon America.

The family traced its roots mainly through the genealogy of three American families—the Alsops, Robinsons, and Roosevelts—stretching back at least 250 years in the New World. The Alsops had arrived from England, the Robinsons from Scotland, the Roosevelts from the Netherlands. They all had merged into what became the New World's Anglo-Saxon ascendancy.

The English were America's substantial majority in colonial times and later, and most other northern European strains blended readily into this majority. The seventeenth century non-English Roosevelts, for example, and other continental immigrants of the time, could scarcely have retained their particular identities for long, since the families with which they were destined to merge tended to be English. And larger non-English but English-speaking elements, the Welsh, Scottish, and Scotch-Irish, had no trouble regarding themselves as part of the prevailing culture. Edgar Allan Poe, who possessed Scottish and Scotch-Irish ancestors, as well as English, felt that "the self-same Saxon current animates the British and the American heart." And across the sea the feeling was mutual. "I refuse to speak or think of the United States as a foreign nation," declared Joseph Chamberlain, the prominent British politician, around the turn of the century. "They are our flesh and blood. . . . Our past is theirs. Their future is ours. . . . Their forefathers sleep in our churchyards."

Such were the currents of sentiment that animated the Alsops, Robinsons, and Roosevelts through most of their New World experience.

Although the Alsops' fortunes waxed and waned through the eighteenth and nineteenth centuries, certain family characteristics remained distinct. There was a strong strain of Anglophilia in the Alsop clan, and a consistent devotion to the politics of moderate conservatism. Displaying a powerful sense of civic pride, they made time to sit on community boards, to help found hospitals and schools, to serve in the Connecticut legislature at Hartford. They favored a life that resembled that of an English country squire, and devoted their leisure to hunting and fishing. Through much of their history, they demonstrated a talent for making money, if not always for keeping it, and for becoming "connected" through friendship and marriage to the prominent families of the day.

The Roosevelts and Robinsons shared many of these traits, and added some of their own. Through wise real estate investments and land development, the stolid Robinson clan became one of New York's wealthiest families. And at the start of the twentieth century, the Oyster Bay Roosevelts, having just sent one of their sons to the White House, had gained national fame to match the family's old wealth. The Roosevelts added a dash of upper-crust eccentricity to the bloodlines that extended down to the Alsop boys of Avon. Among the menfolk could be seen a weakness for alcohol that reached self-destructive proportions for some, while the women were known for their strength of character and force of personality.

The Alsops' New World bloodlines began with Richard Alsop, born in England in 1660. Later Alsops, noting England's Allsopp ale and the similarity between their name and the term "ale shop," speculated that he came from a family of English brewers. Whatever his origins, Richard Alsop settled on Long Island, made a bit of money, married the daughter of a sea captain, and fathered three sons and five daughters.

Two generations later, two of Richard Alsop's grandsons emerged as wealthy entrepreneurs in the burgeoning shipping trade that fueled prosperity in colonial America. One of them, Richard, born in 1726, moved to the bustling Connecticut River port of Middletown and established a successful business based on a shrewd insight. The people of the West Indies, he reckoned, would pay handsomely for ice. The ice could be obtained free in New England rivers and lakes, and insulated during the sea journey with sawdust, also obtained free at nearby sawmills. On return voyages, he could transport rum and sugarcane. The business thrived, and soon Richard was a civic pillar of Connecticut and a representative in the colonial legislature.

Richard's brother, John, emerged as an equally successful shipping magnate in New York. He served as president of the New York Chamber of Commerce and vestryman of New York's Trinity Church, where his wife and daughter were buried. He represented New York at the 1774 Continental Congress in Philadelphia. John Adams of Massachusetts found him to be "a soft, sweet man." But when John Alsop read the Declaration of Independence, drafted at the Continental Congress of 1776, his softness and sweetness left him. As a passionate Anglophile, he refused to sign Thomas Jefferson's treasonous document, and thus became in family lore "John the Non-Signer."

Despite his pro-British sentiments, John Alsop enjoyed renewed business and social success after the war. He was invited to George Washington's first inaugural ball, where his young daughter, Mary, met President

Washington's friend Rufus King, a wealthy Harvard-educated lawyer and future minister to Great Britain. They fell in love and were married within the year.

Meanwhile, Richard Alsop's Middletown shipping business had expanded under the leadership of his son, the first of seven Joseph Wright Alsops extending down to the present. He expanded the shipping trade to South America and China and left a thriving business to his son, Joseph Wright Alsop II, born in 1804.

Possessing what an obituary writer in 1878 would call "a remarkable aptitude for business," the second Joseph expanded the family enterprise into private banking and corporate finance. Moving to New York City, he built a mansion on Washington Square and founded Alsop & Company, which financed such projects as a shipping line to Panama, the Illinois Central Railroad, and the Ohio and Mississippi Railroad. He became a nationally prominent horse breeder, fostered charities, sat on corporate boards, served in the Connecticut legislature. During the Civil War, he was an antiwar "Copperhead" and struck up a close friendship with General George McClellan, the failed military leader who ran for president against Abraham Lincoln in 1864. Alsop was godfather to McClellan's son, and the general was godfather to Alsop's grandson, Joseph Wright Alsop IV.

When not in New York, Joseph II often could be found at his Georgian mansion on Middletown's fashionable High Street, a house famous for its wall and ceiling frescoes patterned after images in the Vatican. He was emerging as the founder of an American family dynasty of the first order. But after his retirement, Alsop & Company managers sought to expand the business through speculation. Caught in the Panic of 1873, they were forced to liquidate the company, and much of Joseph's personal fortune was sucked into this financial vortex. He died a few years later.

There was enough accumulated wealth for the third Joseph Wright Alsop to pursue a life as country gentleman. Born in 1838, he studied at Yale and Columbia College and received medical training at the University of New York. Though addressed throughout his life as Dr. Alsop, he never practiced medicine. Instead, he established a family estate called "Arawana" outside Middletown, and devoted his life to politics and good works. He became Middletown's mayor and served in the state assembly and senate. He traveled widely and devoted considerable time to his twin passions of hunting and fishing. Every fall he organized a hunting excursion at an inn in nearby East Hampton that featured days devoted to shooting partridge, quail, and rabbit, and evenings devoted to abundant quantities of hard cider.

Alsop entrusted the financial management of the family assets to a cousin, who disappeared with most of them. Joseph was forced to sell Arawana and move in with his mother on High Street. In 1890 he was elected Connecticut's lieutenant governor on the Democratic ticket, but the ballot outcome was contested in a partisan fight in the legislature. Before it could be resolved, Alsop suffered a heart attack. He died in 1891 at age fifty-three.

His four children, including fifteen-year-old Joseph Wright Alsop IV, already had lost their mother. Now they lived with their grandmother on High Street. But they came of age in circumstances quite different from those enjoyed by the Alsops of the preceding four generations. For these children, any comforts of life would have to be the product of their own toil. Grandmother Alsop provided a good education, and then they were on their own.

Joseph Wright IV went to Groton School in Massachusetts and studied a year at the University of Berlin before returning to complete an engineering curriculum at the Sheffield Scientific School at Yale. After a few years working for a land and cattle company in Denver, he returned to Connecticut and joined with an aunt to purchase a 150-acre farm near Avon, an agricultural community just west of Hartford on the Farmington River. At Wood Ford Farm, beginning in 1902, Joseph Alsop grew tobacco and maintained a growing herd of dairy cattle.

He was a dour Yankee, tall, confident, elegant, with a dry wit and aristocratic tastes. "He looked distinguished even covered with fertilizer," his wife once wrote. He viewed himself as something of a country squire on the English model, a landed gentleman who tended his farm, devoted himself regularly to the hunt and the stream, and helped run the surrounding community.

In 1905, at the nearby Farmington home of William and Anna Cowles, Alsop met nineteen-year-old Corinne Robinson, niece of Anna Cowles and daughter of Corinne Roosevelt Robinson and Douglas Robinson of New York City. Her uncle was President Theodore Roosevelt. Though not comely, she possessed a lively mind and exuded a kind of sparkling charm. Within four years, on November 4, 1909, they were married at the Park Avenue house of her brother, Theodore Robinson.

Corinne's family background was more than a match for the Alsops. The Scotch-English Robinsons had gained great wealth in the New York banking and commercial trades. They traced their line back to a Revolution-era Englishman named Peter Corne, whose Tory sentiments were even more intense than those of John Alsop the Non-Signer. During and after the Revolutionary War, he kept a portrait of King George III in his wine cellar and led his children down there for nightly vigils before their "master." Generations later, Stewart Alsop was to regard his mother's paternal ancestors as "probably the richest and certainly the most snobbish of all our ancestors."

One of the richest and most snobbish was Aunt Harriett Douglas, who in 1832 built a mansion in upper New York state called Henderson House. It sat on a high headland overlooking the wide Mohawk Valley, an imposing bulk of silvery stone vaguely shaped to suggest a castle in the Scottish baronial style. It contained twelve bedrooms and had a sixty-foot hall. Aunt Harriett was a slightly wacky woman who spent her youth in pursuit of European celebrities, hunted lions in Africa, and displayed her considerable wealth with theatrical ostentation. Her literary friends included Sir Walter Scott, William Wordsworth, and Robert Southey. When Aunt Harriett died childless in 1872, Henderson House went to her nephew, Douglas Robinson. His son, Douglas Robinson, Jr., a broad-faced man with an aristocratic demeanor and a booming voice, married into the Roosevelt family of Oyster Bay and eventually took Henderson House with him into that marriage.

It was not easy adjusting to the vigorous Oyster Bay Roosevelts. Douglas Robinson likened it to being "bullied or ignored or hung on the family like a tail to a kite." But he accepted all that when he married Corinne Roosevelt, sister of the future president. Known in her youth as Conie, she was pert, voluble, intellectually vibrant, adventuresome. When her father surprised his three youngest children with a pony, only four-year-old Conie stepped forward with excitement at the idea of getting on the animal. Her summer reading during her nineteenth year was Gibbon's *Decline and Fall of the Roman Empire*. She loved poetry and was quick to laugh or weep at the vicissitudes of life.

Early in her life Corinne fell under the spell of the cult of TR. The childhood of little Teedie, as he was called within the family, became, of course, the stuff of legend—the bouts with asthma that left him puny and sickly, his determination to get strong in the little gym his father had built for him, his unbounded curiosity and love for books, his enthusiasm for physical challenge and danger. Long before this story entered the national consciousness, it captured the imagination of his parents and siblings, particularly of his two sisters, Anna and Corinne.

Anna, known to family members as Bamie or Bye, had an even more inspirational childhood than Teedie's. As an infant she contracted Pott's disease, a form of tuberculosis that softens and destroys the bones, often leaving the victim deformed. Bamie's fate was a severe curvature of the spine and considerable pain through much of her life. As a child, she was strapped into braces that foreclosed movement and left sores on her back. She never reached normal stature, and her body was left twisted.

Bamie brushed aside this cruel fate as if it were no more than a nuisance. She studied avidly, learned to play the piano and speak French, took care of her younger siblings, and conducted herself as an adult from early childhood. Her father doted on her, but there was no trace of pity in the family's affection. Little Teedie referred to his older sister as "a kind of little feminine Atlas with a small world on her shoulders."

In 1895, when Anna Roosevelt was forty, she married William Sheffield Cowles, a large and courtly naval commander from Farmington, Connecticut, who was nearly ten years her senior. Within three years, Bamie gave birth to a son, William Sheffield Cowles, Jr. Soon thereafter her brother became president, and Bamie established a home in Washington that became known as the "little White House." Theodore rarely made a serious presidential decision without first making his way to the Cowleses' N Street house for consultations with his wise and supportive sister. In middle age, Bamie lost her hearing, and soon the ravages of arthritis left her frequently confined to a wheelchair; yet she never lost the gallantry that had guided her through life. She learned to read lips so well that few knew she couldn't hear; she brushed off the arthritis, and maintained her humor and her passion for lively conversation throughout her seventy-six years.

If Bamie honored the TR myth by matching it in life, Corinne honored it in verse and prose. Imbued with a romantic spirit, she viewed her brother's valor and moral audacity as the quintessence of manly virtue. In fact, the ideal represented by her brother seems to have rendered her incapable of passionate love. Though her family considered the stolid Douglas Robinson an ideal suitor and welcomed the engagement, Corinne was anything but enthusiastic.

In letters to her ardent fiancé, she hinted that her interests went beyond marriage. He was her "dear old fellow," of course, but she really didn't want to give up those nights at home when Theodore would burst through the door after one of his political meetings and regale her with funny descriptions of what had happened. She felt herself incapable of actually saying she loved Douglas. But Theodore took her aside and praised Douglas as an ideal mate. His words were persuasive, and the ceremony took place in April 1882 at the Fifth Avenue Presbyterian Church, with Theodore giving away the bride. Corinne, however, spent a good part of her wedding day in tears. "If you were my brother or cousin," she once had written to Douglas, "how freely I could say I love you dearly. That kind of love I give absolutely."

The man she loved absolutely was brother Teedie. Her writings—a Roosevelt biography published in 1921 and some 170 poems published through the years—are laced with adoring descriptions of his life and character and expressions of homage to what she believed he stood for. In a poem called "To My Brother," she wrote:

> I loved you for the tender hand
>   That held my own so close and warm,
> I loved you for the winning charm
>   That brought gay sunshine to the land.

In her TR biography, Corinne went so far as to suggest that Roosevelt should be viewed as the "brother" of his country, much as Washington was its father and Lincoln its savior. He was the "Great Sharer," she said. "He shared all that he had . . . with all those with whom he came in contact, and especially with those closest and dearest to him—the members of his own family and his sisters."

Despite her early difficulties in marriage and her preoccupation with immaculate family love, Corinne proved successful as wife and mother.

She bore four children—Theodore, Corinne, Monroe, and Stewart. Of these, Corinne came the closest to the Rooseveltian ideal. She was born July 2, 1886, in the sprawling, three-story family home at Orange, New Jersey, and grew up in the family's various houses and retreats—the city home at 422 Madison Avenue, the country house at Orange, the Roosevelt complex at Oyster Bay, and the Robinsons' New York castle, Henderson House. It was a happy life, full of activity and challenge. The Orange place, encompassing seventy-two acres, had a huge vegetable garden, tennis courts, horses and ponies, and at one time a collection of twenty-two dogs of various description and pedigree.

July was spent at Oyster Bay, where Corinne and her playmates learned to swim by getting thrown into the water. From Gracewood, the home of Theodore Roosevelt's aunt, Anna Bulloch Gracie, the children would take a path through the woods to Sagamore Hill, Theodore's huge wood-shingle house, to visit with Uncle Ted and Aunt Edith and play with the cousins. Uncle Ted invariably led the children in vigorous games of hide and seek, windmill climbing, or "obstacle walks," in which they were required to go over or through objects in their way— trees, houses, persons—but never around them.

One hot summer day Uncle Ted led the children on a rowing expedition over the bay to a distant island. His niece Corinne recalled it as "a fleet of little boats, everybody getting horribly sunburned, a mass of mosquitos, cooking what seemed to be a ghastly meal, lack of sleep, and the long row home—and all done with the greatest enthusiasm as if it had been a fascinating Arabian Nights experience."

August was reserved for Henderson House, where Grandmother Robinson presided with austere benevolence. She was a religious woman who could move rapidly from being happy and witty to being exceedingly cross. "It was confusing to children," Corinne recalled, "but we always loved her."

The children liked getting back home to New York and New Jersey in late summer. The horses were there, and tennis courts and a croquet ground where competition was fierce.

A frequent guest at the Madison Avenue house was Corinne's cousin, Eleanor Roosevelt, daughter of Elliott Roosevelt (the elder Corinne's brother). Eleanor's father suffered from the Roosevelt family affliction of alcoholism, which rendered him incapable of caring for his children when his wife died of diphtheria at a young age. Eleanor, then only five, and her brother Hall, known as Brudie, went to live with their Grandmother Hall at 11 West Thirty-seventh Street. It was a bleak existence. Grandma Hall already had raised six children, including two sons who were alcoholics. She insisted on keeping one of them—Uncle Vallie—in her house, and he terrorized the children, on occasion even pointing a gun at them or locking them in the basement. As the younger Corinne observed years later, Grandma Hall "was unable to give anything but a very meager, weary, leftover love." Eleanor, she recalled, was "a pathetic, plain, insecure, lonely little girl." Eleanor frequently escaped her dreary surroundings by staying at the homes of her ebullient Auntie Corinne and Uncle Douglas.

Though the Robinsons spent winters in the city, the elder Corinne opened the big Orange house over the New Year's holidays for a young people's house party and dance. One of these occurred when Eleanor was about sixteen, but it turned out to be just another sad ordeal for the hapless teenager. The younger Corinne and Alice Roosevelt (TR's first child and cousin of both Eleanor and Corinne) wore sophisticated new dresses for the occasion, but Eleanor's grandmother had bought her a short white dress that was completely out of style. "This tall, gangling girl looked like someone at a fancy dress party portraying a little child," Corinne recalled. Her friends begged her to wear one of their castaways, but the stoic Eleanor refused.

Some time later, when Corinne enrolled at Mlle. Marie Souvestre's famous Allenswood finishing school outside London, she found her cousin a changed person. Eleanor was in her last term by then and had come under the spell of the enchanting Mlle. Souvestre, who had adopted Eleanor as her chosen favorite—one in a long line of such favorites stretching back over several decades of teaching. Corinne soon discovered Mlle. Souvestre's force of personality, rapier wit, and extensive connections in the literary world. Her brilliant speech kept her students transfixed, and sometimes she would single out a victim cruelly with sharp and pointed words or a shaft of irony. But to be Mlle. Souvestre's supreme favorite was an intoxicating honor, one that carried the privilege of accompanying her on trips abroad and on social excursions in the London literary world. That was Eleanor's happy fate, and Corinne considered it a mark of her character that she made no enemies through this favoritism.

After Eleanor left, Corinne herself ascended to the position of honor. She enjoyed it, particularly the exclusive access to Mlle. Souvestre's great library and the late night sessions when her special mentor would read aloud from Molière, Racine, and Corneille as the other girls slept upstairs. Inevitably, Mlle. Souvestre would let the book fall to her lap and exclaim how much she missed her *chère Tottie*, the wonderful Eleanor who was so courageous and intelligent and good. Then her hands would go up in the air and fall into her lap as she sighed, *"Mais pas gaie—pas gaie."*

Years later, Corinne speculated that Eleanor's lack of gaiety—and the hardships of life that left her so woeful and serious—helped forge the iron in her soul that the world came to appreciate. And she always found her cousin "an interesting companion." But there was no enchantment of music or painting, or simple gaiety or just plain nonsense. There was no joyful response to the beauty of the world, the fog on the bare trees of winter or the first beckoning of spring. Corinne felt that her cousin was "a far finer woman than I am, but she does not have my kind of fun."

For Corinne, fun was the purpose of it all. Her quick mind, galvanizing personality, sense of irony, and human sympathy all aided her in her determination to attack life in order to embrace it. In her day and at her station, the watchword for women was *class*. This meant more than merely wearing the right clothes and saying the right things: It meant making people love you even as you dominated them. It meant walking into a room filled with people and conquering it. It meant converting Teddy Roosevelt's force of personality to female uses. Auntie Bye had class; so did Corinne Roosevelt Robinson; young Corinne Robinson had it in spades.

And yet while she idealized the kind of life her Uncle Ted personified, she did not always follow it; she was practical, too. The man she chose for her life's companion was in many ways the opposite of Theodore Roosevelt. Joseph Wright Alsop IV passed up tennis, a game for show-offs, in favor of shotgun and fishing rod. He didn't care for visits to Henderson House or Sagamore Hill, but devoted hours to sessions of the Board of Selectmen and the state's Public Utilities Commission. He harbored strong opinions and could be brash in expressing them, but avoided political engagement that had no purpose. He was, after all, an Alsop, part of a clan that had demonstrated through the generations stolidity, substance, a sense of purpose. The Alsops lacked the verve and eccentricities of the Roosevelts; they couldn't match the Douglases and Robinsons in money-making skills. But they made their mark.

The wedding of Corinne Robinson and Joe Alsop in November 1909 was a small affair; the family was in mourning following the death of Corinne's brother Stewart, who had fallen out of a window during a drunken night at Harvard. Corinne wore "an excruciatingly hideous but very expensive fur hat" as the newlyweds departed the Manhattan wedding site on their way to Virginia's Blue Ridge Mountains for a ten-day honeymoon. On the return they stopped at Orange to visit Corinne's parents before heading via train to New Haven to watch the Harvard-Yale football game. Afterward there was a special treat—a ride to Avon in one of the town's two motorcars. They left the game at four-thirty to begin the thirty-eight-mile journey to the farm—and arrived four hours later, following a flat tire and a failure of lights that compelled them to crawl over the primitive dirt roads in the dark. Joe carried Corinne over the threshold and introduced her to the servants. A year later, the first of the next-generation Alsops appeared.

AVON AND HENDERSON

The Long Shadow of TR

TURN-OF-THE-CENTURY Avon, population about fifteen hundred, was an American farm community of a stripe common across much of the nation in those days—bucolic, self-contained, the spirit and image of Anglo-Saxon America. Aside from a small Irish enclave, the townsfolk were nearly all of the Yankee stock. They tilled the soil, produced nearly everything they ate, worshipped in one of the town's two Congregational churches, married among themselves, lived in the same frame houses that had sheltered their parents.

Though Avon was only nine miles by the crow's flight from Connecticut's capital, Hartford, folks didn't get there much. The dirt road to Hartford, intermittently dusty and muddy, wound up the western slope of a ridge called Talcott Mountain, and it was hard going for horse-drawn vehicles or, for that matter, early motorcars. The best means of passage was by rail—first to Plainville, fourteen miles to the south, then by transfer on a funny little passenger train called the *Dinky* coming from Bristol in the west. The trip took nearly two hours.

On Avon's Main Street was a row of dwellings that housed the few townsfolk who weren't farmers—a builder, the store owner, the postmaster, the ministers, and officials of the Ensign-Bickford Company plant, which produced a safety fuse for industrial explosives. Avon was not a rich community. Not a single house in town could match the numerous stately homes in nearby Farmington or Simsbury.

But Avon folks possessed a flinty independence and pride. Thrifty, hardworking, unemotional, they tipped their hats to no one. Although they quickly extended assistance when a neighbor was in need, they greeted newcomers with steely-eyed suspicion. Yet they readily accepted Joseph Alsop when he arrived in 1902. With his expensive clothes, elite education, and distinguished demeanor, he was different from the rustic and plain Avon folk. But, like them, he was a New Englander. He worked as they did, from five thirty each morning until dusk. And he was direct in word and action. Avonites soon turned to him for leadership in the councils of state and local government.

Corinne was different. Born of wealth, from a famous family, a New Yorker, she was not the sort to be greeted warmly by the townsfolk. Shortly after arriving, she accompanied Joe to the annual church fair and supper. Displaying her best Roosevelt smile, she introduced herself: "How do you do? I'm Mrs. Alsop." Her friendly gestures were met with stony stares. But she accepted this standoffishness as a challenge. Besides, she liked "the fine unemotional faces, their lack of pretense and refusal to look as if they accepted someone of whom they had a deep suspicion."

At the town store, where locals purchased everything from small farm tools to patent medicines to calico by the yard, she noted that the town's elderly men liked to gather around the rectangular wood stove in the corner. Seeing an empty chair one day, she walked over and sat down amid bewildered stares from the hot-stove regulars. Though her audacity was shocking to the old-timers, they couldn't ignore her, especially since Corinne acted as if nothing was the least bit unusual about her being there. Slowly, the barriers of suspicion broke down, and Corinne became a regular herself, joining in the stories and laughter that helped warm wintry afternoons. Except for an old man named Mr. Bishop, who never seemed to smile, they all became her special friends. The town's first selectman, Fred Ripley, felt so comfortable with Corinne that he offered to remove his sock so she could see his painful bunion. She declined, but later, after his big toe had been amputated, he had it placed in a bottle and gave it to the astonished Corinne as a mark of esteem.

Corinne never seemed to be intimidated by anything. She loved to meet new people and chat with old friends. She had what her son John called "a strong face"—plenty of character written into her angular features—and displayed genuine interest in the people around her. Still, she possessed a manipulative quality, an apparent need, discernible to a few through the veil of her friendly enthusiasm, to maintain control in every social setting. She loved to gossip and could be withering in her observations about those she didn't respect.

Corinne had been at the Alsop farm barely a year before children began arriving in a kind of "torrential influx." In the early morning of Tuesday, October 11, 1910, she gave birth to her first child, a ten-pound boy. "I felt like some queen or empress who must produce an heir to the throne, as I was the only one who could have a Joseph Wright Alsop the

Fifth," she wrote later. Recalling the sensation of childbirth, she said the pain "has the quality of rhythm like the waves of the sea. . . . Finally, the moment arrived and the child wrenched free, a blasting and pounding, a tornado, an earthquake inside my body, a final tremendous explosion coupled with ecstasy when the baby was born."

In March 1912 came Corinne Roosevelt Robinson Alsop, known within the family as Sis. On May 17, 1914, Stewart arrived. And in August 1915 came John DeKoven Alsop. Years later Corinne recalled her first six years of marriage as "filled with joy, enchantment, adjustment to an isolated farm . . . , spurts of great loneliness, heaviness of body, four babies and two miscarriages!"

Corinne loved motherhood as she loved all other grand aspects of life, but she had no intention of letting her children control her existence. Within nine months of her firstborn's arrival there appeared at the farm a twenty-year-old redhead from the moors of Scotland named Agnes Guthrie, retained through a New York agency to become the Alsops' nursemaid. She was shy and a bit dour and initially didn't take to what she considered Corinne's "pleasant ways." But she loved children, lived in their world, and had a way of keeping them both disciplined and captivated. Corinne delegated the details of the nursery to Aggie as she pursued her varied interests in town.

Joe combined farm duties with civic and political activities, serving at various times in both the Connecticut house and the state senate. He was a strong Republican, but in 1912 he abandoned his party to support his wife's Uncle Ted during the former president's "Bull Moose" White House campaign against Republican President William Howard Taft and Democrat Woodrow Wilson. Roosevelt lost, and Joe's desertion of the GOP destroyed his promising political career as a Connecticut Republican. Thereafter he confined his civic attention to various boards and commissions, including Avon's board of selectmen. Joe was not particularly taken by squirmy babies, but his interest in the children intensified as they became big enough to respond to his companionship.

Even as a baby, little Joseph displayed a strong will, furious temper, and rare intellect. He refused to talk until he could string sentences together at age two, and then he often strung them together in the form of commands. Once, distraught because Aggie had left him in his crib while she prepared lunch, he screamed between sobs, "Meet me here, Aggie Guthrie, meet me here!" He developed an early passion for books, particularly those about animals, and he would spend hours listening to Corinne or Aggie read from them.

Once when Corinne took three-year-old Joe to the zoo in New York's Central Park, she happened upon an exotic animal she had never seen before. "Let me read what it says on this sign over here, darling, so we can find out what that is," she said to the toddler.

"That is a nilgau," he replied matter-of-factly. He was referring to an antelopelike animal described in Kipling's *Jungle Book*.

When Joe was not quite five, Corinne sought to explain to him where babies come from, in preparation for the arrival of her fourth child. She talked of the farmyard cows, explaining that she would be providing the little baby with milk just as the cows did. He remained silent, so she proceeded to discuss the difference between these animals and birds, which lay eggs and don't provide their babies with milk.

"What about the duck-billed platypus?" he asked. As Corinne pondered that response, Joe remained silent for some seconds before speaking again.

"Very hard for a buffalo," he mused.

As for Stewart, the family developed grave concerns about his health. He suffered from allergies, like his great-uncle Theodore Roosevelt, and was a sickly child for much of his early years. His rashes slathered with cocoa butter and his body wrapped in gauze, "he looked like a small, rather wizened mummy," as brother Joe wrote years later. Several times Stewart almost died from asthma attacks, and many a night Corinne and Aggie shared the task of holding him until morning, keeping his head up so he could breathe, reading or singing to distract him from his discomfort. Corinne took Stewart to a New York allergist who determined that the child was vulnerable to nearly all common allergens. He could never be brought up on a farm, the doctor said. Corinne dismissed the advice, but she took care to protect him from undue exertion and farmyard danger areas. "When we wanted to get away from Stewart," his sister recalled years later, "we just ran into the hay barn."

WHEN THE ALSOP children were small, old Route 44 from Hartford to Avon was blacktopped. For the first time, Avonites had quick and easy access to the city, and soon automobiles could be seen crowding the two-lane road. Corinne bought a Ford Model T "cabriolet," which looked like a black box on wheels, and Joseph replaced his old Fiat with a grand Stutz Bearcat.

The highway encouraged the elder Alsop to expand his business. He bought an adjacent farm with a large Guernsey dairy herd and a milk route, and soon his Wood Ford Farm dairy truck was transporting cream and milk to Hartford hospitals and schools. His income grew, and he expanded it further by entering the insurance business, first as head of a cooperative to protect tobacco growers from hail damage, and later as president of a small insurance company called Hartford County Mutual. With the highway, he could manage the farm and still commute daily to the insurance office.

Around the same time the population mix in the town began to change with an influx of Italian families. They came first in small numbers, recruited by Joe Alsop as farm labor during a European trip he and Corinne took early in their marriage. Arriving from the northern Italian area around Lake Garda and Arezzo, they lived in small shanties on the farm or in a tenement house along Route 10 that had been a roadside inn decades earlier. At the busiest times of the year, the farm required up to thirty farmhands, and Alsop considered these sturdy northern Italians to be excellent workers. Soon their relatives began arriving, and then relatives of the relatives. By the 1920s, Avon's Italians outnumbered the Yankees. Like so much of America at the time, Anglo-Saxon Avon found itself adjusting to a different people with new attitudes and folkways and a different religion. The two groups mingled amiably but kept a distance from one another; there was little intermarriage.

The Italian youngsters were fine companions for young Joe and, later, Stewart. Together, they learned to swim in a nearby Farmington River swimming hole where men and boys chased away the summer heat by romping naked in the muddy waters. They explored the outer reaches of the farm and took long hikes up Talcott Mountain.

Young Joe possessed minimal athletic ability and was developing into an overweight child. He would often flee the insecurities of youth by retreating to his favorite farmhouse armchair, where he would spend hours reading. He began with children's classics but soon graduated to standard literature. The Alsop children all became inveterate readers. For years, the elder Alsop devoted each afternoon to reading sessions with his children, starting with *The Wind in the Willows* and *Alice's Adventures in Wonderland* and moving through Kipling to Thackeray's *The Rose and the Ring*. On Sundays, Corinne gave the children long Bible lessons, bringing to life the dramatic stories of the Old Testament.

The nursery, a large dormitory upstairs, was Aggie's domain, and it was always a mess. Joe loved to paint pictures, while Stewart developed a talent for wood carving, and the nursery often looked like a painter's studio in a sawmill. Once when Corinne was away, Aggie wrote to say that the children were potting weeds. "We have fifteen pots up in the nursery now, and Sis says to tell you that they are the champion weed planters in the world." Corinne visualized the scene and decided she was glad to be away.

The household staff generally numbered four—Aggie, as well as a cook, a waitress, and a chambermaid. But Aggie was first among equals. She was to become an integral part of the family, sharing all the ambitions, joys, pain, and love of the close-knit clan. Corinne considered her a kind of "beneficent Pied Piper" with invisible pipes in her heart that only children could hear. She was strict, but in the ongoing struggle between children and adults she sided with the children. If they wanted to stage a play, she wouldn't hesitate to find costume material from among Corinne's fine slips or Joe's good shirts. She once made a dashing beard for Stewart out of his mother's "quite expensive false hair." If the children had a complaint about their parents, she helped them give vent to it.

In the early 1920s the Alsops remodeled and expanded the old farmhouse, adding to the single bathroom and making the place more comfortable. The old nursery became the parents' bedroom, with a dressing room for Corinne, and the children resented it. As nine-year-old Stewart wrote to brother Joe, who by then was away at school, "Mother's 'budwar' is ready it looks as if it were a millionairs blace . . . i have to do all the painting of our own few kitchen chairs wile 'they' rest in lovely kowches and lucksurus arm chiars and they go roun with their noses up in the air." Corinne wrote years later that "the orthography was Stewart's, but the inspiration was certainly Aggie's."

Later the farmhouse would be expanded still further to encompass twenty-eight rooms. A large dining room would be added, with a book-lined study behind it. Just off the newly enlarged kitchen a big pantry and maids' gathering room would be provided, as well as five maids' rooms. Upstairs would become a warren of sleeping quarters, including a bedroom with bath for each of the children, and two guest rooms.

In 1918, in anticipation of female suffrage, Corinne founded the Connecticut League of Republican Women. When suffrage came two years later she won a seat in the legislature, which she held for three terms. She served twenty years as Republican Party chairman in Avon and enjoyed wide influence in GOP circles throughout the state. She was never so happy as when she was mingling with neighbors and playing politics. As her son John recalled, "I can still remember twitching at her overcoat to try to get her away from the hundred and one people she wanted to talk to on her way out of the town meeting." She also loved to entertain guests at the farmhouse or socialize at dinner out in the community. An Alsop cook, Anne Anderson, recalled many a night when Joe Sr., who enjoyed quiet evenings at home, would stop off at the kitchen on his return from the fields and ask about the evening meal. "You're out tonight, Mr. Alsop," she would say, and he would bolt through the door yelling, "Goddam it, Corinne . . ."

Corinne frequently visited her family in New York, and she and her husband traveled extensively during winter months. "We sort of assumed that in January and February we wouldn't see them," John Alsop recalled. The children would remain with Aggie or be sent off to stay with their Grandmother Robinson or other relatives. When the parents were home in Avon, they maintained an adult world that often excluded the children. Corinne and Joe dressed formally for dinner each evening, met in the small study for cocktails, and dined by themselves. Only upon reaching the age of eleven did the children join the adults.

The parents were demanding. "Father made it clear: We were supposed to look after ourselves and . . . be successful," recalled John Alsop, who remembers his father as a kind of "benevolent dictator." The children viewed Corinne as a "tough cookie" who expected the best in anything they pursued. Childish pranks didn't bother her, particularly if they reflected spirit and moxie. She made no effort to protect her children from the world, but let them learn through experience. "Her idea of the proper role," explained John Alsop, "wasn't to go around with an umbrella over our heads, but to follow us with a scrap basket to pick up the pieces after we got into trouble."

But underlying her approach to child-rearing, unspoken yet ever-present, was the cult of TR, the challenge to pursue excellence, adventure, and success in all aspects of life, to prevail in everything from vocabulary building to the development of moral courage. Uncle Teedie had died in 1919, when Joe was eight and Stewart only four, and there was now little recollection of the family's former eminence. But what he had meant to the family, as understood and articulated by Corinne's mother and Auntie Bye, guided Corinne in her guidance of her children.

There was plenty of warmth and closeness in the family. Joe Sr. took the younger boys on frequent hunting and fishing excursions. Corinne taught the children to play bridge. Evenings at Avon were spent in the living room playing cards, talking, or reading the afternoon papers. Joe Sr. would puff on his pipe and ceremoniously struggle with the *Hartford Times* crossword puzzle as the two dogs, a black German shepherd named Albert and a spaniel obtained at Stewart's insistence, lounged on the floor. There was always plenty of lively talk, particularly political talk, and the children were expected to speak up if they wanted to make a point.

When they were young, the children tended to pair off while playing around the farm. Joe and Sis would play together, while Stew and John had their own games and activities. But Joe was very much the older brother who looked after his siblings and demanded their unqualified respect in return. He loved to demonstrate the breadth of his knowledge and judgment. "We looked to Joe for advice," John Alsop recalled. "He was always our ready helper."

When Joe was six, Corinne enrolled him in the red one-room schoolhouse across the road from the farm. There, thirteen children in eight grades were taught by a single teacher. Joe was promoted rapidly through the grades, but with the influx of the Italians, many of whom could barely speak English, Corinne feared Joe wouldn't get adequate attention in the public school. At age eight he was enrolled at Kingswood School in Hartford, a private day school, where Stewart and John also would study. Sis attended Hartford's Oxford School for girls. They traveled to class each morning in the Alsop milk truck on its regular Hartford run.

At Kingswood, Joe and Stewart excelled academically, but neither made much of a mark in sports. Joe's weight problem worsened as he got older, and he showed little coordination on the playing field. Stewart's asthma had slowed his physical development, and even as his allergic reactions lessened he fell ill often. But he excelled in all his classes except arithmetic. "He is faithful, conscientious and thorough, and he has a very good mind," a school official wrote as Stewart completed third grade. As for Joe, headmaster George Nicholson expressed confidence in his intellect but some hesitation about his social and physical development: "In mental power Alsop is much in advance of his years. . . . His reading, particularly in history, is unusually wide, and his interests (which in natural history and design represent real power and promise) are the despair of any ordinary school curriculum. It follows that Alsop stands outside the usual preoccupation of the 'normal' boy. His physical development, though perfectly healthy, is not athletic, and his skill in games is negligible."

Joe took pride in his intellect and enjoyed showing it off, but he harbored deep insecurities about his obesity and lack of athletic ability. These were most clearly manifest when he left the protected environs of the farm each August for the annual monthlong stay at Henderson House, by this time under the matriarchal domination of Corinne Robinson, the Alsop boys' maternal grandmother. The place teemed with children of all ages during the summer, and the emphasis was on rough-and-tumble activities—tennis, swimming, riding. Joe was too slow and cumbersome to play tennis, had never developed even a passing proficiency as a swimmer, and was afraid of horses. Years later, the memory of these feelings of inadequacy returned to him in the vision of his cousin, Douglas Robinson—"lithe, handsome, patronizing and superior, mounted on a splendid and spirited horse, from which he looked down upon me with an understandable sneer."

Despite his feelings of insecurity, Joe never allowed himself to be intimidated by the other children. It wasn't so easy for the shy and reflective Stewart, whose asthma kept him from active athletic competition in the early years at Henderson. "All the cousins would be there, and there was such a great deal of emphasis on athletic competition," recalled Dorothy Robinson Kidder, an Alsop cousin. "Stewart was horribly handicapped."

But Stewart gained a measure of respect from his peers for his abilities as a bridge player, and as his asthma receded he involved himself more in Henderson activities. By the age of nine, he was riding one of the Henderson ponies, which pleased his father. "I am perfectly delighted that you are now allowed to ride and feel sure that it will not make you wheez," wrote Joe Sr. from Avon. Father was wrong. Even years after, when Stewart had graduated to one of the big Henderson horses, a long ride would bring on hay fever and force him back to the house, wheezing.

Despite their difficulties at Henderson, the Alsop boys loved the place. "I've never had a more perfect time than I did this summer at Henderson," Stewart wrote his grandmother after an early childhood visit. Grandmother displayed all the warmth, enthusiasm, and flamboyance that she had loved so dearly in her brother Theodore. She reigned over Henderson with the spirit of a fairy godmother who could summon up an enchanting breakfast or a tennis tournament or a swimming excursion with the wave of the hand. In place of a wand she had housemaids, parlor maids, laundresses, cooks, and a rotund chauffeur named Courtney.

The day began precisely at eight thirty with breakfast, to which the multitude was summoned by the senior parlor maid's rendition of the Scottish ditty, "Up with the Bonnets of Bonnie Dundee," on a set of chimes in the pantry. Side tables would be piled high with cereals, heavy cream, fruit, oatmeal or hominy, eggs, bacon or ham, and the day's special, deviled kidneys or chicken hash. Years later Joe and Stewart recalled that guests were expected to attack this offering "with a maximum of noise and gaiety, exchanging gossip, shouting jokes and even arguing about politics over the coffee all around the big table." Grandmother normally took her breakfast in her bed upstairs, but if the breakfast table downstairs didn't generate sufficient animation she somehow would get wind of it and appear suddenly in her dressing gown "to stimulate a suitable commotion."

Afterward there were riding sessions for the children and a tennis party for adults before guests of all ages made a foray to the Henderson lake for swimming. Then came a large luncheon, tennis for the children and walking or riding for the adults, an enormous afternoon tea, and a "somnolent interlude" before the chimes signaled time to dress for cocktails and dinner. After dinner there were either cards or charades, and the adults would enjoy a nightcap session before bed.

It was a milieu of competitive conversation in the Roosevelt tradition. Participants were expected to join in and make a mark on the proceedings. Those who didn't were left behind, and Grandmother didn't concern herself with any self-doubt that might be felt by those who couldn't keep up.

But when Eleanor Roosevelt appeared unexpectedly during one particularly raucous evening, Grandmother feared she would be ostracized by the Henderson revelers, and so she asked young Joe, then a teenager, to entertain his mother's cousin by engaging her in conversation. The Oyster Bay Roosevelts, all TR Republicans, didn't care much for Eleanor's increasingly vocal liberalism or the Democratic identity of her husband, Franklin, the promising politician from the Hyde Park side of the Roosevelt family. On top of that, Eleanor had campaigned against her own first cousin, Theodore Roosevelt, Jr., when he had run for the New York governorship, and had even suggested during a statewide tour that young TR had been connected to the Teapot Dome scandal.

Joe devoted himself to Mrs. Roosevelt, as his grandmother had requested, and she in turn responded to the youth's precocious understanding of politics by discussing with him the pressing issues of the day. But their efforts at conversation became increasingly difficult as the surrounding house party grew more and more riotous. The end came when dancing started after charades "alarmingly full of double meanings." Then Uncle Teddy, the aggrieved former gubernatorial candidate, stripped off his jacket, stood up on one of the couches as if he were about to dive from it, and announced that he was "going to swim the Channel to dance with Eleanor." At that point, the solemn political discussion between Eleanor and young Joe ended abruptly, and Eleanor hurried off to bed.

Henderson left a deep impression on the Alsop children, giving them a sense that they were part of something grand that extended beyond their Avon world. It also forced an awareness of the competitive challenges posed by life outside the cozy confines of farm and family. For Joe, Henderson created an awareness of the disparity between his family's economic circumstances and those of his mother's family and most of his parents' friends. Years later, toward the end of his life, Joe began a biographical discussion of his childhood by noting this disparity. Even as a child, he seemed preoccupied with money and the symbols of status associated with it. At age eight, he wrote his Grandfather Robinson to suggest that, while Mother fed his empty stomach, Grandfather should feed his empty purse. "So give me please everything you have. . . . I will give you a little each year for food."

As for Stewart, his physical development was improving, and he took pride in his academic performance at Kingswood. But Corinne and Joe Sr. were beginning to note in him a disturbing lack of self-confidence. He seemed to crave encouragement and praise.

He got both at Avon. Aggie was always there to tend to the children's needs, psychic as well as material. And Joe Sr. mixed fatherly sympathy and understanding with his demands for excellence in the children's worldly pursuits. Corinne was more parsimonious with her praise. She sought to enforce high standards by bombarding the children with penetrating questions about what they had done, what they planned to do, how they planned to do it. Corinne's niece, Dottie Kidder, recalled that she spoke "very urgently" and that "she had a quality of being able to look right through you, and whatever you were trying your hardest to hide, whatever insufficiency, she could just get it out of you." Corinne directed toward her children an intensity of interest that nothing else in her life commanded. But the intensity could be intimidating.

Nevertheless, it was a family whose members enjoyed being together, joking with each other about their respective foibles or the absurdities of life in the community, arguing heatedly about the fate of the country or relaxing with a rubber of bridge or the evening newspaper. Looking back, Joe and Stewart would always think of the Avon years as a special preserve of the memory, the wellspring of their self-definition.

3

GROTON

In the Image of
the British Boarding School

ON FEBRUARY 12, 1929, Joseph Alsop IV sat down at his typewriter to compose a letter to Sherrard Billings at Groton School in Massachusetts. Billings, a headmaster, had written to complain about young Stewart, then fourteen and a bit of a problem at the school.

"I am free to say that I do not understand Stewart, nor apparently does any other master," Billings had said. "He keeps a good deal to himself and . . . has not yet learned to get on easily and cheerfully with his fellows." Stewart, Billings had suggested, harbored some kind of inferiority complex "which tempts him to assert himself in some way popular to the crowd."

The boy's father had read many such letters during Stewart's unhappy school years, and a few during Joe's earlier Groton stay as well. Almost always he had acknowledged the problems, and had accepted much of the Groton masters' harsh judgments on his sons' shortcomings. But now he was not so sure. Perhaps part of the problem was Groton itself. Perhaps the masters, dedicated though they were, had contributed to Stewart's troublesome behavior. The elder Joe was not without insight into the matter; he had, after all, attended Groton himself a generation before. He wrote to the schoolmaster:

When I went to Groton I was probably one of the most disagreeable boys that existed. I had been brought up without a great deal of guidance in a small country town in which I learned a great many things that I should have learned in a different manner and where I had been the "cock of the walk" on account of my family. The result was, that I passed . . . the three only unhappy years of my life. . . . My feeling has always been, that while it was natural that I needed a good deal of correction and discipline when I got to Groton, that if I had not been made to feel that there was something wrong with me, as to my basic character, that I would have made much more of my time there. As after all I was not a bad little boy but I was shy and covered it up by bravado.

Joe Alsop's letter captured the dual and often conflicting sentiments of parents who entrusted their sons to Groton in those early decades of its existence. They knew the school was run by dedicated men of the highest character. They knew it offered a classical education designed to prepare the sons of the Northeastern establishment for the mantle of national leadership. But they knew also that the place was tough on boys who didn't measure up to the expectations of the masters. It was hospitable to youngsters who excelled at sports and breezed through their lessons without much skepticism; but it could be an ordeal for those of limited athletic ability or of inquiring intellect. For Joseph and Corinne Alsop these competing sentiments marked the ten years of their three sons' enrollment at Groton.

Tucked away amidst the rural New England landscape about thirty-five miles northwest of Boston, Groton was created in the image of the granite-faced Endicott Peabody, a strong-minded Episcopal minister with a square jaw and penetrating blue eyes. Born in 1857 in Salem, Massachusetts, Peabody possessed a New World genealogy similar to that of the Alsops. His great-grandfather had made a fortune by sending a fleet of fast merchant ships into the trade routes to China and India. Endicott developed into a young man of serious mien and strong conviction, but with a mischievous side as well, a twinkle of the eye. He spent five years at Cheltenham school in England, then attended Trinity College, Cambridge, where he rowed, played cricket, and developed a taste for British humor, British manners, and British ideals. Upon his return to Massachusetts he entered the Episcopal ministry, and in 1884, at age twenty-seven, he founded his American boarding school patterned after the Cheltenham of his youth.

He wrote at the time, "Every endeavor will be made to cultivate manly, Christian character, having regard to moral and physical as well as intellectual development." Like boys at England's Eaton, Harrow, and Cheltenham, Groton boys dressed for supper in white shirts and ties. They used the British spelling style—*flavour, colour, centre*—and the British term *form* as a substitute for the American *grade*. They played the British handball game called "fives" and in cheerleading sounded off with *"Hip, hip, hurrah."* They washed with cold water at long communal sinks.

The rector, as Peabody was called throughout his Groton years, drew the line at the British boarding school tradition of fagging, in which upperclassmen used the younger boys as servants. But senior students were allowed to discipline their juniors in a brutal manner, cramming errant boys into footlockers and pouring water into their mouths in a lavatory ritual called "pumping." Peabody approved of such peer-group enforcement of school standards as an efficient tool of discipline and a test of moral strength. He personally selected the class and school "prefects," who reigned as the school's student autocracy.

Peabody was a stern man and built his school upon a rock; that rock was Jesus Christ. The day began with chapel service and ended with evening prayer. Every boy took a course in "sacred studies" each year. And when the rector took to the pulpit he delivered sermons brimming with moral admonition. The devil, he warned, lurked in the temptations of pride, hypocrisy, and irreverence. Swearing, telling religious jokes, misbehavior in chapel, betting—all were punished severely at Groton. A headmaster, Peabody often said, "has to be a bit of a bully."

The rector believed that family values and family strength fostered good people and the good society, and he viewed his institution as a large family. At the center was his own family, including his buoyant and warmhearted wife, Fanny. Whenever they were in town, the rector and Mrs. Peabody would pass through the dormitories evenings to wish each boy a good night. Like the fabled Mr. Chips, Peabody took an intimate interest in each of his boys, maintained an active knowledge of their home circumstances as well as their school progress, invited them in for individual chats, and corresponded with them throughout their lives.

He took an avid interest in the school play, the debating society, the Grotonian literary magazine. But his primary passion was athletics. He particularly loved football because it demanded courage and toughness, and boys selected as prefects were likely to be star football players or, at the least, standouts in some other sport. As Peabody's biographer, Frank D. Ashburn, wrote, "The way of the non-athlete . . . was not so much hard as inconsequential."

Into this milieu in 1923 came young Joseph Alsop, hardly likely to become the beau ideal of Groton society. On his application form, to answer a question on what was regarded as the young man's "most serious fault, weakness, or tendency to be guarded against," the elder Joe had written, "physical largeness." Under "personal ambitions, hobbies or interests," the father had listed simply drawing and history. Joe's passion for reading didn't rank high at Groton. When Corinne drove young Joe to the school and discoursed a bit with the rector about the boy's reading habits, Peabody replied firmly, "That's all right. We'll soon knock all that out of him."

Young Joe entered Groton's second form (equivalent to the eighth grade), and soon he was competing for the best marks in his form. In an early letter to Grandmother Robinson, he wrote, "My weeklies were fairly good. They were English B-, Latin B+, Mathematics B, French A-, History A-, Biology B+, Sacred Studies B+. I think Mother will be quite pleased." But he seldom got better marks than classmate Erastus Corning from New York, who went on to graduate with top honors and eventually become mayor of Albany.

Though successful academically, Joe's early months at Groton proved a social calamity. As he recalled years later, "I was overweight, I was physically timid, and I had not the dimmest idea of how to get on with my contemporaries." He had only one friend—Dickie Bissell, tall, well-spoken, and confident but, like Joe, not much of an athlete. Young Richard M. Bissell, Jr., whose father was a successful insurance executive and whose mother was one of Corinne's closest friends, had known Joe all his life. Joe's letters from Groton were filled with references to his friend. "Dick Bissell's family," he wrote to Grandmother Robinson, "have disappeared to the West Indies, leaving his brother in charge. His brother says that he will supply Dick with money, fire-arms, and spiritous liquors, if Dick says the word."

But this friendship carried a price for Joe. Young Bissell's was a dominating personality, and no one felt the force of it more than Joe, who had nowhere else to turn. One evening before dinner Bissell placed a powerful stink bomb in Joe's study. As the boys were decorously having their supper in the large Hundred House dining hall, the bomb began to cast its powerful stench throughout the study quarters. When the rector opened the dining room doors, he and the boys were greeted by the offending smell. The windows were thrown open as the boys rushed through the building in search of the infernal device. When Joe found it in his study he flew into a rage, and when he realized Bissell had been the offender he attacked his old friend with fists flying.

Upon returning to Groton for his second year, Joe declared his independence from Dick Bissell. This, as he explained years later, was a serious step. "It meant that I abandoned any form of human company except semi-hostile human company." Throughout the fall and into the bleak New England winter, he lived a life that was "grim beyond imagining." He felt out of place, a nonconformist in a society where conformity was highly prized. Joe became the "butt of teasing," Bissell recalled years later, because of his love of reading, his fat body and lack of coordination, his "almost ladylike interest in people's clothes and things of that nature." It was the only time, Joe confessed years later, that he ever thought seriously of taking his own life.

Then toward spring he learned an "enormous lesson"—that young people like to make new friends if the friendless will only make a sincere effort. Slowly, he became more outgoing, and discovered to his delight that his ready wit could break a lot of social ice. He still spent plenty of time alone, hidden away in Groton's impressive library with yet another book. But he was becoming part of the group, and finding this much to his satisfaction.

His efforts to account for himself on the athletic field still proved unsuccessful, however, and Joe Sr. worried that the school was making a spectacle of his son. During Joe's second year, his father wrote to the rector complaining of the school's policy on athletics. Noting that he normally refrained from suggestions in the belief that school authorities knew best, he said there was one area in which he felt constrained to express himself.

It seems to me perfectly ridiculous to make a boy of Joe's physical make-up go through the motions of trying to play baseball. When any lot of boys are started at that game any person familiar with athletics can immediately pick out quite a number that have a natural aptitude for it, a still larger number in whom it would seem possible to inculcate skill at it and a few who under any circumstances whatsoever could not be good at all. Joe is clearly one of this latter class and it seems to me rather foolish to let him spend his spring term doing what practically amounts to nothing and not only that but making himself ridiculous.

But Joe was finding his niche in other areas. He joined the underclassmen's debating society—the Ciceros—and proved himself an effective contender. "I have just had my debate and I won, by a large margin, so the judges said," he wrote his grandmother. "I might even have a chance for the captainship of the Ciceros next year, but I doubt it." The next fall he did in fact become the Ciceros' captain, and the team of Alsop, Bissell, and a boy named Francis Lindley scored a victory over Belmont Hill School, convincing the judges that the United States should interfere in Latin American countries when the lives and property of U.S. citizens were endangered. The three became Groton's top debaters and represented the school in one particularly tense twelve-hour debate with another champion debating team. The question: Should the United States immediately withdraw its marines from Nicaragua? The judges deliberated for half an hour and returned with a unanimous decision for Groton.

In the Civics Club, designed to keep members up to date on current events, students were assigned various areas of study, and Joe's subject was art. He became particularly interested in Chinese art, and wrote a paper suggesting that Westerners often fail to appreciate Oriental painting. "Chinese line and plane design, in particular, are peculiarly fine in the hands of a master," he wrote. In his later Groton years, Joe also joined the Dramatic Association, and portrayed a portly Mrs. Kent in a play called *Kathleen.*

But Joe's extracurricular triumph was his work for the *Grotonian,* a student-produced literary monthly containing editorials, sports coverage, essays, poetry, short fiction, and book reviews. Toward the back were ads for products of particular interest to young boys of the upper classes, including stylish clothes (Brooks Brothers was a regular) and backpacking trips to the Rockies. Joe wrote extensively for the magazine and became a literary editor during his final year.

The *Grotonian* reflected not only the school itself but the social milieu that sent its sons there. Its pages brimmed with the idealism, patriotism, and commitment to national service that Groton instilled in its young charges. But the magazine also reflected the snobberies and prejudices of the upper classes. One short story published during Joe's school years depicted a London pawnbroker named Isaac Goldstein, and recounted how he was outsmarted at his own game by an Englishman and his American friend. "Well, Bill," exclaimed the Englishman at the end of the story, "I guess we foxed that old Jew."

Most of the *Grotonian* literature, though, simply mirrored the concerns of young boys testing themselves as writers and coming to terms with a world they were only beginning to understand. Joe's work betrayed an erudition rare in the *Grotonian*'s pages. In "The Bells," he described the scene in Saint Petersburg when Russia mourned the death of the Empress Elizabeth and braced for the rule of the mad Peter. "The great bells of the Alexander Nevskii monastery boomed out across the light, crisp snow," he wrote, "and the deep-voiced, throaty tones of the Cathedral of Saints Peter and Paul joined them." In a lighter piece, he exclaimed about buttered toast and poked a little fun at himself in the process: "When I consider the charming modulations of its lyric browns, the golden semi-fluid butter floating happily on its upper surface, I am filled with elation. Sometimes I feel that, if some one wished to poison me (as I have no doubt some do) that they might mix aconite and hellebore, and if they poured it on a piece of buttered toast, I should swallow it with gusto."

Joe's facility with descriptive prose came through in an essay depicting plantation blacks gathering atop a South Carolina hill for a sermon during an eclipse of the sun:

> Suddenly from a group of old men, serious, dignified elders, who sat a little apart from the crowd, a strange figure disengaged himself.
>
> Bent, puckered, wrinkled, he was dressed in white cotton, which contrasted strongly with his mahogany skin. For a short space he went from group to group speaking with the people. . . . Quickly the old man straightened himself and stood up from his talk. Noise ceased; the crowd was at attention. "Brethren," he said, "the Lord has sent an eclipse upon the sun. Repent ye, ye sinners. He has darkened His sun from the earth, so that ye may know your sins. The shepherd is waiting; come unto the fold."
>
> The crowd rocked rhythmically to and fro; a woman shouted "Hallelujah," and those around her took up the cry. Some prayed

already. The sky blackened perceptibly, but the old man preached on. . . . The people rocked on, now shrieking repentance, now sobbing for forgiveness. A woman wept quietly, while a child at her side screamed in terror. The preacher chanted, pointing wildly at the corona flaming through the parted clouds. "Look ye, look ye, ye wicked. The flames of Hell are in the sky. Remember your sin before it is too late." Terror redoubled. The rocking had ceased and most of the congregation were prostrate. The old man moaned on, but the darkness was slowly diminishing.

The people quieted slowly. An occasional sob, a gasp, a rustle; except for these there was complete silence; deeply still. Then the clouds parted again and the sun shone out. The reawakened land seemed to smile a rich assurance to the draggled congregation. . . .

Joe viewed the world through what at the time would have been considered a prism of realism. Though respectful of the plantation "darkies" and their religion, he looked upon them as a kind of exotic people, given to flights of unconcealed superstition. It was essentially a paternalistic outlook toward what he considered quite different people, reflecting attitudes prevalent in his time and within his class.

As JOE BEGAN his sixth-form year, Stewart arrived at Groton as a second-former. Kingswood officials had offered an optimistic assessment of his prospects—character, "splendid"; industry, "good"; ability, "very superior." They said intelligence tests had placed his IQ at "around 130." But the application form prepared by Joe Sr. noted some concerns: Stewart's asthma limited athletic activity; and under the heading of "most serious fault, weakness or tendency to be guarded against," Stewart's father wrote, "severe lack of self confidence."

Joe, always the paternalistic older brother, looked after Stewart on the train to Groton and during the final automobile ride from the rail station to the school. The car was crowded with Groton boys, and Stewart sat with two suitcases on his lap while Joe insisted that he write down the names of his new schoolmates so he wouldn't forget them. Joe helped get Stewart settled, talked with his dormitory master about Stewart's needs, counseled his brother on proper dress, visited him in the school infirmary during a winter illness. "Joe, as usual, has been very nice to me," Stewart wrote home. The younger brother seemed to adjust easily to the school, made friends quickly, and expressed contentment in his letters to Avon. He even showed some ability in sports; he scored both goals for his team in an intraschool soccer match.

By spring, however, school officials had taken a dim view of Stewart's performance. In March, Peabody wrote Joe Sr. to say the boy was making slight effort academically, and was untidy in his schoolwork and careless in dress and manner. Joe Sr. took the matter seriously but speculated that Stewart's apparent freedom from asthma after so many years had "caused him to go on a bust." He predicted improvement.

The following year, Joe departed for Harvard, and Stew was placed in the upper-form dormitory called Hundred House. Things immediately got worse. In the fall he was caught looking over another boy's paper. "He is clearly not as thoroughly determined to do right as we hoped," the rector wrote to Avon. In December Peabody wrote again complaining that Stewart's work was "mediocre" and that he displayed a "carelessness in dress and in most other things." In February it began to look hopeless.

Stewart was reprimanded for fooling around in chapel, picking strings from a bandage and placing them on Douglas Auchincloss's dark suit. A day later he was back in trouble for "having in his possession what is popularly known as a 'stink bomb,' " as Sherrard Billings put it. Billings threatened to send the boy home, he reported to Avon, but Stewart "begged me in tears to give him another chance." One more such disturbance would get him expelled, Billings warned.

Young Joe arrived from Harvard about this time to assess the situation. He talked to Stewart and some of his friends and to the schoolmasters he knew best. He later wrote to his father that Stewart was suffering from the isolation he felt from being placed in Hundred House—away from his peers. Ignored by the upperclassmen of Hundred House, "Stew has been given too much time to be alone," young Joe wrote. "Consequently he thinks too much, and his whole mind has been slightly warped."

The answer, said Joe, was to get Stewart into Brooks House with his peers and to impress on Groton officials the need for "a small dose of encouragement." The result was Joe Sr.'s February 12 letter of admonition to Sherrard Billings. "I know the boy pretty intimately," the father wrote, "and I am thoroughly convinced, that basically he has the finest character of any of our children. He is a boy that needs a good deal of sympathy and encouragement as his first reaction about everything is, that he cannot do it."

Peabody responded by placing Stewart in Brooks House. His school marks improved, and the severe disciplinary problems diminished. But the letters of complaint continued, focusing on the boy's laziness, indifference, and lack of ambition. When Stewart showed a marked improvement in his grades, bringing his half-term average to 83 and ranking tenth in his form, Billings remained in a carping mood: "Fairly good. I hope he will grow less reserved and more frank and open."

It was too much for Joe Sr. "I had looked forward to being able to show Stewart his report with some encouraging remarks from you," he wrote to Peabody. He was particularly struck, he wrote, by the praise Billings had directed toward his youngest son, John, who had scored an average of only 79 and ranked seventeenth in his form. It was a telling complaint, and Peabody responded: "I am quite prepared to believe that you are right. I will certainly bear in mind your wish that the boy should have encouragement and will act accordingly."

Stewart, meanwhile, repeatedly expressed regret in letters home that he couldn't do better. "I do not believe my next monthly will be good," he wrote. "I have been getting rotten marks lately. I am collecting demerits rather fast." When he saw a 67 average coming on one term, he wrote to Corinne, "Somehow, I've done a horrible thing. . . . Tell father not to be too mad. . . . I'll work harder next term." His confidence was low. "We begin our exams today," he wrote at one point. "I am very scared."

But Stewart's letters also reflected a sense of security about the foundation that Avon and his family represented in his life. Often he was quite jocular, even in letters of remorse about his grades. "The news of the school is as follows: Babies: It was bruted abroad that Mrs. Lynes was to have a new one, but it was found to be no more than a full dinner. . . . Music: A Russian came up and sang folk songs to us. His wife was with him and talked too much. Father would have sympathized. . . ."

Like Joe a few years earlier, Stewart slowly took hold as a Groton boy. After being placed with his form peers in Brooks House he became more sociable with his fellows and eventually more responsive to his schoolmasters. His grades improved, though academic consistency eluded him. He never managed to break into varsity athletics, but increased his activity in intraschool sports. He won a leading role in a school play, receiving favorable notices from the yearbook, and he joined a group called the Groton Gaiety Players, which performed humorous skits to wide acclaim. He contributed to the *Grotonian* and became literary editor in his sixth-form year.

Stewart's *Grotonian* writings displayed neither the erudition nor the stylistic flair of Joe's work, but he demonstrated a robust imagination and a budding passion for politics. With the Depression in full force, his writings betrayed an anger at the "ruling classes" and sympathy for those most hurt by the economic collapse. In a short story called "Defeat," he portrayed with some satisfaction the corporate demise of a "grand old man of Wall Street" who was swept away at a shareholder's meeting and died of a heart attack on the spot. In a review of Edgar Lee Masters's *Lincoln: The Man*, he assailed the author for failing to render an impartial portrait: "This one-sided portrayal of one of our greatest presidents cannot be considered good biography."

As his Groton years neared an end, Stewart set his future sights on Yale. Joe Sr. was pleased, and the rector suggested the boy's interest in literature would be well rewarded by the university's fine English department. So in 1932, as Joe was completing his studies at Harvard and casting about for a suitable calling, Stewart made his way to New Haven and the next stage in his education.

FOR JOE AND Stewart the Groton experience had been seminal. Both had struggled to meet the school's standards and ideals, and despite their difficulties neither ever questioned the validity of the institution as a beacon for well-born youngsters. Though Stewart often rebelled in indirect ways, causing exasperation among Peabody's masters and aggravating his difficulties, his letters home never challenged the school's authority over his thinking, development, or behavior.

Both Joe and Stewart ended up taking a great deal of Groton with them when they left. The school's deep-seated Anglophilia reinforced a sentiment they had grown up with and gave it expression and life. It was apparent in the curriculum, as Stewart noted years later when he wrote that he had received five years of English history at Groton, and no American history. All the boys knew that during the Great War the rector had supported the Allies with every fiber of his being, and Billings had volunteered for duty in France as a chaplain. It was drilled into Grotonians that 475 graduates of the school had served in the war, out of some 680 who were eligible for service. Sons of the school had received 160 decorations or citations. Six had been killed in action, eighteen had died in service, and thirty-six had been wounded. All this, the boys were given to understand, was to protect the Motherland, Great Britain, the wellspring of nearly all of Groton's traditions and ideals.

There was a political undercurrent as well, though this was less explicit. Groton stood for democracy, including American democracy, but its democratic ideals were of a decidedly traditionalist nature. The faculty viewed democracy as the hope of the world, and believed in equal justice, equal opportunity, free speech, and rights of conscience. But there was a suspicion of unchecked masses, and unchecked egalitarianism struck most Groton masters as dangerous political mischief. They placed their faith in a democratic system guided by a dedicated, intelligent, and honest aristocracy fostered by institutions such as Groton. As biographer Frank Ashburn put it, the Groton philosophy "objected to the theory that the average or mediocre is as good as the best."

Nearly every boy who left Groton in those days had it stamped onto his consciousness that the school represented the best. They were the people who would inherit the country and fan out into the upper echelons of politics, finance, law, industry. The evidence was clear. Theodore Roosevelt sent his sons there, as they sent theirs in turn. Franklin Roosevelt was a Grotonian. Many Whitneys and Morgans attended, as did diplomats Sumner Welles and Joseph C. Grew. Scores of less famous graduates ascended to the top levels of the financial and corporate worlds. In the early years, nearly 90 percent of Groton students came from families listed in social registers.

The Alsop family was not listed in the highest social registers, and the boys didn't enjoy the kind of wealth that most of their Groton schoolmates took for granted. But their family heritage and their parents' teachings had imbued them with a sense of the country's natural aristocracy, its training for leadership, and its disinterested commitment to service. Groton was part of all that. And they, being part of Groton, were part of it too.

HARVARD AND YALE

The Search for Identity

TOWARD THE END of his Groton School days, Stewart took up James Boswell's 1,300-page *Life of Samuel Johnson*. Plowing through this masterpiece of biography, he was haunted by a question. Dr. Johnson—the autocratic lexicographer of eighteenth-century London, famous wit, man of a million opinions—reminded Stewart of someone, but he couldn't quite think who it was. Then it came to him. It was his brother Joe. Aside from Johnson's religiosity, Joe Alsop and Sam Johnson seemed whittled from the same timber. Perhaps, thought Stewart, Joe would become "another literary dictator."

Joe had gone through a transformation since enrolling at Harvard in 1928. Though still overweight to an unsightly degree, carrying 230 pounds on his five-foot, nine-inch frame, he had developed a persona that complemented his physique. He became the campus wit for a growing contingent of former boarding school chaps who arrived at Harvard the same autumn. Like Dr. Johnson, he always had an opinion on any topic, and usually expressed it in amusing terms. He made a point of knowing what was going on around campus—who was who, what was considered appropriate dress and behavior, where the parties were—and passed such valuable information on to his friends. He developed a taste for alcohol and discovered its value as social lubricant.

The change was so marked that many of Joe's friends believed he had consciously set about to reinvent himself. He began to accentuate the things that made him distinctive—his theatrical mannerisms, the tossed-off witticisms, and the diction of the British upper classes with elongated vowels and clipped consonants. And he discovered that his peers responded to him now in a way he had never experienced at Groton. They found him amusing, and he reveled in the attention.

Joe lived in a campus dormitory at first, but later moved to one of the fashionable boardinghouses in an area of Cambridge known as the "Gold Coast" because of the relative luxury of its student quarters. On the $200-a-month allowance provided by his father, he could cover all his college expenses and still have plenty left over for socializing around Cambridge or weekend trips to New York and Connecticut. Dick Bissell, who had gone off to Yale to study economics, remembers spending a weekend during his freshman year at Connecticut's New London boat races. There he found Joe, bleary-eyed but exuberant, his seersucker suit rumpled and stained, his shirt wrinkled, his Panama hat askew. Alsop needed a shave and was nursing a hangover. He had been up all night in revelry with his Harvard friends. "He set himself to live the life of the fashionable Harvard undergraduate, to outdo his peers in that department," Bissell recalled.

Probably no campus in America better suited Joe's resolve to redefine himself. Founded in 1636, Harvard was the country's oldest university and probably its most distinguished. Names that rolled off its attendance scroll read like a biographical index of New England: Adams, Leverett, Saltonstall, Sumner, Lowell, Prescott, Coolidge, Peabody, Oliver, Wendell, and Holmes. When Joe arrived, some twenty years after Charles W. Eliot's historic reign as Harvard's president, the perspective was still essentially the one that had informed Eliot's "golden age"—pro-British, partial to social and economic elites in a democratic society, conscious of the Anglo-Saxon role in shaping the country, and wary of the new waves of immigration heading for American shores. It wasn't much different from Endicott Peabody's world view up at Groton.

But Harvard's role was not merely to confirm the standing of America's old families; it was also to confer that standing on new families. Over the years, even as far back as the nineteenth century, there had been a slow but constant decline in the proportion of Harvard men from the country's private prep schools, as the college brought more and more promising high school graduates into the elite it represented. When Joe arrived, prep school graduates accounted for less than 60 percent of the college's enrollment, down from 80 percent in the 1880s.

Like most of his prep school friends, Joe didn't pay much attention to the high school kids, whom the preppies considered socially inferior. This was pure snobbery, of course. But for Joe there was another reason. He had found a formula for social success, which gave him a sense of personal security. When he was in his own circle, he knew he was accepted and appreciated even when he was at his most outlandish. But outsiders might find his pronounced mannerisms and affectations odd, and thus they might reject him. So Joe rejected them first. Toward those he considered friends, Joe was caring, thoughtful, sensitive, dutiful. Toward others, he could be dismissive, insensitive, rude. Most often this behavior went by the name of arrogance, but the more discerning were likely to attribute it to insecurity. Whatever the origin, it would remain with him throughout his life.

Joe's Johnsonian persona was new, but he also continued to cultivate the reputation for precocious erudition that he brought from his Groton days. He had been the first young man ever to get a perfect score on the writing exam Harvard used as part of its entrance criteria. The grading was based on the subjective perceptions of three judges, and that all three had rated an essay as perfect was so startling that Endicott Peabody promptly declared a half-day holiday at Groton to honor Joe's achievement. Stewart and younger brother John, both enrolled at Groton at the time, were pleased at the recognition this brought to their family.

Majoring in English literature, Joe set about getting through all the English classics he had not yet read, along with many of the well-known moderns. He possessed what may have been the only copy on campus of James Joyce's controversial *Ulysses*. Among his English classes, Joe particularly enjoyed the creative writing course taught by Bernard DeVoto, the essayist and critic known for his histories of the American frontier and for his fiction written under the name of John August. Joe honed his abilities with the French language by pursuing French writers in the original—Corneille, Racine, Molière, Proust, Rabelais, and Balzac. He took special delight in the essays of Montaigne, and he even read some of the "enchanting" eighteenth-century pornography of the younger Crebillon, who as literary censor at the court of Louis XV had the happy prerogative of being able to publish just about anything he pleased under his own name.

In the spring of his sophomore year Joe received an honor that demonstrated just how successful he had been in reconstructing his social image. He was tapped for Harvard's hallowed Porcellian Club. At the pinnacle of campus society were the exclusive "final clubs," and at the pinnacle of the final clubs was the Porcellian, the undergraduate citadel of patrician Anglo-Saxon society. Run largely on funds from a hefty endowment, the club owned a spacious building with a large banquet hall complete with a set of lovely porcelain from Paris for four hundred guests. The china displayed the club's boar's-head crest, and throughout the building could be seen quaint porcine figurines in various poses. The drinking exploits of club members were legendary.

Through the years various Cabots, Lodges, Saltonstalls, Roosevelts, and many others of the country's Northeastern elite had been tapped for the Porcellian. When Theodore Roosevelt made it, he wrote to his sister, "Of course, I am delighted to be in, and have great fun up there. . . . My best friends are in it." A generation later, when Roosevelt's daughter Alice married Nicholas Longworth, TR wrote proudly to Germany's Kaiser Wilhem, "Nick and I are both members of the Porc, you know." Franklin Roosevelt, who never made it, once confessed to a friend that missing out on the Porcellian was one of the great disappointments of his life.

But Joe did make it, and present at his first February dinner and breakfast were Massachusetts state Representative Leverett Saltonstall (later to become governor and U.S. senator), U.S. House Speaker Nick Longworth, George Whitney of J. P. Morgan and his brother Richard, president of the New York Stock Exchange. Paul Nitze, who had left Harvard the year Joe arrived and taken a Wall Street job with Dillon, Read and Company, attended the dinner, met Joe, and immediately developed an affection for him. "He had enormous breadth of knowledge," recalled Nitze. "He devoured information—on the arts, on culture, on literature, the world. He was the most civilized, joyous kind of person you could find."

During that February weekend, Joe was assigned to look after Speaker Longworth, now an Alsop cousin through marriage. Though a bit intimidated by the assignment, Joe turned out to be a match for Longworth's famous wit, and the two got along well, aided no doubt by the nine bottles of champagne Longworth bought during the festivities. Following the Sunday events, Joe saw a thoroughly inebriated Longworth off on the overnight train. The next day he read in the evening paper that the speaker had shown up bright and alert for a Monday breakfast meeting with President Hoover.

Through Joe's Harvard connections, and particularly those from the Porcellian, he gained entrée to another exclusive institution of that period and that social stratum—the Long Island dances. These were the extravagant "coming out" parties for the young ladies of social distinction out on Long Island's North Shore. For these spring and autumn celebrations the invitees might number as many as a thousand—all the prominent debutantes of the season, plus at least three young men for each deb, plus all the friends and acquaintances of the parents—all turned out in their most formal finery. A huge tent would be erected in the garden of one of the great North Shore homes, flowers and decorations would be brought in, a large dance floor and bands provided, and champagne and a lavish midnight supper served. An army of waiters, attendants, and cooks would be needed to bring the whole thing together. The cost, according to rumors of the day: from $50,000 to $100,000 in Depression-era money.

Joe was so busy pursuing knowledge and social enjoyment that he had little time or inclination to maintain his personal affairs in anything approaching an orderly manner. His finances were such a hopeless mess by the end of his junior year that he dreaded having to report to his father on the state of his checkbook. He solicited help from the meticulous Dick Bissell, and the two set up a table on the porch of Dick's parents' house. They waded through a box filled with budgetary tidbits of the year past—receipts, check stubs, invoices, unpaid bills. The idea was to go through the contents and somehow bring order to Joe's financial chaos. It took days, but finally they thought they had it pretty well pieced together.

They were wrong. The elder Joe, a shrewd money manager, quickly perceived that the whole thing was a sham. He delivered to Joe a stern lecture on the rudiments of personal finance, but the boys' arduous effort to re-create a nine-month budget retroactively from such a jumble of data became the subject of some ongoing mirth at Avon.

All in all, the Harvard days were happy ones for Joe. He cherished the new friendships he had made and took pride in the identity he was creating for himself. He still wasn't, and never would be, like his cousin Douglas Robinson, the confident athlete and horseman who had intimidated him so knowingly during earlier days at Henderson. But Joe now had a feeling that he knew who he was, and he rather liked who he was.

As Joe's Harvard days approached their end, the question arose in the family: What was he to do now? He had arrived in Cambridge at the height of the Roaring Twenties, when times were good and opportunity abundant. Now, as he approached graduation, the Great Depression gripped the land. Professional opportunities were scarce for young men, even those with impressive academic credentials. And there was the reality of Joe's own temperament and demeanor. Given his difficulty with numbers and finances, it wasn't likely that he would make a success in business. Nor did he seem well suited to the law. What, then?

All this was the subject of a family conference, called without Joe's knowledge, at Grandmother Robinson's big home in Manhattan. Nobody seemed to have any particularly good ideas until Corinne Robinson spoke up. The boy could write well, she observed, and he certainly knew a lot about a lot of things. Perhaps he was suited to the newspaper business. Grandmother noted that she was a close friend of Helen Reid, whose family owned the New York *Herald Tribune* and who pretty much ran the newspaper's business departments. Perhaps she should give Helen a call about the possibility of Joe becoming a reporter at the *Herald Trib*. And so in the summer of 1932, as the Great Depression dragged on and President Hoover struggled to hang on to his job against a political assault from Joe's Roosevelt kin, the young man took his diploma at Harvard and moved to New York to begin a career in the news business.

THREE MONTHS AFTER Joe left the Ivy League to make his way in the world, Stewart arrived. But for Stewart there never was any other school but Yale, the alma mater of his father and grandfather. Indeed, Joe actually had felt it necessary to ask his father's permission before applying to that other Ivy League college up in Cambridge. Given Stewart's difficulties at Groton and his often-thwarted desire to please his parents, he was elated when Yale accepted him, and so was his father. And so in the autumn of 1932 young Stewart, well-meaning as ever and just as prone to trouble, made his way to New Haven.

Yale College in those days brimmed with the spirit of competition. If Harvard taught young men to wear the robes of power with dignity and gentility, Yale's mission was to teach the art of accumulating power—in finance, politics, business, and society generally. As Yale graduate and professor Henry Seidel Canby put it, "[Yale] educated specifically for the harsh competitions of capitalism, for the successful . . . pursuit of the individual of power for himself, for class superiority, and for a success measured by the secure possession of the fruits of prosperity." Canby noted that for Yale undergraduates, the competition for social awards was fiercer even than the competition for academic marks—fiercer, in fact, than anything known in the business world.

And the social awards went to those who rose to the top in campus activities. At Harvard, when the time came to judge potential initiates into the Porcellian and other exclusive clubs, it mattered more who you were, meaning who your parents were and your grandparents. But at Yale more emphasis was placed on campus accomplishment. As that fictional Yalie Dink Stover put it, one had to do something to be someone.

Notwithstanding this nod to the idea of meritocracy, Yale remained an institution for the elite, a preserve of the country's old Anglo-Saxon majority. During the 1930s, fully 75 percent of its students arrived from the nation's Northeastern prep schools. And the underlying philosophy along Grove Street wasn't much different from that of those elite academies. But the tough competitive spirit at Yale was leavened by a strong belief in fair play and an idealistic approach to religion and patriotism. In rising to the top, the aim was to remain worthy not only of the ascent but of the social position that was the final prize.

Stewart arrived in New Haven with seven Groton classmates (twenty went on to Harvard, four to Princeton, and six elsewhere), and the group quickly decided to stick together. They all joined Zeta Psi fraternity. "In the matter of prestige and kudos it's tied for about third on the campus," Stewart wrote to Avon. But when Pa, citing financial pressures born of the Depression, balked at paying the $285 fraternity charges, Stewart felt stung. "I don't know if you helped Joe with his Porcellian initiation, and anyway I realize that that was a different situation because this is such a lean year," he wrote home. "If your tightening of the purse strings is due to disappointment that I didn't make either of the big shot fraternities, rather than to honest penury, I can only say that I really did my best in utilizing whatever slight talents I may have, and nobody can do more than that."

The letter typified Stewart's characteristic lack of confidence. It turned out that his father already had deposited $200 to his account to help cover the fraternity fees. But he advised in his next letter that they "really ought to have a talk on the whole situation" the next time Stewart was home.

The elder Alsop took pains to avoid adding to Stewart's sense of inferiority. At the same time, whenever Stewart disappointed his father, Joe Sr. made sure his son understood why. When Stewart's negligence led to a mixup on an important payment to Yale, his father chastised him. "Had you paid any attention to my remark to you that I had not received the bill," he wrote, "the expense of the telegram and the trouble might have been avoided." He also complained that Stewart had left his car in the yard when he had departed for school, and Joe Sr. had had to go out and put it away. But he closed his letter with a kind of paternal wink: "All the above makes you very popular with your affectionate father . . ."

Stewart declared English literature as his major subject and pursued French as his second language. His marks were respectable, but not much more. "None of us really applied ourselves terribly hard," recalled Dillon Ripley, a classmate and friend who went on to become head of the Smithsonian Institution in Washington. In his freshmen year, Stewart scored 85 in history, 80s in English, French, and Latin, and 70 in biology.

Stewart took learning seriously, but concentrated more on his social life. At the start of his sophomore year, brother John arrived from Groton, and the two became inseparable on the undergraduate social scene. They lived in a house called Davenport College and shared many friends there. The brothers refined an old skit they had developed for relatives during summers at Henderson House, and soon they found themselves in demand at parties as a kind of instant vaudeville act. It was a parody of Robert Browning's dramatic idyll "Ivan Ivanovitch," the story of a Russian woman and her children hurrying home to their village in a horse-drawn sleigh. In the dead of the frigid night she is beset by a pack of wolves, and to save herself she sacrifices her children, one by one, to their hunger. When she finally arrives childless in the village, her enraged husband buries a carpenter's ax in her head.

Stewart would begin their parody with an introduction rendered in an authentic but comical Russian accent and filled with irreverent asides. Then, playing the Russian mother while John played the wolves, he and his brother would gallop around the room enacting the tragic events and tossing off funny lines as they went. In their highly theatrical impersonations, the more seriously they seemed to take the whole thing the funnier they became. The humor generated by the skit stemmed in part from the socially outrageous effort to make light of such a serious story—to puncture Browning's intent to shock—by demonstrating just how unrealistic the tale seemed, at least to privileged young Americans gathered over cocktails and laughter in New Haven or Manhattan drawing rooms.

Stewart enjoyed performing before an audience and continued his interest in dramatics at Yale. He had significant parts in nine college performances during his college tenure, and he served on the executive board of the Dramat Club during his senior year.

Like Joe, Stewart and John took delight in the New York social scene, particularly at "coming out" time in the spring and fall. They would travel to Manhattan by car or train and make contact with their cousin and friend from Henderson House summers, Dottie Robinson. Dottie had attended a fashionable finishing school in Virginia called Foxcroft, and she always had plenty of her school friends at her mother's big house on Seventy-ninth Street. Dottie's attractive debutante friends and the carefree Alsop boys hit it off instantly. She recalled years later that she frequently received phone calls from friends planning a group excursion on the town. They would ask, "Do you have a free Alsop for the evening?" Dottie's house often served as a tea-time meeting place where the young people would plan the evening's activities.

Stewart's social exploits sometimes got him into trouble. As a freshman, he was placed on probation for exceeding his allowance of absences from class. On another occasion he and a friend met two young ladies at the York Athletic Club in New Haven and offered to drive them to Bridgeport in search of adventure. Influenced by large quantities of the York AC's free-flowing gin, Stewart drove erratically and a bit recklessly. Attempting to pass a truck, he veered too close and scraped the outstretched arm of one of the girls. After he had driven her to the New Haven Hospital, her two brothers showed up in angry pursuit of the "college punks," and the two Yalies beat a retreat to the sanctuary of campus. The evening's exploits caused Joe Sr.'s insurance rates to double.

In his senior year, Stewart twice was suspended from campus. In November he joined a group of drunken undergraduates who broke into a fraternity house "and made a nuisance of themselves, to such an extent that the Campus Police had to eventually interfere in the affair," as Dean Clarence Mendell wrote to Avon. Stewart was sent home for a week.

In late May, as the campus was preparing for the end of the term and the big 1936 commencement, Stewart took a young woman into a closed fraternity house at five thirty a.m. Both, as Dean Mendell reported to Avon, were "under the influence of liquor." Stewart was suspended for a month, which meant he couldn't graduate with his peers and had to wait until fall to get his diploma.

Thus Stewart's college career ended with a whimper. His four years at New Haven had been marked by a resolve to kick up his heels in a manner never allowed at Groton. Stewart didn't rise to the upper reaches of the academic register; nor did he emerge as a social standout as measured by entry into exclusive clubs such as Skull and Bones, Yale's answer to Harvard's Porcellian. But he absorbed learning easily, and the expansion of his knowledge was greater than was evidenced by his academic marks. In his major subject, English, he consistently was placed in honors courses; in his junior year he ranked third among honors English students.

And Stewart was highly popular among his peers. These included many with bright futures. The Class of '36 included Robert McCormick of the Chicago McCormicks, Whitelaw Reid of the *Herald Tribune* Reids, future famous writers Brendan Gill and John Hersey, future foreign policy expert Walt W. Rostow, and a young Quaker named David Dellinger, who three decades later would emerge as a leading antiwar activist.

Unlike Joe, who had left Harvard four years before with a clear sense of who he was and what he wanted to do, Stewart, in his search for identity, hadn't found much of a direction through his college experience. Not only did he leave Yale without a diploma, he left without any clear sense of how he was going to attain the Rooseveltian ideal of success that Corinne had tried so long to impress into his consciousness.

Yale's 1936 yearbook reported that Stewart harbored an ambition to enter the advertising business, or perhaps to practice law, "in which case he expects to study at the University of Virginia." He did not follow either of these career courses. Times were tough and jobs scarce in 1936, and it proved necessary for most young men to land where they could. For Stewart, that would mean the book-publishing business in New York, where Uncle Ted Roosevelt had become vice president of a big publishing house called Doubleday, Doran. In the summer, Stewart moved to Manhattan, where Joe had arrived four years earlier. But now Joe was gone; his career path had led him south to Washington.

5

THE *HERALD TRIBUNE*

Mastering the Elements
of the Reporter's Trade

OF ALL THE newspapers in America in 1932, none had a pedigree to match that of the New York *Herald Tribune*. Its journalistic genealogy stretched back to 1835, when James Gordon Bennett founded the New York *Herald* as a lively penny paper fueled by a passion for fresh news and an eye for the latest production technology. Bennett paid his reporters well enough to recruit the best, and ran up huge telegraph bills to assure the hottest information. He pioneered coverage of New York's high society, and sent fast boats to intercept Atlantic passenger ships and return with the latest European news. Later, the founder's impetuous son sent a reporter named Stanley after a lost African explorer named Livingstone. And the *Herald* scooped all competitors on the 1876 Custer massacre, getting fifty thousand words into print before any other paper even got wind of the story.

If Bennett's paper gave the *Herald Tribune* its heritage of newsgathering aggressiveness and sprightly demeanor, Horace Greeley's *Tribune*, founded in 1841, gave it an image of seriousness and civic propriety. To Greeley, the central role of a newspaper was that of conscience for its time. Greeley's aim was to monitor public men and instruct readers on the imperatives of civic enterprise. He attacked the Mexican War, jabbed at Tammany Democrats, railed against the evils of slavery. Greeley spoke in the language of moral outrage and moral courage, and when the Republican Party emerged as a political force in the 1850s it quickly became his chosen instrument of national salvation.

By the 1930s, nearly a century after its founding, the New York *Tribune* had had just three editors: Greeley; Whitelaw Reid, who bought the paper in 1872 upon the founder's death; and Reid's son, Ogden, who took over in 1912. Ogden Reid, distinguished-looking and well-meaning but largely ineffectual, had the wit to marry a diminutive firecracker of a woman who had been his mother's personal assistant. It was Helen Rogers Reid, vice president of the newspaper and its guiding force on the business side, who in 1924 negotiated the purchase of the *Herald* by the *Tribune*. The $5 million purchase sum was provided by Ogden's mother, Elisabeth, whose vast wealth had kept the *Tribune* alive through decades of relentless red ink.

In 1932, the paper was on the threshold of its highest glory. Daily circulation had grown to more than 300,000, with nearly half a million readers buying its fat Sunday editions. The paper actually was turning a small profit even as the Depression ravaged the nation's economy. It was also cutting a large swath through the city. Though its circulation was only about 70 percent of that of the metropolitan leader, *The New York Times*, it generally was considered better written than the Times, more diverse in its coverage, more vibrant in capturing the sometimes raw, sometimes heroic, sometimes absurd life of the city.

At the big *Herald Tribune* building on West Fortieth Street, Geoffrey Parsons was considered the city's best editorial writer. Stanley Woodward ran the best sports section in town, if not the country. The paper had recently acquired the influential voice of columnist Walter Lippmann. The city editor, Stanley Walker, was a legend in American newspaper circles. The *Herald Tribune* could boast of an extensive foreign staff, with well-known bylines coming in from Moscow, Berlin, London, Paris. From Washington came the analytical dispatches of author and historian Mark Sullivan. And the paper's feature writers were famous for crisp prose and a novelist's eye for detail.

Into this journalistic milieu in 1932 waddled young Joe Alsop of Groton and Harvard. City editor Walker, surveying the young man's girth, fancy tailor-made clothes, and affected British mannerisms, suggested to an assistant that the foppish Alsop was "a perfect example of Republican inbreeding." He inquired about whether he had any discretion as to the hiring of the young man. He didn't, and so on July 5 Joe reported for work as an $18-a-week reporter.

Joe's introduction to the business was not auspicious. He spent days just gaining a proficiency with the typewriter. Sent out on assigment into New York's darker reaches, he recoiled at such proximity to the canaille of the city. An inevitable focus of the resentment of legions of copyboys who had toiled for years in hopes of landing a reporter's slot, Joe heightened the resentment by treating them like servants. "Boy, get me a pencil," he once yelled to copyboy Barrett McGurn, later a leading *Herald Trib* foreign correspondent. As Stanley Walker reminisced a few years later, "For two or three months he floundered."

One day Joe was given the routine assignment of writing a "canned" obit of Mrs. Benjamin Harrison, the former president's wife. Alsop studied the contents of the paper's obituary page, researched his subject, and tossed into the copy basket a tidy account of the woman's life. Grabbing the piece some time later, night editor Lessing Engelking read it with puzzlement. He called Alsop over.

"When did Mrs. Harrison die, anyway? Or did she die?" he asked.

"I assume so," said Joe.

In fact, the woman remained very much alive. Joe, misunderstanding the assignment, had neglected to indicate on his copy that it was a canned obit and shouldn't run until after her death.

Yet he showed early promise as a newsman. He couldn't be intimidated, even by the most highly placed of public figures. He had a fine eye for the telling detail that captures a situation or a personality. He was relentless in pursuit of a story. And he demonstrated a natural facility for highly literate and descriptive prose. "Suddenly, he found himself," recalled Walker.

The city editor, a tough and tireless Texan with a sardonic wit and a taste for Scotch whisky, particularly liked good features that captured the flavor and tempo of his vast and yeasty city. They added spice, he felt, to the otherwise serious coverage that packed the paper's pages. Joe quickly grasped the elements of feature writing—the human interest focus, the revealing detail, the light touch, the wry overstatement, an occasional hint of satire.

On September 16, 1934, he filed a simple tale about a magistrate and his young daughter, "a pretty, black-haired girl, who is one of the principal ornaments at grade 5-B at Public School 186." The daughter, sitting in court behind her father, "watched the flotsam and jetsam of the variegated petty law breakers of the city pass before the bench." She perked up when a young newsboy named Rubal Cohen, who looked like a "Broadway racing tipster," pleaded guilty to the crime of shooting craps in the street. Joe's effort won him a byline and front-page display the next day:

Magistrate Benjamin E. Greenspan, long a specialist in the dramas of the courtroom, took his daughter, Sarah, ten years old, into the supporting cast yesterday to help him illustrate a lecture to a dice-shooting newsboy with apt references to the immortal works of the late Horatio Alger . . .

Mr. Greenspan was cast for the biggest talking part. Miss Sarah's advice-giving was all the more effective for being generally unobtrusive. . . . [Upon hearing Cohen plead guilty, the magistrate became agitated.]

"I'm amazed to have a newsboy plead guilty to such a charge. Why, newsboys have risen to some of the most exalted positions in the land—Governors, Mayors, Supreme Court Justices, big business heads. Think of them."

Cohen, a middle-sized youth with a slick knowing face and a Broadway cut suit of clothes, stood in apparent thought, at a loss for a reply.

Meanwhile, the sleeves of the magistrate's ample black robe seemed to be violently agitated. The top of Miss Sarah Greenspan's head appeared above the desk parapet. Her father bent down to her in response to the tugs. . . . There was whispering. At length, Magistrate Greenspan straightened himself, visibly inspired.

"Do you know Horatio Alger?" he inquired.

"No, sir. I never heard about him," replied the slightly bewildered Cohen.

"What?" cried Magistrate Greenspan. "You never heard of Horatio Alger. You never read the story, 'From Newsboy to Bank President'?"

"No, sir, I didn't ever," said Cohen. More sleeve pulling ensued. The Magistrate bent his head to whisper to his miniature Portia and bobbed up once more.

"Do you mean to say you've never read the story of 'Ragged Dick'?" said the newly informed magistrate.

"No, sir," was the only answer.

"Young man, I would advise you to read those great books of Alger's, to study and mark them well," Greenspan went on.

[Greenspan then tells of another newsboy he knew when he was a probation officer.] "It was a tragic story. He died in the electric chair because of a fondness for shooting craps. It came about one day that he had no money to play, and he committed a hold-up in a store. Accidentally, he shot and killed the poor proprietor. He was arrested, tried, and convicted, and he went to the electric chair and burned because he wanted to shoot dice. Do you want to die in the electric chair?"

The magistrate's periods had rolled out more and more sternly, until his final question seemed to be more a prophesy than a request for information. The by-now definitely be-fogged Cohen was too worried by the perorations to make his "no, sir" more than a whisper.

"Well, then," said Magistrate Greenspan, "let this be a lesson to you. I will suspend sentence on you . . . , but don't let me catch you at it again."

[Cohen and three accomplices] emitted an audible and simultaneous sigh of relief, and . . . departed at top speed. As they walked out of the court, Miss Sarah Greenspan was observed gently patting her hands together. So delighted with the little moral scene was she that she sat on til recess at 12:30 without a fidget.

Joe spent his afternoons and evenings on such assignments. He visited Central Park "Hoovervilles" where homeless Depression victims had pitched tents and erected tarpaper shacks; handled the "color" pieces at political picnics; interviewed celebrities in their posh hotel rooms. He wrote profiles of Gertrude Stein and Henri Matisse—the French painter amused him with his heavily accented French and excited expressions of appreciation for the Central Park Zoo's black panther, which he considered the most beautiful thing in New York. Joe interviewed actress Tallulah Bankhead at the Waldorf-Astoria as she nibbled on caviar retrieved from the flank of an enormous ice-sculpted fish. With an amusing but unflattering profile of Louella Parsons, he won the undying enmity of Hearst's famous Hollywood writer. And he was rewarded with a regular flow of bylines in a newspaper that parceled out such recognition with parsimony.

Joe also branched out into other parts of the newspaper, particularly the Sunday book-review section. His erudition and literate style made him a natural critic, and even before he emerged as a top feature writer he was getting occasional bylines over book reviews on Sundays. A young reporter named John Bogart, whose desk was directly across the aisle from Joe's, recalled him poring over a new multivolume translation of Proust's writings and pecking away at his typewriter. Bogart was duly impressed when the review by this studious young man received prominent display in the book section a few weeks later.

Joe enjoyed his work at the paper and the recognition it brought him, but he knew the real *Herald Trib* stars were those who wrote stories about momentous events, not lighthearted features or heavy literary meditations. He yearned to apply his journalistic talents to the coverage of politics. Henry Cabot Lodge II had suggested such a channel for Joe's ambitions, before Lodge left the *Herald Trib*'s editorial-page staff to return to Massachusetts and a political career. He had said that Joe possessed a natural talent for political news and should seek opportunities in that direction.

But Joe didn't quite know how to go about it. At one point, after he had filled in for veteran feature writer Ben Robertson for several weeks and seen his own byline more and more frequently, he worried that his exposure in the paper would decline upon Robertson's return. Perhaps that would be a good time to seek a clean break. "Had I best just go along as I am, which will be rather less satisfying anyway, since Ben gets back today, or in three or four months time, when I really begin to know the ropes, ask Mr. Walker to let me have a crack at political stuff?" he wrote to Lodge. He felt a bit inadequate to the challenge of general news, and worried that he might give up a good thing for something less satisfying. "Perhaps features are more repaying than general news," he mused in his letter to Lodge. "I do feel that I need an enormous amount of practice in general news, however, which is more likely to come my way now since the feature supply for me will decrease . . ."

Despite his frustrated ambitions, Joe continued to enjoy his work. He made many friends at the paper and took delight in entertaining them at his spacious apartment on Manhattan's East Eighty-fourth Street. He shared the three-bedroom, three-bath apartment with Bill Patten, one of his closest friends from Harvard. Patten was working as a runner on Wall Street, and together they hired a Japanese man named Buto to look after the place and cook for them. The apartment cost $85 a month.

This was not much of a financial stretch for Joe despite his meager *Herald Tribune* salary. His father provided him an allowance of $100 a month, and as his writing gained notice in the city he managed to supplement his income with freelance articles written for various middle-brow New York magazines. Eventually these activities enabled him to make ends meet even without the paternal allowance; his *Herald Tribune* salary served as little more than pocket money. Besides his lavish entertaining, he wore expensive gabardine suits and handmade shoes.

Since Joe's workday began in the afternoon, he could have friends in for lunch at Eighty-fourth Street before he headed to the office—if he could get up in time following his social exploits of the night before. Richard Bissell remembers arriving for an appointed luncheon to find Joe shaving in preparation for the meal.

"Buto," he yelled intermittently throughout their conversation, "I need another brandy."

His evening parties brought his *Herald Tribune* friends together with Patten's Wall Street friends and the flatmates' holdover companions from Groton and Harvard. The Scotch would flow, the meals were always prepared with special flair, and after dinner the guests would linger for hours over poker or crap-shooting games of the kind that Magistrate Greenspan considered so threatening to the character of young men.

When not entertaining at home, Joe was likely to be found taking his supper at a venerable midtown institution known as Bleeck's, officially labeled on the sign outside as the Artist and Writers Club. Located at 213 West Fortieth Street, it served as the quasi-official clubhouse for *Herald Tribune* writers, as well as for notables from the literary and drama worlds of the day. Novelist John O'Hara called it "a kind of cave inhabited by giants of journalism." To Lucius Beebe, the *Herald Tribune*'s drama critic and resident boulevardier, it was "an arena fragrant with the souvenirs of mighty contests with bottles, wits and fists." To legions of *Herald Tribune* reporters, it was known simply as "downstairs."

Bleeck's featured mahogany-paneled walls, a stuffed sailfish purportedly caught by banker J. P. Morgan, furniture in what one wit called "early Butte, Montana, style," and the best broiled chicken in town. It was run by owner John Bleeck (pronounced "Blake"), a ruddy, white-maned Dutchman who wouldn't hesitate to keep a national celebrity waiting for a table if a lowly *Herald Tribune* reporter needed one at the same time. Stanely Walker could round up a team of eager, if slightly inebriated, scribes to cover a late-breaking story by just calling down-stairs—assuming he wasn't there already knocking down Scotch with his charges. Even Ogden Reid, the shy owner and editor of the paper, could be seen in the place with predictable frequency, buying drinks for his reporters, projecting his booming laugh over the din of the establish-ment, getting a sudden idea for an editorial and ceremoniously reaching for his pen so he could write it as he stood at the bar.

Joe loved the place. There he could be found with his closest *Herald Trib* friends—John Lardner, Lardner's cousin Richard Tobin, movie critic Richard Watts, and others—happily running up the tab as his companions polished off their drinks. Though his friends found him so-ciable and generous, others considered him haughty and unpleasant. "He was arrogant in an Alsopian way," recalled Homer Bigart, the chief copyboy who later became one of the century's leading war correspon-dents. "He never went out of his way to be likable." As always, Joe di-vided people into two groups—his friends, for whose friendship the price was never too high, and all others, for whom he had little time or courtesy.

He always had plenty of time and courtesy when Ogden Reid stopped by Bleeck's. There was a touch of the sycophant in young Alsop, and he frequently managed to maneuver himself into the editor's conver-sation to make sure the head man knew who he was. One evening at dinner, Reid, under the spell of too much spiritous liquor, collapsed face-down into his soup. Others around the table hesitated to rouse him for fear he would regain consciousness amid embarrassment at having been saved from drowning at table by one of his own reporters. But Joe reached over with an air of confidence and compassion and pulled the editor's head out of the soup.

It was easy to have compassion for Ogden Reid, a kind and sociable man who never looked down on others despite his immense wealth and uppercrust breeding. He carried himself in his role as owner with a bearing that bespoke a deep regard for his newspaper as a public trust, as an institution of a free people that transcended the lives of individ-ual citizens, even such as himself. But he was a limited man—limited by an ordinary intellect, by shyness and lack of human spark, and by a hopeless addiction to alcohol. The *Herald Trib* folks at Bleeck's liked old "Oggie" Reid, even appreciated him, but he didn't command respect.

Helen Reid was something else entirely. Tiny, energetic, imaginative, she drove advertising sales to ever-new heights and kept the business de-partments running smoothly. She founded a nationally known annual forum on public policy problems, and added to her newspaper's fame in the process. Though Ogden kept her at a distance from the city room, she managed to wield enough influence to refashion the image of the newspaper, from one of hidebound conservatism to what might be called progressive Republicanism. This she accomplished by pushing for the elevation of various gifted personalities into key roles at the paper— Walter Lippmann and Dorothy Thompson as columnists, Irita Van Doren as literary editor, Geoffrey Parsons as editorial-page editor.

As the New Deal took shape, the *Herald Tribune* became the voice of loyal and responsible opposition, a political outlook that recognized that naysaying required proposals for reasoned alternatives. Defender of internationalism and American free enterprise, the paper was the voice of the Eastern Republican establishment, as hostile to New Deal liberalism as it was suspicious of Midwestern isolationism.

The paper's philosophy matched the political outlook of the elder Joe Alsop and Corinne up in Avon, and of grandmother Corinne Robinson and most of her Roosevelt kin. Joe Jr. was generally sympathetic as well—but he found himself increasingly intrigued by the New Deal initiatives of his mother's distant cousin in the White House. On weekend trips home he argued endlessly with his father over Franklin Roosevelt's policies and programs, and soon he discovered that his political outlook was changing. Back in New York, he longed to get to Washington to cover the fascinating ramifications of New Deal policy.

His break came when Walker sent him to Flemington, New Jersey, as part of the *Herald Tribune*'s team covering the sensational murder trial of Bruno Richard Hauptmann, accused of stealing and killing the tiny baby of American aviation hero Charles A. Lindbergh and his wife, the poet and writer Anne Morrow Lindbergh. For six weeks beginning in early January 1935 the trial progressed, followed in every detail by more than three hundred newsmen. The Hearst organization alone sent thirty reporters, plus a contingent of photographers. The nation's attention was riveted on the daily dispatches from the little Hunterdon County Courthouse, as a juggernaut of prosecutorial talent homed in on the hapless German immigrant, and the flamboyant defense lawyer, Edward J. Reilly of Brooklyn, struggled to keep his client's accusers off balance. The *Herald Tribune* devoted three or four advertising-free pages to the trial nearly every day.

Joe's job was to observe the verbal combat between lawyers and witnesses and produce sidebar material capturing the scenes, personalities, and tensions of the crowded courtroom. These stories would accompany the daily leads produced by veteran reporter Joseph F. Driscoll. With so little courtroom space for the news contingent, second-stringer Alsop found himself sitting on a radiator throughout most of the trial.

Joe produced eight bylined stories during the trial, including two that represented substantial reporting skill and aggressiveness. He rendered a detailed description of Hauptmann's breakdown back in his cell after he had been sentenced to death. And he recounted in riveting detail the police methods used in tracking down Hauptmann over the course of a two-and-a-half-year manhunt. But most of his stories were what the news business calls color pieces. When defense lawyer Reilly called a flamboyant Bronx taxi driver to the stand, Joe captured the man and the moment:

> FLEMINGTON, N.J., Feb. 6 — A song-writing taxi driver, noted in his Bronx circle as an amateur actor and dancer, was the ticketed offering of Edward J. Reilly, chief defense counsel, on the witness stand this morning. His name was Philip Moses; his list of occupations was so long it had a faint flavor of the old butcher, baker, candlestick maker game, and only chance prevented him from giving an imitation of Will Rogers to edify the courtroom where Bruno Richard Hauptmann is on trial for the murder of the Lindbergh baby.
>
> He did actually get as far as pulling his hair down over his forehead in the famous Rogers manner, but a hurried question from Attorney General David T. Wilentz prevented him from going into his routine.

When a pathetic Mrs. Hauptmann took the stand, Joe wrote:

> FLEMINGTON, N.J., Jan. 29 — Mrs. Anna Hauptmann, a woman prematurely aged by hard work, hard saving and the sudden crumbling away of her respectable little world, worked hard today to defend her husband, Richard, as she calls him, against a charge of brutal murder. . . . She did her humble best, and when Hauptmann rebuked her for a mistake during a recess, she answered with a docile "I'll try to do better next time."

And when Hauptmann himself took the stand, Joe brought to his profile not only the literate style for which he had become well known, but also a penetrating grasp of what passed before him:

> FLEMINGTON, N.J., Jan. 24 — Bruno Richard Hauptmann, so long publicized as the dark "mystery man" of his own trial, stepped down from the witness stand today still something of an enigma, but one of a new sort. Instead of a creature of inhuman malevolence, he seemed no more than a simple Bronx carpenter of German extraction, fond of music and the outdoors and given to saving money in a penny-pinching way. The enigmatic thing was the great pall of suspicion hanging over such an ordinary-appearing man.
>
> After all the talk of the strangeness of his eyes and the sinister composure of his demeanor, his testimony had exactly the effect that would be produced if the actor cast for Hamlet's tragic attitudinizings suddenly began playing Polonius.

It was a plum assignment. After a day on the courtroom radiator and an evening of writing, he would announce to anyone within hearing that he must go and change his "linens." Shortly thereafter he would re-emerge from his rented room to lead a contingent of New York reporters on a new adventure in locating a decent eating place. His best success was in finding an ancient country inn serving old-fashioned family-style dinners as well as a drink made with applejack called a "stone fence." The stone fences were "thoroughly lethal," as he recalled years later, which only served to draw the gang back for repeat adventures.

Joe's Flemington performance gave him added stature back in the *Herald Tribune* city room, and before the year was out he was on his way to the capital to cover the U.S. Senate. It turned out to be a momentous development in Joe Alsop's career, for in Washington he discovered the perfect environment for his particular blend of interests, traits, and talents.

JOE GOES TO WASHINGTON

"He Is Himself a Roosevelt"

When Joe arrived in the nation's capital in late 1935, he encountered two intertwined cities, political Washington and social Washington. Political Washington was a city of change, spreading a governmental revolution across the land. It was dominated by Franklin Roosevelt, the cunning, determined, good-natured president called forth by the crisis of the Depression. The fervent New Dealers he had set loose on the country were bent on remaking the nation, and three years into the Roosevelt presidency the New Deal party remained firmly in control. Congress and the courts had brought some restraint to the new regime, but a robust momentum still inspired the Roosevelt "Brain Trust." The new bureaucracy of alphabet soup agencies was in harness. Labor, organized and militant, was on the march. "Economic royalists" and "malefactors of great wealth" served as administration whipping boys. As the 1936 elections loomed, Roosevelt divided voters along economic lines to an extent rarely before seen.

Social Washington was a city suspended in time, almost impervious to the larger societal and political forces engendered by the Great War and the Great Depression. It was the domain of a local elite known as "cave dwellers," a hundred or so families, mainly of Anglo-Saxon heritage, with immense wealth and social standing in major world capitals. They stood for the preservation of the mores and folkways that had guided their forebears for generations. They lived in grand houses overlooking the circles and parks of urban Washington, and held sumptuous dinner parties that unfolded according to protocol stretching back for generations. They lived confidently in their world of tradition and continuity, with little thought that this world might soon be gone, that their great houses would be sold, donated to charitable causes, or pulled down to make way for office buildings.

Joe quickly gained access to the upper reaches of both Washingtons. Entrée to political Washington was his blood relationship with the occupants of the White House. Corinne Alsop, though a steadfast Republican, had maintained friendly relations with her cousin Eleanor and developed a fondness for her distant cousin Franklin that had deepened with the advance of his career. Not even Corinne's decision to second the presidential nomination of Kansas Governor Alf Landon at the 1936 Republican convention had dampened the friendship between Corinne and the president. At social gatherings, the two sparred in mock political outrage, and often they could be seen in a corner laughing uproariously at each other's political humor and gossip.

Even Joe Sr., who despised most everything Franklin Roosevelt stood for, enjoyed having a friend at such a lofty station. In a "Dear Franklin" letter to the president in early 1933, Joe had suggested that Roosevelt's farm policies might ease the plight of New England's tobacco growers. The president had written back inviting Joe to discuss the matter with his agriculture secretary and Federal Farm Board chairman. "If you show them this note I know that they will be very happy to see you," Roosevelt wrote. "I hope, too, that when you come to Washington you will run in and see Eleanor and myself."

The Alsops did visit the White House whenever they were in Washington, and often enjoyed social evenings with the First Family and their friends. Once, after dinner, Cousin Franklin led his guests down to watch a movie in the White House theater, and Corinne ended up seated next to him. After the film, when the lights came up, Corinne and Cousin Franklin immediately struck up an animated conversation while the other guests, observing protocol, remained glued to their chairs, waiting for the president to rise. Finally Joe Sr., visibly angry, pried his wife away from her friend.

Upon his arrival in Washington, young Joe was invited to a New Year's Eve celebration at the White House. There he mingled with important New Deal figures in the upstairs oval room as the jaunty president scooted across the floor in his wheelchair and mixed cocktails for his guests. When Joe was asked to join the First Family each year for Christmas dinner, it posed a dilemma. He hated to miss those wonderful Avon Christmases that Corinne made so jovial, but a White House yuletide was not to be passed up. "On the whole I like better coming up for a family week-end, and then, on Christmas, making my annual expedition into the family life of the White House," he wrote to Avon.

Social Washington also opened its doors to Joe. He came under the tutelage of Mrs. Dwight Davis, a grande dame in Washington society who had been a close friend of the Alsop family and a leading figure in the women's movement against Prohibition. Pauline Davis taught the young man how to dress for a formal dinner and how to observe the required etiquette. Joe nonetheless looked a sorry sight in his ill-fitting rented white tie and tails as he made his way to his first Washington party at the Sheridan Circle home of a Mrs. Keep. Determined to avoid embarrassment, he struggled with the social customs of the day. He learned that at the door he was to take a small card instructing him on whom he would "take in" when guests entered the dining hall, two by two, in a long line called a "crocodile." He learned that no drinks were served until the last guest had arrived; glances of opprobrium greeted the poor soul who came late. Seating arrangements at table always followed a stringent protocol, with the most distinguished company seated at the ends and guests of uncertain rank congregated at the center.

At the Keep mansion, Joe mingled with Chief Justice Charles Evans Hughes, numerous senators and diplomats, and an elegant old gentleman who turned out to be the son of General George McClellan and hence the godson of Joe's great-grandfather. After dinner, the men retreated for brandy and cigars and political talk. The guest of honor, observing form, departed promptly at eleven o'clock, after which the usual bridge games and abundant flows of champagne commenced.

Joe became a regular on the circuit of social Washington. His large frame and conversational dexterity gave him an appearance of maturity that exceeded his twenty-five years, and the older ladies developed a fondness for him. Corinne's cousin, Alice Roosevelt Longworth, daughter of Theodore Roosevelt and widow of House Speaker Nicholas Longworth, took an instant liking to the fat young man given to flourishes of expression and a biting wit. "Mrs. L," as Joe called her, displayed a savage wit herself and delighted in turning it upon the high and mighty of Washington. She filled her large Massachusetts Avenue house with the most amusing of the town's leading lights, and frequently included young Joe among her guests.

Joe's social progress became a matter of interest to other Washington grandes dames whose names dotted the newspaper society pages and who possessed the power to confer social status. Virginia Bacon, whose forebears included the fourth earl of Dunmore and a colonial governor of Virginia, presided over a mansion at 1801 F Street where Chief Justice John Marshall had once lived. Her husband, Robert, descended from an early New England family, lived on inherited wealth and served in Congress through most of the 1920s and 1930s. Edith Eustis, daughter of a former New York governor and U.S. vice president, lived in a mansion called Corcoran House overlooking Lafayette Park. One of her nephews was Charles E. Bohlen, known to his friends as Chip, who had been a few years ahead of Joe at Harvard and a fellow Porcellian. Joe and Chip became acquainted through club functions and developed a close friendship. At one point Joe wrote to Chip, "I have just taken a tiny little house in Georgetown with a double guest-room which I am tentatively naming Bohlensnest."

Edith Eustis took a particular interest in Joe because of his Bohlen connection. Though by all outward appearances a woman of propriety, she had a penchant for mischief. During the First World War, she had made her country home available for afternoon trysts between young Franklin Roosevelt, then assistant navy secretary, and his mistress, Lucy Mercer.

Another of the grandes dames, Mildred Bliss, presided over Dumbarton Oaks, a forty-three-acre estate on the northern edge of Georgetown. Her husband, Robert, a Harvard man, had served major diplomatic assignments in posts such as Paris, Saint Petersburg, and Buenos Aires before moving to Washington in 1933. The Blisses' wealth was of relatively recent vintage—Mildred was related to the West Coast Barnes family, which gave the country Castoria, a major laxative of the day—but they mixed comfortably with the old-wealth cave dwellers and gained respectability through generous charitable giving.

Joe's travels through social Washington were fueled by his connection to the country's old-family establishment. The key was lineage; members of the Anglo-Saxon ascendancy stuck together. And through his access to this society, Joe emerged as a young man of note around town, and became friends with some of Washington's most powerful figures.

Although he frequented the great houses of the city, his own quarters were modest. He took a room in an old boarding house at 1718 H Street presided over by an elderly couple known simply as James and Julia. Another boarder was Michael Straight, a young, British-educated State Department official whose parents had founded *The New Republic* and whose eccentric mother maintained a famous literary salon in New York. George Summerlin, the State Department's chief of protocol and a social gadabout, lived there, along with a banker named Major Heath. James prepared breakfast every morning and placed atop each napkin a copy of *The Washington Post*, which the boarders read over coffee to the sounds of Major Heath swearing over yet another New Deal outrage.

The *Herald Tribune* office where Joe reported for work was a cramped suite of rooms in the old National Press Building on F Street, presided over by a kindly journalistic pro named Albert L. Warner. Like Stanley Walker, Warner greeted the overweight and foppish Alsop with ill-disguised skepticism. But he sent Joe to the Hill to cover the second installment of the Nye hearings on the country's munitions merchants and their Wall Street backers. The hearings reflected and reinforced the isolationism that represented the country's prevalent foreign policy sentiment of the day.

The star of the show was Gerald Nye, Republican of North Dakota and chairman of the Senate Munitions Investigating Subcommittee. He was a rustic progressive, an advocate of nationalizing troublesome industries, a tireless friend to thousands of German-born Dakota farmers still angry about America's role in the Great War. Nye wanted the country to avoid foreign conflicts, and so he attacked the forces he viewed as promoters of war—the big arms manufacturers ("merchants of death") and international bankers who financed the purchase of armaments and then, as Nye viewed it, fomented war to ensure a return on their investment.

The first round of the Nye hearings in 1934 had produced a national spectacle and a piece of important legislation. The spectacle was of the once-dignified figure of J. P. Morgan reduced to ridicule before news cameras as a prankster placed a circus midget onto the hapless banker's lap. The legislation was the Neutrality Act of 1935, which placed America on the sidelines of all international conflicts. It required the president to proclaim the existence of any foreign wars and prohibited American vessels from carrying arms to or for belligerents in such wars.

The second round, in early 1936, conducted amid efforts to strengthen the Neutrality Act, probed more deeply into the role of international arms merchants and their financial backers. Interest ran high on Wall Street, and the *Herald Tribune* devoted plenty of space to Joe's coverage. It was a fine debut, and by the time the hearings closed in late February he had become one of the paper's leading reporters. Soon his Senate coverage was earning him page-one bylines with impressive frequency, and he was becoming a well-known figure around the Senate and throughout political Washington.

Joe tended to agree with Nye and his anti–Wall Street crusade. But up at Avon the elder Joe was appalled—at Nye and at Joe Jr. The world, he would declare during his son's visits, was far too dangerous for such isolationist impulses.

"For God's sake, Joe," he thundered at one point, "you don't even seem to read your own newspaper, or to know that there's such a man as Adolf Hitler. And I warn you that in four or five years, you'll be beating the drums for the repeal of this damfool act."

JOE HAD BEEN in Washington less than a year when he received a call from the Philadelphia-based *Saturday Evening Post*. The *Post* had heard about Joe from a Hollywood scriptwriter named Nunnally Johnson, former newsman and *Post* writer who had known the young reporter during his New York days. "On the subject of new writers," Johnson had written, "you might keep an eye on Joe Alsop, of the Herald-Tribune's Washington Bureau." The editors did and then invited Joe to lunch. A few weeks later they gave him his first assignment—a long profile of Senate majority leader Joseph Robinson.

The *Saturday Evening Post* was the great American magazine in 1936. It traced its lineage back to Benjamin Franklin's *Pennsylvania Gazette*, which later merged with other publications to become the *Post*. It had presented the work of such literary luminaries as Edgar Allan Poe, James Fenimore Cooper, and Harriet Beecher Stowe. After the Civil War it fell on hard times and almost died before magazine magnate Cyrus H. K. Curtis bought it for $1,000 at the turn of the century. Curtis brought in a young preacher's son named George Horace Lorimer to run the publication, and then sat back and started counting his money.

Lorimer dropped the *Post*'s price from ten cents to five to boost readership. He splashed color onto the cover, and amply illustrated every article. He bought the work of the country's leading writers, including Stephen Crane, Bret Harte, and Joel Chandler Harris. He infused the magazine with articles dedicated to what he called "the romance of business." Lorimer possessed an instinctive feel for the American heartland, and he molded his journal each week into a package that reflected the idealism and innocent optimism of a nation just then emerging as a world power.

The results were astounding. Circulation, which stood at a skimpy 33,000 in 1898, leaped to 97,000 in a single year. It hit half a million in 1903, a million in 1909, 2 million in 1913. Then came advertising in record increments as young manufacturers searched for national markets. From a base of only $8,000 in 1898, advertising revenue at the *Post* rose to $1 million in 1905, $5 million in 1910. By the end of the 1920s, the *Post*'s ad revenue exceeded $50 million a year, more than a third of all advertising dollars spent in American magazines at that time.

By 1936, the *Post* was reaching more than three million American homes each week, providing reportage from around the world, tidbits of humor, cover illustrations depicting down-home American scenes, fiction from writers such as William Faulkner, Agatha Christie, Erle Stanley Gardner, Stephen Vincent Benet. The magazine dispensed travelogues depicting faraway places or distinctive corners of the nation, and nearly every week it offered a forceful dissent against the encroachments of the New Deal. "Government," one editorial declared in October 1936, "has become a parasite that sucks billions from wages, profits and savings of all classes, from the lowest to the highest." Altogether, it was an ideal mix for vast numbers of Americans struggling to maintain the ways of old amid signs of profound change born of economic travail.

Joe was thrilled to have access to the *Post*'s national audience and an expansive outlet for his writing. But he was nervous, too. He wasn't sure he could pull it off, and he didn't want to risk failing and losing this opportunity to write for the *Post*. So he recruited a collaborator named Turner Catledge, a rising young star at *The New York Times*. Catledge had grown up in the rural South and attended Mississippi State. He was a slow-talking Mississippian with a penchant for the rustic turn of phrase and a gift for storytelling. Catledge had worked his way up from a county weekly to the *Memphis Commerical Appeal* to the *Baltimore Sun* to the *Times*. Now, at age thirty-six, he was the *Times* Senate reporter.

Though far different in temperament and background, the two proved a successful team. One would sit at the typewriter while the other wandered about the room, and they would toss out ideas and phrases until they could reach agreement on the wording of a paragraph. Joe was the stylist, throwing in literary references and lingering over their prose until it had a lilt. Catledge inserted the more rustic touches, a kind of hominy style that gave their writing a colloquial flavor. Catledge quickly learned to check the final wording whenever Joe sat at the typewriter, lest he type in his own version rather than the one they had negotiated.

The five-thousand-word Joseph Robinson piece appeared September 26, 1936. It was packed with anecdotes reflecting the vagaries of Capitol Hill life and insights into the characters of the majority leader and his colleagues. In a regular feature called "Keeping Posted," which offered inside glimpses of the *Post* operation, the editors introduced Joe to their readers: "He is stout, witty, works slowly and carefully, and is very popular with other reporters." The page featured a photo of Joe looking over a piece of copy, cigarette in hand. More important than the praise and exposure was the money—$1,200, a substantial sum in those Depression days even after it had been split two ways.

A month later, Joe was assigned by the *Herald Tribune* to cover the Roosevelts on election night at their Hyde Park retreat in New York. At around nine thirty he and his colleagues were invited into the president's political war room to congratulate him on his smashing reelection victory. There was Cousin Franklin, sitting at a dining table, surrounded by aides, poring over long slips of ticker tape that revealed the details of the election outcome. When the president saw Joe, he motioned him over and began digging into a pile of tape in search of a sliver of wire information. Finding it, he handed it to Joe with an expression of satisfaction.

"How will Corinne like that?" he asked triumphantly.

Joe looked down to see that the wire copy revealed his hometown of Avon had gone for the president, voting Democratic for the first time in memory.

"There's a telephone out in the hall; go out and call your mother," instructed the president. "Let's find out how Corinne is taking it."

Enjoying Roosevelt's amusement, Joe called his mother and learned that she had anticipated the president's strength. She had spent two weeks instructing Avon's Italian families in the art of ticket-splitting, and her Republican friends had won their seats even as Roosevelt carried the town.

"You can tell Franklin that . . . we still sent Mr. Woodford to the state legislature by just as good a majority as Franklin got for the presidency," said Corinne.

When Joe reported back, the president laughed uproariously.

"I knew Corinne was a professional," he said.

By the start of 1937, Alsop and Catledge were spending as much time writing *Saturday Evening Post* articles as they were covering the Senate for their newspapers. A stunning move by Franklin Roosevelt provided dramatic material for the new team. Probably no politician in American history had held such sway over the nation's political apparatus as did Roosevelt in the wake of the 1936 election. The opposition Republicans, reduced to only seventeen seats in the Senate and eighty-nine in the House, posed no serious threat. Meanwhile, organized labor and the thousands of new patronage jobs in the federal bureaucracy gave the president powerful political leverage. The breadth and intensity of Roosevelt's own popularity, reflected in his 523-to-8 electoral-vote victory, generated a steady flow of political power. As Alsop and Catledge were to write, "Who was there to say him nay?"

The answer was the U.S. Supreme Court. A majority of justices viewed most of the president's aims and goals as unconstitutional. Already they had struck down nine of eleven major New Deal initiatives, leaving intact only the Tennessee Valley Authority and the devaluation of the dollar.

And now, as the president looked to his second-term agenda, he saw the court standing in his way. Major foundations of his New Deal, including Social Security, the Wagner collective bargaining law, and the Utilities Holding Company Act, were working their way up for judicial tests, and the court might very well strike them down. Roosevelt's solution was simple: to promote legislation allowing him to appoint a new justice, up to a total of fifteen, for every justice who refused to retire at full pay within six months of reaching age seventy. This was enough power to remake the court, given the justices' ages: Brandeis, eighty; Van Devanter, seventy-seven; McReynolds, seventy-five; Sutherland, seventy-four; Hughes, seventy-four; Butler, seventy; Cardozo, sixty-six; Stone, sixty-five; Roberts, sixty-one.

When Roosevelt unveiled his plan on February 5, 1937, first to aghast members of Congress and then to reporters, he invited a political struggle far beyond anything he had anticipated. What followed were 168 days of political maneuvering, intrigue, backroom bargaining, and furious oratory as the president pressed his plan with all the force and cunning he could muster. Meanwhile, his opponents, including many Democrats and New Dealers, moved to check his power grab. Senate majority leader Joe Robinson, known as Old Reliable for his devotion to Roosevelt's causes, threw himself into the fight with added gusto born of a fond hope that Roosevelt would reward his efforts with one of the new court seats. But at the height of the drama in July, a depressed and tension-beset Robinson, in his mid-sixties and haggard from the legislative wars, died in his bed of a heart attack. Roosevelt's court-packing scheme died with him.

Following the story from beginning to end were Catledge and Alsop, whose daily dispatches demonstrated access to the inner precincts of power. They then captured the drama in a three-part series for the *Saturday Evening Post*, which began in the September 18 issue. The reporters shaped the story into a kind of Greek drama, with the president cast as the hero of the realm brought down by his own arrogance.

"Suddenly," they wrote, "the shabby comedy of national politics, with its all-pervading motive, self-interest, its dreary dialogue of public oratory and its depressing scenery of patronage and projects, was elevated to a grand, even a tragic plane. Suddenly the old Greek Theme of Hubris and Ara, of pride and the fall that comes after, dominated the play." While the Alsop-Catledge articles exposed Roosevelt's errors of judgment and tactics, they left little doubt about their friendly inclination toward his cause. Introducing the Rooseveltian character in their drama, they wrote:

> His agreeably handsome face, his friendly but imposing presence, his rich, perfect voice with the odd trace of an aboriginal Bostonian flatness—these made his admirable exterior. His great daring, his acute sense of political timing, a taste for power which encouraged him to shoulder the gigantic responsibilities everyone wished to be rid of—these helped him to sponsor a new kind of national government.

And yet Roosevelt was not spared the lash of critical analysis. Defeat, they concluded, had left him "sore and vengeful" and left his judgment "as badly distorted now by the bitter aftertaste of failure as it had once been by the intoxication of success."

The series drew acclaim in Washington. "Nothing but praise has yet been forthcoming," Catledge wrote to Joe. "Even New Dealers think the articles were accurate and fair." It drew attention from New York book publishers wanting to put the story between hard covers, and the two authors didn't take long in choosing Doubleday, where Stewart Alsop worked and Uncle Ted Roosevelt served as a vice president. They settled for a flat payment of $1,800 (no royalties), but Uncle Ted felt confident they would win the next year's $2,500 prize for the Theodore Roosevelt Memorial Book Award. "I don't see how anyone can shriek nepotism," he wrote to Joe, "because after all, I am only one member of a committee of five." He was right about this last point, but only because the other four voted to give the prize to another candidate.

The book, entitled *The 168 Days*, was favorably reviewed and made a number of best-seller lists. Rexford Tugwell, a Roosevelt partisan and early member of the FDR Brain Trust, called it "one of the most brilliant accounts of a complex political occurrence ever written."

JOE LOVED THE attention he was getting and his growing reputation as a rising star among the nation's journalists. But he worried increasingly about his health. He felt tired and listless much of the time, and he woke up mornings with his heart sounding like "the random banging of a loose shutter on a very windy day." He went to see a doctor, and the diagnosis was grim. His heart was beginning to buckle under the strain of his immense frame and his tendency toward overeating, overwork, and excessive social drinking. The doctor urged him to slow down and lose seventy-five pounds; if he did not, he might die within a year.

Joe was alarmed, and when he told his mother she went into a panic. Corinne offered to pay for a sophisticated new diet program at Baltimore's Johns Hopkins University Hospital, and without argument Joe went for intensive treatment under the direction of a pioneer dietitian named John Eager Howard. The food, totally devoid of fat, was tasteless but plentiful—lean meat cooked without butter, fruits and vegetables served without butter or sugar—but despite this bulk, the diet was just this side of starvation. It was administered in the hospital because errors in caloric calculations could be harmful. Joe also underwent a rigorous exercise program to rebuild muscles that had atrophied from lack of use.

In three months, he had dropped sixty-five pounds. He returned to Washington a new man, bent on staying trim and telling his story to the world. He produced a piece for the *Post* entitled "How It Feels to Look Like Everybody Else," and spared no descriptive phrases in relaying just how grossly overweight he had been. For years, he said, merely crossing his legs had made him feel like a penguin. But now, he added, "I'm not merely lighter on my feet. I'm lighter-hearted and lighter-headed." His wallet was heavier; he received $1,200 for the story.

Joe's friends found the new Joe thrilling. "I'm dying to have a long look at your magnificently diminished self," wrote a friend named Maxine Davis. After leaving Johns Hopkins, Joe cut back drastically on the fat content of his diet, and whenever possible he eschewed auto transportation in favor of long walks through Washington. Never again did he balloon to dangerous proportions, but his battle with unwanted poundage proved to be a lifelong struggle.

The autumn of 1937 brought another major change to Joe's life. The North American Newspaper Alliance, a kind of cooperative syndicate run by and for a number of the country's leading papers, was looking for a team of columnists to cover Washington and national politics. Jack Wheeler, head of the alliance, approached Joe with a proposal that Joe and Turner Catledge team up for the job. Joe was thrilled, but Catledge demurred. His future at the *Times* looked bright. So Joe approached fellow *Herald Tribune* reporter Robert Kintner, the paper's chief economics writer. Kintner, a year older than Joe, was a Pennsylvanian, a Swarthmore College graduate, and a relentless reporter with an almost unquenchable thirst for information. A slight, disheveled young man, he had emerged as one of the few reporters who truly understood the economic policies of the New Deal, and he was well connected in the growing federal bureaucracy. Kintner leaped at the opportunity.

The Reids tried to counter the NANA offer by carving out a role for Joe as a Washington columnist, but this would have required him to give up his magazine writing, and a substantial portion of his income. Besides, Joe was more comfortable with a collaborator; the idea of a solo column frightened him a bit. Still, he took pains to depart in the most cordial manner possible. "I cannot forebear from writing you . . . personally, to express all my gratitude, all the deep regrets I feel on leaving the *Tribune* . . . ," he wrote to Helen Reid. "All I can say is that I shall always be grateful to you and to the paper, and that I shall remember my five *Tribune* years as very happy ones and very valuable ones to me personally."

The NANA contract, dated October 20, 1937, called for six columns a week. Each writer would receive $150 a week, and the two of them would split 60 percent of revenue brought in through syndicating the column to non-NANA papers. They would be paid up to $50 a month for office expenses, which just about covered the rent at the National Press Building. The syndicate would pay up to $30 a week for other expenses, until the columnists' share of revenue from non-NANA papers reached that level; then they would have to cover their own expenses. They called the column "The Capital Parade" and promised that it would be the product of hard reporting and sharp political analysis, with plenty of high-level Washington gossip thrown in.

With the column, Joe had arrived. He now had carte blanche to pursue any major story in town and to inject his strong opinions unabashedly into his writings. With sixty papers using his column, and with his exposure in the *Saturday Evening Post*, he was becoming a journalist of national prominence. What's more, his income from the column was three times what his *Herald Tribune* salary had been, and with his *Post* earnings his annual income approached $14,000.

Joe also moved to a higher social plane. He rented a house at 2709 Dumbarton Avenue in Georgetown, hired an interior decorator to help him get it into shape, and began acquiring heirloom furniture from members of his family. Almost immediately the house became a gathering place for influential New Dealers, prominent politicians and diplomats, New York literati, and assorted celebrities.

Through Alice Longworth, Joe met Alexander Woollcott, wit, playwright, *New York Times* drama critic, and one of the country's leading gossips. Soon Joe was spending vacations at Alec's private island in

Vermont and meeting his celebrity friends—playwright and satirist George S. Kaufman and his wife Beatrice, British dramatist Noël Coward, actress Ruth Gordon. Whenever these people came to town, Joe made an effort to "trot out the commissars," as he put it. Noël Coward found the "select" dinner guests to be filled with knowledgeable opinions and witty observations on weighty topics of the day. But "there were jokes as well and lightness of touch and delicious food and wine."

Joe pursued lively dinner guests with the zeal of an ardent suitor, looking for people who combined substantial learning and a social wit with strong traits of character. He had a tendency toward hero worship and often gushed embarrassingly in correspondence with his heroes. He quickly developed an affection for Ben Cohen, a brilliant Harvard-trained lawyer from Muncie, Indiana. In the administration, Cohen was a formidable force, who joined with young lawyer Tommy Corcoran to draft the most important domestic initiatives and to serve as leader of the ardent New Dealers. Joe "admired Ben Cohen beyond words," recalled Isaiah Berlin, then a young attaché at the British embassy and a frequent dinner guest at Joe's house. "Joe totally trusted Ben Cohen . . . [and] would be impressed by whatever Ben said."

Joe felt much the same about Felix Frankfurter, the Viennese-born professor who had come to America as a child and grown up to become one of the country's leading legal scholars and judicial activists. Frankfurter also played a role as the country's civic recruiter, drawing the brightest young men he could find into government service. Corcoran and Cohen were both Frankfurter protégés, and Joe longed to be one, too. After an extended conversation with Frankfurter at Cohen's home, Joe wrote the professor, "I shan't soon forget our long talk. . . . It was a meeting which I have long hoped for, and one which, unlike most such meetings, fully justified all my anticipations." Frankfurter responded warmly to Joe's flattery, and became a close friend and mentor. After his appointment to the Supreme Court in 1939, he was a frequent dinner guest at Dumbarton Avenue.

One day Joe summoned "the little judge," as he called Frankfurter, after Ruth Gordon had sent word that she would be in town for the opening of her latest film, *Abe Lincoln in Illinois*. She arrived, as Joe later wrote to Woollcott, "surrounded by co-stars, press-agents, Moss Hart, Max Gordon, chauffeurs and maids." At dinner, attended by Joe, the Gordons, and the Frankfurters, the captivating but willful actress insisted on recounting for the justice the details of a Hollywood libel case that soon would be argued before the Supreme Court— "notwithstanding the fact that no case before the court has ever been discussed in a Justice's presence in the memory of living man," as Joe later wrote to Woollcott, adding: "Mrs. F and I roared with laughter." They enjoyed the evening so much that, on the way home in Ruth's huge RKO limousine (which inspired the little judge to remark, "Odi profunam vulgus et arceo"), they all decided to meet again the next day for lunch. Two weeks later the same group took the limo to Baltimore to see Ruth's friend, Lillian Gish, perform in *Life with Father*.

Meanwhile, the Alsop-Kintner team's journalistic successes generated ever greater demand for their work. In July 1938 they received word that *Time* magazine founder Henry Luce wanted to talk to Joe about a series of profiles for his wildly successful new magazine, *Life*. Founded just two years earlier, *Life* had captured the national imagination by bringing to its readers new photographic technology in the form of large, vivid, candid pictures. Within a year, circulation had soared to a million, and projections suggested five million. By January 1937, a thousand advertising pages had been sold for the year, with another four hundred promised. But Luce and some of his advertisers worried that readers didn't spend enough time with the magazine—too many pictures, not enough words. He wanted some serious journalism from around the world, including Washington.

Over lunch in New York, Luce outlined a plan for a series of Washington profiles to be written by Joe and Bob, with Luce's famous research department providing most of the background material. Joe suggested $500 per story as a fair price, given the backup support, and the team set to work on a profile of postmaster general Jim Farley, Roosevelt's political fixer.

When they got into the project, however, they discovered that the research material didn't help much. "We had to do precisely the same kind of investigative job we should have had to do for a full length Saturday Evening Post piece," Joe wrote to Luce's assistant, Ralph Paine, adding parenthetically (and disingenuously) that the *Post* paid $1,500 for a full-length article. "Of course, for the present article, the matter is entirely in your hands," he wrote. "We named the sum and agreed to go ahead on that basis." Luce liked the Farley piece so much that Paine sent down a check for $1,500, along with a request for more articles as soon as possible. Joe sent a letter of thanks, noting that the Farley piece received "a great deal more response . . . than we usually receive on the *Saturday Evening Post* pieces." The hard-edged Luce style was making *Life* a more serious product than its old-fashioned competitor.

But *Life* wasn't above light features, and its editors felt Alsop and Kintner would be the ideal team to write one on the Roosevelt family. In July 1939, Joe wrote to Cousin Eleanor requesting an interview for a "light, cheerful sort of piece" and asking if he could stop by Hyde Park in early August on his way to Henderson House. "I know you well enough to know that you will tell me frankly whether or not you want to see me," he wrote, "and whatever your answer, I shall be wholly satisfied." She replied that she would be "delighted" to have Joe stay at her Val-Kill Cottage at Hyde Park—"for the night if you wish or for any length of time you can stay."

The result was a glowing *Life* article called "The Roosevelt Family Album"—a compendium of family profiles, with subtitles such as, "The

President's Father: A Period Piece"; "The President's Brother: Edwardian Gentleman"; and "F.D.R.: Child of a Vanished Race." The authors said the Roosevelt family, having flourished in the pre–Civil War era of easy-living gentry, found itself "quite overwhelmed in the big business age." It was little wonder, they wrote, that Franklin Roosevelt had "struck out on his own course."

Although Alsop and Kintner enjoyed writing for *Life*, they knew the *Saturday Evening Post* still paid a lot of their bills, and Joe set about the chores of diplomacy with the *Post*'s leaders—editor Wesley Winans Stout, a genial but rigid-minded intellectual with a strong conservative bent, and his deputy, a rubicund little man named Martin Sommers. With *Life* paying $1,500 for a short profile (based on Joe's false statement that the *Post* guaranteed $1,500), Joe suggested an arrangement whereby he and Kintner would continue to write long articles for the *Post* (for which the writers normally received $1,200). They would stop writing their shorter ($1,000) pieces for the *Post*, and devote those energies instead toward *Life*. There would be no *Life* contract: "We do not wish to be tied to them, and above all, we don't want to sever our *Post* connection," he wrote. Stout expressed satisfaction with the arrangement, and the Alsop-Kintner team set to work on their next *Post* project.

It was a three-part story, and eventually became another book. The series traced the moves, personalities, and conflicts of the Roosevelt inner circle, spinning the tale of the political revolution brought forth by the New Deal. The magazine noted, in the "Keeping Posted" feature, that the authors were friends of many of the major New Deal figures. "If there is bias in their judgment of men and motives, that bias is likely to fall on the side of the men whom they admire. But they are reporters first of all, telling a set of facts as objectively as skilled reporters can."

It was a matter of some concern to Joe and Kintner that more and more people around Washington associated them with those administration officials known as New Dealers—the liberal intellectuals and activists who had led the Roosevelt revolution in the early 1930s. These included, besides Corcoran and Cohen, Interior Secretary Harold Ickes—"the man of wrath," as Joe and Bob called him in a *Life* profile; Harry Hopkins, former relief administrator, now commerce secretary and widely considered the president's best friend in Washington; and Frankfurter, who was well known as a behind-the-scenes manipulator.

There was no denying that the two columnists were sympathetic to the New Deal. In a 1940 book entitled *The News and How to Understand It*, Quincy Howe, a top official at Simon and Schuster, flatly included "The Capital Parade" among "the pro-Roosevelt columns."

But their zeal as reporters often took precedence over their New Deal leanings. Their fascination with the intricacies of competitive politics drew them to all the various combatants. And Joe's inclination toward sycophancy certainly wasn't confined to his New Deal friends. After writing a *Life* profile of Michigan senator Arthur Vandenberg, then a towering Republican figure, Joe wrote to the senator, "It is very rare, in my experience, that your estimate of a man is higher after writing about him, but if it is not impertinent to record the fact, I should like to say that both Bob Kintner's and mine of you is just that."

The Alsop-Kintner team was particularly attuned to subtle shifts in the political winds, as Roosevelt played New Dealers off against more conservative elements in the government. Kintner proposed a *Saturday Evening Post* story on the quiet but profoundly important work of Treasury Secretary Henry Morgenthau, Jr., the wealthy Hudson Valley farmer who had come to be regarded as the administration's leading conservative, and who was a frequent target of New Dealers. The result, in April 1939, was a three-part series on the most arcane of subjects, government finance. By bringing in their standard fare of anecdote, personality, and narrative, however, the writers crafted a compelling story that reflected a perspective far beyond the outlook of the New Deal. "Being cautious, yet devoted, Morgenthau is ideal for his place," they wrote, "for Roosevelt could not brook an unyielding conservative, and would get into trouble with an extreme New Dealer at the Treasury."

Using sensitive documents provided by Morgenthau, the writers rendered the first public account of how the world's leading finance ministers moved quickly in September 1936 to stem an accelerating flight from the French franc and avert an international financial crisis. Not surprisingly, the French were furious at this breach of diplomatic secrecy, and they blamed Morgenthau, who emerged in the series as a financial hero. When French economic adviser Jean Monnet visited Washington a few weeks later, William C. Bullitt, Roosevelt's trusted diplomat, advised the president to exclude Morgenthau from his initial conversation with Monnet. "The *Saturday Evening Post* article . . . has made everyone believe that even the most confidential communications with Henry will be published by him," said Bullitt.

For Alsop and Kintner, this only added to their stature. Quincy Howe, in his book, pronounced "The Capital Parade" to be Washington's "best written and most authoritative column." That the two young columnists could "steal a march on some of the most consistent Roosevelt boosters in the national capital," said Howe, was attributable to Joe's ties to the "Eastern aristocracy" and his family connections. "He is himself a Roosevelt," Howe wrote. With their expanded fame, Alsop and Kintner also enjoyed increased financial success; the two reporters now were each making $20,000 a year.

But Joe was concerned about the heavy schedule he had to keep in order to maintain that income. Sometimes he was forced to shut himself up for weeks, toiling twelve hours a day over the typewriter. Though he managed to stay reasonably trim, his heart once again started its erratic patterns. After a checkup at Johns Hopkins, a doctor warned that his work schedule was causing real strain, that he might be headed for some kind of collapse. He began thinking about dropping the NANA column or cutting back on magazine work. He asked Stout at the *Post* about a contract to write exclusively for the magazine. Stout demurred, saying that the column served to enhance Joe's magazine work—and, besides, the *Post* wasn't inclined toward exclusive contracts. Meanwhile, in the fall of 1940, Jack Wheeler at NANA insisted on a contract renewal that provided only a $25-a-week raise, not enough to permit Joe to curtail his magazine writing.

The solution came from the New York *Herald Tribune* syndicate. The Reids wanted their wayward reporters back, badly enough to offer a contract that offered the columnists a higher income if their column sold widely in the newspaper market. Alsop and Kintner accepted, and within weeks the column was providing the syndicate with $32,000 a year. Joe saw his syndication income rise from $10,400 to a guaranteed $13,650. This allowed Joe to cut back his magazine work to the occasional *Life* profile or *Post* article that would take him and Kintner into new areas that fortified the column.

The letter to *Post* editor Wes Stout was a painful one. "You have always been so generous, frank and considerate with Bob and me that I know of no way for us to repay you," Joe wrote. "It has been both a pleasure and privilege to work for you." Stout noted in reply that Joe had "offered honest wedlock more than once" and added that "bigamy not being what it is cracked up to be, we neither wonder nor complain at your base desertion of us for Helen Rogers Reid's many and manifest charms." But Joe would "find the kitchen door conveniently unlocked" if he cared to "slip in now and then via the alley."

To the Reids, Joe was effusive in his gratitude. "It is like coming home again," he wrote to Ogden, with whom he had negotiated the arrangement. "I think you will find Bob and I will work hard for you . . . as much from a desire to do a good job for the paper we have never quite ceased to feel a part of, as from our human hope to be successful ourselves." To Helen Reid he wrote, "It is very wonderful to be back on the *Tribune* . . . and it has meant an immense amount to both of us to find, on our coming back, that you have such generous confidence in us." The Reids responded by inviting Joe to New York for a gala dinner featuring Wendell Willkie, then riding high as the 1940 Republican presidential nominee.

STEWART IN NEW YORK

Fun, Frolic—and Drift

ONE SUMMER DAY in 1937 Corinne Alsop traveled to New York City to shop and visit with Stewart, who was then twenty-three years old and about a year into his editorial job at Doubleday. In looking at her son, Corinne did not like what she saw. He didn't look very respectable. He was sloppy in dress and demeanor, and he lacked that crisp self-assurance that had always paved the way for his father. To Corinne he seemed a bit out of control. She was distressed to hear that Stewart had lost his wallet containing nearly an entire week's pay.

Corinne nurtured lofty ambitions for her children, and it bothered her when it appeared they might not fulfill her hopes. She didn't need to worry about Sis, her daughter, who in May 1932 had married Percy Chubb of the wealthy New Jersey insurance family. And John impressed his parents with what seemed like effortless success at just about anything he attempted. Even at Groton John had excelled, becoming a football star, head of the *Grotonian*, and Endicott Peabody's chosen senior prefect. "John," the rector had written to the elder Joe in 1931, "is like the well trained western horse that stands without hitching." But Corinne felt it really was time for Stewart to begin demonstrating a higher level of maturity.

So when she got back to Avon, she sat down and dictated a letter to Stewart. "Darling," she wrote, "it was lovely to see you looking very well, but slightly inconsequential and somewhat dirty. You must begin to have a less tenement-house-attitude about your way of living, it is just as important as for Joe to reduce 65 pounds and would show real character in doing so."

Stewart had begun his job at Doubleday, Doran in the summer of 1936 at a meager salary—$25 a week—but of course his father supplemented that with a $100 monthly allowance. Stewart took an apartment on East Fifty-seventh Street with Yale friend Bill Rand and immediately set about connecting with the set of young people he knew from earlier days who had gravitated to the city. At Doubleday, one of the country's leading publishing houses, he began an eighteen-month training program and quickly proved to his superiors that he possessed special talents as an editor. He was highly literate and had a flair for making manuscripts both readable and dramatic.

Stewart's progress was watched over by Uncle Ted Roosevelt, whose career had taken a few turns since his unsuccessful bid for New York's governorship more than a decade earlier. During the Hoover administration, Ted had served as governor general of the Philippines, but that job had ended abruptly when Franklin Roosevelt entered the White House. FDR had no intention of retaining in office a man, even a relative, who had campaigned against him in a national radio broadcast from Manila, as Ted had done.

Once at Doubleday, Stewart received no favoritism. "He was terribly bright . . . (and) spoke with authority," recalled Ken McCormick, editor in chief at the time. "When we got someone like that in editorial, we tried to keep him there."

Initially the job called for him to read manuscripts and write reports assessing their literary merit and market potential—"just the kind of thing I like to do and think I am most gifted for," he wrote to Avon. Asked to critique a Kipling biography that had been cleared by the British writer's own daughter, Stewart quickly found a host of errors in the manuscript. "He brought real erudition to the job," recalled McCormick.

But his work, while enjoyable enough, was not a motivating factor in Stewart's life. He didn't see himself working in book publishing indefinitely, but he also didn't know what he would rather do. So he devoted himself to his many New York friends and to the Manhattan social scene. The aim was to have as much fun as possible. Stewart and brother John, who had taken a Wall Street job upon graduating from Yale in 1937, began with the social circle they had spent so much time with during the debutante seasons of previous years. Dottie Kidder continued to gather together a number of impressive young Foxcroft women at her mother's huge house on Seventy-ninth Street, and the young men were likely to show up there around tea time to begin an afternoon and evening of rollicking fun. There would be cocktails in the big library at Dottie's, then out to dinner and often a late-night foray into the dark and romantic sanctum of LaRue, a nightclub where the drinks were cheap and everybody knew everybody.

The men drank liquor in huge quantities, often becoming uproariously drunk, but the women generally abstained from drinking until they were married, or at least engaged. In those times and in those circles, it was assumed that young brides came to their weddings as virgins, and most did.

Among Dottie's friends was a young woman named Susan Mary Jay, whose influential forebears of Revolutionary War days had entertained the Alsop forebears at the Jays' elegant New York table. Susan Mary, poised and self-possessed, was a young woman of considerable beauty, as well as impressive ancestry, and as Corinne got to know her during weekend house parties at Avon she concluded that Susan Mary would make an ideal bride for Stewart.

But Stewart preferred the carefree life. He expanded his social circle every week and drove friends around Manhattan, or up to Avon, in his 1932 Ford convertible coupe. He was constantly falling in love with somebody new, then just as abruptly falling out of love and transferring his affections to yet another young woman. He was not particularly smooth, had not developed the social charms that impress older people. But he was loads of fun to his peers, always ready with a quip or funny story. And the Russian skit that he and John had developed at Yale became so well known among Manhattan's younger set that *Vogue* magazine ran a brief item about it. That of course increased demand for the skit at social gatherings, and after a few drinks the call would go up, "Hey, let's have the Alsop boys do that Russian peasant thing." It didn't take much coaxing.

Stewart frequently would drive to Avon for weekends, often bringing a carload of friends. Sometimes Joe would be there also with his friends, and the two groups would mix amiably. Joe's friend Paul Nitze recalls the brothers' mother kneeling on the floor for hours shooting dice with a group of young people; to make it lively she allowed bets of five or ten cents per roll.

There was a special atmosphere during these weekend house parties. For Susan Mary Jay, a frequent visitor, the farmhouse lacked the elegance of the Long Island homes she knew so well, but it was full of warmth and lively political talk, and the food was delicious, if somewhat more simple than the fancy cuisine served in the big New York homes. "It was so congenial, so relaxed, and the boys were so funny and amusing," she recalled years later. Corinne, always in charge, would orchestrate midday tennis games and afternoon bridge games. On Saturday Joe Sr. often would play golf and take a contingent of young people with him. Joe Sr. inspired awe in Stewart's friends because of his powerful presence, but he always managed to make Avon guests feel comfortable.

In the big L-shaped living room, the center of family activity, Corinne would hold forth near the fireplace, which on winter afternoons was always ablaze. Tea was served at four-thirty, and after tea everybody would rush upstairs to dress for dinner. Mr. Alsop generally wore a velvet smoking jacket to dinner; the young men wore black tie. Cocktails were served at six-thirty; dinner followed at seven-thirty. The political talk, always raucous and entertaining, focused largely on the New Deal. The young people favored it, and Joe Sr. would taunt them with harshly expressed anti-Roosevelt sentiments.

One Saturday afternoon, following a long bridge game in the living room, Corinne turned to Stewart.

"Stewart," she said, "why don't you take Susan Mary out to the barn and show her the fine Alsop dairy cows." The young people looked at each other in amusement.

"Oh, Ma," said Stewart, as Susan Mary looked on expectantly, "Susan Mary doesn't want to go out to the barn, I'm sure."

Corinne insisted.

"But Ma," protested Stewart, as Susan Mary became faintly amused and slightly embarrassed, "it's almost supper time."

But the irrepressible Corinne was not to be put off, and so the two rose from the table and headed out to the barn, casting sidelong smiles at each other on the way.

Once in the barn, Stewart felt obliged to follow through on the expedition by dramatically expressing undying love for Susan Mary. But his expressions sounded so forced and out of place amid the cows that they both burst into laughter.

"Well," said Stewart as their laughter subsided, "I guess we've been out here long enough for Ma; we can go back now."

A failure at matchmaking, Corinne remained resolved to improve Stewart's appearance. She and the elder Joe sent him Christmas money in 1937 for an excursion to Brooks Brothers. "With a wide selection of examples of your generosity from Brooks, I should no longer be a figure of fun, but a son, in appearance at least, to be proud of," the grateful Stewart wrote home. A few months later Corinne and Joe sent him a new suit for his birthday.

These were happy days for Stewart. Courtesy of his father, he belonged to the Yale Club, where he went often for exercise. Afternoons he would drop by the River Club, where many of his friends gathered for cocktails. The elder Joe bought him a series of shooting lessons to improve his hunting skills and then invited him to accompany an Alsop hunting party to South Carolina. Stewart loved the trips to Avon and the social whirl that dominated his life. He also took pleasure in brother Joe's growing success and fame, which enhanced his own self-esteem. "Joe has gotten to the stage where everything he touches seems to turn to gold," Stewart wrote home in late 1937. He was even more impressed whenever he traveled to Washington for one of Joe's dinner parties, where famous people were sure to be in attendance.

And with his mother's Cousin Eleanor in the White House, he experienced the thrill of dining there. One Roosevelt family dinner, he complained, was nonalcoholic except for the punch, which "tasted like Hexylresorcinol." Stewart sat next to Eleanor's Aunt Elizabeth Hall, with Franklin seated on the other side of Aunt Betty. The president leaned over and inquired after Joe, who couldn't attend because he was suffering from something called "bursars." Stewart, somewhat ill at ease, replied that Joe had "housemaid's knee." The president "looked puzzled and unconvinced, but he let it pass," as Stewart wrote to Avon. All in all, he added, "I had quite a time with the President, et al."

Despite such heady experiences Stewart came to feel that his life lacked meaning. Professionally and financially he seemed stuck in a low-level job that was going nowhere. All this became the topic of a somewhat drunken conversation between Stewart and John one night at the bar at the restaurant "21." The bartender, a young friend of the Alsops, looked on in amusement as the brothers blamed their father for blundering in the way he had brought them up.

"Here we are," said John, "the product of all that he has made us, including the champagne tastes he's instilled in us, and yet we're stuck with the necessity of living on these beer budgets."

"Let's write him a letter," suggested Stewart.

"A good idea," said John.

Stewart asked the bartender for a pen and some writing paper. They pushed away their beer mugs, and Stewart set pen to paper as they composed a letter of criticism to Joe Sr., which said he should have given them a better understanding of how to live as ordinary white-collar workers mired in a Depression. Upon completing their composition, the brothers obtained from the smiling bartender an envelope and stamp. They addressed the letter to Avon and asked the bartender to post it in the morning. Father never mentioned it. "To this day," recalled John Alsop many years later, "I never knew whether the bartender sent that letter."

Politically, Stewart was on a slow journey away from a flirtation with radical leftism that had begun during his Yale days. Back then, he had considered himself a "Marxist liberal," and his cocktail-party Marxism had seemed to illuminate nearly all the events of the world. In this view, men starved amid abundance because goods were produced for private gain and not for public good. Wars were a product of the capitalist need for new areas of exploitation, given that capitalist nation's own resources were exploited to the limit. Fascism had been invented by the wily capitalist to enslave the masses in the name of greater profits.

Up at Avon, where politics were always served with dinner, such views would enrage the man at the head of the table.

"Why don't you go back to Russia, where you came from?" the elder Joe would shout.

Though young Joe's political views remained much more conven-tional—part of the prevailing liberal mainstream that kept Franklin

Roosevelt in power—Father didn't like his outlook much better. He would rail against "that crazy jack in the White House" and rage against Joe's wrongheaded liberalism. Corrine, no less conservative than her husband, was more quiet about her views—and more stealthy. She insisted that the boys vote as Avonites by absentee ballot and send the envelopes to her for transmittal to polling officials. The boys suspected that she tossed the envelopes away in presidential election years, and yet they dutifully sent their ballots to her as she requested.

As Europe began to heat up, however, and America moved closer to war, Stewart's views changed. At the beginning of 1941, he struggled to collect his views in a magazine article, which he sent off to *The Atlantic*. The highbrow national monthly published his musings in the spring. In the piece he confessed that he had once been a Marxist, but now felt contempt for such thinking. It was foolish, he wrote, to believe that the coming world war would create a new order in which the beautiful truth of socialism would be known and practiced all over the world. "Today," he wrote, "the Marxist liberal of yore feels a little like the college senior who comes unexpectedly on the diary he wrote when he was thirteen, filled with the embarrassing inanities of adolescence."

As Stewart was rejecting Marxism, he had already rejected fascism. The secular faith that motivated German youth was a "vicious" ideology, wrote Stewart, and the American government was correct in committing the country to the defeat of the Axis powers through Lend-Lease and other indirect means of aiding the British in their lonely stand. And yet the isolationist sentiment that gripped the nation in the midst of world crisis led to a kind of "bloodlessly bellicose double-talk" in which "the leaders of American thought, from the President on down, can shake oratorical or editorial fists at the aggressors to their hearts' content . . . but can never so much as breathe that some American boy might get hurt in the process."

The problem, as Stewart viewed it, was that America's youth lacked a guiding faith, "something to believe in, to live for and die for." Though the idea of making the world safe for democracy had galvanized the last generation, it could never serve a second time, especially given the crisis of democracy spawned by the Depression. "A kind of democracy that leaves somewhere between nine and sixteen million unemployed for ten years in the richest nation on earth hardly seems worth imposing on the rest of the world." The national imperative was clear: Give America's youth the dream of a nation in which a man who is willing to do his honest share will receive his honest share; give them the dream of a world in which the global plenty is fairly distributed.

"If this is Bolshevism or red radicalism or un-Americanism," wrote Stewart, "then so be it. America is today face to face with the greatest war of her national history. Without a great faith, we shall lose that war. With faith, we shall win it."

It was a naive bit of leftist idealism, born of Stewart's growing conviction that America must rush to Britain's aid in her hour of travail. *The New York Times* noted with interest the "complete disillusionment" of this obscure young man, and zeroed in on the soft analysis undergirding the piece. In a discursive, unsigned column called "Topics of the Times," the paper pronounced the presentation of Stewart's case "odd" and suggested the dream he called for had already been put forth—by the Founding Fathers, who had created an American democracy free from the kinds of ideological frenzy that ruled in the Soviet Union and Germany alike. "With all due respect," said the writer, "we have had this American dream from the first, provided one will think of a dream as a goal, something for which one strives but from which one humanly falls short."

Down in Washington, Joe dismissed his brother's thesis. America, he believed, didn't need a dream; it had the New Deal. And the goal of saving the British Empire from extinction was sufficiently idealistic to justify America's entry into the war. The country simply needed the will to get on with it.

Meanwhile, Stewart's drift continued, and so did the pursuit of fun and frolic that characterized the lives of Stewart and John in Manhattan. In the fall the boys and a couple of friends decided to host a bash in keeping with the spirit of the times. They sent out postcard invitations:

COLLAPSE OF CIVILIZATION PARTY

Come to 320 E. 57th Street and witness the moral decay of the nation's youth. Intimate glimpses of utter degeneracy, horrible examples of corpusculence, skulkery, scrabacity, flabbery, and advanced morbi-sinestrosis! Come and gambol while Rome burns.

A. Draft Dodge

Scabbery Oliver-Alsop

J. Decay Alsop

Fester C. Cavanagh

The time of the party was "5:30 p.m. til total collapse." The date was November 3, 1941.

Civilization did not collapse that night; but in barely more than a month the America of Stewart's youth would be dead. With brutal precision on the morning of December 7 the Japanese attacked America's forward naval positions in Hawaii, then proceeded to sweep through the Pacific with ferocious martial force. The long period of drift was over—for the United States and for Stewart Alsop.

8

THE WAR ISSUE

"Deeply in Accord with the President's Policy"

IN THE EARLY morning of September 1, 1939, a diplomatically bankrupt Europe plunged into war. As dawn arrived in Poland that historic day, the German war machine cracked into action. The battleship *Schleswig-Holstein* opened fire on the Polish garrison at Danzig. Stuka dive bombers screamed across the border and destroyed Polish warplanes before their pilots could rev up their engines. The Luftwaffe attacked Gdynia, Lwow, Krosno, and Warsaw as General Heinz Guderian's panzer divisions enveloped Polish territory.

At two forty that morning, Washington time, the telephone rang at the presidential bedside. The call was from Franklin Roosevelt's ambassador to Paris.

"This is Bill Bullitt, Mr. President."

"Yes, Bill."

"Tony Biddle has just got through from Warsaw, Mr. President. Several German divisions are deep in Polish territory, and fighting is heavy. Tony said there were reports of bombers over the city. Then he was cut off . . ."

"Well, Bill," said the president, "it's come at last. God help us all."

The war had begun. But in America it would be a war of words, a political conflict over how the country should respond. Isolationists quickly took to the airwaves with arguments against American involvement. Two weeks after the Polish invasion, Charles Lindbergh, still a hero throughout the land and one who could compete with Roosevelt himself for the public's attention, spoke to a huge radio audience, warning against American intervention. "Our safety does not lie in fighting European wars," Lindbergh declared. "It lies in our own internal strength, in the character of the American people and of American institutions." In Congress, the call of isolationism went up from North Dakota's Gerald Nye and his allies—crusty William Borah of Idaho, fiery populist Hiram Johnson of California, the forceful Arthur Vandenberg of Michigan, Montana's Burton K. Wheeler, and a rising star from Ohio named Robert Taft.

On the other side was Roosevelt. He wanted flexibility to help the Allies fend off Nazism. For this, he needed repeal of Nye's Neutrality Act. But the politics of the issue were treacherous. The country wanted to avoid any action that in any way could lead to war. Thus, Roosevelt was caught between his devotion to the Allied cause and the political risks engendered by that devotion. "I am almost literally walking on eggs," he wrote to a foreign official. "I am at the moment saying nothing, seeing nothing, and hearing nothing."

Throughout the year leading up to the Polish invasion, there had never been any doubt about where Alsop and Kintner stood. They viewed the rise of Nazism as a threat to Britain, and anything that threatened Britain threatened the United States. Joe Alsop had grown ever angrier at the appeasement policies of British Prime Minister Neville Chamberlain, who had effectively delivered Czechoslovakia to Adolf Hitler at the famous Munich conference of September 1938. In 1939 Noël Coward, "very Young Tory, belligerent and anti-Chamberlain," as Joe described him, visited Washington and gave Joe a pointed portrait of the prime minister. Chamberlain, said the famous playwright, "behaves exactly as though he were still mayor of Birmingham and as though Hitler were the mayor of Wolverhampton, and he would talk him round about sewage disposal by taking the tram over and laying all his cards on the table."

With the loss of Poland and with Germany at war with Britain and France, Joe became even more convinced that America could no longer afford isolationism. Americans, he believed, needed to understand the scope of the crisis, the instability of the world. This called for a magazine piece, or a series, employing the famous Alsop-Kintner narrative style, with glimpses behind closed doors and dramatic portrayals of powerful personalities. They decided to detail the emergence of the country's foreign policy from the Munich conference to the invasion of Poland—from autumn 1938 to autumn 1939. Wes Stout and Marty Sommers at the *Saturday Evening Post* encouraged the columnists, though they expressed concerns that the final product might conflict too directly with the *Post*'s isolationist leanings.

The writers proceeded. Joe knew that the events he wanted to write about were so sensitive, and so recent, that he and Kintner would encounter difficulty in getting people to talk freely, particularly the president. So Joe approached Cousin Eleanor in the hope that she would intercede in his behalf.

In a letter to Eleanor, Joe noted that Bob Kintner and he were "deeply in accord with the President's foreign policy" and believed "that the articles can be both vastly exciting and extremely useful in dispelling many foolish speculations, vague rumors and idiotic misapprehensions which now have a wide currency." He acknowledged a certain presumptuousness in his request. "But I do think if the articles are written they may prove mutually advantageous." The *Post*, he said, "has one of the largest, and certainly one of the most wrong-headed audiences among the magazines," and such a narrative treatment could prove quite effective in influencing readers. He added, "We should of course expect, if the President consents to help us, to submit our finished product to him before sending it to the *Post*." And the president's involvement would be totally shrouded by the writers. "Certainly," said Joe, "we would be most anxious to conceal it, for we wish to avoid like the plague any imputation of propaganda."

Joe's letter represented a blatant effort to have it both ways: to present himself as an independent newsman and not the New Deal stooge that some critics had suggested he was, while at the same time currying favor with the White House by secretly declaring his fealty to the president, and even denigrating the readers of his own magazine. Typically, Joe's tendency toward tactical sycophancy had lured him into the realm of hypocrisy—but he got the desired response from Cousin Franklin.

Joe also obtained a vast store of information from Treasury Secretary Henry Morgenthau, who had been intimately involved in U.S. foreign policy throughout the previous year. But getting him to open up wasn't easy. Joe proposed an elaborate arrangement under which he and Kintner would obtain access to sensitive Treasury information. When Morgenthau balked at elements of the plan, Joe grew angry, and his complaints reached such a pitch that Morgenthau's men threatened to cut him off altogether. The pushy Alsop quickly turned accommodating. "Bob and I are now very sorry that we were so vehement," he wrote to Morgenthau. "I cannot close without apologizing for taking so much of your time and for trespassing so greatly on your good will and helfulness."

The new approach worked better. A revised arrangement was negotiated under which Morgenthau would make available to the columnists the records of the incidents that interested them; then they would prepare a précis of what they would like to use. The précis would be submitted to Morgenthau, who would edit it as he saw fit. "Only when you have laid aside your blue pencil, will we be free to use the remaining material," Joe wrote to the secretary.

But Joe then pressed for an interview with Morgenthau to discuss the sensitive subject of secret U.S. airplane sales to France. Joe complained that he was not being treated fairly, and argued that it was not sensible from Morgenthau's own point of view to refuse to discuss the story. Once again, he pushed to the breaking point, but when Morgenthau expressed impatience he quickly pulled back.

Morgenthau liked Joe and was amused by his often mercurial behavior. He found Joe difficult to resist because of his White House ties and because the columnist so thoroughly prepared himself and knew so much about the topic at hand. He concluded that if he had such difficulty keeping information from Joe, his lieutenants must be experiencing even more difficulty. He instructed his staff to refuse all interviews with the snoopy columnist and refer all questions to himself. He also offered some advice on how to handle the irrepressible reporter: "You can say, 'Now, Joe, don't get ugly. Don't pound the desk. It is no use going into a tantrum, Joe, because you are not going to get anywhere. . . . Don't jump up as if you are going to leave the room or anything else. You are not going to get the answer.' "

The Alsop-Kintner team completed the series in late January 1940 and submitted it to the *Post*. But Stout rejected it as being too much a New Deal tract. Joe was furious and felt embarrassed that his White House intrigues should come to naught. He insisted that Stout write a letter to the president explaining the decision. In uncharacteristically rough language, Stout replied that Joe had known when he commenced the project that he had no guarantee the articles would be published. "It is true that I said and believe that the White House stacked the cards on you," he wrote. "The only alternative assumption is that you, believing in the rightness of the President's policy, stacked the cards on yourself by an unconscious process of selection and elimination. I should prefer not to repeat this in a letter intended for the eyes of the White House."

Though angry, both sides quickly sought to defuse the controversy. The *Post* paid the writers for their unpublished work, and Joe wrote to Sommers, "I know that you and Wes were both extremely generous to us and that you could only do as you thought best."

The writers next submitted the series to *Life*, but Henry Luce's reaction was precisely the opposite of Wes Stout's; he felt the narrative lacked sufficient point of view. That left *Collier's*, "which nobody reads," as Joe lamented in a letter to Alec Woollcott. The ever-tenacious Joe then hit upon the idea of publishing the thirty-thousand-word narrative in book form, as a kind of pamphlet of contemporary history. By March 19, 1940, the authors had a contract with Simon and Schuster. Produced in large type on tablet-sized paper, *American White Paper* ran to just 104 pages and sold for $1 a copy. The advance was modest—$500. But almost immediately the *Ladies' Home Journal*, published by the *Saturday Evening Post*'s parent, Curtis Publishing Co., bought the serial rights for $7,500—$5,500 to the authors, and $2,000 to Simon and Schuster, which the company promptly invested in a promotion campaign for the book. "So ... the poor Curtis Publishing Company is going to have to print the damn thing after all," Joe wrote to Woollcott.

Published on April 22, 1940, *American White Paper* caused an immediate sensation. Loaded with behind-the-scenes drama, complete with quotations attributed to top U.S. officials in private conversation, the little volume spun a tale of a government struggling to forge a foreign policy that served the country's geopolitical interests while passing muster with a wary electorate. The authors sprinkled the manuscript with salty expressions from Secretary of State Cordell Hull, Undersecretary Sumner Welles, and Assistant Secretary A. A. Berle, Jr., as well as Roosevelt. They quoted copiously from Berle's private diary. They even provided a facsimile reproduction of the longhand draft of Roosevelt's proclamation of a limited national emergency following the September outbreak of war. The dramatic predawn phone conversation of September 1, 1939, between Bullitt in Paris and Roosevelt in the presidential bedroom first saw print in *American White Paper*; it served as the book's lead anecdote.

In a concluding chapter called "Into the Future," the authors suggested that the nation likely would have to decide whether to aid the allies "by methods no longer short of war" or take the consequences of a German victory in Europe. Defeat for Britain and France, they asserted, would force the United States to "treble our Navy, radically alter our economic system, and meet the ultimate issue between us and the dictatorships bent on dominating the world." Such a challenge, they predicted, would force the country to "bid farewell to the historic freedom for which the founders of this Republic toiled and fought."

It was a doomsday analysis, in character for the intellectually excitable Alsop. In looking at events, Joe tended to extrapolate outward, drawing stark conclusions as to where particular developments were likely to lead. This analytical framework often led him to a deeper understanding of the news than most of his journalistic colleagues demonstrated, but it sometimes left an impression that he suffered from a kind of Chicken Little syndrome. He may have been correct about the consequences of a German victory in Europe, but few Americans at the time were prepared to accept such an analysis.

Reviewing the book for *The New York Times*, Ralph Thompson said the authors had "pulled off a journalistic stunt of the first order." He called the volume "astonishingly informed" and "extraordinarily interesting," though he questioned some of the direct quotations in conversations the authors never heard, such as the Bullitt phone call to Roosevelt. "It is highly unlikely that Messrs. Alsop and Kintner, of all places they could have been hiding that fateful morning, were hiding under the presidential bed." In a long article the same day, the *Washington Star* said the authors obviously had access to "reliable 'inside' information" and suggested the book "apparently is an effort to provide a basis for intelligent formation of public opinion by explaining dramatically and in clear language the problems arising from the war."

Some critics characterized the book as no more than a propaganda vehicle for an administration that wanted war but wouldn't dare say so. They noted a private conversation recounted in the book between Vermont's Republican senator Warren Austin and Roosevelt. "I think we should indicate our purpose to support the democracies and legislate with that in mind," said Austin; replied the president, "I am glad to hear you say that, but I can't say it myself."

Within a week the book had sold more than 12,000 copies; over the next weekend, 5,264 sales were recorded; the following Monday morning, 5,103. Then the president weighed in. Asked about the book at a news conference, Roosevelt pronounced the volume "extremely interesting" and added, "If it were not for the fact that it might be considered advertising someone else's wares, I would say that I enjoyed reading the book." When those remarks went out over the news wires, sales shot up further. Ultimately, the book sold nearly 90,000 copies, bringing the authors $7,547 in royalties. Altogether, with the $5,500 from the *Ladies' Home Journal* and $1,500 from the *Saturday Evening Post*, Alsop and Kintner each earned $7,250 from the venture.

Even Joe could not have foreseen, when he wrote his letter of entreaty to Cousin Eleanor, what a wonderful symbiosis the venture would be for himself and the president. Using Joe as a kind of front, Roosevelt was able to communicate to the American people just how hard he was working to manage a diplomatic crisis that threatened to engulf the nation. And using Cousin Franklin as a premier background source, Joe was able to add considerably to his wealth and fame.

But in Europe the crisis deepened, and so did Joe's depression. "I wish to God that some wise rooster could convince me the sky isn't falling," he wrote to Woollcott in the spring.

Then the sky did fall, as the Germans pushed west, circumventing the French Maginot Line defenses, trapping a British army at Dunkirk, and, in a forty-day lightning war, conquering Belgium and France. "It seems to me extremely probable," Joe wrote to Woollcott in August 1940, "that within a space almost too short to let one catch one's breath, the whole world and way of life we know will be swept utterly away. If England goes under as rapidly as many of our military and naval experts fear she may, we shall be virtually powerless to defend this hemisphere."

For Joe, events in Europe reflected two geopolitical realities. One was that when all was said and done America's loyalty lay with England, the country's democratic motherland, and not with Germany. The other was that American isolationism was untenable in the face of a military power bent on destroying the European democracies and stretching its influence around the globe.

But many powerful forces denied the global realities that stirred Joe and the administration. Arthur Vandenberg, the strong-willed but level-headed senator from Michigan, believed it was simply impossible to stop what was going on in Europe without going to war. And hence this "treacherous idea" of employing "methods short of war" was just so much hypocrisy. "My quarrel," he declared, "is with this notion that America can be half in and half out of this war." Even in the wake of Germany's stunning continental victories, Vandenberg and his allies held the political whip hand.

But they faced two relentless adversaries in Alsop and Kintner, who emerged among the nation's most expert laymen on matters of military preparedness, the country's capacity for producing tools of war, and Britain's strategic need for particular armaments. In talks with Morgenthau, the writers learned that in January 1939 the United States had been producing airplane engines of 1,000 horsepower or more at a rate of 7,000 a year. By summer of 1940, when the interviews took place, the production rate was up to 21,000, and by January 1941 it would climb to 28,000. But each warplane needed two engines, and so engines caused a great production bottleneck. That led to a series of Alsop-Kintner columns promoting greater production efforts.

When Walter Reuther, a major official of the United Auto Workers, proposed converting unused auto-plant capacity to the production of airplanes, Alsop and Kintner promoted the idea. When William Knudsen, the production wizard who had headed General Motors and now ran Roosevelt's Office of Production Management, sought to let the Reuther plan quietly die, the columnists exposed the former industrialist's maneuver. Joe found, toiling away in one of Washington's obscure preparedness agencies, a bright young lawyer named Joseph Rauh, who was only too happy to keep the columnist apprised of behind-the-scenes activities related to war production. Rauh had been at Harvard with Joe, but as one of the Midwestern "high school boys" he had been all but ignored by preppy Alsop and his friends. Now Joe treated Rauh and his agency allies with respect. "We leaked our socks off," Rauh recalled years later.

Joe and Kintner fought for a conscription law to supply American forces with sturdy young men. They advocated sending "surplus" American destroyers to Britain, and promoted efforts to bring endangered British children to American shores. They pushed for the Lend-Lease program to aid the British warmaking effort. Their column heaped praise on allies of the cause, such as Bill Bullitt and Republican presidential nominee Wendell Willkie, whom the columnists considered a man of the hour for smiting his party's isolationists at the GOP's 1940 Philadelphia convention. "By nominating Wendell Willkie at Philadelphia the Republicans firmly rejected the English-model appeasement program insistently offered them by the adherents of Sen. Robert A. Taft," they wrote.

In June 1940, Joe joined a small organization called the Century

Group, a collection of Eastern establishment figures bent on sounding the tocsin for war preparedness and the dire need to aid Britain. This august assemblage included lawyers Dean Acheson and John Foster Dulles, clergyman Henry Sloane Coffin of Union Seminary, publisher Henry Luce, businessmen Will Clayton and James Warburg, and several prominent college presidents—James Bryant Conant of Harvard, Henry Wriston of Brown and Ernest Hopkins of Dartmouth. At thirty, Joe was the youngest member of the group.

One summer evening in Washington, he received an unexpected visit from an attaché at the British embassy named John Foster, who revealed an exchange of secret cables between Roosevelt and Britain's new prime minister, Winston Churchill. Churchill had warned that his lack of destroyers could permit a German landing on British shores and begged for a contingent of spare U.S. ships to help patrol the English Channel. Roosevelt's reply had been discouraging. Foster asked Joe for help in mobilizing American opinion, and Joe turned to the Century Group. The group assigned Joe to determine the Royal Navy's plight and the availability of U.S. ships. He learned that the British had only sixty-eight battle-worthy destroyers, while American destroyers outnumbered all others in all the navies of the world.

But Roosevelt, bent on a third-term candidacy, didn't wish to stir up the isolationists, while Willkie felt obliged to keep his party from splitting apart on the issue. Federal law forbade the transfer of naval armaments unless the chief of naval operations certified that it wouldn't damage the country's national interest. Joe proposed that the Century Group ask both candidates to state jointly that such a transfer of destroyers would serve the national interest, thus nullifying the issue in the presidential campaign. A Century Group delegation called on the president, who suggested a radio broadcast in support of the idea by General John J. Pershing, hero of World War I. The committee kicked into action. Columnist Walter Lippmann helped draft the speech; Joe arranged for air time; another Century Group member, Herbert Agar, approached Pershing. On Sunday evening, August 4, Pershing delivered a national radio address exhorting the country to save Britain by sending surplus destroyers. "All the things we hold most dear are threatened," he said, adding that such a move would help prevent, rather than hasten, American involvement in the war.

Roosevelt received a legal rationale for the destroyer transfer when Dean Acheson and a group of other distinguished international lawyers published a letter in The New York Times suggesting that the president didn't need congressional approval for the destroyer transfer. Churchill, meanwhile, promised, as a quid pro quo, U.S. access to certain British territory in the Western Hemisphere for naval and air bases should the need arise. Willkie promised to withhold any political attack, and on September 3, 1940, Roosevelt announced the deal to the public. The reaction was surprisingly mild. Joe, who initially had felt that the Century Group's efforts would be largely futile, was elated.

Mixing journalism and political activism brought complications, however. In the summer of 1940, Joe had visited Admiral Harold Stark, chief of naval operations, and sought information on naval policy. Saying he represented the Century Group, Joe had asked if the navy's leadership favored release of the destroyers. Only with assurances that the navy approved, he told Stark, would his group promote the destroyer deal. When Stark demurred, noting the political and legal difficulties involved, Joe pressed on. If those difficulties could be smoothed out, he continued, would Stark and his top brass approve the deal? Stark replied ("not without solemnity," as Joe recalled later) that in those circumstances he would consider the destroyer transfer to be in the national interest.

A month later Joe began pushing the destroyer deal in the column. "If England is not to be defeated," he wrote, "the English Channel must be held. To hold the channel, destroyers are vitally necessary." Debunking a "widely disseminated theory" that naval officials opposed the transfer of fifty destroyers to Britain, Joe wrote, "The highest naval officers join the President, and virtually every other man in the government to whom the facts are known, in firmly believing that the needed destroyers ought to be made promptly available." The NANA column, in addition to running on editorial pages throughout the country, also was carried in the news columns of *The New York Times*.

The next day that paper's Arthur Krock, a leading isolationist among American newsmen and to Joe a consistent annoyance, appended a note to his regular column disputing Joe's characterization. The Alsop-Kintner column was written, said Krock, "specifically to contradict repeated statements in this space that the Navy's high command opposes the suggestion on several grounds. A recheck among the highest staff men at the Navy Department today brought confirmation that the opposition still stands."

The passage angered Joe, but anger turned to rage when Krock revealed that his source for the item was Admiral Stark. Writing to Stark, Joe said he had been "gravely injured professionally" by suggestions that his column had contained a "pure fabrication." He informed Stark that he felt a necessity to defend himself in a letter to the *Times*, which he enclosed with his correspondence to Stark. "You will observe that the letter omits your name, and does not mention any connection with any group, which it seems unnecessary to bring into the controversy," wrote Joe. "In common justice, since you have discussed the matter with Mr. Krock already, I think you should . . . assure him privately that the statements in the letter are substantially correct."

In Stark's view, Joe had violated an understanding under which Joe had accepted the conversation with Stark purely as background and promised to avoid any reference to the admiral. "In my humble opinion you have not observed this promise even though you have not specifically mentioned my name," he wrote to Joe. In his letter to the *Times*, Joe defended his journalistic integrity by providing the outlines of his visit with top naval officials. "I asked a question in the plainest possible terms," he wrote, "and received what seemed to me the plainest possible reply. And that reply, it also seems to me, was quite adequate foundation for the statement Mr. Kintner and I subsequently published." The letter never made it into the *Times*; either Joe thought better of sending it, or the paper declined to run it.

Just what accounted for the disparity in Stark's statements to two prominent journalists is difficult to determine. In a letter to Helen Reid, Joe said that the admiral was "a nervous Nellie of a man, unwilling to make any decision, however small, without consulting higher authority." Joe revealed to Mrs. Reid that he had noted, in his talk with Stark, that Navy Secretary Frank Knox had expressed support for the destroyer transfer. Stark apparently hadn't wanted to contradict his civilian boss—although the admiral had been expressing totally different lines with people of different views. "I have no regrets about it," wrote Joe, "for while I am not yet sure what Stark's real views may be, I know that what I said about them was more than justified by what he told me."

The letter to Mrs. Reid reflected a deep conflict that Joe had stumbled into. As a journalist, he should have considered Stark's real views to be paramount. If Stark's statement to Joe had been born of intimidation rather than conviction, then Roosevelt and his allies on the destroyer issue still faced the problem of the navy's true outlook. All that was news, and Joe's readers expected him to provide news, whatever it might be. But as a political partisan with strong views on a major issue, he had a different interest entirely: to push events in the direction he favored. By writing that the navy brass supported the destroyer deal, even if it didn't, Joe could help force the issue and perhaps nudge the brass in the desired direction.

That Joe knew he was vulnerable on the matter was reflected in his *Times* letter, in which he implied he had visited Stark as a newsman rather than as a political partisan. "I told the gentlemen to whom I had applied, who were qualified in every way to speak for the professional personnel of the Navy, that I wished to say nothing and write nothing unless they believed the release of the destroyers to be in the national interest," he wrote, finessing the fact that he actually had visited Stark as a representative of the Century Group. As an opinionated citizen, perhaps Joe could take satisfaction in what he had done; as a newsman, he had brought discredit upon himself.

ALTHOUGH THE WAR in Europe remained Joe's central preoccupation, he still had time for other concerns. One was clothes. Joe devoted abundant time to ensuring that he had one of the most impressive wardrobes in town. He ordered dinner jackets, trousers, and suits from London, and grew anxious in late 1939 lest the war interrupt his ability to get such items from E. Tautz and Sons on Oxford Street. He issued specific instructions on what kind of dinner jacket and trousers he wanted, should Tautz still be in business: "The material should be the thinnest available among the plain, unpatterned stuffs for evening clothes, and in color of the darkest midnight blue you have." He wanted it to be double-breasted, with a shawl collar faced in satin. The trousers should have "a very broad single stripe of satin braid." Tautz should send the clothes airmail, "as I need new clothes rather badly."

He was disappointed in the shirts he received from E. & E. Hummel & Co. Ltd. on London's Bond Street: "I like my shirt fronts plain, without a pleat, and the points of the collars spread rather too far." And he had to return several items ordered from Brooks Brothers in New York—a set of evening shirts with cuffs that were too large, a pair of shoes that didn't fit, and a "day shirt" that didn't button all the way down the front. But he still liked to do business with Brooks Brothers, and ordered seven new shirts. "Your custom department will give you my sleeve length and neck size."

Joe was, as always, resplendent when he traveled to the two political parties' summer nominating conventions. In Philadelphia, where the Republicans congregated, Joe paid $9 a night to stay at the Drake Hotel. He flew to the Democratic convention in Chicago on American Airlines, paying $64.80 for the round-trip ticket. But the cost of staying at the downscale Hotel Stevens was only $4 a night.

At the beginning of summer Joe felt that the likely Republican nominee, Wendell Willkie, would defeat his Cousin Franklin in November, and he bet Pennsylvania's Senator Joseph Guffey $25 on the election. But as summer wore on, his views changed, and he hedged his Guffey bet by placing nearly $200 on Roosevelt in various wagers. Joe's predictions on the election were tied closely to war news from Europe. And in June 1940, as Britain prepared for the furious air battle for control of her skies, Joe's mood was dark. As Hitler's bombers and fighter escorts descended upon the island in the thousands, attacking shipping, aerodromes, war production plants, and even civilians in their homes and offices, England's fate and destiny hung in the balance. Never in nearly a thousand years had the English been so threatened by an external force.

But by August it was becoming clear that the resourceful pilots of the Royal Air Force were winning the Battle of Britain. Hitler had failed to get command of the skies, and without it he could not launch an invasion. Businessman William J. "Wild Bill" Donovan, a World War I hero and a trusted adviser to Roosevelt despite his Republican affiliation, returned from a trip to England with an optimistic assessment of the air war. On August 10, the Alsop–Kintner column provided readers with an inside account of Donovan's "glowing report on England's chances." Soon Joe's military intelligence sources were echoing the Donovan view. "So [the British] seem to have at least an even chance to hold out," Joe wrote to Frankfurter on August 21. "At least there are grounds for hope."

JOE'S INTERVENTIONIST CONVICTIONS dominated his social persona as well as his column, and his increasingly well-known outspokenness was never far from the surface. At a Georgetown dinner given by a Massachusetts congressman named Richard Wigglesworth, Joe found himself in conversation with a German embassy official named Herbert Scholz. Scholz, along with his lovely Bavarian wife, enjoyed prominence on the Washington social scene, and was a tireless defender of the Third Reich to increasingly skeptical Washington audiences. To introduce a point about the German–American relationship, Scholz posed a question to Joe.

"Well," he said, "suppose your country goes to war with Germany. What's the first thing you would do?" Joe paused for dramatic effect, then spoke up in a voice audible across the entire dinner table.

"The first thing I would do," he said, "would be to arrest you and put you in a concentration camp."

The German responded with uneasy laughter, and the host quickly changed the subject.

By this time Joe had emerged as a leading journalistic friend of the defense and foreign-policy establishment. Its top officials—Cordell Hull, Sumner Welles, Henry L. Stimson—never became close to the brash young man with the zeal for saving Britain. But he enjoyed close relations with the younger men who arrived in town and coalesced into a corps of pro-British enthusiasts as Roosevelt's New Deal liberalism gave way to foreign-policy demands.

Many of these friendships were rooted in Joe's tribal past and hereditary connection to the Anglo-Saxon sodality. Dean Acheson, son of a prominent Episcopal bishop, a Grotonian and Yalie, had grown up near Avon at Middletown, Connecticut. His family and Joe's were connected through an intricate pattern of friendships that stretched back a generation or more. James Forrestal, a Princeton graduate from a prosperous Hudson Valley family, met Joe through his friend Sheffield Cowles, who was Joe's cousin and stockbroker. Sheff Cowles was the son of Joe's Auntie Bye, the handicapped but forceful sister of Teddy Roosevelt. From New York came Archibald MacLeish, the new Librarian of Congress, whose family had been friends with the Alsops, and whose wife Ada came from a Connecticut banking family that the Alsops had known for years.

Through these interlocking alliances, Joe met other influential policymakers in Washington. At the War Department were John McCloy and Robert Lovett, right-hand men to War Secretary Henry Stimson. Lovett—"outstanding boy" in his class at the academically prestigious Hill School near Philadelphia, and a member of Yale's Skull and Bones— was the son of a wealthy railroad executive. After a successful career on Wall Street, he had moved to Washington to help in the quiet effort to prepare America for war. McCloy, who had grown up poor in Philadelphia under the guiding hand of his widowed mother, went to Amherst and Harvard Law. He was a testament to the readiness of the nation's ruling establishment to open its ranks to aspiring young men from the outside, if they accepted the values of the elite along with its wealth and power.

Joe delighted in meeting with these friends and other prominent people for dinner parties at the F Street Club or at his lavishly decorated Dumbarton Avenue house, which he had purchased in the autumn of 1940 for just under $20,000. Soon foreign dignitaries were added to the guest list: Isaiah Berlin, the British embassy's brilliant attaché, who was becoming one of Joe's closest friends; French financial wizard Jean Monnet; and T. V. Soong, a rich banker and brother-in-law of Chinese leader Chiang Kai-shek. Soong was in Washington seeking U.S. financial assistance for his country's desperate struggle against the invading Japanese.

The center of attention often was Justice Frankfurter, the avuncular mentor to the young interventionists of Joe's circle. Frankfurter "was very much one of us," recalled Isaiah Berlin years later. "He had the right views, he was fond of Roosevelt, he was jolly and amusing, and he had a Viennese coffeehouse kind of persona." Frankfurter also brought other young protégés into the circle. One was Philip Graham, a brilliant young man from rural Florida who had gone to Harvard Law School and served a Supreme Court clerkship before marrying Katharine Meyer, daughter of the publisher of *The Washington Post*. Joe had met young Katharine Meyer a few years earlier when her parents persuaded her to invite this rising pundit and social gadabout to one of her "coming-out" parties in Washington society. Joe had appeared at the Meyer home at his most rotund, and young Katharine had been startled to find herself being escorted by such a fat young man. "I was taken aback," she recalled years later. "It wasn't exactly what I had planned on for my coming-out party." But now Joe was more presentable, and he formed a close friendship with both Katharine and Phil Graham.

Joe also became a friend of presidential confidant Harry Hopkins, a former social worker and son of an Iowa harness maker. Hopkins was so close to the president that he had his own suite of rooms at the White House. For years a top domestic policy liberal in the administration, Hopkins now was emerging as a power on foreign policy, a crucial communications link between Roosevelt and Churchill, and a partisan in the delicate effort to aid the European democracies. Joe cultivated Hopkins as friend and source, and Hopkins responded by accepting Joe's Georgetown hospitality and slipping him information about White House goings-on.

Joe also maintained his close ties with Eleanor and Franklin, who appreciated him all the more after the success of *American White Paper*. As usual, they invited Joe to the family quarters for a Christmas Day celebration in 1940, and he found the president looking happy and "full of life" following his third presidential election victory and a much-needed vacation at Hyde Park. Still, Joe was concerned that the president's "color was not as good as might have been wished," as he put it in a letter to Avon. Young Franklin, the president's son, told Joe that his father looked better than he had after the rigors of the fall campaign. He had taken to afternoon naps, and the family was "pleased and satisfied by the way in which he had been picked up by his little vacation."

During the celebration, Joe and Cousin Eleanor led sixteen couples in the Virginia reel, and the old-fashioned dance seemed to stir a flight of nostalgia in both Eleanor and Franklin. They spent a substantial time in a corner, drinking the awful White House punch and talking with Joe about the old days. Eleanor said she had learned her fondness for such amusements as square dancing from Grandmother Robinson, and she went on at length about the wonderful parties Grandmother had given for the young people at Orange, New Jersey.

"There will never again be such women as Grandmother Robinson and Auntie Bye," said Eleanor. The president readily nodded his assent.

As the party was breaking up, Joe quietly invited young Franklin and Harry Hopkins home for a nightcap. After the short cab ride to Georgetown, Joe pulled from his refrigerator a bottle of champagne and the three nursed the contents as they discussed the political situation. Joe's guests provided an update on the president's leanings.

"The temperature at the White House is rising fast," said Hopkins. Now that the election was over, he added, the president was determined to have a final showdown with the isolationists. Joe was thrilled.

A few weeks later, Roosevelt celebrated his third inauguration, and Corinne came down from Avon to join in the festivities. Joe got a good seat in the press section and found himself stirred powerfully by the occasion. The air was crisp, the sky a cloudless blue, and the president's speech struck Joe as "magnificent." Afterward he and Corinne went to the White House for lunch and mingled with the high and mighty of official Washington. Joe spent considerable time with Justice Frankfurter, who was full of animation and bounce as he buttonholed guests and carried on his erudite banter. Mrs. F., as Joe called the justice's wife, seemed "rather souffrante" with a cold, but otherwise cheerful. The food, of course, was lousy—"three pieces of cold meat each, with a scoop of dank vegetable salad, and a cup of tepid coffee," as Joe described it later.

That night Joe and his mother crossed over to the other side and joined a dinner party at Cousin Alice Longworth's big home on Massachusetts Avenue. Among the guests were some of the city's leading isolationists—Senator Robert Taft, New York *Daily News* publisher Joseph Patterson, Mrs. Hanna Simms, who in earlier days had married into the family of Chicago's fiery press lord, Colonel Robert McCormick. Joe felt "like a mongoose in a whole nest-full of cobras."

As 1941 wore on, the president seemed to get his way more and more. As early as September 1940, Congress had given Roosevelt a selective-service bill that enabled the military to call up enough men to fill nine infantry, four armored, and two cavalry divisions, while increasing the strength of eighteen National Guard divisions. The following March Joe rejoiced as Congress passed the Lend-Lease measure, which made available billions of dollars for Britain's war effort. As Roosevelt signed HR 1776, Stimson knew privately what Vandenberg had said publicly—that it was only a matter of time before America's young men would be "offering their own bodies to the flames," as Stimson wrote in his diary.

But to the impatient and excitable Joe Alsop, events weren't moving fast enough. Luftwaffe bombs continued to rain on London. The battle for the Atlantic intensified as the German U-boat fleet grew from twelve to thirty, and approached fifty by August 1941. Luftwaffe planes destroyed nearly ninety ships in the first three months of 1941, while German ships accounted for another thirty-nine sinkings from January to July. Soon British ships were being sunk at three times the rate of construction.

For Joe these events posed a personal crisis. How could he, at age thirty, spend nearly all his waking moments seeking to nudge his country into war, thus forcing perhaps millions of young Americans into the terrors of combat, while he blithely enjoyed all the comfort, fame, and fortune that had come his way? He possessed his share of human flaws—the calculated sycophancy, the petty hypocrisy, a capacity for selective self-delusion—but on basic issues he could not escape a basic truth learned at home: Character counts.

He was, after all, a Roosevelt as well as an Alsop. Perhaps, as Franklin and Eleanor had suggested, there wouldn't be again any such women as Grandmother Robinson and Auntie Bye. But there was Corinne. The sisters of Theodore Roosevelt had had a profound influence on Joe's mother, and she served as a pretty close approximation of those powerful women. She had drummed into the consciousness of her sons, in ways direct and indirect, the cult of TR that had so captivated her mother and her aunt: Be true to your ideals; principles must beget action; the meaningful life is the one guided by considerations larger than one's self; the greatest of the virtues is courage. Soon Joe was making plans to give up all that he had built for himself in Washington—the column, the magazine work, the large income, the ringside seat at the pavilion of history. He had decided to become one of history's participants.

Part Two

WAR

DISBANDING THE COLUMN

Adventure and Adversity
in the Far East

BY SUMMER 1941, the European war was making its way across the Atlantic and lapping at American shores. War news, war debates, war preparations now dominated the American scene. Joe knew that events could not remain in drift for long. But he was tired of waiting.

"This fat life here, at such a time as this, is now more than I can bear," he wrote to Cousin Eleanor in a letter asking for a reference vouching for his "moral and mental character." He had decided to apply for an officer's commission in naval intelligence. Cousin Eleanor gave him the reference, and on June 10 he was accepted. Immediately he set about shutting down the column, renting out his house, and preparing to head for India as a naval lieutenant. Bob Kintner, who had been married a few months earlier, joined the army as a commissioned officer and maneuvered himself into a Washington desk job.

It seemed remarkable that two men who enjoyed so much success and influence would make such a decision. Franklin Roosevelt told friends he believed Alsop and Kintner could do him more good as columnists than as military men. But for Joe it was a necessary move. Just about every formative influence in his life—the family heritage, the TR mystique, Pa's sense of duty and Ma's sense of moral courage, the Grotonian devotion to English ways and traditions, Harvard's attention to the burdens of class, and Joe's own connection to a president struggling to lead his country in what he considered the proper direction—pointed him toward this course.

"A few weeks ago I became convinced that this country was either going to do something soon or let its last opportunity slip," Joe wrote to Wes Stout at the *Saturday Evening Post*. "In the first case I knew I should want to be in service anyway; and I considered the . . . second so appalling that I did not wish to be in Washington if that happened."

News of the column's breakup attracted letters from all over the country. "I salute you both and send my best wishes," wrote the assistant executive editor of the *Chattanooga Times*. Ben Reese, managing editor of the *St. Louis Post-Dispatch*, asked for a first option on the column in St. Louis "when and if it is resumed." A *Post-Dispatch* reader named Helen Newman noted in a letter to Joe that he had been "referred to many times in print, as 'that zealous Anglophile,' " and hence she wasn't surprised by his decision. But she added: "I shall miss your column," which she labeled "darned good reporting." The *San Francisco Chronicle*'s Paul Smith wired Joe, "Terribly sorry to lose the column but congratulations to you and Bob on your action." And Joe Regan, who had taught all the Alsop boys at Groton, wrote, "You've done a grand job which I hope you'll be back on again after you've done one on Adolf."

Joe replied to all such letters, but reserved his warmest expressions for Wes Stout at the *Post*. "My association with the *Post* has been the pleasantest of my business life, and . . . I shall always be grateful for your unfailingly kind and generous treatment of me," he wrote. "It is very difficult to convey in words the very real satisfaction that such an association gives."

Joe rented out the Dumbarton Avenue house to William Coolidge of Boston for $325 a month, furnished. He purchased a ceremonial naval uniform, complete with sword belt, sword, and Colt .45 pistol. Proudly displaying his new finery, Lieutenant (junior grade) Alsop made his way to San Francisco and shipped out by Pan American Clipper for the Far East, where he was scheduled to assume his intelligence duties as a "naval observer" in Bombay. In Honolulu, he stopped by to visit with Admiral Husband E. Kimmel, the obscure commander of Pearl Harbor whom fate would soon rob of his obscurity, along with a substantial portion of his fleet. Joe displayed his ignorance of naval matters by commenting on the sleek lines of the "destroyers" lined up in the harbor. "Those are battleships, sir," exclaimed the admiral's aide.

From there it was on to the Philippines, and then to Hong Kong via a slow Dutch boat. In Hong Kong, Joe took note of "those wonderful British women . . . who have healthy red faces, no matter what the climate may be, wear healthy British clothes, no matter what the effect may be, and somehow manage to carry with them their own healthy, right little, tight little atmosphere, no matter how exotic their surroundings." In a letter to Avon Joe suggested that "their limitations, and the exactly similar limitations of their menfolk, are their principal source of strength. . . . I suppose if you have more imagination, you are also more timid."

Joe could see that Hong Kong certainly was not timid. The military had placed the island city in the best possible defense posture, considering the inherent weakness of its geographic position. But, while talk of the Japanese threat was much in the air, the unimaginative British colonialists, preoccupied with making money, felt a Japanese assault on European enclaves was really inconceivable. Not surprisingly, Joe felt contempt for those who failed to understand the dangerous realities of the fast-changing world. "They could not see that a policy of appeasement in the Far East would certainly mean the eventual total liquidation of their position," he wrote to Avon.

But he took heart in the fact that the new Churchill government in England was shaking up Britain's complacent Far Eastern diplomats. Now the reins of power were in the hands of a different type of Englishman—men like Sir Archibald Clark-Kerr, British ambassador at Chongqing, whom Joe considered "imaginative, full of intellectual curiosity, with an eye for the future rather than for the dividends."

In Hong Kong Joe encountered an eccentric *New Yorker* magazine writer named Emily Hahn, known to her friends as Mickey. Hahn insisted on taking Joe to a Hong Kong opium den, which turned out to be a dreary brothel in a run-down part of town. Upon telling the madam that they didn't wish to go upstairs, they were ushered into a dingy cubbyhole of a room with two lumpy old couches and two naked electric lightbulbs hanging on wires from the ceiling. A cheerful, plump girl with a peasant's face cooked the opium over a lamp until it bubbled, then skillfully molded half a saltspoonful into a pipe for the patrons to smoke. As the drug took effect, time contracted and expanded oddly, and everything seemed simple and pleasant as the two writers talked on about China and the world. "The entire bout of dissipation, including the massage, cost three dollars in our money," Joe wrote to Avon. "If one had not heard so much about it in the contrary sense, it would have seemed a rather innocent way to spend an evening . . . mildly agreeable, and really hardly worth the trouble involved."

From Hong Kong Joe made his way by plane to Chongqing, China's provisional capital, and into the Asian war. An ancient city perched atop a long narrow bluff at the convergence of the Yangtze and Chialing rivers, Chongqing had become China's capital through the dictates of war and geography. When the Japanese army in 1937 burst forth from its enclave of conquest in Manchuria, it quickly took Beijing and Tianjin in the north, then pushed south to take Shanghai after a brutal three-month siege. From there the Japanese moved easily to the capital at Nanjing, forcing Generalissimo Chiang Kai-shek and his wife to flee just two days ahead of them. As the Japanese continued their advance and the Chinese people rushed into their country's interior in one of the greatest mass migrations of all time, Chiang moved his government first to Hankow and then to the geographically protected city of Chongqing, which overlooks the great rock gorges that separate central China from the interior.

Now, nearly four years later, in the summer of 1941, the city still stood sentinel over the land routes and riverways that could bring an enemy west into the Chinese heartland. The fog and rain cast their seasonal pall over the inhabitants, and left behind residues of slime on the stone stairways of the city's back alleys and of its entry points. Chongqing was filled now with the human debris of war—government officials, shopkeepers, street peddlers and streetwalkers, aristocrats and peasants and the ruling elite—who crowded into its walled precincts and into the bamboo suburbs downriver. From 200,000 at the war's beginning, the population had swelled to a million.

Every day the million contended with conditions of life contrived by the Japanese to crush their spirit. Joe soon discovered that at least once a day, sometimes several times, enemy bombers would swoop down on the city, depositing lethal cargo and sending people scurrying into shelters. Coats of plaster dust lay over everything, and it became nearly impossible to keep the inhabitants supplied with the bare necessities of life.

Joe had been in Chongqing barely a day when the shrill air-raid bells signaled urgently. Following instructions, he grabbed a water bottle and flashlight and joined the townsfolk in a dank, smelly shelter. There he crowded against other inhabitants in mutual discomfort as the drone of bombers drew near. Everyone sat still, many with their hands over their ears and all with their mouths wide open to diminish the impact of concussion on their eardrums. "The astonishing thing about it all," he later wrote to Avon, "is the aching boredom of the whole performance."

In Chongqing, Joe sought out contacts who could introduce him to the upper levels of the government and diplomatic corps. Through T. V. Soong, still in Washington, Joe met Pei Tsu-yi, manager of the bank of China (and father of the future famous architect, I. M. Pei), who promptly invited Joe to spend a day at his mountaintop retreat outside Chongqing. Unfortunately, much of the day was spent in the banker's private bomb shelter, but the Japanese afforded enough of a respite at midday to allow a "perfect lunch" of kidneys and mushrooms stewed in wine, eggs scrambled with tomatoes, and salted fish with rice.

With a letter of introduction from Washington friends, Joe made contact with Britain's Ambassador Clark-Kerr, who invited the wayward navy man to a dinner at his villa. Joe even managed an invitation to a garden party given for the generalissimo and Madame Chiang. Joe sized up Chiang as "a very great man, with a knack even surpassing the President's for keeping in balance all the forces whose support he requires to do his job." He viewed Madame Chiang as a "striking but rather sinisterly polished woman."

At the garden party Joe encountered Claire Chennault, former U.S.

Army aviator and now Chiang Kai-shek's air minister. Chennault was a tough and blustery Louisianan whose pockmarked face and impaired hearing bespoke the many hours he had spent in open cockpits throughout a turbulent army career. Joe sized up Chennault as something of a "gamecock of the wilderness" reminiscent of the Jacksonian epoch. Though seemingly rough-hewn, with homespun demeanor and old-fashioned American humor, he had "a peculiar home-made learning" that manifested genuine intellectual depth. Largely because of his poor health, but also perhaps for his heretical views on air power, he had been forced out of the army in 1937 and found his way to China, where he won the confidence and friendship of a desperate Chiang Kai-shek.

The result was the American Volunteer Group, which consisted of a handful of battered P-40 fighter planes and a collection of undisciplined but courageous American pilots who had been allowed to resign from the U.S. military in order to help China fend off the Japanese advance. Chennault had forged this group, known through legend as the Flying Tigers, into what a China observer called "one of the most spectacular single striking groups in the history of aerial warfare." Chennault, clearly a tactical genius of air power, had created an elaborate warning system that kept him informed whenever a Japanese plane took to the skies. He carefully studied Japanese aerial tactics and the capabilities of their fighter planes, so that he could mold his own combat tactics to maximum advantage. He honed his pilots' aerial skills to so fine a point that their kill ratio reached ten to one. Soon Chennault would take command of the China skies and end the daily bombing ordeal at Chongqing and other major cities.

Joe wanted to join this rugged air commander's campaign to stave off further Japanese conquest. Though he had been mainly preoccupied with events in Europe, for years Joe had decried the Rising Sun fervor of Japan and the threat it posed to Britain's and America's Pacific interests. In Washington he had helped his friend T. V. Soong obtain U.S. aid for the Chongqing government, by working behind the scenes to set up meetings between the Chinese financier and top U.S. officials.

Even before he left Washington, Joe had discussed prospects for a transfer to the AVG with friends Jim Forrestal and Bob Lovett, rising stars in a government increasingly preoccupied with the war. They had explained that the presidential order creating the AVG and allowing American servicemen to resign from the military in order to join the U.S.–sponsored military unit would apply to Joe if Chennault wanted him in his command. They also suggested it would be more exciting than being stashed away in India as a naval observer.

At the garden party, Joe and Chennault talked at length and agreed to meet again later at Chennault's headquarters in Kunming, to the south. After a long discussion at Kunming, Chennault offered Joe a position as "his aide and odd job man," and Joe accepted. He wired his resignation from the navy before sundown, and set out next morning on the ten-day trip over the famous Burma Road to Rangoon, where Chennault ran a training camp and where Joe planned to execute the paperwork to leave the navy officially.

Joe made the trip with a *New York Times* reporter named Tilman Durdin in a large sedan automobile made available by Pei Tsu-yi and his Bank of China. Their guide was an obsequious Chinaman named Mr. Kao, whose conscientious ministrations often became overbearing. Day after day they proceeded on the 712-mile route through Yunnan province, over rocky dirt roads, up steep mountainous terrain and then down again into what looked like jagged holes in the earth. After twelve or fourteen hours on the road, they would reach their evening destination—a small town with a Bank of China facility where bank officials would provide a meal and a bed, which usually turned out to be merely a board with a blanket.

At the town of Pao-shan, which they reached at seven p.m. after thirteen hours on the road, bank officials had prepared what they presumed to be a special treat—Western–style cooking. They were ushered into a small room off the bank's courtyard, where they found Ovaltine and stale British biscuits. Only after an hour and a half of chitchat with the local bank superintendent did the main meal arrive—roasted poultry, including a plate of pigeons roasted whole, with their heads still on. The guests were given only chopsticks to eat with, and the challenge turned out to be an ordeal for the ravenous Americans.

A few days later, when the party arrived in the town of Lung-ling at midnight in a torrential downpour, the springs on the sedan were gone. So Joe and Durdin abandoned the vehicle and proceeded by bus. They reached Rangoon a few days later via a combination of bus and river steamer and promptly checked into the Strand Hotel, the best hotel in Burma.

But Joe soon discovered that naval officials in Rangoon had no record of his Kunming telegram. After waiting around for ten days he was instructed to proceed to Bombay. There, after wiring several pleas for help to his well-placed friends in Washington, he received word that he would be released from the navy as soon as his records could be audited. Disgusted and depressed after a week of waiting, Joe decided to let the navy take care of the matter on its own. Risking a court-martial, he returned to Rangoon to join Chennault.

In mid-October he was assigned staff secretary to the AVG, which meant he would act as Chennault's foreign secretary within the intricate structure of command and support in which the unit operated. Though it was sponsored by both the Chinese and U.S. governments, and though it operated at several British bases, the AVG was directly responsible to no government, and none assumed direct responsibility for supplying Chennault's tactical and logistical needs. Hence, the commander had to beg, cajole, and browbeat authorities of three nations to get what he needed. And the man who did most of the begging, cajoling, and brow-beating was Joseph Alsop. He drafted cables, prepared memoranda, wrote letters, set up requisition lists, and worked out plans. He traveled to Singapore to establish ties with British officials, and headed off to the Philippines in search of crucial spare airplane parts. In the Philippines he met for an hour with General Douglas MacArthur, who struck Joe as a man of brilliance undercut by vanity.

The next morning he took a Pan American Clipper flight to Hong Kong for further supply foraging among British military leaders. The date was December 7, 1941.

Joe didn't know it when he climbed into the airliner for the trip to Hong Kong, but he had managed to get the last commercial flight to leave Manila before the American protectorate would be besieged by a Japanese military machine that would swarm throughout the Pacific. One of the earliest advocates of American entry into the war was about to become one of the war's earliest American victims.

Upon arriving in Hong Kong, Joe learned of the Japanese attack on the Seventh Fleet at Pearl Harbor. The war he had long expected now was reality, and though he was appalled by the carnage in Hawaii he felt a measure of satisfaction that America's military and industrial might now would be applied to the Allied cause. He didn't have time to savor this powerful turn of events or dwell upon its implications, however. Japanese troops were swarming toward Hong Kong, and the specter of being captured by the Japanese and imprisoned as a combatant hovered over him. He needed to get out of Hong Kong as quickly as possible.

But every other Westerner felt the same imperative, and the result was chaos as people scrambled for a seat on any airplane flying out before the expected siege. Joe finally booked passage on what he figured would be one of the last planes out, scheduled to depart on December 12. Then at the last minute he was bumped from the flight. Madame Kung, Chiang Kai-shek's sister-in-law and one of the famous Soong sisters, had taken the seat for her large dog. It was indeed the last seat on the last plane out. Joe was trapped.

Within hours Hong Kong was under siege, and there was nothing to do but wait for the imminent arrival of the enemy, and probable incarceration by the Japanese. Joe cabled home word of his predicament.

It took nearly two weeks for the Japanese to arrive, and in the meantime Joe helped the St. John's Ambulance Corps with the grim duty of caring for combatants who were wounded trying to forestall the Japanese advance. The ambulance corps also helped Chinese civilians injured by Japanese strafing at the waterfront, where the Chinese customarily gathered for their rice rations. Joe spent his off hours at the old Gloucester Hotel, where many of the English and Americans gathered. He received some excellent advice from a U.S. colonel named Mid Condon, who told Joe to destroy any evidence of his association with the AVG. He should try to pass himself off as an American newsman, said Condon, who speculated that military prisoners were in for a rough experience, whereas civilians might get better treatment, and might have at least a chance of being repatriated within a reasonable time.

Joe burned his uniform and passport, along with all other identification papers, and obtained from the U.S. consulate a certificate of identification saying he was a newsman. He then purchased a store of canned food and pieced together makeshift bedding from a large blackout curtain and two chair cushions taken from the city's American Club. He asked Mid Condon's mistress to sew into his coat collar a collection of second-rate sapphires he had purchased in Burma. He reasoned that the sapphires, along with a sizable wad of cash in his possession, would come in handy on the prison black market. Joe, Condon, and Condon's mistress sat quietly in her dimly lit room as she sewed. Soon they could hear the sound of military bands leading the victorious Japanese army into the city. By morning—Christmas Day—the enemy would have Hong Kong.

Joe retained a measure of freedom for nearly a week, as the Japanese left most Westerners alone while they mopped up their victory. Meanwhile, Joe huddled with a hundred or so other Americans in the American Club, sleeping on the floor at night, suffering the weight of anxious boredom by day.

Then, on a warm winter morning lit by pale sunlight, the Japanese ordered all British, Dutch, and American nationals to report to the Murray Parade Ground with such personal effects as they could carry. The scene that morning on the broad city street that ran past the parade ground bespoke the utter transformation of the Asian world. More than 3,500 Westerners—men, women, children, old, young, sick, healthy—trudged up Queens Road, clutching suitcases and makeshift bundles, stopping intermittently to ease their fatigue. Throngs of Chinese lined the street, looking on in amused wonderment. At the parade ground the Westerners mingled in mutual anxiety until, at about noon, the Japanese gendarmes and interpreters arrived. They briskly lined up the assembled into columns of four and marched them away in shifts. Joe had a larger store of provisions than most—a bag of food, a cot, his heavy curtain and cushions from the American Club. The Japanese didn't mind, but an old-fashioned English trader turned on Joe, suggesting he would "lose face" if he appeared to be hoarding provisions for imprisonment. Joe replied tartly that the foreign community in Hong Kong didn't have enough face left to worry about, and the trader stormed off.

Joe and his contingent were marched a mile and a half to an old brothel called the Stag, which was to house 140 Westerners—up to four or five per room, in cubbyholes that previously had housed single prostitutes. There was no heat, no light, and no bedding beyond what the prisoners had brought themselves. The food was bad and scarce—an official ration of two cups of rice and two cups of gruel daily, plus whatever could be obtained on the black market from "brothel runners" who spent considerable time out in the city.

It was a bleak existence, but what struck Joe was how easily he and his fellow internees became accustomed to it. A kind of prison society emerged, along with a camaraderie born of the fact that all were equal in their misfortune.

On the seventeenth day, occupants of the Stag were herded out to an alley, aligned four abreast, and marched to the waterfront. As they waited for a boat to take them around the harbor to their permanent prison, a crowd of Chinese began milling about. The Japanese gendarmes barked orders and strutted menacingly to control the crowd, but one hapless young Chinaman didn't get the message. As the startled Westerners looked on, he was dragged into a clearing by a gendarme and struck brutally with a bamboo carrying pole.

The gendarme then tried to make the man kneel for a formal beating, but, crazed with fear and pain, the Chinaman rolled around on the ground in an instinctive effort to avoid further punishment. The gendarme beat him mercilessly. Then another gendarme ran up and joined the attack, using a steel golf club. Finally, the Chinese gave a convulsive shudder and was still. The gendarmes returned to their posts as the crowd stood frozen in stunned silence.

At last a large harbor boat arrived, and the internees were herded aboard for a short ride to Stanley Peninsula, a narrow finger of land running out to a hill on which stood what had been known as Stanley Fort. Nearby was a prestigious British boarding school where a samurai warrior had sliced off the head of a schoolmaster as he attempted to greet the conquering Japanese peacefully in his library. When Joe, as a member of an advance team to inspect the Stanley area, came across the schoolmaster's decapitated body, he immediately helped himself to as many of the dead man's books as he could cart away, for perusal during the long, boring weeks ahead. Though he was criticized at the time for his hard-heartedness, Joe could never see anything inappropriate in his behavior. After all, no action on his part could have helped the poor dead schoolmaster.

The two central realities of Stanley Prison were the wretched living conditions—overcrowded and lacking anything remotely resembling normal amenities of life—and meager food rations. The internees attacked the first reality by making the prison as habitable as possible, cleaning up the area, repairing dilapidated furniture, finding uses for materials that would have been discarded in any normal society. The second reality was a constant; the rations provided by the Japanese constituted a policy of slow starvation.

It turned out that Joe had been wise to take into prison the sapphires and as much cash as possible. The guards inspected newcomers casually, in hopes that valuables not confiscated from prisoners would make their way into the prison black market—and eventually into the guards' own hands. Joe's cash and other valuables served as currency for the purchase of extra rations of food, which protected him from beriberi and other ailments tied to malnutrition. Joe took pains to share any black market food that came his way, and often organized "pathetic little parties" where attendees would each get a small ration of biscuits and a cup of weak Nescafé, which was considered "a great delicacy."

The internees, moving quickly to establish a prison hierarchy, elected two China Coast traders—one British, the other American—as chairmen of their respective communities. Simultaneously, they chose block committees, established communal kitchens, organized working parties, and formed a camp welfare committee. Joe was amused, as he later wrote, to see the familiar features of any political structure—the jockeying for position, the political promises and weaseling, the perquisites of office, the murmurs of discontent, and the "final, fumbling accomplishment of most of what had to be done."

Joe established a prison routine that sustained him through most of his time at Stanley. He would spend half the morning monitoring the black market, then take a lesson in the Chinese language from a prisoner friend named Charlotte Gower. After lunch he would study Chinese, handle his laundry (the only time in his life that such mundane chores fell to him), and mix with his fellow prisoners. In the American bachelors' quarters he participated in a kind of in-house coup that ousted two oilmen who had appointed themselves inmate bosses and replaced them with a burly navy warrant officer called Jingles. The oilmen, in the view of the coup plotters, had become too friendly with the Japanese.

Joe witnessed the extremes of human nature under pressure of adversity. He was disappointed to see one member of the Mickey Hahn circle become an informer for the guards in exchange for extra rations. But watching Elsa Stanton, a cheerful woman who was rumored to be among the richest Westerners on the China Coast, was an inspiration. Though she entered the prison with a broken leg and moved about only by dragging her large cast behind her, she spent long hours attending the sick and wounded. When the guards gave each prisoner a duck egg in celebration of Japan's sinking of the British battleships *Repulse* and *Prince of Wales,* a controversy erupted between those who wanted the eggs distributed to the Western children in the camp and those who felt each person should be allowed to keep his own egg. A decision was reached to allow those who wanted to give their eggs to the children to do so, while those who didn't could keep them but would have to eat them raw.

The hunger problem was accentuated by the fact that Cheng, the Chinese strongman who ran the prison as a kind of concession, was stealing part of the internees' food before distributing it. The result was that nutritional diseases were becoming rampant. Finally one of the internee chairmen managed to sneak out to issue a protest with the high gendarme officers across town. The officers sent in a man named Yamashita, a former barber at a Hong Kong hotel, as Cheng's assistant.

After the new man verified the complaints, Cheng was dismissed and Yamashita installed as prison superintendent. The situation improved, but regular food rations were still barely sufficient to sustain a healthy life. The average meat ration was five ounces per week per person, including buffalo bones.

Once, feeling close to starvation, Joe made his way to a black market exchange in a hidden, dank room to barter some gold jewelry for a little oatmeal. He got the oatmeal but was disgusted by the disagreeable scene of human meanness and degradation that he witnessed in the process. A black market thug negotiated the deal while fondling two young girls on a dirty bed, as a lavish evening meal was cooking on a kerosene stove.

The days passed in routine ways—the task of staying clean and keeping the surroundings tidy, the exchange of petty gossip, the traffic in rumors. People didn't seem to have much energy or inclination for much else. But, despite the privation, Joe felt fortunate to be where he was and not in one of the more notorious prison camps throughout occupied Asia. Survival was at least possible at Stanley.

MEANWHILE, BACK IN the United States, the anxiety and anguish at Avon were nearly more than Joe's parents could bear. Corinne called Pa Watson, Franklin Roosevelt's assistant, and requested one of her "little chats" with the president. Traveling to Washington by train, she spent nearly an hour with Roosevelt, enlivening him as of old but also imploring him to do whatever he could to ensure that Joe's name would appear on the country's prisoner-exchange list. Roosevelt assured his irrepressible cousin that he would do everything he could to help her son.

In late July word reached Joe that Stanley prisoners were to be exchanged. By Japan's inexplicable logic, American civilians in Hong Kong were considered innocents because it had been a British "imperialist area," just as British civilians captured in the Philippines were released because it had been an American area. Joe and his fellow internees were jubilant.

A Japanese ship carried them to Portuguese East Africa, whence they returned to America aboard a Swedish hospital ship called the *Gripsholm*. It was a particularly enjoyable journey; Joe's old friend Chip Bohlen also was on board, returning to America after his own detention in Japan following Pearl Harbor. Chip had been a member of the U.S. legation in Tokyo when the war broke out. During the long journey to New York Harbor the two savored the lovely expectation of homecoming.

"I shall never be able to tell you how I have missed you," he wrote to Avon. For nearly eight months he had received no news of home, except for a *Harper's Bazaar* photograph of Corinne as leader of the Connecticut Land Army. Back in America, he rushed to Avon for a rousing celebratory welcome during what seemed to him a particularly lovely and lush Connecticut summer. To Brother John, he looked as if he had been dragged through a keyhole, but fit and strong.

Joe could hardly believe his luck to have returned home in such good shape. Many prisoners who actually had been newsmen had suffered serious abuse. Some had been tortured, and one had lost half of each foot to gangrene. Yet he had managed to get off with "nothing worse than a cuffing and a pair of broken glasses," as he put it in a letter to Avon. He felt more hearty and healthy than he had felt for years. "I left the damn place better than I have ever been," he wrote home.

Joe's first hope was to return to Chennault, who by now was a general in the U.S. Army and whose AVG had been absorbed into America's Far East war effort. Joe wanted to get an army commission so he could serve his mentor as military aide. To his embarrassment, he failed the physical exam. He had contracted syphilis in China, and he was ineligible for military service until after he could be treated successfully. Determined to return to China in some capacity, Joe went to see his friend Harry Hopkins. The White House potentate got him assigned to Chongqing as chief of the Lend-Lease mission under administrator Edward L. Stettinius, Jr., a fast-talking, fast-rising former industrialist whose direct supervisor was Hopkins. Joe's new salary was $7,500, not bad for a wartime job in a place where even Americans on low incomes could live like tycoons. By late autumn of 1942 Joe was on his way back to China and to the war that had engulfed his country and the world, as he had predicted it would.

STEWART'S WAR

"In Other Words, He's Found Himself"

SHORTLY AFTER PEARL HARBOR, Stewart rode the train to Washington to visit the military attaché at the British embassy. His aim was to join the British army. It wasn't that Stewart preferred the uniform of the motherland to that of his own country. For months, even before the Japanese attack, he had tried to join the American military. But his history of asthma and a problem with high blood pressure had kept him out. Even Joe's effort to help by trading on his Washington contacts had proved futile.

Now, as America mobilized for war, Stewart's only hope was a direct commission for "limited service" as a desk-bound military bureaucrat. He couldn't accept that, so he decided to test the British service's reputation for being less demanding on physical standards.

The attaché was a tall, thin major with a large mustache and the mumbling manner of a nineteenth-century British colonialist.

"Eyes all right?" he asked, upon hearing that Stewart had been turned down for U.S. service. When Stewart replied that he had 20-20 vision, the major promised to have the young man on his way to England within weeks. Stewart would be joining the King's Royal Rifle Corps, an infantry unit that had originated in colonial America as the Sixtieth Royal Americans. The major offered some advice that demonstrated the gulf then separating the old ways from the new. "Be sure to take a dinner jacket, and a shotgun for grouse season," the major advised. "And, if you can manage it, ship over a small runabout—very useful for weekends."

No runabout was in evidence when Stewart's parents and brother John drove him to the Hartford train station on April 15, 1942, for his two a.m. departure for the port city of Halifax, Nova Scotia. There was a last-minute family get-together at the station coffee shop before Stewart boarded the *Montrealer* and headed off to war. Much of the talk inevitably centered on concerns about Joe, who was then imprisoned in that faraway Japanese camp. Years later, John remembered the night as "terribly depressing."

But a sense of meaning helped transcend the feelings of depression. Pearl Harbor had given America—and Stewart—precisely what the young literary editor had called for in his *Atlantic Monthly* piece a few months before—"something to believe in, to live for and die for." Now the war would come first, and it would be fought not only over something as simple and profound as the Anglo-American tradition of democracy and freedom, but for national survival itself. Stewart possessed qualities needed in that great cause. He had shed most of the insecurities of his Groton career and the slovenliness of his early New York years. At twenty-seven, he was six feet tall and weighed 170 pounds, with a sense of purpose and the demeanor of a leader. He had plenty to offer—and now could keep up with his more successful older brother.

As Joe languished in that Hong Kong prison, he continued to lead the way for his brothers, as he had done all their lives. Stewart and John had never resented Joe's successes or his tendency to play the role of their guidance counselor. They felt no sibling rivalry where Joe was concerned. He had always offered thoughtful gestures to show how much he cared about them. He repeatedly had invited them down to Washington to participate in his high-powered dinner parties, and when they turned twenty-one he had arranged expensive soirees at which their obscure friends mixed with his famous ones. The boys loved to tell the story of how Joe took Stewart aside just before his coming-of-age party to warn with avuncular earnestness about the dangers of too much alcohol—and proceeded to become the first celebrant to pass out under the table from too much drinking.

Yet, for all the love and lack of resentment, it was sometimes difficult for Stewart to be in Joe's shadow, to watch Joe shine as Stewart struggled to establish himself in a manner befitting his family background and his parents' expectations. The war gave him a chance to do that, and Stewart embraced the challenge with enthusiasm and confidence. "Although I am as usual pessimistic in a general way," he wrote in his first letter home to Avon, "I'm very optimistic about the Alsop family specifically. Somehow I'm perfectly certain that no harm will come to any Alsop."

The freighter voyage across the Atlantic in a protected convoy proved uneventful, save for a few submarine sightings and an occasional practice depth bomb. Stewart found himself beguiled by the "English-ness" of the officers and men. But there wasn't much to do except read. He read all of Jane Austen and a number of books on war—Crane's *Red Badge of Courage*, Hemingway's *The Sun Also Rises*, and an obscure period piece which, as he put it, told "how to Make Good in the British Army."

When Stewart arrived in London in late May for a few days of sight-seeing, the devastation that had been visited upon war-ravaged London had a sobering effect on him. "The first time you see places where block after block is completely wiped out, your stomach really turns over," he wrote. "It's really difficult to evaluate the tragedy in human terms—small businesses wiped out, homes wrecked, people killed—because the ruins themselves are so impersonal."

He would be stationed at Winchester, Hampshire, in the red-brick Victorian barracks of the Sixtieth Rifles. Tom Braden, another Ameri-can, who had arrived earlier from Dubuque, Iowa, via Dartmouth Col-lege, was sent to pick up the new man at the train station. He found Alsop sauntering back and forth along the platform, cigarette in hand, overcoat over arm, nattily dressed in a pin-striped suit—"very Brooks Brothers kind of guy," recalled Braden.

"Hi, Yank," Braden shouted, adding immediately, "got any ciga-rettes?" The bombing of Liverpool had disrupted supplies, and the men of the Sixtieth Rifles had been dying for cigarettes. Braden figured the new guy might have a carton or two he could spare. Stewart carefully drew from his pocket a crumpled pack of Chesterfields, took out a single smoke, and handed it to Braden.

"My bags are over there," he said.

It was not an auspicious beginning for what was to become a thirty-two-year friendship. "I thought he was the biggest horse's ass I'd ever met," recalled Braden years later. But Braden and Alsop quickly became part of a gang of Yanks that came together for fun, adventure, and the kind of fraternal commiseration that helps stave off homesickness. The circle included Ted Ellsworth, also from Dubuque and also a Dartmouth graduate, a comical sort with a penchant for irreverent fun; George Thomson, whose parents had been friends of the Avon Alsops and who had a genius for getting himself well connected with the upper-class fam-ilies of England, particularly those with eligible daughters; and Harry Fowler, a New Yorker and Ivy Leaguer who went by the nickname "Plowboy" because of a rustic appearance.

Life was hard in the regiment. In the barracks, thirty-seven men slept—on straw mattresses on the floor—in a space designed for nine-teen. One man's face crowded another's feet. Food was often coarse and sometimes scarce; an egg came along twice a month. Cigarettes were ra-tioned at thirty-five a week. Water was cold except for two days a week. "I never thought I could work so hard and live," Stewart wrote, noting he typically trained for twelve hours a day or more. Evenings often brought a forced march—half running, half marching, with full pack and rifle—of twelve miles in two hours.

But the group had plenty of nights out. Stewart and his friends discovered Rosa Lewis's famous Cavendish Hotel on London's Jermyn Street, which became a social base camp for excursions of legendary gaiety. Rosa, a kind of cockney socialite, had been both cook and mistress to Edward VII when he was prince of Wales, and she had slept with a fair number of the prince's noble friends also. Her culinary abilities were famous, and the Cavendish had been one of the world's great luxury hotels. By World War II, however, it had become a bit raffish, as all manner of people would gather there to escape the worries of war. Rosa, endlessly entertaining, insisted that Stew was the bastard son of someone named Peebo Gardner, but she never explained who Peebo Gardner was.

Stewart spent a weekend with an old family friend named Elizabeth Herbert in Taunton, where despite the war he saw "perfectly kept grounds, eleven servants, huge masses of food, all the trappings of English country gentility." The family palace had been turned into a hospital, and the family lived in a space about the size of a small New York apartment. But, Stewart wrote, "it is all, everything considered, astonishingly pleasant and comfortable."

In June he went with Elizabeth Herbert to a Queen Charlotte's ball, a charity event that was the social occasion of the season for young aristocrats. It was reminiscent of those deb parties in New York and Long Island: "The girls looked exactly like the girls at the Senior Holidays, and there were the same complications about the unpopular ones." Such socializing became more difficult after Stewart and his friends arrived at a training camp in York, the cathedral town in northern England. Though weekend leaves were allowed, they lasted only thirty-six hours, and officer candidates weren't permitted to travel outside a ninety-mile radius. Stewart wrote home asking if his parents or their friends knew anyone within that territory who might be willing to put up a lonely Yank for a weekend.

Just such an excursion materialized in August when George Thomson managed an introduction to the premier baron of England, the Baron Mowbray and Stourton, who owned a place called Allerton Castle. The premier baron, as Stewart later explained in one of his books, "is the baron whose ancestors were barons before any other baron's ancestors were barons." Allerton Castle was not far from York, and Thomson received entrée there for a summer weekend. Asked to bring a friend, he chose Stewart.

Though the castle turned out to be a monstrous structure erected in Victorian times, it was surrounded by "incredibly lovely" grounds, and inside were magnificent Regency furnishings and family portraits by such painters as Romney and Van Dyke. The baron, who had bulging blue eyes, a large nose, and a recessive chin, initially seemed a bit of a stiff. "Good God," he said when the boys appeared at his door, the auto that had delivered them parked behind. "Always had a rule here, back to my grandfather's time. No motor cars. No Americans." But he invited them in nonetheless for what they expected to be a terribly dull time.

Not so. Martinis began flowing at once. A lovely dinner for twelve ensued, replete with salmon, lamb (probably illegally obtained), and hundred-year-old port. There were also the baron's pretty daughter Patricia and her friend of the same name, Patricia Hankey, who was only sixteen at the time but looked several years older. Following a drunken early-morning revel on the baronial lake, during which Thomson's boat sank to the bottom, Stewart lured the lovely Tish Hankey into the garden room and kissed her. "Urged on by 10 glasses of port, soft moonlight, and the scent of roses, I proposed marriage around 1:15 a.m.," he wrote his parents. He added that for the first time following such escapades he didn't wake up in the morning feeling like jumping into the artificial lake. "She really is utterly charming," he wrote. "The whole weekend, what with love and solid comfort combined, was wonderful."

This love didn't blossom immediately, largely because of Tish's young age and the protective instincts of her parents. Besides, Tish wasn't sure she felt the same about this fun-loving American as he seemed to feel about her. And she came from one of England's oldest Catholic families—"none of whom," as Stewart wrote home, "has married a Protestant in eight or nine centuries." But the young officer trainee clearly was smitten. In letters home he compared her to a Trollope heroine, "one of the really nice ones," and she appeared in his letters as Miss Moonlight and Roses.

Training at York was arduous. One maneuver entailed five nights of open-air sleeping in a bog. Stewart had purchased a serviceable sleeping bag and managed quite well, but several mates suffered frostbite; some required hospitalization. Actual conditions of warfare were simulated in training, with plenty of exposure to live ammunition. Stewart learned to ride motorcycles in daredevil fashion, repair automobile engines, handle a field wireless, fire a mortar, lead a platoon into battle, and behave according to regulation in the officers' mess.

He was impressed with his British mates when a stray German plane located the training camp and dropped two bombs on the premises. Though he felt like jumping into the nearest hole, he wrote, "nobody else paid the slightest attention. 'Hullo, bombs,' somebody said, and we proceeded to tea in a leisurely fashion."

In the summer, when word arrived of Joe's release, Stewart's letters burst forth with joy. "It's the most wonderful news I've ever had," he wrote home in July. Though he was naturally reserved in expressions or gestures of affection, Stewart freely expressed his love in letters to Avon. In correspondence with Joe he recalled a late-night conversation, after one of Joe's Washington soirees, in which the somewhat drunken older brother had said the only people he really gave a damn about were the family. "It really shocked me at the time," Stewart recalled, "but I find there's a lot in it." He added that the only people he really missed were his Avon clan—including, of course, the family's longtime nursemaid, Aggie. In a letter home, written as he contemplated combat, he confessed, "I want to say what I'm so bad at saying, how much both of you, and Avon, and all that goes with it, mean to me. It took a war to make me find out."

During his training period Stewart enjoyed a number of encounters with relatives who had made their way to England. Uncle Ted, Stewart's mentor at Doubleday, had become a U.S. Army general stationed in England, and Stewart made contact with him several times. "It's always well to have a general on your side," he wrote to brother John. And he saw Cousin Eleanor during one of the First Lady's 1942 London visits. He chatted with her at the Savoy Hotel in October, and though she remained in bed with a migraine "she babbled on in her usual amusing bird-like fashion," regaling Stewart with tales of her diplomatic exchanges with the British.

A month later the First Lady arranged for Stewart to be invited to tea at the home of Ambassador John Winant. Anthony Biddle, Jr., U.S. ambassador to Poland when the Germans invaded, was there, dressed extravagantly in a dickey with horizontal stripes and square-toed patent-leather shoes. He addressed Stewart as "old boy." A Lady Reading, who looked "like a dilapidated Spanish adventuress," came in with a crumpled piece of Spam, the canned "ham" produced to feed the troops, which she held up as an example of the marvels of Lend-Lease. The First Lady nibbled on the proffered morsel, "making appropriate appreciative cooing noises the while." As young Alsop reached over to take a cup of tea from Cousin Eleanor, a large brass button popped off the fly of his uniform trousers and noisily rolled across the room. It was a bit embarrassing, but "the tea was a great success," Stewart wrote to Joe.

As 1942 neared its close Stewart noticed an appreciable difference in British morale. In October British General Bernard Montgomery had scored a decisive victory over General Erwin Rommel at El Alamein in North Africa, and on the night of November 7 Allied forces had stormed ashore in Morocco and Algeria. Soon it became clear that the crucial ports of Casablanca and Algiers would fall to the Allies. "It's amazing to see what the news from Africa has done for the British Army's morale," Stewart wrote to Joe in mid-November. "Now we're all convinced that given half a chance we'll be more than a match for the Germans."

On December 17 Stewart and his friends became lieutenants in the King's Rifle Corps and began a celebration that lasted through most of their allotted two-week leave. The highlight was a Saturday-night bash at a high-toned London hotel that included a select group of twenty— the five Yank compatriots, a female member of Parliament, and no fewer than three ladies of title. One of the titled invitees was Lady Patricia

Mowbray and Stourton, daughter of the eccentric premier baron of Allerton Castle. Her young friend, Miss Moonlight and Roses, was barred by her protective parents from attending. "Her family," Stewart complained in a letter to Avon, "turns out to be pre-Victorian in its stuffiness and obviously regards me as a big bad old Protestant wolf bent on deflecting their jewel from the straight and Catholic path to some pagan doom."

With Stewart's commission came a new assignment to a British army service battalion, where he took over a platoon and continued training for war. He found himself in a company stationed "off in a horrible little industrial town" in Yorkshire, far from his Yankee buddies. Though the surroundings were depressing, he did enjoy the perquisites of rank, not least his monthly whiskey allowance and his army "batman," an enlisted valet assigned to minister to an officer's every worldly want. Alsop called his batman "a kind of alter-Aggie."

Though the calls of duty crimped Stewart's social style during these weeks, he did manage to get away for another Queen Charlotte's ball in London. He attended with a young woman who gave him "that moonlight and roses feeling all over again." Noting that his earlier affair of the heart had largely "petered out" as a result of the age difference and parental opposition, he wrote, "This new one is very promising. . . . The lady is blonde, the beautiful (peaches and cream type) daughter of a baronet, intelligent, politically liberal, twenty-one, no stuffy parents, and great fun." But at the ball he encountered Tish Hankey, who was "coming out" that spring, and soon he realized he wasn't prepared to give up entirely on the original Miss Moonlight and Roses.

Shortly thereafter, in June 1943, came word that the five Yanks could volunteer for duty in North Africa. Though there wasn't much of a war left in that theater, it was at least military action of a sort.

After more than a year in England, Stewart's appreciation of the British had deepened. "The more I see of them," he wrote to Joe in November, "the greater is my affection for England and the English. . . . In their own odd way, they're really a wonderful people." But, judging from the Eton boys he encountered, he concluded the character of the upper classes had deteriorated in recent decades. He found the Etonians snobbish, shallow, seemingly unprepared for the world as it was being transformed by the war.

Yet Stewart couldn't help sharing some of the upper crust's reverence for the golden days of gentry life. "My New York pink friends would be horrified by the statement," he wrote to Avon, "but the fact remains that an English country village dominated by a good huntin', shootin', fishin' squire is often a remarkably happy place, much pleasanter for all concerned than any proletarian paradise." As he prepared to head out for battle, Stewart mused that "there's something about the English of all classes that makes you rather reluctantly love them—their tolerance, their good humour under the most unpleasant circumstances, their kind-liness and goodness of heart, even their tacit assumption that you realize how unlucky you were not to be born English."

He was less reluctant in his love for Miss Moonlight and Roses. Af-ter Stewart encountered Tish Hankey at Queen Charlotte's ball that spring, he began writing to her and renewed his efforts to see her, though her parents forbade any real dates. "Our dates were lunches, not night-clubs and dancing, which is what he had in mind," recalled Tish years later. "By the time of North Africa, he had made up his mind that he wanted to marry me. I was about halfway there."

In July, after a two-week embarkation leave notable for the quanti-ties of alcohol consumed, Stewart and his four wartime friends linked up with a Sixtieth Rifles major named Puggy Powell, an army careerist straight out of Kipling, who regaled his young officers with tales of ad-venture from his earlier days in the Sudan. He had had six servants there, he recalled, five to look after him and another to look after the five. Before leaving port, the group smuggled on board a case of Scotch and a German shepherd puppy named Watling Street. The dog was dis-covered on board two days before they were to leave port, and that kicked up a lively controversy. Telegrams were dispatched to the War Office, launches were sent out for the stowaway (successfully hidden in the carpenter's cabin), orders were received by blinker light: "Dog must be removed or destroyed immediately." The entire ship soon squared off into a large pro-dog faction and a smaller but highly vocal anti-dog fac-tion. Finally the resourceful Puggy Powell hit upon the idea of designat-ing Watling Street the regimental mascot, which mollified military authorities offshore, and the group of seven—major, five Yanks, and dog—sailed for Africa.

After landing in Algiers, they made their way to a desert transit camp before a long, hot, uncomfortable trip in open-air boxcars across the sand to Sfax. "We just about died from the heat," Tom Braden recalled. They slept on their baggage and subsisted on hot tea made with water from the train's boiler, along with melons and hard-boiled eggs pur-chased from native Arabs, whom Stewart considered "incredibly dirty and ragged."

From Sfax the group sailed to Tripoli and Eighth Army assignments as platoon leaders. Braden and Ellsworth shipped out together and took Watling Street with them. They encountered a little action—"mostly skirmishes, not very heavy," as Braden described it years later. The other four found themselves squatting on the sands for weeks, awaiting or-ders. Finally Stewart was sent to a training course to master the Vickers machine gun, which led to a platoon assignment with a regiment that languished in the desert sun for several weeks near Alexandria.

In the fall of 1943, Stewart's unit shipped out for Italy, where the war was heating up quickly. The Allies had invaded in early September, with the British Eighth Army streaming across the Strait of Messina on Sep-

tember 3 and U.S. General Mark Clark landing four divisions of his
Fifth Army at Salerno on September 9. The campaign to push the Germans up the peninsula went well at first, but by late October it had
bogged down. Stewart arrived in mid-November, and by the time of his
first letter home from the campaign he had experienced the hazards of
mortar fire, a dive-bombing, and a machine-gun attack. He spent many
nights sleeping in an open orchard in torrential rain until he located a
small cave.

He was enjoying the relative comfort of a farmhouse one dark night
in November when word came that his unit in the field was the target of
a shelling attack. He quickly made his way through a deep, winding ra-
vine for about a mile until he reached his men. "No shells came anywhere near me, but I was perfectly certain that each one was carefully
aimed at me personally," he wrote to Avon. "I was delighted to hear at
last the cheerful cockney voices of the men, most of whom I like and admire more and more."

And then he experienced his first real battle. He was moving north
with his unit when suddenly the silence was broken by the crackle of
rifle and mortar fire. Stewart found himself "horribly nervous" at first,
and also "horribly tired" since he had had little sleep for days. He
moved his men into position, and they threw everything they had at the
enemy. "Once the whole thing actually got going," he wrote to Avon,
"with everything under the sun, including an enormous number of
rounds from my guns landing on the Germans, it was so wildly exciting
that I forgot to be either tired or scared." The enemy quickly retreated,
and the firefight proved to be brief and benign. There were no casualties
in Stewart's platoon.

Soon it became clear that the Allies were winning the campaign. Axis
troops, many of them Czechs or Poles inducted into the cause at the
point of a bayonet, or German kids of seventeen years or so, were being
captured in increasing numbers; for every shell the Germans lobbed the
Allies returned fifty. The Allies also dominated the air; the sound of aircraft overhead caused hardly a stir among Stewart's troops, who assumed the planes would be Spitfires. All this, coupled with news of the
German retreat in the Soviet Union, convinced Stewart that the war was
beginning to turn in the Allies' favor. "Tell Aggie to prepare my Christmas stocking for next year," he wrote home.

Still, field life was rough. Stewart came to treasure more and more
the gold cigarette case he had received the previous Christmas from Sis
and Joe. "When my morale is really low," he wrote to Avon, "when I'm
wet through, and sleepless, and I haven't changed my clothes for a week,
or had a hot bath or used a toilet for a month, my gleaming and luxurious cigarette case somehow reminds me that I am, after all, a civilized
human being."

In December, Stewart enjoyed a visit at battalion headquarters from
Uncle Ted. His uncle had not changed much since his days at Doubleday,

when he caused eyes to roll with his theatrical self-importance and his penchant for demonstrating at wearying length his ability to recite poetry. Word had circulated that Ted had lost an earlier command because of his inability to conquer the family affliction of alcohol—but he still enjoyed his lofty rank to the hilt. Upon arriving at Stewart's headquarters, he stopped his jeep dramatically in a cloud of dust, drawing a volley of shellfire from the entrenched Germans nearby and stirring some ire among the junior ranks.

Lunching with Stewart and some fellow officers, he was "tremendously Teddish . . . never stopped roaring for a moment—snatches of verse, vastly exaggerated tales of his experiences in battle or elsewhere, corny pronunciamentos." Once the audience had dissolved, he became more intimate and sympathetic. He suggested that Stewart seek a liaison job at the front, helping coordinate joint American-British activities, and offered his good offices to assist him in getting such a post.

Ted later wrote to Corinne of her son's circumstances and performance. He was thin, reported the general, but looking well and clearly standing high with his fellow officers. "He said," wrote Ted, "this war had done one thing for him: he knew now he could take care of himself no matter what conditions were—in other words, he's found himself."

Some weeks later, Stewart's unit was ordered out of the line. Getting back wasn't easy—"a bloody drive in the dark, and my truck turned over on the way"—but the return to relatively civilized living was decidedly agreeable.

After weeks in limbo, Alsop and George Thomson set off for General Dwight Eisenhower's headquarters in Algiers in search of a transfer to the U.S. Army. They arrived with letters from Uncle Ted and their British battalion commander recommending them for U.S. service. Looking at these papers, the colonel in charge of personnel exclaimed, "Jesus Christ, you two guys sure as hell are out of channels." He informed them that the U.S. Army was accepting no more transfers from foreign armies except for doctors, dentists, and flyers.

They put in for leave in London, where Stewart resumed his pursuit of Tish, while Thomson sought out his own pleasures. In London they encountered a U.S. Marine officer named Hod Fuller who told them about Operation Jedburgh, a highly classified joint operation of French, British, and American soldiers whose mission was to provide arms and liaison to the French underground, the maquis. The Jeds, as they were called, were taking volunteers, and the two Yanks quickly signed up. By spring they had a new unit and a new mission. Jed teams were trained to parachute into occupied France and join the Resistance. The idea was to assist the advancing Allied army after Eisenhower's expected invasion of France had opened up a second front. John Alsop, who had arrived in England as a second lieutenant in a military police unit, also joined the Jeds that spring, as did Tom Braden.

Operation Jedburgh was one of the most successful wartime missions of the Office of Strategic Services, which became the first full-fledged American strategic intelligence service. Its leader and guiding spirit was Wild Bill Donovan, the stocky Irishman whose optimistic reports from England had cheered Roosevelt at the height of the Battle of Britain. In constructing his intelligence operation, Donovan surrounded himself with men of the Eastern Ivy League establishment whose Anglophilia was easily discernible. These men in turn often hired underlings of similar background, all the way down to the London-based colonel whom George Thomson and the Alsop brothers visited in early 1944 in their efforts to get transferred into OSS—"a Wall Street lawyer like most of the senior OSS officers," recalled John Alsop. The colonel quickly signed up the three Ivy Leaguers.

Training was at a handsome base called Milton Hall in Peterborough, about sixty miles north of London. Stewart found his fellow Jeds an interesting lot—high-stakes poker players, randy as young goats—who reveled in the relative lack of discipline at Milton Hall. They were downright disrespectful when subjected to the officious pronouncements of officers who hadn't experienced the war in any serious way. One hapless "civilian in uniform" made the mistake of expressing how deeply he wished he could join the young men in the field rather than remain at the desk to which, upon orders straight from Donovan, he was chained.

From the back of the room, one American Jed quietly murmured, "Fifty-five."

From a few feet away came a more loudly uttered "Fifty-six."

Then, in a rising crescendo, with more and more Jeds joining in: "Fifty-seven, fifty-eight, fifty-nine, BULLSHIT!"

The startled OSS man hurried from the room as the Americans laughed and the more sedate British and French Jeds looked on in "mixed admiration and amusement." Soon the British and French were joining the chorus.

In April, Stewart went off to an eight-jump parachute course along with the other members of his three-man mission team, a French Resistance fighter named Richard Thouville and an American radioman named Norman Franklin. The parachuting was "quite something," he wrote home. "I don't think I've ever been so scared in my life." Describing the contrast between the pre-jump nervousness and post-jump exhilaration, he wrote of "the weak grins, the sickly jokes, the strained faces, and then loud cries of slightly idiotic laughter, and the general air of happy relief on the ground."

About this time, Stewart's interest in Patricia Hankey had deepened into love. Shortly after returning from his Algiers excursion, he wrote home:

I've been in England for four or five days, and I've seen Tish everyday, and practically all I can think of is how much I love her and how utterly wonderful she is and how much I want to marry her. . . . Besides being lovely looking, and intelligent and great fun to be with, and with a good strong mind of her own, she has a quality of translucent honesty and downright niceness about her that I can't describe. . . . Everyone who's seen her for five minutes has told me that I've obviously somehow gotten hold of one girl in a million. . . . I realize that all talk of waiting til after the war was so much pish-tush, and that the only sensible thing was to marry her immediately before she realized what a dope I really was, and changed her mind.

The word to describe Tish Hankey was "self-contained." When John Alsop met her, it struck him that she "exuded a certain coolness," an appearance of being worldly beyond her seventeen years. In addition to being lovely, she was stylish and gracious, and she smiled easily. Though naturally quiet, she enjoyed being surrounded by the youthful revelry so prevalent in London in those years. And she seemed confident of her ability to handle any situation. "You felt as if she could run anything," said John, recalling how she had taken charge of the evening when he arrived in London for the first time to meet her. But, of course, beneath the surface calm and the air of confidence resided the normal insecurities of any woman her age.

Early in the war, Tish had lost her only brother in the North African campaign. She was also tossed into the world of work much earlier than she would have been had her country not been fighting for its existence. But her coolness and self-assurance went beyond the circumstances of war. In school, she had moved quickly through the grades, leapfrogging over her peers and getting her high school certificate at age fifteen. Though the war had interrupted her schooling, her intellectual precocity had quickly been recognized and appreciated by Stewart.

For her part, Tish found Stewart to be immense fun. He didn't strike her as particularly good-looking, but he was always laughing and joking with his mates, and a certain glamour attached to him in those intense times when the dark realities of war swirled constantly around London. He refused to take anything very seriously and seemed bent on rushing headlong into the next social adventure. It all struck Tish as an exciting ride. As his ardor increased, she found herself falling in love with equal intensity.

But there were problems. Tish's parents weren't keen on the idea of an immediate wedding, if indeed they accepted the idea of a wedding at all. Tish was their only remaining child, and the prospects of her marrying an American and going off far from home were not pleasant to them. Besides, they didn't really know anything about this fun-loving American parachutist who was a dozen years older than their daughter. What were his family connections? What kind of financial security could he offer?

Though born into a landed family, Tish's father wasn't particularly well off. An old Etonian and one of nine children, he had made his way to Gibraltar, where he had run a shipping company. The war had disrupted his business, and subjected the family to financial difficulties. He was a "typical cartoon Englishman" who loved to shoot, ride, hunt foxes, and play polo. Since he could do all these things inexpensively in Gibraltar before the war, he had typically played polo three times a week and hunted twice a week in season. He had frequently taken Tish riding along the local beaches, until she went away to an English school at age thirteen. Tish's mother, half English and half Spanish, came from a long line of Gibraltareans who, for some two hundred years, had made their way largely as artisans and shipbuilders.

When war came and civilians were evacuated from Gibraltar, Tish and her mother sailed for England, where Tish completed her studies at the convent school, took a subsequent secretarial course, and then found a wartime job in the British Secret Intelligence Service. Her cover was the passport control office.

Prenuptial discussions between Stewart Alsop and Arthur Hankey did not go well. Stewart took Tish and her father to lunch at the Berkeley Hotel one spring Sunday in 1944, and then the three proceeded in the tube to Kew Gardens. When Tish conveniently wandered off to feed the ducks, Stewart pressed his case for Tish's hand. Hankey, "writhing with embarrassment" at the need to discuss Stewart's financial position, was horrified to learn that the young man had an annual independent income of less than $2,000 and didn't know what he would do after the war. It really wasn't enough, Hankey suggested. He had to be assured of Tish's financial security should she be left a widow. That set in motion a three-way negotiation among father, suitor, and suitor's father back in Avon.

Ultimately, Joseph Alsop came through with a generous package. He increased Stewart's monthly allowance from $150 to $200, which augmented his army pay enough to ensure a decent living standard. He bestowed $7,500 as a gift in 1944, with $6,000 promised annually thereafter as an advance on Stewart's inheritance. Those sums, combined with an anticipated trust distribution due the following year from an uncle's estate, and assets Stewart held in the States, proved sufficient to mollify Mr. Hankey.

But Stewart still had to contend with Mrs. Hankey, whom he considered "something of a dragon." It didn't go well when he presented his case during a country weekend with the Hankeys. Mrs. Hankey clearly looked down on the non-English, and Stewart just as clearly showed his defensiveness. Tempers appeared short. Then brother John showed up, just in time to save the day. He treated the dragon with extreme deference, tossed out casual references to Alsop family connections and ancestral acres, and demonstrated a solicitude that Stewart was incapable of affecting. Though Mrs. Hankey took Tish aside and asked why she didn't marry the younger Alsop, she was won over sufficiently to permit a marriage to the older one.

There wasn't much time for wedding plans. Stewart's jump into France had been put on hold because Thouville had sprained an ankle in a motorcycle accident. That provided a last opportunity before the bridegroom-to-be would be swept away on his mission. With Stewart at Milton Hall, Tish herself had to get her ring and a marriage license and make arrangements at her parish church, St. Mary's on Cadogan Street. The ceremony took place as planned on June 20, 1944, with a small group of relatives and friends in attendance and buzz bombs screaming overhead. With John Alsop away at parachute school, George Thomson served as best man.

Then began a honeymoon that was bizarre even by wartime standards. The newlyweds took the bridal suite at the Ritz for four days, and established themselves as host and hostess for a parade of friends and acquaintances who trekked through to help celebrate the happy event. John hurried down from parachute school, bringing his jump partner, Reeve Schley. Thomson stayed around for the festivities, as did assorted other friends. Rosa Lewis came by, bringing in tow a collection of friends and Cavendish guests, as well as her Scottie dog, Kippie. At one point, Tish asked if they couldn't get away by themselves for an evening.

"Why?" asked Stewart.

"Because it's our honeymoon," said Tish.

Replied the groom: "Tish, this is my leave."

It was an expensive four days, but Sis and Percy Chubb had sent over $1,000 as a wedding present, and that just about covered the bill at the Ritz. Then it was back to Milton Hall for Stewart and back to the passport office for Tish. After he was placed on standby alert to fly out from a military airfield near London, the relaxed OSS command allowed Stewart to spend evenings in London. Each morning the newlyweds would part not knowing whether they would be back together that night. Three times Stewart was told his jump day had arrived, and each time the mission was postponed. Then in mid-July, shortly after his requested transfer to the U.S. Army finally came through, the fateful night arrived.

At the airfield Stewart's team, dubbed Jed Team Alexander, was escorted onto a Lancaster bomber, along with an O-group—coup de main specialists whose mission was to blow up an important bridge. Team Alexander, armed with slung carbines and entrenching tools for burying parachutes, was to jump into the area of Aubusson and Guéret in central France, where the Germans maintained a generally light hold on the towns. This was barely a month after the Allied invasion, and every German soldier who could be spared was at the Normandy front. Finally, the big bomber roared into the moonlit midsummer sky.

The flight to the drop zone—Dee Zed in British military parlance—lasted four hours and included a rough passage through German antiaircraft fire. As the plane circled in search of Dee Zed, the jump team was placed in position. Stewart, as the first to go, sat with his legs dangling over an open hole in the floor of the plane. The others sat behind, each with legs around the man in front. The neophyte jump master told Stewart not to wait for the normal verbal signal but to jump as soon as he saw a light flash. Some time later a light flashed, and Stewart plunged into the night.

It was a mistake—and the kind of mistake that could claim a jumper's life. Someone had thoughtlessly begun fiddling with a flashlight, and Stewart had leaped from an airplane flying much faster than any recommended jump speed, at an altitude of two thousand feet rather than the standard seven hundred. Though he had been in peril, Stewart didn't know it as he floated toward earth and landed in a tree that broke his fall just above ground. But shortly after his landing he realized his error—and his peril. Struggling to control his fear, he set out through the hazardous night in search of safety. Approaching a village, he triggered a frightening chorus of barking dogs and retreated back into the woods to smoke a cigarette and consider his situation. "Face it, Alsop. You're in trouble," he said to himself.

He was indeed in trouble. With much fanfare Hitler earlier had announced that anyone caught working with the Resistance would be shot as a spy. Stewart made his way to a road and watched from the bushes as various cars and trucks passed. On a hunch he decided to present himself to the occupants of a rickety truck that seemed too old to be a Gestapo vehicle. Miraculously, it turned out to be a maquis truck. The occupants welcomed him and took him to a château where he ate excellent French food and drank old wine until dawn. Soon he was reunited with his Jed mates.

After moving from château to château for several days, the team was ordered into an area of the French Périgord region that hadn't had any maquis presence. At that time the Germans controlled the big towns, main roads, and routes nationales, but the maquis controlled villages and small roads. So they made their way, stopping often to ask the locals if any Germans had been seen in the area, and making quick dashes across the routes nationales.

It soon became clear that the Allies were winning the European ground war; the Germans increasingly found themselves on the run. Many Jed operatives ended up serving more as staff officers and military journalists than as spies. With his radioman, Stewart dispatched to London tactical information to be used by the advancing Allies. The team also witnessed a number of small battles, with lots of firing but little damage, as the Germans opted for retreat over engagement. There was plenty of wartime comfort, as the maquis made sure they were well accommodated in châteaux or villas. Stewart spent only one night in his sleeping bag.

In October, Stewart reemerged in London to report to OSS and receive orders for his next assignment. Two weeks later he returned to France, but this time no jump was necessary. He and Braden penetrated the ragged German lines in a Jeep. The mission was modest—to help the maquis put military pressure on a German unit holding out in a western port. "It wasn't much of a war—three shots a day would be about the average," Stewart wrote. Life consisted mostly of enjoying the gaiety of a people being liberated after five years of occupation. He was in London once again by late November.

By this time Tish was pregnant, and Stewart moved to arrange her passage to America so that the baby could be born there. Now that he was to become a father, Stewart hoped for an OSS desk job in Washington. Otherwise he would be on his way to China, where brother John already was headed. Intent on seeing Tish comfortably settled in Avon before the baby's arrival, Stewart booked passage for her on what turned out to be an unfortunate convoy ship with twenty-eight passengers. Caught in fog for ten days, it took nearly a month to get across the Atlantic. Tish spent both Christmas and New Year's aboard ship, before finally arriving in New York harbor on January 4, 1945. Waiting at Pier 94 was her new mother-in-law, who insisted that Tish tidy herself up in the nearest ladies' lounge. Then it was off to Manhattan's Colony Club for lunch with five of Corinne's New York society friends—a fitting if somewhat intimidating introduction to the ways of Corinne Alsop.

It turned out that Stewart, on a faster ship, had already arrived, though he was tied down by military duties. He had wangled a stateside assignment in Washington, at least until the birth of his child, and the couple moved in with Sis and Percy Chubb at their Georgetown home.

Stewart, with Tom Braden, was assigned to write a series of articles recounting episodes of OSS derring-do during the war. The project had a special purpose for Donovan, who wanted the OSS continued as a permanent intelligence agency. Others in the government wanted it disbanded, and to generate public support for his plan Donovan had the Alsop-Braden writings distributed to newspapers as feature articles.

Events moved in quick succession during these months. The Alsops' first child, Joseph Wright Alsop VI, was born July 30. In August, Stewart and Braden received orders for an OSS jump into Thailand. That same month, the United States dropped atomic bombs on the Japanese cities of Hiroshima and Nagasaki. The Japanese surrendered to General MacArthur aboard the U.S.S. *Missouri* on September 2. The orders for the Thailand parachute mission were rescinded. And Stewart and Tish Alsop, with their infant son, were tossed into the social ferment of postwar America.

IT WAS A far different Stewart Alsop who emerged from the hard tests of war, with a Croix de Guerre with Palm from Charles de Gaulle, to face the challenges of civilian life. When he had turned thirty back in England in May 1944, he had written that his life certainly hadn't turned out as he had planned or anticipated. "I remember when I was in college and expected to be married with two or three children at the age of thirty, commuting to a $10,000-a-year job in a respectable Buick," he wrote to Avon. Now he was prepared to pursue such a life in earnest.

As it usually does to men, war made Stewart much more worldly. His intellectualism now was leavened by experience. And his experience in war had left him even more of an Anglophile than he had been before, all the more committed to the concept of Anglo-American alliance in the postwar world, and more receptive to Joe's grand perceptions of world politics and the balance of power.

As for the future, Stewart knew he didn't want to return to book publishing or to New York City. He liked Washington, where his brother had made such a splash before the war. He even thought about joining the U.S. foreign service. And he was intrigued by Joe's suggestion, made on several occasions in letters from China, that the two brothers join forces in the column-writing business. Whatever he might choose to do, Stewart felt confident that he would do it well, and that he was ready for the new adventure of civilian life.

11

JOE AND VINEGAR JOE

War and Intrigue in China

JOE'S SECOND CHINA trip in late 1942 followed a route far different from that of his 1941 voyage. This time he went the entire way by air—south to Miami, then to Brazil, across the South Atlantic to Africa, across the Dark Continent to the Persian Gulf, and over the Gulf of Oman to Karachi, the ancient Indian port on the Arabian Sea, later to become Pakistan's capital. At Karachi, Joe addressed to his friend Harry Hopkins a long letter filled with anguished warnings about the Allied effort in the China-Burma-India (CBI) theater. "A situation exists which is grossly dishonoring to the Army, to the President, and to the country," he wrote, "and if further investigation . . . supports the impression of what I have learned already, I neither care to stay in China, nor accept a commission, nor do anything else but return to the United States as rapidly as possible, put the competent authoritics in possession of the truth, and go into the service as a private."

In dispatching such mournful musings, Joe entered a battle that would consume him for nearly three years, as it consumed some of the most highly placed figures of the Allied cause. It was a bureaucratic battle waged in councils of war, in backrooms of officialdom, in memoranda and letters sent across the oceans in diplomatic pouches or by "safehand."

In part it was a battle over military tactics—whether the central Allied salient in the CBI theater should be General Stilwell's infantry or

General Chennault's aerial attack. Ground power versus air power—the debate had raged since before Billy Mitchell's famous court-martial in 1925. Seldom had it raged more heatedly than it did in wartime China.

In part it was a battle over geopolitical strategy—one that hinged on the question of how the United States should regard China's Generalissimo Chiang Kai-shek. Some viewed him as China's best hope for stability and development, others as a corrupt and inept reactionary blocking all hope of progress for his people. Closely related were questions surrounding the Chinese communists pushed up into a strategic enclave in northern China's Yan'an. Did they offer hope for a modern China or pose a threat to Asian stability and the world balance of power?

Above all, it was a clash of personalities, big men with famous names caught in the vortex of the greatest war of all time: Stilwell, Chennault, Chiang, Marshall, Mountbatten, Hopkins, Soong, Roosevelt. And behind the scenes, playing the role of bureaucratic busybody, was Joe Alsop.

The story comes into focus through the character and aims of the central players, starting with that leathery and plainspoken soldier, Lieutenant General Joseph W. Stilwell. From March 6, 1942, when he arrived in China at the behest of his mentor and patron, U.S. Army General George C. Marshall, Stilwell wielded immense CBI power. He was theater commander, and also Chiang Kai-shek's chief of staff, responsible for distributing all military goods for supply-starved China. Stilwell was a West Pointer, a World War I hero, a leading expert in infantry tactics. He spoke fluent Chinese and had witnessed at close range much of China's violent twentieth-century history. Approaching sixty when he arrived for wartime duties, Stilwell had become famous for his tart tongue and instant judgments. His troops called him Vinegar Joe.

But Stilwell viewed the world in simplistic terms, devoid of subtlety or nuance. His idea of a wonderful movie was Walt Disney's *Dumbo*, which he enjoyed so much when he first saw it that he immediately sat through it a second time. His range of vision was narrow and colored by intense prejudices. He favored the underdog by instinct, and hated the rich and privileged. He disliked the British and hated Chiang Kai-shek and his governing Kuomintang.

Claire Chennault was the temperamental opposite of Stilwell. A cavalier Southerner, he was hot-blooded, self-confident, accustomed to swaying people through his force of personality. And, unlike Stilwell, he believed the future of warfare was written in the skies. By the time the Americans entered the war, Chennault and his Flying Tigers had become legendary, the subject of magazine articles and theater newsreels. The American Volunteer Group's seven-month effort had been a stunning success. The Tigers had destroyed 299 Japanese planes, with another 153 probable hits. Only ten AVG pilots had been killed in the air, while three had died from enemy bombing and ten from accidents. Chennault had lost only twelve planes in the air, sixty-one on the ground. Even Marshall, who despised Chennault, considered the flamboyant Louisianan to be "probably a tactical genius."

After Pearl Harbor, Chennault's AVG had been drawn into the U.S. Army, along with Chennault himself. The Flying Tigers had become the China Air Task Force (CATF), and Chennault had become a lieutenant general.

Chennault's success endeared him to his boss and patron, Chiang Kai-shek. During Chennault's years with Chiang, the two had developed a mutual respect and appreciation. Chiang liked the fact that Chennault maintained a proper deference and avoided involvement in court intrigue. The two viewed events and circumstances in much the same light, and as China's predicament deepened in 1942 they came to share a strong feeling that Joe Stilwell wasn't up to his job.

For Chiang, the turning point came with Stilwell's failed Burma campaign in the spring of 1942. The Japanese had taken Rangoon in February and had moved troops into position to capture the entire Burmese land mass and close off the Burma Road, over which crucial supplies came into China. That would cut China off from all land and sea supply routes from the outside world. Stilwell's job was to take command of two Chinese armies, link up with two British divisions, and dislodge the Japanese from their positions in southern Burma. The effort failed. The Allied armies were cut to shreds, and Burma was lost. China's survival now depended on a single precarious thread of supplies delivered by air from India over the jagged mass of Himalayan rock and glacier that Allied pilots quickly dubbed "the Hump."

Stilwell blamed Chiang and his generals for the Burma debacle. The generalissimo, Stilwell believed, had proved indecisive and arbitrary during the heat of battle, ordering troop movements and then reversing himself. Worse, some top Chinese commanders had ignored Stilwell's orders for attack, while others secretly countermanded various Stilwell commands. Stilwell reacted in the worst possible way, ignoring Chiang and keeping him in the dark on battlefield developments, then insulting him with blunt anger. Chiang questioned Stilwell's judgment in declining air transport out of the disintegrating Burma theater and instead leading a small party out of the jungle on foot. The dramatic three-week trek helped establish the Stilwell legend back home, but Chiang felt the general should have flown to safety in order to hasten the reorganization of Chinese resistance. Chennault agreed and later called Stilwell's actions "a startling exhibition of his ignorance or disregard for [his] larger responsibilities."

In the aftermath of the Burma defeat, Chennault had still more serious differences with Stilwell. The stubborn ground commander, bent on a return engagement in Burma, began stockpiling supplies for that campaign. This meant Chennault couldn't obtain enough fuel and spare parts to keep his air force in action. As he saw it, the most successful military operation of the CBI theater was being shut down in favor of a ground force that had failed and was ill prepared for the more awesome mission Stilwell had in mind for it.

Such was the state of affairs as Joe Alsop made his way to China in late 1942. He soon heard tales of bureaucratic infighting within the CBI command, of intrigues against Chennault, of incompetence among ground commanders and a lack of respect for the potential of air power. As Joe described it to Hopkins, Chennault's reward for military brilliance was "to be subjected to an endless petty persecution, to be spied upon, to be traduced, and to be constantly though obscurely hindered in the application of his superb tactical imagination . . ." Joe requested "most earnestly" that Hopkins get him ordered back to Washington within two months. In the meantime he would investigate the matter so he could report his findings to appropriate officials back home. Of course, he would "retain a wholly open mind" during his inquiry, but there seemed little doubt that things were seriously amiss. Joe added a personal note: His request for home leave was motivated in part by his desire "to end this war in uniform." He planned to seek a commission while in China, but he thought his prospects would be brighter if he could pursue the matter from Washington as well.

Joe arrived in Chongqing in mid-December and found a nice room in a big house occupied mostly by young Englishmen, whom he considered "a little dim in spots, [but] pleasant enough by Chungking [Chongqing] standards." The house came with a cadre of servants, including an excellent cook, and Joe was pleased to report to Avon that it even had functional plumbing. For $6 a week in gold, he got the room, adequate coal, three copious meals a day, a ration of gin, a valet, "and the privilege of having guests when I please."

Joe immediately set about cultivating contacts in Chongqing. He called at Stilwell's headquarters, met with the British and U.S. ambassadors, dined with his old friend T. V. Soong. He spent Christmas with Chennault at his headquarters in the lovely Kunming Valley to the south. The old chief greeted the young civilian with a three-day feast that included dove pie, roast sandhill crane, wild duck, and Burma goose. Despite the vast difference between the Alsop persona and that of Chennault's young aerial warriors, Joe enjoyed them immensely; he found them "all handsome, all pleasant and all oddly foppish" in their silver-gray uniforms embroidered with silver insignia, and their large sapphire rings.

During Christmas dinner, a courier reported that the Japanese had sent a large reconnaissance force over a vulnerable airfield in Chennault's forward perimeter. The chief fired a few questions at the messenger—how many planes had come over? what time? what altitude?—and then fell silent for nearly an hour as his officers chatted and laughed over dinner. Suddenly he interrupted: "I think they'll come again tomorrow. There should be between fifteen and twenty-five bombers, probably twenty. And my guess is they'll be over the field at about 3." He then ordered two missions: a raid against a Japanese field where he felt enemy planes might be found on the ground, and a scramble of fighter planes to protect the U.S. field he feared would come under attack. Sure enough, the next morning twenty-one bombers arrived as expected, and Chennault's men knocked eight of them out of the sky.

Between pleasant repasts and aerial adventures, Chennault poured out his frustrations to Joe. He was being persecuted by Stilwell's people, he said, and thwarted in his efforts to make a significant contribution to the war effort.

"I wouldn't give a damn about the other business," he told Joe, "if I only had a chance to do the job I'm here for." He said he felt like just going home to Louisiana.

But of course he couldn't do that. Claire Chennault would bide his time, apply the levers of bureaucratic politics, and expose the folly of Stilwell's strategy whenever the opportunity presented itself. And with Joe Alsop at his side, the opportunity would present itself frequently.

Chennault's interest in young Alsop went beyond his Washington connections. Joe was ideal to have around in a command beset by political intrigue. He traveled with ease in Chongqing's diplomatic circles, and his friendship with T. V. Soong, now Chiang's foreign minister, gave him connections at the highest levels of the Kuomintang. As an accomplished gossip, he always knew what was going on in the inner reaches of the labrynthine Chongqing court and at the various Allied offices. Besides, Chennault genuinely liked Joe, enjoyed his amusing habits of speech, and appreciated the loyalty and tenacity he showed in the tough bureaucratic battles at hand. Also, Joe's refined intellect offered a welcome outlet for Chennault's more rough-hewn but vibrant mind.

During his brief Chongqing visit, Joe fired off another letter to Hopkins, painting a picture of hopelessness hanging over Stilwell's plans for a ground offensive in Burma. Chinese leaders, bowing to Stilwell's control over the supply train, had sold Chennault down the river, promising ever greater powers for Stilwell in exchange for a larger share of the tonnage coming over the Hump. Thus, Chennault's air operation was getting squeezed out. What's more, the men around Stilwell treated the local Chinese as "so many thieves, traitors, incompetents and savages"; and Chiang's agents lurked everywhere and reported back all they heard to the generalissimo. Thus, it seemed unlikely that the Chinese and the Westerners could work cooperatively in a complex ground operation. Such a campaign couldn't commence for at least a year, anyway, because of the level of supplies over the Hump. Even if the Allies could reopen a supply road over northern Burma's rugged terrain, such a tortuous mountain trail couldn't provide the quantity of supplies Stilwell would need for a sustained ground operation. All this argued for an intensive air campaign, with its vastly more limited supply requirements.

In late February 1943, Joe received word that he was wanted at Lend-Lease headquarters, and by March 1 he was back in Washington working at the headquarters building on Twenty-second Street and pursuing his intrigue on the China matter. He was there when Chennault and Stilwell arrived for a high-level showdown at the Allied military council known as Trident, which was called primarily to set the time and place of a European invasion, and secondarily to devise a military strategy for the CBI theater.

Alsop had two goals in Washington: to get a commission, and to support the war aims of Claire Chennault. Chennault had become a major general by this time, and had his own independent military command, the Fourteenth Air Force. Joe knew that the order for this change had originated in the White House. He also knew that the White House was hearing from others in the Far East who saw the situation much as he did. Madame Chiang Kai-shek, visiting the United States in late 1942, had praised Chennault to Hopkins and Roosevelt, while making clear that her husband didn't like Stilwell. And General Henry H. "Hap" Arnold, air force chief, had told Hopkins in January that he doubted the wisdom of Stilwell's plan to open the Burma Road and favored strengthening Chennault's air forces for a major bombing campaign against the Japanese.

Joe discussed China at length with Hopkins and briefed Cousin Franklin on the Stilwell-Chennault situation in the Oval Office. The president listened intently and asked many questions. But Joe knew it would not be easy for Roosevelt to embrace Chennault's case over that of his superior officer, Stilwell, particularly given Marshall's unyielding support for his China commander. Joe set forth the Chennault case once more in a twenty-one-page memorandum sent to Hopkins in early March. Forceful in argument and filled with political insight, the document set forth the situation in China as thoroughly as it had ever been presented in Washington.

By the time T. V. Soong returned from Washington in the fall of 1942, wrote Joe, the situation looked hopeless, but Soong stepped in to negotiate a kind of concordat between the two headstrong leaders. His motive was the need to maintain a flow of materiel to the Chinese army, not only for use against the Japanese but for the postwar struggle that Kuomintang officials foresaw with the communists and the Soviets. Also, Stilwell had frightened the generalissimo's people with a blunt threat that he would cut off their supplies entirely if they didn't submit to his authority. Under terms of the concordat, Stilwell promised to bolster Hump airlift capacity and increase China's allotment, while Chiang agreed to certain military steps designed to support Stilwell's plans for a Burma campaign.

Emboldened, Stilwell flew to India to secure a British commitment to attack the Japanese in southern Burma as he launched his own northern Burma campaign. But the British field marshal, Sir Archibald Wavell, refused, saying he lacked sufficient shipping for such an action. He also warned Stilwell against any go-it-alone offensive, given the strong Japanese supply situation, the enemy's fortified positions throughout central Burma, and the unreliability of the Chinese army. Though Chiang had his own reservations, he felt bound by the concordat, and so preparations began for a massive ground offensive. It proved impossible to get into position before the rains came, but in the meantime Chennault had been starved of supplies as Stilwell channeled goods into an offensive that lacked any chance of success.

In his memo Joe sought to explain why he and Chennault believed so much could be done in China with a small investment. Japanese-controlled territory didn't extend beyond their fortified bases and long supply lines, he argued, and hence those bases and supply routes were highly vulnerable to surprise attack; Chennault's aircraft often were overhead before they could be detected. But Chennault could use the expanse of unoccupied territory to maintain a sophisticated warning network that kept him informed whenever the Japanese set forth over the vast countryside to mount an air strike. Chennault's specialized combat tactics had rendered Japan's sophisticated Zeros vulnerable to his P-40s; his kill ratio often reached ten to one.

Chennault's plan was to control the skies, then attack at will the crucial Japanese positions in the Yangtze Valley, the port cities along the coast, and shipping in the sea lanes of the Formosa Strait. If the enemy neglected to defend these vital strategic areas, Chennault's assault would stab him in the belly; if Japan sent in air strength to defend them, Chennault would destroy it systematically. Answering the argument that the Japanese would only redouble ground attacks on Chennault's air bases to eliminate the threat, Joe said they couldn't succeed without control of the skies, and Chennault owned the skies.

Joe urged the administration to stop trying to browbeat the Chinese into complying with a questionable ground strategy and cease insisting on American control of Chinese forces as a condition of supplying China. Instead, the United States should mount air offensives to disrupt Japan's supply lines, prevent the enemy from exploiting the riches of the Asian mainland, and strike at his air capacity. Joe added: "As General Stilwell is firmly committed, both to holding the air effort to a minimum, and to pursuing the Dutch Uncle or tutelary policy to its bitter end, logic would suggest he might be transferred."

For two months before the Trident conference, Joe promoted the Chennault case throughout Washington. In late April 1943, after Stilwell and Chennault arrived, Joe made sure Chennault enjoyed himself on the Washington social circuit. In addition to official visits with Roosevelt, Winston Churchill, General Marshall, and Harry Hopkins, Chennault rubbed shoulders with a host of Joe's social friends: Walter Lippmann and Leland Stowe of the *Herald Tribune,* William Bullitt, Felix Frankfurter, and Henry Morgenthau.

In the official discussions of Trident, Stilwell was curt and surly, seemingly bitter that he should be called upon to defend his war plans. The Stilwell case rested on the assumption that operations in China needed to be linked with the campaign in the southwestern Pacific, and that that in turn required a land-based supply route into China. He continued to believe that a major air offensive would simply beget a Japanese ground attack against Chennault's forward bases. In making his case to Roosevelt on April 30, however, Stilwell sat humped over, with his head down, muttering complaints about China's lack of fighting will. Roosevelt wondered aloud to Marshall whether the man wasn't perhaps ill.

In another session, as Stilwell waxed furious about the poor quality of Chinese leadership, Roosevelt cut in to ask what he thought of the generalissimo.

Said Vinegar Joe: "He's a vacillating, tricky, undependable old scoundrel, who never keeps his word—"

"Chennault, what do you think?" asked the president, turning to the air commander, who was sitting in a corner.

"Sir," replied Chennault, "I think the generalissimo is one of the two or three greatest military and political leaders in the world today. He has never broken a commitment or promise made to me."

It is doubtful that Stilwell could have prevailed even if he had managed a better performance. Roosevelt's central purpose in China was to keep Chiang in the war. On May 2, the president informed Marshall and the Joint Chiefs that the proposed air offensive was to be given high priority. He directed that Hump transport be boosted to 7,000 tons monthly, with Chennault getting first priority on 4,750 tons. Stilwell would get the next 2,250 tons, with any excess beyond 7,000 tons to be split between the air and ground efforts.

Stilwell reacted with bitterness. To Marshall, he dismissed the plan as being based on "total misapprehension of the character, intentions, authority and ability of Chiang Kai-shek." To his diary, he suggested the president and his government had been suckered by Chiang, whom he described in a subsequent letter to his wife as "a grasping, bigoted, ungrateful little rattlesnake." Marshall also reacted with anger and directed his most bitter denunciations at Alsop, whom he considered an intriguer and far too much of a Soong loyalist.

Chennault and Joe were elated by the president's action. Further, they were heartened by the easy rapport the general had established with Roosevelt, and the president's remarkable invitation to Chennault that he write directly to the White House on China developments.

Joe was not so successful in his effort to secure a commission. A military physical in Washington showed that his syphilis had cleared up, and the War Department recommended a waiver on his only other defect, his poor eyesight. But then the surgeon general stopped the paperwork by declaring Joe unfit for China service "in view of the record previous to the (most recent) physical." Evidence suggested this was a retaliatory move against Chennault and Joe by War Department officials stung by the Trident outcome, but Joe had an alternate plan. Now that Chennault headed an independent command, he could grant Joe a field commission in China. Although that could put him at the mercy of his adversaries at the Pentagon, Joe felt confident he could trump that threat: during his White House visits, Joe had secured a promise from Roosevelt that if he got into uniform the president would ensure him assignment to Chennault's unit.

In June, Joe set off once again for China, this time as T. V. Soong's $10,000-a-year assistant at China Defense Supplies. He soon discovered that the Trident conference had had little impact on the endless intrigues. On July 2 he reported to Hopkins that the "petty harassment" of Chennault continued, and that the schedules outlined at Trident had come "unglued." He learned also that Stilwell had declared Joe unwelcome as an officer in the CBI theater. Nevertheless, he continued to hope that his application would go through unimpeded.

As Chennault waited for the Hump tonnage he had been promised, the China situation deteriorated rapidly. The Japanese took up positions on the southern banks of the Yangtze from Hankow to Yichang, permitting them to use the river as a major supply route for a possible assault on Chongqing. With sufficient planes, spare parts, and gasoline, Chennault felt confident he could cut this supply route easily, but he wasn't getting what he needed.

More important was the accelerating disintegration of the Chinese economy. Inflation was raging, and famine was spreading. On July 2, Chennault wrote Hopkins of a peasant uprising in Gansu. And in Guangxi, he wrote, where many of his forward bases were situated, the farmers were eating bark and leaves, and children were being sold. Availing himself of Roosevelt's invitation to keep the president informed, Chennault wrote to say that his supply flow had not reached the levels agreed upon at Trident. "The effect of all these unexpected delays will be to postpone the opening of my all out offensive against the Jap aircraft and shipping in China."

Then a communication from Chiang Kai-shek rocked the White House. The generalissimo requested that he be allowed to name Chennault chief of staff of the Chinese air force to increase the general's stature in the theater and to bolster efforts to forge his air corps into an effective force. He asked further that General Clayton Bissell, Stilwell's air commander and a Chennault nemesis, be removed as commander of the Tenth Air Force in India and replaced with "someone else who can work harmoniously with General Chennault."

Roosevelt's response was to pronounce the China situation to be "an awful mess [that] ought to be straightened out at once." He called a conference of his top military advisers—Marshall, Admiral William D. Leahy, General Brehon B. Somervell—along with Hopkins for the next morning in his bedroom, and he spoke bluntly. He expressed dissatisfaction with the effort in China and particularly with Stilwell. Echoing the words Joe Alsop had been funneling into the White House, he noted that Stilwell apparently hated the Chinese, that his cablegrams dripped of sarcasm, that he made no effort to hide his feelings from the generalissimo. The generalissimo, he said, obviously disliked Stilwell.

Marshall defended his CBI commander, but reluctantly accepted Chiang's requests. He vigorously dissented, though, when Roosevelt suggested giving Chennault an independent command, free of Stilwell's control. Marshall argued, correctly, that this would create an unworkable command structure. Besides, Chennault had worked for Chiang and hence was under the undue influence of the generalissimo. Stilwell, unaware of how close he had come to losing control of the Fourteenth Air Force, reacted angrily to his loss of Bissell. "He is . . . a good soldier," he wrote Hap Arnold. "Regrettable that he must go for the reasons involved."

Despite these victories in the bureaucratic struggle, Joe Alsop felt as combative as ever. He worked the gossip circuit, collecting information as if he were back in his columnist's trade, developing confidential sources, piecing together a broader picture of what was going on. He gathered his findings in an ill-advised memo to his new boss, T. V. Soong, who had remained in Washington after the Trident council. Painting a dismal picture of incompetence, Joe criticized Stilwell's command structure, intelligence operations, and training techniques, and quoted freely from a report by one of the theater's bombardment groups. "I am shocked by the extent to which the internal situation appears to have degenerated," Joe wrote. He enclosed an unsealed letter to Hopkins, for Soong to read and pass along. "As I am now your man," he wrote, "I don't wish to have any direct correspondence with him on subjects of this type . . . without sending it through you."

Along with Joe's letter, Soong passed along the memo, though he first excised the last paragraph, in which Joe pronounced himself Soong's "man." Subsequently, Soong also submitted a copy to Britain's Lord Louis Mountbatten, supreme allied commander of the Southeast Asia Command in New Delhi, as part of his effort to get Stilwell fired. General Somervell, present at the Soong-Mountbatten meeting, also had access to Joe's memo, which eventually made its way to Marshall's headquarters in Washington. The bureaucratic struggle was intensifying.

Though based in Chongqing, Joe often made his way to Kunming to stay with Chennault. The general's house, resembling an American beach bungalow in a rice field, was a beehive of activity. The large staff, including three Chinese helpers known as Gunboat, Steamboat, and Showboat, lived in a kind of commune in the garage, and their wives and children were everywhere. The chauffeur had a little daughter named Wong who traveled in the general's car wherever he went. While Chennault didn't care much about elegance, he did like comfort, and he managed to ensure that his table was piled with all manner of Louisiana dishes. Cornbread was served at every meal, and there was an occasional offering of ice cream. He insisted that his house staff maintain a garden with okra, sweet potatoes, and strawberries. The general himself wandered off as often as possible to hunt various indigenous fowl for the table.

In Chongqing, a morning errand took Joe to the mountaintop house of the generalissimo and Madame Chiang, where he was offered a dish of coffee ice cream. Madame was "very pretty and smart, except that, strangely enough, she had let her silk stockings down around her ankles." She complimented Joe on the "extremely useful job" he had done in China and said he looked "much better, harder and not so soft" as when he had arrived two years earlier.

Not long afterward a group of senators passed through, and Joe had a chance to visit with his old friend Cabot Lodge of Massachusetts. The senator had plenty of gossip, including the sad news that Uncle Ted Roosevelt had been relieved of his command in Europe because of alcoholism. "I shudder to think what will happen to him now," Joe wrote home. Lodge also reported that, in London, Churchill had told the senators that he foresaw a day when Americans and Englishmen would have a common citizenship—"in which case," wrote Joe to Avon, "I expect he will run for president."

But the best news of all was the announcement of Stewart's engagement. "I am more excited than I can say," Joe wrote to Avon. He found he didn't mind Stew's fiancée being a Roman Catholic, though he faintly hoped she would not turn out to be very devout, and that her offspring "will not cling to their church with overmuch determination." As for the young lady, he expressed a certain sympathy for her, marrying into such a tribe. "For her sake, I trust she has a good, loud voice, enjoys eating, and will not be too appalled by violent arguments." Joe was filled with brotherly pride in Stewart's wartime accomplishments. "I admire what he has done more than I can say." His excitement at the news of Stewart's engagement stirred him to purchase a $10,000 life-insurance policy and name his brothers as beneficiaries.

As summer passed into autumn, it became clear that Chennault wouldn't get what had been promised. The level of supplies ordered by Roosevelt was coming in, but the corollary commitments of personnel, airplanes, and weapons were being ignored. "If the promises made in Washington last May had been anywhere nearly lived up [to], the job would be halfway done now, and you would be seeing the entire strategic situation in the Far East changing before your eyes," Joe wrote to Hopkins on September 1.

Four days later, Chennault sent Roosevelt a status report, written by Joe. Of the six elements in the Trident commitment, he said, only one had been fulfilled. "We have not had the tools to do our job," Chennault said.

These warnings had their intended effect. "I am terribly disturbed about the Chinese Air Force," Roosevelt wrote to Marshall on September 27. Echoing one of Chennault's specific complaints (included in a Hopkins memo that Roosevelt received the same day), the president noted that "the number of airplanes in China makes it impossible for Chennault to do any real work." He admonished Marshall to "get behind this again and vigorously push our agreed plans." Three weeks later Roosevelt prodded again. "Almost everything seems to have gone wrong with our program for supporting Chennault," he wrote, adding that he would like General Somervell, then on his way to China as a troubleshooter, "to give this whole business his special consideration and attention."

About this same time, Soong arrived back in Chongqing with a White House promise, probably delivered in the form of assurances from Hopkins, that Roosevelt would fire Stilwell if the generalissimo asked him to. Chiang was ready; he had had about as much of Vinegar Joe as he could take, and word quickly spread through the generalissimo's court that Stilwell soon would be on his way out. At this point, the Americans' long and bitter bureaucratic intrigue collided with the even more intense but far more covert court scheming that permeated the generalissimo's government. If the American feud centered on questions of strategy and personality, the Chinese intrigue concerned nothing less than who would control the destiny of the nation and whether the governmental elite would enjoy the spoils of leadership.

Chiang's Kuomintang, never a defender of the peasant class, represented the rural gentry and the progressive commercial classes in the large cities and along the coast. Within that ruling coalition was an ongoing struggle between two powerful factions. The modernists were linked intellectually to America and dedicated to China's national development; largely American-educated and fluent in English, they viewed the United States as a kind of national ideal. They had been largely responsible for the commercial and industrial progress in China during Chiang's brief heyday before the Japanese invasion. In contrast, the traditionalist faction harked back to the warlord tradition that gripped China after the disintegration of its last great dynasty, the Manchu, and to the anti-Western sentiment that had bubbled to the surface intermittently since Manchu days. This faction represented old-school politicians who supported nepotism, unquestioned governmental power, and the use of official position for the enhancement of personal wealth and power.

This bitter struggle was personified by the Soong family, for years rent by political differences and petty jealousies. There was T.V., China's leading modernist, educated at Harvard and Columbia, a banker and financier of acknowledged brilliance. As Chiang's finance minister in the early days of the Kuomintang, he increased tax revenues tenfold in two years and instituted successful reforms in city after city as Chiang spread his influence over China in what became known as the Northern Expedition. *Time* magazine called him "China's Alexander Hamilton." And there was H. H. Kung, the fat, money-loving former Shanxi banker who had married T.V.'s sister Ei-ling. Known among his cronies as "Daddy," the wily Kung represented the traditionalists. But in truth, he was the puppet of his strong-willed and self-seeking wife, who hated to see power and influence accrue to her brother, T.V., and his modernist allies. She was joined in this sentiment by her sister, Mei-ling, the imperious Madame Chiang, who sought the aggrandizement of the ruling family.

Throughout the Kuomintang, as within the Soong family, the power struggle was played out in subtle intrigues and inscrutable maneuvers. For the modernists, China's relations with America were crucial. As pro-Western advocates of strong ties to the United States, they felt the need to prove that their approaches were effective. In the period when Lend-Lease was extended to China, when loans were offered and the American Volunteer Group was organized, the modernists' prestige grew.

Even after Stilwell's Burma defeat in 1942, the modernists enjoyed major influence. T.V. held the post of foreign minister. The enlightened General Chen Cheng was given command of one of Stilwell's Chinese armies, a post from which he could compete with his hated rival, the reactionary and incompetent war minister, Ho Ying-chin. But when China's fortunes plummeted after Stilwell cut off civilian Lend-Lease and relations between him and Chiang deteriorated again, the modernists suffered a rapid loss of prestige.

Now T.V. appeared to be swaying Chiang on the crucial issue of Stilwell. Alarmed, Mei-ling and Ei-ling initiated a subtle intrigue designed to keep Stilwell in place. They invited the general to afternoon teas, fed him gossip, tickled his ego, offered to influence the generalissimo on his behalf. Their underlying agenda was to sow doubts in Stilwell's mind about leading modernists such as Chen Cheng, and to promote H. H. Kung and other traditionalists. Stilwell relished the regular sessions at Mei-ling's house, adopted nicknames for his new friends (May and Ella), and viewed them as "fellow co-conspirators." Lacking subtlety and devoid of political instinct, he concluded that the "two intelligent dames," as he called them in his diary, had been told by T. V. Soong to get behind the U.S. effort.

In fact their motive was to keep T.V. at bay. Soon Madame Chiang was arguing strenuously at court in Stilwell's behalf. She warned Chiang that Marshall had threatened to cut off China aid if the generalissimo couldn't get along with Stilwell. She said she and Ei-ling had been working with the general and could handle him. Then Somervell arrived to confirm that Marshall would be angry if he were forced to pull Stilwell from the theater. Mountbatten, in Chongqing for a round of planning discussions, weighed in to defend Stilwell, whom he knew only as the single American general who spoke Chinese. The generalissimo wavered, and the sisters quickly rallied. They called for Stilwell and told him he could salvage his job if he would show humility toward Chiang and acknowledge mistakes. Late on October 17, Stilwell went over and "put on the act" as Chiang lectured him about the duties of a chief of staff and the need to avoid arrogance in dealing with the Chinese. "This was all balderdash," Stilwell wrote in his diary, "but I listened politely."

As October 18 dawned, Joe felt confident that Stilwell was on his way out. That had been the word from Soong through the previous evening. But on his way to Soong's house that morning, Joe encountered a group of reporters, who gave him the news. Soong had angered the generalissimo; he was out of favor. "Joe was so shook that he looked as if he might collapse on the spot," recalled Annalee Jacoby, a correspondent for *Time*. Hurrying to his friend's house, Joe found Soong in tears. He had berated the generalissimo that morning for reversing his decision, and the furious Chiang had threatened him with a summary death sentence. Soong's career was in tatters, the traditionalists were in control, the modernists faced a purge. Soong was virtually placed under house arrest.

Joe viewed this as a disaster for China, and also for himself. As a Soong employee, he had been effectively neutralized. "I cannot continue to do useful work . . . owing to the misfortune which . . . overtook a common friend of ours," he wrote to Hopkins in December.

When it became clear that the army's refusal of a medical waiver for Joe stemmed from Stilwell's objection, Chennault personally intervened with Stilwell and sent Alsop up to have a heart-to-heart chat with the general. Stilwell withdrew his objection, though he probably did so with the knowledge that in the meantime the right of air force officials to commission civilians had been withdrawn. Now only the president and the secretary of war had such authority.

On December 27, Chennault formally requested a presidential commission for Joe. "It will be a criminal waste if Alsop's special qualifications are not turned to account here," he wrote to Roosevelt. Chennault also wrote to air force commander Hap Arnold, explaining that he had taken the liberty of writing directly to Roosevelt "as the President has expressed a strong personal interest to me in Alsop's case." He added: "I hope you will approve."

Arnold had no intention of approving. A draft reply memo (apparently never sent) fairly bristled with indignation at the letter Joe had sent T. V. Soong the previous summer (which Soong had used to bolster his case against Stilwell in the fall). Alsop, said the memo,

> is a civilian columnist and is not accepted as a military authority. To include such a man in the military organization whose chief he condemns is contrary to the fundamental rule for military force and deliberately cultivates a fatal disloyalty to the military effort

. . . to commission a man who by written evidence has been one of the most destructive agents to the intentions of the Chiefs of Staff is going too far.

General Marshall is determined that everybody in uniform will be a soldier and not a subversive agent and will be held accountable accordingly. He has reached the point where he will not tolerate any further evidence of divided loyalties. By this I mean he will make the issue of his own position against any offenders who may feel that they have the influence to overcome it. He is aware of Alsop's relationship to the President. That makes no difference whatever to him. We are either to have an Army of soldiers or he will not accept the responsibility for the Army.

It took Roosevelt six weeks, but in mid-February 1944 he ordered a commission for Joe. The order angered Marshall, who wrote the president a memo of compliance that also expressed objection to the commission. Revealing the infamous Alsop letter to T. V. Soong (a copy of which he attached to his memo), Marshall said the letter showed that "Alsop is either more competent as a commander than Stilwell . . . or that he is a seriously destructive force." Roosevelt did not respond to the Marshall memo and didn't even keep it on file at the White House. He sent it back to the War Department so that it would reside in Marshall's habitat and not his own.

Word of the commission reached Joe while he was away on the frontier visiting a friend. Elated, he managed to hitch a ride through the mountains in a jeep, reaching Kunming in time for a late-night dinner of celebration with his once-and-future chief. "I am extremely cheerful," he wrote to Avon. The slight regret he felt at losing his status as a free agent, he wrote, "is as nothing compared to the relief of being no longer a civilian when all my contemporaries and friends were in uniform." Sworn in as a first lieutenant the next day, he immediately sent a letter to his parents asking them to send the general a case of bourbon and subscriptions to *The New Yorker*, *Time*, *Life*, and the Sunday *New York Times*.

In Chennault's command, Joe worked seven days a week, often twelve or fourteen hours a day. He was given a dual assignment—to the plans office and the unit mess. As mess officer, he was particularly concerned about the officers' mess, which had confined its offerings largely to the standard army diet of buffalo meat and carrots. By "interminable negotiation" Joe got a more varied fare, without—he insisted in a letter home—slipping into the dangers of special privilege. For $20 a month, he managed to place on the officers' tables such delicacies as snails, brains, eels, crabs, local hams, Chinese mushrooms, and various fruits and vegetables.

In the plans section, Joe worked with Colonel Howard Means, but mostly his job was to serve as staff officer to Chennault, who used Joe to help draft letters and memoranda, deal with the press, handle VIP visits, and serve the general's interests in official and diplomatic circles. Joe traveled with Chennault wherever the general went, often braving hazardous flying conditions with nonchalance. Once, during an inspection tour in Chengdu, a thick fog engulfed the airfield by the time Chennault was ready to depart. Visibility was zero, but the general declared, "Let's take off anyway." He ordered his pilot to drive the length of the airstrip in a Jeep and inspect it for obstacles. When the pilot returned to say it was clear, Chennault ordered a blind takeoff. "I was sweating," recalled Seymour Janow, an Alsop colleague who was along on the trip. "But Joe seemed oblivious to the danger."

Though even colonels in Chennault's command had to share quarters with roommates, Joe lived in the general's house and thus enjoyed special comforts. This naturally stirred some envy, and Joe did little to endear himself to his fellow officers. "He was terribly arrogant," recalled Janow, who himself was a close friend of Alsop. "Most of the staff disliked him."

Joe left behind an impression of such arrogance on one inspection trip that the sergeants and enlisted men at several air bases got together to write a letter of complaint to the War Department alleging that Joe treated them as if they were bus station porters. Hearing of this development, Chennault hurriedly sent Janow out to retrace Joe's route and mollify the angry soldiers before any letter could be mailed. Janow developed a line that seemed to work: "Look, you have to remember this guy is Eleanor's cousin. He can't help it. He doesn't know how to behave as an army officer. Actually, he isn't an army officer. He's just Joe Alsop in an officer's uniform." It worked, much to the relief of Chennault, who knew Joe couldn't afford to have such letters in the hands of his Pentagon adversaries.

In early spring 1944, Chennault's pilots noticed ominous signs along the Yangtze and at the Yellow River bend—growing concentrations of Japanese troops and heavy equipment obviously massed for an eastern China offensive. "China is in mortal danger," Chennault warned Stilwell, but Vinegar Joe didn't want to hear it. The previous November, shortly after "May" and "Ella" had saved his job, the ground commander finally had launched his Burma campaign, and now he was inching his way down the Hukwang Valley toward Myitkyina, carving a narrow road into the mountainside as he went. By now the spirit of Trident was dead; Stilwell had cut Chennault's Hump tonnage to a trickle so he could supply his jungle advance. "Owing to the concentration of our resources on fighting in Burma," Chennault wrote to Roosevelt, "little has been done to strengthen the Chinese armies and for the same reason the Fourteenth Air Force is still operating on a shoe string." To Stilwell he wrote, "Stopping anticipated Jap offensives in China is so vital . . . that I feel impelled to place problem before you frankly."

Stilwell replied, "No possibility of improving your supply situation. . . . You will simply have to cut your operations down to the point where you can be sure of reserves for an emergency." But the emergency was nigh, and Chennault wasn't the only military man who knew it. Responding to a Chennault warning, Hap Arnold wrote on April 24 that top air force officers agreed that Hump tonnage for ground forces should be reduced so that Chennault's could be increased. "However, as you know, the decision rests with the Theater Commander." Stilwell held the cards.

On April 16, six days after Stilwell's intelligence command reported that "Japanese do not have offensive capabilities in Yellow River area," three Japanese divisions crossed the Yellow and poured across the flat Henan wheat fields. Chennault had an operational strength of only ninety planes with which to disrupt enemy supply lines and slow the advance, and the poorly supplied Chinese army could only retreat. Soon the Japanese were pushing toward the rich rice fields of Hunan. Throughout the summer, the enemy pressed forward, gobbling up some of China's most productive agricultural lands. The impact on the Chinese economy was devastating. On August 9, 1944, after a long siege, Hengyang fell for lack of ammunition, and when Chennault proposed that Stilwell divert some of his Hump tonnage to the Chinese land forces so they could retake the city, the general refused.

Writing to his wife as the Japanese continued to advance in eastern China, Stilwell said, "If this crisis were just sufficient to get rid of the Peanut without entirely wrecking the ship, it would be worth it." Stilwell hungered for complete command of the Chinese military. Fed up with Chinese generals who wouldn't fight, he also wanted to strengthen the communists for greater participation in the war. In his diary, Stilwell suggested that the communists represented "the only visible hope" for China.

In June 1944 an emissary from the White House arrived in the person of Vice President Henry Wallace, the Iowa farmer and former agriculture secretary who was on a worldwide inspection tour for the president. He came to China in "full fig," as the most important imaginable VIP, accompanied by the chief of the State Department's China section, John Carter Vincent, and Owen Lattimore of the Office of War Information. In Chongqing he met with Chiang Kai-shek and Stilwell, and saw Joe Alsop for the first time since their prewar Washington days. He greeted the former columnist warmly, and they renewed their friendship as Joe escorted the vice president down to Kunming, where he quickly rounded up a gang of airmen for vigorous rounds of volleyball. Only after sufficient exercise did Wallace get down to the task of discussing the China situation with Chennault and Joe.

What he heard disturbed him. Chennault, in an extensive map talk, spun a tale of military crisis in eastern China. When Wallace took Joe Alsop aside afterward to seek his private advice, all of Joe's pent-up vehemence poured forth. He told Wallace that China faced the disintegration of Chiang Kai-shek's government and a communist takeover unless Stilwell was fired at once. The impetuous Wallace quickly agreed and decided to wire a memo of recommendation to Roosevelt. Joe sat down at his portable typewriter and pecked out the words as Wallace and Vincent collaborated in dictating the message. The memo was in three parts: it reported on Wallace's talks with the generalissimo and outlined China's military-political crisis; it urged Stilwell's recall; it suggested General Albert C. Wedemeyer, then serving as assistant to Mountbatten in New Delhi, as Stilwell's replacement. Joe was overjoyed. Wallace was "surprisingly astute," he wrote to Avon. "It took him an incredibly short time to grasp the position here in China."

But the Wallace memo had no impact in Washington. Chennault and Alsop were losing the bureaucratic war; Stilwell and Marshall were winning. With Chiang's government near collapse amid widespread famine and economic chaos, with military disaster looming in eastern China, with Stilwell urging a strong hand to avert the worst, Roosevelt found himself moving toward the Marshall position. In the fall he sent Patrick J. Hurley, flamboyant Oklahoma millionaire and former secretary of war, to China to help negotiate a new allied arrangement. His job was to bind Chiang to a series of new commitments: Stilwell was to get supreme command of all Chinese armies; he would exercise complete control over distribution of all Lend-Lease military supplies; he would bring the Chinese communists under his command umbrella. To pave the way, Roosevelt promoted Stilwell to full general.

Chiang had accepted Roosevelt's terms in principle, but had raised a host of troublesome details that needed to be worked out. It was a job tailor-made for Hurley, a master negotiator, who quickly decided to keep Chiang and Stilwell away from each other as the talks progressed. Stilwell remained in Chongqing as the negotiating parties convened at Chiang's big villa at Wanxian to draft an agreement. The generalissimo brought in T. V. Soong to help in the talks.

And T. V. Soong brought in Joe. Arriving in Chongqing to serve as a kind of secret consultant to Soong, Joe surveyed the contours of the agreement and concluded that it spelled the generalissimo's doom. Soong agreed, but said Chiang had been so weakened by the military defeats in the East and by the hideous famine that he had no option but to capitulate. Joe settled in at Soong's house overlooking the Chialing River and waited for developments.

Well into September, Chiang still was quibbling over control of Lend-Lease (he feared Stilwell would cut him off and direct all supplies to his communist rivals) and the details of command. Stilwell was getting irritated. "If the G-mo gets distribution [of Lend-Lease supplies] I am sunk," he wrote in his diary. "The Reds will get nothing." Joe, with long hours of idle time on his hands during Soong's absences, devoted himself to lolling in his dressing gown, drinking coffee, writing letters, and reading. One afternoon, he casually picked up a "delightful little volume" called *The Care and Feeding of Infants*. Soon he was engulfed in this new subject, wondering how his parents had managed to bring up four children without mishap. "I finished it and now know the whole subject from breast-feeding to impetigo," he wrote to Avon.

Then the talks blew up. Roosevelt, impatient with Chiang's intransigence on minor matters, and perhaps stirred by back-channel prodding from Stilwell (through Marshal), fired off a sharply phrased message to Chiang, to be delivered through Stilwell. The general leaped with joy. "F.D.R. has finally spoken plain words . . . with a firecracker in every sentence," he wrote in his diary on September 19. He drove to Wanxian to deliver the message. But Hurley intervened. He admonished Stilwell not to deliver the telegram; it would upend the talks. Stilwell insisted that he must present the president's message. Admitted to the conference room, he ceremoniously read the message aloud in Chinese, thus attacking Chiang's dignity in the presence of his underlings. Chiang cut him off and held out his hand for the message. He quietly signaled the meeting's end.

Stilwell returned to his home in triumphant glee. But the tables were turning against him. Soong summoned Joe to the villa of their banker friend, Pei Tsu-yi. Arriving there, Joe found Soong in a state of great agitation and impatience. T.V. recounted the conference-room episode. After the Americans had left, he related, the generalissimo had broken down in tears and announced he could not allow such an insult to go unanswered. Stilwell would have to go.

Soong presented to Joe a draft communiqué Chiang had written for Roosevelt, and asked Joe to review it. Ignoring the proprieties that went with his military position, Joe set about to help Chinese officialdom communicate with his own government. He suggested that Chiang declare Stilwell persona non grata and the person to blame for China's mounting national and military woes. The approach finally adopted was to have the generalissimo accept every provision negotiated by Hurley, but then state flatly that the American commander to enjoy all those powers would have to be someone other than Stilwell. The message was accompanied by an aide-mémoire to Hurley, drafted largely by Joe, outlining the bill of particulars against Stilwell. "T.V. undoubtedly wrote the thing, which was just a personal attack on me," Stilwell was to write in his diary after seeing the document.

Roosevelt sought a compromise. He wired Chiang on October 6, 1944, that Stilwell could be dismissed as the generalissimo's chief of staff and would be removed from Lend-Lease responsibilities. But he proposed to keep him in command of Chinese troops in India and China's Yunnan province to help facilitate transport of supplies between the two places. Chiang wouldn't budge, and Hurley, stung by Stilwell's insistence on disrupting his delicate negotiations, cut the general loose as well. "Chiang Kai-shek and Stilwell are fundamentally incompatible," he wired Roosevelt on October 10. "Today you are confronted by a choice between Chiang Kai-shek and Stilwell. There is no other issue between you and Chiang Kai-shek."

Roosevelt responded by requesting names of persons Chiang could accept as Stilwell's replacement. Joe pressed for Wedemeyer. Mountbatten's assistant, Alsop told Soong, was known to be close to both Marshall and MacArthur, was an admirer of the generalissimo, and had strong credentials as an anticommunist. Wedemeyer got the assignment. After nearly three years of acrimonious command, Stilwell was fired. As he left China, he poured into his diary more of the bitterness and penchant for blaming others that had characterized his stormy tenure. "F.D.R. proceeds to cut my throat and throw me out," he wrote. "To hell with them."

The long bureaucratic struggle was over, and Alsop rejoiced. He was particularly pleased about the Wedemeyer assignment. "The new man," he wrote to Avon, "is . . . the soundest and ablest of all the scores of American military grandees I have had to make drinks for, run errands for, and generally play nurse to, while at my boss's. He comes close, I suspect, to being a great man." The assignment required a measure of greatness. Wedemeyer's arrival on October 30 coincided with the ongoing military disaster in the East, political chaos throughout the shrinking Kuomintang-controlled area, and a climate of suspicion and fear throughout the theater.

Wedemeyer quickly proved that many of these troubles could be addressed with Stilwell out of the picture. A native Nebraskan and a West Point graduate, Wedemeyer had an intellectual bent and a capacity for strategic thinking. He quickly established an easy and pleasant relationship with Chiang Kai-shek, based on mutual respect and a shared hostility to the Yan'an communists. He wooed Chennault—and boosted morale within his command—by signing a stack of Fourteenth Air Force gallantry medals that Stilwell spitefully had allowed to pile up. He promptly saw that Stilwell's cherished Ledo Road through northern Burma was a folly, requiring a prohibitive amount of labor and supplies just to maintain. He concentrated on bringing supplies in over the Hump, and quickly boosted volume to the 100,000 tons a month that Chennault had been advocating for years. He employed a combination of toughness, compassion, and wiles—"using honey instead of vinegar," as a Chinese historian later put it—to win the respect and devotion of his Chinese commanders, and soon he had whipped twenty divisions into shape and created the nucleus of a modern army. He secured for Chennault a bomber force that soon was sent with devastating effect against the big Japanese airbase at Hankow and other crucial targets.

Marshall, who had misinterpreted the internal struggle in China from beginning to end, warned Wedemeyer to be alert for intrigues from Chennault and Alsop. But they never came. "It is most gratifying to me, and I know it will be to you," Wedemeyer wrote to Marshall, "to learn that General Chennault loyally and effectively carried on the Theater policies which I had initiated. I cannot in fairness fail to register my complete satisfaction with his fine work." He added that as far as he could tell, Chennault and Alsop "were not indulging in intrigue against me with the Chinese." With abundant supplies channeled to the Fourteenth Air Force, Chennault was too happy—and too busy—to bother with internal politics. His pilots savaged the overextended Japanese armies in eastern China, cutting off their supply lines and thwarting an offensive planned for the summer of 1945 against Kunming and Chongqing.

But Chennault was a marked man. When Wedemeyer returned to Washington for a planning conference in February 1945, Marshall made clear that Chennault's career was frozen. He accused the air commander of disloyalty toward Stilwell, and of contributing to the military failure in eastern China. He questioned Chennault's honesty and vowed never again to approve any promotion or decoration for the rustic Louisianan. Wedemeyer, a man of direct honesty, relayed Marshall's words to Chennault and suggested that the air commander should begin preparing for his departure from the service.

All this while, as the unit's aerial activity increased, Joe began to gain notice as an astute plans officer. With two colleagues, he punctured the flawed logistical plans devised for a new combined command encompassing the Tenth and Fourteenth air forces. Though Joe's calculations angered the new commander for the combined air force, Major General George Stratemeyer, they impressed Wedemeyer, who moved Chennault's headquarters to Chongqing so it could function as his air staff. He also tapped Alsop and Colonel Howard Means, Chennault's plans staff, to rewrite the China theater logistical tables.

In December 1944 Joe was promoted to captain. And in late January, John Alsop arrived in China "in splendid form" for another OSS assignment in the netherworld behind enemy lines. He and Joe talked for hours, and Joe subsequently invited his brother to Chennault's house for a day of long talks and a night of revelry. "It makes me immensely happy to have him here, but it also increased my homesickness," Joe wrote to Avon.

As Chennault made plans for his inevitable departure from China, so did Joe. One bit of unfinished business was to obtain for Joe the Legion of Merit award. Chennault put in the paperwork, but the awards committee—made up of people who no doubt had suffered the slings and arrows of Joe's arrogance—wouldn't approve it. Chennault sent Janow off to visit with each committee member and unfurl his little speech: He is the cousin of Eleanor; he doesn't have normal manners; he doesn't know how to behave as an army officer; but he really does deserve it, and the general wants him to have it. It worked, and on July 20, 1945, Joe received the decoration for "exceptionally meritorious conduct in performance of outstanding service." By then he had received orders relieving him from service in the China theater and ordering him back to the United States. He was to accompany Chennault through the war-ravaged capitals of Europe on his triumphal way back to the East Coast.

THE CHINA EXPERIENCE was a pivotal development in the life of Joe Alsop. Throughout his remaining life he was to be dogged by vague allegations of wrongdoing and explicit suggestions of supreme wrongheadedness in his promotion of air power in China. He would recoil in anger as journalists and historians would lionize Stilwell and quote the most vehement and embarrassing portions of his letters to Hopkins. Ultimately, in his memoirs, Joe acknowledged the questionable propriety of many of his actions during those years. Certainly, it is impossible to justify an American citizen helping a foreign power gain leverage over his own government, as Joe did when T. V. Soong and Chiang Kai-shek enlisted his assistance in drafting replies to Roosevelt's communications. Joe himself, years later, conceded that such actions constituted a form of "subversion." Certainly, such insubordination and disloyalty would have gotten a less well connected man court-martialed.

But history suggests that Joe and Chennault saw the strategic and tactical imperatives of the CBI theater more clearly than did Stilwell and his admirers. Stilwell's preoccupation with Burma was folly, and so was his famous Ledo Road, which never brought into China a volume of supplies sufficient to justify the blood and treasure expended on it. His approach to dealing with Chiang was guaranteed to turn a bad situation into a hopeless one, and his flirtation with the Yan'an communists constituted a strategic miscalculation of the first magnitude. Stilwell's refusal to respond when the Japanese unleashed their devastating offensive in eastern China brought into question his military acumen and his character. Though the capability of air power was relatively untested then, and has since been shown to have severe limitations, the peculiar circumstances of China, so assiduously studied and clearly understood by Chennault, suggested that this was one vast theater where air power could be a potent factor. Chennault's extraordinary aerial accomplishments—first on a shoestring budget during Stilwell's tenure and then on a larger scale under Wedemeyer—suggest he was right, but Stilwell never gave him so much as a respectful hearing.

Indeed, the whole unfortunate episode never has received anything approaching a dispassionate hearing in American discourse. The emotions of the moment lingered on for years, making impossible any detached assessment. The issue helped to ignite an even greater explosion of historic dimension, the emotion-laden McCarthy era. The animosities of the Chennault-Stilwell battle ticked away quietly, like a time bomb stashed away under the nation's floorboards, until detonated by the powerful question: Who lost China?

Joe Alsop's convictions about America's role in the world deepened through his wartime experiences. As a leading exponent of American involvement in the global war, he had based his advocacy on the need for balance-of-power stability in a dangerous world and his respect for the British Empire as a stabilizing force. Now he saw a new threat. The Soviet Union stood poised to inherit vast expanses of China, he wrote to Avon in the summer of 1944, and this, accompanied by "the inevitable extension of Russian influence in Europe, will polish off the remains of the world balance of power, producing a situation of the most precarious possible kind." And the empire of old, so potent as a world force for so long, now appeared spent. "The British ... are already quite drained," he wrote to Avon in late 1942. "They will be impotent to do anything very positive after the war."

So the big question was America: Would it shoulder the world role that followed logically from its wartime labors, foster an Anglo-American partnership, and seek to become a powerful influence around the globe? Or would it hunker back into the confines of its own well-protected territory and retreat to some kind of postwar "normalcy"? Joe favored the first course.

All of this brought home to Joe a central reality of his time: that the world had been changed dramatically in the crucible of Depression and war, and that it would never again be the same, for his country, for his class, or for himself. Joe found his thoughts turning to those old football games between Groton and St. Marks, with Ma and Pa up to see the fun, "and all your friends and all their sons looking so sure of themselves and the world, and the air so bright, and the New England fall so fine." Vivid recollections rushed into his mind of Avon weekends and of his first dances, with Corinne looking so wide-eyed and himself being so silly.

"How much *over* all that is," he wrote to Avon. It had been over since 1932, actually, but this was so much clearer now. He had seen it himself, around the big table at Harvard's Porcellian Club, in the change in atmosphere between the time of his first dinner there and the time of his commencement luncheon. "For in that interval the persons round the table had been transmuted from owners into ex-owners of the world." It was going to be harder now to move the country in the directions it must take, to overcome the prejudices of the Colonel McCormicks and the Bob Tafts, and to feel a part of the national fabric as of old. But of course there were Avon and Ma and Pa and Aggie. In a rapidly changing world, this would have to do. "You two and Avon are all the security and coziness we all have left," he wrote home in a mood of pensive reflection, "and you and Aggie ... must keep it for us."

It was August 8, 1945, the day before Nagasaki's destruction, when

Joe left China with Chennault and headed home. On October 18, after six weeks of "terminal leave," he reverted to inactive status and set about to reenter the reporter's trade he had left more than four years earlier amidst signs of chaos and war. He looked ahead now to the chaos of peace.

Part Three

PARTNERSHIP

HOME FROM THE WAR

Work and Play in Washington

PEACE CAME TO America first as celebration, then as stark reality. The war had transformed the world, and the nation had changed with it. With one foot planted in the heart of Europe and the other upon the islands of Japan, America truly bestrode the globe like a colossus. The carefree days of yore were gone; whether the country liked it or not, the American Century had begun.

As the country changed, so did its capital city. Washington remained in many ways a small town, but now it was the most important small town in the world. Decisions there reverberated around the globe with a force unmatched anywhere else. This new Washington scene captured the fancy of many of the nation's most brilliant young men, including scions of the leading Anglo-Saxon families. These men would have thrived in normal times as Wall Street financiers, corporate lawyers, or bank presidents. Now such careers struck them as too boring to contemplate. The world was America's oyster, and Washington was theirs.

Some emerged during the war and stayed on (or soon returned) to help wage the peace: Bob Lovett; John McCloy; James Forrestal; Joe's old friend from the Porcellian Club, Paul Nitze; and that Alsop family friend and Yale-educated economist, Richard Bissell. Others flocked to Washington from military service or from Bill Donovan's intelligence network: Frank Wisner, graduate of the University of Virginia and its law school, a former naval commander and deputy assistant secretary of state; Tracy Barnes, of Groton, Yale, and Harvard Law, married to an

Aldrich, and a former Jedburgh operative; Desmond FitzGerald, handsome lawyer from Long Island, married to the granddaughter of Groton's founding rector, Endicott Peabody. Still others came and went according to the dictates of their foreign service careers: Chip Bohlen, George Kennan, David K. E. Bruce. Averell Harriman returned from service as ambassador to Moscow in order to join the cause.

That cause was nothing less than the forging of a new order to replace the one that had been smashed in the First World War three decades before. These men and their compatriots faced the challenge with sober resolve and fun-loving exuberance.

At their side, cheering them on, was the new journalistic team of Joseph and Stewart Alsop. The brothers were natural allies of the fresh foreign-policy elite in postwar America. They had, after all, gone to school with many of these people, and shared with them friends, experiences, and culture. They shared also a desire for a strong, interventionist America allied with Britain and bent on maintaining a balance of power among nations.

The story of the brothers' postwar column begins with Joe's return to Washington in the fall of 1945. As usual he brought with him a collection of friends and a lot of commotion. Stewart and Tish were living in a small Georgetown house on Twenty-sixth Street when Joe appeared with Emily Hahn and Charlotte Gower, who had been his fellow prisoners in that Hong Kong camp in 1942. A long night of celebration began. Though rationing was in effect, Tish managed to get a huge steak from an admiring grocer down the street. Joe was in top form, spinning stories, issuing pronunciamentos, dropping withering quips at every opportunity. Thrilled to meet his new sister-in-law, he showered her with attention and affection. Stewart was deeply moved to be back in the compelling presence of his big brother after five years. The two men traded war stories through the early-morning hours. Tish, for her part, felt intimidated by Joe, but drawn to him nonetheless. She was struck by his argumentativeness, his sweeping statements on his likes and dislikes, his resolve that everything he did must be the best.

She discovered Joe the Connoisseur as he staggered upstairs in a predawn stupor following their night of revelry.

"Joe," she called to him, "what would you like for breakfast when you wake up?" Said the brother-in-law, "I should like poached eggs, darling, on anchovy toast and strawberries with kirsch. And I don't like just any anchovy paste, darling; could you find me a bit of Gentleman's Relish?" Gentleman's Relish was the top British brand—quite unobtainable in Washington at war's end.

Before his Washington arrival, Joe had stopped by the New York *Herald Tribune* to discuss his column and the idea of bringing Stewart into partnership. The Reids had reacted favorably, although it certainly was unconventional to draw into column-writing a man with no journalistic experience. Stewart found the idea heady—and frightening. He knew it wouldn't be easy working for his forceful and mercurial brother, and he had no way of knowing whether he was suited to the reporter's trade. But he also knew it was too good an opportunity to pass up.

This ended for Stewart a period of drift that had begun with the Japanese surrender. He had taken the exam for the U.S. foreign service, though Tish considered such a course "ridiculous," since Stewart never seemed willing to conform to authority. Tom Braden had hit upon the idea of going out to Hollywood to write screenplays, and the two tossed that around for a while. Stewart and Tish discussed, and rejected, a return to the book publishing business. They liked Washington, where Stewart had encountered many friends from earlier days, and neither had any desire to live in or near New York.

Meanwhile, Stewart and Braden had decided to write a book on the OSS. The propaganda stories they had written for newspaper distribution on OSS derring-do had generated considerable interest throughout the country and bolstered Donovan's effort to create a permanent U.S. intelligence service. Why not forge their tales into a book?

But first they needed the blessing of Wild Bill himself. They met with him in the general's office. The young Jedburghs stood smartly at attention as Donovan inquired about their wartime careers and nodded when they thanked him for the opportunity to serve their country as intelligence operatives. Then Stewart casually tossed in the purpose of their visit.

"By the way, general," he said, "we thought we might write a book about OSS."

"A book?" asked the general, his pale blue eyes betraying quickened attentiveness. Then he relaxed, perhaps thinking of the value of such an enterprise to his own agenda.

"Well, go ahead, boys. Just don't mention money."

The two operatives promised never to print anything about the practice of allowing agents to turn in their operational scratch at favorable exchange rates. News of such cash windfalls for OSS officers could generate some political hostility. With this conditional permission, Alsop and Braden worked furiously for several months—first pulling their research together around the Alsops' little kitchen table in Georgetown, then repairing to Avon for a writing blitz. The result was a 237-page book published by Reynal & Hitchcock, and selling for $2.50. *Sub Rosa: The OSS and American Espionage* was a breezy narrative full of anecdotes and real-life tales, the first attempt to write a history of the U.S. intelligence services.

War stories were in hot demand in postwar America, and the Alsop-Braden book made the *New York Times* best-seller list. It also received favorable notices. The authors, wrote General Donald Armstrong in the *Saturday Review*, "reveal enough to fascinate any reader who enjoys bizarre adventures and the struggle of brave men against great odds."

The book would enhance Stewart's credibility as a neophyte columnist, but he knew he was yet to be tested in his new trade. Joe had insisted on a clear senior-junior arrangement, etched into their contract in the form of a sixty-forty split of the column's proceeds. Joe also took the lead in defining the column and positioning it in American journalism.

"The *Tribune*," he wrote in a prospectus for the syndicate, "believes the Alsops have found a pattern for their column which is fresh, important, and certain of high readership value. . . . It will be a column of information . . . setting the most significant events of the day against their background, and interpreting [them] in terms of the influences, large and small, which have brought them about and of their present and future meaning." The brothers, added the prospectus, would focus a large part of their efforts on global forces and America's role in shaping them.

To find an appropriate name for the column proved vexing. "The State of the Nation" sounded pompous, "The Course of Events" too courtly. "Here and Abroad" didn't impress syndicate chief Harry Staton. "Washington Watch" left unmentioned the column's foreign focus. Staton and Joe finally hit upon "Matter of Fact," which was general enough to encompass the international focus and specific enough to convey the hard factual reporting that would be the column's foundation. Joe had a strong sense of what he wanted to accomplish—to break news, stir up controversy, wield influence over the course of events.

The contract with the *Herald Tribune* syndicate called for four columns a week, for which the brothers would draw $25,000 a year, with $7,500 of that for expenses. After the syndicate earned back the $25,000, the brothers and the syndicate would share equally in the proceeds. It was not a lot of money, particularly for Stewart, whose 40 percent share guaranteed him only $7,000. Joe's guarantee of $10,500 remained well below his prewar income of nearly $20,000. But the brothers felt confident that the column eventually would bring substantial income. And for Joe, being back with the *Herald Tribune* was a significant reward in itself.

"I cannot adequately express my thanks to you," he wrote to business manager William Robinson upon completion of contract negotiations, and added his thanks to Staton, *Herald Trib* managing editor George Cornish, editorial page editor Geoffrey Parsons, and, of course, Helen and Ogden Reid. "You have all been so kind to me; and you have all shown such heartwarming confidence in me that although there is nothing I dislike more than settling matters of business, I shall always look back on my talks with my chiefs at the *Tribune* as a really happy and memorable episode."

With the contract signed, Joe set about getting himself settled into his Dumbarton Avenue home. Then came a flow of goods from the Orient, the fruits of Joe's endless search for bargains during his China days. They were transported by military aircraft in coffinlike wooden boxes— carpets, oriental screens, statues, paintings, jewelry, "box after box in an endless caravan," as Tish recalled.

Joe also needed a butler and a maid. On one of his rounds through Washington he met a Filipino taxi driver named José, to whom he took an instant liking. He hired the man on the spot, as well as his wife, Maria, for $25 a week. Known to Joe's friends simply as José and Maria, they were to remain with him for sixteen years, serving the functions of housekeeper, maid, cook, and butler. Joe worked them hard but showered them with affection, and they responded with devotion. Years later Katharine Graham teasingly asked how Joe could keep such wonderful employees on what he paid them.

"Love, darling. I give them plenty of love," he replied.

Stew and Tish, meanwhile, soon got themselves ensconced in a long, narrow town house about four blocks up Dumbarton from Joe. It had four bedrooms, a library, a red door, and a nice atmosphere for small gatherings. They would need the bedrooms; a second child was on the way.

The end of the year came quickly, along with the beginning of the column—and the pressures of producing four quality pieces each week of every year. The first "Matter of Fact" column, appearing December 31, 1945, described President Truman as "an average man in a neat gray suit" in whom simple virtues were combined with serious limitations. The column branded Truman's ever-present cronies as inadequate to the task of ensuring presidential success. It was an open question, they said, "whether the American machinery of government can any longer be controlled by an average man."

They greeted Congress's January 1946 return by suggesting the Truman administration was "not far from coming apart at the seams. . . . Everyone agrees that the president's appeal to the people over the heads of the lawmakers has only served to confirm the congressional attitude of patronizing . . . indifference to the wishes of 'good old Harry.' "

To many in early 1946, Harry Truman did indeed appear hapless. The transition from war to peace brought severe economic dislocations and big political demands. Americans wanted the boys home, which meant rapid demobilization. Consumers clamored for more meat, more gasoline, more goods. Workers demanded higher pay to stay ahead of the inflation they expected. Business demanded an end to controls on production and prices. Veterans demanded jobs. Everyone wanted an end to the long sacrifice. And out in the world, new storm clouds were gathering. Within months of war's end, on March 5, 1946, Winston Churchill, in Fulton, Missouri, would unfurl his memorable phrase, warning that an "iron curtain" had descended across the face of Europe.

The brothers moved quickly to grasp these rapid developments and establish their journalistic voice. They chided the president whenever they detected a lack of resolve, as when he showed an "uncertain attitude" in dealing with growing labor troubles. But when Truman named New Dealer Chester Bowles to head the new Stabilization Board, they applauded this setback for Truman's business-minded cronies, who they believed favored business interests too avidly.

The Alsops developed an early interest in the emerging candidates for the 1948 Republican presidential nomination, particularly former Minnesota governor Harold Stassen, whose aim was to wrest control of the party from Ohio senator Robert A. Taft, the Republicans' leading isolationist. The brothers delved into questions of how best to organize the government to meet the nation's postwar challenges; they promoted the idea of a unified military to supplant the separate War and Navy departments, and pushed for Bill Donovan's dream of a permanent intelligence service.

Even before Churchill's "iron curtain" speech, the brothers had issued strong warnings about Soviet imperialism, and urged U.S. action to check the spread of Soviet influence around the world. On January 3, 1946, they called for a State Department reorganization to meet "the new Soviet imperialism which is now being so strikingly manifested in Iran and Turkey." Though the gravity of this situation wasn't generally understood, the brothers wrote, key figures at State believed the Soviet purpose was to attain a position that could threaten the West's lifelines to its vital colonial enclaves.

THE ALSOPS ALSO moved to establish themselves socially in Washington. Guests at Joe's first postwar dinner party included the chic French ambassador, André Bonnet, and his wife, Ely, Supreme Court Justice Felix Frankfurter, and Senator and Mrs. Lodge. Tish served as hostess, a role that was a bit intimidating for a nineteen-year-old who never before had attended such a dinner. Seeing her nervousness, Frankfurter solicitously engaged her in conversation, but the dinner took a bad turn after the third course—salad and cheese. Following what she thought were Joe's instructions, Tish rose from the table to lead the ladies to their separate discussion, but it turned out to be premature.

"Darling," shrieked Joe in horror, "we have not yet served dessert!" Tish found herself slinking back to the table in an agony of embarrassment.

Joe quickly gained a reputation as a Washington host of verve and style. He was brutal in assessing people's social finesse. According to his formula, a party of twelve could absorb a single bore, and a party of twenty could absorb two. He normally had twelve or sixteen guests at his table, and very few bores. The food, prepared by José at Joe's direction, always was exquisite. Joe "had an extraordinary sense of what goes into a good dish, though I doubt if he ever boiled an egg," recalled Warren Zimmermann, who married Joe's niece, Corinne Chubb. Joe's leek pie and terrapin soup became famous around town.

But it was the guest list that gained the most attention. Often Joe's closest friends would be invited, but always there would be at least one of the capital's most important officials. "Your dinner will please everyone more if there is a lion or two to roar away at the head of the table," Joe once wrote. "And it is also useful to a reporter to feed the lions." Joe fed the lions constantly. In the first four months of 1946 he gave twenty-one dinner parties that brought to his table European diplomats, Supreme Court justices, leading senators and journalists, as well as dozens of lesser lights. Frequent guests included Supreme Court justices Frankfurter and William O. Douglas; senators Leverett Saltonstall, Arthur Vandenberg, and Henry Cabot Lodge; journalists Arthur Krock, Walter Lippmann, and Phil Graham; and close friends Chip Bohlen, Richard Bissell, and Ben Cohen. And of course there were Stewart and Tish.

But the lion roaring at the head of the table most often was Joe himself. He insisted on lively conversation and often stimulated it by throwing out outrageous observations, or forcing a raucous debate on an unsuspecting official who had arrived expecting nothing more than a typically serene Washington dinner conversation. Guests were encouraged to cast off their inhibitions. Charles Whitehouse, an intelligence officer who later transferred to the State Department, once arrived at Joe's to find Chip Bohlen standing on a stool, with a mop on his head, singing a song in French.

Stewart and Tish, meanwhile, set about making their own social contacts, though they entertained less frequently and less ostentatiously, Stewart formed friendships with many of the Young Turks making their way to Washington policy jobs. Among these was Tracy Barnes, whom Stewart had known at Groton and in wartime London; he and his wife Janet became close friends of the Alsops. Barnes worked at the War Department before moving to the new Central Intelligence Agency. Richard Bissell, who had just relinquished a big job with the Office of War Mobilization and now worked as a corporate consultant, frequently stopped by for dinner, along with his wife, Annie. Bissell soon would be back in government service. Stewart rekindled friendships with two intelligence men, Bob Joyce (who later transferred to State) and Bob Amory. Llewellyn Thompson, a rising young sovietologist at State, also joined the group.

The brothers' two social worlds came together in a peculiar institution that became known as the Sunday Night Supper, weekly potluck get-togethers held at various homes on the servants' night out. It started with the Bohlens, the Joyces, and Frank and Polly Wisner; Frank was now a top CIA operative. But soon the Alsop brothers and Tish were included. The host couple furnished a hot dish, while the others brought salads and desserts. Each of the regulars would invite a guest couple. "The theory was that we all had small kids but enjoyed having people in, and this was a convenient and inexpensive way to entertain," Tish recalled.

The suppers became a huge success. Gossip columnists from the local papers wrote about them. People called seeking invitations. The evenings grew so raucous that Joe renamed them the Sunday Night Drunk. The liquor flowed, the arguments became increasingly heated, and often the more indefatigable guests carried on until three a.m. Joe's voluble self-assurance increased with drink, and he would hold forth with theories on governmental goings-on in hopes of eliciting from officials there a shred or two of information. He sometimes would get carried away and invite more than his allotted guests, which generated some irritation among members. But he was firm about maintaining standards. The Alsops' cousin, Dottie Robinson (now Kidder), moved to Washington during these years with her husband, Randolph, a foreign service officer. They were invited once, but only once; Joe loved Dottie but found Randy boring.

The Sunday Night Supper reflected a fundamental change in social Washington since the beginning of the war. Old Washington, the habitat of those "cave dweller" families who were preoccupied with class and heritage, and who had entertained so lavishly when Joe arrived in 1935, was nearly gone. In its place was a social hierarchy more closely tied to actual accomplishment and proximity to power. Washington was a world capital now, and the quaint conceits of the old elite didn't carry much weight anymore. The new elite encompassed people with the intelligence and passion to lead America to its postwar destiny.

A subcategory of this emergent elite later became known as "the Georgetown set," a group of government officials and journalists who combined brains, ambition, style, and a thoroughly modern view of America's role as world power. Not all of them lived in fashionable Georgetown, but many did, including Dean Acheson, Felix Frankfurter, Walter Lippmann, and Phil and Katharine Graham. And many of the Young Turks from the nation's intelligence and foreign services, the Alsops' natural friends and allies, gravitated there as well. The Sunday Night Supper constituted a small part of the Georgetown set in embryonic form.

So did another friendly institution called the Cooking Class, organized to enhance the wives' culinary skill. It was started by Margaret Walker, whose husband John would later become head of the National Gallery of Art. Margaret, Tish, Avis Bohlen, Jane Joyce, Annie Bissell, Polly Wisner, and Emily Lodge would get together each Monday to cook up a fancy lunch, then invite the menfolk and some of their diplomatic friends in to sample the result. Annie Bissell was friendly with a rising young culinary expert named Julia Child, and frequently the women would try one of Child's creations, including a twenty-six-page lobster recipe. John Walker was a regular. Stewart and Joe appeared only occasionally. Frank Wisner got kicked out for breaking the one inviolable rule, which was that the food could never be criticized or ridiculed.

The Alsops also became part of what was known as the Dancing Class, a series of highly exclusive quarterly balls that were a relic of the day when the "cave dwellers" dominated social Washington. When Stewart and Tish first received an invitation to join, at Joe's instigation, they didn't understand what it was.

"Do you want to join this thing called the Dancing Class?" Tish asked Stewart when he got home from work one day.

"Dancing Class? No," he replied distractedly. So Tish wrote a note declining. Joe was shocked when he heard about it.

"Oh my God, darling, how awful!" he exclaimed, and immediately set about to get them back on the list.

Meanwhile, in the brothers' partnership, Joe took the lead. He dealt with the key figures at the *Herald Tribune*, devised strategy for their reporting efforts, determined which brother would undertake which tasks. Stewart chafed a bit when he felt Joe's bombastic style getting in the way of his more easygoing approach to interviewing, but sometimes the two played off each other effectively. On one occasion Joe arrived late to an interview the brothers had scheduled with Harold Stassen. As Stewart proceeded with the interview, chatting amiably in an effort to get Stassen to open up, Joe stood against the door, twirling a keychain, looking disgusted.

"Harold," he roared, "would you cut out all this bullshit?" It worked. The governor stopped mumbling nonanswers and began talking in earnest.

Joe usually took the lead in handling sources, and he quickly resumed his habit of sending notes of flattery or outright support to those he wished to cultivate. "I hope," he wrote to General Dwight Eisenhower, then chairman of the Joint Chiefs of Staff, "that you will think I wrote helpfully and constructively" on manpower matters they had discussed. "At any rate, that was my intention." Writing to his old friend Jimmy Byrnes, newly named secretary of state, Joe strongly urged the country's leading diplomat to cultivate a number of influential reporters in order to bolster his public image. Joe didn't make the suggestion from any personal motive, he assured Byrnes, "but only because I feel affection and admiration for you." He had become concerned, he wrote, about an "unsympathetic attitude" toward the secretary that he feared was becoming more and more widespread. Upon hearing that James Forrestal would stay as secretary of the navy, Joe expressed pleasure at the prospect. "The loss of one of the two or three really able and farsighted men in the government would be nothing less than a tragedy," he wrote to Forrestal.

Also, there were the inevitable notes of apology for his occasional flights of intemperance in dealing with sources. "I feel I must apologize," he wrote to an Atomic Energy Commission official named Carroll Wilson, who had declined to answer questions, "for having been so unforgivably sharp on the telephone last night." Although it had struck Joe as "ostrich-headed" for Wilson to decline to concede "truths which are universally known, and must become the foundation of American policy," he wrote, "the responsibility of decision is yours, not mine; and . . . I had no right . . . to forget to mind my manners."

For his part, Stewart loved his new job. He worked until eight o'clock or later each evening, and struggled to keep pace with Joe's awesome work habits and prodigious accumulation of information. But he learned fast and emerged as an equal partner earlier than Joe had expected. "He has just recently found his feet more or less completely," Joe wrote to *Herald Tribune* managing editor George Cornish in May 1946, "and several of our best columns in the last two or three weeks have been written by him." Four months later, Cornish echoed the sentiment in a letter to Stewart. He had been inclined to attribute particularly good columns "to that older brother of yours," said Cornish, but Stewart's recent offerings had proved "that you have been carrying your full share of the load."

Stewart took the lead in an area of increasing interest to the Alsops: communist infiltration of the trade unions and other American institutions. The brothers felt that American liberalism was in danger of losing political legitimacy over the communist issue, and as liberals they hated to see the movement giving way to conservatism and neo-isolationism. Stewart became particularly fascinated with the question of communist infiltration of the huge labor federation, the Congress of Industrial Organizations. He took notice when CIO secretary-treasurer James Carey failed in efforts to replace the communist leadership of the Electrical Workers, and he wondered how communists, a tiny minority of the membership, managed to accumulate power so successfully.

In September, Stewart portrayed CIO president Philip Murray as hopelessly indecisive in the face of communist infiltration of trade unions. Murray's heart may have been with noncommunist leaders such as James Carey and the United Auto Workers' Walter Reuther, Stewart acknowledged, but "there is equally little doubt that he has refused to commit himself on the communist issue chiefly because he values unity." It was time for Murray to join those labor leaders who saw "deep danger in . . . leaving a large segment of the labor movement under the control of a minority group whose one major aim is furtherance of the dubious objectives of the rulers of the Kremlin."

A week later Murray appeared at the Chicago Conference of Progressives and issued a stinging rebuke to American communists in the progressive movement. He said he had "no damn use for American communists."

Covering the conference from Washington by telephone, the brothers alleged that "progressives" at the meeting had been unduly influenced by Kremlin policy on U.S.-Soviet nuclear control negotiations. They blamed Commerce Secretary Henry Wallace, who, they said, had switched his position on the U.S. negotiating stance after Soviet diplomat Andrey Gromyko rejected the U.S. stance, and after American

Communist Party officials announced their opposition. "This is . . . not to say that Henry Wallace was ever consciously playing into Mr. Gromyko's hands," they wrote. "No doubt he has acted throughout with the kind of muzzy sincerity which finds hard facts and evident self-contradictions no obstacle. Yet it does seem plausible that Mr. Gromyko knew that his allies, the American Communists, had started an all-out drive against the American plan."

Not surprisingly, conference leaders responded angrily, calling the column "a shocking combination of invidious innuendo, unfounded rumor and misstatement of fact." The brothers responded in letters published in the *Herald Tribune* and *Washington Post*, saying that Americans who believed in "strong trade unionism, social planning, social welfare, civil liberties and a one-world solution of the international problem" had a duty to name names when they saw the party at work. "Unless American progressivism expels the communists from its midst, the communists will end by destroying the whole progressive movement."

The brothers followed up with an extensive two-part series, written largely by Stewart, in Joe's old flagship magazine, the *Saturday Evening Post*. Reporting the story in New Orleans, Detroit, New York, and Chicago, Stewart became an expert in the internal politics of the American labor movement. The series dramatized the struggle by portraying the key players on both sides and probing their motives and strategies. What emerged was a picture of a tiny but highly motivated communist minority brilliantly leveraging its organizational acumen amid general membership apathy to gain dominance over a number of major trade unions.

The Alsops felt so strongly about the communist threat to liberalism that they joined efforts to refurbish the country's leading noncommunist left organization, the Union for Democratic Action. James Wechsler, a liberal reporter for the *New York Post*, lingered with Joe after dinner one evening in November 1946 to suggest ways to bolster the group. The first need was cash, it was agreed, and the next day Joe wrote Averell Harriman, then secretary of commerce and inheritor of his father's vast railroad fortune, to suggest that he discuss the problem with Wechsler.

The brothers later attended a Washington organizational meeting of the UDA, along with leading New Dealers Ben Cohen and Eleanor Roosevelt, key labor leaders Walter Reuther and James Carey, and prominent politicians of the day, including Franklin D. Roosevelt, Jr., and the rising young mayor of Minneapolis, Hubert H. Humphrey. The result was a successor organization called Americans for Democratic Action, which considered itself "a declaration of liberal independence from the stifling and paralyzing influence of the communists and their apologists in America."

Though strong conviction led to the Alsops' interest in ADA, neither brother maintained any real connection with the group. They had agreed to avoid conflicts arising from involvement in political or interest groups. Besides, they didn't have time. In addition to writing four columns a week, they supplemented their incomes with magazine writing. Henry Luce's *Life* wanted all the material the Alsops could deliver, and Joe was anxious to reestablish a formal association with his old friends at the *Saturday Evening Post*.

The *Post* had changed a bit since the beginning of the war. Editor Wesley Winans Stout, increasingly out of touch in twentieth-century America, was fired in 1942 after he somehow allowed into print a piece called "The Case Against the Jew." Cancellations of advertising and subscriptions rolled in, and the magazine rushed an apology onto its editorial page, along with the announcement that a new editor had taken over. This was Ben Hibbs, a tall, gray-haired native of Pretty Prairie, Kansas—"easygoing and quiet but with iron in his soul," in the words of Norman Rockwell, the artist whose down-home *Post* covers helped make the magazine what it had become. Hibbs reduced the emphasis on fiction and hired a stable of aggressive, world-traveling correspondents to write about the war and its aftermath. He spent extravagant sums for blockbuster articles by and about celebrities, and launched a circulation war against *Life* and *Look*. Circulation nearly doubled during his twenty-year reign, from 3.3 million to 6.5 million, and revenues shot up as well, from $23 million to $104 million a year.

Joe found he liked Ben Hibbs, appreciated his courtly manner and his quiet determination. He was also pleased that Marty Sommers remained at the magazine and would, as foreign editor, work directly with the Alsops. Sommers offered $2,000 for an acceptable article, and asked for as many contributions as the brothers could provide.

They produced five pieces for the *Post* in 1946, including the first truly authoritative exploration of American security in the age of atomic weapons. "Your Flesh Should Creep," which ran July 13, 1946, was an eye-opener. It was the product largely of Stewart's close association with officials of the Pentagon's Operations and Plans Division and a high-level study committee headed by Undersecretary of State Dean Acheson. The hardheaded assessments of these military professionals proved sobering in the extreme. Though "our oceanic moats and our sea power have protected us" through history, wrote the brothers, those days would soon be gone. "In a mere instant, as history counts years, we shall cease to be the sole great power beyond range of effective attack." *Post* editors were so pleased with the six-thousand-word piece that they featured the brothers in the "Keeping Posted" column, where they noted that this was the twenty-third *Post* piece written or co-written by Joe. *Reader's Digest* snapped up the article for reprint.

As the year wore on, Joe increasingly feared that magazine efforts were siphoning away too much time from the column, which was picking up newspapers at an encouraging rate. He announced to Sommers that he and Stewart would confine themselves to four magazine articles in 1947, all produced for the *Post*, if so desired. He also suggested a kind of consulting arrangement whereby the brothers would produce weekly memos updating the magazine on national and international developments and outlining ideas for future articles. "We like the idea," replied Sommers, who offered $2,000 a year as a consulting fee. Joe accepted, but suggested their consulting services were worth more. After six months, Hibbs and Sommers raised the fee to $4,000.

"Matter of Fact," meanwhile, had become the fastest-growing column in the country. By November 1946 it ran in fifty-seven papers, and had picked up twenty-nine in just four months during the summer and fall. The column appeared in many of the best papers in the best markets, including the *Los Angeles Times*, the *Louisville Courier-Journal*, the *St. Louis Post-Dispatch*, the *Boston Globe*, the *Milwaukee Journal*, and the *Philadelphia Bulletin*. In addition, the column was picked up by *The Washington Post*, which had overtaken the staid *Washington Evening Star* in journalistic cachet and would soon surpass it in circulation as well.

The column was certainly a success journalistically. With each partner interviewing at least three officials a day face to face, and working the phones incessantly, they managed to break their share of news. They were first to outline Secretary of State Byrnes's new foreign policy of "firmness and patience," first to forecast the seriousness of the Soviet-induced Iran crisis, first to report Truman's decision to trim federal spending, first to report a Soviet offer for the unification of Germany, first to reveal Stalin's son's acknowledgment that the Soviet leader was ill. They caused a stir in Western intelligence circles by reporting, for the first time anywhere, the name of the head of the British secret service, and they revealed the substance of Michigan senator Arthur Vandenberg's important London conference speech two days before it was delivered. They kept their focus on broad trends and clashes of the day: the conflict between the West and Soviet communism; the rising conservative trend in the United States; the conflict over the role of organized labor in society; the powerful strategic and political challenges wrought by atomic weapons; the friction between government planners and free-enterprisers.

All in all, it had been a promising first year for the Alsop brothers. Income from the column and their magazine work had reached $44,300. Operating expenses amounted to $14,817, including $2,840 for business entertainment ($2,383 for Joe and $457 for Stewart). When all the accounts were settled, Joe received $15,991 for his year's work, while Stewart earned $10,660.

THE YEAR 1947 began on a sad note. On January 3, Ogden Reid died of complications from throat cancer. He had directed the *Herald Tribune* for thirty-five years, though his stewardship had been unsteady at times as he struggled with his alcoholism. Over the decades he had seen his paper grow from an also-ran in New York's morning field, to one of the world's leading newspapers. The year just past had been the paper's most financially successful ever. Ogden Reid willed his *Tribune* stock to his wife, with the proviso that at her death it would go to their two sons, Whitelaw and Brown. Mother and sons would continue to run the paper.

Whitie Reid asked Joe Alsop to serve as an honorary pallbearer at Ogden's funeral. Joe wired his acceptance and made plans to fly up with James Forrestal on a military plane. But it wasn't to be; he got fogged in at the naval air station. "In a sense I am not sorry," he wrote to Helen Reid the next day, "for the long wait gave me time for reflection." The letter continued:

> What, I asked myself, was Mr. Reid's essential quality, which earned him the respect and affection of everyone who knew him? My answer, after long thought, was ... a singular mixture of courage, honor, kindliness and integrity, a mixture in which each element complemented the others. . . . All working together transformed an essentially simple man into a deeply effective public servant and an important contributor to the history of his times. . . . There is no use my telling you that you have my deep sympathy, and that in these days my thoughts are much with you. You know that already; for I think you must know of the affection I have always felt for you both, and my abiding sense of my great debt to Mr. Reid and yourself.

Joe's association with the *Herald Tribune*, like his association with the *Saturday Evening Post*, was cemented by a powerful sense of loyalty. Just as he never forgot where he came from or the heritage of his forebears, he never forgot that his career was built upon two journalistic institutions deeply rooted in the soil of the country. "It gives me considerable pride, being a *Tribune* man myself," he wrote to Helen Reid, "to feel certain that in the decades of Mr. Reid's direction of the paper, he made through it a very great contribution to the welfare of these United States."

13

GLOBAL CHALLENGE

"We May in the End Be Defeated . . ."

IN LATE JUNE 1946, Joe flew off to Paris to cover the coming session of the Council of Foreign Ministers, where Secretary of State James F. Byrnes and Soviet Foreign Minister V. M. Molotov would resume broad peace negotiations that some policymakers had come to consider futile. Upon arriving, he sought out old friends Chip Bohlen and Ben Cohen, both highly placed in the State Department, and the three headed for dinner. For Joe, the evening's agenda was good company, good food, and good information.

Joe had made reservations at a famous Paris restaurant, Larue's, where the men sat on dusty red banquettes and drank champagne that the proprietor had managed to hide from the Germans during occupation. After a goodly flow of the vintage, Bohlen opened up with his analysis of the session's likely results. He said nobody should expect anything positive, for the Soviets had no incentive to negotiate seriously. They could continue their process of consolidating power throughout Eastern Europe as the little negotiators in big chairs talked on and on. As he spun out his scenario of woe, Cohen acted as a kind of Greek chorus, lamenting the realities of the world, as the old, pouch-eyed waiter hovered over the scene with an air of melancholy alarm.

Consider, said Chip, Bulgaria. The Soviets had promised to withdraw from that Balkan country within ninety days of a peace treaty. But that wouldn't be until next spring at the earliest, and meanwhile the Soviets already had organized a highly efficient secret police there, and were about to take over the military. Serious opposition to the communists soon would be extinct in Bulgaria. The same process was unfolding, though a bit more slowly, in Romania and Hungary. The West seemed just about willing to write off Romania, and hopes for Hungary were dwindling as the economy collapsed and the nation's desperate leaders felt constrained to offer ever greater concessions to the communists.

For Joe, the evening provided more than an excellent repast and good company. Filing a column by wireless on June 25, he echoed the Bohlen scenario, and added: "It is these realities which tell the truth about this conference. . . . It hardly seems likely that an accommodation will be found if the occupants of the plush chairs do not begin to discuss their problem in realistic terms."

The column and the trip—five weeks in Paris, a fortnight in London, three weeks in Berlin—represented the style and substance of Joe's postwar journalistic venture. The column would provide international reporting of the first rank, on-the-ground surveys of diplomatic and military situations throughout Europe and around the world. The idea was that each brother would travel abroad, for eight, ten, perhaps even twelve weeks at a time, filing stories from the battlefronts of a world struggling for stability amid the ruins of war. In Washington, too, the column would focus much of its firepower on the country's evolving foreign policy.

This journalistic challenge required not only a detailed and highly nuanced knowledge of postwar realities, but also an unremitting effort to develop and nurture top-level sources throughout the world. The Alsops seized the challenge, and soon they had become intermittent fixtures in all the major capitals—London, Paris, Bonn, Tokyo—as well as in hot spots such as Yugoslavia, Greece, the Middle East, and China. It was a far cry from those prewar days when the sluggish U. S. economy and corporate penny-pinching had precluded serious journalistic travel, even within the United States. Now the tentacles of American power stretched everywhere. The dollar was the monarch of currencies. And anybody with a U.S. passport and a decent expense account could traverse the international scene like a panjandrum. As never before (or after), it was great to be an American set loose upon the world.

Theodore H. White, a rising young journalist and political rival of Joe's during their China days, arrived in Paris shortly after war's end to discover that a dollar bought 500 French francs on the black market. For 1,000 francs—a mere $2—he could purchase a fine meal in a lavish Paris restaurant such as Larue's. A large apartment in a fashionable neighborhood a block from the Champs-Élysées rented for only $100 a month. And Joe discovered he could fly to Berlin from Paris, stay a week at the Hotel Ritz, take most of his meals in the hotel dining room, and fly back to Paris—all for $175.78.

What's more, wherever he went, Joe encountered Americans exercising immense influence over the course of world events. In Paris there was General Lucius Clay, military governor of the American zone and a kind of benevolent dictator of the conquered power. In Tokyo there was his old Kunming officemate, Seymour Janow, as well as numerous other holdovers from China days. General Chennault soon was back in China running an airline company.

And in Paris there was Joe's old friend from Groton and Harvard, Bill Patten, now a foreign-service reserve officer and husband of the former Susan Mary Jay, the lovely and well-connected friend of Stewart and John during their carefree days in New York before the war. The Pattens had arrived in Paris shortly before war's end and immediately appeared on the diplomatic social circuit. Susan Mary was a poised and accomplished hostess—"stylish, intelligent, loving and good, and very funny," as her friend Marietta FitzGerald put it. Before the war she had been a $75-an-hour model, and in Paris she looked ravishing in the latest designs by Dior and Balmain, who allowed her to wear their dresses as a courtesy on the theory that it was good publicity and bait for other customers. Joe and Susan Mary enjoyed each other tremendously, and the three—Joe and the Pattens—were a lively trio.

Susan Mary organized a large charity costume ball that coincided with the June peace conference, and Joe was there, mixing with diplomatic lions and their women until five a.m. Bohlen stayed with Joe until the end, and the normally sobersided Ben Cohen raised a smile or two by carrying on a flirtation with the duchess de Bricsac, who was dressed in skin-tight silver from head to foot, including a silver mask that matched her silver wings.

In Paris Joe stayed with the Pattens at their home at 21 Square du Bois de Boulogne, a charming old house that had belonged for years to Susan Mary's Aunt Harriet Aldrich and now was owned by Aunt Harriet's three daughters. There Joe could relax as if with family. He lounged around mornings in his dressing gown, drinking coffee and gossiping with the Pattens about their many mutual friends throughout Europe. Through the Pattens, Joe met many new friends, some highly influential, others merely famous. Among them were the British ambassador to France, Duff Cooper, and his stylish wife, Lady Diana.

The Pattens' circle was a lively set, as Susan Mary's subsequent letters to Joe would attest. "Paris is full of English," she wrote at one point, citing Pam Berry, wife of Lord Hartwell; Pam Churchill, the American wife of Randolph Churchill and daughter-in-law of Sir Winston; Laura Waugh, wife of novelist Evelyn; and spy novelist Ian Fleming's wife Ann—"with the usual complement of snarling husbands and would-be lovers." She also told of a garden party at Chantilly, the Coopers' weekend home, in honor of Canadian diplomat Charles Ritchie. "Twenty-five friends suddenly sprang out of the woods after lunch dressed in Negro masks and did a dance to a record . . . played on the Victrola while Diana distributed stamped ties saying, 'This is Ritchie Week'. . . . You will have to believe me when I say it was fun."

Whenever Joe or Stewart traveled to European capitals, they joined in the fun. But work came first. Always on the prowl for sources, Joe applied his standard technique of flattery whenever it seemed likely to succeed. "I want to wish you the very best of luck in the enormous enterprise which you have undertaken," he wrote to Lucius Clay shortly after interviewing him in Berlin. "There is no public servant of the American government whom [sic] I think is more worth giving the trifling backing within my power." When he wanted to master a subject, Joe would seek out leading governmental experts and solicit hours of interview time, often adding lunch or dinner to the schedule. He exhibited unrivaled patience in efforts to interview heads of state and top ministers. Once he spent an entire day sitting outside the office of French president Charles de Gaulle, patiently reading a Dickens novel and waiting for an audience. At day's end he had the interview.

These efforts soon paid off, as the brothers became well known in government circles throughout Europe. "In Paris, Joe was famous and distinguished," recalled Susan Mary years later. The brothers' stature was enhanced by the prestige of the Paris-based European edition of the *Herald Tribune*, which became increasingly important to Europeans as America's role in the world grew. The Alsop column could be found regularly in the Paris edition, and top governmental officials throughout Europe turned to it avidly. *The New York Times*'s chief foreign correspondent, C. L. Sulzberger, based in Paris, wrote Joe to congratulate the brothers on their performance: "I . . . look forward enthusiastically to the Paris *Herald* each day in the hopes that you or your brother's column will be printed. You will be glad to know . . . that your columns are having an increasing influence all over Europe."

Joe was the forerunner and mentor in foreign reporting, but Stewart—aided by abundant letters of introduction from Joe—was learning fast. The brothers brought to the column a depth of conviction that went beyond mere anticommunism and Joe's balance-of-power realpolitik. To them America and the West were facing a crisis of epic proportions, as Joe emphasized in a speech delivered to the Nieman fellows at Harvard shortly after war's end. It was an eloquent testament to the Alsop view of the world struggle then unfolding.

Joe began the Harvard speech with the tale of the Battle of Thermopylae in the Greek-Persian wars. The details, he said, "come back to us, across a span of two millennia, with the freshness and beauty of an heroic dawn." It was a disaster for the Greeks—three hundred brave warriors slain, the last approach to the Peloponnese open to the invading Persians. But the three hundred killed twenty thousand Persians before they themselves were overwhelmed; it was a heroic chapter scarcely equaled in lore ancient or modern. Joe retold the story of the two comrades, Eurytus and Aristodemus, Spartans on sick leave, who, upon hearing of the looming disaster, had to make their decisions. Eurytus, half blind, returned to the battlefront pass and died a hero. Aristodemus went home and found himself ostracized, a national villain until he expiated his disgrace by dying a hero at Plataea.

The choices that faced Eurytus and Aristodemus 2,400 years before, warned Joe, now faced the peoples of the West. Like the Greeks in the Persian wars, they were themselves in "one of those vast continuing conflicts between different ways of life, which seem to recur in history with a certain cruel monotony." Yet in many ways it was more ominous in 1946. While men and women of the West nearly all held to the central tenet of Western society—the idea of the dignity of the human individual—they also suffered from a certain disability, "a sickness of the soul—a loss of certainty—a failure of assurance." The West "must somehow deal with a vast, ominous and perhaps inexorable historic process, and deal with it wisely and in the best sense humanely despite this loss of assurance that afflicts us all."

Many assumed, said Joe, that the moral superiority of the West would prove decisive in the end, but he dismissed such optimism. "Power," he said, "is the raw material of politics," and power begets its own rationale. He cited the students of philosophy at Sparta, who responded to their state's growing power by forsaking freedom in the interest of service to the state. The stark question was: Should we regard Soviet society as riding the wave of the future, and submit to a world empire that would at least promise an end to global competition and war? No, said Joe, the way of Eurytus was preferable. "We may in the end be defeated. . . . But it is better to be defeated after a hard struggle than simply to give in and die anyway."

There it was in all its harshness—the Alsop vision of the struggle of the age. Casting aside moral superiority and the vague idealisms of the day, Joe looked squarely into reality and saw a death struggle that would dominate the lives of all the men and women of all the Western nations until one side or the other prevailed. The key to survival, in the meantime, was that old concept that had animated Joe's thinking on geopolitical matters for a decade—the balance of power. Force must be countered by force, power by power, resolve by resolve.

All this was in the early days of the struggle, and such views were not shared by most Americans, particularly the intellectual classes. The Soviet Union, after all, had been the country's ally in arms, and public opinion was coming around only slowly to the idea that one global struggle had merely been replaced by another. Among liberals, there remained a strong affinity for the stated goals and aspirations of the communist revolution. The Alsop view inevitably generated controversy.

The controversy was heated even within the *Herald Tribune*, that bastion of moderate Republican internationalism. Helen Reid had begun to question what seemed like the brothers' obsession with Soviet communism. She expressed her concerns during a Saturday session with Joe in February 1946, where she noted particularly that their column seemed to lack any suggestions about a policy to meet the crisis they so portentously proclaimed. A more positive tone was needed, she said. Defensively, Joe explained that Byrnes, Acheson, Cohen, and Bohlen all believed there was little hope that an all-out confrontation with the Soviets could be avoided. Meanwhile, he said, the younger men at State argued for a strong policy to halt Russian imperialism immediately. "The first job," said Joe, "is to arouse people to the fact that a crisis is in progress." But he agreed with Mrs. Reid "that one wants to present the constructive side of the situation, as well as sound the tocsin and ring the alarm."

The next day Joe interviewed Byrnes at length and received a copy of an internal memo outlining the government's growing concerns about Soviet intentions. Casting propriety aside, he sent a copy to Mrs. Reid. "I want you, particularly, to see what it is . . . that is getting me down," he wrote. Noting that he had engaged in a "breach of confidence" in sending the memo, he asked her to show it only to editorial-page editor Geoffrey Parsons, and to destroy the document thereafter. Helen Reid seemed satisfied that the brothers were reporting the emergent policy of the government.

The debate also raged outside the paper, perhaps most intensely at a dinner party at Joe's house in early 1946. Among the guests were Ben Cohen, Supreme Court Justice Hugo Black, Commerce Secretary Henry Wallace, and William Gaud, a former China hand who had just become executive assistant to the new war secretary, Robert Patterson. As soon as the men left the ladies, Gaud suggested that America should "kick the Russians in the balls" and check them at every turn. Wallace disagreed, saying the Russians should be granted free access through the Dardanelles, whereupon Gaud retorted that that was "crap." Wallace replied that Gaud's statements were crap, whereupon Gaud declared himself and Wallace "even" on that score. Black agreed with Wallace without incident, but when Cohen agreed with Black, Joe pronounced his viewpoint "a barrel of horseshit." Joe drew an analogy between the Soviet Union of 1946 and Germany of 1938, saying it was imperative that the United States know and understand Soviet intentions. Wallace dismissed that, saying he felt Joe and like-minded people simply wanted to pull the British Empire's chestnuts out of the fire. He said the cost of war with Russia would be infinitely greater than the value of any Mideastern oil, and the country shouldn't even consider going to war over Azerbaijan or the Dardanelles.

Then Chip Bohlen appeared. "Now we have a real expert on Russia," exclaimed Joe. Attention turned to Bohlen, who frankly outlined a policy that seemed pretty close to what Wallace had characterized as pulling Britain's chestnuts out of the fire. As Wallace wrote later, "It is very clear that the policy of the United States, judging from Chip Bohlen's statement, is to maintain the lifeline of the British Empire, even though it means disagreement with Russia."

As the national debate unfolded, Joe concluded that American liberalism was turning sour. He and Stewart contracted with Henry Luce's *Life* magazine to write a piece of advocacy called "The Tragedy of Liberalism." Appearing on May 20, 1946, it caused an immediate stir.

As they so often did, the brothers began with a telling anecdote. American military authorities, they recounted, had decided at the end of the war that the United States needed a ring of outlying Atlantic bases to ensure American security pending the emergence of an effective world organization. Accordingly, U.S. diplomats had commenced negotiations with Iceland for a ninety-nine-year lease on U.S. wartime military facilities there. The matter was delicate; Icelanders were a proud and independent people, and they wanted assurances that the proposed arrangement wouldn't infringe upon Icelandic sovereignty. Nevertheless, the talks were progressing nicely.

Then Henry Wallace "blundered onto the stage of this small but significant international drama." In an interview with an Icelandic journalist, Wallace attacked the idea of forward U.S. bases in the Atlantic and condemned the Iceland arrangement as a provocation to the Soviets. Senator Claude Pepper of Florida echoed the Wallace view on the floor of the Senate, and congressional liberals such as West Virginia's Senator Harley Kilgore and California's Representative Helen Gahagan Douglas characterized the American program for overseas bases as aggressively anti-Soviet. The result: Iceland pulled out of the negotiations.

"By an irresponsible intervention in a matter of great delicacy and seriousness," the brothers wrote, "Wallace defeated his own government's policy." The whole thing reflected "the terrible confusion which now afflicts American liberalism." Surveying the Soviets' global positioning in Europe, the Middle East, the Mediterranean, Korea, and Manchuria, the brothers added, "One can only admire the Soviet leaders' iron nerve and precision of execution, but one must also wonder whether they will ultimately be satisfied with less than dominion over Europe and Asia."

All this apparently eluded the understanding of American liberals, because they were captives of "the ideal picture of the Soviet Union which they cherish in their minds."

Herald Tribune syndicate chief Harry Staton was so impressed with the piece that he sent copies to fifty nonsubscribing newspapers to promote the Alsop column. But one letter writer to *Life* suggested, "The boys are little more than parlor politicians. These two grand admirals of the order of the armchair have virtually sewed up the problems of the world for us. . . ." And Walter Lippmann, in conversation with an upset Henry Wallace, suggested that Joe had become the mouthpiece for a

clique of State Department hard-liners that included Chip Bohlen—
whom Lippmann described as too young to understand the complexities
of foreign policy.

The New Republic picked up on the debate, and invited the Alsops
and liberal journalist Max Lerner to go at each other in the magazine's
pages. The disagreement between the establishment, West-leaning
Alsops and the liberal idealist Lerner proved instructive. While Lerner
insisted that he held no truck with Russian imperialism, he saw little difference between it and the British model then seemingly coming to an
end—or, for that matter, the budding American variety. "We must slap
down both," he wrote, "and as decent Americans we must oppose
American expansionism, too, which can operate more subtly and
smugly than the Russian because it operates by its economic power and
by backing the status-quo groups." Lerner's sense of idealism was offended by such questions as, "Who will control the Middle East—
Russia or Britain?"

In the realm of realpolitik and balance of power that was the Alsops'
intellectual habitat, however, that was the fundamental question. Soviet
control of the Middle East meant a mortal threat to Europe and the
West, and the only way to parry that threat was to consolidate power in
the region under the auspices of the West. Indeed, the central reality of
the postwar world was the decline of British power, and the question
was whether the vacuum thus created would be filled by the United
States or the Soviet Union. The key, as the Alsops viewed it, was the
Anglo-American alliance, a partnership designed to sustain Britain as a
world power operating under the economic umbrella of the United
States.

America seemed slow to grasp these concepts. Joe wrote to Geoffrey
Crowther of the *Economist* that the United States seemed to be moving
toward "honest, nonimperialistic internationalism." But he questioned
whether it would get there soon enough to deal with the "deteriorative
process" in the world. In a letter to a reader in Ithaca, New York, Stewart wrote, "We have assumed world leadership, or rather . . . it has been
thrust upon us. The question is whether the American people, and more
especially the American Congress, will realize that fact in time."

Joe's passion on the issue erupted in mid-1946, when he went to see
Henry Wallace after the commerce secretary had delivered a speech at an
Averell Harriman dinner in New York. Joe considered the speech an attack on the hard-line foreign policy of Secretary of State Byrnes, and he
was "very much disturbed," as Wallace recalled later. Joe suggested that
the secretary was advocating a foreign policy in conflict with that of
Byrnes and Truman. When Wallace retorted that the president had read
every word of his speech, Joe was "completely floored" and said that
simply proved Truman was a much smaller man that he had thought.

"I think you are in a completely indefensible position in the Cabinet," Joe told the secretary.

"So you are going to try to write columns to get me out?" replied Wallace.

"No, Henry," said Joe, "I am your true friend. I agree completely with you on your domestic policy, but I think your foreign attitude is altogether wrong."

"I think," replied Wallace, "that yours is altogether wrong and that it leads inevitably to war."

Such matters were much on the Alsops' minds in 1947 as Stewart began his first overseas reporting trip—a three-month excursion, from mid-February to mid-May, taking him to Ankara, Athens, Tehran, Baghdad, Jerusalem, Cairo, London, and other points. In Athens he came upon a big story.

Stewart knew the situation in Greece was precarious, that communist irregulars from the wartime anti-Nazi campaign had coalesced into a twenty-thousand-man army strongly backed with money and manpower from communist governments to the north. He knew the British had been laboring to stave off a communist takeover and return the disordered nation to stability. What he didn't know was that Greece had become the center of a major crisis spawned by a momentous new development in the Cold War.

He encountered two State Department officials working hard in Athens. Mark Ethridge, head of the American delegation to the United Nations Commission, and Paul A. Porter, chief of the American economic mission to Greece, informed Stewart that just three days before, on February 22, 1947, the British ambassador to Washington, Lord Inverchapel, had walked into the office of the new secretary of state, George Marshall, with an ominous message. His Majesty's government, facing financial collapse at home, could no longer afford its efforts in Greece and Turkey. Britain was pulling out and relinquishing responsibility there within thirty days. The United States would have to take the lead if the West were to halt the spread of communism into the eastern Mediterranean and beyond. Ethridge and Porter told Stewart that their job was to fashion a plan for a massive infusion of American cash into Greece to stem the communist tide.

Stewart dispatched a column sounding the alarm. The United States must act to bring order out of the political and economic chaos in Greece, he wrote, "or Greece is . . . certain to become another Soviet-Balkan puppet, with the profoundest effect on the whole world balance of power." Reading Stewart's dispatch, Joe rushed to the State Department to find Assistant Secretary of State Will Clayton working against time on preliminary plans for a new foreign policy doctrine and a Greek-Turkish aid bill. Within two days, Joe reported "something very close to panic" in the administration sectors "most closely in touch with the foreign situation." He reported a brewing debate within the administration over whether to go public and initiate a kind of "politico-economic fire brigade" to meet the crisis.

President Truman opted for the fire brigade, and within two weeks had fashioned a plan for $400 million in military and economic aid to Greece and Turkey, as well as for American missions to direct the rebuilding of the two nations' economies and armed forces. The president fought hard for the plan, and saw it through Congress by mid-March. In the process, he gave expression to what would become known as the Truman Doctrine declaring America's commitment to the defense against communism. Growing out of this was a broader vision of an America that would wield her economic might to bolster Europe's defenses in the Cold War. As a commencement marshal at Harvard that June, Joe heard George Marshall outline the "Marshall Plan" to Harvard and the world.

For Stewart, the Athens dispatches were a journalistic coup of the first rank. Geoffrey Parsons wrote to Joe that Stewart's work from the Mediterranean had been "beyond belief admirable. He has such a clear, straightforward way of putting things that you see them exactly as he sees them and you are confident that you are seeing them as they are." Joe wrote back that, having picked Stewart as his partner, he felt like the man who puts fifty cents into the slot machine "and is almost overwhelmed by the disproportionate return."

As always the brothers kept up their probing magazine writing. They generated considerable interest with a September 6 *Saturday Evening Post* piece entitled "Are We Ready for a Push-Button War?"—the first serious look at the technology and strategic implications of intercontinental ballistic missiles, which would be part of the Cold War standoff within a decade. The *Post* called the piece "perhaps the most desperately important message the *Post* will publish this year."

Stewart took the lead in a subsequent piece on the strategic challenge posed to the United States if Europe fell to the communists. Entitled "If Russia Grabs Europe—," it ran in the December 20 issue and identified the threat posed by developments in Italy and France, where economic and political deterioration threatened to bring to power tough communist leaders with close ties to Moscow. If this took place, a kind of domino effect would ensue, as mounting geopolitical pressures drove first the smaller countries (Belgium, Holland, Scandivania), then the rotten regime of Spain, and finally Germany—"the key to Europe," as Lenin long before had described it—into the communist sphere. Such an eventuality, wrote Stewart, would force the United States into a state of war readiness unparalleled in its history, with higher taxes, a lower standard of living, and a massive "defensive screen" of bases in the Atlantic and in other critical spots around the globe.

Cultivating sources throughout Washington and the world, the brothers became adept at piecing together fragments of information accumulated through long and arduous reporting. In the end they found themselves returning again and again to two men who served as their most reliable and willing sources: Chip Bohlen and George Kennan. The two sovietologists didn't always tell the brothers what they wanted to know, and sometimes when they did they swore them to secrecy. But they revealed what they could, and found the Alsop column an excellent vehicle for conveying to a sophisticated audience subtle developments in the evolution of U.S. foreign policy.

From Bohlen in early 1948 Joe heard of a strange episode in which an "extremely high Russian official abroad," in disguise, approached an American official, pulled off his fake beard, and voiced hopes for an accommodation between the two countries. Declaring himself a follower of Kremlin strongman Lavrenty Beria, he said that the Politburo was divided, and that if the Marshall Plan passed, Molotov's hard-line approach likely would give way in Russia to a more accommodationist attitude represented by Beria. The conversation lasted five hours, as the "Beria man" sought assurances that the West would not rebuff a Soviet overture if one could be engineered by the Beria faction. "There have been other, comparable incidents, but this one is regarded as having been [of] pretty decisive importance," Joe wrote to Marty Sommers. The Bohlen information produced a January column reporting cryptically that American officials had received concrete information that Molotov's hard-line policies may be "faltering."

Shortly afterward, Chip gave Joe the inside details of the violent coup that Stalin had engineered in Czechoslovakia in early February. He suggested he might be willing to release this information later for publication in an Alsop column or magazine article. (He never actually did so.) In April, Chip told Joe that if trouble came he expected it would be in Greece; he said it was merely a "guess." But it wasn't a guess. Joe learned later from another source that U.S. intelligence had picked up reports of severe restrictions on civilian rail travel and virtual stoppage of air travel in next-door Yugoslavia—"signs of mobilization under normal conditions," as Joe wrote to Sommers.

Joe was sitting in Kennan's office in June when a diplomatic communiqué arrived to inform State of the break between Stalin and Yugoslavia's Marshal Tito. The head of the department's policy planning staff became so jubilant that he grabbed his Russian guitar and began strumming along with the conversation. The break seemed to be the first solid evidence that Kennan's famous "Mr. X theory" of the Cold War might be borne out. This widely discussed postulate, the underpinning of the government's "containment" policy, assumed that if the West built up its own area and contained the Soviets, sooner or later something would crack somewhere within the Soviet sphere. This, said Kennan, was the first crack. "It will, I think, be exploited by cautious advances towards the Yugoslavs," Joe wrote to Sommers, echoing the policy advice Kennan was giving within the government.

Joe's column on the development also echoed Kennan. Alsop wrote that the break confirmed the basic theory of American foreign policy set forth in Kennan's Mr. X theory.

By this time the Soviets had forced a crisis by blockading Berlin, and fears of war mounted. The atmosphere in Washington, the Alsops reported, was no longer postwar. "It is . . . a prewar atmosphere." Lumping the Soviet drive for Berlin together with "the rape of Czechoslovakia, the drive for Finland, the pressure on Scandinavia and the struggle for Italy," they called the blockade "the most dangerous development to date." Bohlen told Joe in early April that he felt the Soviets were bluffing. "We should soon know," Stewart wrote to Sommers. "The plan seems to be to use airlift escorted by fighter planes. If any are shot down, there will be a clear casus belli."

In mid-June 1948 Truman ordered the airlift. The president had concluded that the future of Western Europe hinged on the outcome of the Berlin crisis. Increasingly, top U.S. government officials believed Stalin's aims in Berlin "must be linked to the Kremlin's overall plans" to consolidate the Eastern European satellites into the Soviet Union itself, the Alsops reported from Washington on September 17. But was it a bluff? The Alsops didn't think so. They viewed the Soviet moves as an effort to tip the scales against the West. Either the Western powers would back down—in which case there would be a rush to the Soviet bandwagon in Italy, and the Russian position in Germany would be secured—or there would be a general war, which would come at a time of maximum strength for the Soviets, before the Marshall Plan could succeed in strengthening European defenses.

Fears of war increased further through the summer. "The situation is growing extremely dark," Joe wrote to Sommers. All week long he had heard top government officials seriously discussing the possibility of war. "G. Kennan wants to call up the National Guard; Chip is distinctly worried. Lovett is pretty grim, and so it goes." He added that they were "all losing their confidence that the Soviets don't want war."

In the end, of course, these fears reduced themselves to questions of money. James Forrestal, now secretary of defense, said he needed $17 billion to $17.5 billion to meet the Soviet threat. Over in the White House, the president's closest advisers felt $15 billion was all the country could afford. Joe immediately rushed to the offensive, not only in the column but also in private discussions with key administration officials.

On November 30, Joe hurried off a column outlining what he considered the disastrous implications of the $15 billion defense ceiling in the face of the Soviet threat in Europe. That night at a dinner party he encountered Clark Clifford, a rising star in Truman's White House, and promptly got into a bitter argument with him over defense spending. The next day Joe followed up with a four-page letter seeking to explain why he had become so vehement. It was, he said, "because of the bitter shock of disappointment which the . . . president's rigid budget ceiling has administered to my faith in human nature." All through the presidential campaign that fall, Alsop noted, Clifford had argued that the Republicans would subordinate defense needs to big business calls for budget cuts. But now Truman himself, "whom I have regarded as morally and politically committed to a more courageous course," was yielding to budget pressures. The $15 billion figure, wrote Joe, "casts the blackest suspicion upon the president's emergency message of last year."

Joe's persistence with Clifford seemed to have an effect. "He has got into the picture now, and will probably be on the right side," Joe wrote to Sommers. But now that Truman had won his 1948 reelection bid, the political dynamics surrounding such decisions had changed markedly; the big fight over defense spending was just beginning. In the meantime, a new perception emerged in Washington policymaking. The Marshall Plan—or European Recovery Program, as it was officially called—seemed to be tilting the balance of power toward the West. If the Soviets didn't force a war soon, their hour of greatest strategic opportunity in Europe would be lost. War fears in Washington began to ease.

At year's end, with this new optimism in the air, Joe once again headed for Europe. After a stop in Avon for "fond farewells to the family," he boarded a military plane for Germany—the beginning leg of a ten-week trip that took him to Berlin, Wiesbaden, Paris, Rome, Belgrade, and London. His first column was a paean to the ingenuity, resolve, and bravery represented by the massive Berlin airlift. After hopping a flight from Wiesbaden to Berlin's Tempelhof Airport aboard a giant C-54 cargo plane, *Big Easy 103,* Joe captured the human drama of the historic operation.

He described the steely haze that hung over the steel-cold ground at Wiesbaden as German workers clapped their chapped hands to warm them and their truck moved away from *Big Easy 103.*

"We're ready to roll," said the pilot briskly, his C-54 now loaded with ten tons of canned applesauce, dried apricots, cement, and roofing paper.

Touching ground at Tempelhof, the big plane taxied to a long line of C-54s waiting for unloading. Finally it was in place, and a truck pulled up and discharged fifteen shivering Germans who flung themselves upon the cases of goods—as though, wrote Joe, their lives depended upon speed, which indeed it did. "And another air cargo had been delivered to the beleaguered city of Berlin."

Returning to Rome for the first time in fourteen months, Joe was heartened to discover a slippage in communist support among workers, and a growing sense of stability since the communists had lost national elections there. In London, he found a "miracle" of economic renewal. All this led to a rare display of optimism. "In Europe," wrote Joe by way of summing up, "a stalemate has been reached in the world struggle between the West and the Soviet empire." It was a "perilous victory" but a victory nonetheless.

The trip was not all work, of course. As always, Joe sought out many friends along the way, beginning with the Pattens in Paris. He arrived in time to be on hand at the christening of their newborn son (and Joe's godson), Billy. "Though I have 14 godchildren already, this new addition makes me proud," he wrote a friend. Arriving on Christmas Eve, he contributed to a lively evening of merriment and a pleasant morning of gossiping in dressing gowns and opening presents, as Susan Mary later recalled. Always generous with friends, Joe presented the Pattens with two jardinieres and two haunting small pagan statues. The statues, Susan Mary wrote later to Joe, "have taken possession of the house. I noticed people glancing at them and becoming riveted."

Joe also spent abundant time with David Bruce and his lovely young wife, Evangeline. Always inclined to foster friendships among his own friends, Joe asked the Bruces to have the Pattens to lunch, which they did along with Duff and Diana Cooper. "Joe had so many friends— British, Americans, French," recalled Evangeline Bruce years later. "He revelled in the atmosphere." In Rome he socialized with U.S. ambassador James Dunn and his wife, Mary, who were good enough friends that he didn't hesitate to ask them to forward in a diplomatic pouch some silk shirts he had purchased for Bill Patten. The Dunns readily complied.

Joe's arrival in London was "the excitement of the hour," as Pam Berry wrote to Duff Cooper. He dined with Sir Stafford Cripps, chancellor of the exchequer, and Lady Cripps. In gratitude, Joe later wrote to say how much he admired "the superb job" Cripps was doing. Word reached Susan Mary that Lady Sybl Colefax had crawled from her bed in pain in order not to miss a dinner for the itinerant reporter. As for Joe, he found his visit to England "wonderfully good fun and utterly exhausting." The highlight was a stay with Liz Cavendish, of the grand old Whig family, in her small fifteenth-century country house in Derbyshire. Her husband, a duke, looked rather like a retired gamekeeper making dry flies, and Joe concluded that here at last he would get a rest. Not at all. The duke insisted on staying up drinking and talking until three a.m. Next morning, when Joe awoke at seven to use the bathroom, the butler assumed he was getting up and ceremoniously attended to his rooms, closing windows, opening curtains. "I timidly supposed I was being aroused for early family breakfast, and so, after four hours' sleep, had two hours' nice walk around Derbyshire before I could get any coffee," Joe wrote to Susan Mary.

The entire party also made a visit to the grand old Cavendish home of Chatsworth, where the window frames were gilded and the kitchen was a brisk ten-minute walk from the nearest of four dining rooms. When Joe inquired about these details, the duke said that gilded window frames were economical because they required no repainting. He added that until 1930 or so, the house had had 122 servants, and dishes had been carried from kitchen to dining rooms by footmen in relays. The discomfort had been increased by the rule that all menservants could have as much meat and strong beer as they wanted, resulting in "the footmen smelling very strong and being always drunk." Recounting all this to Susan Mary in a letter, Joe apologized for "sending . . . this drivel." But it amused him, he explained, and, besides, he usually had to keep such things to himself "to avoid the appearance of name-dropping."

14

THE TRUMAN CRONIES

Leading the Charge for Military Preparedness

ON NOVEMBER 3, 1948, Harry Truman surprised the nation with a reelection triumph that almost nobody predicted. The next day, Joseph and Stewart Alsop expressed a proper measure of embarrassment: "There is only one question on which politicians, poll-takers, political reporters and other wiseacres and prognosticators can any longer speak with much authority. That is how they want their crow cooked."

The only consolation for the Alsops lay in the fact that just about everyone had underestimated Harry Truman in 1948. To Joe and Stewart, it didn't seem natural that a man of such ordinariness could be sitting in the White House, especially after such a one as Cousin Franklin. After FDR's death in 1945, twenty-two army trucks had been needed to move Cousin Eleanor out of the White House; the Trumans needed just one to move in. The Roosevelts had reigned there twelve years, from the time Joe was twenty-two until he was thirty-four, and it had seemed that they belonged there. And why not? They were part of the nation's longtime governing elite, the same elite that had produced the Alsops themselves and their forebears.

But then the White House had been taken over by a failed haberdasher with ties to Kansas City's Pendergast political machine, a man who spoke like a Midwestern farmer and seemed unduly preoccupied with his daughter's questionable singing career. The brothers appreciated Truman's judgment in bringing into the government so many men they admired and considered friends—Acheson, Bohlen, Kennan, Forrestal, Bruce, Lovett, McCloy. But they saw also a brewing bureaucratic war between these men and Truman's limited and shallow cronies—men like John R. Steelman, former economics professor and labor specialist from Alabama; John Snyder, former St. Louis banker and now treasury secretary; James Vardaman, another former Midwestern banker; and above all Harry Vaughan, the boisterous military aide, a joke-telling presidential pal whose central purpose in the White House seemed to be comic relief.

It wasn't much different in Washington society, where the shining star was a plump, opinionated, rich Oklahoma widow named Perle Mesta. Not even her "warmest admirers," said *Time*, "would credit her with overwhelming charm or notable wit." But ambassadors, senators, and cabinet officers came at her call. The reason: She was a friend of the president's and an even closer friend to First Lady Bess Truman. Her allies in the government included those presidential cronies the Alsops despised.

During the fall campaign, all this had led the brothers to lean toward New York governor Thomas E. Dewey, the Republican candidate. Joe had traveled to New York for extensive sessions with Dewey and his advisers, scheduled a major piece on the governor for the *Saturday Evening Post*, and sought to convey in ways explicit and subtle his sympathy for the Dewey candidacy. "The big article about the governor is very nearly finished," he wrote to Dewey's executive assistant, Paul Lockwood, "and I find myself hoping that you, particularly, will like it."

Joe entered into an extensive correspondence with his old friend Cabot Lodge, a Dewey campaign insider. Spinning the familiar Alsop line that the challenges of the world required commitment and money, Joe advised Lodge on the hard choices Dewey would face—between letting Asia go and formulating an effective China policy; between losing much of what had been gained in Europe and paying the price for a real Western European defensive system; between appeasing the Soviets and risking war; between letting Britain go down the drain and building a new relationship with the commonwealth. Truman, said Joe, could simply be ignored, "for Dewey's object must be not to tear down Truman (poor Truman has done this quite adequately already) but to build up Dewey."

Besides undermining his claim to journalistic detachment, the letter contained faulty political advice. Although there is no evidence that Joe's counsel made its way into the campaign's decision-making circles, Dewey did indeed ignore Truman, did sit on his presumed lead, did seek to say little of substance on the assumption that he could worry about that after the victory. Like the Alsops and so many others who considered themselves informed insiders, the candidate underestimated Harry Truman and paid the price.

The brothers were pleased that the country remained more liberal than they had thought, and that the Democrats had retaken Congress, gaining nine Senate and seventy-five House seats. But they feared Truman's victory would embolden the cronies. Stewart, stopping by the White House to take in a press conference and assess the president's mood, found that "cockiness fairly oozes out of him." Stewart admired the man's courage and honesty, he wrote to Sommers, but like Joe he disliked Truman's "conviction of infallibility" and feared that his taste for mediocre people would extend to foreign policy. "Then we shall be sunk without trace."

Soon after the election, Truman accepted the resignation of James Forrestal, the last cabinet member inherited from Roosevelt, and installed as defense secretary a man *Time* described as "big, beefy Louis Johnson," onetime assistant secretary of war under Roosevelt, and the Democrats' highly successful campaign fund-raiser. This was just the sort of thing the Alsops had feared. Johnson was an able man, a lawyer, veteran of the First World War, former national commander of the American Legion. He was as tough and ambitious as they come. But his elevation represented the triumph of the cronies over the men the Alsops favored. It didn't ease the brothers' concerns when Perle Mesta showed up at a fashion show and blurted to reporters, "Did you hear the news? That stinker Forrestal is out. My man Johnson is in."

Forrestal had wanted out, but his departure was hastened by an emotional breakdown that two months later would lead to his suicide. It was a crushing blow to Joe, a "hideously tragic event," as he wrote to Sommers. Checking on the circumstances of the new secretary's ascension, Joe learned that Johnson had had "the nerve to march into Truman's office and demand, point-blank, to be paid off" for his fundraising feats. Vice President Alben Barkley and Clark Clifford had opposed the appointment, Joe informed Sommers, but it had been pushed by Vaughan, Snyder, and Mrs. Mesta.

The cronies had taken over. Even Air Force Secretary Stuart Symington, Joe noted to Sommers, now echoed the cronies, "and last night he gave me half an hour of shouting about how 'this country can't do the whole job in the world,' etc., etc." The Alsops considered such talk a new brand of isolationism, and it filled them with anxiety.

Their anxiety was heightened by their interpretation of the Soviet challenge, which reverberated in their writings and found detailed expression in a letter from Joe to Sommers. The West, he wrote, triumphantly had passed through the first phase of the Cold War, which was the struggle for Europe. The success in checking Soviet advances in Greece and Turkey, the salutary impact of the Marshall Plan, the Soviet failure in Berlin, the decline in communist control of European trade unions—all had contributed to a "hair's breadth" victory for the West.

But now a new era was beginning, marked by two East Bloc salients. First, the Soviets would "probe and drive against the weak and vulnerable colonial flanks of the Western world," initially in the Far East and eventually in the Middle East. Their aim would be to attack the

West by unraveling its positions in various troublesome and dangerous regions—China, Southeast Asia, Korea, Egypt. Secondly, the Soviets would seek to consolidate their positions throughout their own empire—concentrating on armaments and strengthening their hold on the satellites—as a means of girding themselves for the protracted conflict.

The Alsops felt that Truman and his gang had failed to grasp these new realities. Making things worse was the departure from the administration of some of the brothers' most respected friends. When Bob Lovett, then undersecretary of state, followed Forrestal into private life, Joe wrote to say he had "never seen another public servant whom I so much respected." When George Kennan departed for a temporary stint in academia, Joe wrote to him, "You have served this country as have very few other men in my time. I hardly know how things will go on without you."

But good news came when Truman appointed Dean Acheson secretary of state. THE DUBIOUS FUTURE LOOKS AT LEAST LESS DUBIOUS TONIGHT LOVE TO ALICE, Joe wired Acheson from Paris. Acheson sent a warm reply suggesting they get together upon Joe's return.

Joe sized up Louis Johnson in May, when the secretary invited him to a long one-on-one dinner. Johnson impressed Joe with his commitment to the creation of a unified Joint Chiefs of Staff. But Joe found him "more than usually emetic" when he described the arm twisting the president had administered to get him to take the Pentagon job. And Johnson was "revoltingly pious" about Jim Forrestal. Moreover, he struck Joe as so ambitious that he likely would "make phony economies in the Defense establishment in order to make headlines." Joe considered him "totally unscrupulous but able."

At their dinner, Joe unburdened himself of a long lecture about the need for strong defense, and later wrote the secretary reiterating his views. "You will be judged by the strength and efficiency of the defense machine you create, and not by its annual cost," he said. "And whereas I believe you will be held to be successful even if this defense organization is costly, provided it is not wasteful and is strong enough for its task, I am certain you will be held a failure if its strength is in any way in doubt." Joe apologized for "writing with such frankness," but in his usual fawning way added that he did so "only because I have the success of your work so much at heart."

Johnson ignored the advice. In April he canceled construction of the $186 million supercarrier *United States*. A month later he ordered another $1.4 billion slashed from the military budget. Parrying criticism, he announced with typical bluster that the United States could "lick Russia with one hand tied behind our back."

Worse, Joe heard that Johnson had ordered that all transactions between Defense and State be channeled through him. This would break down the close collaboration that Forrestal and Lovett had worked so hard to build up between the departments. One source told Joe of a National Security Council meeting in which Johnson asked insinuatingly why Acheson had appointed so many "Frankfurter men like David Bruce" to high positions. Cabot Lodge told Joe of an executive committee session on the Hill, with Johnson and Acheson appearing together, at which the defense secretary "took over and treated Acheson like an office boy."

Against this backdrop, a crisis was brewing in Britain. The country's monetary reserves of gold and dollars were dwindling as her overseas commitments brought pressures on the pound. British foreign minister Ernest Bevin and Sir Stafford Cripps, chancellor of the exchequer, rushed to Washington for talks with Acheson and Treasury Secretary Snyder. Acheson was set to chair the U.S. delegation, but Snyder protested to his old friend the president, waving a copy of a recent Stewart Alsop column from London that ridiculed him as "scolding," "purse-lipped" and ineffectual. Soon afterward, Stewart learned from Richard Bissell that the president had agreed to give Snyder the chairmanship as a show of confidence in light of Stewart's derision. To Stewart, this had serious ramifications; Acheson supported U.S. financial assistance to Great Britain while Snyder had expressed doubts about it.

But the Acheson view prevailed, as the crisis generated fears throughout the American foreign-policy establishment about Britain's future. Chip Bohlen told Joe he considered it likely that Britain would collapse as a great power, and feared that the resulting dislocations would lead to an acute danger of war. Stewart uncovered talk of "an Anglo-American partnership [to] do the job which Britain alone did in the Nineteenth Century, of lubricating world trade and acting as the banker for the West," as he wrote to Ben Hibbs. In a column, the brothers suggested that "wiser Americans" foresaw a relationship in which the two countries would share world commitments that the British no longer were able to support alone. The sterling crisis eased after Britain devalued the pound, and it never generated much interest among the American people; but the Alsops considered it a matter of utmost gravity. A collapse of British power would be a disaster for the United States and a precursor of another war, Stewart wrote to a reader.

Then came a stunning announcement. On September 23, 1949, Truman declared that the Soviets had detonated an atomic bomb. The era of America's nuclear monopoly was over. Among U.S. policymakers, there wasn't much surprise that the Soviets had unlocked the atom's secrets, but they hadn't expected the Beria bomb, as it was called (after Kremlin strongman Lavrenty Beria, who oversaw the project), until 1952 at the earliest.

The Beria bomb development added to the Alsops' anxiety as they watched Truman and Johnson impose a military-spending ceiling of $13 billion for fiscal 1951, down from $14.4 billion for the current year. Joe considered the implications "hair-raising." The country's strategic concepts rested on air power, first as deterrent and then to cut the enemy down to size in case of war. The Joint Chiefs had established seventy air groups as the minimum necessary for the country's tactical and strategic air missions. Now this was being cut to forty-eight groups, including a reduction in the strategic air groups to fourteen from twenty.

The Alsops declared war on Truman defense policies and set out to prove that the country was in peril. "It is hard to imagine anything more serious than President Truman's decision to weaken America's defenses in the year of the Beria bomb," they wrote on October 21.

The Alsops' war with Truman and Johnson centered on disagreements about the nature of the Soviet threat. Truman, Johnson, and top policymakers at the State Department (including Secretary of State George Marshall before his departure in early 1949) believed that the Soviets sought expansion not by war but through subtle campaigns of infiltration and subversion. They reasoned that the tools of war were not appropriate weapons in a competition of political intrigue, and the United States could save money by not building weapons of war that weren't called for. Johnson also insisted that much of his budget cutting merely trimmed fat from a bloated Pentagon. But the Alsops believed that the Soviets soon would begin probing for weaknesses in the West's forward positions as part of an ongoing effort to test the will and sap the strength of the Western nations.

The brothers returned to the defense theme with ever greater urgency through the last months of 1949 and into 1950. Louis Johnson came to despise the Alsops and ordered Pentagon reception desks to inform him whenever they set foot in the building. Once, as Stewart chatted with Air Force Secretary Symington in his office, Johnson burst in, closed the door behind him, "and stood there, saying nothing, nodding his huge bald head up and down with the air of a virtuous husband who has at last caught his erring wife in flagrante delictu," as the brothers described the scene later. Making an introduction, Symington sought to finesse the situation by slurring over the Alsop name, making it something like "Ollup" or "Ulp."

"Yes," Johnson replied, "I know MR. ALSOP," enunciating the name with clarity and passion. He continued to stand there, nodding his head, for what seemed like an interminable time. Then he stomped out.

Although the brothers stood with Acheson in his bureaucratic war with Johnson, their association with the secretary of state began to deteriorate. The reason at first seemed to be Acheson's decision to avoid the press. He parried the brothers' written requests for interviews with letters of friendship that begged off temporarily. "It seems a very long time since we have seen one another," Joe wrote in October, requesting lunch or a drink—"at any rate, an opportunity for a talk without the menace of the next telephone call and appointment." Acheson replied that people crowding in on him now weren't always of his own choosing and that he and Alice had been hoping to get away for a vacation soon. "I have missed seeing you," he wrote. "When things settle down, I shall surely call you."

He didn't call. A month later Joe wrote again, more urgently, saying he and Stewart were "greatly troubled by the course our foreign and defense policy appears to be taking." They planned a series of articles on "big questions" and desired Acheson's insights. Joe added that he was sorry his previous letter had been written "as a friend as well as a newspaperman." The two relationships should not be mingled, he wrote, and this letter was "a purely business letter."

Again, Acheson didn't respond, and soon the matter took on the trappings of a feud. One day in January 1950, following a presidential speech, the two found themselves in the same Capitol elevator. Acheson "rather ostentatiously cut me dead," as Joe described it to Felix Frankfurter. Joe heard that Acheson was telling people that, while he had good relations with the "working press," he found it impossible to get on with frisky commentators who always wished to know what they ought not to know. Acheson also told friends—so Joe heard—that Joe and *The New York Times*'s James ("Scotty") Reston no longer liked him because they had been cut off from their accustomed daily diet of special news.

The relationship between government officials and newsmen was a serious matter to the Alsops, and Joe found himself getting into heated discussions on the subject with old friends such as Frankfurter and Paul Nitze. Frankfurter, a close friend of Acheson, angered Joe by referring to the Alsops' "quarrel with the State Department." Joe lashed out at Frankfurter, but later wrote him a letter of apology "for growing unforgivably heated." But he added: "You do me very poor justice, if you suppose that my views about public policy, or my estimates of individual officials, can be influenced by the kind of foolishness the Department is now indulging in." State's poor press relations were harming the department and Acheson more than they were harming the Alsops or other newsmen, Joe wrote.

"I must confess, nevertheless," he continued, "that I am privately puzzled and hurt by Dean's behavior. . . . And since we used to be friends, it seems to me that he might tell me his complaint to my face, before going quite so far as he did."

At its core, the dispute came down to the Alsops' view of American democracy itself and of the electorate's collective judgment. Years later, in discussing their experiences as political reporters, they noted just how ill-informed many voters could be—garbling names of public persons, showing gaps in their understanding of issues. Yet even the most ignorant voters are often unexpectedly shrewd, the brothers observed, and recognize weak and strong points in the characters of the very people whose names they would get wrong. There was a populist streak in the

Alsops' view of democracy, and it came forth—perhaps conveniently, but with force nonetheless—on this issue.

Joe strongly disagreed with Frankfurter's, and Acheson's, view that policy discussions prior to decisions should be kept within government confines. The effort to reduce the flow of information to the public in order to avoid possibly inconvenient or embarrassing disclosures, Joe wrote to Frankfurter, "is a direct attack on the sound working of our society." Petty inconveniences from disclosures "are trifling prices to pay for an informed public, capable of making, with sureness, courage and insight, the great choices on which our society's future depends."

Though the Alsops continued to support Acheson in their column, the friendship remained on ice for the duration of his tenure as secretary of state—and for some time thereafter. The brothers actually harbored private concerns about his stewardship of the department, which they occasionally voiced to friends. As Stewart wrote to Sommers in November 1949, "Joe suspects, and I think rightly, that . . . these days there just ain't no American foreign policy."

The Alsops expressed chagrin when Acheson, bowing to pressures from the French government and elements within the U.S. government, pulled away from the plan for a more formal Anglo-American compact. This indicated, wrote Stewart, a tendency of American foreign policy "to pursue the shadow rather than the substance." He expressed fears that this policy could lead to a collapse of "the whole Western front against Soviet imperialism."

Such alarms reflected the Alsops' tendency to cloak their analyses in portentous terms of dread and dismay. Certainly it wasn't likely, whatever the exact nature of the Anglo-American alliance, that the two countries would become so preoccupied with little spats that the entire Western defense would fall apart. Some critics suggested that the brothers undermined their own case by overstating the consequences of developments they covered.

Also, Joe was gaining a reputation for sometimes being so bent on proselytizing his sources that he didn't listen to them. Bohlen, for instance, was furious when the Alsops misrepresented his position on the issue of Anglo-American relations. Reporting that George Kennan was the architect of the plan for a closer relationship, they implied that Bohlen had opposed it. But Bohlen had argued for something very close to the original Kennan plan. When *Saturday Evening Post* writer Demaree Bess asked Bohlen how the column had turned out to be wrong, Bohlen replied that Joe had a habit of asking "twenty-minute questions summing up his own decided opinions" and then going away under the impression that his source "agrees with him, whereas he has merely been stunned."

Still, the Alsops continued to break news in the column and to produce probing expository journalism in *Post* articles. The big story at year's end concerned United States plans to build a hydrogen bomb, the next-generation weapon a thousand times more powerful than the atomic bomb dropped on Hiroshima. The brothers were at the forefront of the story from the beginning.

On December 2, 1949, they reported that Atomic Energy Commission scientists were working on a nuclear-fission bomb, that the commission was having difficulty recruiting competent scientists to work on such an awesome project, and that the navy was working on technology aimed at defending against nuclear attack. The brothers criticized government efforts to keep secret the alarming implications of the hydrogen bomb, and suggested such efforts were merely cover for a desire "to play 'economy' politics . . . with destiny." Further columns on the subject followed into the new year, as Truman decided to go ahead with the project on a crash basis. The Alsops' reporting got attention. Writing in *The New Yorker*, Richard Rovere said the brothers, "in one of the most remarkable journalistic performances of recent years, forced the hydrogen bomb story into the open."

Joe's sources at State told him that, in approving the H-bomb project, Truman had also instructed Acheson to conduct a review of American policy as a whole, with particular attention to a U.S. resolve that the Soviets must never get both a stockpile of H-bombs and the means of delivering them in quantity. The bomb, Stewart wrote to Sommers, "has apparently shaken Truman at least to some extent out of his euphoric conviction that 'everything is going to be all right.' " After talking to Bohlen, McCloy, and Kennan, Joe also became convinced that Acheson was weighing a decision whether to "fight the Cold War as what it is—a war," as Bohlen put it. Despite the brothers' pain over their falling out with Acheson, they still considered him among the giants. Assessing his first year as secretary, they likened him to "the only sober man on a raft of drunken lumberjacks."

The brothers' work continued to stir interest and gain recognition. In February they learned that they had won the Overseas Press Club award for best interpretation of foreign news.

IN ADDITION TO journalism and politics, the Alsops remained occupied with personal matters. Joe's passion through much of 1949 was the construction of a new house in Georgetown, across Dumbarton Avenue from the home he had owned since before the war. The old house had brought a handsome sale price of $47,000, and for $17,425 he had purchased a double lot suitable for a large home and spacious garden. Construction had cost nearly $50,000—a goodly sum in 1949.

For Joe, what made the place distinctive wasn't its size or expense. It was the fact that he had "committed an outrage against Georgetown charm." His new house, placed amid the French architecture of this increasingly fashionable neighborhood, was of modern design. Drawing upon his childhood interest in architecture and his considerable natural abilities, Joe had designed it himself. He had used the least expensive, and hence the least conventional, materials, which meant materials not suited to earlier architectural conventions. For the outside walls, he used cinder-block masonry, with a patented concrete stucco sprayed on. Inside, a downstairs area included two bedrooms with baths—one for José and Maria, the other a guest room—and a suite of three small rooms and bath. Upstairs were spacious living quarters constructed around the garden in a kind of U-shape. "In these rooms, through the window walls, outdoors and indoors met and mingled," Joe wrote, describing his adventure in architecture for the *Saturday Evening Post*.

Upon moving in, Joe designated the extra downstairs rooms as the office for the Alsops' writing enterprises—thus reducing their overhead and increasing his own convenience. Soon a parade of top Washington officials made their way to Joe's table for breakfast and lunch interviews. Not coincidentally, the new arrangement also increased Joe's control over the fraternal partnership.

Joe's insistence on dominating the partnership was beginning to bother Stewart. Joe took the best assignments and choice interviews for himself, bossed his brother like an old-fashioned city editor, and sometimes even berated him for not meeting Joe's standards.

"Now, *Stoooo*," he would say, "you really should be at the State Department by now. You really *must* get over there and talk to the assistant secretary. What do you think columning is all *about*, Stooooo? What do you think *reporting* is all about? It's about *shoe* leather, my dear boy, *shoe* leather."

Stewart generally accepted his brother's behavior in good humor. He loved his job as columnist, and he knew he owed it all to Joe. Besides, he loved Joe, and had long since come to accept him for what he was. But sometimes Joe's behavior would become unbearable, and Stewart would rise up in his own defense. Then the shouting matches would commence.

Joe couldn't handle being challenged. As he saw it, the column had been his invention; Stewart was in the partnership strictly at his invitation, and that conferred upon Stewart a junior status. Whenever Stewart showed signs of rejecting that outlook, Joe would fly into a rage. According to family lore, he once threw a typewriter at his younger brother in a fit of anger. "I doubt if he really threw it," said Stewart's daughter Elizabeth years later. "He probably just shoved it off the desk or something." But the story reflects a central reality about Joe's behavior and the nature of the brothers' partnership.

Still, they managed to push out four columns every week, and they remained close friends during off-hours. Joe frequently would dine with Stewart and Tish, and Tish could see that the brothers thoroughly enjoyed each other's company. Inevitably the conversation would turn to politics, and that inevitably led to heated arguments. Tish came to conclude that to be an Alsop simply carried with it a need for animated debate. If the brothers agreed on the broad issues of the day, as they generally did, they would find smaller side issues to debate. If they couldn't disagree on small side issues, they would keep talking until they encountered some micro-issue that they viewed differently. Then they would go at each other.

"Goddam it, Stoooo," Joe would shout, then unfurl a dismissive argument.

"Goddam it, Joe," Stewart would reply by way of introducing his own argument.

It was all reminiscent of the dinner table conversation up at Avon, and it never led to any serious anger. "The basic familial relationship was unbreakable," recalled Tish.

Joe took an intense interest in his brother's family. He wanted all the members of the Alsop clan to be the most accomplished, the best dressed, the most impressive people around. He took steps to ensure that result whenever he felt it necessary. He once took Tish on a shopping spree and "badgered her," as Stewart put in it a letter to Arthur Schlesinger, "into buying seven new dresses at great expense (mine)." As Tish recalled, it wasn't that Joe appeared to consider her inadequate; he showered her with compliments and conveyed that she was special and hence deserved special treatment. "It was more that he admired me and this was for the best, rather than trying to make me over," she said.

But she didn't like it when Joe took the same tack with the children. He developed a somewhat conspiratorial relationship with Tish's nanny, a fastidious Scottish woman named Harriett who viewed her task as to ensure that little Joseph was perfectly clean and well turned out at all times. Whenever she felt little Joe lacked the right clothes, she would take him over to his Uncle Joe, and he would give her his charge card for a fashionable Georgetown children's shop. The result was that Harriett kept little Joe dressed in what Tish considered "wretched little white suits." Tish never felt any particular attachment to Harriett, perhaps because she had been hired not by her but by Corinne, who apparently had wanted to find another Aggie for her grandson. Harriett was no Aggie, in Tish's view, and when her second son arrived in 1947 Tish concluded that Harriett couldn't handle two children and promptly let her go.

When a third child arrived in late 1948, it seemed clear to Stewart and Tish that their Georgetown house was now too small. They began looking for a larger house, perhaps farther out in northwestern Washington's fashionable Cleveland Park area, but didn't find anything they liked immediately.

They did find a 160-acre farm in Maryland's rural Howard County, about thirty miles north of Washington. They bought it for $16,000 in 1950 and promptly named it Polecat Park, in honor of the seven skunks discovered in residence in the basement. The house was a tired old frame structure with water pumped up from a spring, and a bathroom of sorts that also served as a hallway between bedrooms. But the family found great enjoyment at their new weekend retreat. Stewart "loved the place," as he wrote years later, and savored it as a much-needed retreat away from his high-pressure job.

But he had no intention of getting away from his friends. On weekends, the Alsops entertained countless couples who would drive out for the day. Always there were children running around, adults chatting and drinking, barbecued hamburgers and hot dogs, quantities of fresh corn, and ice-chilled tubs filled with ice cream and soft drinks. Ball games became regular events, and on hot days many guests would head down to a nearby muddy swimming hole for refreshment. Tish seldom knew who would be coming, because Stewart had a habit of forgetting whom he had invited. Frequent guests included the Barneses, Bissells, Joyces, Bohlens, and Bradens. Joe often showed up too, but didn't usually spend the weekend; he considered the place a little too rustic for overnight stays.

To all outward appearances, Stewart and Tish enjoyed a life to be envied; but the household was not as untroubled as it may have seemed. As husband and father, Stewart provided the family little in the way of affection. Though devoted, he was distant, preoccupied with work, friends, tennis. John Alsop later recalled that Stewart seemed fascinated with his children as infants, but lost interest as they became toddlers. For brief periods he would allow them to crawl over him as he sat in his favorite chair, would tickle them and make them laugh. But then he would quickly return to the evening newspaper or the latest collection of books he had stacked next to his chair. There were no evening "good night" rituals at the children's bedside, no extended periods of reading to them or engaging them in conversation or games.

In much the same way, his relationship with Tish cooled with time. The effusions of love that were sprinkled through his wartime letters to Avon gave way to a marital aloofness that often proved difficult for Tish. Displays of affection were rare, and Stewart seemed quick to place his work ahead of his wife. When Tish contracted pneumonia while traveling with Stewart in West Virginia, he left her there to recuperate alone so he could return to Washington to file his story. "He was devoted to her, and I never saw him even flirt with anyone else," recalled Marie Ridder, a longtime family friend. "But he was tough on her. He didn't give weight to her, and she felt very lost quite often."

Also, Tish often felt intimidated in the social milieu that she found herself thrust into at such a young age. She enjoyed meeting senators and cabinet secretaries and being at the center of events, but frequently she found herself in settings where there seemed to be a requirement to scintillate. She was not by nature a flamboyant person, and found herself haunted by the fear that she wasn't measuring up to the Alsops' rigid standards of social verve and wit. Marie Ridder recalled a private dinner party Joe and Stewart gave during the 1948 Democratic convention in

Philadelphia. It was in the Terrace dining room at the Warwick Hotel, and present were Winston Churchill's son Randolph; Dame Rebecca West, the brilliant English author; Margaret O'Hare McCormick of Chicago; and Arthur Krock. It was a dazzling assemblage, and Marie couldn't help noticing that Tish seemed nervous to be in the midst of it.

Later, as some members of the party tried to hail a cab on the street, Stewart grabbed Tish and thrust her out onto the pavement.

"We'll use Tish to get their attention," he said. It struck Marie as insensitive.

Most family friends didn't know it yet, but Tish had begun to flee her insecurities by turning intermittently to excessive drinking. Stewart was alarmed, but he didn't know what to do. He had little patience with personal frailties. Determined to carry on as if everything were normal, he responded with a kind of indifference. Most often things were normal, and the family enjoyed many wonderful moments. But there were troubling undercurrents in the family.

MEANWHILE, as the Alsop brothers learned more about the state of the U.S. military under Louis Johnson, they decided to write a series of four columns exposing the defense secretary as a liar on matters of national defense. The idea, Stewart wrote to Sommers, "has my palms visibly sweating." It would be the most direct attack on a public official ever waged by the column. Though he was a controversial secretary of defense, Johnson was not without friends. Joe's proposed title for the series was "Johnson Is a Liar," but *Herald Tribune* lawyers suggested it be toned down ("not very far," as Stewart noted) to "Mr. Johnson's Untruths."

The column series began on February 13, 1950. It aroused as much controversy as any Alsop column up to that time. The brothers wrote:

> It is a grave act to charge a high official with deliberately misinforming the nation. But it is graver still for the nation to be grossly and persistently misled about vital matters, as we are now being misled by Secretary of Defense Louis Johnson's smarmy misrepresentations. . . . Johnson has not been telling the truth about the national defense.

The first column cited specific military cuts ordered by Johnson: naval cruisers reduced from 18 to 13; heavy carriers from 8 to 6; escort cruisers from 5 to 3; destroyers from 155 to140; submarines from 79 to 70; attack carrier groups from 14 to 9; the air force stuck at 48 air groups as opposed to the 70 cited by the Joint Chiefs as the minimum necessary. What's more, the air force replacement rate for equipment had fallen to a point where the 48 groups couldn't all be operational together.

Two days later, the brothers accused Johnson of a "confidence trick" in suggesting that his economies didn't affect the country's military muscle. They said he had sought to "create the illusion of national security where there is growing danger." They cited statistics on Soviet weapons production: 15 B-29–type planes a month, added to a fleet of 350 planes, each capable of delivering nuclear weapons around the globe; annual production of 1,800 of the most modern jets, added to a current fleet of 7,500 effective fighters; annual production of 1,000 aircraft designed for ground support, added to a current fleet of 7,500; an overall air fleet of 19,000 planes, with a high replacement rate, compared to the United States' 13,000 planes and low replacement rate; heavy tank production of 1,500 a year, whereas the United States had no heavy tanks; a submarine fleet of 270 craft, versus 130 U.S. subs in commission. "In truth," the brothers wrote, "the growth of Soviet military power is one of the great central facts in the world strategic situation that Johnson so grossly misrepresents."

In the next column, entitled "The Cost of Mr. Johnson," the brothers argued that the U.S. military build-down undermined the country's leadership in Europe. European defense against Soviet strategic bombers was feasible, using first-rate fighters and new antiaircraft guided-missile technology. The Europeans lacked the resources for such a buildup, and only America could provide them. But Johnson's policies made it impossible for America to take up such a role. The final column in the series, "Johnson and the Generals," described how the secretary used an artful system of "favoritism and intimidation" to keep the military brass in his pocket as he gutted the nation's armed forces.

The reaction was furious. *The Washington Post* accused the Alsops of criticizing the secretary "extravagantly" and having "impugned his motives." Saying Johnson merely wanted to hold armed forces expansion in check, the *Post* dismissed the columnists' suggestion that the United States should match the Russians in military hardware. The brothers challenged the editorial on every count. Glossing over their intemperance in suggesting that Johnson was not merely mistaken but perpetrating a fraud, they protested in a letter to the *Post* that they had said nothing about Johnson's motives. They agreed that it wasn't necessary to match the Soviets weapon for weapon, since the Soviets would likely need a three-to-one advantage in armaments to bring off a European invasion. But the columnists thought Western nations should be willing to "maintain a strength ratio of, say, two to Russia's three, without militarizing their economies."

Life magazine, in a major spread on the debate, said the brothers had "nailed Mr. Johnson to the mast." Echoing the Alsops, the magazine said events soon would dictate major decisions on building up national strength—"the kind that will give Mr. Acheson a diplomatic hole card of real power and will enable him to deal calmly and firmly with either phony peace offensives or military threats." In a subhead to an editorial entitled "War Can Come; Will We Be Ready?" the magazine declared: "Louis Johnson talks and carries a big ax, but his words are stronger than his weapons."

Out in Tucson, William R. Matthews, editor and publisher of the *Arizona Daily Star*, which carried the Alsop column, was outraged. "For the first time in my long experience as an editor, I am leaving out a column of political comment," he wrote to the brothers. He said there was a "vast distinction" between justified criticism of public officials "and continuous tirades of personal abuse into which your column seems to be degenerating." He later decided to run the columns, but with a caveat declaring that they "represent such a gross abuse of the use of a column to vent personal abuse . . . that the *Star* believes it should take space to give Mr. Johnson his just due."

The verbal give-and-take over the Johnson columns continued for weeks, but soon the arguments would be lost in the flames of a much more serious conflict. Within months, the United States would be at war—and Louis Johnson would be out of a job.

15

KOREA

From Joe's Garden to the Battlefront

THE NIGHT OF June 24, 1950, was one of those balmy early-summer evenings that give such delight to Washingtonians, in part because they know the sultry season of heat and humidity will soon arrive to cast its oppressive pall over the capital. Joe had just returned from an extensive trip abroad, and as usual he had decided the occasion called for a party. He could not have asked for a more perfect evening to celebrate his return, nor for a more perfect setting than in the stylish embrace of his new Georgetown home.

Guests of honor were Joe's old friend Meyer Handler of *The New York Times* and his wife. Justice Frankfurter was there, along with Robert Joyce, Army Secretary Frank Pace, and Air Force Assistant Secretary John McCone, with their wives. The guest list also included two men (with their wives) whose presence signaled that Joe wanted to talk about the Far East. One was John Paton Davies, a State Department China hand during the war and an expert on the Orient. Though Davies had been a Stilwell partisan during Joe's bitter struggle in the bureaucratic wars in China, his later posting to Moscow had rendered him an ardent anticommunist. The other was Dean Rusk, assistant secretary of state for Far Eastern affairs. Rusk too had worked for Stilwell, and had fought against the Chennault-Alsop call for greater use of air power in China. But now he was a Cold War hard-liner, and Joe wanted to hear what he had to say.

It was a relaxed and pleasant evening. The men took cigars and brandy outside in the garden, under the awning of wisteria that enveloped the terrace. The conversation was turning lively when José, the butler, appeared to say there was a phone call for "Mr. Rush."

"That must be for me," said Rusk, stepping into the house to take the call.

Within minutes he returned, ashen-faced and shaken, to say he must leave. Then came similar calls for Pace and McCone, and they too departed abruptly after murmuring appropriate apologies. There had been, said Rusk, "some kind of border incident" in Korea.

The "incident" turned out to be a full-scale invasion launched by the communist North—the Democratic People's Republic of Korea—against the Western-aligned regime of Syngman Rhee, known as the Republic of Korea, to the south. As the Alsops had predicted, the U.S. policy of containment had collided with the Soviets' temptation to probe and test the West's resolve at the outlying barricades of the Cold War.

President Truman's top military and diplomatic advisers—the War Cabinet, as it became known—quickly concluded that the invasion must be repelled. They moved rapidly to get United Nations support for a resolution declaring the invasion "a breach of the peace" and calling for withdrawal of the invading forces. But they underestimated the threat posed by the North's Soviet-supplied army, which quickly smashed through the ROK defenses along the thirty-eighth parallel and streamed south toward Rhee's capital of Seoul. In panic, the South Korean army's high command ordered the destruction of bridges across the wide Han River, thus inadvertently trapping three divisions of the ROK army in the clutches of the enemy. Within a week of the invasion, Seoul had fallen, and large segments of the ROK army lay in ruins. Only the United States could prevent the North from gobbling up the entire Korean peninsula.

But the arrival of American troops—two army infantry divisions, the First Cavalry, and a regimental combat team—could only slow the enemy advance. Through six weeks of summer fighting, the invading army moved south, pinning the defending armies into the Pusan Perimeter, a five-thousand-square-mile rectangle in the southeast corner of the peninsula. Their backs to the sea, the American and ROK forces managed to halt the communist advance, but their position was precarious. It looked as if Pusan might become an American Dunkirk.

Almost immediately after the invasion, the Alsop brothers used the column to cheer Truman's hard-line actions and to attack any policy-makers who urged caution. To them, the Korean crisis represented only a small measure of the global challenge. In the days after the invasion, with American naval and air forces ordered into action but with ground troops not yet committed, the columnists chided unnamed Pentagon officials for suggesting that no U.S. ground action would be necessary. South Korea, they wrote, "must be held at whatever cost and by whatever means, including the commitment of American troops and strategic bombing . . . in North Korea."

In another column, the brothers praised their friend George Kennan, whom they identified as the architect of Truman's approach. They attacked administration officials and congressional Republicans equally for fostering the national weakness that had emboldened the Soviets to initiate the Korean adventure. And they tied the crisis to a broader Kremlin plan to exploit the West's weaknesses and break its will. If the South fell, they wrote, a "process of crumbling all around the Soviet periphery" would be "surely and rapidly initiated by the simple fact of American failure."

The brothers' outlook needed a larger forum, and as usual it was the *Saturday Evening Post*. Even before the invasion, Joe had suggested to Sommers a "full-dress strategic review" exploring the dangers confronting the West in the face of American demobilization. "Demonstrations of Soviet strength and Western weakness," he wrote, could be expected in all the sensitive and undefended areas of the world as the Soviets sought "to bring whole nations—France, Italy, West Germany, Burma, Indonesia, the Philippines—to a mood of appeasement and surrender."

In France a few weeks earlier Joe had detailed this bleak analysis to Chip Bohlen, then minister in the U.S. embassy in Paris, and Chip had dismissed Joe's views as excessively alarmist. But now, in the wake of the Korean developments, Bohlen was back in Washington with a new outlook on events. "He came in for a drink last night," Joe wrote to Sommers, "and I had the entertaining experience of hearing my own words thrown back at me in a highly authoritative manner." Bohlen had particularly stressed one of Joe's major concerns—the threat to Europe posed by America's need to divert limited military resources to the Korean challenge.

The result of such musing was a *Post* article written under the dual Alsop byline and entitled "The Lesson of Korea." Spanning six pages, it was an "I told you so" account of the events leading to the war, with emphasis on what the brothers considered the crucial turning point— Truman's decision two years before to reject James Forrestal's call for a $17 billion military expenditure. The final responsibility rested with the president, the brothers wrote. But he had been poorly advised by George Marshall, who was "out of touch," and by Louis Johnson, "hell-bent for election as the great economizer." It was bitter, the brothers wrote,

> to think of the influences, so many of them cheap and sordid, that led the president to reject Jim Forrestal's advice. There was . . . Johnson, who considered that he had a mortgage on Forrestal's job. There was Maj. Gen. Harry H. Vaughan, who hated the guts of both Forrestal and Lovett. There was Secretary of the Treasury John Snyder, in alliance with the Bureau of the Budget, who

seemed to believe that the richest nation in the world could not afford the added expenditure which security so clearly demanded. And there was the pervading atmosphere of blindness and complacency in Washington, typified by some leading congressional Republicans.

The piece represented a departure from the probing, fact-based articles Joe had pioneered before the war with Turner Catledge and Bob Kintner—the court-packing series, for example, or the revealing look at Henry Morgenthau's global economic policies. This was an elongated column, filled with opinion and displaying the brothers' growing penchant for identifying heroes and villains in the nation's ongoing public-policy debates. There would be many more such articles in the future, and many would generate substantial controversy. But even given the harsh tone of "The Lesson of Korea," it met with a surprisingly mild response. The Korean crisis had ended the debate about American preparedness. The brothers' outlook was now the majority view. Their adversaries were on the run.

On July 31, with fresh new khakis packed into his commodious suitcases and a copy of Thucydides' *History of the Peloponnesian War* in his pocket, Joe flew to Tokyo to begin an adventure as battlefield reporter. He was forty years old, without experience in war, and nervous to the point of feeling sometimes like a "quaking wreck." But he was determined to prove he could handle physical danger, which was why he pulled rank on Stewart and took the assignment. As for Stewart, he had already proved his courage in the face of danger; besides, he had a wife and three small children, so he was content to let Joe have the story.

In Tokyo, Joe checked into the Press Club at 1 Shimbun Alley and there encountered a number of correspondents who commuted regularly by military transport between Douglas MacArthur's headquarters and the Pusan Perimeter. Joe was pleased to find an old friend from Chongqing days, Carl Mydans, legendary combat photographer for *Life*. He also quickly made friends with Tom Lambert of the Associated Press and Joe Fromm of *U.S. News & World Report*.

Fromm and Mydans acted as guides and helpmates for Joe in his first flight into Pusan aboard a stripped-down transport plane. Joe had shown up at the Tokyo airbase carrying two suitcases, blankets, a folding bed, and an "apothecary case" filled with pills for every occasion and malady.

"Joe, you have five minutes to get down to one bedroll and a backpack," Mydans instructed. Joe complied, Lambert recalled, but not before mixing himself a medical cocktail of some kind. In the air, Mydans listened patiently to what Joe later described as his "nervous chatter," then served as guide during the fifty-six-mile journey to Taegu, provisional capital of the tottering Rhee regime. In Taegu, Joe encountered

Henderson House, in upstate New York, summer home of the
Robinson family. Corinne Roosevelt Robinson presided here
each summer when the Alsop brothers were young.

Family photograph taken in 1889 at Henderson House. From
left: Douglas Robinson II, Monroe Robinson (eighteen months),
Mrs. James Robinson, Mrs. Newman, Corinne Roosevelt Robin-
son, Stewart Robinson (five months), Teddy Robinson, Mr.
Birckhead, Corinne Robinson (age three, on lap), Mrs. Douglas
Robinson, Mrs. Birckhead, Douglas Robinson, Kenneth Robinson.

Corinne Roosevelt Robinson, the Alsop brothers' maternal
grandmother, with little Joseph (right) and Corinne Alsop ("Sis").

Stewart Alsop as a teenager, about the time he went off to Groton.

The Alsops' mother, Corinne, at the Avon farm.

Corinne Alsop and cousin Eleanor Roosevelt, probably when Eleanor was first lady.

The Alsop family in the 1930s. From left, rear: Joe, Joseph Wright Alsop IV, Corinne. From left, front: Stewart, Sis, John.

A "hefty" Joe Alsop in 1937. His makeover came shortly thereafter.

Stewart and eighteen-year-old Patricia Hankey on their wedding day, June 20, 1944. First a British infantry officer, Stewart later became an OSS operative and parachuted behind the lines in France shortly after D-Day.

Avon scene at the end of the war. From left: Tish Alsop, Joe, Corinne, Stewart, father Joe Alsop, John, Sis, and Sis's husband, Percy Chubb.

In 1948, Joe was a
svelte, dapper
"noted" Washington
correspondent.

That same year,
Stewart was in Paris
with Randolph
Churchill.

Ian Morrison of the London *Times,* who had been a traveling companion during some of Joe's European trips. Within days of their reunion, Morrison was killed at the front—a grim reminder that this kind of reporting was no lark.

The Pusan forces of the American field commander, Lieutenant General Walton H. Walker, were a beleaguered lot when Joe arrived. A month earlier, Walker had engaged the North Koreans, in an effort to expand the perimeter and gain some breathing room for his forces. The ill-equipped troops, outnumbered two to one, had proved no match for the enemy and his effective Soviet T-34 tanks. Within weeks, nearly half of the sixteen thousand U.S. troops dispatched to the perimeter had been killed, wounded, or captured. The defensive line held only after Walker issued a "stand or die" order at the end of July.

Shortly after Joe's arrival, Walker deployed his Twenty-fifth Division down to the southwest corner of the perimeter to shore up a particularly vulnerable portion of the line and if possible push back the perimeter, which then was only twenty miles from the port city of Pusan, the entry point for American military supplies. Joe decided to go along.

By truck the division moved out from Taegu in a long, slow convoy, over rocky and winding mountain roads, through the blackness of night, until the contingent finally reached the southern front at dawn. The landscape was rugged and forbidding—a curious piece of land to fight over, Joe thought, as he milled around in an effort to orient himself to this unfamiliar situation. He was unlike any other war correspondent at the front. He was not a hard-bitten man, didn't talk in the idiom of casual profanity that marked many combat reporters. And he made no effort to hide his ignorance of much that was going on. "He was immensely curious," recalled Carl Mydans years later. "He looked at everything with amazement, was always asking questions." Seeing a cluster of funny-looking canisters lying next to some sleeping soldiers, Joe asked what they were.

"Hand grenades," replied Mydans.

"Gee," said Joe, "aren't they rather dangerous?"

But he caught on fast. In talking with young soldiers, he manifested a warmth and sympathy that endeared him instantly to the troops.

He attached himself to the Fifth Regimental Combat Team, an inexperienced unit that had been given the mission of occupying a nearby hill commanding the route of advance along two coastal roads. The outfit had hardly started up the treacherous terrain when it came under intense attack and soon found itself pinned down amid the rocks and sparse pines of the hill. For most of the day and into the night the battle raged, with troops huddled on the exposed rock or struggling to position themselves against the enemy. Years later, Joe recalled some vivid scenes from the battle: an infantry company moving up the hillside while plumes of smoke from the shellfire of Joe's combat team rose from the crest; a big tank moving aside to let pass a Jeep filled with wounded soldiers; sniper fire spraying an area near a group of worried truck drivers consulting with each other on the chaotic situation.

As the battle raged through the night, Joe lay in the dark, waiting for some signal to move on or out, hoping for the banging of mortar fire to cease. Though exhausted, he slept little. By morning the fighting had stopped, and the troops grabbed a few hours of fitful sleep, huddling down on the rocks amid the sapling pines of a dry riverbed. Joe found himself shaken by the experience of war and the fears it engendered; but he also was determined to overcome these fears.

Back in Taegu, he quickly sought a return to the front, this time to the northernmost tip of the perimeter, where the Twenty-seventh Regiment protected the main corridor of attack to Taegu. Commanding the Twenty-seventh, known as the "Wolfhounds," was a thirty-seven-year-old colonel named John Michaelis, the youngest regimental commander in the U.S. force and a man who was becoming well known for his battlefield brilliance. His job was to guard the mountain passes through which the North Koreans could mount attacks, and his troops found themselves constantly under fire as the enemy probed for weaknesses along the line.

Gaining a greater understanding of the hellish trade of war, Joe learned that Michaelis and a battalion commander named G. J. Check had set a trap for the North Koreans. They had positioned their troops to pounce on the enemy if he ventured through a narrow valley—dubbed "the Bowling Alley" by the troops—that led to the main road south to Taegu. Shortly after Joe's arrival, the North Koreans moved into the trap, and triggered a furious battle. "With a happy grunt," as Alsop later described it, Colonel Check began barking into a tangle of field phones as Joe watched from a nearby rock, smoking cigarettes, trying to master his nerves and track the flow of battle as best he could.

The attack reached its peak at three thirty a.m., first with mortar fire, then with powerful explosions and sporadic blasts of machine-gun and rifle fire. By five a.m. the enemy advance was broken, and the North Koreans retreated beyond the Bowling Alley. By then, Joe had discovered the truth in Winston Churchill's observation that being shot at can be exhilarating, provided you don't get hit. It seemed to Joe that the chances of getting hit were pretty slim, as long as he remained a bystander and stayed well protected behind a solid defensive position. But he soon developed a reputation among colleagues and troops as a fearless battlefield reporter.

Joe ventured out to the front on numerous occasions over the next several weeks to gather material. After each foray, he would return to Tokyo to file two or three columns and enjoy a night or two in a real bed before heading back to Korea. On one occasion, he attached himself to a French battalion up from Indochina, just in time to be with the unit when it came under attack. The AP's Tom Lambert, with the Second Division, decided to call the French unit by field phone to find out what was going on. Amazed that he got through during such a heavy battle, he was even more amazed when he heard the voice of Joe Alsop on the other end.

"Joe, what the hell are you doing up there?" Lambert yelled into the field phone.

"I'm watching the war, Tom," Joe replied.

Back in Tokyo for one of his filing missions, Joe learned that "the big show" was coming soon and he should remain there if he wanted to be part of it. Within days he found himself aboard a warship with Keyes Beech of the *Chicago Daily News*, girding for what would be Douglas MacArthur's famous landing at Inchon. The first waves of combat soldiers moved ashore to attack the nearby island of Wolmi at dawn, but Joe and the other reporters didn't get off their ship until well after three p.m. By then Wolmi had been taken, the mechanized battalions were ashore, and the first major battle of MacArthur's offensive had begun. Joe and Beech boarded a landing craft loaded with marines for the short ride ashore. A thick fog engulfed the Inchon harbor, and the craft moved off course toward a huge seawall beneath heavy enemy fortifications. The seawall loomed up suddenly out of the fog, and the reporters and marines had no choice but to scamper up the slippery rocks to their very own beachhead. Luckily, the enemy fortifications had been abandoned as MacArthur's troops moved in.

Turning to a bewildered Lieutenant George Chambers, Joe exclaimed, "Surely, Lieutenant, they put us on the wrong beach." After hours of waiting and exploring their immediate surroundings, the lieutenant concluded they were indeed on the wrong beach. "Well," said one disgruntled sergeant, "no son of a bitch can say he hit this damn beach before we did." There wasn't anything to do but settle down for the night and join the big inland attack at daybreak. With Chambers and Bernard Kaplan of the International News Service, Joe huddled under a poncho through the night to shield himself from the cold rain. By morning it was clear that the landing had been a success. The offensive had split the North Korean forces in half, cutting off their southern troops from the supply lines, and forcing their northern armies into a headlong retreat toward the thirty-eighth parallel.

Joe marched with a marine outfit known as Easy Company as it moved with the rest of its battalion from Inchon to Kimpo Airport just outside Seoul. This remained enemy territory, and there was plenty of action along the way, beginning with an assault by six T-34 tanks and supporting infantry. The marines positioned themselves quickly to rebuff the attack. They left the tanks as burning hulks along the road and killed scores of North Korean soldiers. Passing the burning tanks in march formation, one GI quipped, "If they was C-rations inside, they'd make good hot chow."

Easy Company encountered still more action at the little railroad town of Bupyong, where the North Koreans had dug in to resist the American advance. Slowly and methodically, the American captain led the operation to clear out the resistance. One mortar blast sent a group of enemy soldiers scurrying out of their defensive position, "and the Marines got them with rifles," as Joe wrote in his next column. The marines then swept the town in search of snipers and holdouts. Captured enemy troops were sent out onto the road naked and shivering from cold. The captain, Samuel Jaskilka, led the operation with cool authority, losing his temper only once—when he heard a false report of heavy casualties in the rear platoon.

"Dammit, don't tell me things again that just aren't true," he demanded.

A day and a half later, the marines had pushed the enemy out of Kimpo and found time for some sleep, but a predawn attack startled the slumbering soldiers. Joe described it in a column: "For two hours there was a long, tense confusion of charges by small enemy groups, sharp firing, short lulls and then more firing and more charges." Finally, as daylight arrived, American tanks quelled the attack. The wounded were brought in from outlying battlefronts, along with a small number of American corpses. As Joe boarded an ambulance to ride to the rear, tanks and marines moved up to clear away the last enemy strong point, and the commanding colonel summed up the situation with a genial farewell.

"You can say we've got Kimpo, but you'll have to wait a little before you can say Kimpo is secure," he said with military matter-of-factness.

The next day Joe entered Seoul just as the battle for the South Korean capital was ending. Thousands of civilians had died in the brutal crossfire, and much of the city lay in smoldering ruins. "So our conquering force received a perfunctory welcome," Joe wrote later. "The people of Seoul displayed no overwhelming emotion . . . no great dramatic scenes of ecstatic cheering and brightly tossed bouquets." With the North Korean armies either trapped or retreating, Joe felt the next big issues would be strategic ones decided at headquarters. He returned to Tokyo.

There he obtained an interview with General MacArthur, who received him in a modest little office that contrasted sharply with the grand quarters he had enjoyed when Joe visited him in Manila before Pearl Harbor. Never much impressed with MacArthur, Joe was less impressed with those around him—"insipid men, arrogant with the press, wary of each other, and generally incompetent," as he wrote later. Their tone toward MacArthur "was almost wholly simpering and reverential." The general, basking in the afterglow of victory, welcomed Joe and motioned him to a low chair next to his own higher one. By then U.S. troops were moving briskly up the Korean peninsula, and it appeared the war soon would be over. Though some in the government were warning of a Chinese intervention if MacArthur threatened the Manchurian border along the Yalu River, the general made light of that.

"As a matter of fact, Alsop," he said, "if you stay on here, you will just be wasting your valuable time."

Joe agreed. Intoxicated with the thought of the Kremlin losing its North Korean satellite, he filed a column urging American forces on and predicting total U.S. victory. The goal, Joe believed, must be the "liberation" of North Korea. He was so passionate on the subject that during a heated discussion at the Tokyo Press Club in September, he tossed down his eyeglasses in agitation and broke them. A few days later, he hitched a ride on a military plane carrying Pentagon VIPs back to Washington.

But the general and the columnist were wrong. By the end of November, China, now under communist rule, had entered the war in force, throwing 300,000 battle-tested troops against the American and South Korean armies that were then beginning what they thought would be the war's last mop-up operation. Facing a choice of annihilation or retreat, General Walker pulled back, and the American and South Korean forces eventually established a defensive perimeter about fifty miles south of the thirty-eighth parallel. It was a devastating military defeat, and an even more devastating psychological blow for the nation. The result was to be a protracted, painful stalemate with powerful political repercussions at home.

Joe's foray into war reporting had been a success, however, and his columns generated dozens of compliments. They "give one the real feel of battle and . . . you have never done better writing," said Cass Canfield, chairman of Harper & Brothers. Desmond FitzGerald thought Joe had "taken up where Ernie Pyle left off." Joe's dispatches, he said, "gave the real flavor of combat." George Kennan said Joe's battle accounts "were like Tolstoy's passages from 'War and Peace.' " In Mobile, Alabama, the *Press* ran an editorial saying that "of all the reporting and analysis of the war in Korea and the defense program in Washington, the work of the Alsop brothers stands out." And from Korea came expressions of gratitude. Lieutenant Colonel Check sent a letter to *The Washington Post* praising Joe for professionalism and bravery.

Meanwhile, back in Washington during Joe's Korean adventure, Stewart had followed the War Cabinet closely, with particular attention to the intensifying internal strain between Dean Acheson and Louis Johnson. By October, Johnson was gone, a victim of his own failed policies and his inability to work with his colleagues in crisis. Stewart and Tish were having drinks with Averell Harriman at the downtown Metropolitan Club when word of Johnson's firing reached them. In his exuberance, Harriman did "a fairly lively jig" and gave Tish a warm embrace of celebration. "His reaction was duplicated just about everywhere in Washington," Stewart wrote to Sommers.

THE CHINESE OFFENSIVE in Korea chilled American policymakers with fears that the Soviet-Chinese combine would force the West into either a strategic retreat or a world war. For the Alsop brothers, the euphoria of October quickly gave way to their characteristic gloom. Joe's outlook darkened further when he went to see General Omar Bradley, then chairman of the Joint Chiefs of Staff. When Joe asked how much time the West had to prepare for war, Bradley replied that it would take three to four years to rebuild the West's defenses. But, asked Joe, didn't China's attack in Korea indicate the West didn't have that much time? The general said that "a good many" in the government expected war by spring; "a great many more" thought it more likely to come in two years or so; and "some" still thought it could be held off for another four years. Joe asked what would happen if it came in two years? Bradley replied matter-of-factly that America likely would be thrown out of Europe and would then have to live in isolation in her own hemisphere for fifty years or more. The result, he added, would be the militarization of American society.

As the new year approached, Joe's famous pessimism took on a new dimension. "Never before has this horrible hopelessness overtaken me," he wrote to British air marshal Sir John Slessor. "I am now convinced the whole Soviet timetable has been grossly misestimated, even by such pessimists as I am." The Russians would act, he predicted, "sometime during the next six to twelve months." He desperately wished for strong presidential leadership to rally the country, but it didn't come. "Being in Washington at the moment," he wrote to Bernard Baruch, "is like attending a drunken beach picnic with a vast tidal wave sweeping in from the horizon."

Stewart's outlook wasn't much brighter. "I am feeling pretty low in mind; Joe's doom complex has seized me," he wrote to Sommers. He had begun work on a *Saturday Evening Post* piece that offered justification for the brothers' constant fears of Soviet expansion. It turned out to be a remarkable piece of journalism—a firsthand look at Joseph Stalin, the global chess master. Stewart arranged an extensive, on-the-record interview with a former high official of the Czech government who had escaped the Eastern bloc after Stalin snuffed out Czechoslovakia as an independent nation. The defector was Arnhost Heidrich, a short, beefy, genial man who had been secretary general of the Czech foreign office, the most important Czech official below cabinet rank. The story of Stewart's acquaintance with Heidrich, as recounted in the article, went back to the spring of 1948, when Stewart had requested and received his first interview with that Czech official.

During that interview, Stewart recounted, Heidrich had spoken with surprising candor and considerable brilliance about the world situation. The end of the interview had brought an even greater surprise. As the

Western reporter rose to leave, the Czech official had motioned for him to return to his chair.

"Do you think there will be a war soon between your country and the Soviet Union?" Heidrich asked.

Stewart replied that, on the whole, he thought not—a long armed truce seemed more likely. Heidrich sighed.

"Then there is nothing left," he said. "I must escape."

Heidrich had escaped, and eventually had made his way to Washington, where he and Stewart renewed their acquaintance. Now, after long conversation and a certain amount of drink, he recounted a chilling experience he had had with Stalin in Moscow, where he and three other leading officials of the Czech government had been summoned in that spring of 1948. The summons had come after Czech officials indicated an interest in discussing with the West the possibility of joining the Marshall Plan. Stalin made it plain that such an idea would not be tolerated. In a late-night session in his Kremlin office, the dictator outlined his reasons why.

The main American purpose of the Marshall Plan, he told his visitors, was to foster European markets for American goods and thus to forestall the depression Stalin was sure America soon would be in. The second aim was to assure American dominance of Western Europe. It was America's intention, he said, to create "positions of power"—a phrase he used repeatedly—not only in Europe but throughout Asia. "It is not only not in our interests that the United States should strengthen its positions of power in Europe," said Stalin. "On the contrary, it must be our first task to prevent this." Then, with cool precision, he summarized in two sentences the Soviet strategy toward the United States and the West: "Our first task must be to tear down the power positions of the United States in both Europe and Asia. Once this is done, England and France will be too weak to resist the pressure."

The aim, Stalin repeated, was to work slowly and patiently toward the elimination of American power outside the Western Hemisphere.

The discussion then shifted to Czechoslovakia's economic difficulties, the ostensible reason for the Czech leaders' desire to attend a forthcoming Paris conference on the Marshall Plan. At this point, Stalin became impatient, and tossed out statistics to show that the economic situation wasn't as serious as Czech leaders were suggesting. V. M. Molotov, the wooden-faced hard-liner, then spoke up in his customary harsh tone. "But you must know that you cannot take part in the Paris conference," he said. Stalin, speaking in his more fatherly tone, wrapped up the Soviet position: "You see," he said, "for us it is a question of friendship and alliance between the Union of Soviet Socialist Republics and Czechoslovakia. We expect you to review our decision and communicate your acceptance of it by tomorrow afternoon at four o'clock."

It was, as Stewart would write, "a naked ultimatum," and was followed by a series of events that eviscerated the Czech government and left in its place a clique of Soviet puppets. Of the four ministers who had attended the meeting with Stalin that night, one later killed himself; another decided to do the same but was carted away before he could perform the deed; another became a powerless government figurehead, an onlooker to the destruction of his own country; and the fourth, Arnhost Heidrich, escaped to exile in the West, becoming a man without a country and a witness to the overreaching intentions of the Soviet Union's implacable leader.

Entitled "Stalin's Plans for the U.S.A.," the article appeared July 14, 1951, and proved a considerable journalistic coup. Rarely in those darkest days of the Cold War did a Western newsman manage to catch a vivid, inside glimpse of Kremlin life. Defectors generally did not talk to newsmen, and when they did they almost never discussed official life behind the Iron Curtain. It was difficult to persuade Heidrich to allow the use of direct quotes from Stalin, but these added life and credibility to the article. Stewart also authenticated the story with the CIA, which had debriefed Heidrich extensively following his defection.

Meanwhile, in Korea, the American war effort appeared hopeless. The bold American design to impose a settlement by force of arms had been frustrated by the Chinese intervention, and there seemed little likelihood the stalemate could be broken militarily. In Washington, officials came to the disturbing conclusion that the country was in a war it could not win, could not walk away from, and could not afford to lose. In Tokyo, General MacArthur rejected that view, chafed at the restrictions placed on his forces, and began a political offensive against Washington's "limited war" concepts, which denied him the option of carrying the war into the enemy's "privileged sanctuary" north of the Yalu. The controversy exploded in April when Truman fired MacArthur, taking a tidal wave of political opposition in the process. Stewart saw the firing as a natural consequence of the bitter disagreement between the president and his general. "Either President Truman or Gen. MacArthur had to be fired," he wrote, "and a general cannot fire his commander in chief."

The stalemate continued, frustrating the American electorate, sapping the strength of the Truman administration, and feeding the Alsop brothers' famous gloom. Still, Joe's war experiences had been a personal milestone—confirmation that he possessed the courage to perform in a combat setting. He took pride in conquering one more fear and putting still further behind him the physical timidity of his childhood.

Meeting the test of combat also helped to place his life in harmony with his sense of commitment to Western precepts and Western survival. He was immensely proud of his fellow countrymen on the battlefield— proud of their bravery, their manly virtue, their sacrifices in their country's cause. At one point, following an overnight battle, he had sat up against a rock and looked at a group of five or six sleeping soldiers snuggled up with their weapons. He expressed his pride to Mydans, who had joined him for a cigarette during the lull in fighting. Though Joe now had experienced the ugliness of war, he had not lost his idealism of war. The spirit of Eurytus, that brave Spartan of old, remained with him, and he saw that spirit in the American GIs in Korea. "Far from transforming [them] into the sarcastic or self-pitying cardboard cutouts of the war novelists," he wrote, "their harsh experience seems almost to have enlarged and amplified them."

But the agonies of war pursued Joe even after his return home, and tempered the good feelings left by his Korean success. A poignant letter came from a Mrs. J. J. Brower of Holland, Michigan, who criticized what she viewed as the brothers' inclination to glorify the war and downplay Truman's ineptitude in getting America into it. Her letter left the impression that she had lost her son in the fighting. In reply, Joe expressed sympathy but could not retreat from his views:

> I hardly know how to reply to a letter such as yours. In August and September, I was at the front in Korea, and no experience in my whole life has so deeply moved me. If your son has been lost there, as I assume you mean, I can only offer you the sympathy that one human being can give to another, and express the gratitude that any citizen must feel to one who falls fighting for his country. If there can be any consolation for such a loss, it seems to me that your consolation ought to be that your boy was fighting for his country.
>
> No one has criticized Mr. Truman's ineptitudes more bitterly than my brother and I, but, after all, Soviet aggression has not been the result of Mr. Truman's ineptitudes. It has resulted, rather, from the decisions of the Soviet leadership. And although I know that Korea must seem very far away to you, I think you will find that if we do not continue to resist this world process of Soviet aggression at all costs, it will reach this country in the end, and sooner than any of us think.
>
> This is a poor, lame letter, which I hope you will forgive as being at least sincere in every word.

As 1950 drew to a close, the Alsops looked back on the previous two years with a certain pride. These had been momentous years, filled with events and developments of historic dimension. Throughout much of that tumult the Alsop brothers had been proved right in their assessments and analyses. They had been right about Louis Johnson's demobilization policies and about his personal flaws. They had been right about the nature of the Soviet threat after the Marshall Plan had buttressed Europe's defenses. They had been right in predicting something like the Korean war prior to its outbreak. "We were dead wrong once," Stewart conceded in a letter to Chip Bohlen, and that was on the likelihood of Chinese intervention in Korea. Of course, he added, only George Kennan had been right on that one. Bolstering the brothers' good feelings was their second Overseas Press Club award—"for distinguished journalism and for the best press interpretation of foreign news."

McCARTHYISM

Joining Battle
to Defend Old Adversaries

IN THE SPRING OF 1949, a year before Korea exploded, Stewart made plans for a trip through China. He had been there hardly a few days before events in that tumultuous nation spun out of control. Mao Tse-tung's communist legions, disciplined and deadly, crossed the Yangtze River on April 17 and marched toward Chiang Kai-shek's postwar capital of Nanjing. By April 24, the communists had taken Nanjing, and the Nationalists had fled toward yet another provisional capital in Guangzhou (Canton). It was the endgame in that long and bitter Asian drama in which brother Joe had played such a prominent role a few years before.

From Guangzhou, Stewart had planned to fly to Shanghai for a few days of reporting, and then to Hong Kong to assess the situation further and write a series of columns. But Tish was with him, and events suggested caution. With Mao's armies moving east and refugees fleeing across the mainland, a Shanghai visit carried a high risk of getting stranded amidst chaos. A group of correspondents had been held up in Beijing a few days before, and Stewart didn't want to tempt the same fate with his young wife. They flew directly to Hong Kong, where Tish would remain while Stewart was off alone in Shanghai. From Shanghai, he summed up the situation and his plans in a cable to the *Herald Tribune* Syndicate: DEPRESSED BAFFLED BY APPARENTLY HOPELESS SITUATION HERE HOPE SEND SHANGHAI COLUMNS SHORTLY.

Back in Washington, Joe followed events with alarm. The China story heightened his inclination to play the boss in the partnership, and he wired instructions to Stewart: "Trust last three China columns will deal fairly extensively with Chinese communist future which you have covered only tangentially so far." Big questions needed answers, said Joe: "What will be Mao's power to organize nation under centralized authority with special reference urban corruption . . . and degree allegiance Moscow? What will be Chinese communist attitude towards United States and foreign business generally? What will be Chinese communist policy towards trading Japan?" Stewart's description of the sense of "defeat and decay" within the Nationalist regime, Joe added, had already been adequately emphasized, and he was revising the last two Canton columns to eliminate "excessive elaboration" of the defeatist theme.

When the three columns came in, Joe wasn't pleased. "Know you will wish to be told frankly that . . . concluding China trinity deeply disappointing," he wired. "Faults are repetition, tendency to expatiate on extraneous topics like American governmental weakness and . . . failure either to paint concrete picture of existing situations or to describe concretely what you recommend doing about these situations." Joe said he hated to "send such discouraging wire but know you can do this job a million times better." Stewart wired back: "Agree your strictures on style last three China columns. Arose from mental constipation seeing too many people too many places . . . will attempt to remove gas and rewrite from entirely different angle."

But Stewart's revisions on the three summing-up columns still didn't satisfy Joe. "First column otherwise excellent but rather too light for summing up," he wired, and said he had revised it to place more emphasis on the strategic situation created by the impending communist takeover. "Please please give me two strong columns on Chinese communists without which China series will be Hamletless Hamlet." Stung by Joe's carping, Stewart fought back. "Have had increasingly uncomfortable feeling you peering over my shoulder trying to guide me into line you think you would have taken if you had made this nightmare junket," he cabled. "Know this with best will in world but does make difficulties. For example know that if I could answer your question about Chinese communists would make wonderful columns but no newspaperman, diplomat or businessman in China has yet been able do more than speculate on basis totally inadequate evidence."

When it came to China, Joe's ever-present tendency to take over became even more marked. Ever since his wartime experiences there, he had felt he understood the Chinese puzzle better than anyone else, and had fumed as U.S. policy born of what he considered ignorance seemed only to sink China ever deeper into chaos. Now the revolution he had worked so diligently to forestall was unfolding with tragic finality. The fond hope of a strong, effective, Western-oriented Nationalist regime in China was dead.

Joe felt a growing need to tell the story as he knew it, recounting the follies and intrigues that had led to what he considered a tragedy of global consequence. The urge to speak out became even stronger in the fall, when the State Department issued a controversial white paper purporting to review in detail the China debacle. In 1,054 pages, it blamed the Nationalists' fall on their own incompetence and backwardness, as well as on Chiang's obduracy and self-serving leadership. By extension, it exonerated the Stilwell partisans and other China hands who from the start had favored the communists and worked to weaken Chiang's regime. The white paper infuriated Joe and heightened his resolve to tell his version of what had happened.

The forum, of course, would be the *Saturday Evening Post*. Joe proposed a three-part series with the controversial title, "Why We Lost China." Sommers accepted the idea, and Joe attacked the new assignment with a will.

He traveled to New York to read through Harry Hopkins's China papers, and discovered to his satisfaction that his own wartime perceptions had "not been altogether lacking in foresight." He obtained from General Albert Wedemeyer secret cables that shed light on postwar events in China. And he spent hours one afternoon with John Paton Davies, Stilwell's political adviser during the war and hence Joe Alsop's political enemy. "We were," Joe wrote to Sommers, "just like two elderly, once rival, now retired prostitutes, sitting in our rocking chairs and cackling about our respective triumphs."

But for Davies it wasn't all laughs. With China going communist in the midst of a Cold War that Davies hadn't anticipated during his wartime days in Chongqing, the former China hand could hear the distant hoofbeat of approaching controversy. Since the war, Davies's sympathetic regard for Chinese communism had given way to a much harsher outlook, and he felt a certain regret for his part in Stilwell's intrigues against Chiang and his extensive flirtation with Chiang's enemies. "Poor fellow," Joe wrote to Sommers, "he is exceedingly ashamed now of the part he played, not to say a bit fearful of the effect disclosure of this part may have on his career."

But for Joe also there was a nagging sense of danger. Taking a tough stand wasn't as simple now as it had been back in the war years when Joe was writing those impassioned letters to Harry Hopkins and (over Chennault's signature) to Franklin Roosevelt. Now some people he didn't want to harm could get caught in the crossfire—for example, John Davies.

All this became apparent when Joe called George Kennan, a longtime Davies friend, to inquire about Davies's Moscow experience and the evolution of his outlook. Kennan became heated, refusing to discuss the matter and suggesting that Joe's journalistic mission might bring undue harm to a good man. Joe in turn became angry and ended the call abruptly. Later he wrote a letter of apology for being "crisp" on the phone. "I don't know whether you simply refuse to credit my assurances to you and John that I want to present as sympathetic a picture of what John and the others did in China as the facts will allow," he wrote. "It is on the whole unusual for one party to a controversy to offer to work with the other, so that the viewpoint of the opposition may be presented as sympathetically and fairly as possible."

Later, after he had completed the series, Joe violated *Post* strictures by offering to allow Kennan and Davies to read the articles before publication, "with a view to getting any suggestions you may have for making what I have written as fair as possible." He was anxious, he said, "to avoid the faintest appearance of personal animus or persecution." Both Kennan and Davies declined; Kennan wrote that he would be "happy to let the past bury its own dead."

The series, appearing in January 1950, kicked up the past with a vengeance. Joe dismissed the State Department white paper and stated his thesis with pungency in the first article:

> Throughout the fateful years in China, the American representatives there actively favored the Chinese communists. They also contributed to the weakness, both political and military, of the National Government. And in the end they came close to offering China up to the communists, like a trussed bird on a platter, over four years before the eventual communist triumph.

Joe began the story with Stilwell. Acknowledging the general's qualities as a combat soldier, he vented all his old complaints about Stilwell's condescension toward his Chinese allies, his ignorance of the political dynamics of the Kuomintang, and his counterproductive obsession with the Burma campaign. Alsop revealed that as early as the 1930s, when Stilwell was military attaché to China, he had developed strong prejudices against the Nationalists and strong sympathies for the communists. Davies, who was vice consul at the time, held similar views.

"Essentially," the article went on, "Stilwell and Davies were victims of the then-fashionable liberalism that idyllically pictured the communists as 'democratic agrarian reformers,' and described their guerrilla operations as 'really fighting the Japs.' " Joe described Stilwell's nearly successful effort to gain control over all Allied armed forces in China and the distribution of all supplies. Stilwell could have used this power—indeed, intended to use it—to force Chiang into an unequal partnership with his communist enemies, or, failing that, to make the communists sole beneficiaries of U.S. policy and destroy Chiang Kaishek's regime.

Even after the general's dismissal, Joe wrote, the China hands continued to advocate the abandonment of Chiang in favor of the communists, much as Churchill had abandoned Yugoslavia's Mihajilović in favor of

Marshal Tito. Joe quoted extensively from a series of official reports, "which, ironically, provide the only known documentary evidence of their purposes." John Service, Raymond Ludden, and Davies, the reports revealed, had all pressed the anti-Chiang case in ways that proved deeply significant.

Joe also sought to establish his fair-mindedness on the issue. The positions of the Stilwell advisers reflected a China policy that may have been "injudicious," he wrote, but was at least "logical, defensible and not indicative of disloyalty." He said the policy had been most clearly defined by Davies, who suggested that by "feeding" the Chinese communists the United States could "wean" them from the Kremlin. Thus, Davies advocated a kind of Titoism in China even before the concept had taken form in Yugoslavia.

But the Stilwell advisers' views, wrote Joe, betrayed an emotional bias that was "indefensible." The bias and the anti-Chiang vendetta prevented any serious effort to fashion a workable Chinese government, and rendered the State Department's China policy "palsied and . . . fruitless."

Reaction to the series was swift. Anne McCormick of *The New York Times* considered it "chillingly impressive" and "a telling retort to the White Paper." Stanley Hornbeck, former head of the State Department's Far Eastern division, told a friend. "I'm glad the truth about these things is coming out at last." But Madame Chiang and Madame Kung, portrayed in the series as leaders of a reactionary faction within the Kuomintang, were "outraged." And Dean Acheson was "enraged," as Joe wrote to Sommers, because he felt Joe had "called his good faith into question." Joe dismissed the criticism. One could not write about what had happened in China without offending Mesdames Chiang and Kung, he wrote to Claire Chennault. And Acheson, he suggested to Sommers, was "reaching an advanced state of neurosis in all his relations with the press."

Joe was pleased that nearly all his friends at State said they considered the series fair, even though it may have provided ammunition to some factions within the country whose interest was not so much fairness as political advantage. The loss of China had touched a nerve in the country—and detonated a controversy that would rage for years to come.

The controversy was fanned by various factions that had banded together in the 1940s in what became known as the China Lobby—publishers, writers, businessmen, politicians, all partisans of Chiang Kai-shek and sworn enemies of Chinese communism. They included Henry Luce of Time-Life; his wife, writer and socialite Clare Boothe Luce; New Hampshire newspaper publisher William Loeb; authors John T. Flynn and Freda Utley; senators Styles Bridges of New Hampshire and William Knowland of California; and Congressman Walter

Judd of Minnesota. For years, these partisans had sounded the alarm, attacked the State Department's flirtation with Mao Tse-tung, and decried the influence of communist sympathizers within the U.S. government.

Now China had been swallowed up into the expanding sphere of world communism, and more and more Americans were listening to the persistent China Lobby. Another element soon would be added to the mix. Alger Hiss, accused of passing secret U.S. documents to a Soviet spy, was convicted of perjury on January 21, 1950. It was a signal victory for the House Committee on Un-American Activities, the communist-hunting panel of Congress, and a great embarrassment for all the "respectable" members of the country's Northeastern elite who had testified on behalf of Hiss's integrity and patriotism. Two weeks later the government reported that Klaus Fuchs, a British physicist who had worked at the Los Alamos atomic-weapons facility during the war, had been arrested as a Soviet spy. The *Chicago Tribune* screamed across page one: REDS GET OUR BOMB PLANS! Republican senator George W. Malone of Nevada attacked the State Department as a nest of Soviet sympathizers whose every move since the United States recognized the Soviet Union in 1934 had been "toward strengthening the communists."

And then on February 9, just days after the third installment of Joe Alsop's China series appeared in the *Saturday Evening Post*, a relatively obscure first-term senator from Wisconsin stepped into the breach with an inflammatory speech in Wheeling, West Virginia. "And ladies and gentlemen," said Joseph McCarthy, "I have here in my hand a list of 205—a list of names that were made known to the secretary of state as being members of the Communist Party and who nevertheless are still working and shaping policy in the State Department."

That charge of betrayal, and subsequent pronouncements of a similar nature, catapulted McCarthy to the forefront of the anticommunist movement and transformed the movement itself into a potent Republican weapon in the battles over foreign policy. The discussion of "why we lost China" now took on a new political meaning well beyond the scope of Joe's *Saturday Evening Post* articles. Senate Democrats, attuned to the political dangers inherent in McCarthy's charges, promptly named a special subcommittee of the Foreign Relations Committee to investigate the disturbing allegations. The panel, chaired by Maryland's Millard E. Tydings, a member of the Senate since 1927, began its deliberations on March 8 in the Senate caucus room. Few Americans realized at the time just how long that show, and its successors, would last.

Joe Alsop was on a foreign trip when Tydings cracked his gavel to begin the hearings. But Stewart moved quickly to declare the brothers' opposition to McCarthy's brand of politics. In a March 5 column he referred to the Wisconsin senator as "the big, raw-boned pride and joy of the real estate lobby" and suggested sarcastically that he may have performed a major service to the country. If McCarthy could prove his allegations, said Stewart, he would deserve a vote of thanks for demonstrating that the State Department was riddled with spies. But, he added, it was more likely "McCarthy will get his head so thoroughly washed that neither he nor any of his like-minded colleagues will soon again use this particular vote-catching technique." Although internal security was "a deadly serious issue," as the Hiss and Fuchs episodes revealed, wrote Stewart, "blanket charges like McCarthy's serve to obscure this issue, to destroy morale in the government, and thus in fact to serve the interests of the communists."

The anti-McCarthy tilt of Stewart's column surprised some of the brothers' readers. The threat of domestic communism had been a recurrent theme in their work, beginning with Stewart's interest in communist infiltration of organized labor in 1946. The brothers' anticommunist zeal had reached its highest pitch during the emergence of Henry Wallace as an alternative-party presidential candidate in 1948. The Alsops had portrayed him as a man with "an enormous capacity for self-delusion," a hapless captive of American leftists, constantly playing into the Kremlin's hands. As Stewart had written to a Cleveland reader, "I am sure you are sincere when you say you are not a communist or a communist dupe. However, I strongly believe that if you vote for Henry Wallace, you will be serving communist ends." He called Wallace's Progressive Party "a communist instrument."

After McCarthy's entry onto the scene, however, the Alsops quickly declared their opposition to his brand of politics. "This whole McCarthy thing has as nasty a smell as anything I've run into since I've been here," Stewart wrote to Sommers in late March. The brothers' vehemence on the subject was tied closely to their heritage. Throughout the civic activities of all the Joseph Wright Alsops going back five generations, one abiding principle was the idea of fair play in politics and life. Indeed, this was nearly as much a part of the brothers' Anglo-Saxon background as the Anglophilia that attended their upbringing and Groton years. McCarthy's reckless allegations violated this principle more dramatically than did just about anything else in American politics in recent memory.

The Alsops viewed McCarthy as a political provocateur, a heartland populist stirring up passions against the country's foreign-policy elite. It galled them to see this crude politician threatening their friends with what they considered unfair and cynical assaults. They also viewed McCarthy's attack on the State Department as an attack on the internationalist philosophy that had guided American foreign policy since the war's end. Nobody was saying it explicitly, but it seemed clear to the brothers that if McCarthy succeeded in bringing down the department's internationalists, the result would be a new wave of isolationism. McCarthyism, Stewart wrote to Sommers, "is the final flowering of the new postwar isolationism, and it is perfectly capable of destroying us in the end."

The brothers' first major salvo came when Joe was still in Europe, following the proceedings of the Tydings committee through the *International Herald Tribune*. The committee heard testimony from a number of witnesses, among them a Fordham University professor and ex–Communist Party member named Louis Budenz, who identified particular China hands from the war years as communists. Among those he named were John Service, Owen Lattimore (former adviser to Chiang Kai-shek), and John Carter Vincent, who had been with Joe and Vice President Wallace during the drafting of Wallace's memorable cable recommending that Roosevelt fire Stilwell. Joe decided to send the committee a letter outlining his own experiences in China and vouching for the loyalty of the State Department officials he had known during the war.

He cabled the letter to Stewart, who had it retyped and sent to Tydings with the understanding that it would be released publicly on Monday, May 8. Stewart arranged for the *Herald Tribune* and *The Washington Post* to publish the letter that morning. Having known the situation in wartime China far more intimately than McCarthy or his informants, Joe wrote, "I think it my duty to say that while I disputed their judgment, I never had the faintest doubt of the loyalty of any of the American officials or others whom McCarthy has attacked." They were, he said, "serving the United States . . . with courage and fidelity," and they should be protected from McCarthy's "vulgar attack."

Joe noted with a certain malice that senators McCarthy, Wherry, and Taft, in voting their isolationist sentiments, had "voted the straight communist party line, as laid down by the 'Daily Worker,' ever since the end of the war." If temporary agreement with the party line is a test of loyalty, he suggested, "let these men be called to the bar, to explain their records." The letter concluded:

> I do not attempt to excuse or palliate the grave American mistakes in China, which I have often before denounced. But I submit that we may as well abandon all hope of having honest and courageous public servants if mere mistakes of judgment are later to be transformed into evidence of disloyalty to the state. And I submit further that the members of the Senate who are now persecuting these men who made, as I think, mistakes in China, have far more to explain. . . . I still believe the loss of China was unnecessary. But I think it far more important that we should not destroy the decent traditions of American political life.

The letter brought words of praise from around the world. "I admire your courage and your clear-thinking presentation of your views," wrote Joe's old column partner, Bob Kintner. From the American embassy in Prague, U.S. diplomat James Penfield wrote to say Joe's letter "was not only one of the more cogent comments on McCarthy I've seen but more important it's the only fair and realistic statement of the China years I've noticed."

On July 17 the Tydings committee issued a 313-page report that denounced McCarthy in unusually blunt language, calling his charges and methods "a fraud and a hoax perpetrated on the Senate . . . and the American people." Two weeks later the Alsops discharged their next salvo in a *Saturday Evening Post* piece entitled "Why Has Washington Gone Crazy?" It explored the "miasma of neurotic fear and internal suspicion" that had overtaken Washington in this new era of communist-hunting fervor. State Department officials feared being investigated and having their phones tapped by congressional investigators; members of Congress feared the same from the executive branch. "The government of the United States," the brothers wrote, "is now spending immense time and effort spying on itself or trying to prevent itself from spying on itself." They cited as a "symptom" Joe McCarthy, who boasted that he had "loyal" friends in the State Department secretly furnishing him with information. They wrote:

A visit to the McCarthy lair on Capitol Hill is rather like being transported to the set of one of Hollywood's minor thrillers. The anteroom is generally full of furtive-looking characters who look as though they might be suborned State Department men. McCarthy himself, despite a creeping baldness and a continual tremor which makes his head shake in a disconcerting fashion, is reasonably well cast as the Hollywood version of a strong-jawed private eye. A visitor is likely to find him with his heavy shoulders hunched forward, a telephone in his huge hands, shouting cryptic instructions to some mysterious ally.

"Yeah, yeah. I can listen, but I can't talk. Get me? Yeah? You really got the goods on the guy?" The senator glances up to note the effect of this drama on his visitor. "Yeah? Well, I tell you. Just mention this sort of casual to Number One, and get his reaction. Okay?"

The drama is heightened by a significant bit of stage business. For as Senator McCarthy talks he sometimes strikes the mouthpiece of his telephone with a pencil. As Washington folklore has it, this is supposed to jar the needle off any concealed listening device. In short, while the State Department fears that Senator McCarthy's friends are spying on it, Senator McCarthy apparently fears that the State Department's friends are spying on him.

The brothers also attacked the "vulgar folly" of Republican senator Kenneth Wherry's campaign "to elevate the subject of homosexuality to the level of a serious political issue" on the theory that "sexual perversion," as the brothers called it, represented a national threat.

Though the reference to McCarthy encompassed only four paragraphs in a ten-column story, the senator reacted with anger. In a letter to *Post* editors, which he read into the *Congressional Record*, the senator said it was "extremely disturbing" that elected representatives seeking to remove "sexual perverts and disloyal people from government" should be attacked in the *Post*. He said he knew a number of *Post* staffers, "and frankly I can't believe that Senator Wherry's attempt to accomplish the long overdue task of removing perverts from our government would be considered . . . 'vulgar' . . . to them." But he added that he could understand why it would be considered vulgar to Joe Alsop.

It seemed to be a thinly veiled suggestion that Joe was homosexual, and the senator amplified his suggestion in a later passage attacking the article's use of the characterization "furtive-looking." Though the article had identified the furtive-looking people not as McCarthy staffers but rather as State Department informants, the senator took it as an insult to his staff. He said he found it "almost inconceivable" that the magazine would lend itself to such a "smear." In fact, he wrote, Joe Alsop had never been in his office—"and incidentally never will be." Ignoring a visit by Stewart a few weeks earlier, he wrote that no one from the *Post* had come by except "a fine normal young man called Ollie Atkins, who merely took some pictures." McCarthy described the Alsop article as being "almost 100 percent in line" with official Communist Party instructions "issued to all communist and fellow-traveling members of the press" by party leader Gus Hall.

McCarthy's letter revealed an unusually tough politician who didn't shrink from battles even with those who bought ink by the barrel. The brothers had thrived on political combat, but never had they engaged an opponent like McCarthy. In a letter to Ben Hibbs, Stewart called the senator's broadside "a particularly slimy business." He cited "the sly hint that Joe wasn't 'healthy and normal' like Ollie Atkins," the implication that neither brother had visited his office, and "the stuff about our following Gus Hall's line." Because Joe Alsop was now in his forties, wasn't married, and didn't squire women around town, some in Washington's political and journalistic circles speculated that he was homosexual. Others assumed he was merely asexual. But no one had ever sought to exploit the question for political advantage—until McCarthy. Joe ignored the attack, declined to discuss it even with family members, and demonstrated in everything he did that such tactics couldn't intimidate him.

With Joe abroad, Stewart requested an opportunity to escalate the fight in the pages of the *Post*, but Hibbs declined; so Stewart fired off a column attacking McCarthy. He argued that the senator had assisted the Kremlin by undermining Americans' faith in their government, by telling lies about innocent people, and by promoting the idea that the "cheap pleasures of spy-hunting" were adequate substitutes for the serious business of ensuring national security in a troubled world.

Meanwhile, Hibbs responded to the McCarthy letter by defending his magazine's longtime opposition to communism and pointing out that the *Post* had backed McCarthy on many issues even though it had found distasteful the "wild, unsupported charges" he had been making. The *Post* had criticized the Tydings committee, Hibbs pointed out, "for its job of whitewashing in their communist investigation," and it had criticized government officials "from President Truman on down" for their efforts to hush up inquiries into communist penetration of government. But Hibbs added that McCarthy's "insinuations about Joe Alsop ill become a United States senator." He added, "I know Alsop well, and I know he is a man of high character, with great courage and integrity."

Hibbs's tepid defense reflected a growing political reality; longtime allies were beginning to diverge on the McCarthy issue. Joe Alsop later speculated that at least 30 percent of the *Post*'s readers backed McCarthy, and that Hibbs thus had to navigate a fine line. Just as Hibbs faced this delicate challenge in directing his magazine, so did the Alsops in dealing with Hibbs. Though the brothers proposed a number of McCarthy articles over the next four years, the *Post* turned them all down. Meanwhile, McCarthy responded to Hibbs's letter by attacking the Alsops further and belittling the *Post*'s contribution to the fight against communism. As for his "insinuations," he said that if Joe Alsop wanted to describe McCarthy as being "a victim of palsy," then he should expect "that I may publicly discuss any of his mental or physical aberrations which I see fit."

The brothers continued to jab at the senator in their column, where they matched his pugilistic style. In July 1951, after John Davies had been asked to appear before the State Department's Loyalty Security Board to explain his wartime China role, Joe volunteered to appear before the board on his behalf. Later he wrote a column about his experiences, breaking into the first person for the first time since the Alsop partnership had begun. It seemed all very ordinary, he wrote—the three-man board clothed itself in "no special majesty." But it wasn't ordinary at all. For here was a man preparing for an exciting new posting to Germany, who had been suddenly charged with doubtful loyalty and publicly suspended from duty. "Here was his name blackened, his career perhaps permanently damaged. . . . And for what? To make a burnt offering with a sweet savor in the peculiar nostrils of Sen. McCarthy."

Davies eventually was cleared, but by this time the McCarthy movement had taken on a new dimension. The stalemate in Korea had left the American people stunned and confused. Confidence in the nation's foreign policy—and its foreign-policy elite—had dropped precipitously. Was this what it was all about? After all the sacrifices of World War II and the commitment to world peace, were Americans destined to find themselves pinned down in a faraway land, losing more and more lives every week for a goal nobody could explain? Was this the price of internationalism? Something was wrong, and nobody seemed to be addressing the problem except Joe McCarthy. With each month, the senator's power grew.

The 1950 elections reflected these political shifts and the growing suspicion that the State Department had "played footsie with communists," as *Time* put it. Fifty-two percent of votes cast went to Republicans, only 42 percent to Democrats. Voters cut the Democratic majority in the Senate from twelve to two, in the House from seventeen to twelve. Maryland's Millard Tydings, who had undercut McCarthy, lost his Senate seat. Illinois's influential Democratic senator Scott Lucas suffered a similar fate. The elections, wrote the Alsops, had given "immense new power and authority to the conservative, isolationist Republican group headed by Senator Taft."

As McCarthy's power grew, the brothers continued their attack as if by instinct. They never discussed the risks involved in taking on the Wisconsin senator. As the senior brother, Joe particularly seemed to thrive on the controversy, to derive from it a heightened sense of identity. Once, while in Avon to cover a local political battle involving pro- and anti-McCarthy forces, he spent an afternoon with John Alsop and his wife Gussie at their home up the road from their big Alsop farmhouse. When the telephone rang, Joe picked it up and spoke briskly into the receiver: "Communist Party headquarters."

THE BROTHERS STILL loved to visit Avon, and did so whenever possible. Joe frequently would stop by on his way to or from his sojourns abroad, and at Christmas the family would congregate at the big farmhouse for yuletide celebrations. Aggie, who ran the household and served as helpmate and close friend to Corinne, would decorate the place with festive abandon, and the old house would ring out with the happy sounds of an extended family reveling in its closeness. Years later Tish would remember the "wonderful gaiety of spirit" during those holiday celebrations. The three brothers—Joe, Stew, and John—"had such a damn good time together," and it was clear that the parents loved having them all at home. Often Corinne and Joe Sr. would invite old family friends from the area, or their cousin, Sheffield Cowles, Auntie Bye's son. Sheff brought his own considerable wit to the always raucous farmhouse conversations.

Joe Sr. loved to bait the brothers with provocative quips about recent columns, hoping to stir yet another fiery family debate. Stewart caught on and ignored his father, but Joe never figured it out. He would rise to the bait, and soon a wonderful family row would be at full throat.

On Christmas morning there would be the chaotic ritual of package unwrapping in the big living room, with Stewart's and John's children attacking the task with a vengeance. Afterward Stewart and Tish would take the children to Mass at the local Catholic church—the only day of the year when Stewart attended church services. When the donation plate would make its way down the row, he and Tish would act out a family ritual. Stewart would hold a dollar bill over the plate in one hand, and a twenty in the other. As the children waited to see which bill he would give, Tish would reach over, grab the twenty, and place it in the plate. The children always enjoyed the little game.

At midday, back at the farmhouse, the family gathered in the dining room for a big Christmas lunch, with turkey, creamed onions, brussels sprouts, and trimmings. Joe particularly liked brussels sprouts and was not reticent in suggesting to Tish and Gussie, who oversaw the cooks in the kitchen, how he liked his sprouts prepared.

"Darling," he would say, "they're much better with a little cream at the end."

The family members would have barely recuperated from the large midday meal when an evening meal, almost as varied and fancy, would be served. Corinne insisted on two large meals because they kept the family together in one large conversation, but over the years Tish and Gussie complained that it was just too much for one day—particularly for the two of them, who did much of the preparation and cleanup after the family cooks had left for their own Christmas celebrations. Corinne refused to bend on the issue, but as a compromise she permitted the evening meal to be served on paper plates.

In early 1951, a new battlefront emerged in the war between the McCarthy forces and the State Department. The Senate authorized another investigation into internal security, to be conducted by the new Internal Security Subcommittee of the Judiciary Committee. Heading the subcommittee was Judiciary Committee chairman Pat McCarran of Nevada, a feisty conservative bent on reopening McCarthy's State Department allegations of the previous year. He promptly appointed a McCarthy partisan named Robert Morris as chief counsel, with the sole prerogative of picking his assistants. McCarthy was delighted, the Alsops enraged.

It didn't take long for the McCarran proceedings to draw Joe Alsop into the battle. It began with the testimony of Louis Budenz, the economics professor who had been managing editor of the *Daily Worker* before breaking with the communists in 1945 and becoming a star witness at congressional hearings, trials, and administrative proceedings. He had devoted nearly three thousand hours to helping the FBI unravel communist intrigues, and on the lecture circuit he commanded big fees, grossing nearly $70,000 in one year.

Asked by Morris if John Carter Vincent was a member of the Communist Party, Budenz replied, "From official reports I have received, he was." Joe Alsop launched his own investigation and learned that, through all his hours of FBI interrogation, Budenz had never identified Vincent as a communist. Moreover, he had firmly refused to identify

Vincent as a communist during the Tydings Committee hearings a year earlier. It was another example, said Joe, "of the astonishingly belated recollection and the hearsay accusation of treason."

When he finally did name Vincent, Budenz told the McCarran subcommittee that one of Vincent's special Communist Party assignments during the war was to "guide" Henry Wallace "along the paths" of the party during the vice president's famous wartime trip through China. Joe Alsop had been there in the spring of 1944 when Vincent participated in the discussions that led Wallace to recommend the firing of Stilwell, which Joe considered to have been a heavy blow to the communist cause in China. With Stilwell in place, squeezing Chiang's regime and working to cut off his American aid, the communists had a chance to supplant the Nationalists without warfare; with Stilwell gone, that chance evaporated. The appointment of Stilwell's successor, the anticommunist General Wedemeyer, had hindered the communist cause further. Joe recalled clearly that Vincent had approved the idea of promoting Wedemeyer to Stilwell's job.

In early September, Joe filed a four-column series designed to demolish the Budenz testimony and force the McCarran subcommittee onto the defensive. He recounted the 1944 Wallace-Vincent-Alsop conversations leading to Wallace's cable to Roosevelt, which he called "a profoundly anticommunist document." Quoting from the still classified document, he revealed for the first time details of the cable. He questioned Budenz's veracity and motives. He noted that many responsible persons and publications were saying that if McCarran could prove his case, he would "justify McCarthy." But, said Joe, if the case were proved with false testimony, then the matter would be put "in a very different, not to say a rather lurid, light."

Joe also attacked McCarran committee counsel Morris. Before details of the Wallace cable were revealed, Joe noted, Morris had sought to prove the "Communist influence" of the Wallace trip with a "woolly-headed ten-cent pamphlet" Wallace had endorsed for the left-wing Institute of Pacific Relations some years after his trip. Brandishing the pamphlet at a committee hearing, Morris had demanded, "That's Communist stuff, isn't it?" Joe acknowledged that after Wallace's 1944 China trip the impetuous former vice president "fell, for a while, into the hands of the Communist party," as the Alsops had pointed out repeatedly during the 1948 presidential campaign. But the issue, said Joe, was what Wallace had recommended to Roosevelt in his Kunming cable. Morris easily could have obtained documentary evidence on that question, but he hadn't. He seemed less interested in the truth than in destroying Vincent.

The Alsop columns reverberated with unusual force at two locations—the floor of the United States Senate and the executive offices of the New York *Herald Tribune*. At the *Herald Tribune*, the Reids were becoming increasingly uneasy over the Alsops' relentless attacks on

McCarthy and his friends. The Robert Morris column turned their uneasiness to opposition. Whitie Reid ordered an editorial to run September 15, the day after the Morris column had appeared, disowning Joe and praising the "distinguished lawyers," as well as the chief counsel, of the McCarran subcommittee.

Worse, the paper had held up the first column in the series, explaining the delay to subscribing papers by saying it stemmed from "legal difficulties." The result, said Joe in an angry letter to Whitie Reid, "was to create serious concern in the office of every client paper" about the soundness of Joe's work. He reported that at *The Washington Post*, "the more timid spirits" took alarm at the wire, and there was a discussion that had to be settled by publisher Philip Graham, who quickly ordered the column to be published "without qualification or remark."

The *Herald Trib* syndicate also had accompanied the final column with a wire saying that in the *Herald Tribune* it would be run not as a column, but as a news story. Joe was furious. "You have the right to use our stuff as you please," he wrote to Whitie. "But I think when you in effect indicate your own lack of confidence in us to our clients, and thus undermine their confidence in us as well, you are going very far indeed." Joe insisted the paper had no right to influence the content of the column beyond matters of libel and taste. If the Reids wanted to assume responsibility for what the brothers wrote, said Joe, "that places our entire relationship in a wholly novel light" and "it becomes necessary to negotiate a new contract."

The Alsop brothers found the Reids' behavior particularly disturbing because it was becoming typical. Around the same time, in the fall of 1951, Joe found himself in a long and bitter dispute with the Reids over a controversial series he filed on Pan American World Airways.

The series, part of an extensive investigation by Joe into influence peddling in Washington, identified Pan Am as "the greatest of the empire builders," with "a record that stands by itself." He told of Pan Am's successful effort to remove unfriendly members from the Civil Aeronautics Board—which was supposed to regulate the airlines—and to retain others whom the company liked. He recounted how President Truman himself, bowing to pressure from CAB members friendly to Pan Am and from White House official John Steelman, had intervened to reverse a CAB ruling that had been unfavorable to Pan Am. "In the Washington influence game," wrote Joe, "the ace is the President of the United States," and the Truman ace "was played most spectacularly in the case of Pan American."

T. E. Braniff, president of Braniff International Airways, congratulated Joe "upon the accuracy of your information," adding that Pan Am had built up a political machine so powerful that it was able to override the will of most of the departments of government.

But at the *Herald Tribune*, the Reids withheld the Pan Am columns and refused to send them out to subscribing newspapers. Helen Reid and business manager Bill Robinson conceded their objection was that the columns could hurt their drive to regain big-business advertising. "They stripped the mask off," Joe later wrote to Stewart in Europe. "I have never seen such a display of trembling terror in any newspaper office."

Joe took the position, based on their contract, that the paper could run columns or not, as it chose, but that the syndicate was obliged to send the pieces on to subscribing newspapers. The Reids then discovered a contract clause, intended to protect against libel, which they said gave the paper the option of refusing to send columns out if it so chose. Joe countered that if the paper withheld them he would provide no replacements, would write to all client papers to explain the matter, and would publish the columns elsewhere so that subscribing editors would know what the controversy was about. The *Tribune* yielded, but only after a Monday had gone by without the Alsop column—the last of the Pan Am series. Helen Reid, under pressure from the airline, had elected not to use it, and Robinson had notified the syndicate's customers to that effect.

Joe was furious. He argued that such notification was a direct breach of the contract, which required the *Tribune* to promote the column "by every means possible." In a letter to Whitie Reid, he issued an ultimatum. If the editorial independence of the column couldn't be guaranteed, he wouldn't write it. Helen Reid and Bill Robinson quickly promised to respect the column's editorial independence and to refrain from communications to editors that undermined its sales potential. But the episode had left both brothers with the fear that their great flagship newspaper no longer stood for the journalistic ideals that had guided it for so long under Ogden Reid's stewardship.

This episode, coupled with the Reids' behavior on the Morris column, raised serious questions about the leadership of the *Herald Tribune*. Up at Harvard, Arthur Schlesinger was so dismayed by the paper's disavowal editorial on McCarthy that he dashed off a letter to Helen Reid. "I could not but feel that something was very wrong somewhere," he wrote. "I just do not believe that the *Herald Tribune* would have reacted in this way a few years back."

Meanwhile, on the Senate floor, the day Joe's attack on Morris appeared, Senator Herbert H. Lehman rose to suggest that the Alsop columns on Budenz and the McCarran subcommittee "very clearly reflect on this body." The New York Democrat identified Joe as "a very widely read and influential columnist," and said it must be taken seriously when such a columnist suggests that testimony given before a Senate subcommittee "was demonstrably false." He said he had no knowledge of whether the allegations were true or untrue, but he urged "an immediate investigation" of "these grave published charges against the honor of the Senate."

When Lehman moved that the Alsop columns be read into the *Congressional Record*, Idaho's Republican senator Herman Welker objected under Senate rules requiring unanimous consent for such a motion. Senator McCarran labeled Lehman's call for an investigation "a travesty" and said the New York senator wanted to "sponsor a columnist's charge that a committee of the Senate is guilty of subornation of perjury." Lehman protested that McCarran had put words in his mouth. He had made no such accusation, he said. McCarran retorted that when his subcomittee's hearings were over the people would see for themselves who was right. "All the Alsops from here to perdition can't stop this committee from going forward," he declared.

The next day, President Truman released to the Senate Wallace's secret 1944 cables to Roosevelt, as well as a letter from Wallace describing the cables' significance and Vincent's role in shaping his recommendation that Stilwell be replaced by Wedemeyer. The material substantially corroborated Joe's version of events, and forced McCarran and his subcommittee off balance. A *Washington Post* article observed that the documents showed Wallace's Kunming recommendation "would have been the exact opposite of the pro-communist kind which he, Vincent and others have been accused of advocating."

With McCarran on the defensive, Lehman appeared on the Senate floor determined to get Joe's Budenz columns read into the record—by unanimous consent if possible, but if necessary by reading them on the floor. That stirred a bizarre debate over whether a United States senator could divulge in floor debate the writings of a well-known columnist on a matter of national importance. Through deft parliamentary maneuvering, Maine's Republican senator Owen Brewster and Georgia's Democratic senator Walter George managed to trump Lehman and quash his effort to air Joe's columns in the Senate.

In early October, McCarran's subcommittee summoned Wallace to testify, and Joe turned fearful that his long effort to impeach Budenz's testimony would crumble with Wallace at the witness table. Joe considered the former vice president a naive and muddle-headed man who would be cut to ribbons by Robert Morris in an open hearing. He fired off a letter to McCarran requesting an opportunity to testify, and released his letter to the press in hopes of pressuring McCarran to honor his request. It was granted.

It was a bold and risky move. Joe had some implacable enemies among the subcommittee members and staff. Also, if Wallace crumbled before a hostile interrogation, Joe's credibility could be impugned as well. He contacted Wallace to provide guidance on how the former vice president should conduct himself before the committee. Joe was aghast to learn that Wallace didn't think he would need a lawyer. He planned to ponder the issue at his New York farm, then travel to Washington shortly before the hearing. Joe argued—diplomatically at first, then less so—that Wallace really couldn't show up without counsel at the kind of hearing McCarran and Morris had in store. Wallace finally relented, and Joe set about seeking the right man for the job.

It wasn't easy. He spent half a day calling Washington law firms "for the wretched Henry Wallace," as he put it to Marty Sommers, but nobody seemed interested. He reported to Marty "a remarkable level of cowardice" in the legal profession. As an example, he related how Clark Clifford, Truman's erstwhile adviser, had explained "with great orotundity and self-righteousness why he was debarred from serving." Altogether, Joe was turned down by thirty lawyers. In exasperation, he took his old Harvard classmate, Joseph Rauh, to lunch. Rauh, a leading labor lawyer and anti-McCarthy partisan, offered his services, but Joe said he needed someone who wasn't associated with the anti-McCarthy position. Rauh understood and suggested George Ball, a rising young Washington lawyer. Ball at first expressed doubts about taking on a client "touched with so much folly." But Joe told him Wallace was likely to be "slaughtered," and had been turned down "by every competent lawyer in town." That posed a challenge the feisty Ball couldn't resist.

Ball felt pangs of regret as soon as he began working with Wallace. He liked the man personally, but the "obstinance of his idealism" rendered him incapable of comprehending his own predicament. Wallace had drafted a statement for the committee consisting largely of a "frontal attack," calling the committee members "faceless men" and questioning their motives. Ball argued forcefully that such an approach would be disastrous, and Wallace finally accepted Ball's more temperate statement, a straightforward rendition of events and a denial of the allegations against him and Vincent. The lawyer subjected Wallace to endless hours of rehearsal interrogation to prepare him for the McCarran ordeal.

Then another hitch developed. Wallace had accepted an invitation to appear on a national radio interview show after the subcommittee's preliminary private inquiry but before the public hearing. Ball announced that he couldn't take the risk of representing Wallace if he appeared on the show. But during a meeting at the radio studio among Joe, Wallace, Ball, and Laurence Spivak, the show's moderator, Spivak said he couldn't release Wallace from his commitment because the show could lose its sponsor, Curtis Publishing. Wallace yielded, and Ball, in a "towering rage," withdrew from the case.

Without Ball it was likely that Wallace would be destroyed by McCarran. At Joe's house later that afternoon, the columnist beat on Wallace "as with a very heavy club" and finally got him to agree to withdraw from the radio show if the Curtis matter could be cleared up. Curtis published the *Saturday Evening Post*, so Joe called Hibbs for assurances that Curtis wouldn't pull its advertising from Spivak's show. Meanwhile, Ball had called a cab and was waiting for it outside. Every few minutes he would poke his head in to ask whether the whole silly matter had been cleared up yet. Hibbs saved the day—"in the nick of time," as Joe later put it. Curtis officials said they wouldn't bolt from the show, and Wallace agreed to pull out. Ball sent the cab away and returned to the case.

On October 17, Joe led off the subcommittee session with a statement recounting his China experiences and arguing that they proved Budenz's testimony was "misleading and untruthful." After the statement he came under intense questioning from Morris, McCarran, and other subcommittee members, particularly regarding his repeated suggestions that Budenz had committed perjury. Joe refused to budge.

"Mr. Alsop," asked Judiciary Committee counsel Julien Sourwine, "do you see any difference between testifying that you do not believe a man and testifying that he is a liar?"

"The overwhelming evidence before the committee," replied Joe, "indicates he lied on this occasion." Ball wrote later that Joe handled his testimony "with courage and bravura."

Then came Wallace, "stumbling through his testimony without too much breakage," as Ball later recounted. The lawyer was relieved that the long hours of coaching had paid off. But the grueling testimony left its mark on Joe. Following the session, he found himself in an elevator with a group of reporters and Senator McCarthy. When the senator smiled at his journalistic adversary and offered his hand, a stone-faced Alsop turned away.

The ordeal was over, and McCarran had been denied his triumph. But the issue was not over. With impressive agility, Budenz and Morris altered the story: the real point, they said, wasn't whether the communists liked Stilwell but rather their position on his removal. The Kremlin had had advance notice of his likely removal, the new story went, and hence official instructions to party sympathizers were to acquiesce in that policy. What's more, as Morris put it to the editors of the *Herald Tribune*, "the party had incorrectly assumed . . . that Wedemeyer was in their camp." He pointed out that the *Daily Worker* had editorialized in favor of Wedemeyer at the time. McCarran's allies were heartened that the press gave scant play to the Wallace-Alsop testimony, particularly in comparison to the play it had given Budenz's sensational accusations. Thus, the McCarran subcommittee became more emboldened. It promptly called Vincent back from his post in Tangier for a hearing the next January.

THE ISSUE OF the "loss of China" continued to reverberate through American politics, buffeting the China hands, stunting and in some instances destroying their careers. Vincent was forced out of the State Department in 1952; Davies was fired in 1954; Service was dismissed in 1951 but reinstated by the Supreme Court in 1957. The emotions stirred by the China controversy and its offspring, McCarthyism, also continued to flow through the country's political discourse, generating heat and anger for years to come. For most Americans the two issues—China and McCarthyism—were intertwined into one: Some believed the China hands had been right about Chiang and ended up being persecuted for their foresight. Others held that the diplomats had been wrong about Chiang and deserved whatever punishment politics and history meted out.

Joe and Stewart Alsop stood almost alone in separating the two issues. They never relinquished their view that the China hands had been foolish men, ignorant of history and naive about the realities of human nature at the core of communism. They believed this ignorance and naiveté had contributed to a great tragedy of history. But the brothers never believed the diplomats were traitors, and they became nearly consumed with anguish over their fate. For the Alsops, McCarthyism represented an assault on the American way of government. For another three years they continued to battle the Wisconsin senator and his followers. McCarthy, Stewart wrote years later, was "the only politican or major public figure I ever really hated." The senator was guilty of what, for an Alsop, was a supreme political transgression. "He did not play the game," said Stewart, "according to the rules."

IKE AND ADLAI

Covering the 1952 Campaign

As THE UNITED STATES moved toward the 1952 presidential election, discerning politicians and pundits knew the Democratic Party was a spent force, sagging under the weight of too many years at the helm of government and too many party hacks hanging onto power for self-interest. The second Truman term was marked by policy stalemate at home, military stalemate in Korea, the China disaster, the McCarthy bitterness, petty corruption in high governmental circles, and a general sense of a "mess in Washington." The Democrats, wrote the Alsops, had become "paralyzed" and almost "suicidal" in their prevailing pessimism. If the president were to run again, they felt, he surely would lose; if he were to retire, the party would be plagued by a "shortage of inspiring political leaders with national standing."

Besides, the brothers agreed with Walter Lippmann that the Republicans' long minority status had poisoned their politics and rendered them more and more irresponsible in opposition. That helped explain, the brothers believed, why the McCarthy movement had become such an integral part of the Republicans' political posture.

But there was one Republican the Alsops did not want in the White House: Ohio's Senator Robert A. Taft. The brothers liked him personally, enjoyed his company, and appreciated his stiletto-sharp intellect. They wrote later that Stewart had been so charmed by the plain-spoken Taft that after interviewing the senator he had to undergo a "de-brainwashing" from Joe before sitting down to write. They respected Taft's unrivaled mastery of legislative details and his standing as the unchallenged leader of his party.

But they didn't like his isolationist leanings. In the postwar years he had deferred on foreign policy to Michigan's internationalist senator, Arthur Vandenberg. But nobody doubted that Taft still harbored the views that had made him an unyielding opponent of U.S. involvement in World War II right up to Pearl Harbor. Since the war, Joe wrote in a letter to publisher Basil Brewer of the *Standard-Times* of New Bedford, Massachusetts, the senator had "directly or indirectly opposed every great measure of American foreign policy . . . , with the exception of the (to me) rather meaningless U.N."

And after losing the Republican presidential nomination to Dewey in 1948, an embittered Taft had succumbed to an uncharacteristically harsh brand of politics. He had become more partisan, less accommodating to the majority party, and a willing accomplice of the McCarthy forces. Thus the Alsops believed a Taft presidency would be a disaster on the two issues they considered most crucial—the foreign menace of communism and the domestic menace of McCarthyism.

In their campaign to keep the country safe from Bob Taft, the brothers highlighted what many considered a fundamental weakness in his bid for the nomination—his lack of broad appeal in a general election. They embraced General Dwight Eisenhower as the one man capable of upending Taft's quest for the nomination and going on to capture the presidency. As early as November of the previous year they had identified Eisenhower as "the candidate desired by the great mass of voters" and predicted a call for his entry into the race. The Alsops liked Eisenhower's internationalist outlook, and considered him sound on the crucial issue of national defense. In a *Saturday Evening Post* article they identified the general as his party's "first and greatest asset." They lauded his "character, outlook, past record and hopeful view of the American future," and added, "If Eisenhower cannot cure the Republican neuroses, no one can."

Joe was so certain of Eisenhower's eventual success that he wagered $100 with Clark Clifford that the general would capture the Republican nomination. Since Joe was betting against the field, Clifford gave him two-to-one odds.

When the Eisenhower forces put forth the idea that Taft could not win, the brothers quickly picked up the chant. In order to win, they wrote in early February, Taft "must either break the Solid South, which his warmest friends among the Dixiecrats say he cannot do, or he must pass something of a miracle above the Mason-Dixon line."

By harping on Taft's presumed weaknesses, the brothers angered the senator's backers and some newspaper editors. Jack Craemer, managing editor of the *Independent Journal* in San Rafael, California, wrote the syndicate to complain that the Alsop column had been "aimed at disseminating pro-Eisenhower propaganda more than at impartially informing the populace." He added that his newspaper would likely endorse Eisenhower, but nevertheless he felt the brothers' work "degrades our paper and threatens its reader acceptance." John Hollister, an old friend of Joe's and a partner in Taft's Cincinnati law firm, said Joe's Taft columns showed "a startling ignorance of what is going on in the country."

To Craemer, Joe offered no argument. Assuring the editor that he had "no bill of goods to sell," he suggested that any appearance to the contrary probably stemmed from the brothers' being stuck in Washington for various personal and professional reasons. "I plan an early escape to the grass roots," he wrote, "and if you see the results in the column, I greatly hope they will strike you as being more soundly analytic and directly reportorial." To Hollister he wrote a three-page letter defending his "Taft Can't Win" column. "Sometimes I write a tendentious column," he said, "but the one you object to was entirely honest in preparation and in purpose."

These exchanges reflected a reality of the brothers' 1952 campaign coverage. They wanted Taft stopped, and they would do whatever they could to help stop him. But they wanted also to preserve the image of the column as reportorial and analytical. It was a problem as old as Joe's column-writing career. It was not always easy finding the appropriate balance, and many Alsop readers felt the column lacked balance when it came to Bob Taft.

By April, the brothers felt a growing confidence that Eisenhower would win the nomination. In the New Hampshire primary in mid-March he captured all fourteen delegates, and collected some 47,000 votes to Taft's 36,000 (Stassen and MacArthur shared another 10,000 votes)

But the New Hampshire results on the Democratic side embarrassed the Alsops. It was assumed that Truman's incumbency would enable him to breeze to dominance in the year's first primary, but the Democratic victor turned out to be Senator Estes Kefauver of Tennessee, the homespun Chattanooga lawyer whom *Life* called "the nation's first serious dabbler in a new brand of political magic—the awesome power of TV." With his angular face etched into the national consciousness through his dramatic Senate crime inquiry, Kefauver descended on tiny New Hampshire as a politician-celebrity—the first of that breed to capture the political imagination of important segments of voters in a presidential campaign year. Before the primary, Stewart had dismissed Kefauver, saying it was an ironclad rule that "you simply do not challenge an incumbent president in your own party." He gave Kefauver an "outside" chance of capturing just one delegate.

After the primary *Time* magazine, recalling how the Alsops had written about prognosticators eating crow after the 1948 election, had fun with Stewart's miscalculation. The brothers attributed the faulty prediction to Kefauver himself, who had told Stewart in a not-for-attribution interview that he expected a big defeat in the state. More likely, the wily Kefauver had snookered Stewart with a political ruse that subsequently became commonplace in primary politics—the game of dampening public expectations to make subsequent results look good. Reporters later learned to be on guard against the expectations game, but in these early years of the circus atmosphere that would come to New Hampshire at primary time, they had not yet caught on.

Taft's New Hampshire defeat was repeated in Minnesota and New Jersey. The senator bounced back with victories in Wisconsin, Nebraska, and West Virginia, and enjoyed avid support among party regulars in many key states; but the polls were showing an unmistakable groundswell for Eisenhower that threatened to engulf Taft's support among party professionals. "Even Taft-minded people on the Hill are beginning to say that they just don't see how Taft can be nominated or Eisenhower stopped," Stewart wrote to Marty Sommers on March 29.

But party regulars seemed intent on using their dominance of the GOP machinery in key states to overwhelm Eisenhower's popular support. In April the brothers received a telegram from disgruntled Eisenhower supporters in Louisiana, who protested the "disgraceful un-American tactics" employed by the pro-Taft forces throughout the state. Urged on by his old friend Cabot Lodge, Joe decided to travel into the South to observe this intraparty warfare as it unfolded.

In the Texas hill-country resort town of Mineral Wells, Joe encountered a political drama that offered ample opportunity for indignation. At the old gimcrack Mineral Wells Hotel, where the party was holding its state convention, national committeeman Henry Zweifel had engineered a steamroller movement to keep the party's delegate-selection machinery in the hands of Taft stalwarts. At precinct and county meetings throughout the state, a surge of Eisenhower enthusiasm had overwhelmed the Zweifel forces and threatened their control. In response, Zweifel's state executive committee simply seated a pro-Taft delegation at the convention, which promptly selected a pro-Taft delegation to the forthcoming national convention in Chicago. There was no compromise; the Eisenhower forces were shut out entirely. Quickly seeing the political dynamite packed into such tactics, Joe wrote from Mineral Wells:

> With the on-the-spot approval of Sen. Robert A. Taft's personal representatives, the Texas delegation to the Republican National Convention has been stolen for the Ohio senator. And this steal has been accomplished by a system of rigging as grossly dishonest, as nakedly anti-democratic, as arrogantly careless of majority rule, as can be found in the long and sordid annals of American politics.

Joe offered a case in point—Harris County, which encompassed Houston, and where Eisenhower delegates had outnumbered Taft delegates 18,700 to 3,700. But in many precinct meetings where delegates to the county meeting were chosen, the outnumbered Taft supporters had staged walkouts and rump caucuses, which had then made the results subject to challenge. Then in challenge after challenge, the precinct-level Eisenhower votes were thrown out, usually on grounds that the surge had been engineered by Democrats ineligible to vote in Republican precinct meetings. So Harris County sent to Mineral Wells two competing delegations, and the state executive and credentials committees had to determine which was legitimate. Tracing the Harris County credentials fight from beginning to end, Joe concluded that the deck had been stacked in favor of the Taft delegation headed by Mrs. Carl G. Stearns. Even the Harris County Republican chairman, a Taft man named Joe Ingraham, had defended a delegate breakdown favorable to Eisenhower as the legitimate county outcome.

Throughout Chairman Ingraham's testimony, wrote Joe, "no effort whatever was made to impugn his facts, or to prove illegality in the Harris County precinct meetings and convention." No one, he added, argued that the Eisenhower forces had not carried Harris County by an enormous margin. In the end, "the Zweifel-Taft stooges simply threw out the legally elected Eisenhower delegation . . . and seated Mrs. Stearns' phony pro-Taft delegation." Asked how her tiny minority could legally name the Harris County delegation, Mrs. Stearns replied, "I just don't know. But we just seemed to, and anyway we're going right along with it."

From Mineral Wells, Joe traveled to Dallas, New Orleans, and Atlanta for similar reporting efforts that demonstrated the closed-door mentality of the Southern Republican oligarchs. Other newsmen wrote similar stories during this time, but nobody rang the alarm with greater force or clarity than Joe Alsop. His theme that there had been a delegate "steal" was picked up by Eisenhower forces throughout the country.

The columns about the Southern Republicans were the kind that Joe liked best—pugilistic pieces on controversial issues that generated plenty of emotion and lent themselves to dramatization as clashes of good and evil. "If Taft gets away with stealing the nomination," wrote Frederic Winthrop from Ipswich, Massachusetts, "it will not be because you and Stewart have not done your damndest." Houston oil producer John H. Blaffer, an Eisenhower delegate at Mineral Wells, reported that he could hardly walk down a city block without meeting twenty friends who wanted to talk politics—"and many of them say that whereas they had been for Taft before the convention they are certainly for Eisenhower now."

But Orville Bullington, chairman of the Texas Republican state executive committee and an outspoken Taft supporter, was not pleased. Joe had identified him as "an amiable old gentleman" whose war cry was, "To hell with foreign policy." He had quoted Bullington as saying, "Whoever controls the committee can always barrelhouse 'em through.

You'll see; it'll be the same at Chicago." Bullington contended he had been misquoted. "Either you cannot hear well, or you are a common liar, and if you will come to Chicago I will repeat just what I have said in this letter to you . . . ," he wrote. Joe dismissed the complaint, saying he suspected Bullington had forgotten their convention conversation "in the general emotion of the moment." He said every word he wrote had come straight from his notes.

The Republican convention became a kind of family affair for the Alsops. Sister Corinne Chubb acquired a vast and "insanely expensive" suite in Chicago's finest hotel, the Ambassador East, and the Alsops assembled as a kind of "tribal phalanx," as Joe wrote to his friend Judy Montagu. There were Stew and Tish, Joe, Sis, and Johnny, "all together with cases of whiskey and champagne and other little economical necessities." It was a triumphant hour for John Alsop, a rising political star in Connecticut and the organizer of the Eisenhower movement in the state. He managed to capture every Connecticut delegate for the general. He defied an effort by the regulars to purge him from the convention delegation and won his seat on the floor with a large majority. "He will be governor someday, I think, if there is a someday," Joe wrote to Montagu.

The convention opened July 7, and the "Texas steal" argument immediately became a powerful rallying cry for the Eisenhower forces. The showdown on credentials came when Ike's people brought to the floor their Fair Play Amendment, which required that the Eisenhower delegates from Texas be given the seats "stolen" by Taft delegates. The amendments passed, and essentially destroyed Taft's drive for the nomination. After the vote, Frank Kent of the *Baltimore Sun* told Joe he had almost single-handedly created the Southern delegate issue for Eisenhower.

An ebullient Cabot Lodge, Eisenhower's floor manager during the convention, credited Joe with the victory. "You made the Texas vote-steal issue," he told his columnist friend as they shared a celebratory drink after the credentials vote, "and now we're going to win on it."

They did, and Clark Clifford sent Joe a check for $200. "You are a very good man to bet with," Joe wrote Clifford.

THE FOCUS NOW centered on Eisenhower's opponent, to be chosen at the Democrats' Chicago convention later in July. Truman had left the race. Kefauver had amassed a string of primary victories. Averell Harriman, hankering for a political career, wanted the nomination, as did Senator Robert Kerr of Oklahoma and Vice President Alben Barkley. But the big question mark was Adlai Stevenson: Could he be coaxed into the competition? The Illinois governor's agonized indecision became something of a national spectacle as a parade of friends and party bigwigs rushed to Springfield to urge him to run, only to increase the public agony. Still, the polished reform politician and grandson of a vice president enjoyed wide support throughout the party. President Truman, at a press conference early in the year, had pointedly called him one of the best governors in Illinois history.

Traveling to Springfield in February to meet with the governor, Joe found himself so beguiled that he forgot his standing as journalistic observer. The two men chatted for close to two hours, and afterward Joe sent the politician one of his florid letters of appreciation and praise. "It really is impossible to thank you adequately for your kindness and hospitality," he wrote. "I can quite honestly say I don't remember an experience . . . with an American political leader since the end of the war which has so much stimulated, enlightened and encouraged me."

Joe added that he could not resist repeating his conviction that "in the most dreadful crisis America has ever entered, you are quite obviously the best qualified man to lead the country." The governor's humility—which of course "does you honor"—should not be permitted "to muffle the clear call of duty," particularly since the governor's hesitations only served to heighten the chances of a Taft presidency. Joe speculated that Truman would support Stevenson if the governor made clear his intent to run, but in the meantime the president's White House cronies had been telling Truman that Stevenson didn't want to run. "If I may say so without impertinence," wrote Joe, "I think you also have a duty to the president, to make his decision a little easier by coming here, by telling him that you will be a candidate if he so desires, and by helping to dispel the false impression of your attitude that the president's self-serving advisers are working so hard to create."

Of course it was with considerable impertinence that Joe presumed to counsel a leading politician on how he should deal with the president. It was the kind of impertinence to which Joe would become increasingly susceptible.

Joe's expertise as reporter and political gossip provided some insights into Stevenson's indecision, which was related in part to his ex-wife— "one of those horrid women," he wrote to Judy Montagu, "who are pretty, had accomplishments (bad poetry in her case) and become accustomed early to being the center and summit of the act." As Adlai became the admired and courted partner, "she evidently went off her rocker," and had even been diagnosed by one psychiatrist as suffering from "manic envy." She had threatened to cause "all sorts of scandals" if Stevenson ran for president, Joe reported to Judy, and because his sons were still young the governor remained highly concerned about her behavior.

When it came to women, Joe was a romantic who harbored old-fashioned views about gallantry. He once slapped a friend's hand lightly when the man was about to light his own cigarette before lighting his wife's. He had an idealized vision of womanhood that included specific characteristics—beauty, charm, wit, an appreciation for the affairs of men, and intellectual accomplishment in the areas of taste and culture. When he encountered women who approached the ideal—Susan Mary Patten, say, or Evangeline Bruce, the young wife of diplomat David Bruce—he was instantly smitten. He was dismissive of women who seemed frivolous or slow-witted.

"In dealing with the couples in his social circle, Joe had separate relationships with the women," recalled Katharine Graham. He was argumentative with the men, but never with the women. He took intense interest in their lives—their homes, their food and wine, their furniture and decorating, their children. For many women in social Washington Joe was one of the most beguiling men around.

Joe also harbored strong feelings about personal loyalty, particularly familial loyalty. That a politician's ex-wife would threaten his career with information from their marriage struck him as a tragedy not just for the politician but for the nation as well. "It does seem ridiculous that such a silly and trivial woman [as Adlai Stevenson's wife] can conceivably affect the destiny of this country," Joe wrote to Judy Montagu, "but there it is."

In June Joe profiled Stevenson for the *Saturday Evening Post*, rendering a portrait of an amiable but unprepossessing man with a deep and far-ranging intellect. "He lacks the majesty most politicians aim for, and his manner is as ungrandiose as his appearance," he wrote. But Stevenson possessed a political determination that had served him well as governor, Joe added, and a Stevenson candidacy would be formidable.

In July Stevenson accepted the nomination in Chicago with a speech that drove Joe "literally to drink," as he recalled decades later. Determined to combine their convention duties with the pleasures of alcohol, the brothers had enlisted Tish to keep them supplied. From her seat in the gallery she would attach a heavy string to a large heirloom silver flask that once had belonged to Joseph Wright Alsop III. Then she would reach over the gallery rail and lower it down to Joe or Stewart on the floor. Now that conventions were covered live on national television, such antics could be hazardous. One network camera caught Joe retrieving the flask—an "unbecoming posture," he later confessed in print, but one that made for "an amusing scene."

Joe did feel he needed something strong to drink when he listened to Stevenson's acceptance speech. He was particularly unimpressed when the candidate compared his agony in deciding to run with Christ's agony in the garden following the Last Supper. The governor even used Christ's anguished plea to the Lord—"Let this cup pass from me!"—as the highlight of his speech. Such political vainglory, accentuated by the advent of national television coverage, struck the brothers as all too typical of a man who laced his conversation with copious references to Lincoln. Both Stewart and Joe were developing a dislike for the governor, although they continued to consider him a politician of substance and promise.

As the autumn election campaign began, the Alsops took heart in the fact that the parties had chosen excellent candidates. Both were strong internationalists, firmly committed to American leadership in the world struggle against Soviet expansion. The brothers set out to cover the campaign in as evenhanded a manner as possible, pointing out the strengths and weaknesses of each candidate. "If both sides are sometimes pleased and sometimes displeased, and if our readers are puzzled to know who our candidate is," Joe wrote to an editor from Winona, Minnesota, "I feel we can be reasonably sure we are doing our reportorial job without undue bias either way."

In August the brothers wrote that the big question hovering over Eisenhower was: What would he do about Joe McCarthy? They reported that officials of the general's high command had decided on a "silent treatment" approach toward McCarthy and his Indiana ally, Senator William Jenner—a "cut-rate McCarthy," as the brothers described him, who was up for reelection. The plan was to stay out of Wisconsin and Indiana and to avoid campaigning with either senator, while taking visible steps to appease the party's right wing in other ways. The Alsops predicted that there would be powerful pressures on the candidate to abandon that plan and embrace McCarthy in the name of party unity. "The outcome really depends on whether Eisenhower will remain true to himself," they wrote.

The powerful pressures did indeed emerge, and within two weeks the Eisenhower campaign announced plans for a stop in Indiana, where the candidate would appear with Jenner. Then plans for a campaign appearance with McCarthy in Wisconsin were also announced. In Milwaukee, Eisenhower had intended to issue some ringing praise for George Marshall, his military mentor and the target of some of McCarthy's most stinging attacks, but at the urging of Wisconsin's Republican governor, Walter Kohler, Jr., he excised the words of praise at the last minute.

The brothers were incensed, but they devoted their column to explaining these compromise tactics rather than attacking them. "It is . . . significant," wrote Joe from the Eisenhower whistle-stop train, "that the general's personal staff, and presumably the general himself, have frankly detested such sacrifices of principle." In fact, the brothers had allowed their distaste for McCarthy to cloud their political judgment. It was naive to think that Eisenhower and the men around him would initiate a civil war within their party in the heat of a campaign. Whatever the general thought of McCarthy, he was a Republican, and Ike wanted active support from every Republican. The brothers should have known that in the end the candidate would embrace the Wisconsin senator in the name of political expediency.

In Springfield, Illinois, meanwhile, Stewart visited the Stevenson campaign, which he described in a column as "the most intellectual and literate of any waged since the days of Woodrow Wilson." But Stewart also felt it had an antiseptic quality, divorced from the sweaty and slightly raucous milieu that normally was the spawning ground for major political movements. He couldn't find the cigar-chomping Irishmen with their encyclopedic knowledge of voting blocs and political geography, or the labor leaders and farm specialists and minority representatives.

Traveling to Hartford to hear a highly literate but turgid Stevenson speech on atomic energy, Stewart remarked to brother John that Stevenson's impressive turn of mind seemed to captivate many intelligent people who normally considered themselves Republicans. "Sure," said John, "all the eggheads love Stevenson. But how many eggheads do you think there are?" Stewart incorporated the conversation into a column and thus added a word to the country's political lexicon and common speech. Soon *egghead* became a widely used political term denoting the intellectual vote. John later said the word had simply popped into his head, invoking "a mental image of a bald head with a thin and fragile bone structure, and mush inside." Years later Stewart regretted having given the term currency since it had become "a favorite epithet of all anti-intellectuals."

As the campaign progressed, the brothers began to feel that the truly big issues confronting the nation weren't being discussed. Top defense and diplomatic planners were sharply divided, they reported, over the results of a recent review of the West's strategic situation. The West was growing stronger, according to the review, but the Soviet empire was growing stronger still. Policymakers were arguing over whether America's security policies should be shaped by estimates of Soviet capabilities or of Soviet intentions. It was a fundamental debate and yet, the brothers complained, no echo of it could be heard on the campaign trail.

That gap, plus Eisenhower's flirtation with McCarthy and Stevenson's lack of political verve, left the brothers dissatisfied with the campaign. In a letter to Isaiah Berlin, Joe compared the election contest to "a trip through the Paris sewers." He added that he didn't consider Eisenhower qualified to be president, "although perhaps I make too little allowance for the inevitable compromises of any political campaign." Although he considered Stevenson "admirably qualified for the White House," he lamented the lack of anything approaching a Rooseveltian image.

Still, the brothers enjoyed traveling, seeing the country's vastness and richness at first hand. "You forget the splendor, the variety, the largeness and the dynamism of this country if you just sit here in Washington," Joe wrote to Susan Mary Patten in Paris.

But when you do a cross-country trip, you are suddenly confronted with the Shasta Dam—almost as beautiful, in its peculiar way, as the Parthenon; pure and perfect, noble and exact in design and in detail, making rich land of a desert, and bringing power to a province. Or you run into a man like Wilbur Renk, the Eisenhower leader in Wisconsin—and his family, Swiss-German pioneers, who have been a hundred years on their land—the farm now 2,700 acres of the very best in Wisconsin—the family's fortune perhaps three million dollars—the man himself about my age, but irritatingly looking about fifteen years younger—discovered with his brothers and old father doing the very dirty job of shearing his prize-winning sheep for an auction—then sitting down in his rather ragged farmer dungarees to talk politics as wisely and bluntly and liberally as anyone I can remember.

When the votes were counted on November 4, Eisenhower had won big, with 55 percent of the vote to Stevenson's 44 percent. He also brought with him a Republican Congress, though not by much. The GOP House margin was only eight; the Senate had forty-nine Republicans and forty-nine Democrats, but with the new vice president, Richard Nixon, to break tie votes, the Republicans had a bare majority there. After twenty years, the GOP was back in power.

Joe voted for Eisenhower. Stewart couldn't bring himself to do so, although he wasn't displeased with the electoral result. Both brothers felt it was time for the country to set out on a new course, and both harbored high hopes for the new administration, mixed with concerns about how it would handle what they considered the McCarthy menace.

LIKE THE COUNTRY in 1952, the brothers took stock of their situation and their futures. After the grueling campaign, and another foreign trip that Joe took immediately afterward, he began feeling that he was working too hard for the income he was getting. He asked Whitie Reid for a contract that would permit the brothers to concentrate mainly on the column, while holding magazine articles to only two a year. Reid offered a raise of $7,500 annually, hardly enough to allow a major cutback on magazine work. Joe began to feel that he was on a treadmill.

Still, it was better than most treadmills. Joe was earning nearly $35,000 a year, while Stewart was getting close to $30,000. Both lived comfortably in fine homes with live-in help. Both traveled the world and rubbed shoulders with the high and mighty.

Wherever Joe went, he encountered close friends and many potential new friends. The persona he had cultivated so carefully in his youth took on an added aura as he reached middle age. He was the character in any gathering, the man who could say outrageous things and get away with it. His sweeping pronouncements and comic antics were becoming the stuff of legend in world capitals far and wide.

Of course he had his detractors too. Many people despised Joe, talked bitterly of his arrogance and snobbishness. Often these were people who didn't know how to deal with him, didn't know how to get him to warm up to them. They didn't know that he had rejected them for the simple reason that he feared they would reject him first. "I just laughed at Joe and his arrogance, his mannerisms and his demanding front," recalled Robert Donovan, the *Herald Tribune*'s Washington bureau chief, who added that Joe treated him with respect and affection. He remembered an incident in Paris one evening when Joe refused to eat in one of the city's most famous restaurants.

"What's wrong with it?" asked Donovan.

"My dear boy," replied Joe, "I happen to know that in this establishment they don't rotate their wine bottles in the racks according to a proper schedule."

On another occasion, when the two decided to have lunch together, Joe insisted on taking Donovan to a restaurant far from their hotel even though Donovan was on a tight schedule. After they got into a cab and Joe issued instructions to the driver in French, Donovan could see they were going farther than he wanted.

"Joe," he said, "there are plenty of fine restaurants on the Champs Élysées. Let's go back there."

"Oh, no, no, no, my dear boy," replied Joe. "It's the Métro." He explained in great detail how the vibrations caused by the Paris subway shook the wines, affected the sediments, and bruised the vintage.

Another part of Joe Alsop's persona was his unshakable pessimism. But this, too, to some extent, was merely part of the pose. One afternoon Joe stormed into the Paris offices of the *Herald Tribune* and issued a pronouncement to anyone within earshot.

"It's the end of civilization as we know it."

"Oh, Joe," said Nathan Kingsley, a *Herald Trib* editor in Paris (later its syndicate chief), "it's much worse than *that*." The response pleased Joe immensely.

Many people enjoyed playing along with Joe the poseur. At the *Herald Tribune* offices in Paris, he would tense up when under deadline, biting his knuckles until they bled, then wander around the newsroom flailing his arms in frustration, muttering to no one in particular. After experiencing this spectacle, one night editor exclaimed, "This is a historic moment for me, something I can tell my grandchildren about. I have just been bled upon by Joseph Alsop."

While Joe could be intellectually snobbish, his snobbishness never took on a petty cast. Once he made a lunch date with old friend Joe Fromm, who was in Washington from his Far East posting for *U.S. News & World Report*. When Fromm showed up at Washington's august Metropolitan Club wearing a sharkskin bush jacket and no tie, club officials frowned on his attire. Indeed, Fromm's editor, David Lawrence, later expressed disapproval. But Joe Alsop didn't seem to notice.

Fromm liked Joe Alsop, but felt more comfortable with Stewart. Joe often let his opinions get in the way of the conversation, but Stewart never did. Like Joe, Stewart often took Fromm to the Metropolitan Club for lunch during the *U.S. News* reporter's Washington leaves. The aim was to pick his brain on Far Eastern goings-on. "Even when he disagreed with me, Stewart remained unemotional and detached," recalled Fromm.

Nathan Kingsley recalled Stewart as "one of God's gentlemen." When Kingsley had some concerns about the column, he didn't bother discussing them with Joe, because he knew Joe would simply get his back up. But Stewart always listened carefully. "He was unfailingly courteous."

At the end of 1952, Stewart and Tish paid $58,000 for a new home for their large family. Located on Springland Lane in northwestern Washington's fashionable Cleveland Park, it was a sprawling frame house with eight bedrooms, set upon an acre of land carved out of the side of a hill. Originally it had been the caretaker's house for what had been a big farm, but in the 1930s two wings had been added. It had a living room spacious enough for the large paintings of Alsop ancestors that Stewart had collected over the years. Two of them, of Aunt Harriett Douglas and her brother William, were large enough to cover the two sides of a doorway that Stewart considered extraneous. The dining room, complete with fireplace, easily accommodated a rosewood dining set that seated sixteen people.

Tish loved the place, but Stewart came to feel it lacked character. Nevertheless, it was perfect for entertaining. Soon Stewart had a tennis court built on a terrace down the hill. By this time the Alsops had four children— young Joseph was seven; his brother Ian, five; sister Elizabeth, known to the family as Fuff (after little Ian's rendition of his baby sister's name), was four; and the baby was Stewart Johonnet Oliver, Jr. All showed signs of being precocious.

Stewart delegated to Tish the basics of child-rearing, and she in turn had nannies to help her. Often they spoke only Spanish, which gave Tish, who was fluent in the language, an edge over Stewart in the running of the household—which he didn't want any hand in anyway. When not socializing or playing tennis, he loved to read. The books would stack up next to his big chair by the living room fireplace—recent biographies, histories, and political tracts. He seldom read contemporary fiction but regularly turned to the English classics, including his standby favorite, Shakespeare. In the shower, in lieu of singing, he would recite extensively, in his booming voice, from Shakespeare's soliloquies.

On March 17, 1953, Stewart received a call from Corinne in Charleston, South Carolina. Pa had suffered a heart attack during his annual winter hunting trip, she said. It had been a mild attack, but his weakened condition had left him unable to fight off a cold that quickly developed into pneumonia. Now he was in bad shape. Stewart should hurry down to Charleston.

Stewart and Tish packed up their old 1942 Buick and drove straight through. They were on the road more than twelve hours before they arrived, early in the morning.

John and Gussie were already there. They had hopped a plane and were in Charleston in time to see Pa alive. He hadn't said anything or shown any recognition. He had died quietly in his sleep shortly before Stewart made it to the bedside.

Joe had been on a reporting trip when he heard the news. He too hurried to Charleston; he too arrived too late to see his father alive.

Corinne, John, and Gussie had been at Joe Sr.'s side when he died. Corinne had gently placed her hand on his.

"Oh . . . my Joseph," she had whispered with a sigh. There were no tears.

An era had ended in the saga of the New World Alsops. Joseph Wright Alsop IV, seventy-six years old at his death, had been the transitional figure in the family history. His life had resembled the lives of his forebears stretching back five generations, more than it would resemble the lives of any of his descendants. His was the last generation that could truly live the life of the New England country squire.

The family quickly pulled together. Corinne impressed everyone with her strength and determination to oversee the impending arrangements. She was very loving toward her sons.

That evening, after the brothers and wives had settled in at the lavish Yeaman's Club on the outskirts of town, they all went for dinner at the grand antebellum home of Nicholas and Emily Roosevelt, distant family relations. Corinne, who was staying at the house, went upstairs to drop off some items she had purchased that afternoon, and Tish went with her. Upon entering the bedroom Corinne burst into tears. Tish had never before seen her cry.

"I can't cry in front of anybody else," said Corinne. Then she promptly collected herself and headed downstairs, displaying her hallmark demeanor of strength and control.

At dinner, the talk centered on Pa. The Alsops mourned by reminiscing, trading stories from the outer reaches of their memory about the man they had just lost. There was plenty of laughter mixed with the pain.

The next day the three brothers called on a local mortician. Typically quiet-spoken but smooth, the mortician quickly sized up the Northerners as men of means. He took them to his cellar and showed them some of the most luxurious caskets the brothers had ever seen. It didn't occur to him that these frugal Yankees weren't about to spend that kind of money on the dead. John noticed the color rising in Joe's face.

"Goddam it," said Joe, "we don't want any of this stuff. What we want is a plain pine box."

"Oh, I'm very sorry," whispered the mortician. "I'm afraid we don't have that."

"Don't you have poor people around here?" asked Joe. The mortician didn't respond.

"Sir," said Joe, "could you give me the name of the nearest Negro undertaker? I'm sure he will have what we want."

The mortician suddenly remembered that he did have one casket that might fit the brothers' needs. And so the boys' father returned to Avon in a simple and inexpensive box.

Once there, Corinne had the casket placed in Joseph's little study at the back of the house. It was his private sanctum, where he had gone for solace, to be surrounded by his books, his guns, and framed prints of his prize cows.

John went into Corinne's study to telephone relatives and friends. Gussie went in to see if she could help, but quickly retreated. John had tears in his eyes; she had never seen that before.

Then Ted Manion, the Avon postmaster, came by.

"You know, John," he said, "a lot of people here would like one last look at your father." The Italian townsfolk were accustomed to open caskets.

"Well," said John, "he's not tarted up." But he accepted the idea of opening the casket if his mother didn't object. She didn't, and so Manion and John took a screwdriver and removed the casket lid.

Tish was horrified. "All my English blood rebelled at the idea," she recalled. But Corinne explained.

"I don't believe in it," she said, "but the townspeople want it. And they did love him so much."

And so Joseph Alsop lay in his study in an open box as hundreds of local folk filed past. There were no candles, no religious overtones.

The next day, mourners from across the state jammed the Avon Congregational Church for the simple funeral. There were many hymns but no eulogies. The three brothers were pallbearers, along with brother-in-law Percy Chubb and a few family friends. Then the family accompanied the casket in a procession to Middletown, where Pa was interred in the Alsop mausoleum.

All the major Northeastern newspapers carried obituaries capturing the elements of Joseph Alsop's career: leading New England cattle breeder, pioneer in modern dairy farming, successful insurance executive, local politician, civic leader. Joe received more than 120 letters and telegrams of condolence from friends throughout the world; all reflected the feeling that this had been indeed a life worth noting. "He had a good life," Stewart wrote to Marty Sommers. "He was a very special New England breed, a vanishing breed, I'm afraid."

18

IKE'S WASHINGTON

Declaring War on
Business as Usual

THE EISENHOWER ADMINISTRATION had been in power scarcely three months when Stewart proposed to Marty Sommers what he called "an amusing, malicious piece"—a story about Georgetown under the Republicans. It seemed that the new regime did not take to the gilded residential area that had been so fashionable during the Truman years. The Republican wives shied away from the place, in part because a gossip publication called *Washington Confidential* had portrayed it as a haven for effete leftists. And the president himself, according to the day's instant legend, had actually admonished his top officials to stay away from the trendy enclave.

Stewart never wrote the piece, but his story suggestion reflected the fact that a new breed had taken over. The Republicans, said Stewart in his memo to Sommers, "are dull fellows who work late and go to bed early." The new cabinet consisted mostly of corporate managers who were bent on bringing order and purpose to the sprawling federal government. *The New Republic* called the team "eight millionaires and a plumber," the nonmillionaire being Labor Secretary Martin Durkin, who had been head of the Chicago plumbers' union. The brothers doubted the ability of these corporate bureaucrats to grasp the complexities of the federal government and the issues confronting it.

Besides, the newcomers weren't exactly the Alsops' kind of people. Most were narrow in scope, a bit stuffy, and suspicious of Washington and its social elites. They lacked the flair that had become associated with Georgetown's social caste—the Frankfurters, Achesons, Bohlens, Bruces, Bissells, Wisners, and Grahams. The new Eisenhower folks gravitated to neighborhoods such as Spring Valley, farther out in northwestern Washington, with their manicured lawns and spreading elms.

"Eisenhower's Washington will, I think, be unbearably boring, although rich," Joe wrote to Diana Cooper in January. "Everyone I am fondest of is going away, and no one I like very much is replacing them."

It soon became clear that the giants of the administration would be Secretary of State John Foster Dulles, architect of foreign policy, and Treasury Secretary George Humphrey, domestic policy czar. The Alsop brothers moved quickly to establish relationships with both.

In February 1953, Stewart spent two and a half hours with Humphrey, an engaging Ohioan who had been president of a large Cleveland-based conglomerate called the Mark A. Hanna Company. Stewart found Humphrey to be a man of intellect and force struggling with the new challenge of government. "Taking this job," Humphrey told Stewart, "is contrary to all my beliefs." Stewart found it "extraordinary to see his mind wrestling with towering problems of which he was almost wholly unaware." The result of that session and several others was a major *Saturday Evening Post* profile entitled "The Man Ike Trusts with the Cash." The brothers called Humphrey "the best test case in President Eisenhower's daring and deliberate experiment in turning over the management of the American Government to men who have brilliantly managed great private enterprises." His power, they noted, derived from the fact that he was the money man in the cabinet, and all great decisions ultimately would come back to money.

It was a highly favorable profile, and Humphrey liked it. "This is too complimentary, but that is your fault," he wrote to Stewart. The easy relationship the brothers established with Humphrey emboldened Joe to write the secretary about his latest defense-policy concern—the need for an air-defense system. Joe had become almost obsessed with what he considered the Soviets' growing ability to launch a first strike against the United States. "I am quite sure that if we are to have shield and spear when we shall need them, the work should start at once," he wrote to Humphrey.

As for Dulles, Joe had known him since his arrival as Republican adviser to the State Department in the Truman years. Dulles was a natural for his new job—first in his class at Princeton and at George Washington University Law School, a top partner at the prestigious Wall Street law firm of Sullivan and Cromwell, one of the country's most successful international lawyers.

The Alsops viewed Dulles as immensely bright but limited by intellectual rigidity. A man of unwavering views and character, he seemed unable to bend with changing circumstances. But they took seriously the need to cultivate the new secretary of state. Joe wrote to congratulate Dulles on his "good beginning" and to request an interview. "Stew and

I both want to support you in the small way that is within our power," he added. When Dulles cleared John Carter Vincent in a pending loyalty matter held over from the Truman days, Joe wrote to congratulate the secretary "from the bottom of my heart, with all the warmth at my command for your wise and courageous decision—"

Even as they made these efforts to curry favor with the new administration's power brokers, the brothers were feeling a growing disenchantment with Eisenhower's government. The budget director, Joseph Dodge, seemed convinced that national solvency—limited taxation and a balanced budget—was more important to national security than defense spending.

The brothers fretted over what the administration would do about an air defense system designed to protect the country from long-range Soviet nuclear bombers. They learned of a high-level task force called Project Lincoln, sponsored by the air force and directed by the Massachusetts Institute of Technology, which had reached some disturbing conclusions: The existing and planned American air-defense system was capable of intercepting only 10 to 30 percent of incoming Soviet bombers. Within three years the Soviets would have four hundred or so atomic bombs and the long-range air power to deliver a massive attack on the United States. Unless major steps were taken the country would be vulnerable to a level of destruction that would render retaliation impossible.

On the other hand, Project Lincoln scientists concluded, a series of technological breakthroughs had rendered a sound defense quite possible, although expensive. It would take a sophisticated radar network, stretching as a kind of picket fence of interlocking radar stations, from Thule in Greenland to Fairbanks in Alaska. It would require a new arsenal of high-technology weapons, including interceptor fighters, ground-to-air missiles, air-to-air missiles, and pilotless aircraft, all capable of supersonic speeds and incorporating the latest homing devices. The cost would be $16 billion to $20 billion over several years.

The Alsops became the country's leading journalistic advocates of Project Lincoln. In March, Stewart and a nuclear physicist named Ralph Lapp collaborated on a piece in the *Saturday Evening Post* entitled "We Can Smash the Red A-Bombers." Then the brothers filed a three-column series that revealed the Eisenhower administration's interest in the Project Lincoln recommendations, and urged that the project be undertaken. The brothers reported that Eisenhower had told a group of congressional leaders that his dilemma was "giving him sleepless nights." With typical extravagance of language, they wrote that "few if any graver choices have ever confronted an American president."

On March 17, the brothers broke the news that the Soviets had been flying reconnaissance missions over Alaska and northwestern Canada. It was ominous, they wrote, that these missions had never set off the air force alert system because the country's warning network lacked the sophistication to detect the intruding planes. U.S. experts learned of the reconnaissance only through the jet contrails left behind by the Soviet aircraft. "To all intents," the brothers wrote, "our Northern approaches are a defensive vacuum." The *Herald Tribune* ran the column on page one.

Not everyone shared the Alsops' anxiety. *Time* reported that, when other reporters checked the Alsops' story, the suggestion that Project Lincoln was the government's prime concern "collapsed like a pricked balloon." The magazine quoted high-level officials saying the Lincoln study was not under active consideration, and added that, even if the country had an extra $20 billion to spend on armaments, most strategists would use it to buy bombers rather than for an elaborate air defense system. "There isn't any line you can hold in the air," said one unnamed air force officer. The magazine entitled its piece "Maginot Line of the Air" and included a photo of Joe with a caption: "Worried by insomnia."

Stewart labeled the *Time* piece "lousy reporting," and told Sommers that the air force's Strategic Air Command, which was responsible for the country's offensive air strategy, "fears and dislikes the whole project, for obvious reasons." Joe called Henry Luce to describe the complexities and urgencies of the issue, and later he and Stewart wrote a letter for publication in *Time*. Published April 13, it said that the Lincoln report had been on the agenda for five of the seven National Security Council meetings held since Eisenhower had become president. The matter, said the letter, also was under active study by two advisory groups "whose verdict the president has indicated he will probably accept." The brothers added that the United States would never strike a first blow, and thus the lack of an air defense concedes to the enemy the opportunity to devastate U.S. cities and industry, and perhaps even the Strategic Air Command. The country's only response to attack would be "to retaliate after being devastated. Surely this cannot be accepted."

The air-defense columns generated interest throughout the world. Joe's friend Blair Clark of NBC wrote from Paris, "Great éclat in the French papers, as you doubtless know, over your air defense pieces. I thought they were the first serious journalism done about what faces Eisenhower, not to mention America." But others felt the series reflected the column's increasing tendency toward pessimism and doomsaying. The *Pittsburgh Post-Gazette*, which had been running Joe's work since the first Alsop-Kintner days, dropped the column in April. Publisher William Block wrote to Stewart that his news executives felt he and Joe "constantly see the end of the world coming in each column," and that this "crying wolf" had become tiresome. The *Daily Times* of Davenport, Iowa, also canceled, objecting to the column's know-it-all tone. "We do not share their views that . . . President Eisenhower is a half-witted babe in the woods who needs the Alsops' advice to get in out of the rain," wrote editor M. A. Fulton to Willet Weeks, manager of the *Herald Tribune* Syndicate.

Even before the air-defense series, Weeks had communicated his concerns about the column to Joe. He said he worried about the trickle of cancellations and the fact that they weren't being offset by enough new sales. He attributed the attrition to the column's gloomy tone at a time of national optimism and faith in the new president. "There is an unusual unanimity among the editors with whom I talked in their assertion that the column tends to be negative and somewhat pessimistic," he wrote.

Joe's first reaction was to treat Weeks's concerns seriously. "If we impress our readers as gloom merchants, we must try to do better," he wrote. "We are trying to do better, within the limits imposed by these not very hopeful times in which we live." But then he went on for two and a half pages in a flight of pessimism about the difficult global challenge facing the country, and the frivolous Washington confidence in Eisenhower's ability somehow to "combine a strong national defense, a creative foreign policy, a balanced budget and lower taxes." The air-defense story, he said, "is more important than any that has been leading the papers in recent months," except for the inauguration and the recent death of Stalin. "What are Stew and I to do—throw away this news story, because people think we are too fond of what is grim? My instinct is to play the news for as much as it is worth."

It was a remarkable response, running contrary to all that Joe knew he should be saying and what he had intended to say. But he couldn't help himself. Joe was a pessimist by nature, and he viewed the ongoing events of his time in apocalyptic terms. Every national decision was a crossroads decision, confronting America with a choice between survival and extinction, between the only right course and the utterly wrong. Occasionally, Joe would express a more robust view of American democracy, seeing it as an ongoing process by which the nation sets its path through fits and starts, trial and error, faulty and brilliant governing decisions. He would reveal on occasion a view of democracy as an essentially self-correcting system that usually manages, somehow, to rise to the most pressing challenges of the day. But that was his intellect talking; his heart fed him pessimism and gloom. Reading over his letter to Weeks, Joe knew it was the wrong thing to say. So he stashed it in a file and suppressed the urge to justify his dark political outlook.

Stewart, meanwhile, had developed a more philosophical view of the country and its future. Seldom did he disagree with his brother on fundamental issues—the need for a strong defense, the Soviet threat, America's role as protector of the West, the evils of McCarthyism. And he possessed the same capacity for outrage, which seemed to be an Alsop family trait. But he didn't share the emotional sense of national urgency that so often agitated Joe. Joe was the senior partner, and he set the tone for the column while Stewart went along without dispute. But discerning readers and close friends detected subtle differences in outlook between the brothers.

In fact, Joe's domineering temperament was taking an ever greater toll on Stewart. Tom Braden recalled a morning when Joe came down to the office in his silk dressing gown, hung over and feisty, at about ten o'clock. Stewart was there, working.

"Now, Stoooo," said Joe, "I simply *caaaan't* work today; I simply *caaaan't*." His evening with the ambassador, he explained, had simply taken too much out of him, and he would have to stay in his room. In his arrogant way he issued instructions on how Stewart should handle the day's reporting chores, and then disappeared up the stairs. Stewart watched him go, then muttered under his breath.

"That son of a bitch; that son of a bitch."

Stewart's underlying anger grew over the years, and the brothers reached a point where a tiny spark could set them off. A typical flare-up occurred after Corinne decided to distribute some Alsop family heirlooms. Joe, feigning generosity, said that all he wanted were two vases he had long admired. They happened to be the most valuable of the possessions, but Corinne readily agreed to let him have them.

To save time, her Avon chauffeur dropped off the entire lot at Springland Lane, and Stewart, not realizing the vases were intended for Joe, placed them on prominent display in the living room. Visiting for supper one evening, Joe spotted the vases and exploded.

"Goddam it, Stew, those belong to me!"

"The hell they do," Stewart shot back. "Ma sent them down here to me."

In an instant the brothers were screaming at each other as Tish, who knew the facts and could have settled the matter in a few seconds, tried unsuccessfully to get the brothers' attention. Joe yelled to Tish, "Order me a cab," and he stomped outside to wait. But it was snowing, and the cab never came, so Stewart had to drive him home. Stewart's anger and the slippery pavement led him to smash his car into a retaining wall next to his driveway; he knocked loose three bricks.

Such fights didn't bother Joe, who viewed combat and controversy as tools of manipulation. After an explosion at work he would go upstairs, take a shower, and head out to his evening social whirl refreshed and emboldened. Stewart, however, hated friction within the family, and the bouts of contention left him dispirited. He often would return to Springland Lane in the evening and sigh, "I just don't know how much longer I can put up with this." But he continued to put up with it.

Even Helen Reid experienced Joe's ornery streak in July, after one of Joe's columns mentioned a leading anticommunist combatant named J. B. Matthews. Joe referred to a controversial statement by Matthews in which he had said that the Protestant clergy included seven thousand communists, fellow travelers, communist dupes, and secret agents. The statement had caused such a fuss that Matthews had been forced out of his job as executive director of McCarthy's Government Operations subcommittee. Joe Alsop had misinterpreted Matthews, and wrote that he had suggested there were seven thousand secret "communist agents" among Protestant clergymen. It was an unfortunate error, and it gave Matthews's allies an opportunity for counterattack. One, an anti-communist writer named Eugene Lyons, fired off a letter to the *Herald Tribune* accusing Joe of "wild falsification."

Helen Reid wrote to Lyons expressing "great regret" for the misquotation, and suggesting that Joe surely would feel the same way. Helen sent a copy of her letter to Joe along with a cover letter calling the misrepresentation "unfortunate."

Joe lost his temper. "I feel great regret, myself," he wrote to Helen, "that you should have apologized on my behalf to a man of the character of Eugene Lyons," whose point Joe dismissed as "a distinction without a difference." To Lyons, he wrote, "I do not feel obliged to quote a man of the character of J. B. Matthews in extense."

Sensing an opportunity, Lyons sent Joe's letter to Mrs. Reid, along with his own suggestion that Joe considered himself "under no obligation to write accurately about those whose 'character' he happens to disapprove." He called this "a record in self-righteous smugness." Taking the bait, Joe fired off an even more intemperate letter to Lyons, a former Soviet sympathizer, saying he had considered Lyons "a dangerous fool" in the days when he wrote loving paeans to the Soviet Union. "The danger into which Folly and Treason brought this country has now produced a condition of hysteria, in which it is necessary for honorable men, who were neither fools nor traitors, to defend decent citizens from slander."

Mrs. Reid, believing Joe to be responsive to clear expressions of disapproval from higher authority, sought to calm him down. "It was a shock to discover a certain loss of balance as well as temper," she wrote to him. "I shall always answer letters to me if I choose to do so." Joe's second letter to Lyons had distressed her, she wrote, and she added: "Your comment in the area of name-calling only makes people angry without helping the cause of clear thinking."

Joe would not back off. Of course he would not try to limit Helen's letter-writing, he said, but her letter to Lyons had embarrassed him, and he had never seen any point in being polite "to the enemies of this republic." Helen tried once more to get the point across: "Regret for an inaccuracy should not ... be a basis for 'embarrassment.' I believe in supporting accuracy," she wrote.

Joe finally got it and conceded that the misunderstanding had been his fault. It had been a remarkable exchange, a teapot tempest that served no purpose for Joe and that could have been avoided had he simply acknowledged his lapse. His journalistic arrogance was gaining intensity.

Through the summer and fall of 1953, the Alsops followed the internal administration battle between the budget balancers and the air defense proponents; by September the budget balancers appeared to be losing. The Alsops revealed in a column that Eisenhower intended to initiate a public-education campaign called Operation Candor, to pave the way for a big defense buildup. But the budget balancers rallied, and Eisenhower retreated. Operation Candor turned into "a mush of platitudes," as Stewart described it after hearing the president deliver a major national security address.

Behind the public confusion was a doctrinal disagreement that the brothers covered closely in their column. The Eisenhower administration had decided to shave $5 billion from the $40 billion military budget in fiscal 1955 while at the same time building up offensive air power and air defense. The administration insisted that this could be done through a "new look" in the military that replaced manpower and conventional firepower with atomic firepower. It was assumed that America would introduce atomic weapons into any conflict larger than a "brushfire war," and thus would realize big savings in conventional weaponry and enlistments. This theory, which generated plenty of controversy inside the military services, came to be known as "a bigger bang for the buck."

The "bigger bang" concept led directly to Dulles's doctrine of massive retaliation—the idea that the West should develop the will and means to retaliate instantly against open communist aggression with massive force, and should strike where it hurt most. Throughout the Eisenhower years the Alsops remained skeptical of both doctrines, fearing they served as an excuse for reductions in both conventional forces and strategic defense while curtailing U.S. flexibility in responding to Soviet adventurism. "There are plenty of informed officials and officers," wrote Stewart, "who privately believe that the requirements of the budget came before the requirements of national security."

While Stewart chased the defense story, Joe headed to the Far East for a protracted reporting trip along the great border between the Soviet and Western spheres. He was particularly interested in Indochina, where French forces were struggling to retain their historic hold in the face of a relentless communist insurgency. Even before arriving, Joe feared that a French defeat in Indochina would confront the United States with a brutal choice between military involvement and a communist Vietnam. He feared the loss of Indochina would set off a "chain reaction of disasters," including communist takeovers in Thailand, Burma, possibly Malaya, and eventually all of Asia.

Arriving in Saigon in early November, Joe found it an enchanting city with bustling streets, crowded markets, and numerous French soldiers on furlough. There were avenues lined with flame trees and French villas in the Louis XIII style. Joe enjoyed taking in the atmosphere of an evening as he lingered at one of the many sidewalk cafés and savored his favorite Vietnamese dish, soupe chinoise, a tangy mix of noodles, seafood, ham, and vegetables in a thick and spicy chicken broth. But under the placid surface were signs of impending doom. Real estate ads in the newspapers told of growing numbers of French colonials bent on getting out as soon as possible. It didn't take much reporting to discover that the communist Vietminh regiments had burrowed into the life of the countryside, and that it would be a long and costly job to get them out. Already the French had been fighting the Vietminh for nearly seven years and had little to show for their sacrifice of lives and treasure.

Joe went north to a battle zone in Tonkin, where the French had seized a crossroads on the vital Vietminh supply route from China to two communist divisions south of the Tonkin Delta. One enemy division had retreated beyond reach, but the other had stood and fought, and the French had managed to maul two of its regiments. Now there was a final drive northward against the third regiment at the town of Phu Nho Quan, which also was the Vietminh provisional capital. Flying from Saigon in a small plane with a French general, Joe reached the battle zone at dawn and proceeded with a battalion of Moroccan *tirailleurs* as they approached Phu Nho Quan through rice paddies. In the distance, the town looked less like a village than like a thicket of bamboo, papayas, and banana trees.

Suddenly shots rang out, and several Moroccans fell to the ground. A French major quietly issued orders for two companies, escorted by tanks, to move out in a flanking maneuver. The firefight continued for several minutes before the Vietminh quietly dissolved into the jungle. Not a single enemy soldier had been spotted during the entire skirmish. But as the battalion moved forward, intermittent shots could be heard in the distance. "It's always like that," said the major with a grin. "The enemy in front, on both sides and in the rear too. That's our war here."

On the advance into the village, several pools of blood could be seen, testament to the Moroccans' marksmanship and to the Vietminh's devotion to their dead and wounded. One of the tanks neatly killed two Vietminh soldiers who had been observing the French advance from a crag across the river. But the engagement was over as nightfall arrived, with the Vietminh dug in across the river and the French forces ensconced on their side. Joe settled in with the troops, enjoying a campfire dinner and raucous military conversation that lasted into the night. With daybreak came a stream of French aircraft, and a large unit of French parachutists dropped out of the sky to help in the advance across the river. By the time the troops got to the other side, the enemy was gone.

A few days later Joe joined up with a Foreign Legion battalion in Bak Ninh and watched from a tank as the French experienced yet another consequence of their lack of battlefield mobility. The battalion had learned of an enemy presence in the village of My Thai, but as the legion moved in at one end of the village, the communists streamed out the other. "The tanks and the artillery had a fair shoot," Joe wrote, "but the widely dispersed, rapidly moving enemy force was not a very satisfactory target." At the legion's command post, a fortified monastery perched atop a lonely crag, Joe mixed with the troops and enjoyed the customary rituals of life in the legion—the evening songs, the elaborate rites of the officers' mess, the haunting sounds of the reveille and the retreat.

Back in Hanoi, Joe filed a column on the Vietminh soldier, hardly ever seen but always nearby. "This omnipresence of the enemy is the real heart of the problem," he wrote. The French did not have enough troops to pacify the crucial Tonkin Delta while at the same time neutralizing the six communist divisions threatening the delta from without. One of these urgent tasks always had to be sacrificed to the other, while Vietminh strength seemed to be constantly growing. The brilliant Vietminh leadership had succeeded in cutting the nation in half, and the only answer was more troops and more materiel. Joe believed both should be supplied by America. "Unless the American government wants to risk losing all of Asia by losing the war here," he wrote, "it is time to take a wholly new and very much bolder look at the situation in Indochina."

After a month in Indochina, Joe flew to Paris in December 1953 and went directly to see Georges Bidault, the foreign minister, and Marc Jacquet, the minister with jurisdiction over Indochina policy. Jacquet said the French people would force a withdrawal from Indochina within six months unless allied reinforcements were provided. He had in mind American financial aid to support French-led volunteer units comparable to Claire Chennault's Flying Tigers in China. But Bidault said there wasn't enough time for such an effort. He predicted that the French would abandon the Indochina effort "in a matter of weeks" unless America provided ground troops to fight alongside the French. Joe also reported that pressures were mounting in the French cabinet for a negotiated settlement with the Vietminh, a move that Joe considered the equivalent of surrendering Indochina outright. "The whole country is already thoroughly infiltrated by communist troops," he wrote. Within a week after a cease-fire to negotiate, six additional Vietminh divisions would be in position, "and after that there will be nothing to negotiate about."

The *Herald Tribune* played the story on page one. "It was one of the major news developments of the day," wrote managing editor George Cornish to Joe. But in official Washington, where Eisenhower and his top leadership had been counting on the French to stabilize the Southeast Asian flank, the column caused dismay. Clearly, Bidault had used Joe to communicate to Washington informally what had been too delicate to communicate formally. Telegrams flew back and forth across the Atlantic. The French foreign minister blandly suggested that Joe must have misunderstood his comments, which had been expressed in French, and the American government quickly seized on the Frenchman's explanation, ignoring the realities of Joe's Indochina columns and Bidault's underlying message. Upon his return, Joe encountered the smug smiles of his colleagues and many a joke about his proficiency in French.

Any smugness in the White House soon gave way to horror. On January 27, the brothers filed a column entitled "Where is Dien Bien Phu?" revealing that the French government officially had requested American troops for service in Indochina. The request was modest—only four hundred mechanics to meet an emergency at the Hanoi and Haiphong airfields. But its significance was as immense as the emergency was ominous. Dien Bien Phu was the remote jungle valley that commanded the approach from Laos into northwestern Vietnam. The French had fortified the valley as a launching point for attacks on the main Vietminh supply roads; but now the French army at Dien Bien Phu was surrounded by Vietminh General Vo Nguyen Giap's crack divisions, armed with heavy artillery that Giap's forces had managed to drag over the mountains and into devastating positions overlooking the besieged French.

"The future of Asia may well be at stake in this remote and obscure engagement," wrote the brothers. "No wonder, then, that the National Security Council has been anxiously debating the problem during these last days." The column forced the Vietnam story into the open, and soon other papers, including *The New York Times*, were chasing leads on the subject and reporting them on page one. Joe took pride in his news beat. "When we can drag one of these subjects . . . from the back rooms, where it is being discussed, onto the front pages, where it has been so much neglected, I consider that we are doing our job," he wrote to Bill Weeks. The *Times*'s Cy Sulzberger wrote to say he had thought Joe was crazy when he filed his Paris story on Bidault's outlook. "You were right. I was wrong," he said.

Three months later, the brothers again scored a news beat on the story with a report that the Eisenhower administration had decided to send troops to Indochina if U.S. allies would go along. The plan was canceled only after the British cabinet rejected British involvement. The story, which made page one in newspapers across the country, signaled Eisenhower's anxiety over events in Southeast Asia. Within days the beleaguered French force at Dien Bien Phu was forced to surrender. An international conference soon would convene in Geneva to determine the fate of Vietnam.

A month later, Joe visited with British diplomat Julian Harrington, who had just been posted to Vietnam as ambassador. Harrington spun out a tale of woe. "The whole countryside is penetrated by the Vietminh," he told Joe. With the French defeated and the communists in control of the North, it was evident that the West was in retreat, and the Eisenhower administration had no plan to reverse the trend. Indeed, the Alsops considered the disastrous events in Indochina in mid-1954 to be a direct result of what they called the "false peace" in Korea a year earlier, when the administration had renounced all-out victory and accepted a communist North Korea. Before the settlement, the brothers had disagreed on the proper course; Joe had argued for a military drive to victory, while Stewart favored a negotiated peace. But after the truce they agreed that the administration had settled for far less than it needed to, and had been disingenuous in portraying the compromise as a strategic triumph.

John Foster Dulles added to the brothers' gloom during a long interview with Joe in late 1954. According to the secretary's dark assessment, the communists in Asia now seemed prepared to push everywhere to the maximum of their ability, by means of indirect insurgencies. The situation in divided Vietnam was ominous. The communists in Thailand were preparing a major initiative. The pressure on Burma was increasing. And the secretary himself felt helpless.

"There's nothing I can see we can do about it," he said. "We can't get Americans to fight for these areas, if there is no direct aggression—just penetration and infiltration."

Joe challenged the secretary on the "massive retaliation" concept, and suggested there were weaknesses in the policy. Wouldn't the Soviets' growing ability to respond to the U.S. bomber force with nuclear weapons ultimately neutralize our Strategic Air Command?

"There is no doubt about that," replied Dulles.

Then perhaps, Joe suggested, it would be better to fight sooner rather than later, while the SAC remained unchallenged.

Dulles disagreed; any war at that time, he said, would be a disaster. But when Joe suggested the United States seemed to be reaching the Chamberlain stage—fight or surrender—Dulles replied that this "could not be ruled out." Then he asked mournfully, "How would you like my job?"

The conversation didn't bolster the Alsops' confidence in the Eisenhower administration, which for them had brought a series of disappointments. The budget balancers had gained the whip hand. Operation Candor was dead. There would be no major air defense initiative. The Korean settlement betrayed a status quo mentality. The West had been, in effect, thrown out of Indochina. "Our policy in these last eighteen months, viewed from the present vantage," Joe wrote to Sommers on June 25, "strikes me as an unending succession of false slogans, phony promises, disastrous decisions and petty backbiting."

THE OPPENHEIMER
AFFAIR

The Triumph of
Journalistic Outrage

IN THE SPRING of 1954 a quiet Washington drama opened in the hearing room of a drab government structure known as Temporary Building III. Through the weeks of April and May some forty distinguished American atomic scientists and educators filed before a solemn board of inquiry and gave witness to the background and character of one of their own. In the balance hung the career of J. Robert Oppenheimer, the tall, angular-faced genius who for a dozen years had served as midwife to nearly all the great nuclear developments of American science. Soon this quiet inquiry would explode into the most bitter security fight of the era—for some a cause célèbre to rival the French Dreyfus affair, for others a desperate effort to protect national secrets from the hands and eyes of hostile agents.

At the center of the struggle were the brothers Alsop, their juices of righteousness flowing as seldom before. For years Joe had considered himself a close friend of Oppenheimer's, had served with him on Harvard's Board of Overseers, and had marveled at his intellect. "I really do miss talking to you very much, and am most anxious to see you again," Joe had written to "Oppy" in 1948. Three years later, at the height of the McCarthy tumult, he had described Oppenheimer to a friend as "a very great American, but vulnerable because of family connections." Now this vulnerability threatened to destroy him, and Joe rushed to the defense.

Oppenheimer was born in New York in 1904, the son of prosperous and cultivated Jewish parents. He went to New York's famous Ethical Culture School, then at age sixteen to Harvard, where he showed promise as a physicist. He was graduated in 1925 after only three years, and went on to study physics at Cambridge and at Göttingen, where he took his doctorate in 1927. After further postdoctoral study abroad, he returned to America in 1929 to take up a dual teaching post at the California Institute of Technology at Pasadena and the University of California at Berkeley.

As Oppenheimer's teaching career began, America still lagged behind Europe in scientific research. He advanced rapidly as a leading American exponent of the New Physics, which was based on world-shaking advances in quantum theory, nuclear physics, relativity, and other fields. Soon his brilliance and intensity placed Oppenheimer at the center of the country's largest school of graduate and postdoctoral study in theoretical physics, and he enjoyed a following that spread far and wide from his West Coast campuses. As the Alsops later wrote, he "took the lead in naturalizing the New Physics in this country."

To those who knew Oppenheimer in those days, he was a captivating man, but also rather strange. There was a head-in-the-clouds quality about him. He read widely in the classics and literature. He learned Sanskrit. He socialized with campus intellectuals—scientists, classicists, artists. But he knew almost nothing of the contemporary world, owned no radio, read no newspaper or current magazine. "To many of my friends," he wrote later, "my indifference to contemporary affairs seemed bizarre . . . I had no understanding of the relations of man to his society."

All that changed in the late 1930s, when he developed a "smoldering fury" about the treatment of Jews in Germany and a growing anger about the lingering Depression. Through his students, many of whom couldn't find jobs after graduation, he began to understand the impact of political and economic events on people's lives. He developed a need to participate in the life of the community.

But he had no framework of political conviction and hence no perspective. Like so many intellectual idealists of the time, he embraced the politics of the radical left, and contributed time and money to such groups as the Spanish Loyalists or American migrant workers; he often gave the money through communist-front groups. He joined political organizations aligned with communism. He fell in love with a troubled young woman named Jean Tatlock, who was always joining and leaving the Communist Party, and through her he met and mingled with many West Coast communists and their sympathizers. His brother Frank and Frank's wife, Jackie, were communists, and Robert himself clearly was one of those referred to as "fellow travelers."

Oppenheimer's marriage to Katherine Puening in 1940 further connected him to the worldwide web of communism. She was a serious-minded woman from a solid, conservative family who had had a disastrous previous marriage to a dashing romantic named Joe Dallet. A fervent communist, Dallet had lured Katherine into the party. She had soon rebelled against the dreary communist discipline and Dallet's worldwide pursuit of leftist causes, and had left Dallet in Paris. He later died at the Spanish front, and she returned to America, where she met and married Oppenheimer.

By then, according to Oppenheimer's account, his own ardor for leftist causes had given way to concerns about his country's fate in the wake of Pearl Harbor. He was recruited into the Manhattan Project, the highly secret national effort to develop an atomic bomb. He created and led a special scientific task force in Berkeley, working with such masterminds as Hans Bethe and Edward Teller. He suggested the establishment of a centralized laboratory at Los Alamos, New Mexico, and when it was established he was named its director. John McCloy, then a top official of the War Department, had said Oppenheimer "was the only American physicist fully qualified for the job."

As new laboratory buildings went up on the Los Alamos mesa, Oppenheimer recruited eight thousand workers, half of them scientists and technicians. He led his team through its arduous and dangerous tasks, past barrier after barrier, into and out of a multitude of dead-end experiments. It all culminated in the exciting and terrifying success at Alamogordo, where the first of the "absolute" weapons was detonated in July 1945.

Throughout this wartime period, Oppenheimer had become all too familiar with U.S. security. As a potential risk, he had been under constant scrutiny. The Los Alamos security officer, Colonel John Lansdale, interviewed him repeatedly and at length about previous connections with communists and communist causes. Oppenheimer had to accept the fact that he was under surveillance, his mail opened by security officials, his phones tapped. Although some officials harbored doubts about Oppenheimer throughout the war years, Lansdale developed a firm faith in his loyalty and discretion, and he put that faith on the line in supporting Oppenheimer whenever critics sought to dig up his past.

After Alamogordo, Oppenheimer went on to a kind of scientific stardom as the high priest of American nuclear physics. He received the prestigious Medal of Merit. In 1947 he was named director of the Institute for Advanced Studies in Princeton, an independent research group that served as the locus of study for such luminaries as Albert Einstein and George Kennan. As director, Oppenheimer reported to a board of trustees; the board's president was Lewis Strauss.

Lewis Lichtenstein Strauss (pronounced "Straws") had been a successful investment banker, a partner in the New York firm of Kuhn Loeb, and financial adviser to the Rockefellers. During the war he had served in the Navy Department, where he rose to the rank of rear admiral in the naval reserve and received the Legion of Merit with gold star. After the war he served four years as a member of the Atomic Energy

Commission (AEC), and proved a shrewd analyst of the new military realities. He advocated a crash program to develop the hydrogen bomb at a time when such thinking put him in the minority; and he successfully pressed for a long-range detection system that could warn of Soviet atomic and thermonuclear testing. He left the AEC in 1950, but in July 1953 Eisenhower appointed him to another term and named him chairman.

As chairman he became a source of controversy on the commission. He treated other commissioners dismissively, as if they could not be trusted with serious responsibility or official secrets. Stewart Alsop, spending an evening at the home of commissioner Henry Smythe, heard a series of woeful tales about Strauss's stewardship. "It's certainly true." Stewart wrote to Marty Sommers afterward, "that the bitterness against him since he took over has built up to a venomous point." To many who had known Strauss well, this was not surprising. There was something of the peacock in him. Short of stature, he dressed impeccably and walked with a strut. He seemed to have a constant need to dominate others, and in policy debates he was rigid and dogmatic. He emerged early in the postwar years as a leading advocate of government secrecy in matters of strategy and weapons. Thus, his views had come to clash with the Alsop brothers' belief that Americans should be kept informed on issues of national security.

For years the brothers had worked cordially with AEC officials in getting agency clearance for their sensitive *Saturday Evening Post* articles on nuclear warfare. But now, with Strauss at the helm, it became increasingly difficult. Joe lost his patience with Strauss one day after the new chairman had called him in for a chat. Arriving with hopes for a candid discussion on serious matters of nuclear policy, Joe found Strauss bent on focusing the conversation entirely on chitchat, punctuated with transparent flights of flattery about the brothers' reporting. After failing repeatedly to turn the discussion toward serious issues, Joe finally stood up in exasperation and terminated the conversation.

"Admiral," he said icily, "you have just wasted half an hour of my time." The story of Joe's rudeness gained wide currency throughout Washington and contributed to the chairman's growing enmity toward the Alsops.

The Oppenheimer affair began quietly enough, behind the closed doors of officialdom, just four days after Strauss became AEC chairman. On July 7, 1953, the commission initiated steps to remove certain classified documents from Oppenheimer's custody.

Then a former secretary to Congress's Atomic Energy Committee, William L. Borden, dredged up many of the old stories and suspicions about Oppenheimer's past affiliations and collected them in a letter to FBI Director J. Edgar Hoover. In the letter he accused Oppenheimer of being a loyalty risk and probable spy. Hoover forwarded the letter to pertinent security agencies, and to Strauss, who initiated a meeting with

President Eisenhower to discuss the matter. The president directed that "a blank wall be placed between Dr. Oppenheimer and any secret data," and that the AEC pursue proper investigative procedures.

On December 23, Strauss quietly suspended Oppenheimer's security clearance, and the AEC issued a harsh statement of charges. The next day, security officials arrived to remove all classified material from the scientist's possession, and by year's end Strauss had initiated an inquiry to be conducted in secret by a special three-man board. The board was composed of Gordon Gray, chancellor of the University of North Carolina and former secretary of the army; Thomas A. Morgan, former head of the Sperry Gyroscope Company; and Ward Evans, well-known chemist from Loyola University. For AEC counsel in the case, Strauss chose Roger Robb, a man aligned with the McCarthy movement and with radio commentator Fulton Lewis, Jr., whom the brothers later described as "McCarthy's chief journalistic incense-swinger." The inquiry proceeded day after day behind closed doors, and nothing of its deliberations reached the public.

Then in early April 1954 Joseph McCarthy delivered a radio address suggesting that his next target would be the country's leading physicists, who were responsible, he said, for a tragic eighteen-month delay in the development of the H-bomb. Curious as to what had prompted McCarthy to signal a move against the scientific community, Joe picked up the journalistic scent, and soon the brothers were on the story.

On April 13, they reported exclusively that the government had suspended Oppenheimer's security clearance and was conducting a secret inquiry into whether he was a security or loyalty risk. The long article, the lead story in the *Herald Tribune* that day, detailed the background of the hearings, the allegations against Oppenheimer, and the stunned reaction of the scientific community. The next day the brothers ran a column suggesting that, while Oppenheimer could anticipate a fair hearing from the Gray board, it would be a different matter if McCarthy applied his method of attack. They conceded that Oppenheimer had been naive in his early years and during the H-bomb debate. But somehow it did not seem likely that the United States was "ready to cast its greatest physicist into outer darkness, as punishment for the woolly headedness of a decade and a half ago."

The brothers were wrong. In early June the board recommended that Oppenheimer's security clearance be revoked. The problem, said the board's two-man majority of Gray and Morgan, was not loyalty. "We find no evidence of disloyalty," said the report. "Indeed, we have before us much responsible and positive evidence of the loyalty and love of country of the individual concerned." Nor was discretion a problem: "It must be said that Dr. Oppenheimer seems to have had a high degree of discretion reflecting an unusual ability to keep to himself vital secrets."

While the board found Oppenheimer to have been an "active fellow traveler" before the war, it also dismissed these past connections as unimportant. But the board concluded that Oppenheimer had "repeatedly exercised an arrogance of his own judgment with respect to the loyalty and reliability of other citizens to an extent which has frustrated and at times impeded the workings of the [security] system." This seemed to mean that he had continued to see and advise friends whom he knew to have highly suspicious communist backgrounds. These connections, said the board, suggested a "susceptibility to influence" when these friends solicited Oppenheimer's help in personnel or security matters. The board questioned whether Oppenheimer had been totally candid in his board appearances, and it concluded that Oppenheimer's 1949 opposition to the development of the hydrogen bomb had demonstrated a willingness to let personal convictions interfere with national security. This, they said, was "sufficiently disturbing" to raise doubts about whether his future participation in national-security decision-making "would be clearly consistent with the best interest of security."

Ward Evans, dissenting from the majority opinion, said that the board action would be "a black mark on the escutcheon of our country." He disputed the suggestion that Oppenheimer had hindered the development of the H-bomb, and said the physicist's testimony during cross-examination showed him to be "still naive but extremely honest." Oppenheimer seemed to be less of a security risk in 1954 than he had been when he was cleared by a Truman loyalty board shortly after the war. "His judgment was bad in some cases, and most excellent in others," wrote Evans, "but, in my estimation, it is better now than it was in 1947, and to damn him now and ruin his career and his service, I cannot do it."

The board sent its report to the full commission amid a whirlwind of controversy and debate. Nearly everyone accepted the sincerity and good faith of Gray and Morgan, but many questioned their conclusions. Particularly controversial was the idea that Oppenheimer's position on the H-bomb should become a security consideration. "The idea of 'enthusiastic support' of a government policy as a security criteria," declared the American Civil Liberties Union, "runs contrary to the whole democratic concept of a free society based on free thought."

The Alsop brothers lashed out at the Gray board on several counts. In a column they said the board had sacrificed the crucial need for a concerted national defense program on the altar of faulty security concerns. They accused the board of making this sacrifice "to satisfy the personal spite" of Strauss. They added: "What scientist, and indeed what ordinary sensible man, will wish to serve a government that is not content with unquestioned loyalty, perfect discretion and vast and unrepaid past services?"

The column shrouded the anger that seethed within Joe's moral consciousness. On June 2, he sent a two-sentence letter to Gray, whom the brothers had known well during his days as army secretary: "Since we have been friends, and since I intend to express my opinion to others, I must express it to you also. By a single foolish and ignoble act, you have cancelled the entire debt that this country owes you." The next day, on June 3, Joe called Gray to discuss the case, and the two carried on an amicable conversation. On June 4 Gray received Joe's letter. He was incredulous that a man of Joe's background and position would write such a letter, and incensed that he would then call and seek to carry on a normal telephone discussion. "In all candor," he wrote to Joe, "I think I must say that, had the letter arrived first, I would not have taken your call."

Gray said that Joe certainly was at liberty to consider him foolish. But he added, "I must caution you about the use of the word, 'ignoble,' as applied to the discharge of my duties, as I saw them in my own conscience and in my own heart." He noted that his dictionary defined the word as "not honorable; base; mean"—a definition he considered actionable. "You cannot fail to know the implications of these words," he wrote.

Joe wrote back, retreating from his personal attack but otherwise sticking to his guns. "You are entirely right—I should never have telephoned you after sending such a letter." He explained that it had been written in the heat of "shock and indignation." He had never intended to send the letter, because upon reflection he had seen that it questioned Gray's motives. "I suppose," he said, "I must have signed it unintentionally, in the middle of a batch of routine mail. I greatly regret the error."

It was a blatant lie, lacking all credibility. Joe's explanation seemed to be intended as a kind of mock apology, acknowledging the inexcusability of his arrogance without acknowledging his intentions in sending the letter. In two typewritten pages of polemic, Joe demonstrated that the fires of passion that had forged his previous letter still burned hot. He harbored no doubts about Gray's good motives, he said, and did not consider him "ignoble." But he felt that the atmosphere of the time and the country's security system had combined to entrap Gray "into doing an ignoble thing in the precise dictionary sense."

> And what of all those, the president of the United States and the secretary of defense among them, who share the criminal responsibility for leaving this country naked of any sufficient air defense? . . . When the time comes for us to pay for our nakedness—and it is coming now—are the president and Mr. Wilson to be debarred from public employment? I disagree with Robert Oppenheimer's stand on the hydrogen bomb, and I have disagreed with this administration's approach to the air defense problem. But I must point out that Robert Oppenheimer's motives were decidedly more admirable, and the results of the administration's folly are proving immeasurably more damaging.

Not surprisingly, the Washington gossip mill soon buzzed with discussion about Joe's intemperate letter to Gray. Three people mentioned it to Arthur Krock of *The New York Times* within a week's time. When Joe heard that Krock himself had repeated the story around town, he wrote a note to the *Times* man suggesting he had gotten the story wrong. Krock wrote back to say he had expressed himself on only one point: "To characterize any act of Gordon Gray as 'ignoble' seems to me both intemperate and unfair, particularly when it is made by one who knows Gray as you do." In reply Joe sought to draw a distinction between Gray himself, whom he described as having pure motives, and the board's action, which he called "a dishonor and disgrace to the United States."

On May 27, the Gray board's findings went to AEC general manager Kenneth Nichols, who two weeks later recommended to the commission that it accept the board's conclusions. On June 28, the commission voted four to one to rescind Oppenheimer's clearance. The next day the decision and the five commissioners' separate opinions were released to the press, and J. Robert Oppenheimer's career of government service ended in humiliation.

In fashioning the commission's rationale, Strauss dismissed the Gray board's concerns about the H-bomb debate; the scientist, he said, had a right to take whatever position he chose without fear of retribution. Strauss also made no attempt to refute the board's conclusion that Oppenheimer was loyal and discreet. He rested his case on what he called Oppenheimer's "substantial defects of character," his tendency toward "falsehood, evasion, and misrepresentation." To support his indictment, Strauss cited six examples of what he labeled false statements by Oppenheimer, some from as far back as 1943. To Oppenheimer supporters, most of these examples seemed petty and artificial; but one of them could not be easily dismissed even by the most fervent backers of the beleaguered physicist. That was the famous Chevalier affair.

Haakon Chevalier was a professor of romance languages at Berkeley, one of a group of communists and fellow travelers who had gained some notice in the Bay Area before the war, and a close friend of Robert Oppenheimer's. Shortly before the Oppenheimers' final move to Los Alamos in 1943, Chevalier visited their Berkeley home for farewells. In a private kitchen conversation, Chevalier told Oppenheimer that a friend named George Eltenton, a well-known West Coast communist, had spoken to him about getting technical information for transmittal to Soviet intelligence. Oppenheimer replied sharply that he wouldn't discuss such a thing, and the matter was dropped.

Later, Oppenheimer was to say that he took no further action on the matter because he felt Chevalier was merely an unwitting tool for Eltenton, and he did not wish to implicate his friend in what seemed like an innocent overture. That was the time, after all, when the Soviet Union was working in concert with the United States to destroy German

Nazism, and many American intellectuals saw no conflict between their loyalty to their country and their devotion to Soviet communism. Oppenheimer said he felt he had discharged his obligation to security by rejecting the overture so coldly.

It was a grievous error, and grievously was Oppenheimer to answer for it. The following summer at Los Alamos, Oppenheimer heard from Colonel Lansdale that security officials at Berkeley had become concerned about possible espionage activities of a leftist union called the Federation of Architects, Engineers, Chemists and Technicians. Knowing that Eltenton was a member of that union, Oppenheimer felt a need to warn security officials at Berkeley about him. But he also wanted to protect his friend Chevalier. When he was questioned about his warning by Boris Pash, chief security officer at the radiation laboratory at Berkeley, he spun out what he later called a "cock and bull story" about Soviet espionage, secret microfilm, and three unnamed persons who had been approached by Eltenton as part of a broad espionage operation. Two months later, when Oppenheimer was told firmly that he would have to supply names, his story collapsed, and he implicated Chevalier for the first time.

In judging this episode, AEC members noted that even after Chevalier had caused so much trouble for Oppenheimer, the physicist still didn't break off relations with his left-leaning friend. As late as 1953, when the Oppenheimers were in Paris, they lunched with Chevalier and his wife.

To those who followed the case closely, there was no doubt that the Chevalier affair had been the linchpin of Strauss's judgment against Oppenheimer. To many, it demonstrated at the least an almost hopeless political naiveté and faulty judgment. To others it was a serious lapse, but the result of an understandable desire to protect a friend while trying to satisfy the needs of security. Oppenheimer had, after all, stepped forward of his own volition to warn security officials about Eltenton. Even General Leslie Groves, head of the Manhattan Project, felt Oppenheimer's lapse represented merely the "typical American schoolboy attitude that there is something wicked about telling on a friend."

The debate over the AEC's Oppenheimer action raged for weeks, and the Alsops devoted numerous columns to the subject. But the column didn't afford a sufficient opportunity to lay bare the episode in all its drama and ramifications. Only a magazine article would suffice for such a challenge. They hoped to see such a piece published in pamphlet form also; officials at Houghton Mifflin expressed interest in the idea. But Marty Sommers rebuffed Stewart's suggestion for a piece in the *Saturday Evening Post*, which long had shown a kind of editorial solicitousness toward Strauss. Joe then called Jack Fischer at *Harper's*, a monthly magazine that reached a relatively small but highly literate audience. He proposed a tough exposé with the title of "We Accuse." Fischer expressed interest and asked for an outline.

Joe, fueled by passionate anger and his affection for Oppenheimer, quickly took over the project. Stewart tended to be more detached on the matter, more inclined to view the physicist as a flawed man who had, at least in part, brought this tragedy upon himself. Joe would have none of that, and Stewart, ever loyal to his brother, went along with Joe's pugilistic approach. Ignoring Fischer's request for an outline, Joe pushed forward to produce a finished article, and by August 5 the brothers had produced more than fifteen thousand words. In a cover letter to Russell Lynes at *Harper's*, Joe called the piece "the most important thing I have ever done" and "the most readable serious piece" he and Stewart had ever produced. The piece was a frontal attack on Strauss and the entire U.S. security system, written in a tone so accusatory as almost to invite a libel suit. It began:

> The title of this report is borrowed from Emile Zola, whose "J'Accuse" marked the turning point in the case of Captain Dreyfus. It is a proud title, for it is still the symbol of one of our era's rare triumphs of the liberal spirit over organized injustice. It is a title, indeed, that one must be presumptuous to borrow: and we only dare to do so because we too accuse.
>
> We accuse the Atomic Energy Commission in particular, and the American government in general, of a shocking miscarriage of justice in the case of Dr. J. Robert Oppenheimer.
>
> We accuse Oppenheimer's chief judge, the chairman of the Atomic Energy Commission, Admiral Lewis Strauss, and certain of Oppenheimer's accusers, of venting the bitterness of old disputes through the security system of this country.
>
> And we accuse the security system itself, as being subject to this kind of ugliness, and as inherently repugnant in its present standards and procedures to every high tradition of the American past.

The brothers dismissed all but one of Strauss's six examples of Oppenheimer's character defects, crediting only the Chevalier episode. Even on the Chevalier incident, they accused Strauss of distorting the facts in his report by suggesting that Oppenheimer's lies had intertwined his entire report to Boris Pash in Berkeley, and by ignoring the fact that Oppenheimer himself had come forward to voice his concerns about Eltenton. "Strauss left out the heart of the matter. He omitted every other explanatory and extenuating fact. . . . And so he achieved no mere caricature of the truth, but a gross and flagrant distortion."

The brothers noted that Oppenheimer's security status had been reviewed by the AEC seven years earlier, and that he had been cleared routinely, although the Chevalier affair had received thorough examination. In fact, the Alsops said, the most recent inquiry had not uncovered anything of significance that hadn't already come up in Oppenheimer's 1947 proceedings. And the AEC's most active member during that time was none other than Lewis Strauss. Strauss had not only voted in 1947 to grant Oppenheimer clearance for the most sensitive scientific post in the U.S. government; he later had nominated Oppenheimer to the directorship of the Institute of Advanced Study, which he served as board president. The "glaring contrast" between the Strauss of 1947 and the Strauss of 1954, said the brothers, posed a puzzle.

The answer to the puzzle, they suggested, could be found in Strauss's tendency toward self-importance. The Alsops resurrected an incident from years before, when Strauss and Oppenheimer, testifying together before a congressional committee, had disagreed over the issue of exporting radioactive isotopes to America's Western allies. Arguing in favor of distribution, Oppenheimer had annihilated Strauss's secrecy arguments; this had induced a visible rage in Lewis Strauss. Other issues also divided the two men, and Oppenheimer had brought to each of their disputes his tendency toward intellectual arrogance, thus further inflaming Strauss's silent enmity. It was impossible, said the brothers, "to avoid the conclusion that this petty, tangled, tragic business of the old friction and disagreement between Strauss and Oppenheimer contains one of the essential clues to the Oppenheimer case."

And Oppenheimer had other enemies who had testified before the Gray inquiry. During the bitter 1949 debate over whether to proceed with a major U.S. hydrogen-bomb project, Oppenheimer's opposition had stirred the undying enmity of Dr. Edward Teller and other H-bomb advocates. Later, in pressing for the air defense system advocated in the Lincoln Project report, Oppenheimer had drawn the ire of powerful air force generals bent on subordinating air defense to their plans for a greater bomber force. Even before the Gray inquiry, the brothers wrote, top air force generals had initiated a campaign to discredit Oppenheimer, and the Gray board became a convenient extension of this anti-Oppenheimer campaign.

So there it was—a dreary Washington tale of sinister motives and petty prejudices coming together to destroy the career of a brilliant but controversial public servant. As portrayed in the piece, Lewis Strauss was not merely mistaken or wrongheaded or stupid; he had willfully orchestrated the professional demise of a man he had silently despised for years. He could get away with it because of his dominance of the commission he chaired; the loaded nature of the country's security apparatus; help from Oppenheimer's fervent enemies; and Oppenheimer's own flaws and past mistakes.

When Lynes and his colleagues at *Harper's* read the Alsops' attack, they were taken aback. Clearly, it represented brilliant reporting and compelling writing. But they had not expected a finished piece, only an outline, and now they had in hand something a little too incendiary. In a letter to Joe, Lynes expressed concern about the lead. "It seemed to us here," he said, "that your attack on the AEC, the government, Admiral Strauss, and certain other accusers should not sound so extreme at the outset as to arouse a defensive reaction on the part of the fair-minded reader."

Others agreed. Felix Frankfurter, after reading the manuscript, advised Joe to "remove all ingredients which, without weakening the strong intrinsic meat, may be a little too much for tender stomachs." Archibald MacLeish reported that he had read the entire manuscript aloud to friends during a recent evening and that they all had felt the piece had a mean-spirited quality. "You would have squirmed if you had been there," he wrote.

Joe tried to respond to these suggestions, but his heart wasn't in it. Seldom had his natural combativeness and political passion been more aroused, and now he wanted to go for the kill. When *Harper's* associate editor Eric Larrabee sent down a memo containing forty suggested changes, Joe rejected eighteen of them. He also stood firm on the lead, forcing the editors in New York to back down.

But then the lawyers weighed in. Morris Ernst, a well-known First Amendment specialist hired by *Harper's*, pronounced the piece libelous. The problem, he said, was that the article attributed to Strauss motives of personal animus in a quasi-judicial matter, and it was sprinkled with phrases, words, and references that added up to a suggestion of malice. That led to further haggling, and to displays of impatience from Joe. He won many of the battles over wording.

Shortly before publication, Lynes informed Joe that the magazine had sent a copy of the manuscript to Strauss and had decided upon a fee of $1,000 for the piece. "I know this isn't a large sum in your terms but it is a very considerable one in terms of what *Harper's* usually pays," said Lynes. Resorting to the intemperate eloquence he frequently displayed in angrily written letters, Joe accused Lynes of violating their understanding on when the piece could be sent to Strauss, and declared that he and Stewart had made "enormously heavy sacrifices, of time and trouble and money," to publish in *Harper's*. Hence, he considered the proffered sum "grossly inadequate." Given all the trouble and expense, he said, he felt $2,000 was "the very minimum that can be regarded as fair, even after the fullest allowance has been made for *Harper's* usual price scale."

The matter of money was set aside, however, when a lawyer named John Cahill appeared at Harper's to announce that he represented Lewis Strauss and wanted to make it clear he considered the Alsop article libelous on its face. The piece, said Cahill, flatly accused Strauss of "a grave and flagrant distortion of the truth" in dealing with the Chevalier matter. Strauss's lawyer threw down a direct challenge to three top Harper's editors. "If I were in your position I would want to know how it is regarded, and I'd like to ask what your views on the matter are," he said.

Lynes suggested that the article didn't really accuse Strauss of distorting the truth, it merely stated that he had been misleading.

"That is actionable in my opinion and directly so," replied Cahill, "and I think the imputation is of injurious suppression of testimony and is a direct charge of it. It is unfounded, unwarranted and unjustified on the facts related."

Cass Canfield, chairman of Harper and Brothers, noted that Strauss had been offered a chance to reply.

"The answers never catch up," Cahill shot back. He objected that there would be no opportunity to run the reply in the same issue that contained the Alsop article.

"But we're printing something saying that we have offered the admiral space to comment in the following number," said Canfield. "This will be eagerly awaited, believe me."

"I don't think that we are going to reply," said Cahill. "We may take other steps."

"We have bent over backwards to be fair," replied Canfield. "It is certainly not our practice to show a piece before it comes out."

The exchange continued for some minutes until Cahill asked whether there was any possibility the article could be altered before going to press. Lynes hurried out to check and returned with the expected response—the October issue already was off the press and in the bindery. Cahill picked up his hat and briefcase and left.

Lynes immediately wrote Joe a letter recounting the exchange and noting that the editors had never acknowledged any need to change the article, even if it had been possible. He pointedly added that Cahill seemed obsessed with the passage in which the brothers went so far as to "accuse" Strauss of "a gross and flagrant distortion of the truth." It was one of those passages, said Lynes, that Joe had been warned about as a source of possible danger. But, he added, it "was one you felt strongly should be kept in the article, and we think it is only fair to point this out to you at this juncture." He added coldly that if he had not sent the manuscript to Strauss when he did, the admiral would not have had the chance to reply in the next issue and hence would have had an even stronger case that *Harper's* had been unfair. Five days later, responding by letter to Joe's complaint on pay, Lynes suggested that the magazine had just about run out of patience. "We may be mistaken but we believe that no other magazine would have taken on 'We Accuse' and stayed with it, and prayed over it as we have," he wrote. "I enclose our check for $1,000. I wish it were $5,000."

There remained the problem of publishing the piece in book form. After reading the manuscript, Houghton Mifflin opted out, but Simon and Schuster embraced the venture. The brothers wrote an introduction, added a chapter providing further background on the controversy, and included an appendix containing many of the official documents of the case. It hit the bookstores within weeks of the *Harper's* article.

Meanwhile, the response to the original *Harper's* piece was immediate and powerful. Groucho Marx, who had never met Joe, wrote to pronounce it "magnificent," and added, "Since I am one of the remaining relics who still sports a hat, this gives me an opportunity to doff it and make a long courtly bow in your direction." Thurman Arnold, a prominent Washington lawyer, called the piece "one of the most moving and best pieces of writing I have ever seen."

The article also generated criticism. "My main objection to the Alsop piece is its shrill tone," wrote management consultant Peter Drucker in a letter to *Harper's*. "I deplore that the Alsops in treatment of this vital issue have chosen to make a spy thriller out of it."

Strauss and the AEC moved quickly to debunk the Alsop article. A commission lawyer named C. A. Rolander, Jr., prepared a document purporting to refute the central points of the Alsop thesis, and the AEC distributed the rebuttal to hundreds of editors and correspondents. *The New York Times* reported that it was the first time in recent memory that a government agency involved in a controversy had sent out statements of its official views in an attempt to influence how a book was received and reviewed.

The brothers had the last word, though, when *U.S. News & World Report*, a weekly newsmagazine with a conservative bent, published at year's end a seventeen-page spread exploring forty-three major points of dispute between the Alsops and Rolander. On each point, the magazine gave the brothers a final opportunity to refute the Rolander contentions, and the Alsops pummeled the AEC official with hearty rebuttals. By this time the pamphlet version of "We Accuse" had reached bookstores around the country, and the brothers had received a second wave of public attention.

The controversy gained new force with the publication of yet another book, a provocative little volume called *The Hydrogen Bomb*, by Time-Life's Washington bureau chief, James Shepley, and the bureau's military writer, Clay Blair, Jr. Delving into the debates over the H-bomb in the late 1940s, the authors exposed unnecessary delays in the weapon's construction, which they attributed to the opposition of scientists struggling with moral questions surrounding their "sin of Alamogordo." As a result, wrote the *Time* reporters, the United States narrowly avoided losing its nuclear superiority—the country's basic check on Soviet aggression. It was a tale of confusion, indecision, and bad judgment surrounding one of the crucial national-security decisions of the postwar era.

The book dredged up the long feud between Oppenheimer and the brilliant but cantankerous Edward Teller, author of the nuclear innovation that had made development of the H-bomb possible. Even during the war, Teller had argued strenuously that scientists at Los Alamos should abandon efforts to build an atomic bomb and concentrate instead on the hydrogen weapon; his stubbornness on the issue had rendered him useless in the Manhattan Project's main enterprise. After the war, he emerged as one of the country's leading H-bomb advocates, pressing for a concerted national effort on the order of the Manhattan

Project. In both instances, he found himself opposing Oppenheimer, who consistently opposed H-bomb development prior to Truman's fateful 1950 decision to proceed with that project. Indeed, Oppenheimer had been chairman of the AEC general advisory committee when it recommended unanimously against a crash program to develop the H-bomb.

The Shepley-Blair book clearly was derived from Teller's views of events, with considerable assistance from Teller's close AEC ally on the H-bomb controversy, Lewis Strauss. It wasn't surprising that the authors depicted Oppenheimer as a fuzzy-headed moralist who lacked the vision and toughness of mind to see a need for the H-bomb—or that Teller and Strauss were shown as heroes struggling against the zeitgeist to push the country toward a policy that would only later be recognized as necessary.

In their column, the Alsops attacked the book as wrongheaded and full of distortions. They explored at length Oppenheimer's opposition to the H-bomb, and concluded that he had had moral objections, yes, but that these had weighed less heavily than technical and strategic considerations. Until Teller's 1950 "brilliant invention" making possible a large H-bomb with a lithium hydride core, it had appeared that a hydrogen bomb would require so much fissionable raw stuff that it might not be an economical weapon at all. Thus it had made more sense to build more A-bombs. Eventually, the initial H-bomb concept gave way to Teller's brilliant invention and Truman's decision, and Oppenheimer had quickly embraced the new weapon.

Oppenheimer had also believed, said the brothers, that Pentagon strategists relied too heavily on the country's stock of absolute weapons, to the detriment of a balanced defense, particularly an air defense system. He had feared, as the Alsops had feared, that the military reliance on nuclear weaponry would constitute a retreat to complacency.

The controversy raged on for weeks in reviews, editorials, columns, and news stories. At *The Washington Post*, the Shepley-Blair book was reviewed by the paper's president and publisher, Philip L. Graham, who called the AEC's action on Oppenheimer "a major mistake of our time . . . which dealt our true national security a major blow." But *Time*, which by now had abandoned its respectful regard for the Alsops, struck hard. The magazine rushed to the defense of Shepley and Blair, and ridiculed the Alsops' interpretation of the Oppenheimer episode, particularly their suggestion that Strauss's motivation was long-hidden personal animus against Oppenheimer. The article added, "The Alsopian myth that the hydrogen-bomb controversy is part of an anti-science, anti-intellectual crusade could do profound damage in this country." Beneath a photo of an arrogant-looking Joe, *Time* affixed the words: "Columnist Joseph Alsop: Menacing mythology." Joe dashed off an angry letter responding to the piece, but *Time* declined to run it. The *Herald*

Tribune syndicate hurriedly sent copies of the article and Joe's response to subscribing newspapers, to blunt any adverse impact among editors.

THE OPPENHEIMER AFFAIR represented the kind of issue the Alsop brothers liked best—a powerfully symbolic and nationally significant controversy given to interpretation in terms of good and evil. Joe particularly thrived on outrage, and few episodes throughout his career generated more outrage in his political consciousness than the fate of his friend Oppenheimer. Joe's strong sense of personal loyalty, and of the need to muster courage to stand by one's friends, propelled him forward.

The affair crystallized all the anger and disgust the brothers had felt throughout the McCarthy period. To Joe particularly, it was unconscionable that a man could be adjudged both loyal and discreet and still be hounded from public service as a security risk. It was for precisely such controversies as this—and the moral imperatives they generated—that Joe had invented the column in the first place, and fashioned his life as a realistic but righteous journalist.

But the episode also exposed a growing weakness in Joe's approach to his craft. It wasn't enough for him merely to lay bare the tragedy of Robert Oppenheimer, to fashion a compelling account of an injustice wrought upon an individual through the grinding processes of an impersonal governmental system. Stewart was more inclined to tell the story dispassionately, to take more serious note of Oppenheimer's personal flaws and avoid the imputation of base motives on the part of his antagonists. But for Joe, who set the tone for the partnership, there had to be villains—men of evil motive and intent. Otherwise the story wouldn't make sense. The main villain here, of course, was Lewis Strauss. The portrayal of Strauss's motives in the *Harper's* piece clearly was libelous, no less so for the AEC chairman's decision not to pursue the matter in court. More important, that portrayal left the brothers vulnerable, as controversy swirled around them in the wake of the article.

Indeed, the very idea that the Oppenheimer case should be equated with the Dreyfus affair contributed to the columnists' reputation for journalistic hyperbole. As *Time* pointed out, Dreyfus was legally lynched by perjured and forged testimony sustained by "a group of reactionary pinheads." By contrast, the procedures of the Gray board were scrupulously fair, and Gray himself—Oppenheimer's chief judge—was one of the country's most respected academics. "There is no dirtier thing that could be said of Lewis Strauss," wrote *Time*, "than that he set up a Dreyfus case; that for personal motives of the most picayune sort he sought the ruin of a man to whom the country owes so much."

It was unfortunate that the brothers' unstinting defense of Oppenheimer and their compelling critique of the country's security system ended up so flawed and vulnerable to counterattack. The fault rested with Joe, who insisted on high dudgeon and maximum pugnacity. Not even his closest friends could bring him to greater restraint or temperance of tone. Joe's outrage prevailed, as it would with increasing frequency as his journalistic power and influence grew.

McCARTHY'S DECLINE

Crossing the Line
of Journalistic Propriety

IT ISN'T UNCOMMON in the reporter's trade for a big story to begin with a small tip. So it was that Joe Alsop happened upon a big story in the early weeks of 1954. The tipster was a White House staffer who revealed that the army had produced a document revealing the persistent efforts of Senator Joseph McCarthy and his chief lieutenant, Roy Cohn, to bully the army into giving special treatment to a young draftee named David Schine. Perhaps, suggested the White House source, Joe could find out more by talking to army counsel John G. Adams.

Joe went to Adams, who showed him a remarkable fifteen-thousand-word document. Consisting of a series of Adams memoranda describing encounters with McCarthy and Cohn, the document rendered an unsavory portrait of two men abusing their senatorial positions and seeking to intimidate the army in Schine's behalf. Adams would not give Joe a copy of the report, but allowed him to read it.

Joe knew he had stumbled onto what likely would become the endgame in the protracted political struggle between the Republican senator from Wisconsin and the Republican president. Joe pleaded with Adams to let him write the story. The army official demurred, but discussed the matter freely, providing extensive details not included in the report. Joe learned more from Lucius Clay, his old friend from postwar Germany, and also an intimate adviser to Eisenhower. He couldn't write the story; all the information in his possession had been given to him off the record. But he was thoroughly briefed for the inevitable day when the outlines of the story would seep out.

The McCarthy-Eisenhower endgame began in the fall of 1953, when McCarthy interrupted his Caribbean honeymoon in order to open up a new battlefront in his four-year struggle against government subversives. He had fresh information, he declared, of communist infiltration into the Army Signal Corps Center at Fort Monmouth, New Jersey, and his Permanent Investigations subcommittee was on the case. Calling a procession of Army officers before the committee, McCarthy badgered and bullied them, making headlines in the process.

Over in the White House, the McCarthy spectacle raised serious political concerns. When Eisenhower had taken office, his aim had been to neutralize McCarthy—and preserve Republican unity—by demonstrating enough ardor of his own on the communists-in-government issue to keep the maverick senator at bay. Besides, some administration strategists had considered the issue an effective weapon against Democrats for the forthcoming 1954 election.

Attorney General Herbert Brownell embraced elements of the McCarthy rhetoric. He warned that members of the Communist Party had become "a greater menace now than at any time," and praised government efforts to root out subversives. In late 1953, he announced the firing of some 2,200 "security risks." He had caused a stir by suggesting that President Truman had deliberately fostered the career of a communist Treasury official named Harry Dexter White. Though angry, the brothers held their fire as the administration sought to co-opt the McCarthy issue. But when the senator showed signs of taking on the administration, they couldn't resist blaming Eisenhower for his own predicament.

"It is clear by now that to underestimate McCarthy is folly, as the administration strategists who believed they could undercut him by 'fighting fire with fire' must surely have discovered," Stewart wrote on November 27, 1953. "It must also be clear to all but the most fatuous that Eisenhower and McCarthy are indeed in opposite corners, and that a clash . . . is now inevitable."

In early 1954, top White House officials were expressing fears that McCarthy's ultimate target was Ike himself. This new prospect, Stewart informed Marty Sommers, "is by now perfectly obvious to the key men around Ike," including Cabot Lodge and Lucius Clay. This was evident, Stewart added, in McCarthy's new and persistent attacks on army officers. "Who is the most distinguished army officer in the United States?" Stewart asked rhetorically. There was evidence, he said, that McCarthy was threatening Eisenhower with a game of political blackmail.

Meanwhile, the brothers had been accumulating information on the immediate postwar period in occupied Germany, when Eisenhower was supreme commander and there occurred what Stewart called "the most serious infiltration of communists in the American government." From

Nicolas Nabokov, a young political officer on the occupation staff, Joe had learned years earlier of this infiltration. Now, pursuing the story, he pieced together a picture of a communist fifth column that had controlled financial and manpower policy throughout the Eisenhower command, had fostered the communist takeover of some major West German newspapers, and had almost handed control of the German labor unions to the communists.

Joe believed that McCarthy was simply waiting for the opportune moment, following the inevitable intraparty clash with the president, to spring this trap on Eisenhower. McCarthy, Stewart said in his letter to Sommers, "considers an 'investigation' of this period his big stick, his ultimate sanction against Eisenhower."

But it wasn't clear to the brothers that the president's men knew of this political danger. Joe decided to alert them. Through a young man named Charles Willis, he sought a session with White House chief of staff Sherman Adams, the former New Hampshire governor known for his frosty demeanor and abrupt manners. The interview, he emphasized, was not for a story but rather on a matter of personal privilege.

On the cold morning of February 19, Joe marched into Adams's West Wing office, sat down, and produced a pad of paper, which he placed on his knee. He wasn't there to solicit information, he stated, but rather to offer some of a rather serious nature. Reading from his notepad, he detailed all he knew of the communist successes in postwar Germany, then handed the notes to Adams.

"Why do you think I need to know this, Mr. Alsop?" the chief of staff asked after staring at the notes.

Joe outlined the brothers' perception of the political situation, and their suspicion that if McCarthy succeeded in his anti-army crusade his next target would be Eisenhower himself. They were convinced, said Joe, that Eisenhower could reduce McCarthy to political insignificance by standing firm and fighting on the army issue. The brothers were considering publishing the information they had, said Joe, in an effort at political inoculation, since a journalistic revelation would be less dramatic and damaging than a McCarthy attack and a major committee investigation. But, before going with the story, the brothers wanted to know whether the administration intended to fight McCarthy.

"Alsop, we'll fight," said Adams.

"Well, that was all I came to find out, Governor," replied Joe. "Leaving my notes with you, I have forgotten the conversation already."

There was no immediate evidence that Joe's West Wing gambit had any significant impact on the course of events. Indeed, White House actions immediately following Joe's visit left a distinct impression that Eisenhower feared McCarthy far more than the senator had any reason to fear the president. First came the capitulation of Secretary of the Army Robert Stevens, a decorated veteran of both world wars, who had headed a New Jersey textile concern before being tapped by Eisenhower to head the army. Stevens had sought administration support in his effort to resist the indiscriminate subpoenas McCarthy had been serving on army brass in his relentless inquiries—but administration officials urged Stevens to strike a deal with the senator. The eventual deal, worked out in a closed-door session among Stevens and three hard-line committee Republicans, was that McCarthy could subpoena anyone he wished as long as he promised to be polite. For caving in so cravenly, Stevens was pilloried in the press and ridiculed by anti-McCarthyites throughout Washington.

"The worst of the damage," the Alsops wrote shortly afterward, "is irreparable." A week later, they blamed "tin-horn politicians" among congressional Republicans and in the administration for pressuring Eisenhower to appease McCarthy.

Then, prior to a presidential news conference scheduled for March 3, rumors ricocheted around Washington that the president had had enough of McCarthy's assaults on the army and would take the offensive. A record 256 reporters showed up for the expected fireworks, but the president's comments turned out to be mild; he didn't even refer to McCarthy by name. Joe Alsop, who attended the news conference with a sense of anticipation, was disgusted.

"Why, the yellow son of a bitch!" he said under his breath to the *Chicago Tribune*'s Willard Edwards, a leading pro-McCarthy newsman.

But the Eisenhower counterattack actually was in the planning phase, and the ultimate weapon was army counsel John G. Adams's secret document, which had been prepared at the instigation of the White House chief of staff. The John Adams memorandum spun what could only be described as a sordid tale of political intimidation and blackmail. Roy Cohn, McCarthy's committee counsel, was a brilliant lawyer who had received his law degree from Columbia at the age of nineteen. The son of a prominent New York judge, he had developed an early passion for issues of internal security and had joined the McCarthy team in January 1953 at the age of twenty-five. Intense, ambitious, arrogant, Cohn immediately set about the task of elevating McCarthy to ever greater heights of power and influence. *Time* magazine said he showed "contempt for all but the top boss."

Cohn's closest friend was a young man named David Schine, son of a wealthy hotel magnate. An excellent student at Andover and Harvard, Schine now spent most of his time collecting fancy cars, hanging out in nightclubs, and chasing movie stars. In early 1953, Cohn persuaded McCarthy to give Schine a job on the subcommittee.

When Schine received his draft notice, Cohn and McCarthy sought to secure an army commission for him. When that failed, they pressured top army brass to give him special privileges, such as exemptions from guard duty and tough training exercises. Cohn's pressure tactics became more and more blatant, and his behavior toward army counsel Adams more and more obnoxious. Taken aback, administration officials checked into the Cohn-Schine relationship and concluded that the wealthy Schine had been supplementing Cohn's income.

All this was detailed in the Adams memorandum, and in March the administration finally decided it was time to use it. On March 10, Defense Secretary Charles Wilson revealed the report's existence to McCarthy, and threatened to make it public unless the senator fired Cohn. McCarthy refused, and Wilson had the report sent to members of McCarthy's subcommittee and of the Armed Services Committee. Within twenty-four hours, it hit the newspapers.

It caused an immediate stir. *The New York Times* published the report verbatim and announced in a front-page headline: ARMY CHARGES McCARTHY AND COHN THREATENED IT IN TRYING TO OBTAIN PREFERRED TREATMENT FOR SCHINE. United Press called the report "sensational" and said it hit the Senate "like a bombshell."

Joe Alsop noticed something funny about the report. It ran to merely thirty-four pages, about one-third the length of the document he had read in Adams's office several weeks before. Many of the most damaging passages now were missing. That called for a column. Under the headline "The Tale Half Told," the brothers reported on March 15 that the full report had been "censored" by Assistant Secretary of Defense Fred Seaton, and they filled in the gaps.

They wrote that the original document was studded with "disgusting obscenities" that characterized Cohn's dealings with army personnel. The final version hinted at this behavior, but its "naked reality" was not captured. "The unbounded arrogance, the inflated egotism, the Nazi-like sense of power that Cohn displayed, was, of course, derived from his position as McCarthy's chief counsel."

The brothers also noted that the original report went into much more detail on the unusual relationship between Cohn and McCarthy. When alone with Adams, McCarthy had denigrated Cohn and insisted that he sought no special treatment for Schine. But the senator remained silent when Cohn would berate Adams on the matter in McCarthy's presence, and sometimes even added his voice to Cohn's complaints. The implication, said the brothers, was that Cohn possessed a peculiar power over McCarthy. The original document, they reported, quoted McCarthy as telling Adams that he would like to get rid of Cohn but couldn't for unspecified reasons.

The brothers revealed that a leading member of the McCarthyite press, acting as a mediator between the senator and the army, actually had promised top officers that McCarthy would call off the investigation if Schine could have a soft New York assignment.

Soon after the column was published, Joe found himself once again at the center of the storm. He was called as a witness before McCarthy's subcommittee, after Army Secretary Stevens was forced under oath to reveal that Alsop had seen the Adams report before its release. McCarthy even suggested, in grilling Stevens on April 22, that Joe had helped prepare the report. On May 7, Joe was cast in the uncomfortable position of having a hostile Senate committee interrogate him about his dealings with a highly placed source.

Because Stevens and Adams already had revealed Joe's involvement, he didn't feel totally bound by newspaper etiquette on protecting sources. "As a newsman, I don't feel I could go at very great length into my discussions with people as a newspaperman," Joe told the committee, "but I feel I can tell you the things which have been brought out in the testimony." Responding to questions, he sketched the outlines of his dealings with Adams, revealing that he had repeatedly urged the army counsel to release him from his commitment of confidentiality. But when the committee's assistant counsel, Thomas Prewitt, asked if Adams had revealed the existence of monitored telephone calls, Joe quickly realized he was caught in the middle of a political cat-and-mouse game. "I don't feel that I can go on about Mr. Adams's conversation with me as a newspaperman," he said.

Joe took pains, though, to clear up the question of whether he had been involved in preparing the Adams report. "I not only had no part in its preparation; I did not know it was being prepared," he said. At that point, Roy Cohn took over the questioning.

The subcommittee counsel was particularly interested in the passage in the brothers' March 15 column stating that Cohn was financially beholden to Schine. "I assume," said Cohn, "that that is information you gathered from these memoranda or these data."

"I heard that from another source, if I recollect correctly," Joe replied.

"That didn't come from Mr. Adams?" Cohn asked.

"No."

Cohn pressed him: "It didn't come from an examination, certainly, of the written material which he showed you?"

"No. I heard that from another source, I think," Joe repeated. "I am not quite sure, you know. After all, you read—"

"Do you usually print things like that unless you are pretty sure of your source?" Cohn asked.

In fact, Joe was wrong. He had learned of the Cohn-Schine financial relationship from the Adams report, not from another source. And his error posed a danger. The hearing he had participated in was part of a high-stakes political clash in which careers were likely to be destroyed. McCarthy and Cohn would not have hesitated to impugn Joe's testimony if it could have helped their cause. That became clear to Joe when he heard from inside sources that the committee was considering a move to recall him for further testimony. An allegation of perjury was entirely possible.

At the urging of Douglas Hamilton, the *Herald Tribune*'s noted First Amendment lawyer, Joe hurriedly wrote a letter of clarification to Prewitt. His memory during the Cohn exchange had been "extremely foggy," he said, adding that his job required that he deal with so many facts that he could not carry in his head the history of all the statements in all the columns he had written. Joe added:

> Because of Mr. Cohn's questions, I later searched my memory at great length and with the utmost care. . . . The conviction grew upon me that the statement in my column that interested Mr. Cohn did not come primarily from other sources, but was based upon my reading of the Adams memoranda. . . . I have now subjected the result of this further search of my memory to an independent check, and I find that I am correct. The indication that I mentioned was in fact in the documents prepared by Mr. Adams, and must have been seen by me therein.

The letter seemed to have the desired effect; Joe was not called back to testify. And, though he heard from Hamilton that Cohn intended to sue him for libel, no lawsuit was ever filed.

The acrimonious Army-McCarthy Hearings in the spring of 1954 may have marked the high-water mark of the senator's temptestuous career—but they also destroyed that career with dramatic suddenness. Always seeking leverage through accusation, McCarthy impugned the loyalty of a young colleague of the Army's chief counsel at the hearings. The counsel, Joseph Welch, rebuked him painfully: "Have you no sense of decency, sir, at long last?" In the time it took Welch to utter those words, McCarthy's ascendancy collapsed. And the revelations about his abuse of office hastened his decline.

Soon the senator himself became the subject of a Senate investigation. By year's end he was censured by his peers, reduced to political insignificance, and left behind, as the country moved beyond the era that would bear his name. The brothers rejoiced—and harbored to the end of their days a fond conviction that Joe's visit to Sherman Adams had played a part in the beginning of the end of Joseph McCarthy.

21

THE MID-FIFTIES

Washington and the West's
Far-Flung Battlements

As THE COUNTRY moved into the post-McCarthy period, the Alsops' reputation grew. The column now ran in nearly 190 papers, and the trickle of cancellations that had bedeviled the brothers through the McCarthy years ceased. Bill Weeks of the *Herald Trib* syndicate was optimistic. "I see no reason why the expansion should not continue," he wrote Joe in August 1955. "Certainly the Alsop column is the best blend of hard news and good writing available to newspapers."

The brothers' name was becoming a household word among informed citizens across the nation. They even made the *New York Times* crossword puzzle as the clue for a six-letter word in 32 across: "Writers Joseph and Stewart." Their well-known gloom would provide grist for a *New Yorker* cartoon: Amid New Year's Eve revelry at a bar, one patron sits on a stool and frowns glumly into his drink. Another patron assaults the man's gloom. "Just who do you think you are, Mac?" he scolds. "One of the Alsops or something?" Further recognition came from the "We Accuse!" article on the Oppenheimer case, which won a Benjamin Franklin Magazine Award and the New York Newspaper Guild Civil Liberties Award. They also won their third Overseas Press Club award, for "best consistent reporting from abroad," in 1954.

The Alsop brood on Springland Lane was expanding into ever new pursuits. Joe was about ten in the mid-1950s, Ian eight, Fuff seven. And the fourth child, Stewart Jr., was three. Young Joe, a student at the fashionable St. Albans School, was developing a reputation as a kind of scientific wizard. He had a basement hobby shop filled with chemicals and electronic equipment. Once, he hooked up a private telephone line that snaked from his bedroom down through the sewers of northwestern Washington to the home of a friend. He later would develop enough expertise to plant an electronic bug in his sister's bedroom.

At one point young Joe got the idea of enlisting some friends, along with Ian and Fuff, in the task of building a bomb shelter below the house. When he asked his father if he could do some digging on the hill, Stewart replied distractedly that it would be fine. He had no idea of his son's ingenuity.

Joe rigged up a "double-bucket system" that allowed the young crew to transport dirt down the hill on a wire. When the bucket reached the bottom of the hill, it would catch on a board, tip, and empty. When the next bucket came down filled with dirt, its weight would propel the empty one back up. Before long the crew had created a hole nearly ten feet deep and was preparing to dig horizontally to make a tunnel. Then Stewart happened upon the scene.

"Oh, my God," he exclaimed, and put a stop to the enterprise.

The children were on their own much of the time, and established their own rules for getting along with one another in a kind of *Lord of the Flies* manner, as Elizabeth remembers it. They did not eat dinner with their parents, but were served in a small "children's dining room" off the kitchen. Most nights they were put to bed by the nanny. "We were raised at a time when children were seen and not heard," recalled Stewart Jr. years later.

When the parents were out for the evening, as they so often were, the children would conspire to manipulate the household help to get extra perks and privileges. One nanny, a woman named Jessie Mae Jefferson Jackson, liked to step out with her friends while the parents were away. The children offered her a deal. They would not tattle about her evening absences if she would permit them to watch ladies' wrestling and other proscribed television programs.

During the week at Springland Lane, Stewart's routine seldom intersected with that of his children. When they came home from school or afternoon activities, their father was likely to be interviewing a source in the living room, playing tennis with friends, preparing to host a dinner party, or getting ready to go out. He showed little interest in their school marks except to express disapproval when their grades weren't as good as he thought they should be.

During weekends at Polecat Park it was different. There, Stewart connected with the children in ways he hardly ever did in town. An avid gun owner, he taught the children to shoot; sometimes he nailed a paper plate to a tree for target practice with a .22-caliber rifle. He also taught them skeet shooting with a shotgun; years later Elizabeth could still remember vividly his strong voice issuing the command to release the skeet: "Pull!" Occasionally he took the children fly-fishing in nearby streams; upon their return with the catch he insisted the children clean their own fish. And he coached them in the rudiments of tennis. A believer in playing an aggressive game, he insisted they learn to charge the net.

On the ride back to town the family would play word games or engage in quizzes on historical and geographical facts: "What's the capital of Yugoslavia?" "What year was the Spanish-American War?" Often they would stop at a favorite roadside diner for the evening meal before cruising into Washington, and each of the children would drop a coin into the little jukebox at their booth.

Despite Stewart's aloofness and inclination to delegate child-rearing duties to Tish, he was a large presence in the family. He represented high standards of behavior and instilled, through example, a sense of fairness and integrity. The children found amusement in his penetrating humor, flowing recitations from English literature, and penchant for poking fun at himself. They laughed when he would notice he was gaining weight and issue a lament by quoting Shakespeare with theatrical flair: "Oh, that this too, too solid flesh would melt, thaw and resolve itself into a dew."

Tish worked hard to compensate for Stewart's aloofness by providing the children with plenty of attention and love. At intermittent times, however, she would retreat to her room, sometimes for days, and let family affairs run themselves while she succumbed to the escape of alcohol. Tish seldom drank socially, and sometimes months or even years would go by without her drinking problem showing itself. But eventually it would return, and its specter was never far beneath the surface of family affairs.

Relatives and friends speculated that Tish's problem stemmed from insecurities developed when she arrived in America as a young wife and was thrust into the Alsops' fast-lane existence. Some attributed it to Stewart's marital aloofness, which had marked their marriage. The children seldom saw displays of affection between their parents; looking back on his childhood, young Stewart could recall seeing them kiss only once.

The elder Stewart seemed simply bewildered by Tish's drinking binges. Returning home from work, he would ask the children where their mother was, and if the answer was "upstairs" he would know it had started again. He would climb the stairs to see for himself, then return downstairs, go to his study, and call his host for the evening's social event. "I'm sorry that Tish won't be able to make it tonight," the children would hear him say. "She is feeling a bit under the weather. But I will be there."

The children were mystified. No one explained the problem to them, and they thought their mother suffered from some strange disease. Later they would suspect a mental disorder or perhaps depression. Not until they were practically adults would they be told that their mother was an alcoholic. Their father would be shocked to learn that no one had ever told them.

Uncle Joe loved his niece and nephews and worried about them. Partly this was an expression of Joe's preoccupation with symbols of status and class. He didn't think Stewart's children were turned out smartly enough; they didn't wear clothes that were properly distinctive.

"Darling," he would say to Tish, half in jest, "why are you bringing up the children like little savages?"

But part of Joe's concern centered on Stewart's aloofness and Tish's occasional withdrawals, and he showered the children with attention and love to compensate.

"Now the dollar man is here," he would say upon entering his brother's house, and he would hold out four dollar bills as the children would run to him for the reward.

He took them aside and offered to pay $10 for every A they got in school. All four of the kids got excellent marks, and plenty of money changed hands. But Joe issued an exception. He despised the popular practice in 1950s schools of combining the traditional subjects of geography and history into one "social studies" class.

"I don't pay for social studies," he declared.

"But, Uncle Joe," they protested, "that's just history and geography."

"I don't care," he replied. "I won't pay."

At Georgetown's Francis Scott Key bookstore, around the corner from his home, Joe opened up a charge account for the children, and on their birthdays they would go in and buy an armload of books. He didn't impose judgment on their reading habits; so long as they were reading, he didn't care what it was. He seemed pleased with Elizabeth's passion for the Hardy Boys mysteries.

Once a week, on Thursdays, he had the children in for supper at Dumbarton. José's menu was always the same—juicy steaks, mashed potatoes, and peas—and for dessert, French vanilla ice cream. Joe wouldn't eat with the children, as he would be dining out later, but he would sit down and engage them in animated conversation.

"What have you been reading?" he would ask, or: "How is school?" He always managed to elicit detailed answers, and always listened intently. Joe didn't talk down to children, but managed to pull them up to adult-style conversation. The result was that children loved to talk with him. And Stewart's children loved their weekly dinners at Uncle Joe's. There was a sense of security in the ancient furniture and multitudinous knickknacks, the familiar parrot squawking from the garden room, the enveloping attention from their forceful but loving Uncle Joe.

In December 1954, Joe flew off to Vietnam for his second visit there in a year. Much had happened in that time. The French, defeated at Dien

Bien Phu, had been forced into a negotiated settlement at Geneva. The agreement, bearing the imprimatur of the great powers, contained just a few simple terms: Hostilities were to cease in Vietnam, Cambodia, and Laos. Vietnam was to be divided into two parts, a communist North and a Western-allied South, separated at the seventeenth parallel. The French were to evacuate the North, and the communists were to evacuate the South. Partition was deemed a temporary expedient, pending an election in two years to decide the country's fate.

Few expected the election to take place, however, and soon the French were making plans to abandon the country entirely. The leader of the North was Ho Chi Minh, the iron-willed, French-educated leader of the communist Vietminh. Having accomplished the destruction of French colonialism in Vietnam, he now set his considerable intellect to the task of consolidating the nation. In the South, the mantle of leadership went to Ngo Dinh Diem, an ascetic Catholic and a Vietnamese patriot. Diem was given to flights of self-importance, and lacked the intellect for the awesome task that fell to him. He quickly sought the patronage of the United States, and the United States just as quickly adopted him as a surrogate leader.

Joe found Saigon a city divorced from reality. As always, the gangsters who ran the gambling, prostitution, and opium dens also wore the uniforms of the local police. Life went on in this corrupt arena as if the city's fate had nothing to do with the fate of the country at large. Meanwhile, although the communist regular forces had been moving north according to the terms of the Geneva settlement, the relentless Vietminh cadres were spreading their tentacles into the countryside, taking control of life in the villages. "Because of its own inherent weakness . . . the government of President Ngo Dinh Diem has hardly attempted to govern," wrote Joe. "And since there is no counter effort to balance the work of the Viet Minh cadres, village after village passes into Viet Minh control."

In short, the communists were establishing a brutally efficient underground government in South Vietnam in violation of the Geneva accords. Diem's government, locked in bitter quarrels with the South Vietnamese army and unable to fill the power vacuum in the countryside, seemed impotent in the face of these pressing challenges. The Vietminh was particularly well established in the southern tip of the country, in the Camau peninsula (later renamed Quan Long). There the communists had established civil and military authority over nearly two million inhabitants. Joe decided to visit the area.

Through a French correspondent named Max Clos, Joe encountered a Saigon dentist who recently had fallen in with the communists. He in turn put Joe in touch with a lean Vietnamese guide named Hinh, who arranged for a ten-hour car ride south toward the edge of Vietminh territory. At a delta town called Phung Hiep, they boarded a *chaloupe,* a large wooden canal boat loaded with pigs, chickens, ducks, several tons of cargo, and about fifty local peasants "jammed together in overpowering intimacy." About twenty minutes outside of Phung Hiep, Hinh and Joe were joined by a Vietminh partisan named Nha, a proud guerrilla fighter in the standard uniform of black pajamas and solar topee. Through the afternoon and into the night the little barge chugged along the canal, past delta hamlets and endless rice paddies, until it reached Vinh Phong, about seventy-five kilometers inside Vietminh territory. There Joe was taken to a palm hut at the edge of town, allowed to bathe in the canal, and given a fine breakfast of noodles with chicken and hot peppers, along with "strong sweet French coffee."

Then came a Vietminh elder named Dr. Pham Thieu, a distinguished-looking man with an intelligent face and solicitous demeanor. After engaging Joe in friendly and extended conversation, Thieu announced that there had been a grave mistake. Hinh had not had any authority to escort Joe to Vinh Phong. The Vietminh had not guaranteed any safe conduct. Joe would have to remain there until the Vietminh Civil Affairs Bureau decided what to do with him.

Joe was under arrest in communist territory. He defended himself by insisting he had come in good faith, in the belief that his visit had been sanctioned, and he harbored no ill intentions toward his Vietminh hosts. After a day of languishing in the hut, reading a book on ancient history and pondering his fate, Joe was brought before what amounted to a provincial court, presided over by a local Civil Affairs Bureau chief named Dr. Vinh. With extreme courtesy, and seeking to appear as unconcerned as possible, Joe attributed his plight to an unfortunate misunderstanding. He asked for official sanction to remain for a time, but said if that could not be granted he would be happy to return to Saigon.

An argument ensued during which two young adjudicators became hostile toward Joe, suggesting he should be held accountable for his intrusion. Dr. Thieu and Hinh urged compassion. Dr. Vinh said nothing through the debate and sat stony-faced for some minutes after the discussion. Then, as Joe's heart pounded with apprehension, Thieu quietly said, "It is very irregular—but you may go."

On the *chaloupe* that carried Joe and Hinh back up the canal, Joe, wearing shorts, engaged in cheerful banter with the peasants on board, laughing and exclaiming at their smooth, hairless arms as they giggled in merriment at his hairy legs. With Hinh as interpreter, Joe and the peasants shared stories of their lives and passed the hours in friendly banter. Joe's new friends proved useful when they reached a large market town. Local police, inspecting Joe's papers, discovered he had no official seal on his exit permit. Apparently, Dr. Vinh's lieutenants had neglected to place it there, and once again he was threatened with arrest.

But his new friends on the *chaloupe* spoke up in his defense, testifying to his good character and recounting his friendly leave-taking with Vietminh officials at the dock in Vinh Phong. Hinh swore it was simply an oversight. After an hourlong argument among police officials at the pier, one man who appeared to be in authority said Joe could go, and the canal-boat captain quickly pushed off amid cheers from the peasants on board. "So I was saved," wrote Joe years later, "quite literally, by the hair on my knees."

The adventure produced three columns that illuminated the nature of the Vietminh movement. The question on Joe's mind was, "How did the communists do it?" How had these cadres, starting with nothing and working in the teeth of superior French military power, managed to establish and hold this palm-hut empire on the plain of Camau?

Through his conversations with the people of the delta, particularly with Pham Thieu and Dr. Vinh, Joe thought he had some answers. First, he wrote, much of the communists' success could be attributed to men like these. Before joining the resistance they had been successful and privileged—Thieu a teacher and archaeologist, Vinh a lawyer. They lacked any personal reasons for enlisting in the cause that consumed them and that required such personal sacrifice. Their mood struck Joe as being like that of "primitive Christians positively longing to be tossed to the nearest lion."

These men, moreover, discharged their responsibilities with remarkable efficiency "and puritanical dedication." Though they weren't themselves communists, their minds had been molded by the communist outlook and the communist cause. Joe was haunted by the question of how such men had come under the communist spell. He knew part of the answer lay in the communists' astute use of Asian nationalism, but he believed that that was the lesser part. More important was the Western impact. The old order of society from which these men sprang had crumbled under the impact of the West. The French had managed to maintain a kind of armature of order through force and the imposition of Western ways, at least until the cataclysm of World War II. "But fundamentally all values, all relationships, all beliefs and standards were at first transformed and then hopelessly disorganized."

Within this "cultural mush," as Joe called it, the communist party was "the only thing that was hard and certain and utterly organized." Joe knew that organization usually triumphs over disorganization, and that a hard minority will ultimately dominate a mushy majority. This, he concluded, "is the central point of the gigantic problem of halting the onward march of communist imperialism in Asia."

WHILE JOE TREKKED through Southeast Asia during the early months of 1955, Stewart took up a matter of national defense that had been bubbling beneath the surface for months and that now threatened to erupt into a major story. This was the air force's plan to build an intercontinental ballistic missile. Through his sources, Stewart learned that the air force had brought in a bright West Coast businessman-engineer named Trevor Gardner to handle research and development, with special emphasis on missiles. Stewart went to see Gardner and was immediately impressed.

He learned that Gardner had convinced his superior that the ICBM race with the Soviets was one the United States had to win. By gaining big funding increases for his program, Gardner had presided over significant technological breakthroughs, particularly those affecting guidance systems, and now the country was closer to the ICBM age than anyone had thought possible just a few years before. As usual, a big inside battle was being waged over whether the American people should be told about these developments. Gardner favored disclosure, which endeared him to Stewart. Additional reporting by Stewart soon produced enough material for a column—though he worried that he had learned more than he was supposed to know, and feared Gardner would be fingered as his source.

Entitled "The Race We've Got to Win," the column offered good news. The United States had about an even chance of beating the Soviets in the race to develop an intercontinental ballistic missile. This was crucial, because the ICBM, married to nuclear warheads, was the ultimate weapon. "It can be fired from one continent to another to destroy a great city," wrote Stewart, "in much the way that a murderer fires a bullet through his victim's head." Because there was no defense against such a weapon, said Stewart, it was imperative that the United States build up its arsenal before the Soviets could build theirs, so that the adversary wouldn't be tempted to launch a first strike or attempt military blackmail.

The column revealed that the country soon would test a jet-propelled missile called the Snark, which could fly at about the speed of sound and had a range of five thousand miles. Behind the Snark was the Navaho, with a range exceeding five thousand miles at twice the speed of sound. Then, within five years, would come the intercontinental Atlas, which would climb six hundred miles into space before plunging to the kill. Stewart argued that the country could beat the Soviets in this new realm of military competition only if the government fostered "a national sense of urgency, leading to a major effort on a wartime scale."

The column bolstered Stewart's reputation as Washington's leading journalistic expert on matters of military technology. That reputation got a further boost in mid-February when Lewis Strauss, chairman of the Atomic Energy Commission, announced that U.S. H-Bomb tests showed nuclear fallout to be a much larger destructive force than the government had ever before acknowledged. Strauss said the fallout could blanket an area as large as seven thousand square miles with lethal radioactive material. This caused a stir, but only because it was the first official acknowledgment of this important reality. Stewart had revealed essentially the same information nearly a year earlier in the column.

In February 1955, Stewart made plans for a trip to the Soviet Union, which recently had relaxed its visa policies regarding Americans. But the brothers were not among the Kremlin's favorite Westerners. Andrei Vishinsky, the Soviet United Nations ambassador, had once attacked the Alsops as "rapists," "bandits of the pen," and "congenital murderers." Stewart asked Chip Bohlen, then ambassador to Moscow, for help in getting a visa. He also wrote directly to Communist Party Secretary Nikita Khrushchev:

> I am aware that there has been some rather harsh criticism of my brother and myself in the Soviet press. But I assure you that, if I am permitted to visit the Soviet Union, I shall try to report what I see as honestly as I can, as my brother and I always try to do.

It worked. The visa was granted, and Stewart immediately set plans to arrive in the Soviet Union on June 20. Arriving first in Leningrad, Stewart was appalled. "The general bleakness and dullness, the crumbling walls of the buildings, the hideousness of the women's dresses, the execrable taste of the few new public buildings, the grimness of the people's faces—these things filled me with a heavy sense of depression," he wrote later. But the depression soon gave way to fascination as he proceeded through the country in companionship with his interpreter, a tough-minded communist named Victor.

What struck him most was the smugness of the Soviet people. Bombarded by the heavy propaganda of the communist overlords, and feeling a growing sense of security and material well-being under Khrushchev, the people really did believe theirs was the better system. Stewart was struck by the pride expressed in such mundane things as mortgage plans for home buying and gardens for workers at Soviet factories. He recoiled at the ignorance induced in the people by the Soviet propaganda machine.

The phenomenon stirred him to anger one day aboard an old side-wheel steamer as he and Victor cruised down the Dnieper River from Kiev. In a tiny lounge with the inevitable big pictures of Lenin and Stalin on the wall, he engaged a group of locals in what became a political discussion. It started with a bombardment of questions, expressed with formal politeness and betraying strong anti-Americanism: "Why do you refuse to outlaw the atomic bomb?" "Why is your country against peace?" "Why do you encircle our country with airbases to destroy us?" "Why have you organized an aggressive bloc, the so-called NATO, to attack us?" When he tried to answer such questions rationally, Stewart wrote, he was met with "a smugly polite disbelief all the more infuriating for being polite."

To regain the offensive, he asked an impolitic question—whether the real number-one man in the Soviet Union was Khrushchev or Nikolai Bulganin, who was Khrushchev's chief Kremlin rival. The crowd appeared embarrassed by such tactlessness on a sensitive political matter—which had the effect of making Stewart's point. But then a quick-witted young man interjected: "And in your country number one is not Eisen-hower, but Morgan's bank or Ford, no?" Amid laughter from the crowd, Stewart protested that the auto workers' union was at least as politically powerful as any motor company. "And they laughed smugly again," wrote Stewart, "and I got angry and showed it."

In Moscow, at a French embassy reception celebrating Bastille Day, Stewart encountered Khrushchev himself. The Alsops long had been fas-cinated by the man who emerged after Stalin's death as the party's pre-mier strongman. He was a man of many parts—sometimes a kind of joking, champagne-guzzling tosspot; at other times a shrewd, calculat-ing, and daring connoisseur of power. It was the outer person with the unpressed trousers and perpetual grin that Stewart met at the French embassy, where the Soviet leader savored his glory by tossing down glasses of champagne, pulling terrified children of Western diplomats into his thick arms, and passionately denouncing American foreign pol-icy. Khrushchev had initiated the encounter, asking to meet "the Amer-ican journalist, Gospodin Alsop."

When Stewart was ushered into the party secretary's presence, Khrushchev grabbed Stewart's hand in his own two hands, held on tight, and peered intently into the American's eyes.

"I have read what you have written about my country," he said with a grin. Stewart muttered a reply and sought to withdraw his hand, but the Soviet leader held on.

"I do not like what you have written," said Khrushchev solemnly, but still grinning. "Perhaps you will return to my country someday, and then you will write the truth about it."

Stewart replied that he always tried to write the truth, and Khrushchev said nothing as he continued to clasp Stewart's hand and in-spect him up and down "like an amused entymologist inspecting some particularly outlandish bug." When Stewart began asking questions about the forthcoming Geneva summit, Khrushchev quickly cut him off.

"No, no, Gospodin Alsop," he said, keeping in place the perpetual grin, "you are trying to interview me, and that I cannot permit."

It was a brief encounter, but it left a deep impression on Stewart. He saw Khrushchev as a "strangely compelling man"—rather ugly and somewhat intimidating, but with a certain undeniable charm.

Stewart stayed at Moscow's Hotel National, "a somber old firetrap" with a view of Red Square. For three nights in a row he was awakened before dawn by hearty singing at all-night parties on the square to cele-brate the graduations of various high schools and colleges. On these oc-casions he quickly dressed and joined the festivities. They were touching scenes "beneath the pretty yellow and green of the Kremlin and the glinting gilt of St. Basil's onion dome," and they reminded Stewart of the small-town America of two or three decades before. The dancing was the "arm's-length, jiggledy-hop sort of dancing," and there was hardly any drinking. The girls wore long white dresses, while the boys, in ill-fitting jackets and baggy pants, "looked like [American] country boys of a generation ago in their Sunday best."

As sedate as these affairs were, they represented something important then going on in Moscow. In Stalin's time, nobody would have dared dance so close to what Stewart called "the very heart of power and the fountainhead of fear." In the era of good feeling fostered by Khrushchev, these young people seemed liberated by the thought of pushing out into the frontiers of freedom. But on the third night such thoughts evaporated when the blue hats of the MVD (Ministry of Internal Affairs) security police showed up. The officers never displayed any muscle, never laid a hand on anybody. "They simply threaded in and out among the crowd, saying a word here and there, killing the party as effectively as an aggressive bore kills a dinner party."

Perhaps, Stewart concluded, there was in fact a change in the winds blowing across the Soviet Union. But old Moscow hands knew that "the change will not, and cannot, be permitted to go very deep." Americans, he was convinced, should not lose sight of the twofold reality behind Soviet global power—the widespread support the communist regime enjoyed from a people who had never had it so good, and the regime's willingness to funnel huge amounts of national resources into armaments.

That, he wrote, was the crux of the challenge facing the West, which tended to assess national power in terms of the number of automobiles on the street or the elegance of the plumbing. A better index, he said, "is to be found in the remarkable aircraft which now regularly appear in the Moscow skies."

In late July at the Geneva summit, where Khrushchev met with Eisenhower and the leaders of Britain and France, Stewart sensed a kind of "breathing spell" in the West's relations with the Soviet Union. He attributed much of this good feeling to Eisenhower's willingness to listen and approach international problems with flexibility. But another important factor was the enigmatic Khrushchev. Though blustery and threatening, he was more willing than his predecessors had been to discuss serious global matters with the West.

After the summit, Stewart enjoyed a diversion in England and France, where the Jedburgh operatives from his OSS days were celebrating their tenth-year reunion following war's end. Ted Ellsworth, now a successful insurance broker in Dubuque, Iowa, was there, and he and Stewart had a rousing good time. After meeting with Queen Elizabeth in London, the Jeds headed to Sivry-Rance in Belgium, where a long drunken weekend of revelry ensued. Ellsworth, who retained his whimsical sense of humor and his penchant for practical jokes, tied a dirty bandage around his head as a conversation piece. In the local bars, the women gravitated to him out of compassion, and as always he enjoyed the attention. In one bar, he pulled from his pocket an old letter from the war years and flashed it in front of Stewart's face. Recognizing it as a particularly embarrassing relic of his past, Stewart grabbed for it unsuccessfully as Ellsworth taunted him. The two men, closest of friends for a dozen years, ended up in a brawl that nearly destroyed the friendship. Thrown out of the bar, they continued to scuffle until Stewart, so drunk and furious he had to make up words to communicate, yelled, "I'll smash your head like a . . . like a . . . a pumplamush."

Stewart traveled on to Morocco and arrived there as the North African colony edged ever closer to a war of hatred between the ruling French and rebellious Moroccans. In Casablanca he encountered "the smell of sickness, which is the smell of hatred and fear." Just two years earlier, the French had deposed Sultan Sidi Mohammed ben-Youssef, a tawdry, self-indulgent ruler who had become, as a result of his ouster, a national hero and symbol of Moroccan independence. A seething Moorish anger had been building in the colony for months, and everyone expected it to erupt at any moment.

Encountering the *Herald Tribune*'s Barrett McGurn, who had just returned from the countryside, Stewart learned of a threatened uprising near the little town of Oued Zem, some ninety miles from Casablanca. The next day before dawn, Stewart and Blair Clark of CBS News hired a taxi for the ride out. Knowing that McGurn had been ambushed on the same country road the day before and had barely escaped serious injury or death, the two reporters felt tense and alert as the taxi made its way into the countryside. But as daybreak illuminated the gentle hills they tended to forget the danger and began enjoying the excursion.

When they reached the outskirts of Oued Zem two hours later, it became clear something terrible had happened. An odd smell—half sweet, half bitter—filled the air. Smoke was rising from burnt-out shells that had been houses until that morning. In a gas station marked with the familiar Mobilgas logo and the red flying-horse trademark, a grisly scene came into view. Five corpses lay in a tangled mass just inside the door.

Down the road was another corpse so charred it was impossible to determine its race. As they approached some French legionnaires, a middle-aged Frenchwoman with a squirrel rifle in hand ran around a nearby building. She was agitated and crying. "Oh, it was terrible," she sobbed. "It was terrible to hear the children crying. I do not want to die. I do not want to die."

When some scattered shots were heard, a French lieutenant quickly ordered the two reporters out of the town. They grumbled but welcomed the excuse to leave such brutal scenes. On the outskirts they encountered people who related how a large band of Moroccans from the surrounding area had swooped down on the town to slaughter any Frenchmen they could find. They had killed fifty-one French residents and an untold number of their fellow Arabs. They had cut the throats of fifteen children and seven hospital patients helpless in their sickbeds. They had severed the noses and tongues of several men. To Stewart, such acts bespoke "a wolfish hatred unimaginable and inexplicable to the Western mind."

To most Americans, such events suggested that the French should simply leave North Africa and give up the idea of control or colonial settlement there. In a conversation with French Prime Minister Edgar Faure at Geneva, Eisenhower had echoed this sentiment, cutting off Faure's description of his hopeless colonial problems and asking, "But why don't you just free all your colonies?"

Stewart didn't see it that way, as he made clear in a September 5 column from Casablanca entitled "The War for North Africa." After all, he pointed out, there were 400,000 Frenchmen in Morocco and another 1.6 million in other parts of North Africa, mainly in Algeria. Could France simply abandon these people to the mercy of hate-filled Moslems? Besides, the loss of North Africa would devastate the French economy and her military position in the world. "France," wrote Stewart, "would cease to have even the shadow of a claim to the status of a great power, if the essential French influence in North Africa were destroyed." He called on French officials to shake off the governmental paralysis that had encumbered the country's efforts to deal with North Africa, and urged cooperation with moderate nationalists there who were losing influence as more radical elements gained sway.

This may have been a minority view in America, but it reflected the essential world outlook of the Alsop brothers. The foundation of their perspective was the West—their civilization and their heritage—and they felt an instinctive reluctance to accept Western decline anywhere in the world. They saw that the old Western dominion over palm and pine was now severely retrenched, that the British Empire was merely a remnant of what it had been, that anticolonial nationalism and anti-Western fervor were gaining ground wherever the vestiges of prewar Western dominance remained. But they clung to the idea that imaginative Western leadership and resolve could somehow preserve the essence of the old days, that France could maintain its presence in North Africa, that Britain could hold sway over its far-flung trade routes, that America would play the role of military custodian of the West.

On the other hand, Western retreat would create power vacuums around the world—and opportunities for Soviet expansion. Defeat in North Africa, wrote Stewart, "could fatally weaken the Western alliance, and in the long run it could be the prelude to a communist Africa. Such are the stakes in the struggle here." As the Alsops saw it, those were the stakes everywhere, in an endless multitude of struggles confronting the West throughout the world.

22

SUEZ

The Beginning of the End of the Old Elite

IN THE MID-1950s, Washington and London found their interests diverging in the volatile Middle East, and tensions emerged in the Anglo-American "special relationship" that had been a force for world stability in the postwar era. The brothers viewed this with typical Alsopian alarm. For them, the alliance was more than just the foundation of the West's defense against Soviet expansionism. The special relationship preserved for Britain a place in the world that comported with the brothers' lifelong view of the motherland as major power and international exemplar. The Alsops felt it was crucial that the United States bolster Britain's global role, which meant acknowledging her dependence on the vestiges of empire. "The vast majority of Americans have enough sense to realize that we are heavily dependent upon Britain, our chief ally," Joe wrote to a reader from France. "But they do not have enough information to understand that Britain, in turn, is almost absolutely dependent on overseas resources which are, essentially, imperial-colonial in origin."

With this in mind, Joe arrived in London on March 23, 1956, and checked into the Ritz Hotel. His mission was ten days of fact-finding and column-writing to prepare for an extended trip through the Middle East, where British Prime Minister Anthony Eden saw crisis looming. His pessimism proved contagious, and Joe, not surprisingly, became infected.

He attended a dinner in Connaught Square at the home of an up-

and-coming Time-Life writer named Raimund von Hoffmansthal and his wife, Lady Elizabeth. The guest of honor was the prime minister himself. Joe had encountered Eden numerous times at social gatherings in the past, and had interviewed him frequently over the years; the two men shared an informal and comfortable relationship. At dinner the prime minister candidly warned that the perennially perturbed Middle East could explode at any moment. He also revealed a secret that was big news, particularly in America: Eden had sent a personal message to Eisenhower seeking assurances of U.S. support for Britain's efforts to preserve its Mideast presence.

The next day, Joe confirmed the story with the American embassy's chargé d'affaires, Andrew Foster, then rushed into print—and generated something of an international incident. Eden had assumed he was speaking off the record at dinner, although he had not stipulated as much because he felt, as Isaiah Berlin informed Joe later, "that it would really be too chilly and discourteous to an old friend and 'one of us,' as you undoubtedly are regarded."

The column ran April 4, and revealed that Eden had sent his Eisenhower message through a high official at the U.S. embassy. Eden's words were so grave, said the column, that the official had asked Eden for a written summary of their conversation to ensure his report's accuracy. "The hard-driven Eden himself wrote out the informal message on the spot," wrote Joe.

To Stewart and *Herald Tribune* managing editor George Cornish Joe sent an accompanying wire: THE FOREGOING EYE ASSURE YOU DOES NOT RPT NOT OVERPAINT THE ATMOSPHERE HERE STOP IT SEEMS TO ME THAT THE FIRST POINT TO GET ACROSS IS THE ACTUAL GRAVITY OF THE ATMOSPHERE FROM HERE STOP . . . HOPE FOR MAJOR NEWS PLAY FOR THIS ONE STOP. To Stewart he added a request that his brother keep him advised of developments.

The first Washington development soon followed, when Eisenhower was asked about the Eden message at a news conference. He responded with puzzlement. "I am certain it is no recent thing they must be talking about," he said. Asked if the British had pressed the administration to take a firmer Mideast stand, the president replied, "Well, if they have, they haven't pressed me."

Joe was dumbfounded. He wired further details on the Eden message to Stewart, and suggested a piece on the Washington angle. Two days later, Stewart filed a column speculating that the Eden message had been withheld from the president by a protective State Department. Since Eisenhower's heart attack the previous September, said Stewart, his aides had gone to extensive lengths to protect him from unnecessary worry. But this could be hazardous. "A chief executive of the United States," wrote Stewart, "cannot function properly if he is wrapped in yards of cotton batting."

Stewart's reporting revealed deep and growing divisions between the two allies. He informed Joe by wire that Washington viewed Britain's tough Middle East policies as a "hysterical" approach designed to appease the Conservative Party right wing. He added: CONVICTION EXPRESSED BRITISH ARMED INTERVENTION IN MIDDLE EAST WILL ASSURE ULTIMATE SOVIET HEGEMONY IN AREA STOP ON OTHER HAND IF THERE IS ALTERNATIVE AMERICAN POLICY OTHER THAN LET DUST SETTLE HAVE BEEN UNABLE TO DISCERN IT STOP.

The complexities of this international situation are best understood through the personalities and motivations of the powerful men at the center of the storm—Dulles, Eden, Khrushchev, Egypt's Gamal Abdel Nasser, Israeli Prime Minister David Ben-Gurion, and Eisenhower. By the end of the year these men would converge in a powerful drama of war and diplomacy that would transform the Mideast balance of power, the Atlantic Alliance, Britain's role in the world, and the Anglo-American relationship. For Britain—and for the Alsops—it would prove to be a devastating turn of events.

The story begins with John Foster Dulles, a man of powerful whims, whose interest in the Middle East far surpassed his understanding of it. The architect of U.S. Mideast policy for four years, he had been driven by two central motivations that probably were contradictory: a strong moralistic anticolonialism and a desire to keep the Soviets out of the region. The first led him to pressure Britain to give up her huge Suez military base, with its eighty thousand troops. The second led him to tilt American policy away from the Truman administration's pro-Israel stance. Dulles wanted good relations with the major players of the Arab world, particularly Egypt's Nasser. He induced Eisenhower to promise arms to Nasser, but then failed to deliver. Nasser grew impatient—and alarmed. He feared Israel's growing military strength. An alarmed Nasser could become unpredictable and dangerous. All this escaped Dulles's notice. He was a man mired in legalisms and details that never seemed to add up to a consistent policy.

Anthony Eden personified the British upper class, with a record that included Eton, Oxford, the King's Royal Rifle Corps, and a Military Cross for bravery in World War I. He was a man of dignity—tall, well-spoken, with a bearing as correct and straight as his well-manicured mustache. He was also a bit of a pedant, given to poring over matters of routine and ignoring big issues. By the time Winston Churchill finally stepped down as prime minister in 1955, Eden had been toiling as head of the foreign office for most of fifteen years, and his long apprenticeship had dulled rather than sharpened his political instincts.

The prime minister suffered, moreover, from the effects of a failed 1953 gallstone operation that had left him with an incurable infection. He took antibiotics constantly. When his condition led to fatigue, he took amphetamines to shore up his energy. His impeccable demeanor soon gave way to peevishness and irritability, and his judgment turned cloudy.

The driving force of his political life remained his wish to preserve as much of the old empire as possible. He hated the Suez troop withdrawal that Dulles had forced upon his country in Churchill's time. Though he couldn't reverse it, he was resolved to protect Britain's place in the Middle East and the free flow of the region's oil. His vehicle was the Baghdad Pact, a British alliance with friendly Arab countries pieced together under the guise of an anti-Soviet bulwark. The idea was to provide economic and military aid to pro-Western countries and win diplomatic leverage. By October 1955, Turkey, Iraq, Iran, and Pakistan had joined what Eden proudly called "a frontier stretching from the Mediterranean to the Himalayas." But this diplomatic handiwork drew the ire of two men—Nasser and Khrushchev.

Nasser was a visionary with powerful emotions and ironclad determination. The son of a postal clerk, he had grown up with feelings of shame at the presence of foreign overlords in his country. His fiery hatred of the British and of Western imperialism had grown into an ardent Egyptian nationalism. As a young military officer, he had distinguished himself in an undistinguished army and helped form a clandestine group of nationalist officers bent on taking over the country from the corrupt lackey King Farouk. In 1952, Nasser led a coup that forced Farouk into exile and transformed Egypt. By 1956 he had consolidated power and emerged as the strongest Arab ruler of the day—"the embodied symbol and acknowledged leader of the new surge of Arab nationalism," as Joe put it. That surge was gathering strength throughout the Arab lands.

But Nasser harbored fears also. He viewed neighboring Israel as a Western enclave in his region's heartland, and he feared the arrival of throngs of Jews who would force Israel into a policy of expansionism. Nasser bristled when he saw Israel building up her armaments and voting out moderate Prime Minister Moshe Sharett while adding political strength to Menachem Begin's nationalist Herut Party. The Egyptian leader wanted arms. Eisenhower had promised them, but now seemed disinclined to fulfill the promise. So a seething Nasser turned to Moscow.

In Moscow, Khrushchev had dismissed the Egyptian rebellion for years as just another military coup like those that sometimes erupted in South America without bringing any societal change. He couldn't muster much interest in a movement that lacked hostility to the bourgeoisie. But when Nasser began his pursuit of arms from Moscow, the young Egyptian's anti-Western spirit impressed the communist leader. Soon he saw an opportunity: Ship arms to Nasser and gain a foothold in the Middle East. Such a foothold had been a Russian dream since the days of the czars.

Across the great Sinai Desert from Cairo, in the fledgling nation of Israel, sat David Ben-Gurion. Tough and wily, with a jagged square face framed by two spears of silver hair, he was Israel's founding father, the embodied spirit of the ingathering set in motion the day his tiny country began its national existence and promptly threw open its borders to the Jews of the world. From a base of 800,000 Jews in 1948, the Jewish presence in Israel had grown to nearly 2 million, and the Israeli leader wanted that number doubled as quickly as possible. But Ben-Gurion and his people felt threatened by surrounding Arabs who wanted to destroy Israel and push the Jews into the sea. Subjected to constant border incursions by marauding Arabs, Ben-Gurion had developed a policy of terrible, swift retribution. It was a bloody approach, and it often brought international opprobrium, but Ben-Gurion would not retreat. It was a matter of national survival.

Finally, there was Eisenhower. As his press conference following Joe's Eden column suggested, his attentions were not riveted on the Middle East. He delegated Mideast policy to Dulles. But after the secretary of state had engineered the promise of arms to Nasser, Eisenhower had stepped in to countermand that policy. Britain opposed arming the unpredictable Arab nationalist, and Eisenhower's long affection for America's wartime ally had prevailed. At the same time, the president disliked Ben-Gurion's controversial reprisal policy. He was quick to condemn Israel's raids of retribution and to support United Nations condemnations even when they caused him political difficulties among Jewish voters. Eisenhower favored an evenhanded Mideast policy that opposed aggression anywhere in the region and supported the aggrieved party in disputes. The idea was to serve as honest broker, husbanding moral authority and maintaining diplomatic influence in the region.

THE EVENT THAT drew these leaders toward a tangled confrontation occurred shortly before Joe's London visit, when the British adventurer, Lieutenant General Sir John Bagot Glubb ("Glubb Pasha"), was fired as commander of Jordan's Arab Legion. A holdover from Britain's days of empire, Glubb had arrived in the Middle East as a young army officer, resigned his commission, joined Jordan's military, and ascended to his powerful job. From that position he had served Jordan and his homeland with equal felicity, enjoying a close friendship with Jordan's King Abdullah and respectful support from ministers at Whitehall. But when Abdullah was assassinated and his young grandson, King Hussein, ascended the throne, frictions developed between Glubb and his new master.

Now, with Glubb gone and the callow king struggling to govern, powerful forces converged to threaten a coup in Jordan. The threat came from Arab nationalists organized by the communist underground and spurred on by Nasser's fiery rhetoric and harsh radio propaganda. A coup in Jordan would destabilize pro-Western Iraq, and a coup in Iraq would likely put at risk the entire Mideastern oil supply. "What is chiefly feared in London," wrote Joe from that capital, "is the stage by stage loss of the oil sources which are the true lifeblood of these islands."

In his London columns, Joe embraced the crisis outlook of the Eden cabinet and condemned the Eisenhower administration for dithering. "Britain," he wrote, "is like a man who feels an enemy's hard fingers reaching for his jugular vein (which in Britain's case is the Middle Eastern oil source) yet can do nothing to ward off the attack." Threatened with economic ruin in the Mideast, Eden was drifting toward a policy of confrontation. But this probably meant, as Joe put it, "fighting Arab nationalism all-out and without quarter, with the Soviet Union on the other side." Joe argued that such a risky course could be avoided only if America would quickly apply her strength to the problem. "If the British go in over their depth," he wrote in his last London column, "we shall have the unpleasant choice between going in ourselves to bail Britain out, or letting Britain founder, and so permitting the Atlantic Alliance to founder too."

Joe left London for Cairo on April 16. It was a bloody month in the Middle East. Reacting angrily to Arab border incursions along the Gaza Strip, Ben-Gurion had ordered an attack on the town of Gaza; sixty-two Arabs were killed, including twenty-five women and children. Nasser had retaliated by setting loose upon the Israeli countryside his fedayeen guerrillas, who killed fourteen Israeli civilians in ten days of raiding. Throughout the month these skirmishes continued, and Joe found himself sitting down with Nasser just a day after the Israelis had unleashed a shelling attack on Gaza.

"This reporter has never seen any national leader in a grimmer mood than Col. Nasser on the day after the Gaza incident occurred," Joe wrote. Nasser spoke frankly about Arab nationalism and his contempt for the British. The remaining British colonial positions in the Mideast couldn't last, he said, because Arab nationalism would overwhelm them. Noting that nationalism already had overwhelmed the British in Jordan, he predicted the same in Iraq, and he warned that the only alternative to Arab nationalism was communism. "That is the choice for you in the West," he said, "between true Arab nationalism, and communism disguised as nationalism. You must make the choice soon."

In a second interview the next day Joe posed a specific question: What must the West do to come to terms with Nasser and with Arab nationalism? The minimum requirement, Joe knew, was the British liquidation of her semicolonial positions in the Middle East, in which case, he said, America would have to "reinsure" Britain against her losses. But would Nasser guarantee the flow of oil? Would he refrain from an attack against Israel? Would he reinforce his relationship with Moscow if the West pushed too hard on these points?

The Egyptian leader recognized the West's vital interests. Good relations were the best guarantee for the oil, he said, adding that he would not attack Israel unless Israel attacked first. But Joe noted in his column that Nasser's reassuring words didn't correspond with what was coming out of his government and the Egyptian press. Regarding relations with the Kremlin, Nasser remained provocatively noncommittal. The Soviets had always been "correct" in their dealings with Egypt. And no Middle Easterner had ever had any experience with Soviet imperialism, he pointedly remarked.

Joe's Nasser interviews convinced him that the West would have to accommodate the Egyptian leader to preserve order in the region and retain some influence there. "Western statesmanship," he wrote, "will surely miss another last chance if Nasser and Egypt are not aided, by all means possible, to make the choice that best serves the long run interest of Egypt and the West alike."

The ruling factor for Joe, as always, was the Soviet Union. In addition to providing arms to Egypt and promising juicy trade benefits, the Soviets had conducted themselves with the correctness of an old-fashioned hotel concierge. They didn't preach against Arab attacks on Israel. Instead they would say, "Take the oil; it was stolen from you." But the real Soviet aim, as Joe warned, was "to use Arab nationalism as a weapon to cut the oil jugular of Western Europe." Britain would be humbled, NATO destroyed, and the Western alliance crippled. Those were the fuses, in Joe's view, leading to the Middle East powder keg.

Leaving Cairo, Joe embarked on a series of adventures throughout the region, beginning in Saudi Arabia with dinner at King Saud's Jeddah palace. The palace cloister that served as the reception area was a hundred yards long and eighty wide, and the Arab personages gathered there were plump but dignified in their flowing robes and corded headdresses. Orange pop substituted for alcoholic beverages, and the king allowed no smoking inside his grand residence. Leading the evening procession were the blackamoor guards who had been serving the court for a generation. Now they were elderly and fat, hardly intimidating despite the gilded scimitars they wore beneath their black and gold embroidered jackets. Afterward came the king himself, tall and impressive.

Following dinner, Joe had an audience with the king in an anteroom off the dining hall that served as Saud's place of respite with his inner court. Nothing remarkable was said, although the king's expression of friendship toward America seemed sincere. Joe appreciated the king's effort to bridge the past and present, but he wasn't impressed with the country or its court. In a letter to Martin Sommers he called it a "rather monstrous country" ruled by a self-indulgent family. The king's palaces absorbed 80 percent of the nation's revenue, and his latest monstrosity at Ryadh used enough electricity to light up an English town of thirty thousand.

Joe was fascinated by life at court—the slavery and the harems, the lavish expenditures for jewelry and designer clothes worn by harem women in their everyday lives. He told Sommers about the wives of

Saud's American pilots, who were getting rich by importing fashionable off-the-rack dresses from America. They sold them at huge mark-ups to the harem women, whose black slaves would come down to a little hole-in-the-wall shop and purchase armloads of the garments for their mistresses. A Paris jeweler was growing rich through his special privilege of admission to Prince Faisal's harem. On one visit he sold $40,000 worth of jewelry to the prince, who promptly gave it to his bodyguard. Slave prices were $150 for an able-bodied man, $300 for a boy, and $600 for a girl. A first-class hunting falcon, Joe wrote to Sommers, could be purchased for about the price of a male slave.

It all seemed grotesquely backward to Joe, and yet he recognized that Saudi Arabia was in ferment. In little more than two decades it had transformed itself from a country that was three-quarters nomadic into a country three-quarters settled. With so much change, fostered by vast flows of oil money, it was inevitable that Saudi Arabia should become a captive of Arab nationalism if King Saud flirted too much with the West. That would threaten the royal family's life of lavish privilege; so the king nurtured his alliance with Nasser, financed the Egyptian's nationalist agitations, and turned an ambiguous face toward the West. "Saudi Arabia," wrote Joe, "must now be regarded as the captive . . . of the new Arab nationalist movement that presently centers in Cairo."

Traveling to Kuwait, Joe found it to be "little more than a vast oil well with a small town on top of it." Kuwait provided two-thirds of all the oil for the British Isles, and its importance was obvious: It could be held militarily in a crisis and could supply Europe's oil needs for a long time.

In Iraq, Joe encountered a sheikh named Ahmed who had transformed the desert through irrigation into large wheat and barley fields. The sheikh treated Joe to a lavish luncheon of "imperial kousy," a dish as large as a table top, with a mountain of rice topped with two whole roast young lambs, "meltingly tender under the fingers, with their rich stuffing of spiced rice and raisins and almonds and bits of liver lying all about them." Joe called on Nuri Pasha, the British puppet who ran Iraq with a strong will and legions of security officers. But Nuri Pasha's dictatorship was far less severe than that of Nasser's Egypt, and he had built the most generous social welfare system in the region. Britain and the West hoped Nuri Pasha and his pro-Western nation would serve as example and magnet, to attract other Arab states toward a policy less hostile to the West. It wasn't surprising that Iraq served as the cornerstone of Eden's Baghdad Pact.

But Joe could see things weren't working out as planned. "All the nationalist emotions that have gripped the rest of the Arab world," he wrote, "are powerfully surging beneath the surface here in Iraq." Nuri Pasha had plenty of resolve and legions of policemen and Western support and progressive policies, but he still sat uneasily atop his government.

Then it was on to Jordan, where Joe met the young King Hussein and his wild-eyed military chief, Ali Abu Nuwar. He found the new Arab Legion commander—Glubb Pasha's successor after Hussein fired the British adventurer—the more enigmatic of the two. Nuwar was young and handsome, with energy and ambition burning in his dark Arab eyes. He hated the British and felt drawn to Nasser's Arab nationalism. He struck Joe as "quite capable of touching off a war with Israel in his impulsive young way."

As for Hussein, he was hardly more than a boy in years and appearance. At twenty, he still loved to race around the countryside in his fast cars and indulge in other youthful pursuits. Yet he wore the mantle of royalty with a mien of seriousness and confidence. His aim, he told Joe, was to serve as mediator between Anthony Eden's Baghdad Pact and Nasser's nationalist agitators. But he was caught between two powerful forces he could not contain. With Saudi money pouring into his country, and Nasser directing an underground subversion campaign in his cities, the young king had little room for missteps. "The pressures . . . are very terrible and the dangers are commensurate," wrote Joe.

In Israel Joe found himself beguiled. He discovered a nation still living in its own legendary age and quite aware of the fact. Joe was struck by the talk of heroes from the days before nationhood and from the later wars of survival, by the widespread feeling that the individual still counted, by the powerful sense of nationality and need for cultural survival.

In June, after ten weeks abroad, Joe returned to Washington and the task of writing his impressions of the Middle East. "The picture there is ominous," he wrote. "Unless present trends can somehow be reversed the free world must eventually expect a Middle Eastern disaster on the approximate scale of the disastrous loss of China to the communists."

As Joe saw it, Britain was threatened in the Mideast by forces and pressures tearing at the old empire—and at her ability to survive as a world power. There was no doubt in Joe's mind that American foreign policy too would be thrown into chaos if Britain ceased to be a world power. Yet he saw little understanding of this at the State Department. "It is amazing and pretty terrifying," he wrote, "to come home and to discover that the state department's chief parlor game seems to be smug carping at the British."

As for the Middle East, Joe viewed the region with the jaundiced eye of a latter-day colonialist. In letters to friends, he compared the area to a hen run that had been used so long "that it grows sour underfoot, so all the chickens get the roop." In a letter to Lady Elizabeth von Hoffmansthal, he added:

> . . . the only rational people in the Middle East are the ones with no influence whatever. After a certain number of weeks chiefly passed in listening to coffee-colored politicians talking nonsense at

the tops of their voices, you begin to think that the white man's burden may not have been such a bad idea after all.

All in all, it was a triumphant trip. Letters of praise poured in, and even *Time* magazine, which had been battering the brothers regularly throughout Eisenhower's presidency, lauded Joe's Middle East writings. "Alsop's dramatic flair as a reporter in foreign lands seizes surely on color, incident, history and personality to bring a situation crackling to life," the magazine stated. "In this journalistic field he has had few peers since the days of Vincent Sheehan." Henry Luce wrote to say, "I was delighted with *Time*'s tribute to your Middle East reporting."

But friend Isaiah Berlin caught the flaw in Joe's writings and thinking. In a letter he said he couldn't understand how Joe could admire so many people so much when so many of them were in direct conflict with each other. "You call Nasser 'wise,' you are impressed with the Syrians and the Jordanians, you think the Israelis splendid Biblical people, you think British policy fatal but call for support for it, and the refugees in Jordan drive you . . . absolutely mad." If he were asked to read Joe's columns and then devise a Middle East policy for Britain or America, he couldn't do it, said Berlin. "What policy do you advocate?"

Berlin was right: there was a gap in Joe's thinking. But what he had in mind was a policy course he could not publicly espouse. Knowing the West could never return to the old days of colonial rule by might, he favored influencing events by stealth. "The key moves in Saudi Arabia and elsewhere," Joe wrote privately to a Northwestern University professor named M. L. Burstein, "would have to take the form of covert operations; and I have a rooted objection to any public discussion of our covert operations, past, present, or possibly prospective."

Joe's model was the successful 1953 CIA operation in Iran, which had deftly deposed the anti-Western strongman Mohammed Mossadegh and restored the pro-Western shah to his throne. The result had been that Iran's oil spigot, shut off by Mossadegh, had been reopened, and America had gained a large measure of influence in the strategically pivotal country. Through their CIA friends, the Alsop brothers had gained a fair amount of knowledge about covert operations, and they viewed such moves as excellent statecraft for unstable areas.

In the Middle East in the summer of 1956, however, it was too late for clandestine maneuverings. The region was about to explode.

For a year, Dulles had been dangling a sweet deal in front of Nasser—generous U.S. funding for Nasser's dream, the Aswan high dam that could turn a vast expanse of desert into productive farmland. The offer represented Dulles's attempt to buy back Nasser's good will after the previous arms-sale debacle had thrown the Egyptian leader into a Soviet orbit. But Nasser miscalculated. He recognized Communist China—a slap in the face of America and her testy secretary of state.

Dulles abruptly withdrew the Aswan dam promise, and this stimulated anew Nasser's anti-Western fervor.

A week later, on July 26, Nasser struck back. He seized the Suez Canal. The canal was a marvel of Western vision, engineering, and grit, a hundred miles of desert waterway that sliced nearly in half the trade route from the oil-rich Persian Gulf to Great Britain. For a hundred years it had lubricated East-West trade, and for thirty-five years it had served as the energy lifeline of Britain and France. Fully 80 percent of the oil that fueled the economies of Western Europe came from the Mideast through the canal. For decades this crucial Western prize had been protected by Britain's Suez base, but now that pivot of force and counterforce was gone. The last troops had left a month before.

The brothers perceived the seizure as a major threat to Britain's great-power status and a potential threat to the English-speaking alliance. What's more, they predicted, Nasser would now turn to Moscow to finance his dam, and thus hand the Soviets an ideal opportunity to become the region's dominant power.

In a July 30 column the brothers outlined three possible courses of American action, "all hideously unattractive." One was to waffle—"to protest, to denounce, but to do nothing." The second amounted to an economic war against Nasser—to freeze his overseas assets, to undermine Egypt in the world cotton market, perhaps to impose a trade embargo—but this would merely throw him further into the arms of the Soviets. The third was military action—to send in British parachutists and marine detachments, backed up by America's Sixth Fleet. Of course the Egyptians would resist, and the result would be war, perhaps even a very big war if the Soviets decided to get involved.

The brothers speculated that Britain wouldn't use force without American backing, and American backing wasn't likely in an election year, with Eisenhower defending his presidency against an opposition party hungry for an issue. "Thus the betting is about ten to one on a policy of waffling, and the grumbling acceptance of another major setback for the weakening West."

AFTER THE 1956 Republican convention in San Francisco, Joe retreated to a health spa called Bill Brown's and renewed his intermittent battle against excess weight. After shedding eight pounds, and three inches off his middle, he felt better physically but worse about the administration and the election. He disliked Eisenhower and his administration so intensely that he longed to see them cast aside by the voters. Yet the Democrats had once again nominated Adlai Stevenson, and Joe disliked him almost as much. He expected an Eisenhower victory, largely on the strength of the president's "glowing personality." As Senate majority leader Lyndon Johnson had put it to Stewart, the American people would re-elect Eisenhower "even if they have to send him to a taxidermist first."

Meanwhile, Eden and French premier Guy Mollet were hatching plans for military action. They had the will, the troops (scattered in various locations around the Mediterranean), and a powerful reason to confront Nasser. They lacked only a pretext. They knew an effort to retake the canal would be branded an act of aggression by anti-Western voices around the world, and even by Dulles and others in the West. But they hoped they could neutralize Dulles with some kind of international rationale. They found it in discussions with Israel's Ben-Gurion.

The idea was to have the Israelis attack Nasser's fedayeen in the Gaza Strip as an act of self-defense. When war broke out, Britain and France would intervene in the region to restore order and retake the canal, ensuring its use for all nations. Secret discussions took place. Plans were devised and set in motion. The idea was that the whole operation could unfold, and the canal be reopened, before world opinion could generate any real opposition.

The plan was ill-conceived from beginning to end: it was unrealistic to think that troops for such an operation could be assembled from far-off locales without U.S. intelligence noticing. And the planners could not foresee that their bold and risky military adventure would become ensnared with another momentous international drama in Hungary, where the Soviets would bring up tanks to crush an ill-starred independence uprising. As the United States approached election day these dramatic events transformed the campaign into a jumble of moral and geopolitical questions impossible to sort out in the heat of the moment.

On October 30, a week before the election, Britain and France delivered an ultimatum to Nasser: Accept the West's custody of the canal or face war. A day later, British and French warplanes bombed Nasser's military positions along the canal. On November 5, British forces landed in Egypt and occupied Port Fuad and other parts of the canal area.

When the Middle East drama began unfolding according to the predictions of American intelligence, Eisenhower was outraged that his friends the British would take such action without telling him. He accepted Dulles's call for the moral high ground and drew a parallel between the British-French actions in Suez and the Soviet aggression in Hungary. In campaign speeches, the president declared, "There can be no peace without law. And there can be no law if we were to invoke one code of international conduct for those who oppose us and another for our friends."

This faulty reasoning ignored the fact that the British and French wanted to secure an international waterway that had been seized illegally, while the Soviets had used force to keep a neighboring country under their yoke. But Eisenhower's moralistic posture proved devastating, and it helped bring upon the British and French a barrage of invective from the Third World. At the United Nations, the U.S. ambassador joined the verbal assault on America's allies, and the hall exploded in applause and assent.

British and French resolve crumbled in the face of such opposition. On November 8 the British declared a cease-fire, and the next month witnessed a humiliating retreat as United Nations troops moved in and Nasser blocked the canal by scuttling hulks throughout the waterway. Only Israel emerged a victor, having destroyed a large Egyptian force in Gaza.

To the Alsops the drama was a triple disaster—for Britain, Europe, and America. It was further evidence that the West was in decline and that the decline was perhaps irreversible. They could not forgive Eisenhower and Dulles for turning America's back on Britain in her hour of decision. Perhaps, they wrote, the French and British had been wrong to initiate such an adventure, and surely they had been wrong to keep Washington in the dark. "But once the attempt had been started for good or ill, the fate of the Western Alliance automatically hung upon its success," they wrote.

The brothers used the column repeatedly to castigate the administration's handling of the crisis. On November 16 they wrote:

> The most strategically vital region of the modern world has been handed to the Kremlin on a silver platter—with the American government as a rather conspicuous platter-bearer. . . . What must now be expected, therefore, is the progressive collapse of every remaining Western position in the Middle East, under the assault of the Nasser-led Arab nationalist movement. Arab nationalism will now be more inflamed than ever before because of the fruitless attempt to topple its leader. It will be more confident than ever because of the apparent Western surrender to the recent Soviet threats. It will be more Soviet-influenced than ever because not only Nasser, but the Arab nationalists everywhere will now tend to accept the Soviets as their guides and protectors. And the Soviets will use the Arab nationalists, cooly and ruthlessly, as instruments to cut the Western Alliance's oil jugular in the Middle East.

The Alsops found themselves at odds with those who attacked the Anglo-French operation as foolhardy and immoral. *Time* magazine, a steadfast Eisenhower supporter, needled the brothers and other high-profile newsmen by suggesting they had been snookered by the British and French embassies playing "the diplomatic game of foxes and lions to maneuver [their countries] out of a jam." *Time* singled out the brothers as having "swung even more wildly" than other newsmen taken in by diplomatic public-relations campaigns.

But the brothers carried on the debate for weeks, in the column, at gatherings, in correspondence. Hugh Gaitskell, British opposition leader and a bitter critic of Eden's policies, wrote that he had been "pretty surprised" by Joe's recent writings and that perhaps Joe's London sources had been too much on one side of the issue. While there had been "a lot of jingoism and anti-Americanism" in London, he said, he felt certain that "the intellectual and moral leadership in the country has been entirely on our side." In response, Joe lectured Gaitskell: Nasser was not a communist; he was an anticommunist. But everything he wanted to do was what Moscow wanted him to do, which was to destroy the remaining British positions in the Arab world. He added:

> I can foresee a day when, as Labour prime minister, you may be called upon to choose between lying quiet and looking pleasant while Britain's oil jugular is absolutely cut through, or preparing for and ordering the military occupation of Kuwait, plus any other military measures that may be needed to counter the reaction to an occupation of Kuwait by Nasser and the other Arab nationalists. It will be a horrible choice. It will be all the more difficult to make because the American leadership and the British Labour leadership have talked, in these last weeks, in such exclusively moralistic terms.

JOE'S HYPERBOLE, as usual, undermined his argument. The move into Kuwait did not prove necessary (at least not until three decades later), and despite serious efforts the Soviets could not forge Arab nationalism into a weapon against the West's oil jugular. Still, the Alsops saw the Suez crisis with clarity and wisdom. It did indeed mark the end of Britain's role as a major participant in the world's top diplomatic deliberations. Anthony Eden, consumed in the fires of crisis and defeat, soon was out of power, and his successor, Harold Macmillan, sent a cable to his old friend Dwight Eisenhower: OVER TO YOU. Britain was out of the great power game.

The historic Anglo-American partnership was now transformed, the one-voice English-speaking diplomacy now gone. In facing Soviet expansionism and other unpleasantness around the world, America would be on her own.

The decline of Britain also marked the beginning of the end of the Anglo-Saxon elite in America. For generations this element had been the dominant source of American leadership, its rules and values and outlook preserved and fostered not only by such surface institutions as Groton and Harvard's Porcellian Club, but in the profounder aspects of the nation's life. It had been the single most powerful influence in the lives and thinking of Joe and Stewart Alsop, just as it had been for so many of the men then forging and executing American foreign policy. For a time in the postwar era, after America had emerged as the world's dominant power, the old Anglophile elite had continued its influence much as before, and in world affairs was seen as perhaps more influential than ever. The brothers had reveled in their role as its chronicler and cheerleader.

But for generations the elite had drawn inspiration and guidance from its ties to the old country. The American worldview mirrored British policy; twice in a quarter century America had entered bloody wars to protect Britain's world dominance. Underlying this was the conviction that the British empire had been on balance a force for good in the world, that the traditions and principles emanating from generations of Anglo-Saxon successes on both sides of the Atlantic represented hope for wide-ranging peace and prosperity. From such convictions America's Anglo-Saxon elite derived its confidence.

But now the vestiges of empire were gone, and the elite would begin to experience an erosion of confidence. With the old Anglo-American ties broken or strained, a new guiding spirit would have to be found.

It was not surprising that the Alsops would take up the cause, almost by instinct, of Sir Anthony Eden. It was not surprising that they would feel the rising acid of bitterness at the Dulles-Eisenhower abandonment of the motherland—which Stewart years later referred to as America's "matricidal role" in the Suez episode. Of all the men of their class and generation who had been shaped by schools like Groton and who had experienced the formative influences of the Ivy League, they were the elite's leading commentators, who defined in words what had been the essence, purpose, and guiding spirit of U.S. foreign policy for a hundred years. They knew that the Suez events of 1956 were a blow not just to Britain and to the Anglo-American partnership, but to America itself and to the traditions of American decision-making that they had come to regard as beneficent and hallowed.

23

SEPARATE WAYS

"Floods of Tears, Diluted with Champagne"

MIDDLE AGE DID not settle gently upon the frame or the consciousness of Joe Alsop. At the end of 1956, as he reached his forty-sixth birthday, Joe felt old and depressed. His tendency to gain weight grew more stubborn, and only through periodic retreats to Brown's health spa did he manage to maintain himself. He kept two wardrobes in two separate closets— one for those times when his weight crept up on him and one for after his refreshing trips to Brown's.

Professionally, the brothers were an immense success. Joe's annual income had hit $36,000, a princely sum for any newsman at that time. But he felt he was in a rut, with few prospects for significant improvement in his circumstances. He felt life was passing him by. A year earlier he had spent a weekend with Harvard classmates, the twenty-third such reunion since their 1932 graduation, and he was struck by the impact of age on them. "It is a little depressing," he wrote to a friend, "to discover that where we used to be able to go through four days of martinis and tennis and champagne and swimming and whisky and sailing and picnics and sightseeing, we are all destroyed nowadays by one day of martinis alone. . . . Oh dear, I hate getting old."

As for Washington, Joe felt four more years of an aging and listless Eisenhower would bring disaster upon the country. "There is something rancid about this city now," he wrote to Chip Bohlen at the height of the Suez trouble. To Martin Sommers, he compared the capital to "a boatload of happy people, gorged with food, too full of wine even to look out the portholes, hearing only the band playing in their saloon, and steaming full speed ahead toward the rocks." In addition to Suez and Hungary, there was Sputnik, the Soviets' successful launch of a satellite that orbited the globe. Khrushchev's victory in the first leg of the space race had shocked the American consciousness with a sudden sense of inferiority. To the Alsops it was merely a reflection of trends they had been warning about for years.

All this led Joe to conclude that he had to leave Washington and set up shop in Europe as a full-time correspondent. "The tempo of events abroad has now accelerated, and the tension everywhere has now grown, to a point where much more continuous foreign coverage is really essential," Joe wrote to Brown Reid at the *Herald Tribune*. He would become the fireman overseas for a year while Stewart would handle the stateside alarms. Thus they would deliver more columns from the epicenters of events both at home and abroad.

The Reids accepted the idea and even consented to give Joe an additional $4,000 annually for expenses. At the *Saturday Evening Post*, Ben Hibbs agreed to take four articles a year from Joe at the regular rate of $3,500 each; the magazine would continue to accept articles from Stewart at the same rate; and the brothers would continue to receive $4,000 a year for their weekly memos filled with story ideas, observations, and gossip. In addition, Hibbs agreed to pay Joe $6,000 a year for expenses.

Stewart's struggles with life were of a different sort. Still in his early forties, he wasn't experiencing the same age anxieties that plagued Joe. True, he frequently moaned in a joking way about getting older, but he didn't seem preoccupied with it. He enjoyed life and seemed comfortable with what he had accomplished as well as what he had yet to accomplish. Stewart's problem was Joe. The older brother's behavior was becoming unbearable, and his insistence on taking the choice assignments was beginning to make Stewart feel professionally thwarted.

What's more, Joe continued to demand that he get 55 percent of the partnership earnings, and this was grating on Stewart more and more. He felt he provided an equal share of the work and should be equally compensated. But Joe wouldn't hear of it; he wouldn't even discuss it. He had "invented" the column, said Joe, and without him Stewart wouldn't even be in the trade.

"Stoooo," Joe declared at one point, "you have to remember that I am the *senior* partner and you are the *junior* partner."

Tish could see that Stewart was "deeply unhappy." He hated the thought of terminating the partnership, but that's where things seemed to be headed.

And now Joe was proposing to live overseas, and Stewart didn't like the idea. He feared Joe's expenses would cut into their combined income, and that a long-distance partnership would simply spawn new tensions between them. He disliked being shunted to domestic reporting while Joe handled all the international news. When Stewart raised his concerns about the plan, and also noted his longstanding complaints, Joe took the offensive. He suggested that his brother should perhaps embark on a discreet search of professional alternatives during Joe's year abroad.

This was a bluff. Joe expected Stewart to decide that his best option was with their partnership, and he hoped the arguments would now cease. He was wrong. With the partnership being altered to the junior partner's further disadvantage, Stewart concluded that a job search might be a good idea.

JOE RENTED OUT the Dumbarton house for $300 a month, plus gardening and utility bills. The José and Maria team stayed on at $70 a week, paid by the lessor. "Love is the great secret in dealing with them," Joe advised his new tenant. "Love, plus remembering that they are rather competitive, so if you make a present to one you must make a small present to the other, if you praise one you must find some reason to praise the other."

In Paris, Joe found quarters in the Hotel Saint-James et d'Albany on the rue St Honoré, a pleasant but unpretentious old structure conveniently located in the city center. Furnished as a living room, it had a hideaway bed and a large vestibule that Joe used as a closet. The service was good, and the price was excellent: $2,000 a year.

He spent Christmas 1956 with Bill and Susan Mary Patten—lunch at their home with the children, then an "exquisite dinner," on Joe, at one of Paris's expensive restaurants. Later the three went on to a party at the flat of a Paris socialite named Mona Bismarck, at the Hotel Lambert, once a great Louis XIV palace and still in original condition. Joe ended the evening "coquetting with the local reigning beauty," twenty-four-year-old Vicomtesse de Ribes, who looked "rather like the wonderfully pretty serpent dressed by the late Dior." Remembering his flirtation the next morning, Joe confessed to his brother John that he "felt rather a fool."

For New Year's Eve, Susan Mary arranged a quiet dinner party to include Joe; Frank Giles, the Paris correspondent for *The Times* of London, and his wife, Lady Katherine; U.S. ambassador Douglas Dillon and his wife, Phyllis; and Pierre and Elise Bordeaux-Groult. Mme. Bordeaux-Groult, née Elise Duggan, had been a young beauty who captivated Stewart and John in their carefree New York days; her new husband had been known until their marriage as Paris's most eligible bachelor. At Phyllis Dillon's suggestion, they had the dinner at the embassy.

Joe also attended a soiree for the Dillons at the home of Alain de Rothschild, who owned, among many other things, the Château Lafite vineyards. There thirty of Paris's social lions "all but bathed" in Lafite 1900—fifty-seven-year-old claret "still rich and marvelous and in perfect condition." When Joe remarked to Rothschild that it was the best wine he had ever tasted, the baron responded somewhat airily.

"Well, it's all right now," he said. "The last time we tried it was ten years ago, and then it was a little acid. But now I think it's come round nicely."

With the new year Joe flew to Moscow to begin an extended Soviet tour. On the advice of his CIA friends, he decided against staying with Chip and Avis Bohlen for fear of bringing Kremlin disapproval upon the ambassador; but the two friends engaged in some spirited debates, particularly on Suez. Chip had complained to Joe that his columns on the crisis had presented the U.S. position "in the worst possible light."

Joe traveled through Russian Siberia and found himself fascinated by what he saw. The itinerary was a catalogue of unfamiliar and strange-sounding names—Kuybyshev to Kustanay to Akmolinsk (Tselinograd) to Barnaul to Kemerovo. He interviewed local officials and industrialists from early to late each day and filled his notebook with illuminating comments on a land in ferment. In Kuybyshev, a growing industrial city, Joe interviewed two leading factory managers, the banker, the doctor, and the newspaper editor, along with lesser persons. "It has been one of the best reporting days (in the sense of never a dull moment) that I've ever put in," he wrote to Martin Sommers.

He spent a morning with a man named Aleksandr Vassiliev, head of the local ball bearing factory, whom he described as "a human phenomenon of intense interest for anyone who wishes to penetrate at least a little way into the great Soviet mystery." Working devotedly by day and studying engineering at night, Vassiliev had moved up from metal polisher to factory manager. He seemed dedicated to his work and to the system for which he toiled, although he demonstrated little interest in politics.

For two thousand miles Joe encountered no indoor plumbing, and with temperatures often at forty below it was "a really quite remarkable experience," he wrote to Corinne. Most of the hotels were simply large dormitories with no facilities for a bath, and twice Joe shaved with tea because no other hot water was available. In Kemorovo, a city of about 250,000 known for its coal mines, the hotel had eighty rooms and one bathtub, which Joe monopolized.

There was no shortage of hospitality. In Kustanay he enjoyed a vodka and smorgasbord feast lasting two hours, only to be followed by another round of vodka and another smorgasbord and then, at eleven-thirty p.m., by an enormous Kazakh dish called *bisermak*—overdone mutton, mutton fat, and slimy noodles, eaten with the fingers. He wrote to Corinne of "the extreme niceness" of the people, the competence of those in key positions, and "the friendliness of everyone."

Returning to Moscow to write his hinterland columns and line up interviews, Joe spent an evening with a young embassy couple, the Heyward Ishams, and in a quiet Moscow restaurant they encountered two young engineers. After dinner the five wandered off to a milk bar, a kind of young people's hangout where one could buy ice cream, beer, and wine (but not vodka). The place was filled with healthy-looking students whose faces lacked the pallor of those from the war generation who had suffered so much malnutrition. The young people, mostly in American garb, showed great affection for the Americans.

Joe invited the two Russians to join him and the Ishams for a nightcap in his hotel room, where they exchanged pleasant chitchat and avoided politics. "One could . . . feel the longing for a little gaiety, the desire to know more about the West, the rebellion against the airlessness of this system," he wrote Corinne.

For two weeks Joe waited in Moscow for a Khrushchev interview. Then word came that the party leader would see Joe in his big bleak office, nerve center of the Communist Party's Central Committee. Joe was struck by the man's gusto and self-confidence, which had diminished not at all since Stewart's encounter with him two years earlier. Joe was also struck by his ignorance of the outer world. Khrushchev seemed truly to believe everything he said about America's aggressive designs. Joe could see in his demeanor some of the gambler's recklessness that had stirred such concern in the West. His agricultural policies and his plans for industrial reorganization were huge political gambles, Joe wrote to Sommers, "and his foreign policy is even more venturesome than Stalin's."

Khrushchev used the interview to initiate a propaganda ploy. The Soviet Union, said the party boss, desired to "normalize" relations with the United States, and he was prepared to withdraw all Soviet troops from foreign countries to further that goal. All he wanted in return was for America to withdraw its troops from Europe and Asia. In essence, wrote Joe, Khrushchev wanted a "Fortress America" policy as his price for relaxing world tensions. As an effort to force America onto the defensive in the arena of world opinion, it was clever; as a diplomatic initiative it lacked seriousness.

But the gambit generated interest, and Joe's story was splashed across front pages throughout America and Europe. The *Herald Tribune* headlined its story, "Khrushchev Talks to Alsop" and ran a photo of Joe along with Khrushchev's.

Joe's visit changed his views of the Soviet Union. He had previously considered it almost invincible because the regime could use internal as well as external force to achieve its ends, and this perception had fueled his gloomy assessment of the West's danger. Now he saw how difficult it was to manage a highly technical society without freedom. As the Soviets lumbered into the modern age, they would need trained and proficient managers. This would require a first-class education system and confidence that management decisions would not bring down the wrath of state authority. This in turn would force the system to grant greater freedom. But could the Soviet leadership grant a little freedom without having to grant a great deal? "This," wrote Joe to Sommers, "is the inherent conflict."

Joe enjoyed the life of global gadabout, but he sometimes felt his travels kept him from understanding anything very deeply, confined as he was to "the surface aspects of local political situations." In a letter to Katharine Graham, he compared himself to a young Englishman he had encountered in the Middle East who traveled the world selling British woolens. When it seemed they had talked enough about the woolen industry, Joe inquired about the man's impressions of various capitals he had visited.

"How was Djakarta?"

"Demand for woolens was very poor, because of currency shortage."

"And how was Bangkok?"

"That was quite good for tropical worsteds."

"It seemed to me comical at the time," Joe wrote, "but when I thought it over, he struck me as being exactly like myself."

Yet he loved the life and the action, loved being away from Washington and slipping into the social whirl of major world capitals. In April 1957, with spirits high, he began another tour of the Middle East. Two positive changes had occurred since Joe's visit the previous year. First, a discernible American Middle Eastern policy had emerged in Washington. In London, Joe had learned that Eisenhower and Dulles had assured Harold Macmillan, the new prime minister, that America was committed to a policy of pressuring Nasser out of office. "It is a very tricky sort of policy," Joe wrote to Sommers. It involved clandestine operations throughout the Middle East and alliances with leaders in the region who didn't have the masses solidly behind them. The president had outlined his position in what became known as the Eisenhower Doctrine, which promised military aid to any Middle Eastern government that asked for help against communist aggression.

The other development was King Saud's change of heart. The old Saudi monarch had abandoned Nasser decisively, and had clamped down hard on Egyptian infiltrators and Palestinian terrorists. With Nasser slipping more and more into the role of Soviet puppet and with Syria now in the Cairo orbit, King Saud emerged as the key figure in the new American policy.

While in Cairo Joe heard about a coup attempt against Jordan's young King Hussein, and the Amman crisis extracted him from Egypt "like a rotten tooth that leaves the jaw easily." Arriving in Amman, he checked into a dreary old hotel called the Amman Club, which served as headquarters for the pack of correspondents who had flooded into town at the first whiff of trouble.

They found a story of treachery and intrigue, with Hussein threatened from within and without. Pulling the strings were Cairo and Moscow, but the inside accomplice was the king's young friend and military leader, Ali Abu Nuwar. The fires of ambition had lured Nuwar into a plot of betrayal that maneuvered the king into isolation as Soviet puppets took over his cabinet and then attempted a military coup. The aim had been to transform Jordan into an Egyptian satellite.

But the king had stood his ground, courageously refusing to flee Amman and deftly turning his military against the plotters. By the end of the fateful Saturday of April 13, 1957, Nuwar and his band of conspirators had been thwarted and sent off to exile. The immediate danger had passed.

Arriving just days after the coup collapsed, Joe still felt crisis in the air. The Syrians were threatening to intervene, and Western intelligence picked up signals that the Israelis contemplated a campaign to capture Jordan's strategic West Bank. To protect Jordan, King Saud placed his troops under Hussein's personal command, and the United States dispatched the Sixth Fleet into the eastern Mediterranean as a "hands off" warning.

When things quieted down in Amman, Joe traveled to Beirut—"a wonderfully corrupt but extremely agreeable place," as he put it to John, "physically lovely . . . , with the best food . . . in the whole of the Middle East and with an astonishing floating population of American oil men, well drillers who have been making their pile on the Persian payroll, tourists, newspapermen, rich sheiks and other grandees from all over the Arab world." He spent a week at the lavish St. George Hotel, filing three columns, finishing a *Saturday Evening Post* piece, and enjoying evening repasts with his newspaper friends on the St. George veranda overlooking the Mediterranean.

Joe marred one dinner when *The New York Times*'s Sam Brewer gently corrected a column in which Joe had reported a vast amount of Soviet military aid flowing through the Syrian port of Latakia. Brewer, who had visited Latakia, suggested diplomatically that it wasn't big enough to handle the magnitude of shipping reported by Joe.

"You're full of shit!" Joe shot back, stung at being corrected in front of his friends. Brewer calmly replied that he had come for a pleasant evening, not to be insulted, and walked out. Joe tried to ignore the episode, but he clearly was troubled. Later, in the men's room, he raised the matter with *The Wall Street Journal*'s Phil Geyelin.

"So, Phil, what am I going to do about Brewer?" he asked. Geyelin didn't know.

"I can't send flowers," mused Joe. Then he brightened and added: "I know—I'll have a dinner party for him." And he did.

"Joe was always the guy who wanted to keep the party going," recalled Geyelin. "He wanted to be one of the boys, but he was too smart for the boys, and so he always got into arguments."

He always exploded when things didn't go as he wished. Arriving in Damascus a few days later, he found himself waiting in an anteroom for two hours while officials searched a vast network of file cabinets to determine whether he was Jewish. Joe threw a tantrum.

"I must see the foreign minister," he demanded. "I have a very important appointment that I simply cannot miss. I must phone the foreign minister this minute." His fulminations only ensured that he would be held longer.

Between interviews and writing, Joe incessantly worked the phones to seek an extended interview with King Hussein, and finally his efforts paid off. Hurrying back to Amman, he spent the better part of two days with the king, taking his measure and hearing all the dramatic details of the attempted coup. Joe was the envy of his colleagues one night when the correspondents gathered at the gate of the Interior Ministry, which served as state censor. The officers would toss from the balcony the censored pages from the reporters' files, and the pages, littered with red markings signifying extensive excisions, would waft down to the ground and get kicked up by the wind as the hapless reporters chased after them. Then the pages of Joe's story were tossed down—with no red marks. The censors didn't tamper with exclusive royal interviews.

Joe left the Middle East in a rare mood of optimism. The gloom of Suez had receded as Hussein's brilliant turnaround shifted the regional balance in the West's favor. The Soviets had suffered a bad case of scorched fingers, and, with Saud and Hussein now steadfast Western allies, Egypt and Syria found themselves isolated.

In Paris, Joe received a visit from Corinne, and the two went out to dinner with a group that included Phil Geyelin. At one point Joe asserted a point, and Corinne cut him off.

"Oh, Joe," she said, "you don't know what you are talking about."

Geyelin was surprised to see Joe retreat. "She was the only person I ever saw get away with that," Geyelin recalled years later.

Joe was less amused when he was cut off at a high-toned London dinner at the home of Lady Cunard, an American-born expatriate who had married a wealthy Londoner and become one of that city's leading social climbers (as well as mistress to maestro Sir Thomas Beecham). She was "a tough little egg, tough as nails," as Susan Mary described her, and she wanted to be constantly amused. At her dinner she turned to Joe and addressed him in her affected, elaborate manner.

"Now, Mr. Alsop, you come from a very peculiar country, which of course is my own native land as well, and you possess much influence within that country. Tell us, please, of the current fortunes of the strange land from which we both come. Please illuminate this company that has assembled here this evening."

"Well, Lady Cunard," replied Joe, "it is like this," and he commenced to expound his elaborate views on the state of America. But Lady Cunard didn't want a discursive reply; she wanted a quip. She brusquely turned to the other side of the table and addressed another guest in the same flowery manner. Joe couldn't believe he had just been cut off so dismissively. He sat silently through the rest of the evening, and, according to Isaiah Berlin, "he never recovered from it."

BACK IN WASHINGTON, Stewart enjoyed greater leeway in cultivating inner-circle sources who had been Joe's exclusive preserve. He spent considerable time with Lyndon Johnson of Texas, the forceful, pro-fane, and brilliant Senate Democratic leader. Johnson, who for years had been solicitous toward Joe, took a shine also to his brother and regularly invited Stewart to the Capitol for lunch or drinks. Johnson was an excellent source—always generous with political gossip and inside information, although everything he revealed seemed to cast himself in a heroic light.

In November 1957 Stewart and Tish spent a weekend at Johnson's LBJ Ranch near Austin. The senator met them at an Austin fund-raiser, then whisked them into his Lincoln Continental for the hour-long late-night drive to the ranch—with Johnson driving at seventy to eighty miles per hour the entire way. At one point the senator began railing against newsmen, calling them slaves to their publications' advertisers.

"Lyndon," said Stewart, "I'm not an old hack."

"I'm sorry, Stew," replied Johnson. "I didn't mean any insults."

On Saturday morning it was back into the Continental for a tour of the ranch, of Johnson's birthplace, his school, his daddy's home. Then Tish went back to the ranch while Johnson took Stewart to a fishing hole for three hours of fishing mixed with interviewing. Later, while the two couples were driving around spotting deer, the clock hit five p.m.

"It's time!" exclaimed Johnson, and he reached back to his auto bar, poured himself a huge slug of whiskey, and drank it down like water.

"Since my heart attack," he explained, pouring himself another bourbon, "my doctor said I could only drink between the hours of five and seven." He used the time aggressively.

Back at the ranch, Johnson insisted on walking into dinner first, like a sovereign. At table, when he wasn't talking—which wasn't often—he would bare his belly and scratch reflectively. After dinner, he herded the company back into the Lincoln for further deer spotting. Around mid-night they found themselves at a little farmhouse, where Johnson blasted the horn until a middle-aged woman staggered out in her bathrobe.

"These people want to see the scrapbooks," yelled Johnson to the woman, who turned out to be his cousin. So they tromped in and sat down while the cousin produced a huge stack of scrapbooks tracing the LBJ career.

"Okay, Stew, here are the records of my life," said Johnson, and he lay down on a sofa, placed his cowboy hat over his face, and promptly went to sleep.

The next morning Johnson insisted on taking Tish to Catholic mass. Afterward, while the Alsops were packing for their return to Washington, the senator lounged in the pool on a large float, with his telephone alongside on a small one.

Johnson gave Stewart an expensive transistor radio upon his departure, and since he was surrounded by the senator's family, all smiling approvingly, the reporter felt he couldn't refuse the gift. He later returned the favor by sending Lady Bird Johnson a leatherbound cookbook that gave special attention to methods of preparing catfish, a Johnson favorite.

Stewart also developed a warm association with Vice President Richard Nixon. Though Nixon lacked personal charm, Stewart wrote Sommers, he had an "absolutely first rate intelligence and unsurpassed political instincts." Privately, Nixon criticized the White House team for failing to comprehend the political dangers in the Sputnik launch. "He told me," wrote Stewart to Sommers, "that Eisenhower and the Republicans have enjoyed one great central asset—the feeling of confidence in Eisenhower in handling defense and foreign policy matters; and that Sputnik, as a symbol, had dangerously eroded that confidence."

When the Senate took up the first serious civil rights bill since Reconstruction, Nixon gave Stewart insider briefings on the administration's legislative strategy. The vice president also slipped him a nice story about the administration's difficulty in filling major jobs from the ranks of corporate America. This, Stewart wrote to Joe, seemed "calculated to make a newspaperman feel grateful." And when Nixon decided to back California senator William Knowland for governor, the vice president gave the scoop to Stewart, for front-page display in the *Herald Tribune*.

Stewart and Tish also maintained their high-profile social life. During one of Corinne's Washington visits they held a dinner for 26 people, including Tom Braden and wife Joan, who were visiting from California. Braden had become the owner and publisher of a small newspaper in Oceanside, but he and his wife loved visiting Washington and usually stayed with the Alsops when there. Joan, lively and socially ambitious, was something of an "enchantress," as one old friend described her. Chip Bohlen, in Washington between diplomatic assignments, came to the Alsop dinner and stayed until four a.m.—"arguments but no fights, and rather agreeable," Stewart wrote to Joe. Chip was complimentary on Joe's Soviet pieces—"though with the inevitable faint note of condescension." In the fall, Stewart and Tish invited more than 150 to a ball. Attendees included senators, top diplomats, journalistic grandees, and ambassadors from Britain, Italy, Sweden, Peru, and the Netherlands.

In July, Stewart revealed in the column that the Soviets had successfully tested a long-range, multistage missile. He called it an event "of grave international significance," particularly in light of America's failure in her first effort to test such a rocket a few weeks earlier. Pentagon officials pooh-poohed the story publicly, but within weeks it was confirmed in both Washington and Moscow.

Also in July, Stewart broke the story of Defense Secretary Charles Wilson's proposal to hold expenditures for missiles to 10 percent of the military budget in the following fiscal year. At a National Security

Council meeting after Stewart's story appeared, Eisenhower "blew his stack" over the leak, according to two participants at the meeting. The president's penchant for secrecy disgusted Stewart. "It is nobody's business, of course," he wrote to Joe with sarcasm, "if the administration decides to let the Soviets beat us to the ICBM, in order to cut taxes in the next election year."

Stewart's performance on the missile story filled Joe with pride. After the French magazine *Paris-Match* praised the Alsops' consistent scoops on defense stories, Joe wrote, "The praise . . . was entirely earned by you, and it has raised our stock in France in the most dramatic way."

But by fall a series of powerful events in Arkansas yanked Stewart's attention back to domestic politics. Defying a federal court order, the segregationist governor, Orval Faubus, called out the Arkansas National Guard to bar a group of black students from enrolling at Little Rock's Central High. There followed a string of tension-filled days as mobs swarmed around the building to preserve segregation, and black students showed up to enter the school. At one point, the mob rushed two black reporters; this gave nine black pupils an opportunity to slip into the building. The protest turned ugly as the mob rushed police barricades and fought to storm the school to extract the "niggers." Police officers quickly removed the black students to calm the mob.

These events threatened to ignite more violence not only in Little Rock but throughout the South, where white majorities remained bent on preserving the entrenched system of segregation. On September 25, Eisenhower ordered in five hundred paratroopers of the 101st Airborne Division to restore order and enforce the court-ordered integration of the school. By that time Stewart had filed two columns on the crisis from Washington, then rushed to Little Rock to report from the scene.

Stewart's Little Rock pieces reflected a journalistic trait that was becoming a hallmark of his work. He projected himself increasingly as the detached and dispassionate observer searching for fundamental insights into complex social and political developments. He opposed Southern segregation as a blot on the underlying principles of American democracy. And the venom he saw in the streets of Little Rock shocked him. "I have never had before in this country," he wrote to Sommers, "such a queer feeling of being a stranger in a foreign land."

But Stewart resisted being caught up in the emotionalism of the day. He avoided political sanctimony or moralizing and sought instead to describe and analyze, to give readers greater understanding of events. Stewart's interest was in the clash of political forces, and he knew these forces often were deeply personal, cultural or emotional. While he was a liberal on civil rights, he harbored conservative views on the implementation of democracy. When it came to emotion-laden issues, he favored incremental progress and stability over passion.

In Little Rock, Stewart had a depressing look at the race issue close up. He was there on the day of greatest violence, when the black newsmen were roughed up and the nine black children slipped into Central High temporarily. It was a clear, crisp Monday morning when he wandered down to the school to encounter an oddly cheerful scene—crowds of people milling around as they might at any country fair. The men wore overalls and colorful open shirts, while the girls and young women sported the day's standard garb of saddle shoes and wide skirts. As he made his way down the street, he received friendly greetings of "howdy" from the locals.

But when they realized he was a Northern reporter, the townsfolk turned hostile.

"We Southern people don't like to talk to strangers," said a man in a visored hat. Another, noting a newspaper Stewart carried, said, "If you want to stay healthy, you better throw that away. Now, that's just my advice." One large red-faced man shouted at a group of reporters, "Nigger lovers!" A high school boy responded with a snicker.

"Go ahead," he said to the red-faced man. "You can say anything you want. They're chicken."

Later, in the midst of a knot of bystanders, Stewart saw a high school girl with straw-blond hair and red-rimmed blue eyes quaking with indignation. "A damn nigger come into my English class and sat down. Just sat right down there," she said. The people murmured angrily, glancing over at the school. Another student exclaimed, "I just started crying when I heard they'd got in there. I started crying and I couldn't stop." One man looked over at the school with anger in his eyes. "Those nigger kids are gonna have to come out some time, and you just see what happens then," he said with what Stewart called "awful relish."

Recording the scene in graphic detail, Stewart wrote that when the black students were spirited out of the school by police, a palpable sense of anticlimax and disappointment emerged in the crowd. "For it was a crowd with a thirst for violence. . . . And its thirst for violence was by no means satisfied by the beating up of a couple of Negro adults."

Stewart took pains to note that he hadn't encountered the same hatred or thirst for violence among shopkeepers and others interviewed away from the emotional scene around Central High. But the vast majority of Southern whites passionately opposed school integration, and thus those few who welcomed violence could sway events. The withdrawal of the black children from the school, said Stewart, "was a capitulation to the veto power of violence."

That is why the . . . scene at Little Rock Central High School on Monday was a tragic scene. For its meaning was plain. If the American government chooses to use its great powers to force through school integration in the South, it will pay the price of years of bitterness and violence. Yet if the American government does not use its powers to that end, it will be bowing to the blackmail power of violence, and permitting the law of the land to be flouted. Then the price may ultimately be even higher. Thus either course may have disastrous consequences. The country, in short, is faced with a problem to which there is no easy, good, or wholly moral solution, and perhaps no solution at all. That is the tragic meaning of Little Rock.

Stewart's Little Rock columns won high praise. Sommers called them "magnificent reporting," and Joe called them "really brilliant." But two Southern newspapers canceled the column because of Stewart's Little Rock filings, and opted for the more pro-Southern column of conservative David Lawrence. "I do not think what I wrote was anti-South in any way," Stewart wrote to Joe, "but feeling down there is running so high that you either have to write like Lawrence or you're a Yankee nigger-lover."

As THE YEAR unfolded, Stewart's fears about frictions and problems in the partnership proved prescient. The brothers' relationship began to deteriorate almost from the beginning of 1957.

It started with small matters, such as Joe's view that Stewart wasn't communicating with him sufficiently on matters of column scheduling. "It helps me to be kept . . . fully informed of the state of the scheduling so don't let us argue about it any longer," Joe wrote to Stewart after a testy exchange of letters on the subject. Stewart retorted that he had provided adequate information, and anyway it certainly was more communication than he had ever got when he was overseas and Joe had routinely held Stew's columns in reserve for as much as three weeks while replying to inquiries with silence. Stewart noted that he had written Joe seventeen full-length letters while Joe's replies had numbered only six. "It is impossible to carry on a largely one-way correspondence, since I don't know what you want to know," he wrote.

Joe replied, "Goddam it, Stew, you ought to know by now how much this means to me. You have been so grossly inconsiderate about this matter that I now grow passionately angry every time I think about it."

The wrangling also involved matters of coverage. After the Little Rock events, Joe chastised his brother for not getting to the Arkansas capital more quickly. Stewart dismissed the "irritable and irritating" letter by suggesting Joe should have enough confidence in him "to let me make up my own mind on the best time for covering a story like Little Rock." He argued that his timing was "just right."

Joe also lit into Stewart when he learned an accounting system he had set up before his departure had gone awry. Joe had intended to deposit his partnership checks into a domestic bank, as a kind of savings plan, while other income went to his Paris bank for expenses. But the brothers' new secretary, Peggy Puffenberger, had misunderstood and informed their accountant that the partnership money also should go to Paris. Assuming that Joe had changed his mind, the accountant diverted the money to Paris. By the time the problem was discovered, he had funneled $23,666.67 into the Paris account. The amounts in his account had puzzled Joe, but he nonetheless had spent half of it. Now he blamed Stewart.

"I have been grossly misled by the really gross piece of carelessness which completely upset the seemingly foolproof system I took such care to set up," he wrote. "I cannot understand how you can possibly have failed to check Miss Puffenberger's first letters having to do with my affairs."

Even before such exchanges became routine, Stewart's frustrations had reached a breaking point. In February, at a dinner with Marty Sommers, he had broached the idea of a more formal relationship with the *Saturday Evening Post*. Sommers had been receptive, and the two had agreed to let the idea gestate for a few months and resume discussions in the fall. As the issues between him and Joe became more rancorous, Stewart's resolve to depart the column intensified.

But he still harbored strong feelings of loyalty toward his brother and their partnership. In October, he proposed that they adopt a fifty-fifty split on all noncolumn income, such as the magazine work and Stewart's growing lecture assignments, while maintaining the standing arrangement for the column. He also suggested that each brother be allowed two weeks a year for outside assignments that would not be shared at all. "Let me know what you think," Stewart wrote. "In the meantime, let me say that in any case I am grateful, and always will be, for the opportunity you gave me some twelve years ago."

Joe pronounced the fifty-fifty arrangement on noncolumn income "reasonable," although he ridiculed Stewart's preoccupation with the matter. Then he indulged himself in a flight of polemic that escalated tensions to a still higher pitch. He was "absolutely unwilling," he wrote, to make any further adjustment in their partnership beyond the new agreement. "I want to go on with the column," he wrote, "but I don't want you to go on if we are going to have perpetual arguments about participation, feelings on your side that you have been victimized, etc."

He added that at his age he wasn't sure he could continue working at such a pace much longer. He sometimes longed for the relative ease of shouldering just the column. "That of course is my alternative—no outside work or bother of any kind, three columns a week like WL [Walter Lippmann], six months at home and two to four trips abroad of anywhere from three weeks to three months." That, said Joe, would be a "very manageable and profitable recipe."

It was essentially a threat, designed to force Stewart back into a role of subservience. Joe added that he didn't much care for the job Stewart had been doing over the past year: Stewart didn't hit hard enough, didn't show sufficient toughness, didn't bundle up his facts with enough dra-

matic flair. And, Joe said, Stewart was too willing to shelter his work behind that of other publications, such as the authoritative but sparsely
read *Aviation Week*. Joe noted that he had argued many times that they
shouldn't quote from other publications. He added:

> But (and this is why I sometimes feel I might as well shout at a mill-
> stone) I have now just finished reading another column in which
> you sheltered behind both *Aviation Week* and the *Washington
> Post*. It took approximately six paragraphs for you to reach the
> real point of the column, which was that the administration was ly-
> ing. You had ample facts to make the point without sheltering be-
> hind others. Indeed, you had known *Aviation Week*'s facts long
> before they did. Why not then make your point in the lead, and
> prove it with your own facts, in the body of the column?

Joe's critique of Stewart's work contained some truth. Stewart did
lack Joe's instinct for the jugular. But Joe's intemperance and condescension proved incendiary. Stewart replied that he long had felt that Joe
wrote "too shrilly about Washington matters"—and anyway, Stewart
shouldn't have been expected to imitate Joe's style.

Stewart informed Joe by letter that he had discussed with Sommers
the possibility of joining the *Saturday Evening Post* as a contract writer
and that Ben Hibbs had indicated interest. In December he went to Philadelphia for a chat with Hibbs, and together they agreed on the outlines
of a full-time relationship. Stewart would deliver eight articles a year, beginning in April, continue the weekly Washington letter, and in other
ways represent the *Post* in the capital. He would receive $35,000 a year,
plus $3,500 each for additional articles. Stewart would be free to sup-
plement his income by lecturing and appearing on broadcast programs.
Returning to Washington, Stewart wrote to Hibbs. "I am really delighted, Ben, at the prospect of coming to the *Post*, and I feel confident
that I can do a good job for you."

Financially the move made sense. Stewart had been earning just
under $30,000 a year in the partnership. By adding extra magazine ar-
ticles and lectures to his new *Post* base, he felt he could increase his annual income to more than $40,000. And Joe, by going solo with the
column, could look forward to $50,000 a year if he managed to hold his
expenses to $20,000.

At the *Herald Tribune*, Brown Reid accepted the idea, and the paper
agreed to release Stewart from his contract on April 1, 1958. Stewart
was hit by the full magnitude of his planned departure from the column.
"I do feel oddly sentimental at the prospect of our splitting up," he
wrote Joe, "and in my inarticulate way, I really do want you to know of
the affection I feel for you, and the gratitude."

In Paris, Joe suddenly had second thoughts. He wrote to Stewart imploring him to think longer about the move, to put the matter on hold

for at least a year. "For God's sake, don't be in a hurry about it," he wrote. He also wrote to Hibbs, informing him of his admonition to Stew and suggesting the move might not be in his brother's best interest. Joe argued that the column had never enjoyed greater prestige and that it was a mistake to break up the team just when they stood on the threshold of even greater glory.

But Stewart wouldn't budge. "Perhaps I have been very foolish to leave the partnership home," he wrote to Joe. "But I know myself well enough to know that, if I had not done so, I should have become increasingly restive, sour, and in your word (which always irritated me, though I acknowledge that it has been accurate at times) negative." In mid-February he signed on officially with the *Post*, and on March 10, 1958, the move was announced at both the *Post* and the *Herald Tribune*. The brothers announced the breakup in a column entitled "Hail and Farewell," a kind of retrospective on their twelve years together. "A parting in which personal feelings pull one way and practicality pushes the other way is always a sentimental business," they wrote.

Walter Lippmann said in a letter that it was "painful to see the end of a good thing," but he predicted that "separately your influence and your usefulness will multiply by this fission." In Paris, C. L. Sulzberger read the news in the *Herald Tribune* "with astonishment." He wrote to say it had never occurred to him "that anything could terminate the highly successful and interesting partnership." The dean of Columbia University's Graduate School of Journalism, Edward Barrett, thanked the brothers for putting forth "the voice of doom. We have needed it badly—and still need it—amid all these smug complacencies."

Time, reporting the split, quoted from Joe's letter to Brown Reid: "I feel a little bit as though we were a species of minor Greek chorus, which was separating just as the drama approached some sort of climax," but Stew had to put his own career "ahead of the interest of being a Greek chorus." The magazine predicted that, "as a one-man chorus, Joe will keep the doom-crying column's accent on tragedy." In the piece, Joe called the breakup "a great wrench" and added that at a recent family reunion "there were floods of tears, diluted with champagne."

THUS ENDED THE Alsops' brother act. It had been a successful run, punctuated by dramatic scoops, swoops, applause, and high flying throughout the world. Just the previous November, when the brothers' private feud had reached its highest pitch, *Newsweek* had called them "possibly the most influential and provocative . . . newspaper columnists in the business." In a full-page profile, the magazine added that the brothers had "browbeaten, cajoled and otherwise pried timely exclusives out of high-level governmental places."

Naturally there was speculation about the impact of the split on each brother's career. Doris Fleeson, a columnist of modest rank and a friend of Joe's, said privately that she didn't think Stewart's departure would harm the column. Its heart and soul always had been Joe, she said. But the *Herald Tribune*'s Washington bureau chief, Robert Donovan, thought otherwise. Donovan had known the brothers for years, and had followed the column carefully. He had concluded that, while Joe was the more brilliant brother, Stewart served as the partnership's "balance wheel." Donovan wondered how the machine might run now without that balance wheel.

Donovan's perception was closer to the mark. When the brothers' partnership died, the column they had given life to died with it. The column's success had come in large measure through the nature of the collaboration and through the talents and instincts each brother had brought to the enterprise. Joe's greatest contributions were his flair for political combat and his attention-grabbing dramatic touch. Stewart brought a passion for mastering the arcane and the gift of dispassionate analysis. Together they kept watch on their contemporaries great and small and illuminated the affairs of the world. What they saw and pondered they put into words with their own stamp and style. Now that dual byline and unique mix were gone. An era was ending, not just for the Alsops but for their trade.

Part Four

PARALLEL

CAREERS

NEW DIRECTIONS

The East and the Heartland

AFTER THE BREAKUP of the Alsop team in early 1958 the brothers found their relationship changing. Naturally they didn't see each other as often; they no longer worked in the same office. But it was more than that. Joe pulled back. He no longer invited Stewart and Tish to his most high-toned dinner parties, when the guest list was most impressive. Joe seemed to want it understood that, although he was no longer the senior partner in their professional relationship, he was still the senior Alsop in social Washington. He always had a need to dominate and control those closest to him, and if he could no longer dominate his brother through their partnership, he would find other ways.

Stewart was particularly hurt when Joe had his famous dance for Jordan's King Hussein and didn't invite Stewart and Tish. "He was angry about that," Tish recalled years later. "He felt Joe had really delivered a blow."

But generally Stewart accepted the new developments in the fraternal relationship with philosophical detachment. He had his own social life and didn't need Joe to gain entrée to Washington's high and mighty. Besides, he understood Joe and loved him, and he knew his feelings were reciprocated. Joe still came often to Springland Lane for family dinners; the family still gathered for holiday festivities; and the brothers still engaged in their raucous political arguments. Though different now, the fraternal relationship remained, as Tish had noted from the beginning, "unbreakable."

Joe was pleased with his decision to return to Washington and the life he had created there. "In my middle aged way," he wrote to Isaiah Berlin, "I have greatly enjoyed creeping back into the familiar and luxurious cocoon I have spent so many years spinning for myself. José and Maria, the parrot, the orange trees, the garden, the house, the books, the wine, the dinner parties, . . . the friends . . . I love them all."

Joe brought on Rowland Evans of the *Herald Tribune* as a part-time column partner, to write about Washington during Joe's overseas sojourns. The two would meet for breakfast on the terrace at Dumbarton. The younger man was struck by Joe's love for his beautiful garden. One morning, as Joe sat in his bathrobe, talking with Evans and eating breakfast, a gardener toiled away on the task of mulching. Joe kept looking over at him, getting more and more agitated.

"Excuse me," he said, and went over to the gardener.

"No, no, no, no, no," he said. "You don't know how to mulch." And he got down on hands and knees to demonstrate how it should be done.

Joe developed relationships with younger beat reporters around town who could help track important developments. One was the *Herald Trib*'s Warren Rogers, who covered the Pentagon and State Department. Joe addressed the younger man as "Young Rogers," and called him often for information. "He recognized that I knew the cats and dogs, nuts and bolts, nooks and crannies at the Pentagon and State," recalled Rogers later. "He used me, and I liked it."

Sometimes Joe would invite news sources in for afternoon drinks and discussion and ask Rogers and other young reporters to join them. Rogers was struck by the "little touch of the putdown" Joe employed at such times for no apparent reason.

Once the guest was a defense scientist named Richard Ruble, whose name Joe mispronounced.

"Now, Dr. Ru*bell*," he began, "could you tell me . . ."

"Well, Mr. Alsop," replied Ruble, "first of all, I'm not a doctor, I don't have a Ph.D. And, by the way, it's pronounced *Ru*ble."

"Ah, yes, of course," said Joe. "Now, Dr. Ru*bell* . . ."

STEWART'S ROUTINE CHANGED significantly with his new job. Although he had access to the *Saturday Evening Post*'s secretarial staff for a day a week, he worked out of the Springland Lane house. He would hole up in his little study, surrounded by books and government reports, and work the phone or pound his old Underwood typewriter. Tish was struck by Stewart's prodigious work habits. His concentration was so great that the only way she could get his attention was by dialing his study phone from the family phone.

When he wasn't in his study, Stewart would be gathering information around town or conducting afternoon interviews at home in the living room. At noon he could be found at the downtown Metropolitan Club, habitat of the Washington establishment. Often he would stop by the *Saturday Evening Post* offices in the Solar Building on Sixteenth Street to oversee some secretarial work or fraternize with the small *Post* staff.

Upon completing a magazine piece, Stewart would take it promptly to Tish, who was his "guinea pig." They joked that if Tish could understand what he wrote, then the piece was fit for distribution across the country. Tish was direct in her critiques, and Stewart listened seriously to her.

Now that the brothers' professional paths had diverged, they directed their work more and more toward what amounted to specialized audiences. Their flagships—the *Herald Tribune* for Joe, the *Saturday Evening Post* for Stewart—together reflected the mind and heart of an earlier America. The *Herald Trib*'s connection was with the largely Anglo-Saxon elite of the Northeast; the *Post*'s was with the predominantly Anglo-Saxon communities of the heartland.

The *Herald Tribune* had served for decades as an accepted medium of the Eastern matrix of major corporations and law firms, international financial institutions, and top universities—the training grounds and playgrounds of the country's leadership class. Members of this establishment had not imposed themselves upon the nation. They had always been there. It was their duty to serve, and they enjoyed broad support from those millions across the land who shared their heritage and viewed the world in terms similar to theirs.

Those millions, in the heartland, ran their communities in much the same way as the national elite ran the country, dominating banks, civic organizations, school boards, county courthouses, and businesses. They constituted the core readership of the *Saturday Evening Post*, whose old fashioned editorials and Norman Rockwell covers depicting middle-class scenes were regarded by many as symbolic not just of the magazine and of their own families, but of the nation itself.

Joe now devoted himself almost exclusively to the column and his relationship with the *Herald Tribune*. Seldom submitting to the rigors of magazine writing, he focused on the kind of high-impact reporting government officials felt compelled to read. He reached nearly 25 million readers through 190 newspapers, but he wasn't writing for hinterland masses. Through the *Herald Tribune* he was speaking to Washington policymakers and their counterparts in the world's major capitals.

As for Stewart, his journalistic impact in Washington declined sharply when he departed the column. But the *Post*, with its 6 million subscribers and some 20 million readers, provided a forum where Stewart could describe and explain the often mystifying ways of Washington for the country at large. The magazine continued to provide abundant

space for long, probing articles on politics and policy; *Post* editors believed Americans would read such articles as long as they sprang to life
through tight, lucid writing. Stewart, a master of such writing, viewed
the *Post* as the country's "Number One national magazine," as he wrote
to Martin Sommers, the only one with "the reputation, the resources,
and the space available so that a writer like myself [can] really master a
subject."

The first subject he set out to master as a solo newsman was Richard
Nixon, "the second most important political figure in the country," as
Stewart called him. Bent on digging deeper into the man's life than anyone had ever done, Stewart obtained a list of Nixon's classmates at
Whittier College and Duke Law School and wrote them asking for information and anecdotes from the vice president's past. He spent ten days
of interviewing in California and accumulated more than a hundred
pages of typewritten notes.

Then came the first exclusive interview granted by Nixon since he
had become vice president. Stewart had spent hours preparing questions
in the hope that the interview would produce good material to run in
question-and-answer form alongside his profile. On a Saturday morning
in late April 1958, shortly before Nixon was to depart for a trip abroad,
Stewart spent two hours with the vice president at his undistinguished
stone house in Washington's fashionable Northwest section. Drinking
coffee on the porch overlooking Glover Park, they exchanged chitchat
about a new highway to be built through the park, and Eisenhower's
habit of dropping a heaping spoonful of sugar into his coffee; but Nixon
wasn't much for small talk, and they quickly got down to business.
Stewart was struck by the vice president's candor.

Entitled "The Mystery of Richard Nixon," the piece ran July 12,
1958, with an accompanying interview called "Nixon on Nixon." Stewart wrote, "Despite a surface blandness that sometimes makes him seem
quite ordinary, Vice President Nixon is a most extraordinary man." He
noted that Nixon stirred deep emotions, both positive and negative, and
had emerged as a kind of cardboard figure to supporters and detractors
alike. His own feeling, wrote Stewart, had been akin to that of an old
lady from Nixon's hometown of Whittier, California, who said she
couldn't help hating the man even though she knew it was wrong to
hate. To Stewart, Nixon had seemed shrewd, tough, and ambitious, but
not much more. Now he found himself impressed by the vice president's
knack for seeing the political world clearly and being right most of
the time.

Still, Stewart castigated Nixon for "rather sleazy" debater's tricks,
such as the aside during a 1954 speech when he was extolling the virtues
of John Foster Dulles: "And incidentally, in mentioning Secretary
Dulles, isn't it wonderful finally to have a Secretary of State who isn't
taken in by the Communists?" Nixon hadn't said explicitly that

Acheson and Marshall, Dulles's predecessors, had been taken in by communists. "But he implied it," wrote Stewart, "and the implication is grossly misleading."

All in all, though, it was a positive piece, and it stirred emotions in readers in much the same way Nixon stirred emotions in voters. The *Louisville Courier-Journal*, run by the liberal Bingham family, mocked the piece in an editorial as "a publicity blurb" and "one sided puff." As Barry and Mary Bingham were old friends, Stewart was more hurt than angry, but he wrote a letter to the editor: "It seemed to me clear from the tone of your article that your editorial minds are hermetically sealed as far as Nixon is concerned—that you would never believe anything written about him unless he were portrayed with horns, a tail, and cloven hooves."

The piece won praise, too. Columnist William S. White called it "perceptive . . . illuminating and . . . fair," and *Newsweek* ran a two-column article on Stewart and his Nixon profile, which it called "one of the most searching studies yet published on the man." *Reader's Digest* snapped it up for reprint, and in a subsequent California trip Stewart was pleased to learn that "everyone seemed to have read it." Stewart set out to give similar treatment to two other political pooh-bahs, Lyndon Johnson and New York's rising Republican star, Nelson Rockefeller.

As Stewart worked to refine the art of political magazine writing, Joe faced concerns at the *Herald Tribune* that the Alsop column, sans Stewart, might become too alarmist. The paper's managing editor, George Cornish, sent Joe a letter of caution on the subject. Many editors tended to regard Joe as the gloomy Alsop, he said, and they would be sensitive now to any changes in the column's tone. In a reply, Joe agreed that he must be less strident, but then he scribbled a postscript: "But it's hard not to say hard things of such outright lying as Foster [Dulles] has just indulged in."

Joe's zest for controversy was usually more of a plus than a minus, but it wasn't always easy striking the right balance. That became clear early in 1958 when he stopped off in London, sniffed the air, and wrote: "This London, with its rich and charming surface, whose shining courage so recently set an example to the world, is now a city that all but stinks of defeat." For years, he continued, he had witnessed Britain's struggle to maintain her role as great power, but now that struggle seemed to be nearing its end. Britain suffered from too many problems—economic, strategic, diplomatic, military—that were generating "a wholly novel discord of ideas and attitudes."

The column had been intended as a rebuke of the Eisenhower administration, from which Joe wished to see "imaginative and courageous" leadership to stem Britain's decline. But this point was lost on Londoners, who took offense at Joe's stark words. The *Daily Express* attacked the column as an insult to the nation and demanded an apology. The

Economist disputed the notion of British defeatism and attacked Joe's analysis. *Economist* editor Donald Tyerman was so outraged that he couldn't stop talking about Joe at a London dinner party, to the discomfort of other guests.

The controversy deepened when word circulated that before writing the column Joe had lunched with Prime Minister Macmillan at Lady Pamela Berry's and had dined with Hugh Gaitskell at the home of Ann Fleming, wife of novelist Ian Fleming. Speculation grew that these officials may have influenced Joe's thinking. Dora Gaitskell, wife of the opposition leader, slyly wrote to Joe that defeatism in Britain was largely a party matter, meaning a Conservative Party problem, "and I can understand how your Tory friends feel frustrations." Gaitskell himself considered Joe's column "unduly gloomy."

As always, Joe stood ready to rush to the center of world events, and he moved quickly in May 1958 when the French Fourth Republic collapsed. In Algiers, two French generals, fearing they would lose the government's support in their fight against Arab insurgency, seized power and demanded a new French government headed by Charles de Gaulle, who they thought would continue to support French colonialism in Algeria. Rioting had spread to Paris, and France teetered on the edge of civil war. During a dinner party one evening at the Pattens' Paris apartment, conversation turned to whether they should phone Joe in Washington to get him over there immediately. Then the phone rang.

"It's Joe," exclaimed Susan Mary, hanging up the phone. "He's on his way."

On arriving, Joe tried, without success, to learn details of a secret meeting between de Gaulle and beleaguered Prime Minister Pierre Pflimlin. He decided to take Susan Mary on an excursion of the Left Bank in search of news—or, barring that, interesting antiques. The friendship between Joe and the Pattens, always special, had deepened over the years. Despite his respiratory problems, Bill maintained a vitality in life that Joe enjoyed. When not suffering from bouts of ill health, Bill frolicked with his children, Billy and Anne, painted landscapes, and kept up a hectic social schedule. "He cared about people, and it showed," Susan Mary recalled. He particularly cared about Joe—and worried about him when he headed off to Vietnam or other world trouble spots. Once, just before a trip to Vietnam, Joe called Bill to discuss his plans, and Bill ended the conversation with a sense of foreboding. "I wish he wasn't going out there," he said to Susan Mary. "He seems to have a need to court danger."

For her part, Susan Mary loved Joe's visits. She found him immensely entertaining, always well informed on diplomatic matters, and acutely knowledgeable on subjects of taste and culture that other men didn't care about. She enjoyed his erudite discourses on dress styles, furniture, antiques, art, literature. And he was such a connoisseur of gossip.

As for Joe, he reveled in Susan Mary's company. In her late thirties, she certainly still passed his rather stringent tests for feminine beauty, grace, and style.

After an afternoon on the West Bank looking at antiques (but not buying), the two stopped by the *Herald Tribune* office and heard that tensions had intensified after the Socialists had rejected calls for a de Gaulle government. Joe hurried off to his sources and later returned to the Pattens with word that paratroopers from Algiers had encircled nearly all military airports in France, and that government troops might not be able to hold them. Joe arranged for a black-market trader to take checks written in dollars in exchange for French francs—crucial in a crisis. Susan Mary filled the bathtub just in case water was shut off.

The next night, the first warm night of spring, Joe and the Pattens dined with Eddie and Gillian Tomkins in their lovely apartment high above the chestnut trees of the avenue Gabriel. Tomkins was counsel at the British embassy, and his guests included British ambassador Gladwyn Jebb as well as Tomkins's stepfather, a French banker. The talk centered on fears that bloody riots could break out at any time.

Suddenly from the open windows came the sounds of a crowd marching down the Champs Élysées, singing the Marseillaise. The stepfather turned puce, the butler ran in crying, "*Fermez les volets* [Close the shutters]," the spaniels began howling. Joe and Susan Mary rushed outside to see knots of French soldiers, who had been lounging around for a week, now snapping to battle alert. Trucks, rolled up to protect the Élysée Palace, served as cover for a cordon of soldiers with machine guns. Soon it was clear that the marchers were only students, and tensions eased. The two Americans headed into the Champs Élysées amid a scene that reminded Susan Mary of V-E Day—cars overfilled with young people, horns blaring, crowds marching, roisterers waving chestnut blossoms broken from nearby trees. Joe found himself marching arm in arm with a fat blonde singing an old liberation song that Susan Mary recalled from the last days of the war.

The scene turned frightening for a moment when Joe and Susan Mary stepped out of the crowd at the Franklin D. Roosevelt Métro station and saw five paratroopers lurking at the bottom of some steps. The uniforms disappeared quietly into the station, stirring fears that hostilities were about to begin. But nothing happened, and the two Americans returned to the palace, where new throngs had gathered for further revelry. Later, at a crowded bar on the rue de Berri, they joined a group of *Herald Tribune* correspondents exchanging rumors and comparing notes on the night's confusion. Others had seen paratroopers too, but they had not been part of any military initiative. The worst had passed. The crisis would ease; de Gaulle would assume power. In a few days things would become so quiet that Joe could leave for Algiers.

———

BACK IN WASHINGTON, Joe cultivated his high-level Washington friendships and acquaintanceships. Although he claimed not to care for Nixon, he heaped praise upon the vice president in a letter: "It was a very great pleasure, as well as a very great privilege, to share the long, chatty lunch with you. . . . It is far more stimulating than a good drink (and immeasurably rarer) to see a public man whom one can genuinely admire."

With more sincerity he wrote to Lyndon Johnson, "You happen to be one of the half dozen men I have known in American public life whom I have admired almost without qualification." But he expressed concern about Johnson's frenetic work schedule: "Do take care of yourself." Johnson replied, "To you, the door is always open and the welcome mat is always out. You can come to me as an adviser or you can come to me as a man who seeks information. . . . But I hope that you come first and foremost as a . . . friend in whom I find warmth and comfort."

As middle age descended upon Joe, he began to experience the ravages of time—old friends and mentors dying, contemporaries experiencing new difficulties in life, the sense that life was somehow speeding up.

In spring of 1958 he heard that Claire Chennault, his hero and mentor from China days, was dying of cancer. "Is there anything I can do to help?" he wrote the general. "Is there any chance of your coming to Washington so that I can see you again? Is there any way I can make this trial, which you are bearing with such fortitude, at least just a little more comfortable for you?" Chennault replied that he appreciated Joe's solicitude but his battle was "one of those which I must fight alone." He lost the battle soon thereafter.

In May, while Joe was in Europe, Aggie Guthrie died. She had been with Corinne for nearly half a century and had showered the Alsops with a special brand of love. Her death brought anguish to the family, for she was part of the heart and hearth of Avon—friend and confidante to Corinne, executive of household affairs, cheerleader to the boys in their careers. No matter of family importance had escaped her notice or attention. She had filled the family stockings for Avon Christmases, ordered decorations and ornaments from catalogues, maintained the china and silver for special occasions, kept scrapbooks for Alsop columns and articles about the family.

Around the same time, Phil Graham, publisher of *The Washington Post* and a person Joe considered "probably the most successful man among all his contemporaries," was showing signs of mental breakdown. Just two years earlier, he had been a cover-story subject for *Time*, which had described him as "an energetic charmer whose facial furrows and tall, angular frame . . . give him a Lincolnesque look." Now he was given to fits of bizarre antics, outrageous tantrums, and uncontrolled sobbing. Joe attributed Graham's crisis to an inner doubt about his own values. "He was all out for the most conventional sort of success. He achieved it on the largest scale. And then, somehow, it turned to dust and ashes in his mouth," Joe wrote to Berlin. A similar calamity had befallen Frank Wisner, CIA deputy director and longtime friend to both Alsop brothers. Suddenly given to wild mood swings and erratic behavior, he had been sent off to the psychiatric annex at Johns Hopkins University. Now his once-sparkling career lay in ruins.

On the other hand, Joe and Stewart took pride in the blossoming political career of their brother John, who was maneuvering his way toward the Republican nomination for Connecticut governor. Witty, articulate, and dignified, with the typical Alsop zest for a rousing good time, John was the Alsop brother who most resembled the brothers' father, and his life also paralleled that of the elder Joe. Like his parents, John had served in the state legislature. He helped run the family farm, and made a tidy living in the insurance business. He lived the same kind of country squire's life that the elder Joe had enjoyed—farmer, businessman, civic leader, huntsman, fisherman.

The forces of modernity had pressed in hard on such a life, transforming the once-bucolic Avon into a sprawling suburb, and rendering the land uneconomical for farming. John had devoted himself to converting some of the Alsop land to commercial use—a Howard Johnson motel had gone up in early 1957, and a Texaco station had followed within a year. Now he was seeking to sign up an A&P supermarket. From an initial investment of $30,000, the four offspring of Joseph Alsop IV now collected a gross income of $6,000 a year. But they took pains to ensure that they didn't show a profit; the aim was tax benefits first and financial returns later.

At the state GOP's 1958 nominating convention, John led the early floor ballots. But then the party pros coalesced behind an establishment candidate and thwarted the reformist Alsop. "The pros slit his throat, neatly, from ear to ear," Stewart wrote to Martin Sommers, adding that John surely would make another gubernatorial run in four years.

Stewart, at middle age, was happy with life in Washington. The old house in Cleveland Park was a comfortable place, though a little down at the mouth in a sort of fashionable British way. Stewart didn't like spending money on home maintenance and had "an absolute mania for making amateur repairs," as Joe recalled years later. He used glue to maintain one of his favorite possessions—an old and tattered Aubusson carpet.

The two older sons—Joe and Ian—would be off to Groton soon. Elizabeth was demonstrating intellect and discipline at Sacred Heart School and was slated for Miss Porter's fashionable finishing school in Farmington, Connecticut. Young Stewart was bright, handsome, and cheerful. Within a year, a fifth child would appear—a son named Richard Nicholas. His godfather would be Marty Sommers.

The Alsops seemed the ideal American family when Edward R.

Murrow of CBS News brought his cameras to Springland Lane for one of his "Person to Person" interviews over national television. Stewart seemed a commanding figure in his double-breasted suit, with his full head of hair and deep voice. He answered Murrow's questions with slow deliberation and some casualness as he stoked the fire or perched on the arm of a sofa. Tish, wearing a white sweater over a silk dress, seemed a bit nervous but lovely, while the children appeared to revel in the limelight.

"Who's the budding writer in the family?" asked Murrow.

"I am," said Elizabeth. "I like to write stories—animal stories."

Ian said he liked to paint whales. And young Joe explained his passion: "I like to hack around with little motors, electric motors and little balls and buzzers—it's lots of fun."

"What a wonderful family," said Murrow.

Watching from Avon, John considered the children "the hit of the evening." He thought Stewart and Tish "seemed very much at ease and came through it very well," although John was amused at Stewart's efforts to appear relaxed. "It seems to me," wrote John, "that the Alsops . . . are about as well known . . . as any family in America."

Stewart felt relieved to be off the treadmill of column writing, and he enjoyed working with the bright and kindly Sommers. He also welcomed an invitation from *Post* officials to set up shop at the magazine's four-room office suite on Sixteenth Street. Stewart's new office had an imposing desk, an overstuffed leather couch, and two leather chairs. Books lined one wall, and another displayed a collection of photos and memorabilia commemorating Stewart's career.

The magazine in those days enjoyed what its editors considered its greatest glory. Although it purported to be a mirror of America, it was more a mirror of conservative America, later known as Middle America. It pitched its message to the Midwest long after that region had ceased to wield the powerful national influence of earlier days. Never quite able to forgive the presidency of Franklin Roosevelt, the *Post* railed against the Democratic Party and such New Deal inventions as Social Security and unemployment insurance long after these concepts had become standard features of American life.

The magazine also reflected the middle-class culture of the early television age. A cover story on Arthur Godfrey, leading TV personality of the time, sold two million copies on newsstands. That led to a much-heralded "I Call On" series of fluffy features on such luminaries of the day as Bing Crosby, Grace Kelly, Dick Clark, and Marilyn Monroe.

But there was always room for Stewart's sharp-eyed Washington reporting. Stewart also served as broker for articles by Washington writers and others with story ideas. This could be uncomfortable when he found himself having to turn down important people or close friends. Rejected authors included Dean Acheson and Stewart's own mother, who had submitted a memoir of Aggie Guthrie. But the broker role also carried considerable power in Washington, where so many writers longed to see their bylines in the *Post*.

ALL IN ALL, the brothers enjoyed the new paths they had chosen. But they experienced recurrent difficulties in their personal relationship. These stemmed largely from two issues—the settling of partnership accounts, and a book project they had undertaken as the partnership neared its end.

During his year abroad, Joe had added to his private library by buying books on contemporary politics and charging them off to the partnership. Stewart believed that if such purchases constituted a business expense, the books should be considered a partnership asset. Joe regarded them as his personal property. Although it was a matter of only $270, both brothers became feverish over it. "Sometimes I wonder whether you have any memory at all," wrote Joe, noting that his practice of charging book purchases to the partnership had long predated his year abroad. Replied Stewart: "I do not think any fair-minded man examining the list of books you bought last year would agree that they were bought exclusively for business purposes."

Then there was the office furniture. Joe wanted to keep some of it, and he proposed giving the remainder to Stewart, who had no use for it. Stewart wanted the partnership to sell the unwanted furniture and distribute between them any partnership losses from the sale.

As tempers flared over such issues, Stewart sent the partnership ledger to his lawyer, Lloyd Symington, with a request that Symington help obtain an arbitrator. Joe was furious: "Your decision to refer our affairs to Lloyd Symington made me so angry that I did not trust myself to write you before I left for Taipei. I dislike intensely these disclosures of our affairs, when the sums of money involved are too ridiculously small to deserve the publicity of arbitration." The matter had gone on long enough, he said. He outlined his idea of a proper settlement and sent Stewart a check for $305.84 to represent that settlement.

Stewart replied: "I return your check herewith. I certainly shall not accept it as a 'final settlement.' " He suggested that Joe consult an accountant on proper ways of disposing of unwanted physical assets of a partnership, rather than using an "Alice-in-Wonderland" approach. He added:

> But I know you won't, so the Hell with it, and in that case I shall make no further attempt to collect my fair share of the final partnership distribution, or any part of it, and I wish to discuss the matter no further. . . . For the rest, I suggest that to avoid unnecessary talk we maintain at least a superficial appearance of amiability.

Eventually, the brothers came to a settlement they both despised. They both hated such animosity over trifling sums, but neither could break the cycle of anger. Soon their hostility spilled over into their book project.

The book idea had come from New York publisher Eugene Reynal, who suggested in spring of 1958 that the brothers collect columns from their twelve-year partnership and publish them along with an introduction and some political context for each column. The brothers thought the book would need more; they suggested sections describing various aspects of Washington reporting, with anecdotes from their experiences. Reynal liked the idea and paid them an advance of $6,000. They reached agreement with Ben Hibbs at the *Saturday Evening Post* to use at least one chapter, perhaps two. That would bring in another $3,500 or $7,000.

Emotions flared instantly. It was agreed that they would write five chapters encompassing nearly a hundred pages, but when Stewart submitted his portion Joe set about to rewrite it. When Stewart complained, Joe offered to let him out of the project with a payment of 20 percent from the advance and from any royalties—"the rest to be my gamble since you evidently do not wish to make the necessary effort to turn out a book that would have any serious chance of selling, or that I would wish to sign."

Joe was probably right in concluding that Stewart's work needed editing. Pressed for time as the book deadline had approached, Stewart hadn't given the work his usual effort. Still, Joe's insistence on rubbing Stewart raw on the matter only ignited another round of fraternal hostility. After an exchange of bitter letters, the brothers agreed that Joe would get two-thirds of the Reynal advance to reflect his greater share of the work. They would split the magazine proceeds fifty-fifty, and Joe's extra work on column selection would entitle him to 60 percent of royalties. Stewart acknowledged the fairness of this arrangement. "But why in Hell do you have to say things and write letters calculated to put any self-respecting man's back up?" He complained bitterly about Joe's habit of referring to him as the "junior partner," and he changed "junior" to "younger" throughout the manuscript. He also didn't care much for the column mix Joe had selected. Stewart's columns tended to be features, while Joe's were hard news; this gave the impression that Joe was the more functional reporter.

Eventually the brothers managed to simmer down and put much of their bitterness behind them. Joe acknowledged the validity of Stewart's complaints and agreed, at his brother's suggestion, to excise from the book some of the harsh polemics he had directed at Eisenhower (Stewart had feared such intemperance would harm sales). The brothers agreed to identify themselves as Republicans in the book's foreword, largely as an antidote to *Time*'s habit of labeling them New Dealers.

The 377-page book, entitled *The Reporter's Trade*, went on sale for

$5 a copy in October 1958. The *Virginia Kirkus Service*, a library tip sheet, called it a "must book for any ... citizen who can stand the facts," and the *Washington Star* called it a "monument to the 12-year career of Washington's most distinguished reporting partnership." A. J. Liebling, noted press critic for *The New Yorker*, devoted two pages to a discussion of the brothers and their book, and suggested that Joe, or "Alsop Major," as he called him, was really the guiding spirit of the column—just the kind of judgment Stewart had wanted to avoid. Still, even Stewart was pleased to see such an important magazine take notice of the book. *Time*, on the other hand, dismissed the work as merely a collection of past columns. The magazine ignored the extensive fresh material, minimized Stewart's contribution, and ridiculed Joe's "overly pessimistic" view of the world.

The book did not do well. Reynal printed fifteen thousand copies, and had eleven thousand in bookstores for Christmas, but by summer of 1959 the stores had returned four thousand. "I cannot understand the public's reaction," mused Reynal.

The public's reaction was easy to understand. The brothers had thrived on controversy since the first days of their column-writing careers, but they also had always enjoyed the backing of large segments of public opinion. Whether the issue was the need to prepare for World War II, Louis Johnson's military build-down, or Joe McCarthy, millions of Americans had agreed with them. Now, in the midst of the popular Eisenhower presidency, that had changed. The brothers' repeated attacks on the president and his policies struck a discordant note with many readers who did not think the nation and the world were hurtling toward disaster. Among liberal Democrats and intellectuals, it was fashionable to belittle the president as an aging and inarticulate bumbler, but out in the country he was loved because he had succeeded where success counted most—by providing peace and prosperity. In that context, the Alsop outlook was a minority view and, to many Americans, an unwelcome one.

Joe's fame as a leading anti-Eisenhower polemicist caused difficulties after a dramatic development at the *Herald Tribune*. The paper had found itself in a downward spin by the mid-fifties. Circulation plummeted and profits declined. By 1957 it had slipped into the red, and the Reids concluded they would have to find a partner. The partner turned out to be John Hay (Jock) Whitney, ambassador to Great Britain and an Eisenhower intimate.

Whitney matched the Reids as an embodiment of the Eastern Republican establishment. He was a Grotonian and a Yalie. His maternal grandfather had been John Hay, brash young secretary to Abraham Lincoln and later secretary of state. The Whitney side of the family was equally rooted in the American aristocracy. Whitney had parlayed a $30 million inheritance into $200 million by bankrolling fledgling companies, Broadway plays, and Hollywood movies. He maintained a personal staff of a hundred to care for his eight resplendent residences, including a six-hundred-acre estate on Long Island and a thirty-two-square-mile Georgia plantation, to which he frequently invited the president for quail hunting.

Whitney had purchased a minority share of the *Herald Tribune* in 1957, and in the fall of 1958 he took control. "It's an immense responsibility, but that needn't faze you, for no one is better qualified to carry it," Joe wrote Whitney. "Indeed, I can think of no one else I'd rather see at the head of the paper that gave me my start." Joe added, as if he shared Whitney's Republican instincts, that GOP prospects in New York's gubernatorial race looked better than ever, with Nelson Rockefeller gaining on Averell Harriman.

This caused a flap when Whitney told Paul Nitze that Joe's letter had struck a blow for "our side," in contrast to his recent columns attacking the president. Nitze garbled the message in repeating Whitney's remarks to Joe, saying it was understood Joe had called the ambassador's purchase of the *Herald Tribune* a great thing for "our party." Joe moved quickly to explain in a letter to Whitney:

> As it happens, I am and always have been a Republican, and in 1952 I cheered for, worked for and voted for the President. In 1956, I could not bring myself to vote for either of the candidates. . . . I make no apologies for this judgment. . . . It is based on the best assessment of the facts of the defense and foreign situations that I can make. . . . I pray to God my judgment is wrong and your quite opposite judgment is right, for if I am right, the future will be difficult for all of us.

Joe didn't want to sound "prickly," but he was concerned by Nitze's suggestion that Whitney thought he might be trying to truckle to his new chief by putting on false colors. "As I express my opinions on politics four times weekly with considerable vigor," he wrote, "this would be the act of a fool." Whitney replied that he had expressed to Nitze only simple satisfaction. "In absolutely no way did I suggest that you were staining what I imagine to be the whitest nose in Christendom." He added that he expected to argue with Joe vigorously, as he had in the past, but there was no reason to worry about "absentee malice." Joe accepted Whitney's response with "great relief."

As Joe's contract came up for renewal in the fall of 1959, he insisted on major changes: three columns a week instead of four; greater syndicate contribution to his expenses; greater effort to increase the number of subscribing papers. Although he had expected to be making close to $50,000 a year as solo columnist, expenses had brought his income down to below $40,000. He wanted a guarantee of at least $40,000 from the *Herald Tribune*. Whitney accepted an agreement that met most of Joe's terms, and the column continued on a three-a-week schedule. But the contract covered only one year.

Meanwhile, Stewart reached a comfortable cruising speed with his magazine work. He produced a steady flow of political profiles, campaign explainers, and behind-the-scenes pieces on the inner workings of government. His profile of Rockefeller matched the Nixon piece in depth and insight, and *Reader's Digest* reprinted it. Stewart's prewar boss at Doubleday, Ken McCormick, suggested publishing the Nixon and Rockefeller pieces together in a book, to go on sale as the battle for the 1960 Republican presidential nomination intensified. The result was a 240-page volume called *Nixon and Rockefeller: A Double Portrait,* which came out in early 1960. The projected sales didn't materialize, because Rockefeller had withdrawn from the nomination battle by the time of publication: a rueful Stewart remarked that readers could get "one book for the price of two." Still, it brought new literary attention to Stewart as he prepared to cover the 1960 presidential race.

In the fall of 1959, Stewart took a two-month, three-thousand-mile auto trip through Poland, Czechoslovakia, Hungary, Romania, Bulgaria, and Yugoslavia that yielded three long pieces for the *Post*. The tone of the series was optimistic—another sign that Stewart was developing his own independent outlook. His travels followed by only four years the Soviets' suppression of the Hungarian rebellion, but Stewart concluded that the Soviet effort to impose its will upon half of Europe eventually would fall of its own weight.

Stewart was struck by the often wildly friendly welcomes he received throughout East Bloc countries, particularly in small towns, where the state police were less intrusive. He wowed the locals with his magic Polaroid camera, which could produce finished pictures in a minute and was dubbed an "Americanski sputnik." The enthusiastic throngs that gathered around him everywhere seemed stirred by an unspoken but powerful emotion—the lure of freedom. *Freedom* had become a "shabby, tired old word" in the West through overuse and misuse, wrote Stewart. "But spend a few weeks in the countries of un-freedom, and it will become real to you again. . . . It is a word which explains why, unless we in the West are unimaginably foolish and flabby, the race to which Khrushchev has challenged us is a race he cannot win."

25

1960

Covering and Savoring
the Kennedy Phenomenon

THE CAMPAIGN YEAR of 1960 was viewed widely in Washington as a likely watershed. After eight years of grandfatherly guardianship, America wanted change. Though Ike remained popular, his second term had not been a success. Sputnik had shattered the country's faith in its technological superiority and invulnerability to attack, and persistent recession had undermined confidence in the Republicans. The country's GNP had plunged 2.8 percent in 1958, and unemployment had risen to more than 7 percent, the highest level since the Great Depression. The political year would foster a great debate over how to pull the nation out of lethargy and direct it toward a new course.

The budding campaign would stir Joe Alsop to exceed even his usual tendency toward political hyberbole. Presidential politics, he wrote in his New Year's Day column, "have deeper meaning than they have possessed in any peacetime election year in the history of the United States."

Joe welcomed the Democrats' seemingly robust prospects for victory in 1960. He viewed the Republicans as a collection of unimaginative businessmen preoccupied mostly with balancing the budget. By January 1960 it had become clear that Vice President Nixon would be the Republican nominee. While Joe liked Nixon's internationalist convictions and foreign-policy acumen, he felt the vice president seemed politically craven at times. Writing to a friend, Joe said Nixon "does not seem to me to have lived up to my former view of him, which was that he would always take a pretty courageous stand on the big, basic things like defense and foreign policy."

So Joe cast his lot with the Democrats. In April 1959 he had bet a friend $100 that a Democrat would win the White House in 1960. By January of the election year he had become convinced that the nominee would be the young senator from Massachusetts, John F. Kennedy. With two Republican senators—Pennsylvania's Hugh Scott and New York's Kenneth Keating—he wagered half a case of 1947 or 1949 claret each that Kennedy would capture the Democratic nomination. As Joe saw it, the country needed change in 1960, and the man of change was Kennedy.

Joe was smitten by the entire Kennedy clan. The charm, class, beauty, confidence—all struck Joe's fancy and drew him to what would become an American political cult. He had become a family friend since just after the war, when his gadabout life in Europe had brought him into contact with Kathleen Kennedy, known to her friends as Kick. Witty and fun-loving, Kick had married into an old English family during the war; her husband was Cavendish, marquis of Hartington, eldest son of the duke of Devonshire. He later died in battle. In 1948, Kick herself was killed in an airplane crash in France. But in those two years just after the war she and Joe had enjoyed a close friendship.

In spring 1947, when Kick had been in Washington visiting John and her sisters, she had invited Joe for dinner to meet her brother, then a freshman congressman. Joe had arrived at the Kennedys' Georgetown house to find the place in considerable disarray—furniture oddly placed, carpet wrinkled, half-eaten hamburgers on the mantelpiece. Joe concluded he had come on the wrong day, but the maid assured him he had been expected. The young people, she said, had been doing a series of competitive exercises on the floor. So he sat down to wait, "and one by one the occupants of the house, each more astonishingly good-looking than the last, strolled into the living room," as Joe wrote later. They set about straightening up the place and settled down to a lively evening of laughter and political talk.

Joe was struck by the young congressman's gaiety and intelligence. But Kennedy did not seem entirely serious about politics. He once told Joe, with stoic matter-of-factness, that he suffered from an incurable, slow-motion leukemia. "They tell me the damn disease will get me in the end," he said. "But they also tell me I'll last until I'm forty-five." Joe thought this explained young Kennedy's lack of ambition and his casualness toward politics. He seemed more interested in pretty young women. When Kennedy complained about the dearth of available women at Joe's political dinners, Joe stopped inviting him. The two remained friends but ceased to maintain regular contact.

It was not leukemia attacking Kennedy's body, but Addison's disease, which he later controlled through the new drug cortisone. By the time

Joe returned to Washington from Paris in early 1958, Kennedy seemed a changed man. He was married now, to the glamorous Jacqueline Bouvier, and he was also a senator. The Senate had captured his interest as the House never could, and now he showed a true passion for politics, along with a resolve to become president. "The inward seriousness of the man was apparent now beneath the surface wit and charm," Joe wrote later. The Kennedys became frequent dinner guests at Dumbarton, and Joe often was invited to the Kennedys' Georgetown home on N Street.

Joe enjoyed the renewal of his friendship with Kennedy, and encouraged the young politician to develop a strong pro-defense posture in the Senate. In the summer of 1958 a heated debate unfolded in the chamber following press reports that the Pentagon had sponsored a study of how America should handle the coming era of possible nuclear inferiority. The debate's underlying assumption was that the Soviets were likely to gain a large edge over the United States in the deployment of nuclear-tipped intercontinental missiles. Joe suggested to Kennedy that he could gain attention by standing up as one Democrat who would face facts and call for preserving America's capacity for deterrence.

Kennedy liked the idea and delivered a stirring Senate speech outlining the dangers of the so-called "missile gap"—the period of presumed Soviet superiority between 1960 and 1964. He called for a supreme national effort to avert the "peril" of those uncertain years. The risk, he said, was not just from a Soviet attack but from aggressive Soviet diplomacy and adventurism that would flow from superiority: "The balance of power will gradually shift against us. Each Soviet move will weaken the West, but none will seem to justify our initiating the nuclear war that might destroy us."

Having induced Kennedy to deliver the speech, Joe filed two columns praising the senator's courage and wisdom. Kennedy's voice, he wrote, "was the authentic voice of America." Kennedy was pleased with the attention his forceful floor performance had brought him. "I want to thank you," he wrote Joe, "for your very fine columns and your original suggestion."

As candidates for the Democratic presidential nomination began jockeying for position in 1959, Joe found himself in an awkward position. He supported Kennedy with genuine passion, but he didn't want that publicly known because he didn't want to compromise the column. This led to friction between him and his longtime friend and lawyer, James Rowe, a former New Dealer who now was a force behind the candidacy of Minnesota Senator Hubert Humphrey. Joe angered Rowe with a column reporting the "startling news" that Catholic voters in Queens, New York, were preparing to switch parties in huge numbers in order to boost Kennedy's presidential aims. Rowe questioned the methodology of Joe's conclusions, and noted that the pollster used for the survey, Louis Harris, was Kennedy's own.

Joe responded with a column—"Letter to a Humphreyite"—in

which he defended the previous column and declared his "impartial loyalty to the facts." To establish his independence, Joe proclaimed himself a registered Republican and added, with stunning disingenuousness, that he would "most like to vote for Sen. Johnson among the Democrats." But personal preferences "ought not to prevent political reporters from publishing remarkable political facts."

In declaring for Johnson, Joe compromised his column with a lie. He did in fact feel close to Johnson and would have been pleased to see him win the White House. But his heart was with Kennedy, and his nod toward Johnson seemed designed only to throw readers off the scent. Rowe, outraged that Joe would carry their disagreement into print, accused the columnist of creating a phony argument between them in order to boost Kennedy.

As Joe struggled with such controversies, Stewart made the rounds of top campaign officials and potential candidates. Like Joe, he enjoyed Kennedy's candid and unguarded political discourses. In December 1958 he and the senator mulled together the weaknesses of each candidate, and Kennedy acknowledged his own liabilities: he was a senator, and senators seldom got nominated; he was ahead in the polls, and early front-runners seldom won; and he was a Catholic, and no Catholic had ever made it to the White House.

As Stewart described it to Martin Sommers, the others' weaknesses could be ticked off with brutal brevity: Johnson—South, oil, heart attack; Adlai—two-time loser; Hubert Humphrey—"draft dodger" (as LBJ put it) and "too smart for his own good"; Stuart Symington—as Joe had put it, "really too shallow a puddle to jump into."

By March of 1959, however, Stewart too had become convinced that the likely winner would be Kennedy. In a *Post* article exploring the coming nomination race, he said the senator's strategy was to paint himself as the choice of the people, not of the party pros. He would seek to maintain his poll lead by challenging his rivals to primary battles in key states. If Symington and Humphrey entered those primaries and if polls were accurate, wrote Stewart, Kennedy would win and strengthen his lead. If they declined the challenge, "Kennedy's claim to the title of people's choice will be reinforced, and he will painlessly pick up a useful number of primary delegates."

In December 1959 Stewart traveled to New York for a conference of Democratic bigwigs, where the party's presidential candidates were placed on display to perform their "buck-and-wing," as Stewart called it. Harry Truman ruthlessly upstaged the lot, standing beside each as he addressed the delegates, grinning at the wrong moments, fingering his watch, yawning gently, as if he didn't consider any of them capable of filling his shoes. Stevenson got the biggest applause, but Stewart felt the old magic was gone, "even for the eggheads." As Stevenson spoke, Stewart scribbled into his notebook, "This man will never be president." Kennedy and Humphrey performed most admirably, according to the press consensus, but for Stewart they all looked like vice presidential timber.

That evening Stewart attended an exclusive soiree at the Seventy-ninth Street mansion of Marietta Tree, the Democratic Party's leading hostess. Beautiful, well-connected, and rich, she was the granddaughter of Groton's founding rector, Endicott Peabody. To Stewart she seemed "amazingly well preserved—hardly . . . changed since the days when we used to drool and swoon when she visited the Rector at Groton." She had been married to Desmond FitzGerald, the Alsops' CIA friend, but that marriage had dissolved shortly after the war, and later she had married Ronald Tree, grandson of Chicago multimillionaire Marshall Field. Tree, son of an English father and an American mother, had been brought up in England, and had served in Parliament. He had a stately mansion in England called Ditchley, where Ronald and Marietta had lived for a time. But Marietta had longed for America, so they had sold Ditchley and taken up residence in New York and the Bahamas.

Now she was the most connected of the connected in Democratic circles. Adlai Stevenson was an old and dear friend and sometime lover, and she maintained close political friendships with all the major powers in the party. Socially, she was *it*. "If you don't go to Marietta's parties you are nowhere," Stewart wrote to Sommers.

Stewart enjoyed the evening at Marietta's. The place was studded with important Democrats—"the whole gallery," as he put it to Sommers—as well as a host of supporting players. Arthur Schlesinger was there, enjoying his role as literary paladin to the party's mighty. He had written three of the seven candidates' speeches for that day's conference, and earlier had served as intermediary in bringing about a "semi-reconciliation" between Kennedy and Eleanor Roosevelt, who still nurtured ill feelings toward the senator because of his past association with Joseph McCarthy.

As the primaries approached, Joe Alsop suggested that he and Stewart join forces for extensive door-to-door reporting on voter sentiment. They had pioneered the technique in the 1950s (with the help of pollster Harris) in order to find out what was bubbling beneath the political surface. Wisconsin was shaping up as a crucial Kennedy-Humphrey battleground, and the brothers headed there in frigid February for door-to-door canvassing.

When the American hinterland collided with Joe Alsop, the results could be comical. Wearing a Russian fur cap and a fur-lined coaching cloak that had belonged to his Grandfather Robinson, Joe looked like "an angry, large-nosed, bespectacled animal peering out from behind a bush," as Stewart recalled later. Trudging up to a lower-middle-class house in Wausau, Joe rang the bell and waited, clipboard in hand. An Irish-looking woman opened the door, peered at Joe, exclaimed, "Holy Mary, Mother of God!"—and slammed the door. Bewildered, Joe went to the next house, where he encountered a woman with a thick Eastern

European accent. She listened intently as Joe unfurled his prepared spiel in that manner of talking he had cultivated so many years before, a kind of cross between Harvard and Oxford. She answered all the questions, then asked with blunt curiosity, "Ascuse me, meester. Why you spik so broken?"

At another house, Joe's feelings for Kennedy got the better of him. The woman there was a no-nonsense Midwesterner who answered all Joe's questions with matter-of-fact candor. She and her husband didn't care much for Humphrey, but they were Lutheran and would probably vote for him because they couldn't vote for a Catholic.

"Thank you, madam," said Joe. "I think you're a *goddam bigot!*"

But the polling yielded rich insights. The brothers had chosen for their survey the state's pivotal seventh district, where Harris's research showed the two candidates in a dead heat and where the primary likely would be decided. In talking with forty-six voters, the Alsops had determined that Kennedy held at least an outside chance of making a serious race against Nixon there, while Humphrey and other Democratic hopefuls seemed to have no chance. "Although Kennedy's faith cut both ways," Joe wrote, "being a Catholic helped him decidedly more than it hurt him."

After the polling expedition, Stewart hurried off to join the candidates on the stump and witness firsthand their handling of the Wisconsin challenge. He found Kennedy to be "an unexpectedly self-conscious and diffident man" who seemed ill-at-ease as a campaigner. When a group of brightly dressed girls suddenly surrounded the senator to give a well-rehearsed and silly cheer ("Right sock, left sock, rubber-soled shoes; we've got the candidate who can't lose"), the candidate "wore a rather bemused air, as though he had unexpectedly found himself knee-deep in midgets."

Yet he received questions with the demeanor of a teacher bent on providing answers. He never talked down to his audiences, and often tossed off erudite phrases and obscure quotations. In one brief talk at Wisconsin State College at Whitewater, he quoted Aristotle, George Bernard Shaw, Walter Lippmann, Professor Sidney Hook, President Eisenhower, Thomas Jefferson (twice), John Quincy Adams, Daniel Webster, and Abraham Lincoln. The Whitewater talk, wrote Stewart, "was an obviously deeply felt disquisition on the related roles of the educator and the politician in a free society."

The famous Kennedy charm was always in evidence, augmented by that hint of diffidence. The wit was used deftly to beguile an audience or defuse a situation. At one question-and-answer session, he asked for one more question and was rewarded with a long, rambling, unanswerable query from an outraged woman. Kennedy looked stunned for a moment, then said with a wry smile, "I should have stopped a minute sooner." The audience laughed in sympathy.

Humphrey was as different from Kennedy as it was possible to be.

Voluble, excitable, ebullient, he cut through political turbulence like a sleek motorboat through waves. Never diffident, never at a loss for words, he could say just about anything and make it work. "Spontaneity," he shouted to one group, in no particular context. "Spontaneity. That's what you get in this gatherin'—you never know what to expect." It didn't make any sense, really, but it struck the audience as funny, and it struck Humphrey as extremely funny. "He laughed his high, infectious laugh," wrote Stewart, then "answered questions in his usual rapid-fire way, with his usual combination of pugnacity and good humor."

Humphrey's simple, unadorned rhetoric was brilliantly calculated. In one speech the only quotations were from "the beautiful words of Scripture," but his presentation struck Stewart as a "highly expert appeal to the self-interest and the emotions of his farm audience." There was some political corn—"If Muriel and I ever move to Sixteen Hundred Pennsylvania Avenue, it will be a real family place, and you folks would always be welcome. We'd have the coffeepot on all the time." There were well-planned sideswipes at Kennedy's insufficiently pro-farm voting record. And Humphrey ended the fifty-minute speech (for him rather on the short side) with a moving peroration keyed to the theme, "Be proud you're a farmer." Humphrey, wrote Stewart, "looks too much for his own good like the Hollywood version of a politician, and too little like the Hollywood version of a President."

Stewart was taken with the Kennedys more than with the Humphreys; but he never sought to be friends with either, and maintained a reporter's distance. Still, after the Wisconsin trip he asked a *Post* editor for a photo of him in friendly banter with Jack and Jackie. He planned to have it autographed by the senator and affixed to his office wall.

No trophies were necessary for Joe, who included the Kennedys among his closest friends. After returning to Washington from his Wisconsin polling trip, Joe invited Jackie and her sister and brother-in-law, Princess Lee and Prince Stanislas Radziwill, to lunch at Dumbarton. The food was exquisite—noisettes and mushroom rice, caviar and champagne—and the conversation was filled with convivial laughter. Afterward, Jackie made plans for a trip to Milwaukee, and from that city's Pfister Hotel she wrote saying she had been sorry she hadn't dashed off a letter of appreciation before leaving Washington.

> But now I am glad I didn't, as your lunch seems that much more magical with a bit of reality in between.
>
> You were so sweet to do it. I just wanted to tell you that I will miss Lee and Stas so much, and that will remain one of the happiest souvenirs of the time the four of us were together.
>
> The most voluptuous daydream to which I treat myself is reliving every sip and bite. . . . I have a feeling my brother in law is doing the same!
>
> So many thanks dear Joe

When Wisconsin's voters rendered their judgment on April 5, Kennedy collected 56 percent of the vote, and six of ten districts. But the result was too close and too filled with signs of political weakness to ensure Kennedy the nomination. The vote had broken down along religious lines, and word went out from the party's political councils that Kennedy couldn't carry Protestant districts. He would have to proceed to West Virginia and demonstrate that he could beat the Protestant Humphrey in an overwhelmingly Protestant state.

Joe hurried to Slab Fork, West Virginia, a bleak mining town, scurfy with coal dust, tucked away in the state's rugged mountains. It was a poor community, but the Slab Fork Mining Company had brought to town effective management techniques and a kind of corporate benevolence. Its workers could count on steady employment and enough pay to allow a careful man to send his children to college. With the help of Lou Harris, Joe polled more than eighty residents—and came up with astounding results. The survey showed thirty votes for Kennedy, twenty-seven for Humphrey, ten undecided, and the others either not registered, undecided, or Republican. Many Protestant voters, the poll revealed, would vote for Humphrey because he was a Protestant; many others didn't take Kennedy's religion into consideration at all. Joe reported that Humphrey could win only through religious prejudice; a Kennedy win would represent triumph over that prejudice.

It was too much for Jim Rowe. In a letter he called the column "the most disgusting performance I have ever seen in print," and added that he had instructed his secretary to return all files concerning Joe's legal affairs. "I have no longer any desire to have any kind of association with you whatsoever." Joe wrote back to defend the column, but his tone was temperate and he declined to address Rowe's angry withdrawal from their lawyer-client association.

The balloting on May 10 gave Kennedy 61 percent of the vote. Humphrey carried only seven of fifty-five counties. "All in all," wrote Joe, "this Kennedy performance in West Virginia can only be described as formidable."

As KENNEDY AND HUMPHREY campaigned among the crags and dales of West Virginia, a volley of antiaircraft fire half a world away touched off a diplomatic explosion. On the morning of May 1, in Peshawar, Pakistan, a CIA pilot named Francis Gary Powers had taken off in a high-altitude plane called a U-2. His flight plan was a northwest course over the heart of Russia and into Norway. His mission was part of a highly secret intelligence operation to penetrate Soviet military designs through the use of advanced aerial photography. The U.S. government had been making such flights for nearly four years on the calculation that the benefits outweighed the risks. Soviet fighters, it was believed, couldn't get near the U-2's flight ceiling of seventy thousand feet, and hence couldn't knock this remarkable seeing-eye plane out of the sky.

But the Soviets, after chafing for years at the brazen violation of their airspace, now were ready. On the afternoon of that May Day, they brought down Powers's plane, forcing the pilot to bail out. He was captured near Sverdlovsk as a spy—the first acknowledged American spy ever seized by the Soviet Union. The sequence of events that followed was marked by American fumbling, Soviet pugnacity, and diplomatic chaos. The White House first denied knowledge of the episode, then had to recant after an angry Khrushchev waved Powers's confession to the world. Khrushchev used the provocation to torpedo a Paris conference that had been scheduled to commence in just a few days, at which he and Eisenhower had planned to discuss world peace. And the nation braced for a colder Cold War.

"God knows the whole business was handled bumblingly," Stewart wrote to Sommers, but he also felt encouraged. "The fact that we could get away for so long with such an operation won't be lost on the world," he wrote. The mastermind behind the overflights had been the Alsops' friend Dick Bissell, now the CIA's deputy director for plans. After discussing the project with Bissell, Stewart concluded that the U-2 flights probably had provided the basis for the Eisenhower complacency that had so rankled the Alsops as their fears of a "missile gap" had intensified.

In truth, there was no missile gap, as Eisenhower knew from reports received from Bissell's U-2 operation. For years he had boiled with anger at the voices of doom—Stuart Symington, John Kennedy, Nelson Rockefeller, the Alsops—railing about a missile gap and declaring his air force budget inadequate to the Soviet missile challenge. But he could not have silenced his critics without compromising the U-2 program, which showed that the Soviets had the capability to outstrip America in missile production but weren't doing so. Reading the Alsop attacks in his favorite newspaper, the *Herald Tribune*, the president would hurl the paper across the room and unloose a string of invectives. He had called Joe "about the lowest form of animal life on earth." But even now, with the U-2 program exposed by Powers's confession, Eisenhower still couldn't squelch the missile gap warnings.

Throughout these months Joe's world continued to change. He read in *Time* that John McCloy, one of the great architects of the postwar world and a reliable source in those heady days after the war, was retiring as chairman of Chase Manhattan Bank. "I feel sure that the Chase Bank will miss you," he wrote to McCloy, "just as the government has desperately missed you." At Jock Whitney's *Herald Tribune*, George Cornish retired as managing editor after thirty-six years at the paper. His replacement was Fendall Yerxa, "not as nice a man as George, but I would guess . . . tougher and more energetic," as Joe wrote to a friend. He didn't expect any great revolutions at the paper.

In Paris in March, Bill Patten died from the lung disorders he had been fighting most of his life. It was a severe blow. Patten was Joe's age—not quite fifty—and had been Joe's closest friend at Harvard, his roommate in the New York days, the host and companion of so many wonderful times during Joe's Paris visits. To Susan Mary he wrote what she later termed a "sweet, affectionate letter." Scheduled to visit Paris during a forthcoming European trip, Joe fretted about the appropriateness of staying with Susan Mary as in days of old. He asked Cy Sulzberger to approach her tactfully on the matter, and Sulzberger cabled back that she would be "delighted" to stick with tradition. Susan Mary wrote to Joe, "Of course you must stay here on your arrival. . . . All your . . . friends are clamoring to see you & I have every intention of making it a lovely gay time. Bill would have been furious if I had continued to be dreary."

Back in Washington, Joe was seeing the Kennedys as often as possible. In mid-June, during a lull before the Democratic convention, he stopped by their Georgetown house one afternoon for drinks. The senator was ecstatic over news that Mayor Richard Daley of Chicago, one of the country's leading Democratic bosses, had promised his support. It was a giant step toward nomination.

A few days later Joe held a dinner for the Kennedys and fifteen others, including diplomat Llewellyn Thompson and the Bradens. Joan Braden had been introduced to Jackie earlier by Joe, and had become a kind of ex officio press secretary to the candidate's wife, helping her through broadcast appearances and coaching her on appropriate responses to reporters' often raucous questions. Joe's dinner was buoyed by the excitement surrounding Kennedy's apparent lock on the nomination, and by a goodly amount of alcohol—fourteen bottles of wine, a bottle of Scotch, a bottle of gin, and half a bottle of bourbon, according to Joe's expense records.

IN JULY'S FIRST WEEK, in the sunny sprawl of Los Angeles, the Democratic National Convention began. Stewart flew out on July 7, dropped off several of his children with the Bradens in nearby Oceanside, and checked into the Beverly Wilshire Hotel in Beverly Hills. He had with him, in draft form, a discursive inside look at how the nomination had fallen to this forty-three-year-old Catholic who had started out without the support of a single important party leader and with opposition from liberals, labor, farm groups, and black leaders. Stewart planned to update the article as convention events unfolded, then ship it off for quick publication. Interviewing Kennedy in Washington on June 30, he had pressed the senator to concede that he would accept the vice presidential nomination if he somehow missed the top spot.

"Look," the proud Kennedy had replied, "I'll make you an offer. If

I take the vice presidential nomination with anyone, I'll let you have my next year's Senate salary."

His confidence proved justified during the roll call on convention Wednesday. As Wyoming's delegation put Kennedy over the top and pandemonium erupted on the convention floor, Stewart heard one top party official exclaim, "How in Hell did he do it?" Stewart's piece, entitled "Kennedy's Magic Formula," answered that question the next week.

Joe also stayed at the Beverly Wilshire, along with Phil and Kay Graham. Phil appeared to have recovered from the inner crisis of a couple of years before, and Joe lunched with the Grahams every day in the hotel dining room. They ate at a large table they had reserved by slipping the headwaiter a persuasive sum of money. On the day after Kennedy's nomination, Joe told Graham he thought Kennedy should pick Lyndon Johnson for his running mate. Graham agreed. He had supported Johnson for the ticket's top spot throughout the primary season, and now that Kennedy had prevailed it made sense for Graham to promote his man for vice president. The two decided to head over to Kennedy's suite at the Biltmore and put forth their case for Johnson. With Joe in the lead they pushed their way through the convention throngs and into the crowded Biltmore lobby, where they managed to board an elevator heading for Kennedy's hotel office. There they encountered two potent Connecticut politicians, John Bailey and Abraham Ribicoff, impatiently waiting for an audience with the senator. It was a typical scene of political commotion—the room blue with Bailey's cigar smoke, a general sense of chaos, self-important young staffers briskly passing to and fro. With Joe's familiar face as credential, he and Graham were escorted to Kennedy's personal secretary, Evelyn Lincoln. She placed them on the schedule.

They waited in a seedy double bedroom that served as a reception area, then were escorted into the senator's cubbyhole office. Looking fresh and remarkably composed, the candidate invited them to come directly to the point. Joe said he feared there might be a temptation to make the difficult decision on a running mate based on superficial considerations. Noting the groundswell for Symington then sweeping the convention, he added, "You know damn well that Stu Symington is too shallow a puddle for the United States to have to dive into." Kennedy smiled, and Joe surmised he already had dismissed Symington. Joe then recommended Johnson. The big Texan could serve admirably as president should that prove necessary, Joe said, and he could deliver the rich lode of Texas electoral votes to Kennedy in the general election. Knowing that many insiders were predicting that Johnson would reject a vice presidential offer, Joe urged Kennedy to make the offer only if he was really serious. If he made the offer and then withdrew it, said Joe, the resulting blowup would harm his chances in the fall.

Kennedy listened, then turned to Graham, who presented a sweeping analysis of the electoral college and the potential role of Johnson in delivering an election-night victory to the Democratic ticket. Joe sensed that Kennedy already had decided on Johnson, and hence their arguments served merely to bolster his confidence in the choice. But, knowing that Graham was close to Johnson, Kennedy gave the *Post* publisher a list of his secret phone numbers in case the occasion should arise for Graham to serve as intermediary between the two senators.

That proved wise. After word of the looming Johnson choice hit the convention gossip circuit, party liberals rose up in protest; Robert Kennedy, serving as his brother's campaign manager, strongly opposed the choice as well, since he had promised organized labor that the Texas senator wouldn't be considered. With his brother's blessing, Bobby went to Johnson's suite to beg him to withdraw from consideration. Chaos hit the Johnson camp as word seeped through that Kennedy was reneging on his offer. But Phil Graham was among the Johnsonites with John Kennedy's private phone numbers, and he called the candidate to find out what was going on. Kennedy asked to speak with Johnson, and when the Texan came on the line the candidate assured him that the offer was genuine. With his mastery of sweet talk, Kennedy managed to deflate Johnson's anger, and the fateful ticket was forged.

Joe filed a column filled with inside information on the Kennedy-Johnson drama, but he revealed nothing of his role or that of his friend Phil Graham. From there it was all anticlimax, except for a bash at the Beverly Wilshire put on by the Alsop brothers and the Bradens. It got a bit out of hand, as two hundred ravenous party officials and journalists showed up following the final convention session, including Senator William Fulbright, the Harrimans, Bruces, and Radziwills, the publisher of *The New York Times*, the entire *Newsweek* bureau, and a large contingent of triumphant Kennedy people. "You certainly are a most lavish host," wrote Philadelphia Mayor Richardson Dilworth after the party.

The brothers also had a dinner for Eleanor Roosevelt and the Robert Kennedys at a fashionable restaurant called Perino's. Joe had hoped Jackie Kennedy would attend, but the candidate's wife, pregnant with her second child, had decided against making the strenuous journey to Los Angeles. She had expressed her disappointment to Joe in a letter: "I write to say how sad I will be to miss that evening. . . . Please think of me when the suspense [of the convention] gets unbearable."

After a few days back in Washington, catching up on correspondence and laundry, the brothers traveled to Chicago to cover the Republican embracement of Richard Nixon. Checking into the Ambassador Hotel, they found themselves close observers of a political firecracker set off by Nixon on convention eve. To neutralize his major party rival, Nelson Rockefeller, and prevent a messy platform battle, Nixon joined the New York governor in what became known as the "Fifth Avenue compact." Among other things, it repudiated Eisenhower's policy of placing fiscal austerity above defense spending, and it accepted a more aggressive

stance on civil rights for blacks than many party conservatives would
have favored.

The politically astute Nixon, watching the emergence of the
Kennedy-Johnson ticket, knew he must not focus too much on the South
alone, once solidly Democratic but now up for grabs. Republicans had
been dreaming of a "Southern strategy" based on the idea that they
could use that region, increasingly hospitable to the GOP, as a large electoral base. But Kennedy's choice of Johnson seemed to thwart that strategy. Nixon would have to face Kennedy state by state, North and South,
in a political war of attrition. The "compact" was designed to fortify
him for that war.

But it angered the president and party conservatives, who despised
Rockefeller and placed low taxes and balanced budgets above all else.
Joe was elated to see Rockefeller's ideas triumph over what he considered the Eisenhower complacency. "The hordes of Republican fogies,
young and old," he wrote from Chicago, "were naturally enraged to be
jerked into the modern age by main force, at the very moment when they
had hoped to commemorate William McKinley by publicly trampling all
over the wicked Gov. Rockefeller." He later praised Nixon for facing
down angry Eisenhower partisans and steering the platform committee
toward language stating that the national defense effort should be
intensified.

With the convention's end, Stewart joined the Nixon entourage,
while Joe flew to Massachusetts to spend a social weekend with the Kennedys at their Hyannis compound. There he dined with Jack and Jackie,
watched the energetic Kennedys play touch football on the lawn, boated
off Cape Cod. At Eunice Kennedy Shriver's house, Joe seized young David Kennedy, Bobby's son, and whirled him into the air to give the boy
a thrill. But he accidentally whacked his head on the low ceiling. The
young Kennedy displayed remarkable bravery, gritting his teeth at the
pain and refusing to cry out. "It was the bravest behavior by a child I've
ever seen," Joe later wrote to the boy's mother, Ethel Kennedy. To David
he sent a gift as a "gesture of apology."

During the weekend Joe engaged Jackie in a conversation about the
political drama swirling around her. Jackie expressed exasperation with
the demands of the campaign and the intrusions on her family life. She
was appalled by the personal questions fired at her by reporters and the
behavior of news photographers who chased after little Caroline with
their flashbulbs, intent on turning her into "a ghastly little Shirley Temple." It wasn't the first time Jackie had wondered if the whole business
was worth it. A year earlier she had resisted the idea of Jack running for
president and throwing their pleasant life into chaos. But Joe had had a
large impact on her thinking. "It's the only game that's worth the candle," he had said, and gradually she had come to agree. "If Mummy or
. . . my father in law had told me that, I would have been annoyed," she

wrote to Joe. "But you have dimensions they don't have, so I listen to you."

Now she was troubled once more as the political and personal pressures mounted. She told Joe she resented having newspapers relate that she bought her maternity clothes at Bloomingdale's department store in New York, and she felt uncomfortable giving a party for sixty newsmen whom she hardly knew or had never met. When Joe sought to dispel these concerns, Jackie seemed irritated.

Back in Washington, Joe wrote her a long letter offering perspective on the matter. It was a conflict, he said, as old as politics—private life vs. public demands upon politicians and their families. He had seen many wives struggle with it, and some handled it better than others. There was the irrepressible Cousin Eleanor, who could pull off "oddly humorous and even downright fantastic things"—such as appearing as a model at a Democratic fund-raising fashion show. There was sad Pat Nixon, who indulged in "false homey touches" that came across like an "adman's phoniness." And in between were those who could reconcile the private person with the public persona.

Take those stories about Bloomingdale's, said Joe. It really isn't much different from the many stories over the years about Jackie's sister Lee buying her ball gowns at Givenchy. Such stories seemed to be normal publicity, depicting accurately a glamorous life, while the Bloomingdale's piece depicted accurately a political life. It probably helps politically to let readers know she buys off the rack at Bloomingdale's, said Joe. "It's the kind of thing, in short, that can be done for public purposes without any departure from or falsification of your private self."

And there wasn't any reason for Jackie to be embarrassed by the party for newsmen. It was considered normal for people like herself to give parties for people she hardly knew when the purpose was, say, raising money for charity. Why think differently about the party for newsmen? "Maybe this is the right standard to apply," wrote Joe. "Do forgive me for this further intrusion on your privacy."

Jackie replied, saying she was "most touched" that he would write such a long and understanding letter. He was very perceptive to sense what was troubling her. She added:

> You have been of more help than you can imagine. It never occurred to me to look at the privacy problem unemotionally—that the press party is like a charity one—the Bloomingdale dress the same as Lee in *Vogue* posing in all her Givenchys. . . . Now I will be reasonable—thank god you explained how—It makes everything so peaceful. I couldn't bear it if Jack should ever think I was at cross purposes with him. I never will be, as you know, but he couldn't explain it properly.

And there is one more thing you have taught me—to respect

power. I never did—possibly because it came so suddenly without my having had to work for it—(power by marriage I mean)

But if things turn out right—I will welcome it—and use it for the things I care about.

Thank you again dear Joe—for such a needed letter.

Joe's friendship with Jackie deepened through the fall campaign. As he crisscrossed the nation to cover the candidates, he sought to telephone her whenever possible. When he failed, she was disappointed. "It would have been a joyous moment in a frantic day to talk to you," she wrote after two efforts by Joe to phone proved futile. "I think of you often and read you always." Joe wrote to express excitement at watching her young husband launch his autumn offensive. "It really is rather moving, if you don't mind my seeming mushy," he wrote, "to see Jack going into the hardest campaign of the century with his rather special combination of a hard, realistic grasp of his problem and a high heart."

Stewart, assigned to the Nixon camp, found the Republican candidate's performance decidedly mixed. The campaign was "brilliantly organized," he wrote to Bob Fuoss at the *Saturday Evening Post*. And on domestic issues Nixon stated his positions crisply and eloquently. But Stewart felt his stands on foreign and military matters lacked content. "What he says," Stewart wrote to Fuoss, "boils down to, 'everything's approximately dandy, and elect me to keep it that way.' " It seemed that Nixon, having sealed the nomination with the Fifth Avenue pact, now was opting to keep Eisenhower happy during the general election campaign. Stewart viewed this as inadequate for a potential leader of the West—and bad politics. He wrote a tough piece for the *Post* questioning Nixon's approach to foreign and defense issues, but the magazine countered the critique by publishing in the same issue an editorial endorsing the Republican candidate.

AT EIGHT THIRTY, CHICAGO time, on the evening of September 26, the two candidates faced each other in debate at the austere CBS studio in downtown Chicago. The candidates' words and mannerisms were beamed across the country via the television airwaves, and seventy million Americans tuned in. Never before had so many people witnessed an event of such political force, rendered all the more crucial by the fact of those millions of viewers. In the country's living rooms, Nixon stumbled badly. Television portrayed him cruelly as a drawn, furtive, and tired man, no match for the crisply fresh and well made-up Kennedy. Marty Sommers, viewing the debate on his Philadelphia TV screen, felt Nixon looked like "a suspect who was being questioned in the West 47th Street Station in connection with a statutory rape case." But Joe had watched the debate from the studio, and he made no allowance for appearances. He didn't realize that television had undone Nixon and that a new era of politics had arrived. Filing a column on the event before its impact was fully realized, he pronounced both candidates "enormously impressive, each in his different and characteristic way." It was hard to believe, he wrote, that the debate had been decisive in any way.

Within hours of filing the column, Joe called Cousin Alice Longworth, a staunch Nixon backer, to get her reaction.

"Well, Joe," she said, "your man's in, my man's finished."

Slightly embarrassed that he had missed the debate's significance, but elated that Kennedy had won, Joe shared a postdebate celebration with Jack and Jackie in their hotel suite at the Ambassador East. Jackie wrote later, "I will never forget how sweet you were the night of the Great Debate, with your lovely support & what it meant to poor tired Jack. Things have to turn out right for people like you & Jack or there is no justice."

On the evening of October 11, Joe and his friends took a break from politics to celebrate an event of considerable moment to them all. Joe turned fifty on that day, and the Grahams and Stew and Tish organized a memorable bash. Some 150 guests were invited, and nearly 90 showed up, at the sprawling home of Katharine Graham's parents at 1624 Crescent Place. Guests included Mrs. Robert Low Bacon, the dowager of social Washington; Mr. and Mrs. Robert Woods Bliss, old friends from the prewar era; Dean Acheson, who long since had patched up his friendship with Joe; Allen Dulles, Desmond FitzGerald, Tracy Barnes, and Dickie Bissell of the CIA; diplomatic heavyweights Chip Bohlen and David Bruce; longtime intimates Felix Frankfurter and Ben Cohen; and prominent newsmen Arthur Krock, Walter Lippmann, and Cy Sulzberger. Lady Pamela Berry came all the way from London, and of course Marietta Tree, the social lioness of the Democratic Party, was there. The Kennedys couldn't make it, but sent champagne and a note from Jackie: "You know what joy it would give us to spend [your birthday] with you. I cannot express & become tearful when I try—In this supercharged emotional time—how we appreciate your friendship."

At the birthday bash, Phil Graham offered the toast, reminiscing on the time twenty years before when he first visited Joe in his Georgetown garden as he lingered over breakfast with Isaiah Berlin. He was loosely encased in an eccentric and weirdly colored kimono, recalled Graham, and his blasting laugh was shattering windows throughout the neighborhood.

"What I remember of that morning most is how endless was his knowledge," said Graham, "how free of any taint of tentativeness were his opinions, and how overwhelming was his omniscience." He called Joe a paradox: "He is a rasping geyser of bad temper, and he is a gentle fountain of friendship. He is constantly on the brink of fleeing to monasticism, and he is inexorably drawn to involvement in the noisy world. He is cuttingly cynical, and he is splendidly and sentimentally naive."

It was impossible to sum up Joe Alsop, said Graham. "When I knew him only little, his essence was easy to grasp. But the more I know of him I only know there is more of him to know. I hope and believe that is a loving thing to say of a man of fifty, for Kay and I love Joe as all of you do." It was a wonderful evening, full of hearty cheer and sentiment. But there wasn't time to savor the occasion. The next morning Joe rose at dawn to fly south and join Lyndon Johnson's campaign through Florida and Alabama.

Later he rejoined the Kennedy campaign and found himself in Minneapolis, where he ran into a young *Wall Street Journal* reporter named Robert Novak, who would later become a well-known columnist.

"Oh, dear boy, I'm delighted to see you," said Joe, and invited the younger man out to dinner. Novak was puzzled; the Democratic–Farmer–Labor Party dinner and rally was due to start in less than an hour.

"Aren't you going to eat at the DFL rally?" he asked.

"Surely not," replied Joe. "That's just a bean feed." He said they could enjoy a nice dinner and still get back in time for the speeches. Novak was skeptical; the University of Minnesota football team had played at home that afternoon, and he doubted they could get a table on such short notice.

"No, no," Joe assured him. "Don't worry about that."

But the restaurants were all booked. By the third try, Joe was beside himself with frustration and embarrassment.

"I am Joseph W. Alsop," he shouted to the puzzled maitre d' of one fancy restaurant. "This is an outrage."

He and Novak ended up at a downscale hamburger joint.

ELECTION NIGHT WAS not a time of high drama for Stewart, the dispassionate brother, who dubbed himself "Mr. Facing-Both-Ways" in the election and considered the candidates about equal as potential presidents. Even before the ballots were cast on November 8, Stewart had left the country with Tom Braden for a long reporting trip through Africa. The parties had chosen well, he believed, and the country would render a good decision.

But for Joe the stakes were immense. He and the Grahams gathered before a borrowed television set at Dumbarton to watch the returns come in. The first results sent them into shouts of enthusiasm, as Kennedy picked up Connecticut and then delegate-rich Texas. They took pride in their small role in securing Lyndon Johnson and his state for the Democratic ticket. But soon it became clear this would be no runaway. Late into the night, it still was impossible to tell who would win, and it was well past midnight when Kay decided to return home. Phil remained to share the tension and the ample stores of Scotch with Joe. At nine a.m., when he finally left, the outcome was still in doubt. Joe sat riveted to the television set, sipping a Scotch and awaiting the final word. It came with news that Michigan had gone for Kennedy. His man was in. He stumbled off to bed.

THE NEXT DAY Joe plunged into the task of helping to define and shape the new administration. He was at the height of his influence now, with a powerful column, a friend soon to be in the White House, and an administration in tune with his political outlook. Joe was determined to wield his influence to the hilt—through the column, of course, but also through private conversations with the high and mighty of the new government.

He correctly anticipated a protracted battle within the party for the soul of Kennedy's presidency, and he declared himself quickly in favor of Democratic moderates and against the party's more liberal elements. The big question, as Kennedy headed to Florida for a much-needed rest, was whether one of the left's premier darlings, Adlai Stevenson or Chester Bowles, would become secretary of state. Watching the liberals campaign noisily for their "shining shibboleths of virtue," Joe felt their efforts "revealed the persistent flaw in American . . . liberalism. This flaw is an incurable tendency to put shibboleths ahead of practical facts." Joe predicted in the column that Kennedy would bypass Stevenson and Bowles in favor of a man who, like the new president, took a more hard-line foreign-policy stance.

He was right. After Kennedy offered the nonplussed Stevenson a job as ambassador to the United Nations, the liberals pushed Senator William Fulbright of Arkansas for State. When Kennedy sought Joe's advice on Fulbright, the columnist urged caution. Fulbright was vain, he said, and vanity often led to disloyalty. Joe advocated his friend David Bruce. Kennedy bypassed Fulbright and Bruce in favor of Dean Rusk, a competent protégé of the Democratic foreign-policy establishment who lacked the stature to be troublesome. Joe pronounced himself satisfied with Rusk.

Joe also weighed in on the matter of treasury secretary. Party liberals wanted Senator Albert Gore, Sr., of Tennessee, an economic populist, but Joe dismissed Gore as a superficial man who talked too much. He urged Kennedy to name New York banker Douglas Dillon, who had served as undersecretary of state and ambassador to Paris in the Eisenhower years—and was also an Alsop friend. Although a Republican, Dillon would be unfailingly loyal, said Joe. Kennedy chose Dillon.

The president-elect also accepted Joe's advice on George Kennan and Averell Harriman, stalwarts of that early postwar effort to reshape the world. Kennedy wasn't inclined to give either man an important job, but Joe praised both as highly competent and worthy. Kennan became ambassador to Yugoslavia, while Harriman took a key designation as ambassador-at-large.

Inauguration week in Washington was bitterly cold and filled with snow, but the weather couldn't diminish Joe's excitement at seeing the fogies of the Eisenhower camp finally leave town. The city was bubbling with glamorous young people who thrilled Joe, filled him with a new enthusiasm for the Washington scene.

On inauguration night, he served dinner at Dumbarton for the Grahams and Bohlens, and then the five rode together in the Grahams' limousine to the inaugural ball at the D.C. Armory. Snow was falling, the limo moved slowly through the dazzling city, and the party polished off several bottles of champagne along the way.

Joe didn't linger at the ball. After an hour or so, he asked Phil Graham if he and Kay wanted to return to Dumbarton for some drinks. No, said Graham—he was having a good time at the armory. Joe said he anticipated that some close Kennedy friends, Flo Smith and Afdera Fonda, might stop by. Phil still demurred, so Joe headed out into the snow to make his way home—but he couldn't find a cab. Some time later, Phil Geyelin encountered him thrashing about in the snow trying to hail a cab. "He was close to hysterical," recalled Geyelin. "He was desperate to get a taxi." Finally, he managed to get a ride with Averell Harriman's stepson, Peter Duchin.

Thus, Joe was home in time to receive Flo and Afdera—and a multitude of their friends, who had been told that Joe would have champagne flowing for inaugural revelers. The friends included John Kennedy's brother-in-law, actor Peter Lawford, and a bevy of Hollywood starlets.

Meanwhile, at one-forty-six a.m., the new president left inaugural festivities at the Statler-Hilton and entered his limousine for what Secret Service agents expected to be a short ride to the White House. But Kennedy instructed his driver to take him to 2720 Dumbarton Avenue, and so off he went, followed by a carload of Secret Service agents and a half dozen vehicles filled with reporters and photographers. Shortly thereafter, hearing a loud knock at his door, Joe opened it to find a jaunty Jack Kennedy standing on his portico, flecks of snow scattered about his thick hair and overcoat. Behind him was a scene of pandemonium—a traffic jam on the street, reporters milling about, television lights shining brightly, neighbors leaning out of windows in their nightclothes cheering the new president.

Kennedy remained at Joe's for more than an hour before returning to the White House at three twenty-one a.m. Joe subsequently wrote that he had no idea the president would show up at his house on inauguration night—but that seems unlikely, given his agitation at not being able to get a cab at the armory. In retrospect, Phil Geyelin viewed Joe's behavior as reflecting "the ultimate nightmare—to have the president show up on inauguration night and not be home."

In any event, the long, festive night and the Kennedy visit reflected for Joe the transformation of Washington. There was a new spirit in the city, a political and social ferment, as well as the prospect of imaginative leadership in the executive branch. Georgetown once again was fashion-able. Joe now would enjoy easy access to the inner councils of policy-making. He would be invited to the White House for the first time since his cousins had lived there nearly two decades before. He would attend state dinners, interview the president in the Oval Office, exchange gossip with the First Lady. Suddenly it occurred to Joe that turning fifty wasn't so bad after all.

JOE AND KENNEDY

The Public Life,
the Private Life

IN THE LONG friendship of Joe Alsop and Isaiah Berlin, it was common-place for the two to enjoy each other's company late into the night, sharing gossip and laughter and abundant spirits until nearly the first glimmerings of dawn. On one such occasion, Joe unexpectedly turned serious, as if he had something important to reveal. His changed mood was accentuated by his apparent difficulty in revealing it.

"Isaiah," he said, "there's . . . uh . . . something . . . I . . . uh . . . something I am about to tell you."

Berlin raised an eyebrow.

"What's that, Joe?" he inquired, his curiosity rising.

"I . . . uh . . . I . . . uh . . . I am . . . uh . . . uh . . . I am a homosexual."

"Oh, Joe," replied his friend, "everybody knows that. Nobody cares."

Joe seemed taken aback by Berlin's offhand response—perhaps because Berlin had reacted so casually to what was to Joe a serious matter, or perhaps because Berlin had dismissed Joe's darkest secret as no secret at all. "I just wanted to make light of it," recalled Berlin years later. "He thought he was making a tremendous concession to a dear friend. My response was cruel, though not intended as such."

Joe's sexuality detached the person within from the outward persona. He lived, as did most homosexuals of the time, in the closet of a secret life, a life apart and veiled, yet central and fundamental. On at least three occasions the fact of his homosexuality nearly impinged upon his public persona and threatened scandal, but each time the matter was contained and controlled, though not without embarrassment.

The most serious episode occurred during Joe's 1957 trip to the Soviet Union. He had completed his journey through Siberia, and as he lingered in Moscow awaiting word on a Khrushchev interview he had an encounter with a younger man in his hotel room. It was a grievous lapse of discretion. Soviet agents of the KGB had rigged his room, and cameras caught the scene. Within days, Moscow-trained thugs barged into his room and spread out the photographs for his inspection. Their aim was blackmail and espionage. They said they would expose Joe—unless he agreed to become a Soviet agent.

Shocked and humiliated to be caught in such a snare, Joe knew his only way out was defiance. He dismissed the agents with contempt, suggesting they were on a fool's mission if they expected him to turn traitor. He said he appreciated their nice work and inquired sarcastically as to whether he could get extra copies of the photos for his personal collection. As soon as they departed, he went directly to the American embassy to report the incident. His friend Chip Bohlen was ambassador at the time, and Chip offered counsel on how Joe should handle the situation. He said Joe should get out of the Soviet Union as soon as possible and that he should be thoroughly forthcoming with U.S. intelligence investigators, who would want to interview him on the episode.

Joe was debriefed at length by the CIA and required to sign a statement recounting the experience in detail. As an incident of serious espionage risk, it was referred to the FBI for possible followup after Joe's return to the United States. J. Edgar Hoover's agency had jurisdiction over counterintelligence matters involving U.S. citizens, and officials at the FBI discussed whether they should open a case on Joe to determine if he was maintaining contact with Soviet agents. It was decided that wasn't necessary; besides, Joe was living in Paris, beyond the agency's reach.

The incipient scandal disturbed not only Joe; it threatened Stewart too. Stewart worried about his brother's reputation and his well-being, but he also feared disclosure of Joe's sexual orientation might injure or destroy their column. Earlier, Stewart had been involved in an effort to keep secret an incident in San Francisco in which Joe had been picked up by police in a public area that served as a homosexual rendezvous. Those were the days when homosexuals routinely were attacked as "perverts" and careers could be destroyed through exposure. The Moscow incident increased Stewart's concerns.

Most of Joe's friends over the years had supposed he was not particularly active sexually. He didn't seem to live a furtive life; they couldn't recall running into him in unaccustomed places with men nobody seemed to know.

In fact, as far as anyone could tell, most of Joe's family had no idea he was a homosexual. There is no evidence that Corinne ever suspected it, and brother John said years later that he was "shocked" to find out in the late 1970s, after he and his brother were well into their sixties. He had assumed Joe was "asexual." Stewart knew, but for years he never discussed it with other family members, including Tish. That was the way of the Alsops; they didn't gossip about one another or discuss each other's problems.

Many of Joe's friends also considered him asexual. One was Seymour Janow, who shared an office with Joe in Chennault's China command. As far as Janow could tell, Joe didn't seem to have any romantic interest in women or men. After the war, many around Washington, including Joe's friends, speculated that he was homosexual, but few ever knew for sure. Many friends concluded that he confined his sexual activities largely to times away from Washington.

In the 1940s Joe had an extended affair with a handsome young sailor named Frank Merlo, whom he met in New York and who later had a long, tempestuous relationship with playwright Tennessee Williams. Described by friends as a "warm, decent man with a strong native intelligence and a sense of honor," Merlo met Williams in 1947 and a year later moved in with him. He disclosed his previous relationship with Joe to writer Gore Vidal, a longtime Alsop acquaintance, who used the information to twit Joe.

Berlin was not far wrong when he said "everybody" assumed Joe was homosexual and didn't care. But Joe never allowed the matter to intrude into his friendships, never hinted at or invited discussion of the topic. If anything, he tilted the other way to provide extra cover. He used words such as "pansy" and "fairy" with abandon. If the gossip turned to someone who was homosexual, Joe likely would say, "Oh, he's one of *those,* isn't he?" There was never a hint that he himself might be one of those, and he never ventured into areas of conversation that could make his friends uncomfortable. They, in turn, accepted him for what he was.

But Joe had enemies too, and they were less inclined to be understanding. Seymour Janow remembers Joe's detractors in China dismissing him behind his back as a "queer" or "faggot." Joseph McCarthy hinted darkly at Joe's homosexuality in his angry letter to the *Saturday Evening Post,* and Indiana's Senator Edward Jenner, a McCarthy supporter and frequent recipient of Alsop jabs, once broke up an impromptu press conference with a crude reference that many interpreted as an assault on Joe. And the FBI's J. Edgar Hoover, with his perverse curiosity, vast files, and network of agents, kept a close eye on Joe's activities.

Hoover's personal files revealed that during a trip to Germany in 1954 Joe had asked a State Department official to help secure for him a "warmer" for the evening. The official was himself homosexual, according to the FBI report, and provided the services himself. This information was collected in the course of an investigation aimed at rooting out homosexuals from the State Department.

Hoover also made sure Joe's own report on the Moscow incident made its way into the government's upper echelons. He informed top Justice Department officials, as he clearly should have. But he also took Eisenhower's chief of staff, Sherman Adams, aside after a conference to inform him of the matter. "Governor Adams expressed his appreciation for being so advised," Hoover wrote in an internal memo. Of course, White House officials despised Joe for his relentlessly critical columns, and it wasn't long before they were hatching plans to use the information against him.

At a White House reception for reporters in late 1959, Eisenhower's press secretary, Jim Hagerty, collared the *Herald Tribune*'s Robert Donovan, steered him off to an anteroom, and began denouncing Joe.

"We're fed up," he said. "We can't stand the guy any longer." When Donovan said he didn't think the matter really concerned him, Hagerty blurted, "I'm going to lift his White House pass. I'm going to lift his pass, and I can do it."

"How are you going to do that, Jim?" asked Donovan.

"He's a fairy."

Donovan said he didn't think that gave Hagerty any right to deny Joe access to presidential coverage.

"He's a fag, and we know he is," Hagerty shot back. Then he stormed off.

Despite Hagerty's threats, the White House made no move to lift Joe's pass. But the press secretary's outburst demonstrated that Joe's secret resided just below the surface as reality and hazard.

Compounding the difficulty was Joe's desire to share experiences that other people enjoyed, such as the love of a lifelong mate. Near the end of his life, he confided to a friend that his greatest regret was that he had never settled down or developed a longtime, meaningful relationship with a man. An open homosexual affiliation for someone in Joe's position in those days, before "coming out" was commonplace and society lost some of its old animosities, wasn't possible. If Joe was to have a longtime relationship sanctioned by society, it would have to be with a woman.

Since his youth, Joe had nurtured hopes of being married. Such a marriage would have to be platonic, but Joe didn't see why he couldn't find someone willing to accept him for what he was. As a young man, during his reporting days at the *Herald Tribune*, he had thought that that someone should be a young woman named Lily Emmett. She was tall and blond, with an easy manner that bespoke a self-assurance of the kind that Joe lacked. An accomplished painter, she came from an old established Anglo-Saxon family. "Joe absolutely loved her and admired her," said Evangeline Bruce, who recalled that even years later, as an old man, Joe sometimes spoke of Lily with a kind of wistful nostalgia.

To Lily, Joe wrote tender letters of affection, and in one he proposed marriage. It would be a marriage without sex, he explained, but he vowed that they would nonetheless enjoy a lovely life together. Lily declined politely, but they remained good friends throughout their lives.

Later, after the war, Joe proposed marriage to Judy Montagu, a clever Englishwoman, not as pretty as most in Joe's circles, but bright and witty and amusing. She adored Joe, and he loved seeing her whenever he was in London. When she consulted her friend Gore Vidal on whether she should marry Joe, he said yes, if she could be content with a platonic relationship. She decided against it.

During the 1960 campaign, in the wake of Bill Patten's death, Joe decided his ideal mate would be Susan Mary. She obviously adored him, and he adored her. His visits to the Pattens' home in Paris over the years had been among his most cherished times, and the Pattens and Joe had been a lively trio. He also felt a special kinship toward Susan Mary's children, Billy and Anne; he was Billy's godfather. Susan Mary also would be a perfect Georgetown hostess in the giddy new era that Joe anticipated with the election of John Kennedy.

After fifteen years in Paris, Susan Mary, now forty-one, was an accomplished hostess and social presence on the diplomatic scene. "She knew more about French politics than most of the people in the embassy," recalled Benjamin Bradlee, who wrote from Paris in the early postwar years. He added that she entertained conservatives more than socialists, and did it "awfully well, with butlers and decanted wine." Actually, the Pattens entertained above their diplomatic station. Bill's health had confined him to the role of foreign service reserve officer, and his embassy job—dealing with French treasury officials—was not an elevated one; but their charm and vivacity were credentials for entry into the upper circles of society, and their friends included many grandees of the time. Among them were Duff and Lady Diana Cooper.

Duff Cooper, a British diplomat of rare personal magnetism, had been a member of Parliament, secretary of state for war, and first lord of the Admiralty. After the war he was posted to Paris as ambassador. He was of the old school—blunt-spoken, with great charm and large appetites. He was a bit of a rake, and Diana countenanced his affairs so long as she approved of his lovers. Diana, Viscountess Norwich, was a lively free spirit who had caused a sensation in polite British society by running off to America as a young woman and playing in motion pictures. She and Duff made the British embassy in Paris a center of the city's intellectual, political, and cultural life.

When Diana met Susan Mary shortly after the war, she was immediately taken by her poise and beauty. Susan Mary seemed a bit of a waif amid the intense social whirl of liberated France, and yet she managed to hold her own with an impressive mien. As one of Diana's biographers noted, Susan Mary loved the diplomatic and social establishment of postwar Paris, and yet felt no urge to impose herself upon it. She was content merely to bask in its warmth. Diana quickly concluded that Susan Mary would be the "ideal mistress" for Duff, and she set about the subtle task of engineering an affair between the two.

Ultimately she succeeded. The love that grew between them was a powerful force in both their lives, and yet it was shared in the context of the great friendship between the Coopers and the Pattens. Both Duff and Diana appreciated the fact that Susan Mary was utterly discreet and that she assiduously protected her often ailing husband from knowledge of the affair. It lasted until Duff's death in 1953, and close friends concluded it was the greatest love of Susan Mary's life; but she never let it undermine her marriage or her family. Throughout the affair and long after, Susan Mary nursed Bill through the most difficult periods of infirmity and remained with him devotedly until his death.

Some months afterward, in the summer of 1960, Joe first proposed to Susan Mary in a letter. It was waiting for her upon her return to Paris following a trip to the United States with Bill's ashes. Joe informed her of his sexual orientation and said theirs would be a platonic marriage, but promised a happy life together. It was an eloquent letter, but it did not sway Susan Mary. She said years later that she was surprised to learn that Joe was homosexual. She and Bill had never suspected it, had never speculated on the subject. She concluded that it was not the kind of marriage she wanted, and wrote back to decline the proposal.

Still, they remained loving friends. During the summer, when she spent several weeks with her children in the south of France, Joe wrote her amusing letters about the unfolding campaign and the political conventions. In December, Joe came through Paris and renewed his courtship, describing the exciting life they could have together as a grand couple of Georgetown. Susan Mary began to reconsider her decision. After dinner one evening, they discussed the matter further in the living room of her Paris flat. Susan Mary accepted. They made plans for a February 16 wedding in Washington.

In early January, the engagement was announced publicly, and Joe was flooded with good wishes. "What wonderful news it is about you and Susan Mary!" wrote Harriet Aldrich, a cousin of Susan Mary's mother. "I was knocked flat with surprise." Martin Sommers wrote to say he and his wife had spent an entire evening drinking to Joe and Susan Mary's future—"in Scotch; alas, this event caught us with no champagne on tap here." Mary Whitehouse, whose husband was Susan Mary's cousin, called Joe's future wife "the most beautiful, intelligent, courageous woman in the world." In reply, Joe expressed delight at the turn of events. "I am the very luckiest man in the world," he wrote to Harriet Aldrich. "And after fifty years of being rather contentedly alone, I find I can hardly bear to be alone for another single minute." He set about making plans for Susan Mary's arrival and a whirlwind of social activity in the days surrounding the wedding. He also made plans to expand the Dumbarton house, adding bedrooms for the children and a garage for Susan Mary's car.

At three thirty p.m. on January 3, 1961, as a blizzard was beginning throughout the Northeast, Susan Mary landed at New York's Idlewild Airport aboard an Air France jetliner. Joe met her there along with Corinne's chauffeur, who drove the two to Avon just ahead of the approaching snowstorm. After a traditional weekend at the farm—more cozy even than normal because of the snow—they drove to New York for a day of settling business matters. They took a train to Washington Monday afternoon, and arrived in time to dine with Susan Mary's mother in Georgetown.

On February 9 they dined with Phil and Kay Graham; on the tenth, with Vice President Johnson and Lady Bird; on the eleventh, with Alice Longworth; on the twelfth, with David and Evangeline Bruce. On the fourteenth the president himself and Jackie dined at Dumbarton, along with a small circle of friends, including the Grahams and Stewart and Tish. Stewart ribbed Susan Mary lightheartedly, in the process ribbing Joe as well.

"I was married to Joe once myself," he said. "It wasn't easy." He added a word of advice: "Don't ever let him drive your car."

The president's penchant for gossip endeared him to Susan Mary, who was a pretty accomplished gossip trader herself.

"Tell me about Macmillan," said the president at dinner, referring to the British prime minister.

Susan Mary related a sad and funny story about the time Macmillan's wife, Lady Dorothy, had taken up with another man. The whole family rose up and conspired to get the man married off to Lady Dorothy's cousin, and as the wedding neared they all congratulated themselves on how deftly they had managed to solve that messy problem. But then Lady Dorothy accompanied the couple on their honeymoon, and Macmillan, strange man that he was, responded by simply going off to the country for the weekend and being sick intermittently out the train window. The president roared with laughter at the story.

The wedding on Thursday, the sixteenth, took place at All Saints Episcopal Church on Chevy Chase Circle. It was a small affair for family only—Corinne, Stewart and Tish, John and Gussie, Sis and Percy Chubb, Susan Mary's mother. Afterward there was dinner at Springland Lane.

Then it was back to Paris via New York. Joe accompanied Susan Mary to Paris, where he combined reporting with another round of celebration with friends. One afternoon, following a day of reporting, Joe retreated to a hotel bar for drinks with two colleagues, Elie Abel of NBC and Phil Geyelin of *The Wall Street Journal*.

"Come on, Joe," said Geyelin, winking at Abel. "Let's go out and get us a nice dinner."

"No, I can't," replied Joe. "Susan Mary is preparing a light meal."

"Just give her a call," said Abel. "Say you're going out with the boys."

"No, I really can't," said Joe.

It was the first time either man had ever seen Joe pass up an opportunity for an evening out. Geyelin and Abel also were amused at Joe's intense interest in a ballgown that Susan Mary had recently purchased. He went on at length about how it was designed, where the hooks went, the engineering of it. "It was an intellectual interest," recalled Geyelin, "like something very new in his life."

In Washington, Joe and Susan Mary moved quickly to establish the Dumbarton house as a leading locus of society in the Kennedy era. Joe handled the invitations and seating arrangements. They had elaborate dinners every two weeks, usually for sixteen guests, and the house was filled with people in between for various lunches, breakfasts, and smaller dinner affairs. Joe and Susan Mary discovered that they usually shared the same opinions about people, so it was easy to agree on guest lists.

The guests always included at least one major figure from the new administration. The new regulars were Attorney General Robert Kennedy; McGeorge Bundy, a former Harvard dean and scion of the Northeastern elite, who had been named Kennedy's special assistant for national security; Walt W. Rostow, Bundy's deputy; Lawrence O'Brien, Kennedy's political mastermind and head of the Democratic Party; Kennedy brother-in-law Sargent Shriver; and Arthur Schlesinger, who had left his Harvard teaching post to become a presidential assistant. Mingling with these new movers and shakers were Joe's old regulars—the Bissells, Wisners, Bruces, Bohlens, Nitzes, Harrimans, Achesons, and Grahams.

Susan Mary's arrival brought change to the Dumbarton household. José died shortly after Kennedy's inauguration, and Maria, uncomfortable with the maid and cook Susan Mary had brought from Paris, soon left for other employment.

Susan Mary was pleased to see Joe adjust easily to having her children in his household. When Billy went off to Groton, Joe wrote him regularly; and when Anne found herself struggling with her school Latin, Joe reserved two hours every afternoon, from five to seven, to coach her. Susan Mary had no reason to think Joe was pursuing any secret life outside their marriage. "I never saw any indication of his having an affair with another gay person after he was married to me," she recalled years later. "I don't see how he could have got away with a great deal without my knowing it."

Joe treated Susan Mary tenderly in those early months of marriage, and expressed wonderment at the new contentedness in his life.

"Oh, I've never really been happy before," he told her.

JOE'S EXCITEMENT AT the changes in his private life mingled with his excitement at watching Kennedy cobble together his team of tough-minded realists. Many were Ivy Leaguers who reveled in the sport of politics, quoted from poetry, and devastated their adversaries with rapier wit. They met the challenge at hand with a kind of cockiness, and a certainty that they were smarter and tougher than their predecessors. "Born in this century," as Kennedy had noted in his inaugural speech, "tempered by war, disciplined by a hard and bitter peace," they represented the crossing of a generational threshold.

"I wake up every morning to find that two or three really brilliant and capable men have been added to the new administration," Joe wrote to his British friend John Slessor. To George Kennan he exulted over his friend's return to government: "It cheers me up; it reassures me; it greatly reinforces my . . . alarmingly high hopes for the future."

Joe's column reflected these high hopes, as well as his fervent support for the new team. When Kennedy caused a small storm by nominating his brother Bobby for attorney general, Joe wrote that Bobby had accepted the offer only reluctantly and after considerable agonizing. Thus, he suggested, "it hardly reeks of 'nepotism' in any normal sense of that word."

As Joe looked ahead to the new administration, he felt confident that the Republican penchant for Pentagon penny-pinching and for using the threat of "massive retaliation" to maintain world stability would be replaced by a bolder and more flexible approach. "The defense effort will be intensified," he predicted in a column at the dawn of the new administration. "And a very serious effort will be made to negotiate arms control agreements with the Soviets." These approaches were not contradictory, he suggested, but were intertwined in a sound policy summed up in Winston Churchill's famous dictum, "Arm to parley."

Before any serious parleying could take place, however, the administration faced growing trouble in the former Indochina, where a communist insurgency threatened Laos, a tiny landlocked country jammed against China, Cambodia, Burma, the two Vietnams, and Thailand. With Soviet backing and an infusion of materiel and men from North Vietnam, the communist Pathet Lao had captured key positions in the strategic Plain of Jars and threatened the pro-Western regime in Vientiane.

Joe had been alerted to the threat in Laos by his CIA friend Dick Bissell, and even before the inauguration he had written Kennedy a "Dear Jack" letter threatening to oppose the nomination of Chester Bowles as undersecretary of state unless the president or Secretary of State Rusk personally looked into the Laotian situation. The Bowles appointment would energize forces, at the United Nations and around the world, that would press for a soft line on Laos. "I cannot be happy about your verdict, therefore," he had warned, "unless you, or at least Dean Rusk, have found time to study the fairly appalling relevant data in person." Joe's warning had some effect. Kennedy spent more time on Laos during his first hundred days than on any other issue.

On March 6, after *The New York Times* had devoted extensive coverage to events in Laos, Joe weighed in with a hard-line column. The threat in Southeast Asia, he wrote, would pose a "naked choice" for America if the Vientiane forces should fail to hold off the insurgency: surrender the country to the communists, probably under the guise of a negotiation to "neutralize" it; or escalate the conflict, either by sponsoring intervention by the Thai army or through direct action. "Laos," wrote Joe, "is perilously close to becoming another Korea," and the price of surrender would be no less than the price America would have paid had Truman backed away from the Korean challenge.

Kennedy agreed with Joe that a serious threat existed, but he didn't quite see the issue in Joe's stark terms. He wanted to avoid any open-ended commitment in Laos, because he knew America's allies would not go along, and he feared getting mired in a war without end. He favored a cease-fire and negotiations toward a neutralized Laos, precisely the "guise" that Joe felt might shroud an eventual surrender. The trick was to get the Soviets to accept the Kennedy approach. By March 23, Kennedy was ready to threaten the use of force in order to pressure the Soviets. At a news conference, he spoke in tough terms and announced he had moved the Seventh Fleet into the South China Sea, placed combat troops on alert in Okinawa, and sent five hundred Marines into neighboring Thailand. The Soviets promptly accepted the cease-fire.

Joe, arriving in Thailand as events unfolded, promptly filed a column praising Kennedy's determination and willingness to use force. "There was the grimmest sort of hard meaning in the President's decision to intervene militarily in Laos," he wrote from Bangkok. "The first fruits of tough-mindedness are . . . encouraging."

The column cut more slack for the president than Joe probably would have granted Eisenhower, who likely would have been attacked for half measures and for offering Moscow a free hand to subvert the Vientiane regime. Kennedy's actions hardly constituted the tough course portrayed in Joe's prose; there was little reason to believe America was willing to go to war over such a tiny, remote place. And Joe's approval of a policy he had opposed just a few weeks before reflected his willingness to tailor his outlook in support of his favorite in the White House.

Early in the new administration, Joe found himself defending his longtime stance on one of the Alsop brothers' pet issues—the so-called missile gap. The new administration had hardly taken over when Defense Secretary Robert McNamara told a group of reporters that the gap was a myth. Aghast, Joe filed a column calling McNamara's comments "the first bad bobble of the Kennedy administration." The secretary had got himself hoodwinked by the bureaucracy that produced estimates of Soviet missile production, wrote Joe.

But America's first reconnaissance satellite, launched in August 1960, proved that the Soviets had not initiated the massive buildup of intercontinental missiles feared by the Alsops and their sources. In September 1961, Joe acknowledged that the Soviets had fewer than fifty intercontinental missiles, a far cry from the two hundred the Alsops had been warning about, which also was the number needed for the Soviets to pose a serious first-strike threat.

But Soviet missile factories had not been idle. Khrushchev had been producing medium-range ballistic missiles at a furious pace, and by summer 1961 he had nearly two hundred capable of hitting targets throughout Western Europe. This had contributed to his increasingly bellicose oratory, and his menacing joke that the Western European countries were his "hostages." A crisis was in the making.

The crisis arose abruptly in the ornate music room of the American embassy in Vienna, where Kennedy and Khrushchev were meeting for two days of talks in early June. On the second day, after frank exchanges on such matters as Laos and a nuclear test ban treaty, the discussion shifted to Berlin, and Khrushchev suddenly turned belligerent. He threatened to sign a bilateral peace treaty with East Germany that would render untenable the Western allies' position in West Berlin, a divided city locked inside communist East Germany. If America sought to maintain the status quo in Berlin, warned Khrushchev, there would be war.

Khrushchev's ultimatum surprised and shocked Kennedy, who appeared shaken as he prepared to depart for London after the final session. Yet the administration line, delivered in briefings by Chip Bohlen and White House press secretary Pierre Salinger, misrepresented the summit as an "amiable" discussion permitting the two superpower leaders to get to know one another. Joe, who had accompanied the presidential entourage to Vienna, bought this line; but then so did the rest of the press corps. Only James Reston of The New York Times, who interviewed the president himself after the sessions, learned the true story. He revealed that Khrushchev had threatened war over Berlin, and that the president had left Vienna in a "somber" mood.

Joe's first column after the summit, filed from London, missed the mark entirely. American officials had made no attempt, he wrote, to dress up a meeting that changed nothing. But in London Joe attended a reception that followed the christening of one of the Radziwill children, and he was able to gain a new perspective from the president himself. Joe was standing near the door when Kennedy arrived, and the president walked over and backed him against the wall. Seldom had Joe seen Kennedy quite so lost in thought.

"I just want you to know, Joe, I don't care what happens, I won't give way, I won't give up, and I'll do whatever's necessary." Joe didn't know precisely what the president was talking about, but he found Kennedy's words "a little chilling among the duchesses and the champagne."

Joe did not recount this episode fully to his readers. However, after returning to Washington, he filed a tough column saying the president had found his meeting with Khrushchev "chilling" but that there was a certain vigor in the administration as it went about preparing for the coming test of nerves.

The episode confirmed Joe's view of the world situation, the central reality of which was Khrushchev's bold, imaginative, risky resolve to test the West wherever he could. "In situation after melancholy situation," Joe wrote, "a single, simple, central fact stood out. The leaders of the West, apparently including the new leader of the United States, have not found the answer to the new brand of brinkmanship which Khrushchev is practicing."

Joe leaped to Kennedy's support a few weeks later when the president proposed a $3.2 billion defense buildup, including greater conventional forces in Europe. Throughout the summer, Alsop pounded away on the theme that Kennedy's aim was to dismantle the New Look strategy of the Eisenhower years, which substituted nuclear superiority for ground strength in the European standoff between East and West. Now that America's nuclear superiority was in question, he wrote, it was necessary to emphasize ground troops once again. "The new doctrine," he explained, "calls for a really serious, reasonably protracted test with conventional forces."

AS THE YEAR drew to a close, Joe turned his attention to the renewal of his *Herald Tribune* contract. He had misgivings about his longtime relationship with the paper. There was turmoil at the *Herald Trib*. An aggressive new editor, John Denson, had arrived from *Newsweek*, and he was reshaping the product with a vengeance, introducing splashy graphics and bold, interpretive writing. There was a new vibrancy in the newsroom.

But the *Times* still outsold the *Herald Tribune* two to one weekdays and nearly three to one on Sundays, and carried three times as much advertising. Perhaps, thought Joe, Jock Whitney's new team could turn all that around and find the key to getting his paper into the black. But Joe also felt that he wasn't paid enough for what he did, for the arduous days of reporting week after week and the stature he had attained in his trade. He had discussed the matter with Denson, but the results were far from satisfactory. Denson not only had brushed aside Joe's concerns, but had indicated the columnist might have to accept a package even less generous than the current contract. Joe wrote to Whitney, restating his complaints and needs. For good measure, he sent a copy to Ernest Cuneo at the North American Newspaper Alliance, who for years had been trying to lure Joe away from the *Herald Trib*.

In his letter to Whitney, Joe lamented that he never seemed able to get his income much over $35,000 because expenses in producing his kind of column were so high. In 1960, expenses had come to $39,737. He didn't see how he could get that down without cutting into the effectiveness of the column. He revealed that Cuneo had offered him $40,000 a year in expenses, another $40,000 in income, a month's annual vacation, and 50 percent of syndicate revenue above $100,000 a year. He hated to think of breaking his old connection with the *Tribune*, "especially at the very moment when you are giving the *Tribune* the first leadership in which I've had any faith in the whole postwar period." But if the *Herald Trib* syndicate couldn't meet Cuneo's terms, he said, he would be forced to go with NANA.

Whitney responded with a formula he said came close to matching NANA. Joe would get $26,000 a year from the newspaper and 57.5 percent of all revenue from the column's syndication. Based on 1961 earnings, that would guarantee nearly $75,500; if he could hold expenses to $35,000, Joe would have the $40,000 income he wanted. The paper also guaranteed a month's vacation each year.

But Whitney and *Herald Trib* president Walter Thayer introduced two new issues that troubled Joe. During his vacations, the paper would replace him with *Herald Tribune* writers, and any payments necessary for this work would come out of Joe's guarantee—so it remained unlikely he would reach his $40,000 income goal. Also, the syndicate wanted to study the idea of barring *The Washington Post* from running the column. It didn't help the *Tribune* sell papers in Washington, said Whitney, when its most popular features were available in another publication.

Joe knew that his presence in the increasingly influential *Post* was crucial to his Washington standing, and that he never could accept such a blackout. But he signed a two-year contract on the understanding that the company could raise the issue for discussion after a year.

Joe and Susan Mary continued to enjoy Washington's stepped-up social velocity. In December they had the Kennedys in for dinner, along with McGeorge Bundy, Pentagon official Roswell Gilpatric, the British ambassador, the duchess of Devonshire, and a couple of viscounts. In January they entertained Washington's upper caste "in great herds and droves," as Joe wrote to Billy Patten at Groton. They had a lunch for twenty-four one Sunday that led to a dispute between Joe and Susan Mary on whether it was appropriate to serve champagne at midday. Susan Mary said it was vulgar; Joe insisted it was not. He later observed that the guests had "managed to swallow a couple of gallons of vulgarity, and seemed to be all the more cheerful for it when they left."

More champagne flowed at a small White House dinner where the company "gossiped agreeably" and viewed the new Red Room, refurbished under Jackie's meticulous direction. Joe wrote to Billy that the women present were all pretty—"Mummy the prettiest in her red sari dress." Later in January they dined at Lyndon Johnson's huge but unattractive house, where a visit was "rather like going to an opera in which one man sings all the parts." Joe wrote to Billy that he always enjoyed seeing the vice president even though he did all the talking.

Joe continued to worry about Walter Thayer's plan to bar the column from the *Post,* and about his own static income. He discussed the matter with Phil Graham, who came up with a solution. Graham, whose press empire had grown considerably with his recent acquisition of *Newsweek,* was planning to start a new syndication service. He offered Joe a handsome package to switch to the *Post*—$40,000 in guaranteed expenses, an income formula that likely would get him well above his goal of $40,000 a year and an annuity for greater financial security at retirement. Although Joe would be associated with the *Post,* his column would be distributed by the *Los Angeles Times* Syndicate until Graham managed to get his own service into operation. Joe decided to make the move. It would take effect as soon as his two-year contract with the *Herald Tribune* ran out.

It was smart. The *Herald Tribune* was dying, and nothing could save it—not Jock Whitney's wise and temperate stewardship, not Denson's newsroom management and exciting innovations, not the paper's lingering reservoir of high-class and wealthy readers. Newspaper economics were changing, and there wasn't room in the tough new world of publishing for two morning broadsheets in New York. The *Times* was entrenched. The *Herald Tribune* lived on borrowed time.

Its slow, agonizing death marked the end of an era, an era when the Northeast's elite had had its own newspaper that reflected its attitudes, folkways, and aspirations.

It was better now for Joe to seek his professional fortune in Washington, the vibrant center for a new era soon to be dominated by the information industry and the mushrooming government establishment. The *Post* anticipated the future and stood poised to capitalize on it. Phil Graham's empire of tomorrow could offer much more to Joe Alsop than could his old newspaper of yesterday.

27

STEWART AND KENNEDY

The Art of Journalistic Detachment

As SPRING CAME to Washington in 1961, Stewart hit upon the idea of combining his passion for tennis with his aim of establishing contacts among the new Kennedy people. He would bring together a foursome for aggressive doubles matches on the Springland Lane court, then lead the contingent up the hill for drinks, a light supper, and some informal political talk. Bobby Kennedy was an occasional guest, Defense Secretary Robert McNamara a frequent one.

Stewart liked the new administration and enjoyed the special access he got from the president's team. He particularly enjoyed the gala White House party for the Radziwills in March, and was struck by the president's candor in bantering about the Peace Corps, when he suggested in his lighthearted way that, like Stewart, he didn't believe in the idea. Kennedy's "incredible candor," Stewart later wrote to Marty Sommers, was used "quite consciously as an instrument for dealing with reporters—it sort of locks them in." Of course, Kennedy later went ahead with the Peace Corps, steering it through Congress and appointing his brother-in-law to run it.

Among the Kennedy people, Stewart particularly liked McNamara, whom he met one Sunday at Paul Nitze's southern Maryland plantation. He had anticipated a rigid corporate mind and a dull persona, but McNamara turned out to be "a very interesting and likable chap" with a mind that was "sharp and to the point," as Stewart put it to Marty Sommers. He found that the defense secretary agreed with him that the proportion of support troops in the U.S. Army was too large relative to combat troops. For years, Stewart had tried to get Eisenhower officials interested in the matter, to no avail. McNamara, on the other hand, was well briefed on it, and seemed determined to bring the ratio into better balance. Stewart promptly made plans for a *Post* profile of McNamara.

Despite his regard for the Kennedy kingpins, Stewart feared getting too close to them. He was resolved to write the stories as he saw them, not as he wished them to be. Reading Joe's columns, he felt his brother was trimming a bit. He would never suggest as much to Joe, but he did gingerly raise the question of whether Joe might be getting too close to the Kennedy inner circle. Joe brusquely dismissed the suggestion.

The brothers continued to see each other often, at social gatherings around town, at evening or Sunday family meals, and at holiday festivities. As Stewart's children got older, the families stopped going to Avon for Christmas and celebrated instead in Washington. Christmas morning at Springland Lane was a chaotic time, with the children itching to get to their presents, which would be arranged in individual piles in the living room. The rule was that no presents could be opened until after breakfast, and Stewart teasingly would linger over his breakfast for an extended period, as the kids "went crazy." Then he would uncork them to the living room, and the frenzy would begin. Stewart continued his ritual of attending church with the family on Christmas morning.

Then everyone would get dressed up—the children grumbling about the dress code—for the traditional Christmas lunch at Joe's. Of course Joe did it up big, with a huge suckling pig and oyster crab soup to accompany the creamed onions and brussels sprouts. It wasn't food the children liked, and Tish finally asked Joe to include some more traditional menu items, such as turkey.

At age thirteen, young Joe had gone off to Groton, like his father and grandfather, but the experience was not a happy one. He dedicated his electronic brilliance to the task of bugging the headmaster's office. It was a grand caper, and gave the boys a detailed understanding of plans and sentiments at the highest levels of the administration—but the headmaster, suspicious of the boys' inside knowledge, soon discovered the instrument and promptly expelled young Joe.

Although Stewart believed his son deserved to be expelled, he showed understanding about the prank, and initiated an effort to find a new school. He and Tish took young Joe to the Hill School near Philadelphia, which seemed anxious to enroll the young prodigy. But in the interview Joseph was unresponsive and sullen, and the headmaster dismissed him from the room and told his parents the school wouldn't take him. Stewart was furious. "If there is to be any more interviewing," he told Tish, "you can take your son."

With Corinne's help they finally enrolled him at Suffield Academy in Connecticut, where the headmaster, Appleton Seaverns, came from an old Hartford family. He offered young Joe a deal: The school would give him ample opportunity for his experiments under school auspices if he would refrain from private endeavors. Joe accepted.

Ian remained at Groton, but he clearly hated the place. He never really became part of the school, made no lasting friendships, participated in no extracurricular activities. "He just survived . . . and waited for liberation," Stewart wrote years later. Clearly, Groton wasn't what it had been in the old days, or perhaps boys weren't what they had been. In Stewart's day, few had really liked Groton, but nearly all had accepted it. It would have been unthinkable to rebel against it or even question its role in their upbringing. Now the school couldn't command that kind of allegiance.

IN MARCH AND APRIL of 1961, the *Saturday Evening Post* ran three long stories by Stewart on Africa, the product of a seven-week sojourn through the continent in late 1960. He had spent nearly two weeks in the newly independent Congo, and visited Senegal, Guinea, Ghana, Nigeria, Rhodesia, and South Africa. On November 28, 1960, he had arrived in the central African city of Leopoldville to study firsthand the complex forces buffeting the Congo. What he found, superimposed upon the predictable clash of tribal loyalties and postcolonial anti-European fervor, was the same old struggle between the West and Soviet communism.

In Leopoldville he saw Joseph Mobutu, the young general who recently had ousted and arrested the Congo's communist-leaning leader, Patrice Lumumba. Mobutu lived beside the Congo River in a large white house he had taken over as his command post. In the Western press he had been portrayed in deprecatory terms as "the so-called Congo strongman," a pretender who was out of his depth and couldn't last. But Stewart found him to be an impressive leader who knew what he intended to accomplish. In his first weeks in power he had brought the army in the Leopoldville area under control, preventing the kind of bloodletting that had gripped the Congo after independence.

His central mission was the eradication of the communist influences that had gained ground under Lumumba. He had discovered, he told Stewart, that the Soviet "technicians" sent to Lumumba before the coup were actually military officers disguised as civilians. "I have expelled them all," he said with quiet confidence.

But Mobutu was prevented by UN peacekeeping forces from moving decisively against communist rebels in Stanleyville or secessionists in mineral-rich Katanga. Forced by the UN command to confine his troop movements to minor maneuvers, he was losing momentum and prestige by the day. Meanwhile, the Stanleyville communists, under Antoine Gizenga, were on the march. "Mobutu was certainly a sad and harried man when I saw him," Stewart wrote.

Mobutu's principal adversary was a pipe-smoking Indian intellectual named Rajeswar Dayal, who headed the UN command in the Congo and despised Mobutu. He was a follower of Indian Prime Minister Jawaharlal Nehru's doctrine of "positive neutralism," which Stewart viewed as opposition to anything that would give Western interests an advantage over communism. When Stewart went to see Dayal in his air-conditioned office in central Leopoldville, the UN official struck him as a stubborn ideologue with a distorted view of the Congo drama. Dayal portrayed Mobutu as a dangerous renegade who soon would institute a reign of terror in the land unless he was corralled by UN forces.

As Stewart viewed it, Dayal's UN force, subsidized largely with U.S. dollars, was preventing a moderate, pro-Western, anticommunist regime from consolidating its position in the heart of Africa. Meanwhile, Gizenga's procommunist regime in Stanleyville was expanding its power. Stewart blamed Eisenhower's blind support for the UN in the Congo, and hoped the Kennedy team would be more tough-minded.

Stewart saw the Congo through the prism of the Cold War. Khrushchev, that master global chess player, wanted a disciplined communist satellite state there, a glittering prize in itself and also a large stride toward control of vast areas of resource-rich Africa. He had been sending planeloads of money and military hardware to his Congo puppets, Lumumba and Gizenga. As a result of America's inattention and the UN's "neutralism," Stewart concluded, Khrushchev might well succeed.

Stewart's views reflected the position of his CIA friends, who favored covert action to preserve as much Western influence as possible in Africa. As the Cold War moved into a period marked by insurgencies around the world, Stewart came to reflect the CIA viewpoint more and more in his *Post* writings. CIA director Allen Dulles was an old friend and occasional dinner guest at Springland Lane. It was at Stewart's house that Dulles had met Dick Bissell, whom he later hired and promoted to the sensitive post of deputy director for plans. Dick and Annie Bissell were close family friends of Stewart and Tish, frequent bridge companions and weekend guests at Polecat Park. Stewart's old friendships with Frank Wisner, Tracy Barnes, and Desmond FitzGerald further sealed his intimacy with the agency. And of course he had himself been a spook, had learned firsthand the tools and language of the craft.

Like his CIA friends, Stewart rejected the notion that anything resembling democracy could emerge in the Congo, or that the country could coalesce into anything more than a loose federation of tribal satrapies. As for the liberals' view that Lumumba had been chosen democratically by the Congolese parliament, Stewart wrote that the former leader had bought off the parliament's members "at the going rate of $2,000 a head." America shouldn't forget that the people best able to maintain a semblance of order and efficiency in Africa were "those horrid people, the former colonial powers." It was largely through the Belgians, he wrote, that the cities continued to operate, that government finances were kept in reasonable order, and that the Katanga mines functioned:

It is easy for Americans to forget that Africa south of the Sahara is only a generation or so removed from the prehistoric past—literally prehistoric, since there was no writing and thus no written history. The witchcraft, slavery, cannibalism and tribalism which marked that recent, unrecorded past still strongly color the political present. Thus the worst mistake we in the West can make is to see Africa through Western eyes, to judge Africa by Western standards.

Predictably, conservatives reacted favorably to Stewart's call for realpolitik in America's Africa policies. "Patches of blue have opened up . . . in the overcast sky of public opinion," said *National Review*. Praise came from other quarters too. Dean Acheson wrote to say he had heard "much admiring comment," and Connecticut's Democratic senator Thomas Dodd called it "a breath of fresh air."

And over at the White House, Stewart informed Sommers, "most of our new rulers, including number one, have read it, and I think it has had some influence."

"Number one" liked the *Saturday Evening Post*. In fact, the magazine emerged in John Kennedy's thoughts one day when a highly classified report from Vietnam crossed his desk. It had been written by Major General Edward Lansdale, a clandestine CIA operative and the driving force behind the creation of South Vietnam. The report described in moving detail the story of one valiant village fighting off communist commandos in the Vietnamese hinterland. The villagers sustained shocking losses over several years and still never wavered in their commitment to freedom or their faith in the future. "This is a wonderful story," the president scribbled on the document before sending it back to the CIA. "It ought to be published by some big magazine like the *Saturday Evening Post*."

Dick Bissell passed the president's comment on to Stewart, who set about to get the report declassified for publication. Through Bissell, he obtained Kennedy's permission to run the report along with a box explaining how it came to be published. "Behind the official language of the report," said the box, "the president saw a story of human valor and dedication to freedom, a reminder that communism is *not* the wave of the future." The headline: THE REPORT THE PRESIDENT WANTED PUBLISHED. It was a nice coup for the *Post* and a propaganda victory for the president.

IN APRIL 1961, the nation's Kennedy euphoria ended at the Bay of Pigs in Cuba. The administration sent fifteen hundred Cuban exiles ashore there, with covert U.S. support, in hopes they could foster an insurrection against the island's communist dictator, Fidel Castro, and topple his regime. Castro had become a bone in the throat of the American government. Kennedy had played up the issue during the campaign, had jabbed at Nixon and his party for allowing such a menacing dictator to rule just ninety miles from U.S. soil. Now, with expressions of robust confidence from top officials, he authorized the adventure, though with some hesitancy.

It turned out to be a military, political, and diplomatic disaster. Castro nipped the invasion on the beach, killing scores and taking 1,214 prisoners. Washington's secret involvement quickly became known. To the world and the nation, Kennedy looked like a bungler.

Stewart seized on the story, producing a piece called "The Lessons of the Cuban Disaster." It was an inside look at how the unhappy events unfolded: "why certain astonishing errors in judgment were made, and why certain grievous faults in our Government's system of making decisions developed." Stewart pulled no punches, even though some close friends were intimately involved. In the piece, he revealed his long association with Dulles and Bissell.

"They did go wrong. There is no doubt on that score," he wrote, adding that the CIA men, intoxicated by their past successes, had demonstrated "a dangerous confidence." Their emotions became unconsciously engaged in the operation, "and thus their judgment was clouded." This was particularly true of Bissell, wrote Stewart. Moreover, there had been no governmental machinery for an independent assessment of the CIA plan with a coldly critical eye. "The operational CIA men sat in judgment of their own much-loved offspring."

Much the same syndrome was evident in the military, which helped plan the details of the invasion and then became a partisan of its own handiwork. Stewart revealed that the military's support for the plan had been contingent upon the CIA's being correct in two assumptions: First, that the invasion would stir a widespread anti-Castro revolt; and second, that the anti-Castro forces would control the air over the battlefield. Given those conditions, the president's key military officials had supported the plan.

With the old pros in national security all but promising success, the president had turned to his most highly placed civilian advisers, Secretary of State Dean Rusk and national security adviser McGeorge Bundy. Like the president, they felt the plan didn't quite smell right. Yet, Stewart wrote, they couldn't bring themselves to question the solid phalanx of professionals pressing for it.

Within the State Department, Undersecretary Chester Bowles had opposed the plan, but it is doubtful his views ever reached the president. Arthur Schlesinger had sent Kennedy a strongly worded memo of dissent, but Schlesinger was far down on the pecking order. Generally, the skeptics had remained quiet, declining to take on the cocky CIA men and military officers.

But while their skepticism didn't kill the plan, it served to water it down. By the time Kennedy gave the final go-ahead, he had ruled that in no circumstances could the U.S. military intervene, not even to ensure that the rebels would control the sky above the landing places. Stewart's sources told him that an original Eisenhower plan had envisioned American intervention on a contingency basis, particularly to provide air power if needed. Hence Kennedy's ruling, wrote Stewart, constituted "a basic change in the whole nature of the operation." Kennedy strategists failed to reassess the revised plan to test its feasibility under the new directive.

The implications of the fiasco emerged in a sad scene depicted in Stewart's piece. On the morning of April 19, Kennedy and his key aides gathered for final discussions on whether the United States should send in air power to save the beleaguered invasion force. Even though they knew that their decision meant the destruction of men they had sent on a fool's mission, the officials decided against intervention. "That decision," wrote Stewart, "marked the first great Kennedy failure. Bobby Kennedy, who hates failure more even than most Kennedys, . . . remarked, as the meeting ended, that what worried him most was that now nobody in the Government would be willing to stick his neck out, to take a chance, to plan bold and aggressive action against the Communists."

Stewart's was the most thorough piece of reporting on the Cuban fiasco, but it demonstrated the hazards of insider journalism. At a party at Arthur Schlesinger's shortly after publication, Bobby Kennedy deplored Stewart's suggestion that Eisenhower people had planned U.S. military involvement on a contingency basis. It wasn't correct, said Kennedy, even to speak of an Eisenhower "plan," since the previous administration had not produced any final, formal, or approved plan for a Cuban operation.

A few days later, after a barrage of criticism had hit the administration for changing the Eisenhower "plan," Bobby noted in a letter to Stewart that the piece had had "an impact and . . . has been widely quoted." Thus, he said, he wanted to clarify his position: "The fact is, there was no Eisenhower Administration plan or concept or even idea which provided for the use of American Forces on a contingency basis. There was no plan, concept or idea for the use of American planes marked or unmarked." He said he had confirmed this with Allen Dulles and that General Maxwell Taylor had taken up the matter directly with Eisenhower "because your story and Congressman [William] Miller's attacks on President Kennedy along the same lines had caused us some concern." The former president, said Kennedy, "stated the facts as I have related them above."

Stewart had been misinformed—most likely by CIA and military officials anxious to duck responsibility for the Cuban fiasco. "I did some further checking," Stewart wrote Kennedy, "and you are quite right." Stewart invited Kennedy to clarify the issue in a letter to the *Post*, but the attorney general declined. "I would be happy to have the matter dropped," he wrote. Demonstrating his affection, he added he would be "delighted" to have Stewart stop by his office for an interview at any time.

The Cuban debacle left its mark on Washington. Within months Dulles was out as CIA chief, and Dick Bissell's sparkling career as public servant soon ended also. Stewart's old friend Tracy Barnes, Bissell's top deputy, stayed on for several years, but the Bay of Pigs stymied his agency career. The president slipped into a period of depression, which was accentuated in June by the Vienna confrontation with Khrushchev over Berlin. Ethel Kennedy, Robert's wife, told Stewart the president had been "terribly distressed" by his Cuba piece, not so much because he considered it anti-Kennedy or false but because he thought Stewart had managed to learn too much about the inner workings of government. He was particularly upset about Stewart's account of an Oval Office meeting on April 5 attended by the president, Rusk, McNamara, and Dulles. Ethel said the president had concluded one of the three must have spilled a detailed account of the meeting to Stewart. In truth, Alsop had gained his understanding of the meeting by talking to many participants and others who had heard about it afterward.

Stewart learned that Kennedy had become preoccupied by Berlin and his political standing in the wake of Cuba. To Stewart, the president had every reason for concern, and, unlike Joe, he was inclined to place much of the blame on the president himself. In a September piece entitled "How's Kennedy Doing?" Stewart faulted Kennedy not only for Cuba but for the Laos cease-fire, which struck him as likely to lead to disaster. "It will be downright astonishing if Laos escapes eventual and total Communist domination," he wrote. Kennedy's bold talk to persuade the Soviets to accept the cease-fire would look like a bluff. "And our danger will be mortal indeed if Nikita Khrushchev concludes that the President of the United States is a bluffer." In Vienna the Soviet leader had all but called Kennedy's bluff to his face. It was a tough piece.

As the year drew to a close, Stewart's attention turned increasingly to his own livelihood. At the old, gray *Saturday Evening Post*, aging executives were feeling the winds of change and competition. The magazine was in trouble. Indeed, the whole Curtis Publishing Company was in trouble.

Post editors decided that 1961 would be the year of change, and they set about to refashion the magazine. Ben Hibbs, nearing retirement, was fading from the scene, and the redesign fell to his executive editor and heir apparent, Bob Fuoss, who adopted a recipe of splashy graphics, shorter stories, more punchy opinion pieces, and abandonment of the magazine's ancient Republican heritage. The ad salesmen loved the "new look" so much they stood up and cheered when it was unveiled at a Pocono resort in rural Pennsylvania.

But when the new *Post* appeared on September 16, 1961, it bombed. Readers wrote to complain at a rate of ten thousand letters a week. Advertisers, already skeptical of the *Post*'s ability to deliver, wandered off in even greater numbers. Advertising revenue dropped to $86 million in 1961 from $104 million the previous year, and the *Post* took a loss of $3 million for the year. The result was corporate turmoil. Within a few months, Hibbs, Fuoss, and the head of Curtis all would be gone. Rumors of the company's sale began circulating, and a nattily dressed New York broker named Amman Erpf began hovering around in hopes of a fire sale.

Stewart, little schooled in the dynamics of mass-magazine publishing in the television age, didn't understand what was happening. He viewed Erpf as the villain, but there were no villains, only goats. The goats were the people to whom Stewart had assigned his loyalty—Hibbs and Sommers and the top management of Curtis Publishing. They were good men, with lively intellects and plenty of heart. But they didn't understand the changes bearing down on them.

Editors at the *Post* were grasping frantically for a new magazine formula that could keep the company going. Change was in the air, and it wasn't all welcome. Marty Sommers, Stewart's close ally for sixteen years, was sixty-one and thinking of retirement. "All of the turbulence at the office was getting me down some," he wrote to Stewart after returning from a much-needed vacation. It wasn't clear that the magazine could survive much longer. Stewart began 1962 determined to establish a secure future for himself and his family, even if that meant leaving the *Post*.

In January he received a call from John Wheeler of the North American Newspaper Alliance, who wanted to talk to him about a column. For years NANA executives had hoped to sign Joe, but with his move to *The Washington Post* it was clear he wouldn't be available. Perhaps, wrote Wheeler to Stewart, he might want to consider a once-a-week column for starters. Stewart wasn't sure he wanted back into the column business, but he agreed to talk with Wheeler.

When Joe heard about it, he exploded. The idea that his own brother, whose news career he had fostered sixteen years before, would go into direct competition with him was almost more than he could bear. Joe was sure Stewart's reentry into column writing would hurt him financially; some papers would drop his column for Stewart's. "I cannot emphasize too much the harm that such a venture of Stew's will do to both of us," he wrote to brother John.

Typically, Joe's hollering had outpaced his hurt. Stewart managed to calm him down by telling Susan Mary at the Dancing Class that he really had no desire to write a column and appreciated all the arguments against going into competition with Joe. But, given the *Post* situation, he had to look at all options, since his financial responsibility to his family came first. Joe expressed relief when he heard that.

Stewart also had to worry about visibility. He derived about a fifth of his income from ancillary activities such as lecture tours and television.

If he lost the kind of exposure the *Post* provided, much of that extra income would dry up. He could earn a decent living as a freelance writer, but that couldn't match the scope and reach of the *Post*. *Life*'s staff writers produced only three or four pieces a year, and anyway Stewart hated the idea of working for the Luce empire, which had attacked Joe so mercilessly the past eight years. *Look* was a biweekly and didn't produce much serious journalism. *Reader's Digest* probably would take him and would pay well, but that would entail perhaps four three-thousand-word pieces a year written in the *Digest*'s homogenized style. He didn't like *McCall's*, "with that staccato female style they prefer."

Joe suggested that Stewart secure a multiyear contract with the *Post* to include an income guarantee over three or five years. If the magazine folded during the contractual period, he would be protected. Stewart liked the idea and negotiated a three-year agreement guaranteeing him a minimum of $43,000 a year. Anxious to keep Stewart happy in a time of uncertainty, Fuoss also gave Stewart an elevated new title—Washington editor. "You certainly have earned the promotion," Hibbs wrote from retirement. "You have always performed magnificently for the *Post*."

A few months later, Phil Graham offered Stewart the job of *Washington Post* editorial-page editor, and he considered it seriously. He even sought Tish's opinion, something he seldom did on career matters. It was a high-profile job, and it could be lucrative. On the other hand, Stewart didn't like the idea of giving up the independence of a contract writer. Tish feared that working for Phil, whose behavior was increasingly erratic, could be worse than working for Joe. She was "emphatic" in opposing the move. In the end, Stewart agreed with her. "It was, frankly, tempting," he wrote to Fuoss, "since the financial prospects are bright, and the job would certainly be a challenging one." But he preferred to remain with the magazine if the company could assure him it was on a path to survival. Curtis president Matthew J. Culligan quickly wrote to say the company was "truly on the way up."

THROUGHOUT 1962, Stewart kept his eye on political events in Connecticut, where John once again was going after the Republican nomination for governor.

In June Stewart flew to Connecticut to cover the GOP convention for the *Saturday Evening Post* and see John snatch the nomination from his chief party rival on the eighth ballot. His opponents said that he didn't look good on television—nose too large, ears too floppy—and that he was stuffy. But he was effective nonetheless. After the sixth ballot, a key Alsop delegation hinted it was ready to switch to another candidate. John met the delegation leaders behind closed doors, and they emerged looking as if they had been beaten up. Joe, who also attended the convention, was standing nearby.

"Good God, Johnny," he said, "what did you do to those people?

They look as though they'd been poleaxed." John smiled. On the next ballot the delegation stuck with him.

Stewart's *Post* piece, "My Brother Runs for Governor," appeared September 1. "Don't expect me to be objective," he warned. "I think my brother would make a wonderful governor." The piece was a rambling reminiscence of John's earlier days and a discourse on why people enter politics. Stewart thought the political virus was hereditary and that John had it from their parents. From early adulthood, Stewart revealed, John had wanted to be governor.

But John had a strong opponent in Democrat John Dempsey, the incumbent governor. And the reelection race of Connecticut's junior senator, Democrat Abe Ribicoff, a big vote-getter, would bring to the polls large numbers of Dempsey voters. The State's Democratic machine was run by the redoubtable John Bailey, who had been one of the first major local machine politicians to jump on the Kennedy bandwagon; Connecticut Democrats thus could expect all-out support from the popular president.

When the votes were counted, John went down narrowly to defeat. It occurred to Stewart that the outcome reflected the transformation of Connecticut politics wrought by demographic tides. Republicans, he wrote a friend, couldn't prevail in statewide races unless they nominated "a candidate who is a Catholic, preferably with an Italian name." It might even be necessary, he added, to discover the Democrats with their hands in the public till. "In Connecticut politics," said Stewart, "us Yankees are all washed up."

28

MISSILE CRISIS

Stewart versus the Adlai Cult

Autumn arrives in Washington as a tonic, a respite from the oppressive days of high summer. As the city's political classes make their way back into town after relaxed August days at Martha's Vineyard or Ocean City, thoughts turn to the fall social season, the dinners and receptions that seem to celebrate the arrival of Indian summer beside the Potomac.

For Joe, autumn of 1962 brought plans for yet another dinner at Dumbarton, to be attended by Mr. and Mrs. John Kennedy—Joe's third dinner for the president since the inauguration. It was to be Wednesday, October 17, and Joe and Susan Mary planned to have eighteen guests at table, including French ambassador Hervé Alphand and his wife, Chip and Avis Bohlen, Phil and Kay Graham, Robert Kennedy and McGeorge Bundy. The menu was soft-shell crabs, beef in jelly, salad, cheese, and a dessert of crêpes princesses Grand Marnier. The ostensible occasion was a farewell to the Bohlens: Chip was leaving the next day on assignment as ambassador to Paris.

The White House limousine delivered Jack and Jackie to the house, and they scampered up the front steps in a mood of apparent lightheartedness. It was warmer than usual for an October evening, and cocktails were served on the terrace overlooking Joe's green and spacious garden. As guests arrived, greeting each other and mingling, the president casually took Bohlen aside for a chat. Soon they were at the far end of the garden, strolling together back and forth under the magnolias. The guests assumed they were discussing Bohlen's Paris assignment.

But the chat went on far longer than anyone would have expected. What were the president and Chip talking about down there? Alphand seemed particularly curious, then nervous. Susan Mary worried about Avis Bohlen's bad back; Avis had taken codeine in order to attend the dinner, and Susan Mary feared the pain would soon return. She worried also about that roast in the oven. Would her impatient little French cook, Jeanne, have the presence of mind to keep it juicy? And Susan Mary was puzzled. It wasn't like the president to conduct business before dinner.

Finally the two men turned back toward the terrace and walked up the brick path along the boxwoods, joking and laughing as they rejoined the group. The president apologized to Susan Mary for the delay, and they all went in for dinner.

Far from a matter of routine or levity, the president's talk with Bohlen focused on a profound crisis that had engulfed John F. Kennedy and the country. Few knew it yet, but Nikita Khrushchev, that geopolitical chess master, was busy assembling in Cuba a lethal load of surface-to-surface missiles capable of delivering nuclear warheads to the cities of America. His purpose was to gain a decisive advantage in the power balance between the two nations. Kennedy had learned about the Cuban missiles only the morning before, and he and his special executive committee—ExComm, in White House parlance—had been working nearly around the clock on the crisis.

Kennedy knew that an intimate knowledge of the Soviet psychology could be crucial in handling Moscow and averting war. He wanted Bohlen, a leading Soviet expert, to delay his Paris departure so he could provide counsel during the delicate maneuvering ahead. In the garden, Bohlen had cautioned against any change of plans. It would signal to the Soviets that Kennedy knew of the missiles, he argued, and rob the president's response of surprise. Though disappointed, Kennedy had finally agreed that Bohlen should leave for Paris.

But at dinner the crisis remained very much on the president's mind. Twice he asked Bohlen about Russia's past reactions when it had found itself in awkward situations from which it was difficult to withdraw without losing face. In response, Bohlen expounded at length on Russia's history and national psychology. To many of the guests, the conversation seemed hypothetical and somewhat irrelevant. After dinner, when the men gathered in the garden room, the president remarked that the likelihood of nuclear war within ten years, based on mathematical chance, was about 50 percent. Joe found the conversation "chilling."

The next day the president had a date in Connecticut that he couldn't duck, for the same reason Bohlen couldn't delay his departure for Paris. Kennedy was to campaign for Abe Ribicoff's senatorial bid and for John Dempsey's gubernatorial candidacy against John Alsop. The president regretted having to be away from Washington for the five hours he had scheduled for his Connecticut appearance, but he feared a cancellation would stir speculation. So he flew north to enter the political fray against the brother of his dinner host of the night before.

Through the week and into the weekend the ExComm pondered, debated, agonized. Some advocated sudden air strikes to knock out the missiles. Others favored a naval blockade that would give Khrushchev a chance to retreat with some dignity. The ExComm explored every aspect and implication of the crisis, every hard-line option or conciliatory gesture that might help ease the country away from the collision course. By Sunday Kennedy had decided on the blockade, and on Monday he briefed congressional leaders and informed the American people via a nationally televised address from the Oval Office.

There followed six anxious days of cryptic messages and sparring between Kennedy and Khrushchev, of naval confrontation in the North Atlantic, of tensions ebbing and flowing as Kennedy sought to confront and maneuver the Soviet leader. Through it all, the nation held its breath, wondering whether this young president could rise to meet a matter of such unparalleled national urgency.

But he did, and by Sunday Khrushchev had backed down, pledging to dismantle the missiles, crate them, and return them to the Soviet Union. The country sighed in relief, and Kennedy enjoyed the glow of success. It would come to be regarded by most Americans as his finest hour.

Shortly after the crisis ended, Stewart received a call from Charles Bartlett, a Pulitzer prize–winning columnist and one of Kennedy's closest friends in the Washington press corps. Bartlett wanted to write a piece for the *Saturday Evening Post* recounting the dramatic proceedings of the ExComm. Sensing an opportunity, Stewart suggested they collaborate, and Bartlett agreed.

Bartlett and Stewart listed the most promising sources and divided them according to who knew whom best. They soon discovered that many officials were reluctant to talk freely, and their task of reconstructing events became a painstaking labor of piecing together fragments of information parceled out coyly by the participants. One of the more forthcoming sources turned out to be Michael Forrestal, an aide to McGeorge Bundy in the White House, who had had a second-row seat during the crisis. He was the son of James Forrestal, Joe's close friend from the 1940s, and the old connection proved helpful.

Forrestal told the reporters that on the Saturday before the president's decision, as the ExComm moved toward recommending the naval blockade, Adlai Stevenson's soft-line recommendations had raised eyebrows among ExComm members. The UN ambassador had suggested that Kennedy dangle the idea that the United States would abandon its missile bases in Turkey, Italy, and Britain, along with its Guantanamo military base in Cuba, if the Soviets would withdraw their Cuban missiles. He seemed to be clinging to political negotiation over the alternative of military action at a time when the rest of the ExComm had agreed on a military approach.

The reporters knew this would be a vital part of their story if they could get it confirmed, and confirmation turned out to be easier than they had anticipated. It was shortly after the interview with Forrestal that Bartlett and his wife dined at the White House with Jack and Jackie, as they often did, and Bartlett mentioned the Stevenson episode.

"I heard this amazing story about Adlai," said Bartlett, who then recounted his understanding of events.

"Oh, you got that, huh?" replied Kennedy with a smile. "I wasn't sure you'd get that." It was what Bartlett later called "confirmation by indirection," but the president seemed pleased to confirm the story. Later, Robert Kennedy was more emphatic in assuring Bartlett he was on the right track. "He was madder than a jack at Adlai because of what he had recommended," recalled Bartlett three decades later. "The Kennedys thought Stevenson had been hopelessly naive."

Before submitting their finished piece to *Post* editors, Alsop and Bartlett sent it to Ted Clifton in the White House press office, and it came back annotated in John Kennedy's handwriting. The president hadn't disturbed the passage about Stevenson, but he had excised a passage about his speechwriter, Theodore Sorensen, being in the ExComm meetings. Sorensen had been a conscientious objector during the war, and Kennedy feared a political recoil from hard-line conservatives if it became known that the president had sought or received Sorensen's advice during a military crisis.

The Alsop-Bartlett piece, three pages in the *Post*, ran December 8 and brought to life the deliberations of the nine major ExComm participants. Not precisely a chronology, it offered what the authors called "certain untold episodes of the drama which illuminate its true significance."

The atmosphere was "calm but somber," the story said, when ExComm members gathered in the White House Cabinet Room at the very hour that the blockade was to take effect—and as two dozen Soviet ships followed a course toward Cuba. The president sat at the head of the table and fired questions relentlessly. When answers were slow in coming he tapped his front teeth impatiently with his forefinger, "a characteristic gesture." Everyone knew that if the blockade didn't work, a military escalation would ensue that could include air strikes against the missiles or even a Cuban invasion. No one around the table doubted that such steps would be answered with further moves by Khrushchev. And there wasn't anyone in the room, said one unidentified official, "who wasn't pretty sure that in a few hours we'd have to sink one of those Russian ships."

The article related how Kennedy was determined to give Khrushchev time to ponder the crisis while the blockade—"quarantine," as the pres-

When Joe and Susan Mary themselves were married in 1961 (here, they've just been part of the 1968 wedding of Susan Mary's daughter, Ann Patten), they were formidable hosts, called the "grand couple of Georgetown."

A happy Joe wrote the caption: "My brother John and Gussie at their wedding with me as best man."

Stewart's family in 1957. From left: Joe, Elizabeth, Stewart, Ian, Tish, and Stewart Jr. (Two sons came later—Nicky in 1960 and Andrew in 1967.)

Family receiving line during Elizabeth's "coming out" party in 1968. From left: Elizabeth, Alice Roosevelt Longworth, Susan Mary, Tish, and Joe.

Stewart with *Saturday Evening Post* editor Ben Hibbs (center) and foreign editor Martin Sommers. Stewart dealt most directly with Sommers during his long association with the *Post*. "Stew loved Marty," Tish Alsop once said.

The Alsop brothers and Tish receive drinks from Joe's valet and cook, José, in the fashionable Dumbarton living room.

Stewart with Jackie and candidate Jack Kennedy during the Wisconsin primary of 1960.

Joe relaxes after dinner with President Kennedy at the White House. The photo was taken with a flash camera by Jackie Kennedy.

In the middle of the Vietnam war, Joe, an unreconstructed hawk, arrived for a visit aboard the U.S.S. *Coral Sea.*

Stewart and Defense Secretary Robert McNamara following an interview in McNamara's Pentagon office.

Stewart with Lyndon Johnson at the LBJ ranch.

Stewart Alsop died of leukemia in May of 1974. Here, members of the family stand at graveside in Middletown, Connecticut. Second from left is his brother John; sixth from left, with dark-rimmed glasses, is Joe. Joe passed away in 1989 at the age of seventy-eight.

ident called it—was going into effect. He ordered the navy to refrain from intercepting any Soviet ships as long as possible. Then came word that some Soviet vessels had changed course and that others had gone dead in the water. Dean Rusk nudged Bundy and uttered the famous phrase, "'We're eyeball to eyeball, and I think the other fellow just blinked."

But it wasn't much of a blink. American U-2 flights over Cuba revealed that work on the missile sites was proceeding apace. By Saturday—called Black Saturday by ExComm participants—the picture was bleak. Kennedy had received a rambling and self-contradictory message from Khrushchev the night before that included both hopeful signs and expressions of belligerence. When the ExComm met at ten a.m. Saturday, it appeared Khrushchev was playing for time, hoping to avoid a direct confrontation until he could get his Cuban missiles operational. That seemed all the more likely when word arrived that Khrushchev had upped the ante, demanding the dismantlement of American-controlled missiles in Turkey as the price for his removal of the Cuban missiles. Then came further bad news: A U-2 spy plane had been shot down over eastern Cuba by one of the newly installed Soviet surface-to-air missiles—evidence that Khrushchev now had the capability to blind the U.S. intelligence eye while he stalled for time.

The ExComm's morning meeting on Black Saturday, the Alsop-Bartlett piece revealed, was characterized by "short tempers and frayed nerves." It looked increasingly as if Kennedy would have to order air strikes to ensure that the Cuban missiles would not become operational. After a late lunch, the ExComm reconvened in the White House Oval Room at four p.m. It was decided that air strikes would have to come by Tuesday at the latest. Unquestionably, Russians as well as Cubans would be killed—"clearly . . . the next rung on the ladder to nuclear war," wrote Alsop and Bartlett.

It was then that Bobby Kennedy proposed an ingenious ploy. The president, he said, should ignore all the ominous signs of Black Saturday and act as if he assumed Khrushchev's Friday night message had been a gesture of conciliation. Kennedy agreed, and ExComm members quickly drafted a message for the president to send to Moscow. "If I understand you correctly," wrote the president, there could be a deal. Essentially, it was that Khrushchev would remove his missiles and Kennedy would terminate the blockade and promise not to invade Cuba. The letter was sent at eight p.m., the Alsop-Bartlett piece said, and other channels also were used to "make abundantly plain to Khrushchev the nature of the choice he faced."

It worked. The next day, quickly dubbed Sunny Sunday, Khrushchev accepted the Kennedy accommodation. "This was, of course," wrote Alsop and Bartlett, "the final, unmistakable blink" that proved once and for all that Khrushchev was not ready to risk nuclear war over Cuba. The lesson, said the authors, was simple: "If we respond firmly where our vital interests are threatened, Khrushchev will choose 'zigzags and retreats' rather than nuclear war." To know this, they added, constituted a new reality in the Cold War.

In recounting ExComm deliberations during the five days leading up to the blockade, Alsop and Bartlett explained how the president's men had separated into "hawks and doves"—hard-liners who favored air strikes and soft-liners who favored blockade. Hawks included CIA director John McCone, Joint Chiefs chairman Maxwell Taylor, Dean Acheson (brought in as an elder statesman), and eventually Bundy. Among the doves were Robert McNamara, Robert Kennedy, and Robert Lovett (another elder statesman).

Saturday, October 20, saw the emergence of a "rolling consensus" best articulated by McNamara, who argued that the United States must "maintain the options." Pursuing the blockade option, he said, still left open the air strike option; but an air strike would instantly eliminate all other options short of war. Eventually just about everyone accepted the rolling consensus—with one exception. The authors wrote:

> Only Adlai Stevenson, who flew down from New York on Saturday, dissented from the ExComm consensus. There is disagreement in retrospect about what Stevenson really wanted. "Adlai wanted a Munich," says a nonadmiring official who learned of his proposal. "He wanted to trade the Turkish, Italian and British missile bases for the Cuban bases."
>
> The Stevenson camp maintains that Stevenson was only willing to discuss Guantanamo and the European bases with the Communists after a neutralization of the Cuban missiles. But there seems to be no doubt that he preferred political negotiation to the alternative of military action. White House aide Arthur Schlesinger was assigned to write the uncompromising speech which Stevenson delivered at the UN on Tuesday, and tough-minded John McCloy was summoned from a business conference in Germany to work with Stevenson in the UN negotiations.
>
> In any case, the president heard Stevenson out politely, and then gave his semifinal approval to the McNamara plan. He gave his final approval Sunday.

The Alsop-Bartlett article was the most penetrating inside look at the Missile Crisis up to that time and for some time to come. It introduced two phrases into the modern political lexicon—"eyeball to eyeball" and "hawks and doves." But its merits as expository journalism were lost immediately in the explosion of controversy it ignited in political Washington. Among journalists and politicians, Adlai Stevenson enjoyed a cult following, and his disciples rushed to the barricades to defend him. They attacked the article and its authors, making much of the fact that Bartlett was a close Kennedy friend. He had introduced Jack Kennedy to

Jackie and had ushered at their wedding. It had been in Bartlett's column a year earlier that suggestions of White House unhappiness with Chester Bowles had first surfaced; within months, Bowles had been removed as undersecretary of state. Wasn't it reasonable to assume, people were asking, that Bartlett had been used as a White House instrument to begin the process of getting rid of Adlai?

The nation's newspapers splashed the story across their front pages on December 4, including a quotation from a Stevenson spokesman calling the Alsop-Bartlett account "inaccurate and untrue." The spokesman said that Stevenson had never advocated trading U.S. bases for the Soviets' Cuban missiles and never dissented from the ExComm consensus in favor of a quarantine. He said that Stevenson himself had requested the help of Arthur Schlesinger and John McCloy, contrary to the article's implication that Kennedy had forced them on Stevenson to ensure a hard-line approach at the United Nations.

The controversy generated powerful political pressures that focused directly on the White House. The president and his men knew that the press and the American people would want answers on whether Kennedy had provided this damaging information on Stevenson, had seen the story before it went into print, or had cooperated with Bartlett and Alsop in any way. Alsop and Bartlett knew that pressures would mount on the White House to repudiate their account. The first ominous sign came with the first wave of stories, in which White House Press Secretary Pierre Salinger was quoted saying what Alsop and Bartlett knew to be untrue. "Nobody in the White House saw the article before it was printed," said Salinger. He also offered a carefully worded defense of Stevenson.

When the story broke, Stewart was out of the country on a reporting trip through Latin America. He followed the controversy as best he could, via wire reports and telephone, but he couldn't play much of a role in defending his work. That job fell to Bartlett, who didn't relish the part. Stewart later felt Bartlett hadn't been aggressive enough in parrying criticism from the Adlai cult. Bartlett himself had been in New York when the article first appeared, and he decided to go underground to avoid the media bloodhounds braying in pursuit. Every major news organization was calling. NBC's "Today" show wanted to put him on the air. The major newsmagazines were preparing cover stories on the controversy. Bartlett's aim was to avoid being asked directly whether Kennedy had seen the article before it went to press.

From a relative's house in New York, Bartlett called Kennedy to get his assessment of the situation.

"Charlie," said the president, "where are you?"

Bartlett told him, then said, "I'm glad to be up here and out of all that heat."

"Well, that's just great, you son of a bitch," replied the jocular Kennedy. "I'm down here taking all the heat."

And the heat was getting more intense by the day. Columnist Roscoe Drummond called the leak of National Security Council secrets "a grave crime" and said the matter would not rest until "Kennedy himself shows that he is sufficiently disturbed or sufficiently disgusted . . . to discover who is guilty." *The New York Times* joined the call for rooting out the leakers. A popular editorial cartoon depicted a pained Stevenson sitting in a hospital room with a knife protruding from his back. A doctor carefully examines the knife and muses. "Judging by the angle, I'd say it came from above."

Stevenson went on the offensive. On the "Today" show he declared, "This must be some kind of record for irresponsible journalism." In another interview he expressed puzzlement at why Alsop and Bartlett would write such an article. "I couldn't figure out their motives in completely misrepresenting my position," he said. *Newsweek,* in its cover story, accepted without question Stevenson's contention that he had himself requested Schlesinger and McCloy as collaborators at the UN. The magazine also quoted an ExComm member as saying he was "disgusted" by the Alsop-Bartlett article, which he added was "full of inaccuracies." *Time* casually referred to "demonstrable inaccuracies" in the story.

To discerning Washington hands, it was clear that efforts to discredit the Alsop-Bartlett article were motivated largely by the aim of forcing Kennedy to repudiate the piece and thus neutralize its impact on Stevenson's political standing. But Kennedy had problems: He couldn't repudiate the piece without lying about his own involvement in its preparation—or worse, forcing the authors to reveal his involvement to protect their own reputations; and he couldn't ignore the matter without generating widespread suspicions that he had indeed collaborated with the authors. The issue went to the heart of Kennedy's standing with his party's liberal wing, a political force he could ill afford to alienate.

The president did his best to steer safely through the political shoals. Three days after the controversy first flared, he called Stevenson in for a White House chat in hopes this would soften the liberals' dudgeon. It seemed to work at first. Stevenson left the White House West Wing and told reporters that as far as he was concerned the matter was closed. The White House issued a statement saying Stevenson "strongly supported the position taken by the President on the quarantine and valiantly developed the United States position at the United Nations." Stevenson later told a television interviewer that he was "grateful to the president for his generous reference to my participation in the Cuban crisis."

But speculation persisted on the president's involvement, and every word and action from Kennedy was scrutinized for signs of his true feelings. The two men found themselves together on the dais at a Joseph P. Kennedy, Jr., Foundation dinner at which it was master-of-ceremonies Stevenson's task to introduce the president. Stevenson drew laughter by quoting Joseph Pulitzer's observation that accuracy is to a newspaper what virtue is to a lady, then added, "Of course, a newspaper can always print a retraction." The president, as *Time* reported, "made no attempt to match the Stevenson wit—and no attempt to show warmth toward Adlai."

At a news conference Kennedy gave Stevenson "a pat on the back," as the *Washington Star* put it, but he refused to repudiate the *Post* article. He said that while he was responsible for how he conducted himself in office, he wouldn't take responsibility for what his friends wrote.

The issue was fanned anew when *Life* reported that Kennedy had instructed top-level officials, including those at the State Department and the CIA, to cooperate with Alsop and Bartlett. This was untrue, and Salinger quickly repudiated the *Life* allegations. The focus of press attention shifted to the "culprit" who had leaked the information to Alsop and Bartlett.

From South America, Stewart followed all this with anguish. When Clay Blair, the *Post*'s new editor, wired to say they were winning the public-relations war, Stewart disagreed. "On contrary," he wired back. "From everything I read here we are having our heads kicked in, with even wire service reports accepting as factual Stevenson version.... Since my professional reputation deeply involved I feel strongly we should not support Stevenson's position by silence."

Even from such a distance, Stewart saw what others had missed— that Stevenson had cleverly distorted the terms of debate to his own advantage. By insisting that he had never opposed the blockade, Stevenson had set up a straw man, for the Alsop-Bartlett piece did not say he had opposed the blockade. By that fateful Saturday, everyone had agreed the blockade was necessary. Stevenson's suggestion had centered on what Kennedy should do in concert with the blockade. He had suggested introducing into the negotiations, as bargaining chips, the European missiles and Guantánamo. In other words, he had been willing to reward the Soviets for their provocations even before the Soviet reaction to the blockade became clear. That was what had ruffled the Kennedys.

On returning, Stewart wrote a strong defense entitled "Footnote for the Historians," in which he sought to clarify this point. He also revealed that he and Bartlett had had three lengthy talks with Stevenson's official spokesman, Clayton Fritchey, before writing their article. He quoted from his notes extensively to show that he and Bartlett had been correct in their reporting.

Indeed, wrote Stewart, he had called Fritchey and read to him the passage saying Stevenson had been willing to discuss Guantánamo and the European bases with the Communists along with neutralization of the Cuban missiles. His notes indicated that Stewart had asked Fritchey if this was a fair summary, and Fritchey had agreed it was.

Stewart wrote that he believed such a position as Stevenson's might be considered akin to "a Munich" because it contained the seeds of appeasement. Elimination of America's forward bases had been a Soviet refrain since the days of Stalin, and the loss of those bases would upset the world power balance in favor of the Soviets. And Guantánamo was central to the U.S. strategic position in the Western Hemisphere. Thus, wrote Stewart, Stevenson's adversaries "sincerely believed that such concessions as Stevenson proposed . . . would encourage the Soviets, as Hitler was encouraged in the time of Munich, to further adventures in the expectation of further concessions."

But Stevenson didn't want to answer such critics in order to defend his position, wrote Stewart; instead he "used every device to becloud the real issue. . . . He portrayed himself as a victim of a McCarthyite plot, while hotly 'denying' that he had 'opposed' the President's blockade policy—which, of course, we never wrote."

Stewart's "Footnote" set off another round of news stories, editorials, columns, and letters.

Eventually the issue died down and was entrusted, as Kennedy had suggested, to historians. In later years, it emerged that the Alsop-Bartlett article had been correct in most respects but also incomplete and perhaps misleading. By the time the ExComm got to the fateful Saturday discussion in which Stevenson had uttered his controversial positions, everyone had come to feel that the quarantine option, then all but embraced by the president, likely would lead to negotiations with the Soviets. They expected the negotiations to include discussion of the Turkish bases—and probably the Italian ones. Kennedy long had considered the missiles in Turkey obsolete and wanted them out of there anyway. Stewart and Bartlett could not have known, as only a handful of men in the world knew, that Robert Kennedy had rendered an unofficial, personal pledge to the Soviets, made in conversation with the Soviet ambassador in Washington, that the Kennedys would initiate action to relinquish the Turkish bases after a decent interval of five to six months.

The Kennedys' personal commitment to Khrushchev, kept secret even from most of the ExComm, didn't become publicly known until Robert Kennedy's book on the crisis was published six years later (some months after his assassination). This news was heralded by Stevenson partisans as demonstrating that the UN ambassador had not been out of step with the Kennedys or the ExComm during that Saturday discussion. For years it would be cited as evidence of an injustice perpetrated against Stevenson by Alsop and Bartlett.

But this misses the essential point about those delicate and complex ExComm discussions. The Stevenson actions that caused a stir—and some pique—among ExComm members had not been his willingness to entertain the idea of bargaining away the Turkish missiles. It had been his suggestion that Kennedy initiate discussions on the European missiles even before the outcome of the quarantine became clear, and his willingness to place the crucial Guantánamo base on the bargaining table. As Arthur Schlesinger has written, Robert Kennedy felt it was

Stevenson's timing and his Guantánamo proposal, and not the matter of Turkish missiles, "that created his reputation as the supreme dove."

The Alsop-Bartlett article was correct in suggesting that Stevenson's comments had angered the Kennedys. Robert Kennedy had even suggested that they should replace Stevenson at the UN, "as he was such a weak man in these kinds of negotiations." Moreover, the Alsop-Bartlett article was correct in suggesting that the Kennedys had dispatched Schlesinger and McCloy to the UN to keep Stevenson from going soft. As Schlesinger rushed for his New York–bound plane, the attorney general had taken him aside for instructions. "We're counting on you to watch things in New York," he had said. "That fellow is ready to give everything away. We will have to make a deal in the end; but we must stand firm now."

The missile-crisis piece and its aftermath constituted a turning point in the career of Stewart Alsop. The intense national attention it brought him, though harsh at times, removed him once and for all from the shadow of his brother. The controversy beamed a national spotlight on Stewart's particular journalistic talents—inside reporting on dramatic Washington events, and narrative storytelling for a national audience. In addition, the episode demonstrated to the nation that the old *Saturday Evening Post* wasn't dead yet. Up in Philadelphia, *Post* editor Clay Blair pronounced himself "delighted" with Stewart's work.

29

FROM JFK TO LBJ

Early Rumblings of a Distant War

In February 1963, Lady Diana Cooper visited Washington and was the guest of her very good friends Susan Mary and Joe Alsop, who orchestrated an experience for the grande dame that proved memorable even in such a life as hers.

On February 6, they honored her at Dumbarton with a dinner that included among the company Robert and Ethel Kennedy; Senator Edward Kennedy and his wife, Joan; Treasury Secretary Douglas Dillon; Senator John Sherman Cooper; Alice Roosevelt Longworth; and David Bruce, then ambassador to London. The cook prepared terrapin soup, roast saddle of lamb, and a soufflé dessert. Joe served Moët & Chandon champagne and Château Pavie 1945. Diana was struck by the singular focus of the conversation—"politics, politics," as she wrote to her son, John Julius Norwich.

The next day, Joe took her to see Vice President Lyndon Johnson, whom Joe had described as "a frustrated force of nature." Johnson mumbled through the fingers of his huge hand and seemed disengaged throughout the interview. A day later, Diana accompanied Eunice Shriver, sister of the president and wife of the Peace Corps director, on a tour of the White House. "She . . . has the [same] wild originality of countenance and has always been in love with her brother Jack, looks like him, talks like him," Diana wrote to John Julius. In the Cabinet Room, the two women surveyed the huge table with note pads placed before each chair. Eunice, a close friend of Robert McNamara, playfully jotted a Valentine's Day message on the pad in front of his seat. Diana scribbled "Love from Debo" on the president's pad as a message from her friend, the duchess of Devonshire, Kennedy's former sister-in-law.

On Valentine's Day, the president and first lady came to a small Dumbarton dinner to meet Lady Diana. Also on hand were the British ambassador, Sir David Ormsby-Gore, and his wife; Joan Braden; and David Bruce. The menu was caviar blini, veal, rice, puree of peas, endive salad, cheese, and bombe Jeanne d'Arc. This time Joe served Château Lafite 1947 along with the Moët & Chandon. "Nice to see you again," the president said to Diana, although the British aristocrat couldn't remember ever having laid eyes on the young president. They had met in London eight years earlier; at the time she was much more famous than he, and the encounter had stuck in his memory but slipped from hers.

At dinner, Kennedy was seated at the head of the table, with Diana at his right and Joe to her right. Joe served as a kind of interpreter for Diana in her conversation with Kennedy. The president would ask a question, and she would answer; then Joe would lean forward and say, "What Diana means is . . ." David Bruce, who watched this comical spectacle from his seat nearby, could see that Diana wasn't bothered by it. "She was thrilled to meet the president," said Mrs. Bruce years later, "and she knew and appreciated Joe for what he was."

After dinner, Diana enjoyed a long conversation with Jackie, who had read all of Diana's books and remembered them in detail. Diana found Jackie even more beautiful than she had expected, "and a hundred times more of a personality." For his part, Jack Kennedy was thoroughly beguiled by this animated British aristocrat. "What a woman!" he remarked to Joe upon leaving Dumbarton, and he invited Diana to a forthcoming formal dinner at the White House.

Those were heady days for the Alsops. Their social standing had never been higher, and Joe's access to top-level administration officials had never been easier. His ability to lure the president to his table conferred upon him a professional stature unmatched in Washington journalism. His column now penetrated even deeper than before into inner councils of government; it was indispensable for anyone who wanted to know what the Kennedys were doing or planning.

When Charles de Gaulle, the maverick of European diplomacy, abruptly vetoed Britain's entry into the European Common Market, Joe took note. On February 20, a week after the Dumbarton dinner, he broke the story of the administration's "grand review" of European policy in the wake of de Gaulle's action. Kennedy's European ambassadors, including David Bruce, had been recalled for discussions, and they were joined by top administration strategists. Not surprisingly, Joe was much impressed by this effort within the administration he so clearly admired. He noted reverentially that the president himself had directed the operations, presiding in person at various review meetings "and supervising every phase."

Stewart too enjoyed special access at the White House and throughout the administration. He felt Kennedy had the makings of a great president. What struck him was Kennedy's deftness in pushing aside the liberal wing of his party in major policy decisions. "In New Deal terms," he wrote to Bill Emerson at the *Saturday Evening Post*, "Kennedy is actually an essentially conservative president, dedicated to preserving a manageable status quo." He cited the president's devotion to low tax rates, his strong defense posture, his moderation on farm issues, even his Medicare proposal, which Stewart described as adopting "the Bismarckian theory of letting the poor pay for the poor." These views squared with Stewart's own philosophy. But unlike Joe, Stewart was willing to risk Kennedy's anger in his writings.

This was evident in a piece called "The Collapse of Kennedy's Grand Design," a look at ramifications of de Gaulle's nationalistic diplomacy. This was a sequel of sorts to a piece he had written a year earlier entitled "Kennedy's Grand Strategy," for which he had interviewed the president at length. The piece had outlined the president's plan for a true Atlantic partnership and a "centrally controlled" nuclear deterrent, meaning an American-dominated alliance. Those had been the days of Khrushchev's post-Vienna bluster, when he had seemed determined to force the West out of Berlin. But now, a year later, Khrushchev was less bellicose, and Europe was inclined to relax once again. Stewart viewed de Gaulle's Common Market veto of Britain as the death knell for Kennedy's "grand strategy." His article exploring this strategic collapse angered the president, and Kennedy made sure Stewart learned of his feelings. "I fear my stock [at the White House] is not high these days," Stewart wrote Emerson.

Meanwhile, Stewart was having difficulties with his editors at the *Saturday Evening Post*, who increasingly changed his prose without informing him before publication. "I rewrite every sentence of every piece I write at least three times and often more," he wrote to *Post* editor Robert Johnson. "A good editor can often rewrite my much rewritten sentences and improve them in the process, but I don't see why I shouldn't be told about it."

The *Saturday Evening Post* had changed. No longer was it the comfortable and predictable place Stewart had enjoyed for nearly two decades. A new team had come in, moved the headquarters to New York, and injected aggressive new ways into the operation. Marty Sommers, that charming font of sympathy and wise counsel for thirty years, was gone. He had retired in late 1962 and soon thereafter died of complications from a longtime problem with alcohol. Stewart had loved Marty, whose outlook on the world had matched his own; he had cherished the warm camaraderie they shared, and appreciated the keen intellect that lay behind Sommers's gentle nature.

But the new team, led by former Time-Life writer Clay Blair, wasn't inclined to appreciate Sommers's character or intellect. They saw a mag-

azine in turmoil, perhaps in mortal danger, and they naturally blamed the old leadership that had failed to keep pace with a fast-changing world. They wanted greater "relevance," a sharper edge, more hard-hitting journalism.

Stewart's stock in trade already was hard-hitting journalism, and his ability to make sense of Washington's maneuverings established him with the new team. But in another way the changes posed problems. The place was rife with power struggles. Nobody seemed sure what the magazine stood for now or what it wanted from its writers. Stewart found himself fighting with his editors more often and more aggressively than ever before.

In the summer of 1963 Don Schanche, the *Post*'s number-two editor, suggested that Stewart add a regular column, to be called "Affairs of State," to his feature writing. The idea was for a page of about fourteen hundred words that combined explanatory writing with analysis and occasional opinion. Stewart was nervous about the assignment because he would have to file the column nearly three weeks before publication. "This is a sonofabitch of a lead time for a political column," he wrote to Sommers's replacement, Otto Friedrich, requesting that the column be placed on a page that didn't require such advance filing. But the magazine's brass said that couldn't be done.

On September 1, Stewart signed a new contract that encompassed the column assignment and provided a gross income of about $66,000, of which about $8,000 would go for in-town expenses. The *Post* would pay all out-of-town expenses.

The column, first appearing September 23, 1963, was a success. *Post* president Matthew Culligan liked it so much he immediately launched a plan to sell a big ad contract for space next to the column. The ad salesman noted substantial demand for the space.

Stewart often took the column beyond Washington; he made it a forum for exploring the endless and varied patterns that made up the great cultural quilt of America. He traveled to Rome, Georgia, a point of reference for John Kennedy in 1963. The president had carried the town in 1960 by 54 percent, compared to 51 percent in the South generally. Georgia was the only state that had supported the Democratic presidential ticket consistently since the Civil War. If Kennedy could lose Rome, he could lose Georgia; and if he could lose Georgia, he could lose the South.

Stewart found an old man sitting in his undershirt on a rickety porch. He had voted for Kennedy but never would again. Asked to describe the president's performance, he replied, "Just plain rotten." The attorney general's performance? "Rottener." The man squealed with laughter at the sound of his own voice.

On racial matters, the Georgian was even more provocative. "Look, mister, I don't know where you come from. But here in Georgia we know how to handle the Nigra. A Nigra's all right in his place, but you

gotta keep him in his place." The man on the porch would strike many Northerners as a caricature, wrote Stewart, but his views were taken seriously in Rome, Georgia.

In the town Stewart also encountered Mrs. Albert Dempsey, who felt blacks should be accorded full rights of citizenship. Although she was a product of the South and of Southern thinking, she had changed her views when her son, a marine, had brought home a black friend from the barracks. "If we are going to call ourselves Christians," she told Stewart, "then we must look into our hearts and do what's right."

Stewart himself could see no easy solution to the country's race problem, but he believed Mrs. Dempsey's son represented the best hope for eventual accommodation between the races. "But it is a small and distant hope," he wrote. "For the present, the old man on the porch represents a crushing majority, and Mrs. Dempsey and her son an insignificant minority."

Later Stewart devoted a column to what he called "a tale of two cities"—white Washington and black Washington. He enlisted Clarence Hunter, a black reporter for the *Washington Star*, to guide him through black Washington. Together they visited the Platinum Coast and the two Gold Coasts, where the richest blacks lived; the little enclave of the "old line aristocracy"; the vast middle-class areas; and the crime-ridden Second Precinct, where the poorest people lived. They enjoyed a meal at Billy Simpson's, a noted black restaurant, toured an inner-city school, visited numerous blacks in their homes. After seeing what he had imagined would be a largely foreign city, Stewart bundled up his impressions into a kind of travelogue, and concluded that it was a great deal less foreign than he had expected. "Black Washington is for the most part, in fact, just another American city, and its essential Americanness is everywhere evident," he wrote.

It was clear, he added, that some folks in black Washington hated white Washington just because it was white. But those people, Clarence Hunter had assured him, were a distinct minority. They wouldn't remain a minority, Stewart warned, "if Negroes are permanently denied rights of other Americans." But there were still "ties that bind, and it seems reasonable to hope that the two Washingtons, like the two races elsewhere in the United States, can go on living amicably side by side."

Stewart enjoyed writing the column and appreciated the benefits of writing for a major national magazine. He produced a profile of the CIA that inspired a New York publisher, Harcourt, Brace & World, to propose a reissue of *Sub Rosa*, the book Stewart and Tom Braden had written on the OSS back in 1946. Braden wrote a new introduction, and Stewart's *Post* piece served as postscript. The proposed royalties amounted to only 6 percent—"low, but what the hell," Stewart wrote to Braden.

Stewart encountered frustration that same month when he sought to interview the president for a piece on Kennedy's assessment of world af-

fairs. Pierre Salinger had said it would be no problem and said he would call back with a reply the same afternoon. No call. Stewart called twice more and left messages, but still got no reply. He tried going through presidential aide Kenneth O'Donnell, again with no luck. Finally he concluded that Kennedy himself must have rejected the idea of an interview because of emotions it might stir with Adlai Stevenson and his followers—lingering fallout from the missile-crisis article of the year before.

Joe Alsop never experienced difficulty getting access at the Kennedy White House. McGeorge Bundy, the national security adviser, and Secretary of State Dean Rusk were particularly good sources for Joe, as they were for Walter Lippmann; these two were considered by the administration to be Washington's most important newsmen. The two men had been friends and rivals for nearly three decades—and not just as newsmen but also as social hosts. Lippmann, ever the diplomat, found raucous social debates distasteful. At his famous Georgetown salon, whenever he detected temperatures rising at table, he would deftly change the subject to calm the situation. He fostered sedate, learned discussions not just on Washington politics but also on literature and art and goings-on at Whitehall in London or the Élysée in Paris. Though Lippmann's guest lists often overlapped with Joe's, his dinners were a far cry from the argumentative discussions of Dumbarton.

Lippmann's reputation was that of journalistic sage, a writer of erudition who didn't need to wear out shoe leather in order to expound on important events. Joe privately looked down on Lippmann's lack of reporting instincts, but it was the difference in the two men's fundamental outlooks that often stirred emotional debates between them. Lippmann put his faith in diplomacy and abhorred the use of force. Joe viewed diplomacy skeptically, and placed his trust in the use and threat of military power. Both Joe and Stewart delighted in denigrating Lippmann's work, and Stewart once suggested in print that Lippmann's positions on foreign affairs had for years been "consistently and demonstrably wrong." Still, Lippmann enjoyed a reputation as being primus inter pares in Washington journalistic circles, and not even Joe could overtake that reputation.

Joe was known as the leading reporter among the influential columnists. Working the Kennedy administration, he often would seek to elicit information by positing a theory, sometimes a highly unlikely hypothesis on administration goings-on, and then carefully surveying the response. Or he would use what Dean Rusk later characterized as the "hand grenade technique"—storming into the secretary's office, breathless and scowling, attacking what he presumed to be the latest stupidity on the part of the government. "Pretty soon the bristles would begin to rise on the back of my neck," Rusk wrote later. "Unless I caught myself, I'd begin to say, 'Joe, you don't know what you are talking about. Let me set you straight.' "

Joe also had frequent one-on-one chats with the president in the

Oval Office, and even more frequent access to Bobby Kennedy, with whom he often shared private luncheons.

Nor was it uncommon for Joe and Susan Mary to attend intimate White House dinners filled with political talk and laughter. Kennedy enjoyed regaling his friends with tales of what he had to put up with as president. He once pulled from his pocket a sampling of the long letters he received regularly from his stuffy ambassador to India, John Kenneth Galbraith, and read them aloud "with comic emphasis."

Occasionally these White House repasts would include just the Alsops and the Kennedys. The president could be remarkably frank during these dinners, revealing highly sensitive information with the knowledge that Joe would keep it to himself unless given the go-ahead to publish. On one occasion in 1963 Kennedy shared what had been for him a delicious moment—an opportunity to goad his European nemesis, Charles de Gaulle, in the name of protocol.

"Joe, I have the best joke to tell you," said the president. It seemed that a Soviet defector, then in the hands of the CIA at a New York safe house, had revealed that French military intelligence services were riddled with Soviet spies.

"Our people believe him," said the president with a laugh, "and so I had the pleasure of sending our friend de Gaulle a handwritten letter by courier telling him that he had a problem."

Kennedy added that de Gaulle's office had called immediately to request an opportunity to debrief the defector.

"They're sending a top general over next week," he said.

"Who is it?" asked Joe.

"You've probably never heard of him—fellow named Jean Louis de Rougemont."

"Oh," exclaimed Susan Mary, "he and his wife Louise are two of my closest friends."

They all laughed at the small world they inhabited. But for Kennedy the biggest laugh came from the jab he had administered to de Gaulle while fulfilling diplomatic courtesies.

Joe and Kennedy shared great sadness in August, when Phil Graham fired a shotgun into his head. Both men had felt warm affection for the brilliant *Post* publisher with the intoxicating personality. Joe had watched with mounting frustration and horror as his friend had slipped ever deeper into a state of mental and emotional deterioration. He had hoped desperately for Phil's recovery. The loss weighed heavily upon Joe's heart.

But he continued to play to the hilt his role as Washington's leading gentleman journalist. For some around town, it seemed Joe's success and influence had gone to his head. The flamboyant personality he had forged for himself during his Harvard years was becoming even more extravagant, his elaborate mannerisms more accentuated. In the minds of many, including brother Stewart, Joe was becoming something of a caricature of himself. Always quick to anger and to take offense, now he was becoming even more crotchety. Always something of a bully, he was becoming more of a bully. His thirst for controversy grew with his success. Stewart began calling Joe "the terribly tempered Mr. Bang."

The person who bore the brunt of Mr. Bang was Evelyn Puffenberger, Joe's secretary, known to her friends as Peggy and to Joe as "Miss Puff." Joe would stomp into the office each morning, slam the door, and exclaim, "Well, now, Miss Puff, let's get cracking." Of course, Miss Puff would have been "cracking" for an hour or more by the time he arrived. She considered Joe to be "the most interesting person I ever worked for," but also "a born bully." She recalled later, "He would yell, he would scream, he would carry on like a mad fiend at times." Repeatedly she would resign on the spot.

"Now, now, Miss Puff," Joe would say in a soothing and apologetic tone of voice, "there's no need for that, no need for that." And he would promise once again to keep his temper in check.

Many who saw Joe at his worst still considered him wonderfully amusing, but for those who bore the brunt of him at his worst, such as Miss Puff, it wasn't very funny. Now Susan Mary began to feel the lash of his mercurial temperament. About a year after their wedding, Joe began to express displeasure with his wife, belittling her household decisions and berating her for what he considered her faulty efforts to handle their social affairs. She tried her best to respond to his complaints and run the household according to his wishes, but the complaints continued.

Then about a year and a half into their marriage, at the summer home of Kay Graham, Susan Mary had a conversation with Kay that stunned her.

"Joe came to talk with me the other day," said Kay. "He said he feels trapped by marriage."

"My God! He said that?"

"Yes, he did."

Susan Mary desperately wanted to save the marriage. She tried to anticipate Joe's displeasure and avoid setting him off. But sometimes, when she failed, her own stubborn streak would emerge, and then she would defiantly ignore his demands. That invariably prompted Joe to lose his temper. Susan Mary harbored no illusions about her chances of avoiding divorce. She knew it would be a difficult challenge.

MEANWHILE, SOME TEN thousand miles from Washington, in the jungles and rice paddies of Vietnam, John Kennedy had been helping the South Vietnamese resist the insurgent Vietcong, sponsored and directed by the belligerently anti-Western North Vietnamese regime of Ho Chi Minh. By summer 1963, the United States had seventeen thousand military personnel in South Vietnam, trying to forge that country's hapless military into an effective fighting force. Not surprisingly, Joe Alsop supported this effort.

A year earlier, in September 1962, he had written a column from Washington suggesting that the American-sponsored South was beginning to win the war. This came from certain optimistic reports relayed to Washington by the South Vietnamese defense secretary, Nguyen Dinh Thuan, who had predicted the communist guerrilla movement could be "decisively destroyed" after two or three more years of hard fighting. Indeed, according to Joe, the U.S. commander in Vietnam, Gen. Paul D. Harkins, had told his superiors in a Honolulu meeting that a communist defeat could be brought about "within one year after the army attains a fully offensive footing." The Vietnam war, Joe had written, had "the faint, just barely detectable smell" of previous guerrilla wars in Greece and the Philippines, when American doomsayers had predicted disaster right up to the time of dramatic anticommunist victories.

Joe's column had not reflected reality. Far from having found any path to victory, the South Vietnamese army was a military basket case, a day-by-day frustration to the U.S. military advisers in the field who had to deal with its incompetence, its debilitating favoritism and corruption, and its unwillingness to wage war in any serious way. Harkins, who wouldn't countenance negativism or pessimism from his commanders in the field, had insisted upon glowing reports to Washington. It had been a misinformed government whose outlook had seeped into Joe's misinformed column.

Throughout most of 1963, Joe had ignored the Vietnam story as the situation there deteriorated under the erratic leadership of Ngo Dinh Diem and his unstable brother, Ngo Dinh Nhu. Diem seemed incapable of conciliating the various dissident groups within his country, particularly the Buddhists who fostered demonstrations throughout the South and shook the regime with well-staged self-immolations by elderly monks. The photos of Buddhist monks in flames as they sat cross-legged on Saigon streetcorners generated horror throughout the world and brought opprobrium to the Diem regime. Soon young American reporters of the Saigon press corps were portraying Diem harshly, and top U.S. officials were wondering if he could successfully prosecute the war. Diem hurt himself further by unleashing a series of raids on Buddhist pagodas throughout the country. The day after, on August 22, there arrived in Saigon the new U.S. ambassador, Joe Alsop's lifelong friend, Henry Cabot Lodge.

By the time Joe reached Vietnam in mid-September 1963 for ten days of reporting, Lodge had concluded that Diem must go. At the ambassador's invitation, Joe stayed at the embassy, and there he had ample opportunity to hear Lodge decry the misrule of Diem and his brother. Indeed, Lodge already had set in motion a U.S. plan to sanction a coup by the South Vietnamese military.

On two successive days Joe spent several hours in conversation with

Nhu and Diem at their lush offices at the Palais Gia Long. He had become well acquainted with the pair during his many visits to Saigon, and he had felt a strong sense of confidence in their patriotism and judgment. Based on his conversations with Lodge, he was prepared to revise his opinion, but he was not prepared for what he encountered.

He first visited Nhu in his long, high-ceilinged office lined with books and mementos and overlooking the palace gardens. The state councillor, as Nhu was called, motioned Joe to a chair near his cluttered desk and then, pacing back and forth along the length of the office and lighting cigarets in quick succession, commenced a long tirade against Saigon's American press corps, the American government, his own military, and his own brother. He proclaimed himself to be the world's greatest living expert on guerrilla warfare, but said he couldn't bring his brilliance to bear because he was obstructed at every turn by the obstinate Americans and by his brother.

Then Nhu announced that he had been involved in secret negotiations with Hanoi, conducted through the French ambassador, Roger Lalouette. He said he expected to reach a settlement with the communist regime soon, and that he would bring his brother along on any accommodation he found acceptable. When Joe asked what he would do if the communists later reneged on their agreement, as they had done so often in the past, the councillor dismissed the question as unimportant. He had only to go into the countryside and wave a handkerchief, he boasted, and a million men would spring to arms at his back. He was, after all, the world's greatest living guerrilla expert. As Joe put it years later, "Nhu had gone stark, raving mad."

The next day Joe went back to Gia Long for lunch with President Diem, who greeted him cordially. Joe soon discovered that Diem's thinking echoed Nhu's. Diem repeated much of what his brother had said the previous day in almost identical terms, and he seemed just as impervious to reason.

Joe filed a bold column relating his Gia Long experiences and expressing chagrin at the intellectual decay within the Saigon government. Nhu, he wrote, had "lost touch with the real world," and Diem had "lost his ability to see events or problems in their true proportions, no doubt because his natural tendency to be suspicious has been daily played upon by his brother." Joe echoed Lodge's view that success in the war hardly seemed possible with these men in charge. "So there are likely to be changes here," he concluded.

But Joe couldn't let it go at that. He had admired Diem, had considered him a Vietnamese patriot and a hero in the struggle against the communists following the 1954 partition. He couldn't bring himself to blame Diem entirely for the state of things. He attacked the American press corps for writing negative stories about Diem and exacerbating his paranoia: "The constant pressure of the reportorial crusade against the government has also helped mightily to transform Diem from a courageous, quite viable national leader, into a man afflicted with galloping persecution mania, seeing plots around every corner, and therefore misjudging everything."

It was a bizarre column, and it touched a nerve in Washington. Joe hadn't named names, but sophisticated readers knew he was talking primarily about *The New York Times*'s David Halberstam, whose dispatches had been very critical of Diem and pessimistic about the South's military prospects. James Reston, the *Times* Washington bureau chief, phoned Mac Bundy and asked, "Why don't you call off Alsop?" Reflecting the administration's frustration with Halberstam's dispatches, Bundy replied, "Don't you believe in freedom of the press?"

Joe's column was not a product of serious analysis but rather of the emotions he felt as he contemplated the West's experiences in Asia. If a national leader could go "right around the bend," as Joe himself put it, because of foreign press coverage, then he clearly suffered from serious intrinsic flaws.

Back in Washington, Joe went to the White House to brief Kennedy in the Oval Office. He reiterated what he had written in the column, only in stronger terms.

"I don't think this is viable," he said.

Joe didn't know that Kennedy already had concluded the same thing. On November 2, word reached Washington that Diem and Nhu had been killed in a military coup led by General Duong Van Minh and sanctioned by the U.S. government. When he received word of the deaths during an Oval Office meeting that morning, Kennedy rushed from the room white-faced and visibly shaken.

Years later, Joe wrote that he had come to feel some guilt over Diem's fate, for he suspected his Saigon dispatches and his report to Kennedy may have contributed to the coup decision. More significantly, he came to conclude that Diem's overthrow and death had been a tragic watershed in the lengthening Vietnam struggle and in America's involvement there. The assassination created a power vacuum in the countryside that the communists quickly filled; it also established an American moral responsibility for that faraway little nation, which sucked the United States still further into the quicksand. In any event, within three weeks—on November 22—developments in Southeast Asia would be overshadowed by a tragedy at home of overwhelming proportions.

JOE WAS SITTING in his upstairs garden room that Friday when Susan Mary rushed in to say she had heard that the president had been shot in Dallas. He hurried down to his office to listen to the radio and work the phones, frantically calling friends in the government and media to find out the facts. Soon he learned the extent of the tragedy. Miss Puff later heard him sobbing uncontrollably. "I didn't think he had that much emotion in him," she thought. Joe passed the following days in something approaching shock. He had loved John Kennedy, and he could not shake the feeling that the best days of his own life were now behind him.

Up on Springland Lane, where Stewart was in bed with the flu, there wasn't time for shock. Otto Friedrich called to demand a profile of Lyndon Johnson within twenty-four hours.

"Stew," said Friedrich, "it is absolutely forbidden to have the flu at a time like this."

Writing largely from memory and his extensive LBJ file, Stewart produced a full-length profile in the allotted time. He also dug out the transcript from a 1959 interview with Johnson. The magazine ran excerpts from the interview alongside the profile, and added a medical update on the new president's 1955 heart attack. The subhead for the profile read, "An extraordinarily complex man—proud, tough, shrewd—he will be master in his house."

Upon completing the assignment, Stewart visited Cousin Alice Longworth for a brief dinner before going home to bed to shake off the flu. "Goddam it, I'm depressed," he wrote to Friedrich on Monday. "I don't claim to have been a friend of his, but almost everyone who knew him had an affection for JFK." That same day Joe and Susan Mary attended the funeral at Saint Matthew's Cathedral with Cousin Alice. In his column that morning, Joe had called the fallen leader "the worthy citizen of a nation great and free—a nation, as he liked to think, that is great because it is free, and this was the thought that always inspired his too brief leadership of this republic."

Both Joe and Susan Mary moved quickly to offer support to Jackie in the months following the president's death. Susan Mary plunged into the task of answering the ninety thousand foreign letters Jackie received after the assassination. For several weeks she toiled away in the old State Department building, from dawn until dusk, six days a week. Tish also contributed her time. Both Alsop wives received affectionate letters of appreciation from Jackie.

Joe continued his loving correspondence with Jackie. "It all but broke my heart not to be able to see you yesterday, if only for twenty seconds," he wrote her a few months after the assassination, after plans for a get-together went awry. "The truth is that my heart suddenly became all too easily breakable, because all sorts of memories were flooding back upon me." She replied, "People always say time makes everything better—but that isn't true about Jack—just the reverse for me—and the same for you—as your letter . . . showed." She added, "Dear Joe—I am glad you did write to me—It helps to know that someone else feels the same way."

Later, when Joe sent Jackie a book for Christmas, she wrote to say he had served as inspiration for her program to instill good reading habits in her children. "So thank you for that too. . . . You can imagine how much love I send to you & to Susan Mary."

But Joe's thoughts went beyond his slain friend and his friend's widow. He also had to think of the future. He considered himself a friend of the new president, and he set about immediately to solidify his political relationship with Lyndon Johnson. Over the weekend he had dispatched a letter to the White House expressing his confidence in Johnson and offering his support. On Monday morning he called the Oval Office. Johnson avidly took the call, and they found themselves discussing the inevitable investigation of Kennedy's death and the Sunday murder of the leading suspect, Lee Harvey Oswald.

"I appreciate very much your calling," said the president.

"Well," replied Joe, "you know what I feel about you, and you know how I . . . well, I put it all in the letter."

Johnson then outlined his plan for a board of inquiry within Texas to assist the FBI in its investigation. "We don't send in a bunch of carpetbaggers . . . that's the worst thing we could do right now," he said. He had worked on the problem the previous day and had concluded that the federal government's role in the Texas investigation should be confined to normal FBI efforts. The "blue-ribbon panel" he had in mind would be strictly a Texas operation.

Joe sensed that the president's plan could prove controversial. Already he had heard that *Washington Post* editor Al Friendly planned an editorial calling for a high-level federal inquiry, and Joe felt the president should have his press secretary, Bill Moyers, jump on that bandwagon.

"I'm sure you're right," said Joe, "except there's one missing piece." He said it didn't make sense to have the attorney general review the investigation of his own brother's death, that there should be some higher federal involvement in reviewing the FBI reports and presenting the government's findings to the country. To press his case, Joe threw in copious amounts of flattery, all duly recorded on the president's private taping system:

"So that the country will have the story judicially reviewed, outside Texas, and if you tell Bill Moyers to call up Friendly and if you'll get out a special announcement this afternoon, you're going to make a marvelous—well, you've already made a marvelous start. You haven't put a damned foot one-quarter of an inch wrong, and I've never seen anything like it. You've been simply marvelous in the most painful circumstances, but I do feel that there is that much of a gap and I'm sure that if Moyers calls Friendly, you have a terrific support from *The Washington Post* and from the whole of the rest of the press instantly."

Johnson protested that, if he followed such a course, he would ruin the two procedures he already had decided upon—the Texas panel and the FBI inquiry.

"No you won't, no you won't," retorted Joe. The president could just add some men of national stature to the review panel to give it "absolute conviction," while at the same time getting out ahead of the *Post* and others who could be calling for a federal inquiry.

"I hate to interfere, sir," said Joe. "I only dare to do so because I care so much about you."

"I know that, Joe."

"And I have the deepest faith in you . . ."

"Thank you, my friend."

Joe's second column after the assassination was a tribute to the new president, whom he described as a man of "common sense, courage, intelligence, a knack of getting things done and the deep, true concern for his country that President Kennedy himself noted."

On Wednesday, Johnson addressed a joint session of Congress. He announced his plans to keep the slain president's team in place, and issued a call for the completion of Kennedy's agenda. Afterward Joe and Kay Graham lunched at Dumbarton and shed a few tears as they spoke of Phil Graham's great confidence in Johnson and the pride he would have felt at his fine beginning. That afternoon Joe called Johnson.

"I want to [thank] you for that most wonderful—and how grateful I am—for that beautiful article," said the president. "I don't deserve it, but I appreciate it."

"Your speech was a triumphant success," Joe said, and added that it had made him proud of his country. "I kept thinking about how everyone abroad was going to be impressed."

"Thank you, my friend."

"And good luck to you and let me come and see you."

"Sure will, sure will."

Joe had known Johnson for close to a quarter century—since LBJ's days as an aggressive young congressman and Joe's days as an aggressive young columnist. The Texan had been an excellent source. With his close ties to House Democratic leader Sam Rayburn, Johnson had been invited to New Deal strategy sessions at the Roosevelt White House, and he often had revealed elements of the discussions to Joe. Later, feeling that the columnist owed him something for all that information, he had suggested that Joe write a column about him as a rising star in the party. Feeling that he couldn't justify elevating this obscure congressman in his national column, Joe had pacified his friend with an extra column that he had sent out to the syndicate's Texas papers.

Now, so many years later, with both men much older and highly successful, they felt a special kinship. Johnson called Joe at seven p.m. the Friday after the assassination to report that he had decided to take Joe's advice and appoint a federal commission to study the Dallas events.

"That's just fine, sir. I think that's just fine," Joe said after the president had read him portions of a news release announcing the new Warren Commission, named after its chairman, Chief Justice Earl Warren.

Although Joe enjoyed his special friendship with the new president, he couldn't get over his grief for the departed one. "Politics in this city will not be as exciting again in my lifetime," he wrote to the Baron

Philippe de Rothschilds on January 9. To a friend named Mrs. Milton Gendel in Rome, Joe said he was thinking of giving up the column now that the excitement of Kennedy's presidency was gone.

With the column providing less satisfaction, Joe found greater zest in an enterprise he had been working on for years—a book exploring the archaeological riddles of the Greek Bronze Age. It was the product, as Joe said in his preface, of two journeys. The first was a voyage of the mind—a lifetime of reading everything he could find, whether in English or French, on Aegean civilization. The second was an exciting tour, guided by American field archaeologist C. W. Blegen, to the digs at Pylos, seat of power of the great King Nestor of Homer's epic.

The book, entitled *From the Silent Earth: A Report on the Greek Bronze Age*, appeared in February 1964, under the Harper & Row imprimatur. It recounted the great archaeological controversies clouding that distant past of Pylos: whether Homer's *Iliad* was myth or actual events; whether the Mycenae of Homer's epic was in fact a Greek (Indo-European) civilization or perhaps of some other provenance. The persistent German-American archaeologist, Heinrich Schliemann, had answered the first question nearly a hundred years before by unveiling some of the mysteries of old Troy (Ilium); and Professor Blegen, in discovering Pylos and its rich store of written tablets, had answered the second. The tablets proved that the language of the Bronze Age Mycenaeans was Greek, and that this language had formed the basis not just for the civilization of Mycenaean Greece but for that of the Greek colonies around the Aegean and probably also for the later Minoan culture of Crete. "This resurrected Pylos of King Nestor . . . revealed the truth about the first great phase of Greek civilization, and hence, of course, about the earliest high period of our own Western civilization," Joe wrote.

Joe's archaeological foray was more than a dry rendition of ancient names and places. Employing writing techniques he had mastered decades earlier for the *Saturday Evening Post*, he wove personality, controversy, and anecdote into a rich tapestry of history and culture. Using his knowledge of politics and human nature, he rendered a vivid fresco of the everyday life and civic ritual of a time and place long passed by.

A few academics sniffed disapprovingly at the popularly written book in their field of learning, but it received respectful notice in the popular press. *The New York Times* reviewer called Joe "an amateur student of Greek archaeology of near professional learning." In *The Washington Post*, a Yale professor emeritus of Latin wrote, "Alsop has been very respectful of the specialists; they will do well to return the compliment." Friends and acquaintances wrote to salute Joe's scholarship. "How-oh-how did you have time to learn and write all this in your already so full life?" asked Lady Bird Johnson. And a top official of the Greek government wrote to say, "My countrymen are indebted to you for your great contribution."

The book sold more than ten thousand copies, a success in the field. "I enjoyed writing the damned book more than anything I've done for a long time," Joe wrote to Mrs. Gendel.

As LYNDON JOHNSON grappled with the reins of government in the first weeks of 1964, both Alsops felt the "force of nature" would likely become a special president. Stewart, in one of the national radio commentaries that had become a part of his professional routine, proclaimed the president's first weeks to be "downright dazzling." He produced a feature-length piece for the *Post* entitled, "Johnson Takes Over: The Untold Story." It portrayed a man of force and intellect who, in those first delicate hours and days after the assassination, knew precisely what he wanted to do and how to get it done. Stewart went overboard a bit in a May column, suggesting the country was more "rational" in its political mood than it had been for a long time. If the country truly was in a "second era of good feeling," he wrote, Lyndon Johnson, "a born conciliator, is peculiarly suited to preside over it."

In April, Joe sent Johnson a letter noting that the president had "all too many difficult bridges to cross on the road ahead." He expressed confidence that Johnson would "get across them" and take the country with him, too, with "perfect success." Johnson responded with a note of thanks. "I hope to have lunch with you soon and discuss a number of things," the note added.

Both brothers supported the president's efforts to get his party's equal-rights agenda through what had been, until Kennedy's death, an obstructionist Congress. But they did not bring to that issue the same fervor they demonstrated on foreign policy. The civil rights bill that passed the House on February 10 was a monument to political and social change. It was designed to inject into the body politic a greater degree of federal intervention than the country had seen through any single piece of legislation in memory. It was meant to outlaw discrimination on the basis of race in nearly all public accommodations; to open all public tax-supported facilities to all citizens; to empower the attorney general to file suit anywhere in the nation to desegregate schools; to create a federal Equal Employment Opportunity Commission to combat discrimination in unions and employment; and to allow the federal government to cut off funds to states and localities found guilty of discrimination.

"As Americans we have a moral duty to accord equal opportunity to our Negro citizens," Joe wrote to a reader from Alabama. In a March 30 column entitled "The Last, Best Chance" he reported approvingly that the bill's Senate proponents felt confident they would be able to vote cloture on the floor, thus ensuring a vote and the bill's passage. When Senate Republican leader Everett Dirksen maneuvered most of his party's senators into a yea vote for cloture, Joe wrote, "Party and country . . . have rarely been better served." But he didn't use the column to crusade for the bill; indeed, given the bill's import, it was surprising how little he wrote about it.

Joe viewed the civil rights cause from the perspective of the art of the possible. He thought the best course was a slow, deliberative push for equal rights rather than bold initiatives that might drive wedges between the races. He denounced Republicans who advocated a presidential election strategy of exploiting whites' racial fears to forge a coalition of Southerners, frustrated Northern working-class voters, and conservative Westerners. But he was equally quick to criticize civil rights strategists who pushed issues that could help foster this Republican "Southern strategy." His favorite target was the idea of forced busing to desegregate schools in big Northern cities. White parents wouldn't stand for such disruptive approaches, he argued, and would move to nearby suburbs to avoid sending their children on long bus rides to inferior schools in often dangerous neighborhoods.

For his part, Stewart called the race issue "the old, ulcerous unresolved national dilemma." In April he wrote a controversial *Post* column exposing "an empty gesture toward integration," in which Chicago school officials had moved the sixth grade from an all-black school into a predominantly white school near the University of Chicago. The black students were confined to an annex, set off as a kind of curiosity in a strange environment. When their teacher asked them to write about what they liked and disliked about their new school, the result was "a bizarre but revealing explosion of illiterate protest." They wrote of being shut off, of a teacher's ill-concealed contempt, of whites who picked fights and were their "enemies in the same building." About the only thing they liked was the food—which suggested to Stewart that many of them were hungry a good deal of the time.

Seeing the prospect of a growing underclass in the country's major cities, Stewart applauded Johnson's proposals for improving ghetto schools and combating poverty. Without such efforts, he wrote, most of the blacks who would form majorities in many large cities would be illiterate and would hate whites. "Surely," he wrote, "it is worth a reasonable investment to avoid a situation in which our big cities will be ruled by an uneducated, white-hating majority."

But Stewart took offense when he witnessed what he considered black racism. He went to Cambridge, Maryland, with George Wallace, the Alabama governor and segregationist who was collecting surprisingly large proportions of Democratic primary votes in Northern industrial states, and wandered across Race Street to witness a counter-rally orchestrated by a local black activist named Gloria Richardson. There he heard Minister Lonnie 3X of the Black Muslims assail all whites and extol the virtues of black radicalism: "Moderates seek accommodation with whites; radicals seek a showdown. . . . If we want freedom we're going to have to fight for it. . . . There must be a great rising up, a revolt for freedom now." Gloria Richardson talked of "revolution" and "civil war." Then, although she had promised to keep her rally away from the Wallace event, she led a march across Race Street and into confrontation with the National Guard. As she expected and desired, she was arrested.

As she waited to be carted off to detention, Stewart asked her if it would be unfair to write that her rally was as antiwhite as Wallace's had been antiblack. She replied that you had to "sense the mood of the people," to "get in front of them to lead them." But surely she knew that if it really came to a "civil war" between the races, the whites would win. "Yes," she replied. "Yes, I know." then she pressed her hands to her head and sighed, "Oh, God, I'm tired."

AS THE CAMPAIGN year of 1964 unfolded, Johnson held a firm grip on his party and appeared unbeatable in the November election. The economy was growing by a healthy 4 percent a year. Having pushed major Kennedy initiatives through Congress—the Civil Rights Act, a big tax cut—Johnson had demonstrated a zest for leadership and change, a quality the electorate clearly liked. And, despite a growing involvement in Vietnam, the country was still at peace—at least as close to peace as seemed reasonable during the Cold War.

By late spring it seemed clear that the Republican nomination would go to Arizona senator Barry Goldwater, a new-breed GOP conservative whose political philosophy was rooted in the New South and the emergent West. The brothers didn't care much for Goldwater, whose politics they considered harsh and exclusionary. They feared a Goldwater-led party would adopt a Southern strategy of race-dominated politics. Goldwater represented a sharp departure from the only brand of Republican politics the brothers could support—the old-fashioned, moderate, establishment strain that had emerged with the Oyster Bay Roosevelts at the turn of the century, that had been exemplified in the old *New York Herald Tribune*, and that now was represented by GOP liberals such as Nelson Rockefeller and Pennsylvania governor William Scranton, both of whom sought to wrest the nomination away from Goldwater.

But the GOP liberals, despite manners and money, could not change enough minds, and Goldwater captured the GOP nomination at the raucous convention in San Francisco's Cow Palace. The conservative hardliners fashioned a party platform that rejected nearly all positions but their own. They stripped from it the 1960 planks designed to placate liberals and organized labor. They crushed the civil rights plank offered by party moderates. They shouted down Nelson Rockefeller when he sought to address the convention. In a perceptive *Post* piece entitled "Can Goldwater Win?" Stewart suggested that Goldwater's Senate vote against the civil rights bill, coupled with the party's rejection of a mild civil rights plank, all but ensured that race would be an issue in the fall. Goldwater clearly was opting for a Southern strategy.

In the election, Johnson crushed Goldwater in a landslide of historic dimension, winning 61 percent of the popular vote to the Republican's 39 percent. Joe won a bet he had made with the president as they sat along Texas's Pedernales River during a lull in the campaign; Joe had bet that LBJ would win 60 percent of the vote or more, while Johnson modestly had bet against that possibility. "I am sure you will never find a happier debtor," wrote Lady Bird to Joe after the election. In his postelection column, Joe avoided flights of praise, instead warning the president against the kind of hubris that often follows such political victories. Stewart, less restrained, wrote, "We have a first-rate professional country-runner running our country." If Johnson could prove his mettle in foreign affairs as he had in domestic, added Stewart, he "could turn out to be a great president—perhaps, even, one of our greatest."

EVEN BEFORE THE votes were counted and Joe collected on his bet, however, the relationship between the Alsops and Johnson had begun to fray. The issue: Vietnam.

Johnson harbored powerful fears about Vietnam. He knew he couldn't walk away from that small country and its people after his own government's bloody-handed involvement, just weeks before he became president, in overthrowing their leader. Yet he sensed the danger of becoming entrapped in another Korea with all the attending overseas perils and ugly domestic ramifications. Throughout 1964, he remained determined to keep that distant conflict out of the campaign. He wanted to finesse the issue as long as he could.

But the Alsops feared disaster in Vietnam. "The time may be coming," Stewart had written in June, "when direct American military pressure on the communist side will be the only alternative to defeat in Southeast Asia." It was natural, he wrote, that the president would want to avoid the military options then under discussion, such as bombing raids and blockades against the North. These weren't likely to foster a palatable settlement, he wrote, and they could lead to "a lot of American soldiers fighting a very nasty war on the ground."

Joe wanted action. "The situation . . . is ghastly to the point of extreme danger," he wrote in May to a friend named Sol Sanders in New Delhi. "I should not be surprised to see us suffer a final defeat this summer, unless rather drastic counter-measures are taken pretty soon."

Joe traveled to Vietnam twice in 1964, in May and December, and he filed dire warnings each time. In between, he repeatedly sounded the tocsin for action. His penchant for directing his column as a spear toward Washington policymakers had never taken on a sharper point. He aimed the column directly at a single person, the man in the White House, whose ego and aspirations he knew so well. He knew that Johnson feared above all else the appearance of weakness, that the president desperately wanted to prove himself a man of greatness. Joe also knew that Johnson harbored deep insecurities about his humble Texas origins, manifest in his envy of the style and grace of the Kennedys and their Ivy League friends. Joe played upon all these impulses in pressing his case for U.S. military action in Vietnam:

> The United States world position will simply come apart at the seams if the president ducks the challenges in Vietnam, just as our world position would have come apart at the seams if President Kennedy had ducked the challenge of the Soviet missiles in Cuba. . . . A communist victory will be a gigantic American failure; and just as nothing succeeds like success, it is also a rule of history that nothing fails like failure.

A few months later Joe declared that Johnson's hopes of shoring up the Saigon regime through diplomatic efforts had "failed . . . irrevocably." Johnson, he said, faced "a harsh test indeed." In late November he wrote, "As President Truman did in China, President Johnson now faces a situation in which taking action will be bad politics now, whereas inaction will be worse politics later on." When Joe got word that Johnson contemplated no military intervention in Southeast Asia, he wrote:

> It must certainly be underlined that the catastrophe now being invited will also be remarkably unpleasant. For Lyndon B. Johnson, Vietnam is what the second Cuban crisis was for John F. Kennedy. If Mr. Johnson ducks the challenge, we shall learn by experience about what it would have been like if Kennedy had ducked the challenge in October 1962.

Throughout 1964, Johnson became increasingly miffed with these taunts. His first reaction was simply to nudge Joe playfully, a tactic he employed during an intimate White House dinner in June. The invitees were Joe and Susan Mary, the Clark Cliffords, and White House aide Jack Valenti and his wife. After dinner the four men took a walk around the South Lawn, enjoying the soft summer evening.

"Now, just what would you do in Vietnam, Joe?" asked the president. "You are always full of alarm and urgency, but now I want to hear from you exactly what you would do."

It was a subtle needle, but Joe, seemingly unaware of the president's playfulness, launched into a long disquisition on the complex problem, speaking the entire time in generalities. Then the president interrupted.

"Now, that's very fine, Joe, but what the hell would you do at nine a.m. tomorrow morning? Every time I ask one of you experts who write knowledgeably about all the problems a president has—what you would do—you always blow generalities in my face. You tell me we ought to be firm, but you don't tell me how. You tell me we should apply sanctions, but you don't tell me what."

The president laughed and turned to Clifford and Valenti.

"Joe reminds me of General de Gaulle," he said. "When de Gaulle talked about neutralization I said that is very fine. But when you asked him, 'What's your plan, General?' de Gaulle would always wave his hand and say: 'Don't bother me, those are just details.' "

The president laughed again, turned to Joe, and gave him a long, elaborate French military salute. Joe smiled wanly, not sure just how much the president had been putting him on. Then, according to Valenti, the columnist "did something unaccountably strange. He shut up."

But Joe didn't shut up in the column, and soon Johnson's playfulness turned to anger. "LBJ hated to be hedged in," recalled Valenti, "and Joe was pressuring him with the column persistently, like fingernails scratching on a blackboard." During Joe's December trip to Vietnam, a wire photo depicting Joe getting out of a marine helicopter made its way to Johnson's desk. The flight had been a routine military excursion, like those accorded to all reporters covering the war. Johnson flew into a rage to see a man he had come to regard as his journalistic nemesis riding in one of his helicopters.

"Look at that SOB Alsop," he demanded. "How the hell did he get aboard that military helicopter?" He turned to Valenti and roared, "You call McNamara and find out how that happened!"

Soon Joe began hearing rumors of the president's displeasure, and his White House invitations dried up. "I am told that my despondency has given rather bitter offense in some quarters," he wrote to Mac Bundy. Joe lamented the rift and missed his White House access, but he didn't spend much time fretting about it. "I hate to offend people I admire," he wrote to Bundy. "But in my trade the time to retire has come when you stop calling the turn the way you see it."

30

JOE AND VIETNAM

Trapped by the Force of Conviction

IN EARLY 1965, Joe Alsop found himself filled with sadness and nostalgia. The immediate cause was the death of Felix Frankfurter, the "little judge" of Joe's precocious youth of the 1930s, when he and the Frankfurters had tumbled into limousines with such luminaries as Ruth Gordon, Noël Coward, and Lillian Gish for nights on the town filled with wit and laughter.

Dean Acheson organized a memorial service at Frankfurter's apartment, and a hundred mourners crowded in to hear Paul Freund of Harvard read the section from *The Pilgrim's Progress* that speaks of the death of Mr. Valiant-for-Truth: "My sword I give to him that shall succeed me in my pilgrimage, and my courage and skill to him that can get it. My marks and scars I carry with me." A young rabbi gave a recital of the Kaddish, and the apartment was filled with elegiac music by a trio of singers.

President Johnson was there, along with all the members of the Supreme Court and scores of Frankfurter friends who were also Joe's friends—"a quite astonishing assemblage," as Joe wrote later to Jean Monnet in Paris. Mrs. Frankfurter, aged and ailing, was wheeled into the hall just before the service began, and she spoke to no one except the president. "Agonizingly enough," wrote Joe, she lost control just for a moment, at the very beginning.

The service filled Joe with what he described to Monnet as "an almost unbearable sense of contrast between the past and the present." It occurred to him that he had experienced three periods in Washington that could be called "heroic"—the era preceding World War II, the immediate postwar period, and the golden Kennedy years. He considered himself a lucky man to have witnessed those times as intimately as he did. "But it is still very painful to think about them now," he confessed.

To all outward appearance, Joe had every reason for contentment. He had a beautiful wife and two stepchildren he loved. He was at the top of his craft and enjoyed financial security. His professional life was filled with excitement. But Joe was not given to contentment.

His routines were well established after four years of marriage. He rose around seven thirty and took his breakfast in the garden room, amid the potted plants, while Susan Mary enjoyed the luxury of breakfast in bed. Over breakfast Joe attacked the newspapers, reading first *The Wall Street Journal*, then racing through the *Washington Post* and *New York Times* in search of fodder for the column. Miss Puff would arrive around nine thirty, and Joe would issue instructions on matters at hand—interviews to set up, travel plans to arrange, luncheons to organize. Then he would head out for a round of interviewing, or work the phones for two or three hours.

He usually had lunch at home with a source, sometimes in the company of a journalistic crony or two, such as Ben Bradlee, Phil Geyelin, or Rowland Evans. Usually Joe would drink a martini before lunch or wine during the meal. After lunch, if it were a deadline day, he would bat out the column. Otherwise he would head out for interviews. Often he would break away from his routine to speak with Susan Mary about their forthcoming social schedule or the seating arrangement for that evening's dinner. The couple dined with friends nearly every night, either at Dumbarton or out.

On weekends, with no column pressures, Joe would relax, taking Susan Mary to the country or on long walks through Georgetown. Often the couple would enjoy a more informal—but usually raucous—supper with Stewart and Tish. Susan Mary later recalled weekends as "family time"—and "quite heavenly."

There were idyllic moments in the lives of Joe and Susan Mary, but there were difficult ones too. Joe's feeling of being trapped in marriage would come over him with increasing frequency, and it would trigger outbursts and bullying directed at Susan Mary. Even in front of friends at dinner he would belittle her comments and observations, and suggest that she was boring the assemblage. This was in stark contrast to those wonderful days in Paris when Joe always seemed so proud of his old chum Susan Mary and so taken with her wit. It was as if he couldn't allow his wife to shine socially lest she diminish his own luminance.

But Joe's ambivalence about marriage was only part of what burdened his sensibility in these early days of 1965. He was becoming obsessed with Vietnam. For Joe, Vietnam was a test of the entire postwar foreign policy fashioned twenty years earlier as the cornerstone of American strength and world stability. In a column, he touted the so-called domino theory, noting communist insurgencies in Thailand, the Philippines, Indonesia, and Cambodia. The Chinese communists, he wrote, "are not merely hoping for an American defeat. They are . . . preparing to take advantage of it." To Richard Rovere of *The New Yorker* magazine, Joe suggested that a defeat in Vietnam would "poison our national life for a generation."

Joe's relationship with the Johnson administration continued to deteriorate as he pounded away at what he considered the president's complacency in the face of grave overseas danger. On February 17, Joe filed his strongest anti-Johnson column yet, calling the president's growing preoccupation with governmental secrecy "a presidential weakness so grave that it may well turn out . . . to be *the* presidential weakness." He attributed this to Johnson's obsession with his own image, which he considered "almost alarming to contemplate."

Such words stung at the White House. McGeorge Bundy stopped talking to Joe on policy matters, although he took pains to preserve their friendship. Joe wrote to say that Bundy's refusal to discuss Vietnam would harm the president far more than himself. Johnson's secretiveness and inaccessibility had stirred grumbling within the press corps, Joe wrote, and the anger likely would increase:

> Then a time will come when events render the president vulnerable on one flank or another. And when that time comes, large numbers of my colleagues will inevitably seize the opportunity to tear and rend him. I shall not be among the tearers and renders, I can promise you. But it all seems very wasteful and needless to me, particularly because the president could so easily have such extraordinarily good press relations.

Then, during the cold Vietnam night of February 7, 1965, a team of Vietcong commandos raided a detachment of American troops at Pleiku, killing 8 and wounding more than 100. They also destroyed ten U.S. helicopters used to direct patrols against communist infiltration routes. Johnson retaliated with a bombing raid against a North Vietnamese army camp sixty miles above the seventeenth parallel, which divided North and South Vietnam. Two weeks later, on March 2, Johnson ordered an air attack on a North Vietnamese ammunition depot and naval base, and a week later sent in 3,500 marine combat troops to guard the airfield at Danang. Privately, Johnson demonstrated even greater resolve, telling General William Westmoreland, Paul Harkins's successor as commander of U.S. forces in Vietnam, to "assume no limitations on funds, equipment, or personnel" in his mission to repel the communist insurgency. The U.S. troop buildup had begun.

On April 7, at Johns Hopkins University, Johnson delivered a major address on Vietnam, appealing to the North Vietnamese to accept his offer of "unconditional discussions" and participate in his grandiose plans for a huge Mekong development project akin to America's Tennessee Valley Authority. But he declared that America "will not be defeated . . . [or] withdraw." Hanoi denounced the speech as "full of lies and deceptions."

The lines were drawn, and Joe was pleased. The bombing initiative, he wrote on March 5, should dispel any suspicion that Johnson was willing to "subside by degrees into surrender." He called Johnson's address a "great speech."

Still, Joe's long and often bitter debate with Johnson had left him depressed, and even with the two men now in agreement on Vietnam, the wounds remained raw. He missed the Kennedy presidency and the grand Kennedy social whirl, and he couldn't get excited about the Johnson era. He continued his affectionate correspondence with Jackie, and the subject seemed always to come back to Jack. After the democratic convention the previous year, he described how he had lost composure in Alice Longworth's hotel suite when the testimonial movie about JFK had come on the air following the long ovation for Bobby. He was also stirred profoundly by a reminiscence of Jack by a writer named Eddie Folliard—"not brilliant, but so full of the love and sorrow of a simple-hearted man that it made me howl like a dog." She wrote back to thank him for his "sad and touching letter" and added that she too had been affected by the televised movie. "If there was only some hope or consolation. I should never have watched that convention film on television."

Joe expressed even greater emotion a month later. "The loss of the president . . . broke my life in half," he wrote Jackie. "While he was here, somehow, the sunlight gilded every distant hill, and one could hardly wait to get there, in order to see if it was as exciting as it promised to be. Now nothing seems worth doing." In November, on the first anniversary of Jack's death, Jackie took solace in her friendship with Joe. "This November all that's left is love—You help me by loving him too. . . . With my love dear Joe, Jackie."

And now, in early 1965, Joe found that seeing Jackie cheered him up as nothing else could. After she attended a lunch at Dumbarton, he wrote to say it was "perfect heaven to see you again. . . . I enjoyed lunch more than I've enjoyed anything in months." After lunching with Jackie and the Radziwills in New York three weeks later, he wrote another letter of affection, offering advice on a ticklish subject—whether Jackie should accept Johnson's offer of an ambassadorship. With everyone Johnson dealt with, Joe warned, he sought to "get something on them, or to put them under an obligation, or both." Jackie declined the offer.

Joe's preoccupation with the Kennedys stirred him to nurture his friendship with Bobby, who had won a Senate seat from New York in 1964. He wrote Bobby a long letter of advice, prefaced with expressions of embarrassment that he had succumbed to his "busybody tendencies."

He yielded to temptation, he said, only because he cared so much about Bobby's future: "Let me put it that if I can once again vote for a Kennedy for the presidency, it will mean more to me than any other political development I can think of."

Joe became concerned when he detected in Bobby a preoccupation with Lyndon Johnson's repeated efforts to humiliate the Kennedys. When Joe stopped by to interview Kennedy, the senator returned repeatedly to the subject.

"How much do I have to take?" he asked in exasperation.

The answer, said Joe in a letter to Kennedy written the next day, was that he didn't have to take "a damn thing"—didn't even have to give the man the time of day unless it suited his purposes. But it did suit his purposes, said Joe, to take all measures to avoid a breach with the president, or even any talk of friction between them.

"If the row happens," wrote Joe, "this is my written promise to be 100 percent on your side, in public and in private; but don't have it, please, for your own sake as well as for the sake of those who hope much for you."

Joe also advised Bobby on how he could achieve senatorial stature. Dismissing the media-savvy pols who got their names in the papers but never managed to shepherd a serious piece of legislation through the chamber, Joe cited great progressives like George Norris and Robert LaFollette, men intent on influencing colleagues and producing laws. Joe admonished Bobby to take on vast amounts of homework on key issues, particularly those of special importance to New York.

Bobby shouldn't indulge his interest in foreign policy, said Joe. After making a mark on domestic issues, Joe lectured, then Bobby could branch out into international issues. He concluded: "There—Polonius writing to Laertes couldn't have done worse. Forgive the letter of an old fool, who's at least an admiring fool."

Joe's own misgivings about Johnson led him to think wistfully about Harry Truman. He confessed to Dean Acheson that he hadn't appreciated Truman's dimensions during the Missourian's often-beleaguered presidency, and he proposed writing to the retired president to express his second thoughts. Acheson endorsed the idea, and Joe sent off a letter.

On advice of counsel—the very best that cannot be hired—I write this letter with some trepidation. I asked Dean Acheson whether it would merely strike you as ridiculously presumptuous or would please you. He said, very sensibly, that it might indeed strike you as presumptuous but that he thought it would also please you.

My purpose is simply to apologize for the inexperience and bad judgment which led me to underrate your leadership of our country while you were in office. When I look back now, I must say with greater opportunities for comparison, your years in the White

House seem to me a truly heroic period. Nowadays, I never lose a chance to say that in print. But I did not say it then, and that is why I think an apology is owed.

Truman responded warmly, saying Joe need not have worried about appearing presumptuous, and that he rebelled at the thought of "exacting an apology from anyone who has publicly disapproved of me"—particularly, he said, from someone of Joe's talents. "But," he added, "I warmly welcome your reassessment . . . and dare hope that it might be sustained by the ultimate judgment."

Joe couldn't help lamenting the passing of those heroic days as he headed off to Vietnam on May 10 to find disaster in the making. The very day he arrived the communists launched a series of attacks, overrunning Songbe, the Phuoc Long provincial capital, fifty miles north of Saigon. Later they destroyed two South Vietnamese battalions in central Vietnam and raided the South Vietnamese military headquarters at Dong Xoai and a nearby U.S. special forces camp. The South's best battalions were being systematically destroyed by Vietcong forces and by four North Vietnamese regular battalions that had crept into the country despite U.S. air attacks on their infiltration routes.

For the communists, events were unfolding according to the rulebook on guerrilla warfare of China's Mao Tse-tung and North Vietnam's leading general, Vo Nguyen Giap. The rulebook foresaw three stages of war: in the first, guerrilla units are formed, the countryside is destabilized, and the dragon's teeth are obscurely planted; in the second, hit-and-run guerrilla tactics disorient the defending army and destabilize the defending government; and in the third, more conventional forces are fielded for major engagements designed to scoop up victory. By spring 1965 the communists had in place sufficient "main force" elements for the decisive third phase. The U.S. aim was to thwart this third-phase thrust and force the communists back into the classic small-scale, long-term guerrilla warfare of the second stage.

In Washington it was becoming clear that the air campaign wasn't working and that a communist victory was at hand unless the United States sent in large contingents of ground troops. Westmoreland had requested a troop level of 180,000 by the end of the year, and predicted that another 100,000 would be necessary in 1966. Johnson's advisers were debating this request when Joe filed his first column from Saigon.

The column said Johnson's bombing campaign had had a large impact in bolstering the South's morale and busting the momentum of the North. This in turn greatly enhanced chances that South Vietnam's "able and astute political leader," Prime Minister Phan Huy Quat, could stabilize his government. If Washington would keep up the bombing, he wrote, morale in the South would be high and Quat could succeed.

It was a questionable piece, reflecting the dangers in Joe's growing inclination to use the column to influence policy. Instead of ferreting out facts and their meaning, as he had done with brilliance in his earlier days, he fashioned a rationale for the policy he favored. In truth, the bombing policy had not succeeded, and there was no reason to think it could have any impact on the fate of Quat, whose hapless government would crumble within the month.

Joe later contradicted his own words in a column from Danang, where a growing Marine contingent was establishing a large and well-equipped base camp. The tough U.S. troops were a welcome sight, he wrote, because "the outlook is very much more ominous, and the North Vietnamese intervention is very much more flagrant and massive, than anyone seems to imagine at home in America." Though the North had been surprised by Johnson's bombing attacks, he said, such surprises would hardly keep the enemy off balance for long. His assets were greater than was generally supposed.

Joe visited Pleiku, site of the famous commando raid the previous February, and from that beleaguered point the nature of the American challenge was clear. To the right were the jungle-clad mountains of the Annamese chain—solid Vietcong country. To the left were the jungles of Laos, sanctuary for thousands of communist troops. In between was the trough of the high plateau, through which ran Highway 14, the only artery running north through the populated rice fields, small farms, and jungle villages. A U.S. colonel named Theodore Metaxas pointed up the highway and sighed, "The VC can cut that road whenever and pretty nearly wherever they want to!"

Joe's Saigon reporting established a pattern that was to hold throughout the war. He spent abundant time with top American officials, both civilian and military, returning to the same sources repeatedly during his trip. He had dinner four times with Gordon Jorgenson, a top CIA man. He saw Ambassador Maxwell Taylor three times, including once for dinner. He dined and breakfasted with Westmoreland. And he carved out time for his reporter friends, particularly Keyes Beech of the *Chicago Daily News* and Sol Sanders of *U.S. News & World Report*. Joe felt special affection for Beech, a gnarled veteran of war and a tough-minded newsman who fit the profile of an adventurous foreign correspondent. He had fought as a marine in World War II, then had covered Korea, where he had befriended Joe and helped him through his first harrowing days as combat reporter.

Beech had a large apartment at Number 7 Dondat in Saigon, with cook and housekeeper, and every night his friends would gather there for dinner, large quantities of liquor, and spirited talk. Joe frequented Beech's place, knocking down Scotch and tossing his opinions around like spears.

When Cabot Lodge had been ambassador, Joe stayed at the embassy, but he enjoyed no such tribal relationship with the austere Maxwell Taylor, and so he took a suite at the seedy old Majestic Hotel, a relic of the French past where the top-floor restaurant offered stunning views of the city and barely edible renditions of French cuisine. All the waiters knew "Monsieur Alsop" as the man who handed out huge tips upon arrival, then expected unfailing service. "When Joe showed up, all the ancient servants appeared as if out of nowhere," recalled Frank Wisner, Jr., son of the Alsop brothers' CIA friend, who served a stint in Vietnam as a foreign-service officer. The concierge, known simply as "Mr. Ba," would brighten upon Joe's arrival. After getting his up-front tip, he would dote on Joe, bringing him his favorite soups, unpacking his suitcase, pressing his trousers.

Joe was back in Washington for only three months before he headed off once again for the war. By now Cabot Lodge was back as ambassador, and Joe stayed at the embassy for several nights—until Lodge grew tired of his excitable friend. Lodge took aside Barry Zorthian, who headed the Saigon USIA operation and dealt with the press corps.

"Take him off my hands, Barry," said Lodge. "Have him stay with you for a few days."

Zorthian always knew Joe's stays would be memorable. One evening he had dinner prepared for Joe and a Time-Life writer named Charles Murphy, a legendary world-beat reporter who, like Joe, was conservative in outlook and an establishment thinker. Zorthian thought the two would get along famously, but it turned out they had known each other for years and apparently had "some kind of history," as Zorthian put it years later.

Joe and Murphy got into a prolonged argument. After a couple of drinks, Joe suggested to the waiter that he simply bring in the bottle, and the discussion turned nasty.

"You're the epitome of the failed establishment," shouted Murphy.

"I salute the originality of your fascist mentality," retorted Joe.

Zorthian, who couldn't get a word in, finally went off to bed. When he got up the next morning his two guests were gone and the bottle was empty.

Whether Joe stayed at the embassy or with Zorthian, Lodge made sure he received special treatment. Lodge had a car dispatched to meet Joe at the airport, provided convenient transportation for him throughout the city, and gave dinners in Joe's honor. By this time Joe had also struck up friendships with Westmoreland and General William DePuy, the architect of Westmoreland's strategy of creating an American "killing machine" for a protracted war of attrition against the communists. The idea was to engage the enemy through "search and destroy missions" and kill communists until North Vietnam realized it couldn't win a main force confrontation. "We are going to stomp them to death," DePuy had said. "I don't know any other way."

Joe gave a lunch for DePuy early in his stay, then later spent a day with him in the field. He subsequently dined with him in Saigon and lunched with him twice. He also went with Westmoreland on a daylong excursion to survey the massive U.S. deployment. The first stop was

Cam Ranh Bay, once a bustling French port and now reawakening from a post-colonial period of sleepy quietude. A ten-thousand-foot airstrip had been carved out of the countryside, and an engineering group had just transformed a sandspit into a port capable of handling ten thousand tons of cargo a week. "You can get a lot done with a little Yankee ingenuity," said Westmoreland.

Later they touched down at An Khe, between the rich, populous coastal lowlands and the high plateau. The U.S. buildup was in full swing there, as Caribou transport helicopters landed every three minutes and deposited another thirty soldiers of the army's First Air Cavalry Division. The larger Chinook helicopters dropped off even more troops, and truck convoys snaked their way up Highway 19 with tons of supplies. Surveying the scene, Westmoreland remarked to Joe with obvious satisfaction, "Well, I think the balance is changing a bit in this particular part of Vietnam."

Amid such scenes and with men such as Westmoreland and DePuy, Joe suddenly felt the flush of optimism. This was going to work, he thought, just as it had worked in those other times when world stability and the American Century had been challenged by errant forces. At My Tho, in the northern Mekong Delta, he talked with a wiry, lean VC defector who had become disillusioned with the fighting and no longer felt his side was going to win. The man's revelations of diminishing peasant support for the Vietcong, punishing taxes imposed in VC-controlled areas, and greater VC training in "big unit" fighting, said Joe, proved that Giap's plans for a 1965 victory had been foiled.

His spirits high, Joe again visited with young Wisner, now working with two companions in My Tho. They were pacification officers, helping with internal refugees, village development, agricultural policy. They lived like peasants in a small house with a primitive kitchen, an even more primitive bathroom, and "every form of pollution known to man." Joe seemed to revel in the adventure of finding himself in such backward surroundings.

Joe's combat experiences weren't as intense as they had been in Korea, or in Vietnam during the French war, when he had marched at the company level. He was in his mid-fifties now, and less agile. But he regularly visited troops at the battalion level, and his bravery never was questioned. Once he was in a helicopter when the pilot spotted a unit of Vietcong nestled in zigzag trenches. He flew over as his gunners strafed them, and the helicopter took plenty of fire. From his precarious perch, Joe watched the whole thing "like a kid at an amusement park," as the pilot later described it.

"Oh, my word, I do believe we're receiving fire," Joe exclaimed with genteel wonderment.

Back in Saigon, Joe made the rounds of top U.S. and South Vietnamese officials, including the two young generals who had taken over the government, Prime Minister Nguyen Cao Ky and Chief of State Nguyen

Van Thieu. He also made the usual contact with Beech and Sanders, as well as with *The New Yorker*'s Hong Kong–based Robert Shaplen and Beech's *Sun-Times* colleague, Ray Coffey. But he generally stayed away from other Saigon reporters.

A vast generational rift had opened up within the press corps. On one side were the old-timers who viewed Vietnam in terms made familiar by their experiences in World War II and Korea. To them, the war was necessary and winnable. On the other side were the younger men who had concluded that this was a war like no other in the American experience, and that victory was unlikely at best and probably impossible. Their pessimism had been fueled by the fiery infighter John Paul Vann, an Army lieutenant colonel during the Kennedy years and now an AID pacification officer. Vann harbored contempt for army strategists such as Westmoreland and DePuy, whom he considered thickheaded and unimaginative. Their search-and-destroy strategy, reflected in their preoccupation with body counts, was doomed to failure, Vann believed. He favored assiduous pacification programs, greater efforts to bolster the South Vietnamese army, and more attention to fostering an effective and honest government in Saigon.

Vann also had contempt for Joe's reporting, and at one point refused to travel with him. Joe complained to the army brass, who asked Vann to relent. He did, but he remained wary of Alsop. "He gets everything wrong; he doesn't take notes; he screws up the works," Vann told another reporter.

Vann had powerful influence with the younger correspondents, beginning with David Halberstam, the controversial *New York Times* reporter whose dispatches had ruffled Joe back in 1963. Now his outlook could be seen in the dispatches of the *Times*'s Charles Mohr, Neil Sheehan, and R. W. Apple, *Newsweek*'s Merton Perry, and *The Washington Post*'s Ward Just. "Vann truly became the patron saint to those guys," recalled Ray Coffey later. Vann's friend Daniel Ellsberg, a member of General Harkins's pacification team, also served as a valued source for the younger reporters. "He was always leaking to these guys," recalled Coffey, "basically saying we couldn't win."

Most of these younger men despised Joe. They disliked his elitist ways, the special treatment he got when he swooped into the country, and his bold assertions on the war. They thought he had been seduced by military officers who didn't know what they were doing. Most of all, they resented his arrogance, his quickness to assail the motivations of those who disagreed with him. They could talk to Beech, whose views on the war they also disliked, and they could engage him without generating animosity; not so with Joe.

Joe despised most of the young reporters in equal measure. He saw his country at its most fearsome extremity since the Cuban Missile Crisis, and here were these influential reporters, barely dry behind the ears, filing endless stories that hurt the cause. Joe winced at seeing the country's leadership questioned and undermined in war; when he read the stories out of Vietnam he could hardly control his anger.

The lingering rift opened up like a gash on the head shortly after Joe's autumn Vietnam trip. The subject was the bloody November campaign in the remote Ia Drang Valley, where 234 Americans died in one four-day period. The First Air Cavalry had been sent in by helicopter to engage three North Vietnamese regiments and thwart a communist sweep toward the populated coast. The operation was meant to demonstrate the effectiveness of transport helicopters in jungle troop deployments. The Americans also launched devastating B-52 air strikes, thus proving that these huge bombers could be used effectively as tactical weapons in ground combat. Though vastly outnumbered, the Americans managed to extricate themselves with superior mobility and firepower.

Throughout the thirty-four-day campaign, 305 Americans were killed; but according to U.S. body counts, Americans annihilated 3,561 communist troops. This was encouraging news to Westmoreland and DePuy, whose strategic minds fastened upon the twelve-to-one kill ratio as proof that the war of attrition would work. With their highly mobile troops and precision-coordinated bombing, they would dispatch their killing machine and destroy the VC and North Vietnamese main force units. They would bleed the enemy to death.

Joe agreed. He was struck by the efficiency and bravery of Americans facing combat for the first time. "It is . . . something to wonder at," he wrote, "when these green troops take on numerical odds of at least seven to one, and . . . win such remarkable victories on the enemy's chosen terrain."

But after Ia Drang, the three bedraggled North Vietnamese regiments limped to safety across the border in Cambodia. U.S. field commanders wanted to pursue and destroy them, but Cambodia was off limits under Johnson's rules of engagement. Thus, America bestowed upon Giap the discretion of battle. He could engage when he was ready, and retreat when he was not.

Moreover, Hanoi drew lessons from Ia Drang that were the opposite of what America had intended to teach. Far from demoralizing North Vietnamese strategists, the battle had spawned confidence that they could outmaneuver the American killing machine if they would pay the requisite price in blood. And they would. As Giap and his lieutenants saw it, they had a strategy of "people's war." America had the tactics of helicopter warfare. Tactical thinking was no match for strategic thinking. They would not be bled to death; they would bleed the Americans to defeat.

Joe overlooked much of this. He became enraged when he read the news dispatches on Ia Drang, which concentrated on U.S. casualties and ignored the positive battlefield elements. He fired off a letter to James Reston, gray eminence of the *New York Times* Washington bureau, complaining in typically intemperate tones about Neil Sheehan's Ia Drang reports and his overall work. Reston sent a measured reply saying he agreed there had been too much emphasis on U.S. casualties, but he disagreed with Joe's general condemnation of Sheehan. "We are in for a bleak winter, so all the more reason to keep things in perspective," wrote Reston.

Joe wasn't satisfied. He wrote back to recount his own combat experiences in Korea and suggest that Sheehan should spend more time with the troops. The "disgraceful" *Times* coverage, concluded Joe, had missed "the heart of the news."

Maintaining his calm, Reston replied that they were talking about different things. The troops' performance was the heart of the news only if it supported Joe's estimate of the Westmoreland strategy. "You are dogmatic about that; I cannot be," wrote Reston, adding that he had always respected Joe's judgment and courage in such matters, but "for myself, I simply do not know, and frankly I am very skeptical." Perhaps, said Reston, the heart of the news was that the North Vietnamese were more willing to take their multiple losses of defeat than America was to take its one loss of victory. He added:

> Even if we were to base our policy on your confidence and boldness and risk all to save all—which is a policy but a policy Johnson will not follow—history and geography would still be against us and in the end this may be the "heart of the news."
>
> This, at least, is my nightmare. I cannot get over Paul Valéry's "Ultima Verba." I thought of it when you wrote of "victory": "Stop conqueror. . . . Pause at this lofty moment of victory. Be silent for a time and reflect on what to think at this pinnacle. . . . Whenever you re-live this day, may there never come into your mind these cruel words: 'What Was The Use?' " I do not question that we can and have won "victories," but in the end, I cannot believe, try as I do, that we will have a satisfactory answer to Valéry's terrible question.

The exchange crystallized the Vietnam debate with awesome force. Joe may have been right that there had been a victory at Ia Drang that the *Times* had not adequately explained. But Reston posed a pointed question when he asked what ultimate meaning that victory really had. Joe brushed aside the question. He had bought into the Westmoreland-DePuy thinking, and, having bought in, he would never sell out.

With the new year, Joe headed again for Vietnam, "like a very old dog returning to his vomit," as he put it to Philippe de Rothschild. By this time the routine was well established. He would stay with Lodge for as long as the ambassador would have him, spend a couple of nights with Barry Zorthian, then check into the Majestic. He would see the usual sources numerous times—Lodge, Westmoreland, DePuy, Jorgenson, Wisner, his journalist friends—and speak with dozens of others too. He would go out into the field to visit troops and survey battle scenes. He would enjoy the perquisites of his privileged station—embassy transportation, military helicopters, high-level military escorts into the field. He would drink heavily at lunch and dinner, and the drink would call forth his most unsavory blend of superiority and pugnacity.

Joe had developed a peculiar form of interviewing. He would pull out his notebook, position himself as if he were about to scribble away—and then lecture his source on the course and conduct of the war. "As a reporter, he didn't ask questions; his mind was made up," recalled Wisner, who accompanied Joe on numerous sessions with high-level officials. Over drinks one afternoon at the home of William Porter, Lodge's deputy ambassador, Joe nearly lost control. He stood up and stomped his feet.

"You've got it all wrong, Bill," he exclaimed. "You're doing it all wrong."

Porter laughed it off, as he usually did at such moments. Like many high-level diplomats, he had known Joe for years and knew there was no point in arguing.

Besides, for those planning and prosecuting the war, there was no more loyal and supportive newsman than Joe. Throughout his next Vietnam visit, in early 1966, Joe saw signs of American success. He reported that the famous 514th Vietcong Battalion, known as the "ever victorious," was "really in dreadful shape," beset by defeat, defection, and unpopularity in the villages. Using a growing flow of intelligence, wrote Joe, Westmoreland had foiled a major drive planned by the communists and mauled three regiments. The harvest-guarding operation in Phuoc Tuy had produced an enemy body count of six hundred—"the equivalent of another regiment knocked out of the ring." Westmoreland, wrote Joe, had every reason to thank God he was not General Giap.

Yet it was clear that Hanoi's strategy was to accept these defeats and continue bolstering its regular forces, putting ever more main force units into the field and upping the ante in blood and treasure. Joe took note of all this, writing on February 4 that the large infusion of North Vietnamese regulars had threatened to upset the entire balance of the war. The U.S. approach was working, he wrote, but it would be overwhelmed unless Johnson provided more manpower. The Joint Chiefs were preparing a request for a total of half a million troops by the end of 1967, and they assumed this would require a call-up of the military reserves.

Joe favored the call-up as an action that could push the overextended Ho Chi Minh to his breaking point. He didn't see that it also could push America to its own breaking point. In February 1966, during Joe's Vietnam visit, Democratic senator J. William Fulbright of Arkansas, chairman of the Foreign Relations Committee, convened a series of nationally televised hearings to question the president's policy. A group of fourteen senators urged Johnson to maintain the bombing pause he had ordered at year's end and to seek a negotiated settlement. Bobby Kennedy was hinting that he might break dramatically with the president over the war. And college campuses across the country were growing restive as the draft became a dark reality in the lives of nearly all young men. The American public continued to support the war effort, according to opinion polls, but Americans wanted victory and they didn't particularly want to pay a high price for it. The president's political position was precarious.

But Joe Alsop wasn't inclined to acknowledge political realities. His approach was to "risk all to save all," as James Reston had put it. Joe's March 2 column—entitled "The Untold Story: Victory?"—suggested that the U.S. killing machine had decimated the vast Vietcong infrastructure. With more American troops pouring into the country every week, this infrastructure soon would have to support as many as twenty communist main force divisions, double the communists' current troop level. It was too large a load, said Joe. The structure would crumble.

Two days later he attacked what he called "a very great newspaper's successive stories" on a recent American offensive against four target regiments of the enemy. Although Joe didn't name the newspaper, insiders knew it was *The New York Times*, and the stories—one by Neil Sheehan, the other by R. W. Apple, Jr.—reported on a coordinated military thrust involving 25,000 allied troops on the central Vietnamese coast. Sheehan had marched with the northern task force of marines, which had encountered little resistance and failed to engage the target battalions in any serious way. The army task force, in Binh Dinh province to the south, had mauled three battalions, while a fourth retreated with light losses. Although Sheehan noted the successes in Binh Dinh, his story emphasized the disappointment of U.S. commanders who had hoped for a larger kill than they had obtained.

Joe was enraged, and his anger turned hotter when he read the *Times* editorial page, which had become a leading voice of war opposition. An editorial suggested that the offensive proved that "the war cannot be won" and that any statement to the contrary was "deceptive." In his column Joe attacked the editorial as having "all but crowed over this report of failure of American troops in the field." Westmoreland himself, said Joe, had told him that two target regiments had suffered losses that would keep them out of the fighting for three months, and he subsequently learned that another had suffered a "complete collapse." Joe quoted Westmoreland's staff as calling the Binh Dinh campaign "the most successful combined operation to date," and he gave that description credence "unless Westmoreland's staff is playing ducks and drakes with the facts. And who is more likely to play ducks and drakes with the facts—reporters rather obviously reflecting the outspoken preconceptions of a great newspaper, or Gen. Westmoreland, who is one of the soberest and most brilliant field commanders in U.S. history?"

Joe's instinct for attack was taking over. For years he had avoided initiating public spats with news colleagues, but now he was going out of his way to suggest that the *Times* coverage stemmed from a base desire to follow the paper's editorial line. In his attack Joe failed to note that the Binh Dinh fighting had been part of a broader offensive whose overall results had not matched its objective. Sheehan and Apple had placed the Binh Dinh fighting into a broader context. Moreover, some of the statistics Joe used to bolster his arguments couldn't withstand scrutiny.

Sydney Gruson, a *Times* editor, responded to the column by writing to Joe and enclosing a spirited defense by Sheehan, "not to get into an argument with you," as Gruson wrote, but to show that "we do not have to report to reflect the paper's editorial policy." Joe dismissed Gruson and Sheehan. "Nonsense," he wrote to Gruson, taking particular exception to Sheehan's suggestion that his reporting directly contradicted what Westmoreland had told Joe. "I do not believe that it is respectable reportorial practice to call a man in Westmoreland's shoes a liar—and that, of course, is the net of what Sheehan did."

Joe took delight in having "fluttered the dovecotes," as he put it to Isaiah Berlin; but the Vietnam controversy was beginning to take a toll on him. "I cannot tell you how isolated and suddenly out of fashion I feel," he wrote. "The old way of looking at the world in this country . . . is now increasingly outmoded."

Perhaps, Joe suggested to Berlin, his feelings were merely a product of his being "bone tired and sick to death of Lyndon Johnson's Washington." But it was more than that. The Vietnam nightmare had spawned a new political phenomenon—liberal isolationism. Throughout his career, Joe had taken joy in his fight against isolationism—but it had always been a conservative movement emanating primarily from the Midwest of Colonel McCormick's *Chicago Tribune* and Ohio's Senator Robert Taft. These were welcome foes. Joe's own region, the Northeast, had been a bastion of internationalism throughout his life, and the nation's intellectual classes had generally supported the internationalist outlook. Now the editorial board of the Northeast's leading newspaper, and the nation's, had turned against the internationalist cause as reflected in the Vietnam venture. And the intelligentsia had turned ferociously against the war. The nation's campuses had become hotbeds of opposition. The fault lines of political discourse were shifting, and Joe didn't like it.

But these changes couldn't affect his view of the world or of the war. He dismissed his friends who tried to warn him that he courted embarrassment with his predictions of early victory. One was Robert Shaplen of *The New Yorker*, an old-timer who viewed the world much as Joe did. "You are more optimistic than I am," Shaplen wrote to Joe. He felt Joe was underestimating the resiliency of the Vietcong. True, they had been hurt in some places, and the Westmoreland strategy seemed to be the right approach. But victory would require more time than Joe thought, and more resources than Johnson likely would invest.

The mushrooming American bureaucracy in Vietnam, Shaplen argued, was turning the effort into a gigantic Yankee construction project, spawning corruption and undermining the legitimacy of the Saigon government. "Let us say that the role Westy envisages for the Allied forces . . . might, if the Viets can seize the follow-up opportunity, pave the way for a true comeback in the countryside," wrote Shaplen. "I don't, I'm afraid, Joe, yet see the proper application of will and effort on the part of the Vietnamese to meet this challenge." Joe ignored Shaplen's counsel.

Meanwhile, for Johnson, the war's strain on domestic politics was reaching ominous levels. The president's standing in opinion polls was dropping steadily. The American body count had reached into the hundreds every week. The president's growing political weakness found stark expression in the off-year election campaign, when Bobby Kennedy emerged as an irrepressible political force, and a clear threat to Johnson within the Democratic Party.

When the votes were counted on election night, the president's party lost forty-seven seats in the House of Representatives. It was a serious blow to the Democrats and a clear reflection of Johnson's growing weakness.

In late January 1967, Joe received a letter from Bill DePuy saying U.S. forces had completed an operation that DePuy considered "THE turning point in the war." They had destroyed the communists' positions around Saigon, had killed a thousand enemy troops, and taken 388 prisoners. "I suggest you drop everything . . . and get on the first airplane to Saigon," wrote DePuy. "The documentation, the interrogations, the implications . . . constitute the biggest story out of Vietnam since the US entered this arena. This is entirely consistent with what you have been saying." Joe promptly made plans for still another visit to Vietnam.

Meanwhile, the war continued to dominate Joe's life, defining his outlook and his relations with others, taking an ever greater toll on his friendships. In a January 16 column he attacked his old friend Arthur Schlesinger for opposing the war in a book called *The Bitter Heritage*. He called the book "silly" and "a piece of partisan pamphleteering . . . deceptively dressed up as a serious intellectual production." Joe dismissed Schlesinger as a holdover Adlai Stevenson cultist. The column led to a blunt exchange of letters between the two old friends.

A month later, Joe reluctantly criticized Kennedy after the senator had delivered a Chicago speech debunking the Johnson administration's view of the Asian challenge. Kennedy, he wrote, was becoming a cult hero to the Democratic Party's old Stevensonian wing of liberal intellectuals. No doubt Kennedy would enjoy the "privileges and pleasures" of being a cult hero, wrote Joe. He might even get the Democratic presidential nomination one day. "But he cannot seriously hope to reach the White House, for this kind of cult hero can never command a national majority."

Joe didn't enjoy writing the column, but he wanted to coax Bobby away from his party's liberal wing. He sent the senator a courtesy letter informing him of the column's imminent appearance:

> I've just . . . sent off a column which will give you no pleasure at all, although I must confess that I used a restraint which I should have used for no other man in present American political [life]—or in past political life either, except your brother—who had made such a speech as you made in Chicago. I write you now to say, quite simply, that I wrestled with myself a long time before writing such a column—the first moderately critical word I have written about any Kennedy since your father's return from London a thousand years ago. I finally concluded that in honesty, I could not keep silence.
>
> Because I still care more for your future than that of any other man in public life, because indeed you're the only one for whose future I give a damn, I hope you will understand what I've done, even if you don't enjoy it.

As Joe saw it, the country was threatening to rise up and destroy the Johnson Vietnam strategy, if not the president himself, at just the moment when victory seemed to Joe to be practically in hand. The big Time-Life media empire, now without its guiding spirit, Henry Luce, who had died earlier in the year, dramatically turned against the war. Plans were under way among the nation's youth for a massive "march on the Pentagon" in the fall. Joe's own niece, Stewart's daughter Fuff, planned to participate. And an opinion survey reported that 46 percent of the public considered the Vietnam commitment a "mistake," while 44 percent still supported the war.

Joe's frustration at such developments now showed up more and more in his behavior. At social gatherings he was even more belligerent than usual, dominating the conversation and assailing those who didn't agree with him. At the Hong Kong home of diplomat Heyward Isham he got drunk and argued bitterly with Annette Karnow, wife of Stanley Karnow, a leading Asian correspondent. Joe became increasingly strident as Karnow declined to retreat from her view that the Saigon government would collapse without U.S. support. At last he thrust his face toward hers.

"Balls, madame," he shouted. "Balls, madame." Others at the dinner grabbed Joe and escorted him away.

Although such behavior harmed Joe's reputation, the social elite stuck by him. Stanley Karnow, in Washington during the mid-1960s, was invited to Polly Wisner's for dinner, and Joe was there being his usual indelicate self. As they were leaving the table, Polly looked over at Joe and then turned to Karnow.

"Can't Joe be insufferable?" she asked.

"Yeah," replied Karnow, who then asked what seemed to him a natural question. "Why do you invite him?"

Polly looked at Karnow in horror, as if he had just asked why she didn't sell her children into slavery. "Suddenly I was the one who was seen as obnoxious," Karnow recalled years later; class solidarity, he noted, still reigned among such people in those days.

And among such people there was sympathy for Joe. They knew his behavior was a product of the Vietnam agony, as well as the changes then being visited upon America. The assault on authority, the flouting of convention, the loosening of sexual mores, the drug culture, postmodernism in the arts—these all left Joe feeling disoriented. "I cannot understand what is happening to America any longer, perhaps because I have finally become an old codger, frozen in the viewpoints of the past," he wrote to Isaiah Berlin. "The pleasures the young enjoy nowadays seem strikingly unpleasurable to me. The work of the younger artists and writers strikes me as thoroughly ridiculous or boring. . . . And the chatter of the so-called intellectuals has begun to drive me mad with fury."

Still, he kept telling himself that all would be well if the Vietnam victory he and DePuy foresaw would just materialize. He traveled to the war twice in 1967, seeing the usual sources and filing the usual stories. His columns from the second trip, in September and October, gushed with optimism, reflecting the rosy outlook of Westmoreland and DePuy.

But storm clouds of war opposition were gathering despite Joe's best efforts. Only the president could turn away the storm, Joe reasoned; he wanted Johnson to make a strong statement assuring the American people that victory was possible. Joe and the president had rekindled their friendship as their views on Vietnam had converged. Following his autumn trip to Vietnam, Joe posed the idea of a statement to the president. Intrigued, Johnson suggested that Joe work on the idea with his new national security adviser, Walt Rostow.

In early November Joe drafted a five-page, double-spaced statement encapsulating his basic view of the war—and that of the president. It outlined Hanoi's momentous decision to move to big-unit warfare after America had sent in ground troops in 1965. It revealed that North Vietnam had sought to maneuver American troops into position for a battlefield defeat that would "paralyze the United States with fear and dismay." It accused the communists of pursuing sham negotiations during which they would step up their offensive in hopes of a complete takeover of the South. It declared that captured enemy documents showed conclusively that Hanoi was losing the big-unit war. Hence the president would reject the growing chorus for a new bombing pause to foster a negotiated settlement.

Joe sent the statement to the White House, where it quickly got sucked into the maw of bureaucratic haggling and reemerged as a mush of bland statements and observations. Joe wrote the president to plead for the original concept of a forceful statement designed to make news and sway the public. "I must tell you in all frankness that the new draft seems to me just about worthless," he wrote, adding that unless Johnson managed to change the tone and direction of the Vietnam debate, the clamor for a bombing pause and negotiations would grow.

Joe managed to get the statement restored to something near his initial idea, but the president, embroiled in an internal debate stimulated by Robert McNamara's growing doubts on the war, never issued it. The country's leading optimist on Vietnam continued to be Joe Alsop, not Lyndon Johnson. "The enemy," he wrote, "has at last been driven to grope, with some urgency and in a quite new manner, for an easy way out of the bind in Vietnam, which is getting tighter and tighter."

JOE WAS RIGHT, but he was also wrong—and his perceptions, right and wrong, soon would be engulfed by events. Later assessments would show that he was right that Hanoi and the communists were in a bind, that the effectiveness of American firepower and mobility had devastated the Vietcong guerrilla efforts and main force elements. What's more, the war in the countryside had forced nearly a million South Vietnamese peasants into the cities, drying up the source of food, shelter, soldiers, and revenues the communists had relied upon for years. Facing hardship, Vietcong soldiers had deserted in growing numbers. The result was that Hanoi was forced to send more and more North Vietnamese troops into the South, and to blend these inexperienced soldiers with the depleted Vietcong units. Seldom did these mixed units perform effectively.

Joe was also right that Hanoi's military architects understood the difficulties they now faced, understood that they would have to change course. A bold new effort would be needed to shake off this persistent killing machine that Westmoreland and DePuy had created in the South. Otherwise, the communists would have to revert to less decisive guerrilla tactics, as Joe had foreseen.

But this simply wasn't as important as Joe had supposed. Hanoi had enough manpower to carry on the war at existing or even higher levels for a long time. In North Vietnam, 200,000 young men reached the age of eighteen each year, with 100,000 being inducted. Already Hanoi had planned to increase its mobilization by close to 100,000 troops to blunt any U.S. plans for an invasion. Joe was wrong in thinking that Hanoi had reached its manpower breaking point.

Meanwhile, the United States was nearing its own breaking point. Even before the U.S. buildup had reached 470,000 troops toward the end of 1967, Westmoreland was saying privately that another 80,000 would be necessary to bring the enemy to heel within five years. To end the war within three years would have required yet another 118,000 troops, or a total of nearly 670,000. This was politically impossible. Before year's end Johnson had authorized another 55,000 troops, for a total of 525,000, and already the political forces arrayed against the war were reaching dangerous proportions.

The problem was summed up by Democratic representative Thomas P. "Tip" O'Neil of Massachusetts, a longtime Johnson ally, who said, "We are dropping $20,000 bombs every time somebody thinks he sees four Vietcong in a bush. And it isn't working." That perception was taking hold in Congress and in the country. In Congress, McNamara had given testimony before an Armed Services subcommittee that had confounded those who still hoped for victory through Johnson's strategy. Erstwhile war supporters such as senators Stuart Symington, Strom Thurmond, Henry Jackson, and Howard Cannon now raised urgent questions about the apparent quagmire.

It was the same throughout America and in Vietnam itself. Joe's friend Keyes Beech, whose outlook so closely matched Alsop's, nevertheless saw with dismay the dislocations wrought by the American presence and buildup, and their corrosive effects on South Vietnamese society. Beech recognized that the South Vietnamese Army lacked the will to fight. And he saw how the bitter political battle at home was devastating the morale of U.S. troops, who were turning increasingly to drugs and becoming surly to their officers.

Joe had missed much of the significance of all this, had sifted and sorted evidence to support what he wanted to believe and to influence those he considered most in need of belief. His approach to the column since Stewart's departure—the preoccupation with impact, the determination to affect the course of events—had entrapped him, had shrouded fundamental realities from his view. His belief in the Vietnam War as the logical and righteous extension of America's postwar vision and destiny had ensured that he could not escape the trap his deepest convictions had set for him.

31

STEWART AND VIETNAM

"Like a Tethered Goat at a Tiger Shoot"

ON A FALL weekend in the late 1960s, Elizabeth Alsop came home to
Washington from Sarah Lawrence College to join one of the big antiwar
demonstrations that were becoming a regular part of everyday life in the
nation's capital. She brought three classmates with her, and the four students added their voices to those of hundreds of thousands of others
who were chanting, marching, waving placards, bringing into focus for
network television the depth and force of the antiwar movement in
America. They all spent the weekend at Springland Lane.

Stewart had an intense interest in the emotions and thinking behind
the demonstration, and he saw in this quartet of protesters a good opportunity to educate himself. At one point, while the four young women
gathered around the living room fireplace, he took his normal place in
his big easy chair, sipped a bourbon, and engaged the youngsters in
conversation.

"So, why are you down here?" he asked.

When they poured forth their emotional opposition to the war, he
probed and nudged, forcing them to explain their thoughts and feelings.

"Why do you think that?" he would ask, then request specific recommendations on what course of action they thought the president
should pursue. When they said he should simply pull out the troops, he
queried them closely on the consequences of such a course for South
Vietnam and for U.S. foreign policy. He listened intently when they
spoke; he never interrupted. "He didn't suggest the demonstration was

wrong," recalled Elizabeth, "though he certainly thought it was. He argued a bit, but it was never patronizing."

Elizabeth took care to keep her friends away from Uncle Joe that weekend. "I knew he probably would have told them they were traitors to their country," she said years later.

For Elizabeth, imbued with the idealism of the young that fueled so much of the antiwar fervor, discussing the issue with Joe was frustrating and sometimes distasteful. He made her feel stupid, as he railed on about all the secret documents he had seen that proved him right.

"You haven't seen the secret documents," he would say. "You couldn't possibly know what you are talking about."

"But, Uncle Joe," she protested at one point. "99.9 percent of the American people haven't seen the secret documents. Does that mean they have no right to an opinion?"

"Sure they do," he retorted. "But the opinion will be wrong."

From the beginning of Lyndon Johnson's troop buildup in 1965, Stewart's approach to the war differed markedly from that of his brother. Stewart remained detached, analytical, and skeptical.

It wasn't that he questioned the policy of protecting South Vietnam or the government's willingness to expend American blood in the cause. To him, as to Joe and nearly the entire foreign-policy establishment, it was unthinkable to abandon this little client state to Asian communism. Years later it would become fashionable to view the Vietnam adventure as a policy aberration, a national tragedy that could have been avoided if America's leaders had simply seen clearly enough to avoid the commitment entirely. But this would ignore the central reality of U.S. involvement in Vietnam—that it was a natural, and hence probably inevitable, extension of the American global policy established at the dawn of the postwar era.

This postwar American vision had generated powerful political currents in the country. As much as Lyndon Johnson wanted to avoid the dangers of a growing U.S. involvement in Vietnam, he knew that it would be equally dangerous to him politically to allow any new march of communism anywhere in the world. The country would not accept that. If Vietnam constituted a geopolitical trap, the trap had been set twenty years earlier, at the end of World War II.

Stewart was more aware of the trap than Joe. In February 1965, at the dawn of the buildup, he produced a *Saturday Evening Post* column entitled "What's Wrong with Our Army?" The answer: It was top-heavy, sluggish and flabby.

There were 60,000 men in uniform for each of the sixteen combat divisions of around 13,000 men, Stewart observed—a ratio double that of the Soviet Red Army "or any other serious Army in the world." There were too many officers—5,000 full colonels, and jobs for fewer than 200 of them in combat units; 35,000 field-grade officers—major and up—and jobs in combat units for fewer than a tenth of them. With so few actual combat and command jobs, pressures arose to create head-quarters and staff jobs so that high-ranking officers could have "slots" and careers.

This "luxuriant blooming of the Army bureaucracy," wrote Stewart, was all too evident in Vietnam, where a dozen generals commanded 22,000 men and most of the military men had nothing to do with fighting.

Disaster has its uses, wrote Stewart, and perhaps the threatened disaster in Vietnam would lead to a hard new look at the way the army was run. "For it seems reasonable to suspect that the way our Army is run has had something to do with the threatened disaster."

It was a valuable critique—and the kind of thoughtful reporting that Joe seldom did. Dazzled by military idealism, Joe had no inclination to trash the American army or identify its shortcomings. The fact that it was his own country's army, out on the frontiers of the Cold War, was sufficient to ensure his devotion and support. Stewart harbored no such romanticism.

Stewart also was early to question whether the president was up to the Vietnam challenge. Washington, he wrote to the *Saturday Evening Post*'s Bob Johnson in early 1965, had become obsessed with Lyndon. Everyone in town had his own favorite LBJ story, including at least one scatological term attributed to the president. Johnson would toss off such vulgarisms as, "He don't know enough to pour piss out of a boot," or "Even a farm girl knows what's happenin' when she's gettin' it up there."

People were genuinely terrified of the man. Raw FBI files on Washington's leading players were Johnson's favorite bedtime reading (including the FBI file on Joe's unfortunate Moscow episode of eight years earlier). And he unfurled nasty attacks on subordinates in the presence of their colleagues.

The president's weaknesses were all too evident—his habit of equating honest dissent with "subversion," his obsession with secrecy, his vulgarisms. Johnson's "urge to manage the unmanageable," said Stewart, "may be his downfall."

Stewart laid bare the president's weaknesses in an anecdote recounted for *Post* readers in March. At a foreign policy briefing, the president, after listening while his advisers catalogued world trouble spots, exploded in a Johnsonian monologue. Perhaps, he said, this country had been "listening too much to our own propaganda about being leader of the free world." Perhaps it had been too easy for tinpot dictators to blackmail us by saying, "Pay me or I'll go communist." Maybe it was time to "let some people sweat a bit—let them go right up to the end of that street and see what happens." Maybe it was time we let the other side have a try at running the world—"get their libraries burned and their people eaten in the Congo."

Stewart suggested that this remarkable outburst reflected a changed mood not just in Johnson but also in the nation. It wasn't quite isolationism of the prewar stripe, he wrote; but the mood of the country was more "inner-directed" than it had been since World War II. The Eighty-ninth Congress, brought forth by the voters in 1964, was the most liberal domestically and the "least global-minded" since the Marshall Plan. There was growing frustration over the price of America's global commitments, and it was natural that the president would share that frustration. Stewart, viewing all this from his Cold War perspective, declared that the president's primary task was to prevent any unfavorable alteration in the world power balance.

In early 1965, Stewart departed Washington for his first visit to South Vietnam, where he traveled throughout the country in an army helicopter manned by two sergeants with machine guns constantly at the ready. Interviewing soldiers in the field and big shots in Saigon, he discovered many of the same verities seen by Joe in these early months of the U.S. buildup—a U.S. Army filled with martial enthusiasm, a beleaguered Vietcong increasingly bolstered by North Vietnamese troops, military complexities that would severely test American resolve.

At an army prison camp near Saigon he encountered a North Vietnamese private named Nguyen Van Thant, who had been captured a week earlier. Looking intently at this thin warrior, Stewart could see the fear of death still written on his young face. Stewart talked to him in a spare interrogation room decorated with signs in Vietnamese that read: THOSE WHO ARE TRUTHFUL WILL BE WELL TREATED. THOSE WHO LIE WILL BE SEVERELY PUNISHED. Nguyen had been drafted into the North Vietnamese army two years earlier at age seventeen and had infiltrated into the South with 450 other regulars. The trek had been brutal; all he had had to eat was a little rice and dried fish. By the time he arrived he was sick, and soon captured. Stewart asked why he was there.

"We were told that we must fight to liberate our southern brothers," he replied through an interpreter.

Did he think the communists would win the war?

"I do not know, but I do not think so. The Vietcong are very frightened of the helicopters and the armored cars."

After talking with Nguyen, Stewart concluded that he was telling the truth. He seemed to be a victim of historical forces beyond his comprehension; but he also represented a reason why a small war was becoming a much more dangerous war. The infiltration of North Vietnamese soldiers such as Nguyen, some ten thousand of them by the latest estimates, had upset the delicate power balance between the Vietcong and the South Vietnamese army. The war in the South could not possibly be won now without direct U.S. intervention.

That intervention was personified by Captain Robert Alhouse of Brooklyn, adviser to a South Vietnamese major charged with defending the town of Phu Hoa Dong, about half an hour's helicopter ride from

Saigon. The town had been cleared of Vietcong, but the enemy wasn't far away, as Stewart learned when Alhouse escorted him and a group of other reporters to the edge of town. A rifle shot rang out from less than a hundred yards away, and a bullet whizzed over their heads. The group huddled behind a "very large and very useful tree," and Alhouse instructed them to walk back at five-yard intervals "to avoid . . . presenting an inviting target." The experience seemed routine to Alhouse, who said he got shot at pretty much every day. "That's what I get my $55 extra combat pay for," he said.

Alhouse had developed a strong sense of protectiveness for his little town, where the children crawled over him like ants. To Stewart, he represented the best of the U.S. military—dedicated young men offering compassion and Western expertise in a just cause. As long as the supply of Captain Alhouses did not run out and the will of the U.S. government did not falter, reasoned Stewart, the war could be lost only through "the disintegration of Vietnam's will to fight."

As for the Vietnamese army, Stewart was disarmingly upbeat. He encountered a number of tough, dedicated officers like a Colonel Banh, who commanded a beleaguered Vietnamese regiment in Darlac Province, north of Saigon. How long, asked Stewart, could the South Vietnamese army hold on?

"Not forever," replied the colonel, "but longer than you Americans think." He added, "If we are not betrayed, we can fight for a long time." At the threatened provincial town of Ban Me Thuout, Stewart asked a sergeant named Thomas Alfinito to describe the South Vietnamese soldiers.

"Damn good fighters and damn fine men," he replied.

Stewart approvingly reported Alfinito's answer to his readers, and added:

> The honor of the United States has been committed by three presidents to the proposition that those "damn fine men" who have fought the communists so long and so bloodily—as well as the children who crawl like ants over Captain Alhouse—shall not become subjects of the communist empire. It is impossible to see at all clearly how this war might be won. But, whatever the cost, we cannot permit it to be lost—not unless the United States is willing to accept dishonor as well as defeat.

A month later, Stewart wrote another column in support of the military thinking behind the American war effort. U.S. mobility and firepower, he said, would have rendered a Vietcong defeat inevitable, had it not been for the infiltration of the North Vietnamese army, now up to forty thousand strong in the South. That was why Johnson had decided to bomb the North—to force the North Vietnamese to pay a price for their intervention. "If the price is high enough, they may halt the aggression," he wrote. "In that case, . . . the supposedly unwinnable war in Vietnam might be won."

It didn't take long for Stewart to see cracks in his early reasoning. Making the rounds of his sources in defense and foreign-policy circles, he asked how they saw the war ultimately ending. Would there be a conference, with Ho Chi Minh promising not to do what he had never admitted doing—supply the Vietcong with men and arms? Well, no, they replied. Then how? The answers always struck Stewart as "fuzzy in the extreme," as he put it in a radio commentary. "The fact is," he told his listeners, "that short of some sort of concealed surrender to the communist side, the best we can do is to hang on and hope for a break."

By summer of 1965, the peril of Johnson's troop buildup was clear, and Stewart was talking of quagmire. "We might as well face the fact that this small war could turn out to be at least as nasty as the Korean War [or] in some ways . . . a lot nastier," he said in a radio broadcast.

In a September column, he identified the soft underside of the American strategy. He recounted a conversation he had had with an unnamed U.S. general during his February visit to Vietnam, just after Johnson's bombing campaign had begun. He had asked about the results of the bombing, and the general had replied that there was a chance the bombing would convince the North that it couldn't win the war at an acceptable price, and hence it might lead to a negotiated settlement on American terms. But there was an equal chance, the general had said, that the North would respond by sending ever more troops south to aid the Vietcong.

"That would require a large American troop commitment," Stewart had said. "How do you see those troops being used?"

The general had walked over to a wall map of Vietnam. The answer would depend, he had said, on the objective. If it were simply to hang on in South Vietnam, the United States might create strongholds here and there in the South. But it wasn't likely, he had added, that the war could be won with a static defense. Few wars in history had ever been won with such a strategy.

"If you wanted to *win*—" the general had begun, his hand hovering over the map somewhere between the eighteenth and nineteenth parallels; "If you wanted to *win* this war—" Then he had dropped his hand, returned to his desk, and become "briskly uncommunicative."

Stewart noticed that the general's hand had hovered over the narrowest part of North Vietnam, where the long tail of Laos between Vietnam and Thailand was at its narrowest as well. If the United States really wanted to win the war, Stewart elaborated, then it probably would have to use its naval and air superiority to cut off the North Vietnamese invasion—probably with an amphibious operation like the Inchon landing in Korea.

All wars, wrote Stewart, generate their own logic, and the logic of

Vietnam now made clear that it had become what presidents Eisenhower, Kennedy, and Johnson had all passionately hoped to avoid—an American land war in Asia. "The only way to stop the awful logic of war," wrote Stewart, "is to stop the war." But the war could not be stopped unless the North Vietnamese believed the consequences of the war "may be even more terrible for their side than for our side."

It was going to be difficult to persuade them, as Stewart foresaw, with an American strategy based on defense. Even before Westmoreland's search-and-destroy approach had become discernible, Stewart could see that such a body-count strategy was likely to lead to disaster.

Stewart was also quick to perceive that the American people had been dangerously oversold on the value of air power. "Wars," he wrote, "are won bloodily, on the ground, not cleanly, in the air." The widely held view that U.S. air supremacy could bring the North to heel was an illusion that threatened the Johnson presidency. Hundreds of interviews conducted by Stewart and pollster Oliver Quayle showed a widespread feeling that Johnson was "indecisive" and "wishy-washy" in his handling of the war. The interviews and Quayle's polling showed clearly that the American people supported the war, but they wanted it prosecuted with vigor. "It has just not occurred to most Americans that the United States could really be forced to throw in the sponge by a comparative handful of Asian guerrilla fighters," he wrote.

Perhaps that was an illusion, too, added Stewart, but it suggested that the North Vietnamese may also have miscalculated in thinking they could break the American spirit as they had that of the French a decade earlier. With both sides nursing their illusions, the danger was that they would "stumble deeper and deeper into a more and more lethal war."

Though absorbed by Vietnam, Stewart still found time to indulge his interest in the American domestic scene. He traveled to Watts in Los Angeles two months after that black enclave erupted in a spasm of rioting that left 34 dead, 1,032 injured, and property worth nearly $40 million in rubble. The riot had shaken America and pierced the national consciousness with a recognition that underlying all of the efforts to improve race relations was a sump of rage that could threaten the nation's foundations.

Stewart and his guide for the day, Associated Press reporter Andy Jaffe, parked their car across the street from a group of young black men around a bench in front of a shoeshine shop. As they approached, Stewart asked if there was going to be another riot.

"You damn right there's gonna be another riot," said a light-skinned black in dark glasses. "Next time all the depressed people all over the country will be united, and we'll have guns, and we'll get what we want."

"What do you want?" asked Stewart.

"The first thing we want is we'll kill every goddam white capitalist—starting with *Mister* Lyndon Johnson." The words, wrote Stewart later, were as "shocking as a pistol shot in a quiet house."

Stewart drew aside a quiet young black man dressed in a business suit. He was a social worker with two years of college, and Stewart asked if the expressions he had just heard were typical of sentiment among the young in Watts or perhaps merely an attempt to shock white folks. No, said the man quietly, most people in Watts talked that way and thought that way. Stewart asked if he also anticipated another riot.

Yes, he said, there would be another riot, but different. "Next time both sides will have guns. If I see you and you see me, it's just gonna depend on who shoots first." His tone, wrote Stewart, "was one of friendly warning, not of threat." At this point, Stewart added, "I began to understand the depth of the bitterness of the young men of Watts, and the width of the gulf that separates these young men from the secure and comfortable life that most white Americans live."

After talking to dozens of people in Watts—the local black newspaper editor, white police officers, a white social worker, local businessmen, juvenile delinquents—Stewart left with the feeling that the race problem in America was "wholly insoluble . . . like some incurable disease, with which both whites and Negroes must learn to live in pain all the days of our lives."

THE SATURDAY EVENING POST, with its 6.5 million subscribers and newsstand purchasers, still provided Stewart with a fine forum for his special brand of expository writing. As a business, however, it continued to deteriorate. In January 1965 the magazine had abandoned the weekly publication schedule that had been its lifelong hallmark and went to a biweekly schedule to cut expenses. This had required a new contract for Stewart and a pay cut of some $6,000. But the Curtis board of directors gave him stock options, and his lecture tours and radio commentaries made up the difference.

The *Post* was in its death rattle. Tensions between the editorial department and the business side intensified as a power struggle developed between Curtis president Matthew J. Culligan and *Post* editor Clay Blair. All this boiled over when Culligan decided to fire Blair and the company's magazine division head, Marvin Kantor. A dramatic weekend ensued, with Blair's followers meeting in a series of rowdy caucuses and vowing to bring down the magazine.

Culligan, fearing the next issue wouldn't materialize, called three men to New York to ensure publication if necessary. One was Stewart, who flew up, checked into the Regency Hotel, and joined Culligan's other standby firemen, former *Post* editor Robert Sherrod, now a kind of writer-at-large, and Harold Martin, a veteran *Post* writer based in Atlanta. They made their way to an apartment on East Eighty-fifth Street where a palace conspiracy was unfolding. Manifestos were being drafted declaring that Blair and Kantor would have to be reinstated forthwith or the conspirators would all walk out. Tensions were high, arguments rampant. Into this bedlam ventured the three, by now dubbed by one of the conspirators "the goddam triumvirate."

Stewart, wearing the traditional trench coat of a foreign correspondent, struck his editor, Otto Friedrich, as a man with "a rather grand sense of his own importance," but Friedrich considered Stewart an able and likable man. Stewart, Sherrod, and Martin removed their coats and sat down on a sofa. Sherrod, spokesman for the trio, said they had no point of view in the dispute and wanted only to make sure the magazine came out on schedule. Don Schanche, one of the more fiery participants and author of the latest manifesto, interrupted.

"It might be well," he said, "for you to know the latest developments." He handed the manifesto to Stewart, who read it silently until he reached the last sentence.

" 'As a condition of our continued employment,' " he quoted. "That's pretty strong."

"Damn right," said one of the conspirators.

Bill Emerson, second in command under Blair, then took over.

"Listen," he said, "let me ask you one very basic question. Do you have any idea of the charges that have been made against Joe Culligan? Have they told you any of that?"

"Well, no, not in any detail," said Sherrod.

"Then you don't really know what this is all about, do you?" said Emerson.

"We're just writers and editors, just like you," said Martin. He asked if Emerson was going to continue in his job even without Blair.

"I was," bellowed Emerson, "until the three of you appeared on the scene, trying to take over the magazine."

"Hell," said Stewart, "we're not editors, but we don't want to see everything wrecked."

"You're just cat's paws in a power struggle you don't know anything about," Emerson shouted. "You've been swindled and misled and taken in by that bunch to do their dirty work for them. And you're fucking up the last chance we have to save this magazine."

At that point the session erupted into a series of heated exchanges, and the triumvirate quickly rose from the discomfort of the sofa and sought to engage the angry journalists in more civil one-on-one exchanges. Stewart found himself face-to-face with Friedrich.

"Go home, Stew," said Friedrich.

"Jesus Christ! All I'm trying to do is to help keep the *Post* alive."

"Back to Washington, Stew. You don't realize what you're involved in here, and you're better off that way."

A few minutes later, after a heated exchanged between Sherrod and Blair, the three withdrew, and the rump session broke up.

In the end, nobody won the power struggle. Blair and Kantor were gone for good, but Culligan couldn't survive the corporate bloodshed, and soon he was gone too. Blair was replaced by Emerson, an expressive, friendly-faced Georgian with a passion for journalism and a flair for leadership. Still, the old days were gone now, and no editor could stave off the desperate corporate bigwigs bent on tearing down the walls that had protected the *Post*'s editorial sanctity for so long.

WITH THINGS RESTORED temporarily to quasi-normality at the magazine, Stewart traveled to North Carolina in early 1966 to visit with members of the Ku Klux Klan. He rendered a stunning portrait of Raymond Cranford, "exalted cyclops" of a sixty-member "klavern" in Greene County and a prime example of those Southern whites who were "wholly alienated from the comfortable American society that most of us know," as Stewart wrote.

In his profile Stewart didn't condemn Cranford or his fellow klansmen, didn't express shock or display moral superiority. He merely described them in neutral terms and let them talk. The result was devastating.

Cranford was a man who hardly ever laughed and never displayed his teeth when he smiled, and he was given to what Stewart called "brutal monologues" demonstrating his preoccupation with the people he called "niggers." At a desegregated Raleigh lunch counter, Stewart asked if he cared that a black man was seated next to a white across the room.

"If that man sitting next him wants to eat like a nigger," said Cranford, "that's his business. But if that nigger was to come to this table, I'd know how to handle him. I'd say I'd got some alligators I'd like to feed." Then began the monologue, which Stewart presented in excerpt form:

"A white nigger, that's worse than a nigger. A white nigger's a man's got white skin, and a heart that's pumping nigger blood through his veins. If it comes to a fight, the white nigger's gonna get killed before the nigger."

"You come from Washington? I call Washington Hersheytown—ninety percent chocolate and ten percent nuts."

"We don't believe in burning crosses on a man's lawn. If I'm gonna burn a cross, I ram it through the man and burn it."

"I got a daughter, she's nineteen years old. I love my daughter, but I find her with a nigger, I'll take my gun and I'll blow her brains right out of her head."

"You speared this guy," Harold Martin wrote Stewart, "like a rat on an ice pick."

The piece encapsulated the hallmarks of Stewart's column writing—imaginative reporting, human drama, sharp insights into American life. In February 1966 he turned his attention to a phenomenon he called "the Johnsonization of Washington," reflected in the departure of McGeorge Bundy as the president's national security adviser. Bundy, wrote Stewart, was both an intellectual and a member of the country's reigning establishment, and his departure reflected the eclipse of both intellectuals and "establishmentarians" in Lyndon Johnson's Washington.

Stewart defined an establishmentarian as "a person with an Eastern, classical-liberal education, moderate-liberal political views, who is rich enough not to worry about money and is strongly imbued with the notion that 'public office is a public trust.' " He clearly was talking about the Anglo-Saxon elite. Of course this establishment had contributed its share of pompous asses to the Washington scene, wrote Stewart, but it also had contributed many great public servants. He ticked off the usual list, including many old Alsop friends: James Forrestal, Robert Lovett, Dean Acheson, John McCloy, Christian Herter, Allen Dulles.

Now these men were gone, and more people like them were fleeing government. Stewart viewed all this with discomfort. The chief virtue of intellectuals and establishmentarians in government, he wrote, is that they were generally men of independent mind. With their disappearance, "the ultimate effect of the Johnsonization of Washington could be a government-by-toady. It is hard to imagine a surer recipe for disaster."

And disaster was looming. Taking up the Vietnam war in a column, Stewart could not bring himself to criticize the establishmentarians who had engineered the Southeast Asian adventure, and he still insisted the commitment was honorable. But he questioned more and more the McNamara thesis that Ho Chi Minh would cut his losses and seek a settlement when he realized he couldn't win in the South. This thesis, the basic assumption of the government's war strategy, seemed rational and logical, wrote Stewart, but the other side may not be rational and logical. "The other side may be totally unwilling to settle the war as long as they are convinced that *our* side can't win."

By September this insight had become even larger in Stewart's thinking, and he wrote a column entitled "Vietnam: Great Miscalculation?" He recounted how he had posed to a top official his own thesis that perhaps Ho wasn't as logical as American policymakers had supposed.

"You mean you think Ho is an Asian Churchill?" the official had asked with derision. "You mean, 'We'll fight on the beaches'—all that sort of thing?"

Yes, wrote Stewart. After all, any logical, rational person would have advised Churchill to cut a deal with Hitler in 1940 when a German invasion loomed and the Führer had offered tempting peace terms. "Again and again in history," he wrote, "for reasons irrational and even dishonorable, men have fought on when their cause seemed hopeless." As Stewart viewed it, Johnson's policymakers had fooled themselves in sending nearly 400,000 troops to war on the basis of diplomatic assumptions and a military strategy that were wrong.

With these dark thoughts, Stewart traveled once again to Vietnam in late 1966. He didn't find much to cheer him. In the home of the U.S. cultural attaché, Stewart spent an evening with eight male Vietnamese students from Saigon University. The students were all members of South Vietnam's ruling class—not surprisingly, since only ruling-class children could gain admittance to the university and be exempted from military service. The parents of seven were associated with the government; the eighth came from an old mandarin family.

The students argued furiously over such questions as whether the peasants in the countryside hated the Americans by a factor of 90 percent or only 50 percent. They lamented America's failure to bring South Vietnam desperately needed economic and social reforms. But they also considered the Americans too meddlesome, more and more like the colonialist French. "As the talk proceeded," wrote Stewart, "one thing became abundantly clear. Not one of those eight young men . . . felt any sense of commitment to the war against the communists in their own country. The war, in their eyes, was the business of the Americans."

There was something sad about these young men. "They are at the age of idealism and they have nothing to be idealistic about." They knew too much about the Vietcong to be procommunist, and too much about their own system to have any allegiance there. "So they end up against everything—against, above all, the Americans who are fighting their war for them."

Stewart traveled to the Mekong Delta south of Saigon and perceived that the war would be won or lost there, where half the South Vietnamese population lived. By day, the Vietcong controlled a third of these eight million people, by night two-thirds. Stewart could see that the South Vietnamese army, "idiotically trained by Americans only in conventional warfare," was ill-equipped for the guerrilla challenge in the delta.

In fact, the delta was in danger of falling to the communists. American troops had moved in, but the decision to send them in, born of military necessity, could have adverse consequences. Even north of Saigon, wrote Stewart, where the population was relatively sparse, the cumbersome American killing machine had destroyed thousands of what one U.S. colonel called "friendly people." How many "friendly people," asked Stewart, would be killed or wounded when the Americans moved into the populous delta? "And what will be the political consequences, in this most political of wars?"

To answer the question, Stewart visited two U.S. Army officers working in the delta. One was Major Jack Stapleton, a big, beefy regular soldier from Columbus, Ohio, who was a military adviser near My Tho. In one little hamlet, as Stapleton strode through on an inspection tour, a little Vietnamese boy grabbed one of his hands, then a girl grabbed the other. Soon children were hanging onto his belt, his shirttails, and his trousers while others crowded around trying for a handhold. Stewart described the rest:

> "OK," he said, "come along if you want, but I don't see why you want to hang onto a guy who's four feet taller than anybody else" (a pause. The children, not understanding a word, begin to giggle), "with round eyes" (loud laughs) "and a big belly" (screams of laughter) "and a red face" (near hysteria) "who smells terrible" (pandemonium).

Later Stewart encountered a rangy major named Colson, who had moved into the delta about six weeks before with the first American combat battalion. He displayed a chart listing twenty-six VC killed and twenty-four captured, at a cost of only twelve Americans wounded. Stewart asked how Colson could be sure the dead and captured Vietnamese were all VC.

"How do you know?" he echoed. "You catch a civilian with a weapon, or a guy shoots at you, you know damn well he's VC."

Outside battalion headquarters a dozen Vietnamese were lined up, squatting on their haunches. They had been brought in at gunpoint after a battalion sweep that morning during which one Vietcong soldier had been killed and another wounded. During such sweeps, said the major, all males capable of bearing arms, as well as any suspicious-looking females, were brought in for routine interrogation. In the line was a middle-aged woman who had been found with a shortwave radio capable of picking up the battalion frequency. There also was a fourteen-year-old boy whose face betrayed no emotion as he "stared back at the big white men around him with his almond-shaped obsidian eyes."

At day's end all but two young men were released and given fifty cents for their trouble. Stewart wondered what they were thinking after such a day:

> I wish I could have read the expression in the boy's black eyes. Was it just fear? Or was there hatred also? Might he not join the VC now, after a long day squatting on his haunches, surrounded by "round eyes"—the big, well-fed, red-faced, queer-smelling foreigners?
>
> How do you balance the love of the urchins for their protector, Major Stapleton, against the hatred which at least some of Major Colson's "detainees" must surely have felt? That is the key question, as American troops prepare to move into the Delta, and the remorseless Americanization of this small war proceeds apace.

During his Vietnam travels, Stewart often crossed Joe's path. Once, during a visit to the northern I Corps, where the marines operated, Stewart was shown to his sparse quarters—a small tent with a cot. Looking around, Stewart addressed his escort officer.

"Didn't my brother Joe come through here a few weeks ago?"

"Yes, sir," replied the lieutenant.

"Did he sleep in quarters like this?"

"No, sir."

"Well, where did he sleep?"

"The general vacated his quarters, sir."

Stewart didn't enjoy the privileges Joe always managed to wangle during his Vietnam visits, but he packed more reporting into his trips. He asked hundreds of questions in a steady stream and listened intently to the answers, always probing for new angles that could provide new insights into the war. Stewart's visits with GIs in the field left him feeling that this was "the most effective—and the most professional—army ever fielded by the United States," as he put it in a column. That, he said, accounted for the low casualty rate among U.S. soldiers and the high esprit that seemed evident everywhere. Yet the most this highly professional army had been able to accomplish so far was "preventing the war from being lost." The wicked ambiguities of the war seemed certain to begin taking a large psychological toll on the American troops.

A marine battalion comander in the far north told of an old woman caught the night before, signaling with a flashlight to a North Vietnamese unit a few hundred yards away in the "demilitarized zone."

"What did you do with her?" asked Stewart.

"Let her go. What else can you do?"

The commander of an air cavalry battalion farther south described a patrol during which his sergeant had encountered two Vietnamese men squatting against a hut. As the sergeant walked up, one shot him through the head. The officer asked plaintively what the sergeant should have done to avoid such a fate. Should he have killed the men when he first saw them? How could he know whether to befriend or shoot them?

"An old woman or a squatting peasant," wrote Stewart, "can turn out to be the enemy in this war. So can a child."

Stewart's visit heightened his skepticism about the Westmoreland-DePuy strategy. He didn't think that even this highly professional army, with its mobility and firepower, could kill enough communists of the North and South to soften Ho Chi Minh's resolve. The American military advantages were offset by fearsome liabilities: the communists' huge manpower base in North Vietnam; their ability to strike at points of greatest U.S. vulnerability and then scurry back into Laos and Cambodia; the likelihood that America's awesome firepower would alienate the South Vietnamese peasantry; and the lack of any South Vietnamese elite committed to the cause.

Upon his departure, Stewart heard a tale that further stirred his skepticism. On a flight to Hong Kong he sat next to Phil Geyelin, the former

Wall Street Journal correspondent and now editorial-page editor of the *Washington Post*. Geyelin recounted an American operation he had witnessed in his ramblings through the war zone. The idea had been to land an artillery force by helicopter into an area infested with enemy troops. A U.S. infantry battalion would be deposited nearby—at a point known as the "hot LZ"—to draw the enemy into battle. As soon as the enemy showed his face, the well-positioned artillery would blow him away.

Sure enough, said Geyelin as Stewart listened closely, the enemy attack materialized on schedule, and the artillery force killed a large number of communists. But the American infantry force was cut up as well. At a later briefing, U.S. officers with long pointers extolled the success of the operation in their usual clipped jargon. Then a chopper came in with some of the U.S. casualties, and the reporters insisted on viewing the bodies. Most of the casualties had resulted not from small-arms fire but from big explosions. "Their faces had been blown off," said Geyelin. They hadn't died in any firefight; they had been killed accidentally by their own artillery.

Stewart was silent for a time following Geyelin's story. Then he captured the incident with what struck Geyelin as the perfect image.

"Like a tethered goat at a tiger shoot," he said. Stewart seemed stunned that the army would engage in such reckless and self-destructive battlefield tactics.

"I'm not looking forward to going home," he said.

"Why?"

"I can see I'm going to have to break openly with my brother on this war. I'm not looking forward to that."

Back in Washington, Stewart managed to avoid the kind of break with Joe that would generate publicity and cause embarrassment. But throughout 1967, as Joe's optimism swelled to ever higher levels, Stewart's pessimism grew in equal measure. The war took a toll on their fraternal friendship. They argued incessantly over Vietnam, railing at each other in raised voices and heated tones. The arguments were no different from the fiery exchanges they had been waging since the early days of their partnership, and they never got personal or nasty. But soon the brothers discovered that they had each pulled back from the other. They bestirred themselves less now to get together for evening meals or Sunday afternoons. There was never any animosity, never even any overt recognition that they had pulled back. It seemed to those close to them that they had simply decided subconsciously that less contact would keep their passions from becoming overheated. Their affection for each other was too precious to risk.

In May, Stewart went to see Robert McNamara at the Pentagon and came away shaking his head at the picture of confusion he saw. Stewart noted that U.S. combat commanders were saying the communist main forces would be defeated by the end of the year—so why would Westmoreland want to increase U.S. troop strength to 600,000? McNamara agreed that it sounded like a "contradiction"—but Stewart should remember that combat commanders always want more men.

Stewart should also consider the possibility that, even if the communist main forces were not defeated by the end of the year, the U.S. force still might not need more troops. McNamara explained that Westmoreland wanted more troops for pacification efforts, to protect and preserve villages that had been cleared of Vietcong. But the secretary didn't believe U.S. forces were well suited for pacification, and he was disinclined to provide the extra troops.

If the main forces weren't defeated by year's end, Stewart asked, and if Westmoreland got no more troops, how long could the war go on? McNamara had no answer; but he speculated that the North Vietnamese would launch some kind of counterpunch to offset the U.S. war of attrition. "If someone were pounding me telling me to give in, I'd damn well die first," he said. Did that mean Johnson was likely to order a new bombing pause? The secretary said he wouldn't speculate on that, but he hinted the emphasis now was on secret diplomacy.

That, thought Stewart, meant a new bombing pause was likely. It meant McNamara was now operating exclusively in the realm of hope—hope that Ho Chi Minh would see he couldn't topple the American killing machine, that he would negotiate a reasonable settlement. Beyond that, the secretary seemed devoid of answers.

McNamara's confusion and anguish contributed to a column Stewart wrote two months later, as Washington chafed in the summer heat and racial tensions mounted across the land. "There is an erosion of confidence," he wrote, "that you can almost smell . . . in Washington's hot, humid air."

Perhaps, mused Stewart, the country needed new policymakers. The men who needed to ask the tough questions facing the nation, wrote Stewart, couldn't really do so because "the asking itself is a confession of failure." Many of these people were "brilliantly able," he wrote, "but perhaps new men are needed to do the new thinking which now so clearly needs to be done."

It was a remarkable column for an Alsop. It suggested that the old elite had contributed to a period of national failure and it called obliquely for a new government, which meant a Republican government. To Stewart, the country could not continue much longer on its current course.

Stewart's outlook didn't change much after an hour and a half with Lyndon Johnson in late July 1967, shortly after a violent five-day race riot had erupted in Detroit. At six twenty p.m. one Friday he was ushered into a small West Wing office where he found Johnson sitting at a desk wearing his wire-rimmed glasses "and looking more than ever like Foxy Grandpa," as Stewart wrote to Otto Friedrich.

The president gave Stewart a limp handshake, and the reporter told of how his recent interviews with black militants had left him convinced they posed a serious political problem for the president. Johnson didn't respond. It wasn't what he wanted to hear.

Johnson, stung by criticism that he had waited too long to dispatch federal troops to quell the Detroit riot, launched into a long, elaborate explanation of the constitutional requirements to be met for such an action. A huge book on military law was brought in, and the president pounced on the relevant passages. Then the book was whisked away, and a long memo was produced describing the negative reaction that had greeted previous presidential decisions to send federal troops into domestic situations. The memo was placed in front of Stewart, then removed.

A flick of a presidential switch and a bark of command, and soon a huge volume of *The New York Times* was brought in. Johnson turned quickly to June 1943, when Franklin Roosevelt had sent troops into Detroit to quell that year's racial riots. Johnson pointed out that his proclamation had been nearly identical to that of Stewart's cousin.

"This wasn't public relations," said the president. "This was the constitution."

"Yes," replied Stewart, "but you've been in politics a long time, Mr. President, and I've been writing about politics a long time, and surely you agree that it was inevitable that every political writer would put a political complexion on the statement."

Appearing nonplussed, Johnson replied that he wasn't the first president to have trouble with the press, nor would he be the last.

Then aides brought in a huge pile of telegrams. The president handed them to Stewart one at a time—giving him just enough time to glance at each. All were "fulsomely complimentary" about the president's handling of the riot. When Stewart asked about negative responses, a small pile was brought in, placed before him, and snatched away before they could be read.

Stewart brought up Vietnam. He had been reading a speech by Senator John Sherman Cooper, he said, and while he had never been a dove he had been impressed by the Kentucky Democrat's call for a bombing pause, if only to convince friends at home and abroad that the United States was sincere in its desire to negotiate.

Johnson called Cooper "a very fine man," but said he lacked the full picture. Echoing Joe's views, the president said there was no evidence Hanoi wanted to negotiate. The communists would simply use a bombing pause to improve their combat position so they could kill more Americans. "Maybe someday," he said, "I'm gonna have to kill . . . some more of those marines on the DMZ, just to prove we want peace, but I'm not going to do it now."

Stewart said he worried most about the lack of progress in the pacification program. "If we can't pacify the country and the South Vietnamese can't either," he said, "then the war is unwinnable."

Johnson dismissed the point, saying many people back in World War II thought that war was unwinnable too, but they had been proved wrong. Those who said so about Vietnam would also be proved wrong. Then he stood up and said good-bye. Johnson looked well, and he seemed cheerful enough. But Stewart was struck by his obsession with detail, the endless flow of books, documents, and memoranda. "My God, he's president now," wrote Stewart to Friedrich, "and the time wasted with such stuff is incredible." Then there was the president's obsession with the past, the troubles of FDR, the Second World War. "You sense," he wrote, "that he is reaching back to FDR as a crutch, a prop."

Depressed by the confusion he saw at the highest levels of government, Stewart turned his attention to a November column profiling Robert McNamara and his passion for "reason" as the basis for policymaking. It was a typically sensitive Alsop column, yet devastating. Stewart wrote that the secretary's "reason," all wrapped up in his preoccupation with numbers and graphs and quantifications, had been "the light that failed." He added, "One senses that he knows his light has failed, and that its failure troubles him far more deeply than all the harsh things the generals and the senators are saying about him." The light's failure had led to an agonizing self-inquiry by McNamara, and that in turn led to his departure from office, announced just a few days after Stewart's column appeared.

THE ANNOUNCEMENT OF McNamara's departure rocked Washington and the country. Here was the man who had presided over the Vietnam effort from the beginning, who had given no public hint that he lacked resolve or loyalty to his president. Now word was circulating through major news outlets that his leaving had been precipitated by agonizing doubts about the war. It was a devastating blow to those who believed, and wanted others to believe, that the war strategy was working. Among those, of course, was Joe.

But Stewart had seen it coming. Because he never had seen much merit in the McNamara-Westmoreland-DePuy strategy, he had been attuned to subtle developments, such as McNamara's private agonies, in a way that Joe never had been. He had seen the hollowness of the Saigon elite, the failure of pacification, the futility of a war strategy that ceded a safe haven to the enemy. Almost from the beginning, Stewart had viewed this war as likely to be nasty, brutish, and long.

As he had told Lyndon Johnson, Stewart had never been a dove. Like Joe, he had never questioned the need for American resolve in checking communist expansion. He had never recoiled at the government's willingness to shed the blood of its young men to protect South Vietnam. He had never felt the fashionable new foreign-policy moralism creeping up on his cold-eyed geopolitical outlook. He had remained true to his class—the elite that had taken the country into the roiling waters of internationalism and had accepted the mantle of military custodian of the Free World.

What was Stewart's answer? What strategy did he advocate to replace the faulty Westmoreland-DePuy war of attrition? In truth, he didn't advocate anything with much vigor. On two occasions he had predicted that the "awful logic of war" would force Johnson to project ground power into the North in order to cut off the enemy's supply of men and materiel that seemed to render the war of attrition untenable. Stewart's extensive interviewing during the early years of the war had shown clearly that the American people favored a more vigorous war effort, even against the North, to prevent America from getting bogged down.

It is impossible to know whether such a bold approach might have proved more successful than the Westmoreland-DePuy half-measures, or whether it would have invited even greater catastrophe. In any event, the country was stuck with Westmoreland and DePuy, and as more and more people came to question the strategy in the waning weeks of 1967, it came to pose an ever greater threat to the careers and professional standing of those who continued to cling to it. Stewart never bought it, and his brand of expository reporting, informed by his skepticism, was to hold up well when an even more urgent Vietnam crisis erupted in the new year.

32

1968

The Victims and Victors of History

THE NEW YEAR of 1968 arrived amid forebodings. For many Americans, it was clear that the Vietnam ordeal could not continue as a kill-ratio war that defied all traditional rules of military success, and led to no capture of enemy territory or surrender of enemy armies. Frustration, in the tradition of American democracy, was turning into political rage.

In ten months, this rolling sentiment would intersect with that continuous line of succession of power represented by America's presidential elections. Lyndon Johnson's job was on the line. Either he would solve the Vietnam quandary and end the homeward flow of body bags from Asia, or the voters would toss him aside. As the new year dawned it wasn't clear which was the more likely.

The answer came with violent abruptness before the year was a month old.

In the late-January calm of a Lunar New Year cease-fire, seventy thousand communist troops shattered the celebration, attacking more than a hundred South Vietnamese cities and towns. They struck along the coast, at Hoian, Da Nang and Quinhon, until then presumed secure. They shelled the big U.S. complex at Cam Ranh Bay and stormed numerous towns in the central highlands. They attacked the mountain resort of Dalat and invaded thirteen of sixteen provincial capitals in the Mekong Delta. They captured the ancient northern capital of Hue and carried the war into the heart of Saigon—even into the U.S. embassy compound, where four GIs were killed repelling Vietcong commandos.

Ambassador Ellsworth Bunker had to be hurried away in his pajamas as some four thousand communist troops attacked the city from north and south.

The Tet offensive was the most daring and decisive operation of the war. Back home in the United States, Americans watched in horror as the bloody spectacle unfolded on their television screens. For months their government had told them that peace was around the corner, that Westmoreland had the situation in hand. Now they saw firefights in downtown Saigon, communist forces on the march throughout the South, and six thousand marines besieged by two communist divisions at a little jungle outpost called Khesanh. Millions of Americans abruptly changed their views of Johnson's war.

Joe's view didn't change. Events, he believed, confirmed what he had been saying—that Hanoi was desperate, that American mobility and Westmoreland's killing machine had forced the communist forces into a corner. Within a day he filed a column comparing Tet to Japan's desperate kamikaze raids in the final engagements of World War II. Hanoi's central purpose, explained Joe, had been to stir a general uprising throughout the cities of the South that would topple the American-sponsored government and trap the U.S. Army in a hostile land. That did not happen. Hanoi had failed to deliver the decisive military blow that would knock the Americans out of the region.

As usual on Vietnam, Joe was both right and wrong. He was right about Tet's military significance and the motivation behind it. Tet had been a desperation move, and it had been a military defeat for Hanoi, which lost its capacity to wage war in the South, at least temporarily. The communists had lost 10,000 men in the first few days of the offensive, compared to 249 Americans dead and 500 South Vietnamese. As Johnson asked at a post-Tet news conference, "Is that a great enemy victory?"

The answer was yes. Hanoi may have lost the military battles, but it won the psychological war. When the guns of Tet subsided, Westmoreland had run out of credibility and Johnson had run out of political capital.

Joe missed these political ramifications entirely. When he finally realized what had happened, he saw it as a national tragedy of epic proportions. Just when the country was presented with an opportunity for a decisive blow, he felt, it had given up. His disgust for the news coverage of the war turned to rage when he saw Tet's military implications being ignored and the psychological aspects seized upon. To Joe this was merely self-fulfilling prophesy posing as journalism. The psychological blow was heavy, he believed, because the American people didn't know about their army's military successes. And they didn't know about the successes because the news media were fixated upon the psychological blow.

Within twelve days Joe filed four columns exploring Tet's military ramifications. He pleaded with readers to consider not just America's painful problems in the war but also the problems of the communist side, which were even more painful. He reported new information suggesting that Tet had cost the communist forces nearly thirty thousand men killed or captured. America, he wrote, stood at a "breathless moment" that called for "stoutness and resolution."

But the country now was preparing to extricate itself from Vietnam by extricating itself from Lyndon Johnson. Signs of this were visible in New Hampshire, where the year's first presidential primary was scheduled for March 12. The growing antiwar forces within the Democratic Party had fostered the insurgency campaign of Minnesota's Senator Eugene McCarthy, a studious and mordant politician with a force of conviction and a poet's sensibilities. McCarthy hated the war, considered it a drain on the material and moral resources of the nation. His aim was to bring down the president in order to end the war.

Joe had been dismissive of the McCarthy candidacy. In late December he had written that the Minnesotan lacked the fire to ignite the antiwar left and, besides, public opinion was congealing around a growing animosity toward the raucous antiwar demonstrators who were McCarthy's electoral base.

Stewart, writing in the *Saturday Evening Post* shortly before Tet, had shown something close to contempt for McCarthy. When he had pressed the senator to explain his alternative Vietnam policy, Stewart wrote, McCarthy had merely demonstrated a tendency to "hedge, waffle and straddle." He had vowed to stop the bombing except for supply routes, cut back on search-and-destroy missions, evacuate areas held by the Vietcong, and press for negotiations based on a coalition government that would include the communists. What McCarthy really had in mind, wrote Stewart, was "ducking out of Vietnam, wearing any convenient fig leaf, and leaving the communists triumphant."

But it didn't matter that McCarthy lacked a credible policy. Thousands of antiwar youths from the campuses of America swarmed into New Hampshire to seize the national destiny, and the senator captured 42.4 percent of the state's Democratic voters, just 7 percentage points behind the sitting president. And now Robert Kennedy announced he was "reassessing" his decision to stay out of the race. Joe lit into his old friend in a column filed from Vietnam. He decried the "shameful, humiliating and quite irrational defeatism" typified by Kennedy's "talk of a war without end." It was an open break with the man he had hoped to support for president.

As Joe struggled with what he considered Bobby's betrayal, bad news continued to fall heavily upon the president. Then on Sunday, March 31, Lyndon Johnson addressed the nation from the Oval Office. First he announced a new halt in the bombing and a new commitment to peace talks with Hanoi. He talked of the national ordeal. There was a division in the American house, said the president, and the attainments of his presidency must not be allowed to be lost in the suspicion, distrust, and selfishness that now gripped the nation. Then he let loose a bombshell. "Accordingly," said Lyndon Johnson in his nasal Texas twang, "I shall not seek and I will not accept the nomination of my party for another term as your president."

In Vietnam, Joe listened to the speech on the Armed Forces Network with two seasoned army officers, and he reported later that the passages on the bombing halt and peace talks had stirred "gloom, bitterness and scorn" in the officers. "He chickened out," said one. But the renunciation of office had inspired joy. "By God, there's a man," said the officer. "He has no concerns any longer except the concerns of the commander in chief. . . . His hands are free now."

For Joe that summed up the speech's meaning. "He need not listen to the whines of the muddleheaded and the howls of the Defeat-at-Any-Price crowd," he wrote, adding that if Hanoi's leaders went to the bargaining table Johnson could tell them to take it or leave it. "And if they will not take it or if they will not negotiate, he can do what is needed, which is not much, to win the war in Vietnam."

Stewart viewed it differently. He wrote a stark analysis entitled "Defeat?" After Tet, he noted, Radio Hanoi had crowed that the United States would soon experience its first major defeat. "It now seems entirely possible, and perhaps even probable," wrote Stewart, "that the prediction will come true." Ho Chi Minh had never expected to win on the battlefield, added Stewart. He had intended to win on the American homefront, "and that is what he is doing." Powerful newspapers and magazines that had supported the war just a few months before were backing away. Two network news heavies, NBC's Frank McGee and CBS's Walter Cronkite, had pronounced the war unwinnable. Even within the government—at State, in the CIA, in the Pentagon itself—the belief was taking hold that the war was a hopeless cause.

In other words, wrote Stewart, the old resolve was fading fast. "Those who, like this reporter's stubborn and courageous brother, still maintain that the war can and must be won are now a tiny and beleaguered minority."

For Joe, defeat remained unthinkable. In April he went to Landing Zone Baldy in Quangtin Province and witnessed a decoration ceremony for the first battalion of the Sixth Infantry Regiment, descendant of a much-decorated regiment of the War of 1812. The unit's colors were heavy with battle honors from old times, wrote Joe: "Canada, Chippewa, and Lundy's Lane, the Bad Axe River, where they fought the Black Hawk Indians, Vera Cruz, Churubusco and Chapultepec, Manassas, Antietam, Chancellorsville and Gettysburg, Santiago de Cuba and Panay in the Philippines, Alsace-Lorraine, Saint Mihiel and the cruel Meuse-Argonne, a long list from the Second Great War, from Algeria via bitter Anzio to the Po Valley where the Wehrmacht broke at last in Italy. . . ."

At the ceremony, the honor guard's uniforms showed the scars of combat, and the guard commander's hand was messily bandaged where he had lost a finger. "Here," wrote Joe, "all the strains of our America were gloriously represented—Irish and Yankee, Jewish and Puerto Rican, German and Central European and Negro." For Joe it was a touching scene. "Thus vividly reminded of the long American past, thus simultaneously face to face with youthful patriotism and brave endurance and our country's strange accomplishments, an old man's eyes perhaps ludicrously misted." As the chopper lifted him above the site, he found himself asking once again "the question that Vietnam always seemed to raise: Who are the Americans?"

By the time of Joe's return in early May, the campaign for president had reached a high pitch. On the Republican side it appeared the victor would be that old warhorse, Richard Nixon. He had risen from his defeats of the past eight years—the 1960 loss to Kennedy and a subsequent failure to capture the California governorship—to win the New Hampshire primary and position himself for his party's nomination. Nixon looked increasingly formidable against the Democrats as the governing party tore at itself in a bitter brawl for the power that Johnson had relinquished. Vietnam had turned normal intraparty byplay into vicious warfare.

In the Wisconsin primary, McCarthy acquired 56 percent of the vote and a basket of delegates for the Democrats' August convention in Chicago. But his way was not clear. Kennedy had entered the race, presenting himself as the *real* peace candidate. And Hubert Humphrey sought the prize as heir to the Democratic regulars, the city bosses, ward heelers, and labor leaders who constituted the sinews of the party. McCarthy and Kennedy would do battle in the primaries—Indiana, Nebraska, and Oregon in May, California on June 4—while Humphrey would cadge delegates in state conventions and caucuses.

Then there was George Wallace, the bantam former governor of Alabama whose ailing wife now held the job as his stand-in. He represented the so-called Southern strategy in distilled form; the idea that the Solid South, alienated by the Democrats' racial policies, now constituted a crucial swing region in national politics. But Wallace was more than just a regional candidate, as he had proved four years earlier in several Democratic primaries. A significant minority in key Northern areas shared his anger at the rise of racial politics, urban riots, the burgeoning federal government, and the growing power of "pointy-headed bureaucrats who can't park their bicycles straight." Now he was forging ahead with a third-party candidacy, a spoiler role in the fall campaign. His aim was to siphon off enough electoral college votes to deny either major-party candidate a majority, thus throwing the contest into the House of Representatives, with George Wallace as power broker.

Joe considered Wallace to be "the most significant third party contender since Theodore Roosevelt." Stewart, flying to Montgomery to talk with Wallace, found him to be "like a character out of one of those bad political novels or maybe a musical comedy." But there was no doubt, wrote Stewart, that Wallace represented a significant body of political sentiment. As usual, Wallace himself expressed it best: "You people in the Eastern press don't give the average man in the street any credit for intelligence. Take this academic freedom. Does that mean the freedom to burn the American flag or send help to communists who're killing our boys? That's something the average man just doesn't understand. You ask the taxi drivers, or the steelworkers, not here, up North. Ask them about George Wallace. You'll see."

Stewart also spent some time with Hubert Humphrey and concluded that the vice president enjoyed substantial political assets—plenty of money, the status of his high office, and solid support from labor, farm organizations, and the growing contingent of Democratic businessmen. But Stewart wondered if Humphrey had what he called "that presidential smell." The main problem was that Humphrey's obsequious alignment with Lyndon Johnson had made him look like "another man's man"—and a man who looks like another man's man is not generally taken seriously. On the other hand, wrote Stewart, Humphrey was an "oddly reassuring sort of fellow" running at a time when masses of Americans yearned for reassurance about their government and their country.

In early May, Stewart traveled to Los Angeles to watch Robert Kennedy in action, and he was struck by Kennedy's capacity for arousing emotion in youthful crowds. "When he describes with passionate emphasis the awful weaknesses in our rich and complacent society and then adds his laconic signature phrase—'I don't find that satisfactory'—it is genuinely moving." Kennedy conveyed to his young audiences a resolve to bring swift change to American society.

But two things stood out in Stewart's mind. One was that these intense youngsters clustering around Kennedy had "the nasty smell of a mob seized with a mass emotion and out of control"; he likened them to Mao Tse-tung's rampaging teenage Red Guards. And not all Kennedy's solutions seemed practical or realistic. His plan for Vietnam envisioned a "just settlement" emanating from a troop pullback and a willingness to allow communist participation in the Saigon government. But Stewart suggested that history provided no precedent for getting a "just settlement" with communists by reducing the pressure on them. And would it be in character for Kennedy to become the first American president to accept a catastrophic American defeat?

Joe disliked watching Kennedy emerge as a cult hero of the left. When the senator won the Indiana primary, Joe sifted through the tabulations and discovered that Kennedy had lost large segments of white voters he would need in the November election—blue-collar workers from ethnic neighborhoods and middle-class suburbanites. These people, wrote Joe, didn't like Kennedy's fiery liberalism and his glorification of "youth-in-revolt."

A week later, after Kennedy handily captured the Nebraska primary, Joe filed a perceptive column analyzing the senator's strategy of leveraging popular support in the primaries to lure support from party elders in the big industrial states where delegates were chosen by established power brokers. The strategy wasn't working. Despite Kennedy's primary victories, the power brokers didn't trust him. This wasn't surprising, said Joe. Kennedy had been railing against the Democratic establishment for two years, and had allowed himself to be captured by the party's liberal wing.

Joe's analysis proved itself in late May, when the large Pennsylvania delegation caucused and produced a sizable majority for Humphrey. The next day, Kennedy lost to McCarthy in Oregon. It was time, wrote Joe, for Kennedy to retreat from the "new politics" conceit that if he wasn't nominated it would be a result of the sinister machinations of party "bosses" bent on thwarting popular sentiment. "These wicked 'bosses,' " wrote Joe, "are not in politics to frustrate the people's will. . . . They are in politics to win elections, and if they back Vice President Humphrey . . . they do so exclusively for the coldly practical reason that they think Humphrey will help them more than Kennedy."

Still, Joe was not prepared to give up on Bobby. While it was "downright alarming" to watch Kennedy's arrogant entourage in action, he wrote, it was "downright moving" to follow Kennedy through a day of California campaigning. Throughout the day, he wrote, "there ran the . . . basic theme of this man's true compassion, his deep engagement in the problems of our time, his passionate wish to tackle those problems for the sake of this America of ours. These qualities are the core of Robert Kennedy."

In the politics of 1968, Joe's emotions ruled, and his emotions still belonged to the Kennedys. He hoped for the candidate to heed his published warnings; he wanted to vote for Bobby and feel comfortable in doing so. But he would vote for him in any case if given the chance.

He would not get the chance. On June 4, the night of the senator's triumph in the California primary, a twisted Palestinian named Sirhan Sirhan shot Kennedy as he was being whisked through the kitchen of his Los Angeles hotel. He died twenty-six hours later. Once again the nation mourned the violent death of a Kennedy. And once again Joe was grief-stricken. He wired a message to Ethel, sent both to the Ambassador Hotel and to Good Samaritan Hospital, where Kennedy lay dying: "At this dark moment in the story—yours and Bobby's story and our poor country's too—I send you all my affectionate sympathy and fervent prayers for his full and fighting recovery. All my dear love."

Joe and Susan Mary were among those invited to the requiem Mass at St. Patrick's Cathedral in New York. Following the Mass they rode the funeral train to Washington and made their way to the five-thirty burial at Arlington National Cemetery. Joe made no effort to hide his sorrow. One old friend, Daniel P. Moynihan, stood just a few feet away, yet did not say hello. Joe, he wrote later, had seemed "so stricken and inward turned" that a greeting had seemed inappropriate.

Joe and Susan Mary paid a call on Ethel and found their visit "beyond belief pleasurable and entertaining, too," as Joe wrote to her later, adding:

> It made me think, all over again, what a very lucky man I have been. At my age, all men I think begin to look backwards as much as forwards. But most look back a very long way, to the years when they were young and hungrily tasting this world's pleasures for the first time. Whereas my own best years, only just ended, were those in which the main figures were first the president and then Bobby; and they came to me when I had enough experience to appreciate my own good fortune. For that very reason, of course, I find it far harder to bear the fact that those golden times were so tragically and irrationally cut off; and when I think of you, not on the outer fringe but at the very center of those times, my heart swells. Yet I cannot help but feel, too, that all of us, even you who suffered the most cruel loss, must at least thank God for having been part of it all for a while.

Ethel wrote back: "The depth of your affection for him is of great comfort to me now as it was a source of joy to Bobby during all those years in Washington." To a friend named Allen Whiting, Joe wrote, "Despite the block of Vietnam, I was very much a Kennedy man; and his loss was the worst thing that has happened to me since his brother was killed."

Joe had other reasons for feeling down at midyear. His preoccupation with Vietnam and his insistence that the war could still be won had left him open to polemical attacks. Never before had he been in such a minority position on a major issue, and never before had journalistic America taken such delight in attacking him. Now even his idiosyncrasies and character quirks were fair game for parody and ridicule.

In May *The New Republic* ran a piece entitled, "Alsop Lets His Friends Down," by the magazine's Saigon man, Zalin B. Grant. It called Joe "the super-hawk of American journalism . . . the Pentagon's best friend and Westmoreland's bitter-end supporter." Thus it was ironic, wrote Grant, that Joe had violated a Westmoreland-imposed story embargo on the big U.S. offensive in the Ashau Valley that had begun at the end of Joe's latest Vietnam visit. The embargo break, Grant reported, had enraged the Saigon press corps, which had been sitting on the story.

In fact, Joe's embargo violation had been an inadvertent indiscretion;

he had learned of the operation outside of official channels and then filed the story from Hong Kong on his way home. Besides, wrote Joe, the embargo had had nothing to do with military security but with Lyndon Johnson's desire to obfuscate the fact that he too, like the North Vietnamese, had been pursuing a policy of "fighting while negotiating." This would have been a good story for Grant to pursue, suggested Joe.

But Joe was more vulnerable on matters relating to his privileged life in Vietnam and his demands for special treatment. Grant's *New Republic* piece continued:

> U.S. military and embassy officials have washed him with Top Secrets, chauffeured government cars have been put at his disposal and helicopters made his to command. His VIP treatment has become legend. So has his response. On a trip to an aircraft carrier in the Tonkin Gulf, one story has it, he once demanded a plane be made available to fly him to Hong Kong. . . . In Danang, Air Force officers still recount the chewing out he gave a colonel when his private jet failed to arrive on time. On his visits, Alsop commandeers the air-conditioned guest room of Ambassador Ellsworth Bunker's pleasant villa. From there he summons high mission officials for sessions that turn into . . . interminable Alsopian lectures on keeping morale up and pressing onward with the war. . . . Alsop sallies forth to the field where he is briefed by generals and— judging from his reports—laden with captured enemy documents. Occasionally, though, Alsop does see a bit of the action.

Defending himself vigorously in the magazine's letters column, Joe pointed out that as a close friend of Bunker's he hardly needed to "commandeer" a guest room, that he saw as much action in Vietnam as his physical capacities would allow, and that he got no better treatment from U.S. officials in Vietnam than any other newsman of "comparable seniority." But the damage was done, and it was evident that Joe had become an easy mark.

Within two weeks, *Harper's* appeared with a profile by Merle Miller that portrayed Joe as an eccentric curiosity with an awesome intellect and a spoiled child's temperament. Friends called him "imperial," wrote Miller, while detractors considered him "arrogant." Miller gave his own spin to the story about Joe demanding special treatment to be retrieved from a Seventh Fleet aircraft carrier in the Tonkin Gulf. In his version, Joe wanted a destroyer to take him to Hong Kong because, Miller explained falsely, Joe was afraid of flying. Miller also reported that Joe had once called Robert Kennedy's office to denounce the senator as a "traitor." A Kennedy partisan described Joe on that occasion as "completely out of control." A former Saigon bureau chief for *Newsweek*, Everett Martin, was quoted as saying, "Alsop doesn't get briefed by the colonels; he briefs them." Martin said Joe had had his own jet available to him in Vietnam.

Miller described Joe's manner of addressing taxi drivers ("Now look here, my good man"); his French cuffs and hand-tailored Savile Row suits; the silk handkerchief that peered out persistently from his breast pocket. "We all make ourselves up," said an unnamed "friend," "but Joe does it every morning." At the wedding years earlier of the infirm Bill Patten and Susan Mary Jay, wrote Miller, Joe had been heard to predict that Susan Mary soon would make a "lovely widow."

One "ex-friend" was quoted as saying that on the subject of Vietnam, Joe had become what Joe himself detested most—"a b-o-r-e." She added, "A lot of people won't go there for dinner anymore. When the subject is brought up—always by Joe—you can see people raise their eyebrows as if to say, 'How can I get out of here?' "

There was much in the article for Joe to take pride in—Miller's tribute to his intellect and force of personality, tales of his Groton and Harvard days, his wartime experiences, and his early triumphs. But the tone was dismissive, and Joe was not pleased. As always, he fought back.

He wrote a letter for publication in *Harper's* saying that Miller had "such a gift for inaccuracy" that it would be tedious to correct all his errors, "from . . . a grossly incorrect description of a portrait in my dining room . . . to a particularly big and ugly lie about my behavior at the wedding of my closest friend, whose wife became my wife."

Joe also objected to Everett Martin's suggestion that he had received special treatment in Vietnam. He wrote to U.S. Army General Winant Sidle asking him to confirm that his treatment was similar to that accorded with newsmen of his station. "If I have the facts right, I think it's quite important that you support the position I have taken," he wrote. "But of course, if I have the facts wrong, you must say so!" Sidle wrote back to say Joe's treatment reflected the standard pattern for high-level journalistic visitors. "If you are guilty of something, which of course you're not, you have considerable company." Of course Sidle didn't address the privileges Joe had received through his connection with Lodge and Bunker.

Friends jumped to Joe's defense. The *Post*'s Ward Just, who disagreed frequently with Joe on Vietnam, wrote to *Harper's* saying Joe never had his own jet in Vietnam and that he "took more risks than any reporter of comparable age or reputation." John O'Hara, the novelist, wrote Joe to say *Harper's* was a "grubby operation" and that Cass Canfield, who ran the parent company, Harper & Row, was a "horse's ass." In letters of thanks to O'Hara and others, Joe said he would "rather be unpleasantly noticed than ignored," but he was pleased to have the magazine's "unfairness" noted.

With so many influential people dismissing Joe, however, his column lost some of its sting. When he attacked economist John Kenneth

Galbraith and others for "intellectual bankruptcy" on Vietnam, Galbraith issued a statement saying that, next to Lyndon Johnson, Joe was "the leading non-combatant casualty of Vietnam . . . a figure of fun." Galbraith posited what he called the "Rostow-Aesop-Alsop" thesis of military strategy: "There is nothing like a series of really major military defeats to bring a country to the brink of victory."

As Joe's career went into decline, Stewart's was on the rise. In late April, Harper & Row published a 365-page book that Stewart had toiled over for two years. *The Center: People and Power in Political Washington* was a travelogue through the corridors of the capital, with chapters on such pockets of power as the White House, Congress, the Pentagon, the State Department, the CIA, the press, and the Supreme Court. It was a chatty book, filled with telling tales about how things really worked in Washington behind the facade of officialese and day-to-day headlines. In it, Stewart generally avoided serious conclusions, but he ended the book with the somber view that Vietnam and the country's racial problems had shaken Washington's self-confidence, poisoned many personal relationships, and "torn the city apart."

The book was a moderate success; it sold enough copies to justify a paperback edition in the fall. The reviews were mostly respectful. In *The Washington Post*, Phil Geyelin said Stewart's essays contained "more of the real feel and flavor of Washington, more humor and more insight, than any of the efforts at fiction that I can recall." In the *New Leader*, Arthur Schlesinger wrote that the book's "sense of history" gave it a "special distinction." But Washington writer William V. Shannon noted in the *Chicago Tribune* that this was less a muckraker's book than an insider's rendering of people Stewart dined with at the upper levels of Washington society. "Nothing is written here that would prevent the author from being invited back," he wrote.

Then came the biggest move in Stewart's career since his break with Joe. *Newsweek* editor Osborn Elliott asked him to become the magazine's regular back-page columnist, to replace the retiring Walter Lippmann. It was a big opportunity. In the magazine business in the late 1960s, *Newsweek* was known as the country's "hot book," a vibrant, thriving magazine that drew advertisers and avid readers with equal force. For years it had been a bland also-ran in the newsmagazine field, a distant second to Luce's imperious *Time*. Then Phil Graham, in one of his periods of manic fury, had purchased the magazine in 1961 for $15 million, pulling off what was to be called "one of the great steals of American journalism." Graham invested money in the editorial product. He put Elliott in charge with a mandate to assemble a first-class news staff, brightened the magazine's look, and revamped the ad sales team. Circulation and ad sales soared. From 1.4 million in circulation when Graham bought it, the magazine topped 2 million by 1968, and money was pouring in.

Newsweek's circulation was considerably less than the *Saturday Eve-*

ning Post's 6.5 million, but the *Post* had just embarked on a bizarre campaign to slash its circulation in half as an economy move. Besides, it wasn't clear who the *Post* readers were. As far as Stewart could tell, the magazine was read by hardly anyone in Washington of any consequence, and for years he had felt a decline in its journalistic authority. *Newsweek*, by contrast, had impact. It went to many of the most influential Americans in the most influential cities throughout the country. In Washington it was read avidly by the city's political class.

Elliott offered Stewart a contract providing $800 a column, plus whatever expenses he incurred. It represented a bit of a pay cut, but television appearances and lectures could make up the difference. Elliott yielded to Stewart's insistence that he be allowed to bring along his *Post* secretary, Amanda Zimmerman. And so with little regret Stewart pushed off from the beleaguered and sputtering *Post* in early July, after a twenty-two-year association. In a farewell letter to Otto Friedrich, Stewart said he expected to feel a bit lost without Otto and other *Post* editors breathing down his neck.

In early August Stewart reported to *Newsweek*'s twelfth-floor bureau at Pennsylvania Avenue and Seventeenth Street and moved into his office overlooking the White House. He found the place instantly to his liking. Elliott's global newsgathering empire gave him a much fuller sense of being at the center of things than he ever had felt at the *Post*. Washington bureau chief Mel Elfin had assembled a team of bright, aggressive reporters who proved enjoyable company. Stewart quickly established himself as something of a gray eminence in the bureau, always eager to offer advice on a story or help a reporter get access to high-level sources.

His approach to the craft, honed over his ten years as a *Saturday Evening Post* regular, proved ideal for the back-page space he now filled every week. The conversational writing style, the pungent analysis, the telling anecdotes, the human insight—all came together in a showcase forum that provided real impact. At age fifty-four, Stewart was at the top of the trade.

His first *Newsweek* column was a provocative suggestion that the United States was not designed by nature for the role of world leadership. "The 1968 election . . . marks the end of an era—the era that started so hopefully with the Truman doctrine and the Marshall plan, and which is ending so sadly with the unwon war in Vietnam."

Since the birth of civilization, wrote Stewart, the community of nations had always produced its number one. When number one had been reasonably secure—as during the Pax Romana or the Pax Britannica—the world had been reasonably peaceful. "The times of continuous war," he wrote, "have come when the pecking order was changing and uncertain." Now the world pecking order seemed to be heading into a period of uncertainty, and Pax Americana seemed to be coming to a close. Perhaps the result would be a Pax Sovietica; the Soviets had become the dominant power in the Middle East, and were building a navy. They also seemed to have a strong will and abundant self-confidence, qualities America appeared to be losing. "Or perhaps," wrote Stewart, "with the pecking order changing and uncertain, there will be no pax at all."

The column reflected Stewart's view, shared by Joe, that Vietnam was the pivotal experience in American postwar history. As the Alsops saw it, Vietnam was shaping the 1968 elections, which in turn were shaping the American future. It was not a future to their liking.

In early August the Republican convention opened in Miami Beach, and it seemed a foregone conclusion that the nominee would be Richard Nixon. But many Southern delegates supported California's handsome and articulate governor, Ronald Reagan, and party insiders speculated that Nixon would have to move to the right to gain power. Pouncing on this story, Joe wrote from Miami Beach that the single most serious political reality Nixon faced was George Wallace. If Wallace turned out to be as strong in the general election as he appeared, he would be an ominous threat to Nixon—unless Nixon managed to cut into the Wallace base of disaffected Southern whites and meld that bloc with mainstream Republicans.

After a triumphant Nixon chose Maryland governor Spiro Agnew for his running mate and delivered what Joe called a "politically well contrived" acceptance speech, it was clear that Joe had been right about Nixon's intentions. "The words and acts quite clearly mean that Nixon will follow the 'Southern strategy,' " he wrote.

Although Joe believed Nixon couldn't win without a Southern strategy, he didn't like it. To him it was pandering to racial prejudices and sinking to a level that candidates for national office should avoid. Repeatedly in the column he referred to Wallace supporters as "racists," and privately he was even more outspoken, suggesting to friends that an election waged on race issues, however obliquely, would fan the flames of racial animosities and lead eventually to oppression of blacks.

Up in Avon, brother John, Connecticut's Republican national committeeman, disliked Joe's columns on the emerging Nixon strategy. "I am going to have to take public issue with you . . . if [the columns] go on as they are," he wrote. "I beg you to be objective and let what happens happen and then judge it." In reply Joe said he couldn't suppress his fears that a GOP appeal to Wallace voters would have "certain automatic effects at the present terrible juncture in American affairs." He declared the 1968 political contest to be "the most dangerous election in my lifetime." He would have to call things as he saw them.

There was something undemocratic about Joe's views on the Wallace factor, as if he felt the country would implode if politicians addressed political sentiments he considered evil. Stewart, more dispassionate and analytical, set out to learn just who these voters were. He concluded they often weren't the racists many liberals assumed.

If he was an autoworker or steelworker, said Stewart, the Wallace man earned around $8,000 a year, with maybe another thousand for overtime. He probably owned a house worth about $16,000, in which he had equity of around $9,000. Take away taxes and his finance payments, and the Wallace man was not left with much to run a house and a car and to support a wife and two or three children.

Now, said Stewart, consider the circumstances this Wallace man had to face. He couldn't afford to live in safe suburbs; he had to contend with the crime of the central cities. When Wallace vowed that American wives would be able to go to the supermarket without physical fears when he became president, wrote Stewart, "that empty promise means a lot to the Wallace man." When Wallace vowed to support "the inalienable right of a parent to decide where his children go to school," the Wallace man knew this meant he wouldn't have to send his children on buses across town to bad inner-city schools. "It may be illiberal of the Wallace man not to want to send his children to bad schools in the name of integration, but it is not at all unnatural," wrote Stewart. And when Wallace attacked "open housing," the Wallace man knew this was one politician who understood his fear that integration of his neighborhood was likely to cause the value of his house—his only real capital—to plunge.

At the Democratic convention in Chicago in late August, Joe came face to face with a party he could hardly abide. "The place," he wrote upon arriving, "is crawling with youthful draft-protesters and draft-dodgers, amateur secretaries of state recruited from the groves of academe, leftwing intellectuals of every possible stripe, and other similar persona with one unique and total obsession, the Vietnam war." Joe was shocked by the mild reaction of so many Democrats, particularly Eugene McCarthy, to the Soviets' summer repression of Czechoslovakia. "The fatuity and egotism of their responses to the heart-rending death of freedom have had to be seen to be believed," he wrote.

Seeing the antiwar factions gaining sway within the party, Joe concluded that the country was witnessing the end of the Democratic hegemony inaugurated by Franklin Roosevelt thirty-six years before. Liberalism as practiced by Roosevelt, he suggested, was threatened by a new-breed ideology that he called "academic-intellectual liberalism." The new-breed liberals, Joe wrote, possessed no courage to match their convictions. At least the young protesters in the streets freely acknowledged that they didn't care if the United States lost the war.

Out on the streets Stewart watched the unfolding drama of protesters battling Chicago police. Unlike many liberals of the day, he felt little sympathy for the protesters. On Wednesday in Grant Park he heard a lot of youthful oratory incorporating "a four-letter transitive verb, in such brief declarative sentences as '(verb) Johnson,' '(verb) Franklin D. Roosevelt,' and even '(verb) America.' " But the scene appeared peaceful enough, with kids enjoying pot smoking, the mild weather, and participation in a cause.

Then two young men rushed a flagpole and began hauling down the American flag. As it hit the dirt, the police charged, releasing tear gas and bashing out blindly with their billy clubs. There wasn't anything particularly puzzling about these events, Stewart suggested. The cops obviously had orders to prevent the flag from hitting the ground, and the protest organizers knew that. So they brought down the flag to spark a confrontation—"meaning televised pictures of brutal cops beating up unarmed youngsters."

Stewart was puzzled by what he saw as the flag was lowered. All around him were young people cheering, laughing, and smiling with obvious pleasure at this domestic assault on the flag of the country. He scribbled in his notebook, "Generation of jerks."

But that was not really the proper way of looking at this powerful social phenomenon, he thought later. For the emotion behind those cheers, laughs, and smiles had made possible the truly remarkable achievements of the New Left, which had brought down a president, forced a change of course in a major foreign engagement, and now threatened to immobilize the Democratic Party. Perhaps the deadening influence of television had something to do with it, he suggested; perhaps America's affluence was breeding a kind of social decay. He added:

> Yet there must also be something more—some political poison, some Virus X—which has caused this deep loathing for American society, and even for America itself, among many of the young. Perhaps Virus X is beyond the capacity of the middle-aged to understand, or the young to explain. But one thing seems certain. In time, Virus X will work greatly to strengthen, not the New Left, but the extreme right. In Chicago, for the first time in my life, it began to seem to me possible that some form of American fascism may really happen here.

Vietnam had driven a wedge through the Democratic Party, had left it with lacerations so deep that it would take years for the scars to heal. The bloody street scenes, the snarling debates within the convention hall, the bitter residues of the Vietnam issue—all were harbingers of the coming war for the soul of the party. Joe was right. The Roosevelt era was dead. It wasn't clear what would replace it—within the party or the nation. And Stewart was right. The New Left was pushing the country to the right.

Hubert Humphrey emerged from the fires of Chicago with his party's nomination, but it didn't seem to be worth much. Stewart wrote that most presidential nominations were rather like coronations, but Humphrey's had been "more like an execution." His erstwhile allies in the liberal camp, he added, "have performed a really brilliant knife job on poor Humphrey." The media were portraying him as a buffoon, while the Kennedyites and McCarthyites "have been busy slicing [him] into small pieces." It would take a powerful effort by Humphrey himself, wrote Stewart, as well as a lot of help from more sensible liberals and a big assist from fate, "if this decent and honorable man is to have any chance at all of becoming president."

In November, Nixon parried a late Humphrey surge and emerged narrowly as victor. The margin was less than a percentage point in the popular balloting—under a half million votes. Wallace received 13.5 percent of the popular vote.

THE CRUEL YEAR of 1968 chased down many victims—Lyndon Johnson, Hubert Humphrey, William Westmoreland, the nation's hopes for a Vietnam victory, the Democratic Party, Joe Alsop. But perhaps its leading victim was the old elite, the Anglo-Saxon establishment that had played such a role in America's destiny from the beginning right up to the Vietnam war. The foreign policy created by this elite nearly a quarter century before had led straight to Vietnam, and now Vietnam was seen by just about everybody as a failure. Hence the broader foreign policy was seen as a failure too. The bitterness engendered by the war was now directed at the very worldview that the elite had given America at the dawn of the postwar era, when the Alsop brothers had led the cheers.

At the heart of that worldview was a faith in America's righteousness, a conviction that the job of preserving world order, however messy or brutal, was a hallowed national calling. That faith and that conviction, which were supposed to see America through as she endured the pain of power, now lay in tatters. Millions of young people were attacking the war as immoral and America as a global monster injecting evil into pristine regions. The liberal isolationism that had angered Joe at its early stirrings now threatened to capture the entire Democratic Party. The necessary strains of imperialism that undergirded America's exercise of global power now stirred such anger and hostility in the land that the very concept of Pax Americana had become politically untenable.

All this dealt a fearsome blow to the old elite, from which it would never recover. With Suez and the retreat of Britain from the global scene in 1956, the elite had lost its lodestar. Now, in the wake of the Vietnam debacle, it had lost its confidence. An elite without confidence, as Stewart was to write years hence, soon ceases to be an elite.

It wasn't simply a matter of foreign policy. The war had loosed upon America a social and cultural revolution that would remake the nation. The drug culture, the counterculture, the stirring of minorities, the assault on the mores and folkways of old—all constituted an attack on established authority. It was an attack on the authority of the elite and the institutions it had nurtured for decades to guide the nation while also protecting and preserving its position.

When the dust of revolution had settled, profound changes would

touch all the institutions of old—Groton, the Ivy League, the social customs surrounding the "coming out" of well-born young women in the
elite's exclusive preserves at the pinnacles of power and influence. Even
the New York *Herald Tribune* was gone; the old mouthpiece for the
Eastern establishment had been put out of its financial misery in 1966 by
Jock Whitney. Joe hadn't even bothered to write a column lamenting its
passing.

The elections of 1968 reflected another profound change. The nation's political center of gravity was shifting, moving away from the
Northeast and Midwest and toward the South and West. Demographic
patterns now made it possible for a Western politician such as Richard
Nixon to win the presidency without carrying New York, Pennsylvania,
Michigan, or Illinois. A potent new electoral base included California,
Texas, and Florida, states with little interest in the Yankee Northeast. In
putting together his government, Nixon conspicuously passed over scions of the old elite such as New York's Governor Nelson Rockefeller,
and turned to hungry and aggressive newcomers. And the Southern
strategy that had stirred Joe's instant animosity was becoming an ele-
mental part of American politics.

Viewed in this context, it was little wonder that Joe Alsop refused to
accept the nation's judgment on Vietnam, that he nourished hopes that
the confidence that had for so long guided the nation and its reigning
elite could be somehow rekindled. It was little wonder that he was becoming even more argumentative, that he drank more, that he lashed
out at those who couldn't see the issues as he saw them. The world he
had known and cherished was crumbling, and he couldn't bear to suffer
in silence. Stewart shared all these sentiments, lamented the crumbling
with equal sadness. But the differences in the brothers' temperaments
led to differences in their reactions. Ever the dispassionate, detached
observer, Stewart stepped back to study developments and analyze the
profound changes they were bringing.

Each in his own way, the brothers would come to terms with the decline of the old elite. But it would take time. They would have to become
farther removed from the fires and furies of 1968.

33

THE GREAT RETREAT

*Dissecting Nixon's
Dangerous Game Plan*

JOE DIDN'T VOTE for Richard Nixon. But hardly a month after the new president's inauguration he concluded he had been wrong in giving his vote to Hubert Humphrey. "I must say I am now very glad that Nixon was elected," he wrote to General Phillip B. Davidson, Jr., a top intelligence officer in Vietnam. "He has been extremely adroit in lowering the decibel count of the argument about Vietnam, and this will give him much more time than Humphrey would have had."

As Joe explained it to Ellsworth Bunker, the Nixon people had studied all the Vietnam options and concluded that the price of surrender would be high and immediate. Joe pronounced himself "much encouraged."

As for domestic policy, Stewart explored that situation in depth following Nixon's inauguration. A profound development had occurred in America, he wrote: "The *proletariat* has become *bourgeois*." A Marxist would say that was impossible, but there it was. A proletarian, Stewart pointed out, was defined as "one of the wage-earning class," while a bourgeois was "a person with private property interests." And in America a great many wage earners now had substantial property interests, which they intended to defend "as ferociously as the classic capitalists of Karl Marx's day."

Thus a transformation of political attitudes had occurred, as Stewart noted in relating an experience of Connecticut's Democratic senator, Abe Ribicoff. It occurred after his nationally televised spat with Chicago mayor Richard Daley at the Democratic convention. Returning to Connecticut, he visited a union shop and experienced the following exchange:

UNION MAN: We saw you on television, Senator, and it seemed like you were for those hippies. You're not getting our vote this time.
RIBICOFF: Look, suppose your kid was beaten up by the cops, how would you feel?
UNION MAN: Those hippies . . . were wearing beards and anybody who wears a beard, he deserves to get beat up.
RIBICOFF: Christ wore a beard. Abraham Lincoln wore a beard.
UNION MAN: Obscenity.

The next day Ribicoff helped dedicate a high school in rich, Republican, WASP-filled Litchfield County, and he received a standing ovation for his defiance of Daley. The shrewd senator instantly realized that he would lose if he depended on traditional areas of Democratic strength—labor, ethnic groups, the big-city vote. So he cut his losses in the Democratic areas and concentrated his efforts on well-off Republican enclaves. "Those Republican WASPs saved me," he told Stewart with obvious glee.

The center of gravity of American politics had shifted, wrote Stewart. "Now that the working class has become middle class, the ex-working stiff tends more and more to share middle-class sentiments about everything from the flag and law-and-order to beards. He has become, if you will, a bit of a square."

And Nixon was, as Stewart had put it in a previous column, "the quintessential square"—just the man to exploit these powerful shifts in the American political makeup. The new middle class, he wrote, gave Nixon a serious chance of making the Republican Party the national majority party. The key was those voters George Wallace had pulled together into a knot of political sentiment; if Nixon could capture that sentiment he would be a powerful politician indeed.

The brothers moved quickly to establish access in the new administration. Joe took a particular interest in Nixon's brilliant national security adviser, Henry Kissinger. During a presidential tour of European capitals in early 1969, Joe wrote Kissinger to express congratulations on the trip's success: "It all seems so well arranged and . . . so well prepared." By the way, Joe added offhandedly, one of New York's grande dames, Brooke Astor, would be visiting in March, and he was hoping Kissinger could join them for dinner on the twenty-first—"eight o'clock and black tie. She is great fun. She longs to meet you." Joe also wondered if it would amuse Kissinger to meet Isaiah Berlin, who would be visiting also in March. "I don't want to harass you with invitations," wrote Joe, "but he is an extraordinarily interesting man; if you would indeed be amused to meet him, it would be a pleasure to have you."

Still, Joe felt Kissinger needed some instruction on Washington's social mores. When he invited the White House aide to a small dinner for Kay Graham, Kissinger found himself stuck at work with last-minute demands and had a secretary call with regrets. The next day Joe sent a note suggesting it was permissible to be on call to official duties but rude to have a secretary express apologies. "For God's sake, call the hostess yourself." Kissinger wrote a gracious note to Susan Mary apologizing and expressing appeciation for the social instruction. He never committed another such faux pas, and Joe became a close friend.

Stewart also enjoyed easy access to Kissinger, as well as to Secretary of State William Rogers, a leading corporate lawyer who had served as attorney general in the late Eisenhower years. Another source was Richard Helms, director of Central Intelligence since 1966, who shared Stewart's background as OSS officer. Helms told Stewart that Nixon strongly wanted to get out of Vietnam—but Hanoi knew it, and that weakened his hand in the Paris negotiations that had begun during Johnson's last months in office. On the other hand, Nixon's bargaining position was strengthened by the fact that the military situation in the South looked better than it had for years. The communist main force had been decimated in the 1968 fighting, and it would take time for Hanoi to rebuild its forces.

Obviously, said Helms, the negotiations centered on some sort of mutual troop withdrawal. But if North Vietnam merely withdrew to Laos and Cambodia, the settlement would be phony, a formula for a delayed communist takeover of the South. Also, without some U.S. troop presence in the immediate area, the balance of power would shift back to the communists.

Helms reported that Nixon wasn't the voracious consumer of intelligence information that Kennedy and Johnson had been. He was "a one-subject man." If there was a revolution in Honduras, he would wave it aside and say, "Let State handle that." But if Vietnam was involved, even indirectly, he would pounce on it.

In early 1969 Stewart posed a question to Secretary of State Rogers. Even with the improved military situation, didn't Nixon face the same danger of domestic revolt that had doomed Johnson? Rogers acknowledged the danger but expressed confidence that two factors would dampen it. Nixon had no intention of resuming the bombing of North Vietnam, which had stirred such strong feelings in the country. And, unlike Johnson prior to his March 31 withdrawal from presidential contention, Nixon was seriously pursuing an accord. It was Hanoi, not the United States, that was intransigent now, said Rogers.

Stewart asked if Nixon couldn't buy time on the domestic front by bringing home 50,000 or 100,000 troops in the spring and again in the fall.

"I'd rather not comment on that," said Rogers, visibly stiffening. "It's not my department."

In a later conversation, Rogers told Stewart that Nixon had considered, then rejected, an announced withdrawal schedule. That would have undermined the United States bargaining position, said Rogers. Such a schedule did exist, however—"in flexible form, to be adjusted according to circumstances," as Stewart wrote in his notes.

Stewart bundled up this information into a June column summing up the Nixon predicament. The president, he wrote, had devoted most of a recent National Security Council meeting to a disquisition on the following theme: "A great nation that fails to meet a great challenge ceases to be a great nation." The United States, Nixon had said, could not accept a "disguised defeat" in Vietnam. He would not sell out the Saigon regime of President Nguyen Van Thieu in order to strike a deal in Paris and get America out of the war.

Still, Stewart predicted that the president soon would find himself under "savage pressure" at home to strike just such a deal. In the Paris peace talks, the communists were suggesting it would be a simple matter for both sides to withdraw their troops from the South if only the political problem in Saigon could be settled—and it could be settled easily with a coalition government that included the communist National Liberation Front. Already, wrote Stewart, "mounting murmurs are being heard" among Senate doves and liberal intellectuals "to the effect that only the 'corrupt and unsavory' Saigon government stands in the way of . . . an end to the killing." If the war dragged on, "the murmurs are sure to rise to screams."

But history taught that the communists viewed coalition government as merely a subterfuge for eventual conquest, Stewart wrote. He saw Nixon's predicament as an "interesting human equation." Perhaps the president meant it when he vowed that there would be no disguised defeat—but perhaps he would conclude that a Saigon coalition, bolstered by a favorable battlefield situation, could fend off the communist subversion that would threaten. And perhaps, if the war menaced his political survival, Nixon would simply accept the best deal he could get. Meanwhile, the president would talk tough. "For strongly to denounce a disguised defeat," wrote Stewart, "is one way to disguise a defeat."

As CHANGES CONVERGED upon the nation, so did they come to the Alsops. Joe, approaching sixty, was coming to terms with the fact that he needed to take vacations more regularly now, and to pace himself more carefully when he was in Washington. It was getting tougher to maintain his fast-lane existence.

He didn't curtail his drinking, however. "At parties," recalled *Washington Post* editor Benjamin Bradlee, "he would sit and drink until the booze was spilling out of his glass onto the floor." Alcohol had always been an integral part of the Alsop brothers' lives, as it had been part of the daily routine up in Avon during their formative years. Indeed, it played a large role in the lives of most people who made up the Anglo-Saxon elite, a hearty and boisterous breed given to attacking life on occasion with flights of abandon. America's postwar generation, particularly its most successful members in business, the arts, and journalism, had adopted a carefree attitude toward alcohol.

It had always been standard procedure for the brothers to enjoy cocktails before dinner, wine during dinner, a martini or two at lunch—and, as the years progressed, the amounts increased. As Tom Braden remembered it, Stewart would toss down a couple of bourbons before heading out to a social dinner. Upon his arrival, he would have a martini or two; then at dinner, several glasses of wine. After dinner he might have a Scotch or perhaps a couple of beers.

Stewart also made sure he had plenty of alcohol when traveling abroad or around the country. His daughter Elizabeth remembers him filling two or three flasks with bourbon before a trip and tossing them into his suitcase along with his shirts and toiletries.

But even given his large social consumption, Stewart never lost his composure or good-fellowship. He might become a bit more intense in friendly debate, but he always maintained control. It wasn't the same with Joe, who was now drinking more than ever, with the result that more than ever he slipped into the fits of argumentativeness and social aggressiveness that tested his friends' patience and disgusted nearly everyone else. "He got tiresome at times," recalled Evangeline Bruce, "and sometimes his friends got impatient with him." But they never abandoned him.

Those who only saw Joe at his worst couldn't understand why his friends stayed by him so loyally, but for his friends there was no other course. Joe was himself a wonderful friend as well as an amusing companion. He was unceasingly thoughtful, gave generously of his time, and showered his friends with support and affection. Walter Ridder, who had known Joe since the war, always said that if he found himself facing some kind of emergency, the first person he would turn to would be Joe. Kay Graham never forgot how supportive Joe had been after her husband died and she decided to take on the intimidating challenge of leading the vast *Post* empire. "He was wonderful, always sending me notes saying, 'You're doing great,' " she recalled, and added, "Joe was one of the two or three best friends of my life; I loved him."

Of course she could see through him too. When he would write to say he had detected that she needed a rest from her arduous schedule, she knew his real interest was to get her to accompany him on his next trip to a spa. She often went along and found the routine therapeutic as well as enjoyable.

Joe brought a zealotry to his intermittent efforts to get into shape, adhering strictly to an austere diet, avoiding alcohol, taking long walks. He would begin with two or three miles a day, but soon would be walking ten miles. Of course Kay was a captive audience during these walks, and invariably he would pummel her with complaints about something in the *Post*'s coverage or editorial stance. Once he hammered her so incessantly about the paper's position on missile production that she finally lost her patience.

"Goddam it, Joe, what do you want me to do?" she said, only half serious.

"Pull up your socks, darling," he replied. Kay laughed.

Kay liked having Joe and Susan Mary to her weekend place in Virginia, and Joe loved going there. When he learned how casual it was he adjusted quickly.

"Darling, I'd like a little tea," he said at one point.

"Fine, Joe," she replied. "It's in the kitchen."

Thereafter Joe simply went to the kitchen and made his own tea. But he wasn't particularly adept in that environment. Once he poured boiling water into a pitcher used for syrup. It exploded, giving a shock to Joe and providing the Graham family with a story worthy of many retellings. "It was wonderful out there," recalled Kay. "Lots of children, dogs running around, long walks. Joe fit right in."

But Joe's other side was never far away, and some friends became uncomfortable with how he treated Susan Mary. He continued to deride her in public, rudely dismissing her comments at dinner parties. "Oh, that's petty nonsense," he would say. "You know better than that." Susan Mary's reputation as a witty dinner companion during her Paris days now counted for little, and she frequently just clammed up when guests came to Dumbarton.

But sometimes she would rebel, refusing to be put in her place. That made matters worse. "Let's don't talk about that anymore," Joe would say, by way of diverting Susan Mary from her topic of discussion. She would ignore the comment and go on talking about it. "Sometimes she would really get her teeth in his ankle," recalled Kay Graham. Then he would lose his temper, and the sparks would fly.

It was worse at family gatherings. Joe would bicker constantly at Susan Mary. Elizabeth Winthrop, Stewart's daughter, recalled many a family dinner as "ghastly, long and tense." Sometimes Susan Mary would quietly steal off to her room to escape Joe's wrath. Even early in the marriage Joe's rudeness toward Susan Mary was evident at family gatherings. An embarrassing moment occurred at Dumbarton when some of Stewart's children and the Patten kids staged a family play. It turned out to be a parody of Joe.

"Goddam it, Susan Mary!" bellowed the young actor playing Joe, and he railed on in the manner so familiar to family members. The children had planned to put on two performances that night, but the second was canceled "by order of the management," as Elizabeth recalled years later.

Joe also refused to give Susan Mary any serious hand in running the household or planning for social events. If he was out of town and she chose a menu, he would berate her for getting it wrong.

All in all, Joe wasn't cut out for marriage. His need for absolute dominance over his surroundings made him a lousy husband. Still, he loved Susan Mary. When she was away, he missed her and wrote her tender letters. He spoke of her to friends in the most glowing and loving terms. And she loved him despite his worst traits. She hoped he would change, would soften his approach; yet as he got older he got even more crotchety.

When she complained of his behavior he would accuse her of trying to reform him and change him, which he simply wouldn't have in his own house. He would suggest that maybe she should seek a divorce. She would back off, assuming the role of loving conciliator and blaming herself. "Yes, I did try to reform you, I realize now, & it was v. foolish and I'm going to try immensely hard to give up any efforts to change you," she wrote to him. "I do like you very much as you are." On another occasion she wrote:

> I have no one else in the world . . . who I love as I do you, so I think it would be very silly to go on talking about divorce, if it appeals to you not to. You felt trapped, very trapped, and with reason, but I am learning a thing or two, like not minding your long absences, and feeling very grateful for the 6 months or so that we are together. . . . In the immediate future, as you asked me, I have thought about it and I would like to stay married to you, because I love you, and want you and miss you. It was me you asked to decide, but if you decide differently I shall not make a fuss. You took such a gamble and were disappointed, and I shall always feel that I let you down.

So they struggled on, with Susan Mary accepting the burden of adjusting to Joe's bluster and demands. She was gratified that he served the role of father to her two children with affection and interest. He helped get Billy into Harvard, and gave him sound counsel and sturdy support; and he showered Anne with loving attention. As Anne matured, Joe devoted himself to the matter of finding her a good husband. He was elated when she began dating a young man named George Crile, who came from a prominent Cleveland family. "She will never do better," he told family members, and he took young Crile aside to inquire about his intentions. That led to a proposal, and the couple—she at age eighteen, he at twenty-four—were married in 1968.

IN STEWART'S FAMILY, son Joe, having survived his Groton humiliation, had graduated from Massachusetts Institute of Technology and launched a career in the computer business. Ian, a free spirit and product of the growing counterculture, was about to graduate from Dartmouth. Elizabeth, still called "Fuff" by family and friends, was showing promise as a writer at Sarah Lawrence. And young Stewart was attending Suffield Academy, where he had enrolled after convincing his father that he couldn't survive even one more year of Groton.

Young Stewart's Groton experience represented a divide in the Alsop family history. As much as Ian had hated the place, he had stuck it out and was graduated in 1965. But during young Stewart's Groton days the school became a serious issue in the Alsop home. The son felt suffocated by the place, and Tish feared his continuation there might actually prove harmful. At first Stewart dismissed such talk.

"You're *supposed* to be miserable at boarding school," he would say. But soon he had seen that Tish might be right, and they had transferred Stewart to Suffield. The senior Stewart later tried to place some perspective on the matter:

> All three of my boys seem to have decided, in their different ways, that the school was the Enemy, and they either fought it or had as little to do with it as possible. Why? A difference in them? In the school? In the times? I don't know. I think we were somehow conditioned to accept a degree of misery and discomfort—hard discipline, cold showers only, bad food, no girls—that our children's generation is unwilling and unprepared to accept. In any case, while Groton was a net plus for Joe and John and myself, it was clearly a net minus for Joe and Ian and Stewart.

Neither of his younger sons—Nicky, born in 1960, and Andrew, born in 1967—would go to Groton. Thus did another institution of the old elite lose its force for the Alsops and the nation.

By the late 1960s, Stewart and Tish found themselves spending less time at Polecat Park, their cherished retreat of earlier days. The older children no longer liked the place, Tish had grown tired of the primitive surroundings, and Stewart felt less need for a retreat as his professional life eased off. Then, in early 1969, they came across a new kind of retreat—a grand old manor house for sale on thirty acres only fifty miles from Washington in Frederick County, Maryland. Stewart and Tish fell instantly in love with it.

The place was called Needwood Forest. The house, 160 years old, was a huge Georgian brick structure with six bedrooms and seven working fireplaces, including two in the large living room and two more in the master bedroom. There were a spacious lawn, a stocked pond, and acres of forest. Although Stewart and Tish knew they wanted it, they also wanted Joe's advice on what could be done with it before making an offer. But they cautioned Joe, who sometimes let his enthusiasm run amok, about expressing fulsome praise in the presence of the real estate agent, lest they lose all bargaining leverage. Joe stomped through the house, tossing off disparaging remarks about the old woodwork and the overgrown garden and suggesting that the house might be infested with termites. When he got Stewart away from the agent, he grabbed his arm and whispered with excitement, "Buy it, Stew, and don't haggle."

They did buy it, and soon resumed weekend entertaining in the country—now in grand style. With their dividend from the Polecat Park sale, they added a tennis court and a swimming pool.

The Stewart Alsop household had reached a settled quality with the departure of the older children and the purchase of Needwood. Tish suffered from arthritis and would need an operation soon. Her drinking also remained an intermittent problem. Stewart's aloofness continued; the family often seemed to rank for him somewhere below work, social life, and reading. During young Stewart's Suffield days, he turned to his Aunt Gussie for help in getting his dad's attention.

"Aunt Gussie, would you bribe my father to come to parents' weekend?" he asked. When Gussie related the conversation to Stewart, he was taken aback, and he did make it to the next parents' weekend at Suffield. But his attendance at such weekends was a rarity.

Nevertheless, Stewart's force of example and Tish's enveloping affection kept the family together. Years later young Stewart would express appreciation for his father's manner of building his life and maintaining his family, as well as his integrity and sense of fairness. "He was not the most loving person in the world," said Stewart Jr., "but he managed to marry someone who was."

In early 1969 the *Saturday Evening Post* finally folded. Over the years Stewart had written 126 full-length articles and 147 one-page columns for the magazine, and its demise hit him "like . . . the death of an old friend." Good writing, he wrote, "is menaced by television, which threatens to engulf the written word, like a blob from outer space in one of television's own idiot-pleasers. The decay of the written word, of which the *Post's* death is a symbol, is surely a tragedy, and maybe not a very small tragedy either."

Stewart continued to use the *Newsweek* column to provide insights into the fast-changing American society. He traveled to Yale to assess the campus mood. The angry protestors, avoiding war and seeking to tear down his alma mater, infuriated him initially. But he found himself drawn to the idealism, innocence, and "good-hearted nuttiness" of the kids. It occurred to him that much of their radicalism stemmed from the military draft, which grabbed the sons of less advantaged Americans and provided safe havens for the wealthy. One of those havens was Yale, and all Yalies knew that other men their age, less privileged or less bright, were fighting and dying while they avoided the fight. That knowledge, wrote Stewart, was "inherently corrupting." They had to hate the war in order not to hate themselves.

Campus protest, seemingly out of control, was causing a shift in

American politics, and Nixon's delicate game plan for getting out of Vietnam remained threatened by homefront pressures. Calls for an enforced coalition and a big troop withdrawal were gaining force, and Joe's liberal friends felt certain that Nixon would bend to the pressure. But he didn't. After a trip to Guam to meet with South Vietnamese president Thieu, Nixon announced only a nominal withdrawal of 25,000 troops. Joe was elated. He and Susan Mary went to a party at columnist Joe Kraft's, "where the whole bleeding heart newspaper community was unhappily assembled," as he wrote to Ellsworth Bunker. There was hardly a newsman there who hadn't predicted an imposed coalition government and a withdrawal of at least 200,000 troops. "They all looked like quinces," wrote Joe.

In two September columns Stewart sought to explain what Nixon was really up to. The plan, he wrote, was not to win the war; that now was seen as impossible. It was to not lose the war—and somehow to control the domestic opposition so Hanoi could be persuaded that the United States could remain indefinitely in South Vietnam even without any hope of victory. The military approach would revert to what Nixon now called "Vietnamization"—substituting Vietnamese infantry for American infantry so that U.S. combat units could be withdrawn. The result would be a drastic reduction in U.S. casualties and the ultimate elimination of draftees sent to Vietnam. Thus, according to the theory, the passions of dissent would be stilled, and the United States could continue a limited effort sufficient to assure that the war would not be lost.

In short, the president had initiated a massive military retreat, the most difficult of military maneuvers. So far he had been brilliant in camouflaging the retreat with tough talk, denunciations of those who opposed him, and public support for Thieu. But it was a retreat nonetheless, and it could not be reversed.

The flaw in the plan could be seen in the nature of the American military effort in Vietnam. As Stewart had often noted, the ratio of support troops ("impedimenta," as Julius Caesar had called them) to combat troops was huge. The impedimenta outnumbered the fighting soldiers two to one. Nixon planned to bring home the combat troops first, in order to reduce U.S. casualties and blunt antiwar agitation at home. Only by stemming this agitation could he confront Hanoi with the prospect of an indefinite American presence in Vietnam.

This made no sense in military terms. It was dangerous to leave a large contingent of support and supply forces virtually incapable of defending themselves in Vietnam. A year hence, with perhaps 200,000 U.S. soldiers in the country and very little combat capability, this "soft underbelly" of the U.S. Army would be almost hopelessly vulnerable to a Tet-style attack. That, wrote Stewart, "would be an almost irretrievable disaster for the United States, and a wholly irretrievable disaster for Richard Nixon."

For his part, Joe worried that Nixon's Vietnamization plan was just a cover for concealed surrender. During a Vietnam visit in the fall, his second of the year, he suggested that the Nixon program was going well, with both the South Vietnamese army and local self-defense militias becoming much more cohesive and efficient. But Nixon couldn't succeed unless he somehow forced Hanoi to withdraw its troops from South Vietnam and surrounding sanctuaries in Cambodia and Laos.

Joe went to Firebase Rendezvous in the Ashau Valley and learned that North Vietnamese main force units had moved in quickly to fill any vacuum left by the retreating U.S. combat forces. During the Khesanh siege, he noted, Hanoi had had five divisions fighting in the two northernmost provinces of South Vietnam. Within a few months after the enemy's Khesanh defeat, that force had dwindled to just two regiments, "lurking in the remotest mountain refuges." The splendid South Vietnamese 1st Division, plus fragments of the U.S. 101st Airborne and 3rd Marine divisions, had been sufficient to root out the Vietcong structure in the populous Coastal Plain. But now those two Hanoi regiments had grown to four, and six more were poised on the border.

Joe's reporting revealed one of the twin dangers Nixon faced as he struggled to lead his country out of the quagmire. Alsop wanted the president to halt the pullout and launch a major offensive to punish the enemy and force Hanoi to negotiate seriously in Paris. But Nixon knew that such a course could expose him fatally to the other danger— the unraveling of the country's domestic fabric. U.S. casualties in 1969 were likely to hit ten thousand, a number sure to add to his vulnerability. Yet the president seemed steadfast in wending his way through the dangerous thicket he had chosen for his Vietnam exit.

That became clear to Stewart on October 2, when he went to the White House to interview Henry Kissinger and ended up interviewing Nixon also. Kissinger patiently explained why Stewart was wrong in thinking the United States was heading for a disguised defeat in Vietnam, then said, "The president would like to see you." Upstairs in the Oval Office the president waited, seemingly in high spirits, looking thin but fit, his face sunburned, his hair carefully brushed. There was some brief chitchat about a lunch on Fishers Island the two had shared two years before. Then down to business.

"Well, I hope Henry's been giving you a good fill-in," said Nixon.

"Yes, Mr. President—I asked Henry to persuade me we're not going to be defeated in Vietnam. He's done his best, and it's a good best, but I'm not sure I'm persuaded."

"Yes," said Nixon, "Henry can be very persuasive. But I can tell you we're not going to be defeated in Vietnam as long as I'm here."

Nixon said Hanoi assumed he would suffer the same fate as Lyndon Johnson, but there were differences now. They got LBJ at the end of his term, whereas Nixon had nearly three and a half years to go. As long as he was president, said Nixon, he would not accept a U.S. humiliation. And there would be no concealed defeat. Most world leaders understood that.

"We've found that out on our trips abroad, haven't we, Henry?"

Kissinger nodded.

India's Mrs. Gandhi had made clear that she understood why the United States must avoid a Vietnam defeat. And a European prime minister—"you remember, Henry"—had been talking "very dovish for home consumption" but said privately that he appreciated the Nixon policy.

And then there was the impact of defeat on the country itself. "The American people would lose confidence in themselves, they'd lose their self-respect." So he wasn't going to be influenced by demonstrations or polls. Anyway, the polls showed a majority supporting the war.

Stewart interrupted to say he recalled a poll showing a majority supporting Nixon's conduct of office but less support for his handling of the war.

"That was Harris," said the president. "Gallup shows 60 percent, and majority support for sticking it out." He reached into his desk drawer, pulled out a thick folder and leafed through it. "This is a Princeton study—in depth," he said, producing the study. "That's the only kind worth much." It showed a majority supporting the Nixon approach. But he didn't care if the polls dropped to 20 percent. "I'm not going to pay attention to them," he said.

Stewart said that the Nixon policy seemed salable to him, but was the president making enough of an effort to sell it?

"Well, maybe not. Of course we've changed the policy—we've turned it around, we're bringing back sixty thousand men, 15 percent of the combat troops. But look at it this way—I don't want to keep haranguing, I don't want to keep saying that Johnson was wrong and I am right. . . . This could do to me what happened to Johnson, I know that. But I'd rather have that happen than accept a concealed defeat, a national humiliation in Vietnam, because I'm sure that would destroy this country's confidence in itself."

Nixon rose from his chair. Stewart stood up, shook hands as they exchanged brief farewells, and departed.

Stewart felt convinced that Nixon meant what he said when he vowed never to allow a Vietnam humiliation. He scuttled his plans for a column entitled "Our Coming Defeat in Vietnam," and wrote instead a piece recounting his Oval Office conversation. It was the column Nixon wanted to see, just as he *didn't* want to see an Alsop column predicting a disguised Vietnam defeat.

At year's end Stewart left for Vietnam with son Ian, who had taken a reporting job for a small Virginia newspaper after his Dartmouth graduation. Ian had been an antiwar protester, and Stewart thought it might be good for the two of them to survey the war together. Perhaps, he thought, they both would gain some added perspective. In the Mekong Delta, they traveled by car from the southernmost province of An Xuyen to the regional capital, driving eight hours over washed out roads, and passing at one point an artillery battery shooting off into a mangrove swamp from a base alongside the road. Not long before, this area had been VC territory, but now it appeared pacified.

Up in III Corps, where old family friend Charles Whitehouse served as chief U.S. civilian official, it was the same. "I don't think I'm fooling myself," Whitehouse told Stewart. "I really think we have the VC on the ropes." The Tet offensive, wrote Stewart, had forced the people of South Vietnam to choose sides in the war, and they had chosen—not so much for the government, but against the Vietcong. Hence, he wrote, if Saigon could contain the Vietcong threat in the delta and Nixon could contain the threat at home, "the Vietnamese really will have a chance to make it. . . . We can do no more than give them that chance—and no less."

Nixon did indeed seem in command at home. After a massive march on Washington in October, it had appeared the antiwar forces might have him on the defensive; but a November demonstration fizzled after Nixon delivered a November 3 speech appealing to the political stability and wisdom of Middle America. An exultant Joe called the speech "one of the most successful technical feats of political leadership in many, many years." It had defanged the opposition and galvanized a national majority behind the president's Vietnam policy of slow, deliberate withdrawal. Also, by sending out Vice President Spiro Agnew to savage the antiwar elements and their apologists in the news media, Nixon had forced the opposition onto the defensive.

THE YEAR 1970 did not begin well for Joe. Humor columnist Art Buchwald, who had disliked his former *Herald Tribune* colleague since the two had first met in Paris after the war, wrote a play called *Sheep on the Runway*, about a remote little country called Nonomura. In the play a syndicated Washington political columnist named Joe Mayflower, a well-born WASP with tailored suits and elaborate mannerisms, visits Nonomura and quickly detects a communist threat requiring instant U.S. military action. Mayflower throws his weight around, bullies the doves, intimidates generals, plays off his highly placed Washington connections. Soon Joe Mayflower manages to create for himself a lovely little war, which he fans by scurrying hither and yon waving masses of captured enemy documents.

The play enraged Joe, and, as always when attacked, he reacted to excess. He threatened to sue. He declared that anyone who attended the play would never again be invited to his dinner table. He showed his pique in a quote to a *Washington Post* gossip writer. The play was panned in Philadelphia but received a favorable notice from *The New York Times*'s Clive Barnes, which got it a run of a hundred performances or so on Broadway. Bob Kintner, seeing his old friend mishandling the matter, wrote to suggest that Joe should try to ignore it. "While I thought your comment in the *Post* was fine," he said, "I would stop making any statements concerning your portrayal and treat the matter . . . as one of those things." The more he seemed angry, added Kintner, the longer the publicity would continue.

Joe wrote back: "That was an exceedingly nice letter. It came at a bad time. It gave good advice. And I am very grateful for it."

Joe was more pleased than ever to be heading back to Vietnam shortly after the Buchwald episode. Before he left he received a call from Nixon, who requested that he come in for a chat. Joe found the president "extremely cool, collected, and firm," as he wrote to Charles Whitehouse. When Joe expressed concerns about the growing rate of North Vietnamese infiltration into the South, Nixon nodded. If the current rate continued, he said, he was determined to "do something." Since Joe made a point of never asking about future military operations, he didn't pursue the matter.

Upon his return, he wrote a long letter to the president recounting what he had learned and offering advice. He had learned that the North Vietnamese main force units were gaining enough strength to threaten "a showy local disaster . . . say, a rout or murder of all the government's pacification forces" in South Vietnam's two northernmost provinces. This would be politically devastating for Nixon, and thus Joe urged "a temporary deceleration, or a long stretch-out, or even a considerable deferment of further troop withdrawals from Vietnam."

Nixon didn't want to decelerate or defer, but he knew Joe's fears were well-founded. In February the North Vietnamese had launched an offensive across the Plain of Jars in Laos. In March, other units broke out of their sanctuaries in Cambodia. Moreover, by spring the U.S. pullout from Vietnam had reached 115,000 troops, and it was clear that the next increment would cut deeply into U.S. combat strength.

On April 26, the president approved a military assault into Cambodia to destroy communist sanctuaries in the Parrot's Beak area, which plunged into South Vietnam toward the Mekong Delta, and also in the so-called Fish Hook region farther north. On April 30, in a televised address, he announced the "incursion" with bellicose rhetoric, challenging his critics to make the most of it. Twenty thousand Americans, supported by air power, had crossed into Cambodia and were attacking two main North Vietnamese and Vietcong bases. Vast stores of materiel were captured, and twelve thousand North Vietnamese troops were held up in the infiltration pipeline because of the incursion. It was a serious setback for the communists, and it bought time for Nixon's withdrawal policy.

But it came at a grievous price. Campuses across the nation exploded in righteous anger. The nation's intellectual leadership turned on Nixon with a vengeance. The country was stunned when four young people were killed in a confrontation with National Guardsmen at Ohio's Kent State University. Nixon's deftness in keeping the antiwar movement off guard, such a large factor in his success thus far, now collapsed. The domestic war flared again.

Shortly after the incursion, Stewart went to see Kissinger and found him in an expansive mood. He showed Stewart two sheets of yellow lined paper with the president's handwriting—used by Nixon as he had weighed the pros and cons of his decision. One listed the cast of characters within the administration and their views and roles in the drama. It also outlined certain tactical moves designed to deal with the coming political storm. The president had scribbled out a decision to withhold advance knowledge from Senate Democratic leader Mike Mansfield, who predictably would oppose it.

At the top of the list the president had written, "Time running out for sanctuaries"; the coming rainy season and the disposition of communist troops meant the incursion had to come soon or not at all. Another scribble: "Provoke move on Phnom Penh?" The president had feared that his expansion of the war could lead to a full-scale communist assault on Cambodia's new anticommunist ruler, Lon Nol, who had just taken over the country from the feckless Prince Norodom Sihanouk. Further down the page was another series of pluses and minuses on whether to move into the Fish Hook area. Among the pluses: "Reduce impact of sanctuaries on Vietnamization . . . It *may* divert Communists from attack on Phnom Penh . . . It *may* undermine leadership of North Vietnam. . . ." Minuses: "It will create deep divisions in the United States . . . It might lead to a cut-off of the Paris talks . . . It might provoke a Communist attack across the DMZ."

Kissinger told Stewart that he had first seen the yellow sheets on the morning of April 26, when he had discussed the plan with Nixon. He had told the president that, while he never offered views on domestic matters, he did think he knew American university life pretty well and feared the Cambodia move would inflame the campuses. The president had replied, "Believe me, I've considered that danger," and he had pointed to that "minus" item on his yellow pad.

Kissinger explained to Stewart that the president had bought time from his November 3 speech until April, but that the downfall of Sihanouk had "changed the whole ballgame" by unleashing a serious communist effort to conquer Cambodia and Laos. If that happened, American support for Nixon's slow retreat would collapse entirely, and humiliation would be at hand. "Now," said Nixon's closest foreign-policy adviser, "we have time, flexibility, we can move in any direction, and if we can get a negotiation going seriously, with some sort of ground rules, we can get out very fast."

He paused. "If we have two years—"

"Henry," said Stewart, "you haven't got two years."

"No, but we have to act as though we had."

The trick, said Kissinger, was to stage a great retreat and emerge at the other end as still a great power. Stewart noted that it was the most explicit confirmation he had heard of his own theory of what Nixon was really up to.

Kissinger gave copies of the yellow sheets to Stewart, along with explicit ground rules: Any direct quotes would have to be cleared with him before publication, and Kissinger himself could not be named. Stewart readily agreed and hurried back to the office to write a column.

He argued in the column that the scribbles dispelled two widely reported myths. One was that Nixon hadn't discussed the incursion with top defense and foreign-policy officials. In fact, wrote Stewart, he had had extensive discussions with Defense Secretary Melvin Laird and Secretary of State Rogers. The other myth was that Nixon had become so isolated from reality that he hadn't realized his action would touch off a domestic firestorm throughout the country. The scribbles proved that Nixon had weighed that factor carefully.

They also made clear, Stewart added, that Nixon's chief motive was to speed Vietnamization, "meaning to speed the American troop withdrawal." But to many Americans that simply didn't matter. The antiwar movement had turned into an anti-Nixon movement, and was gaining ever greater force on the campuses, among opinion leaders, and in the news media. The president's position was becoming precarious. As Stewart wrote in a subsequent column:

> The spasm of national hysteria induced by the relatively minor Cambodian operation shows how little time the president has left. He must substantially complete his retreat from Vietnam within a matter of not too many months. Otherwise, this fat and flabby country, which was not fitted by history or temperament for the great-power role thrust upon it by the second world war, seems likely to go mad.

Stewart had it right. And the insight of his weekly column was gaining attention. David Warsh, a Vietnam–based *Newsweek* reporter, wrote to say that "it is fashionable on the Saigon cocktail-party-circuit to talk of what a hot ticket is Stewart Alsop." He added that Stewart's recent pieces on the Nixon retreat and the yellow pad had been "astonishingly good."

Stewart's work frequently was compared with Joe's in these times, and it made Stewart uncomfortable. Among the younger reporters in the *Newsweek* bureau, Joe had become an object of ridicule, and when Stewart chanced upon a conversation about his brother he would walk away without a word. Even with close friends bent on discussing Joe's columns, Stewart would say merely, "Well, that's Joe; he'll never change." And he would move on.

Although Joe didn't command in Washington the respect he had enjoyed in earlier days, he still had plenty of friends, as Kay Graham proved in October when she organized a sixtieth birthday party for him that drew 125 guests. Kay, worried about putting so many people in her house, had broached the matter with Joe.

"Do you think you can cut down the guest list?" she asked.

"Quite impossible, darling," replied Joe. So she had proceeded.

Joe considered it "the most beautiful party you can imagine," as he wrote to Isaiah Berlin—"quite knocking the eyes out of assorted Whitneys and Paleys." Stewart and John performed with hilarity, and Kay delivered a thoughtful and amusing toast. Joe loved his birthday weekend. "I don't think I'd ever seen my step-father so at peace with himself," Anne Crile wrote to Kay Graham.

But Joe was never far from adversity in these times. In November, while he was in Vietnam, an ugly incident occurred outside the Dumbarton house. On a car down the street, in front of a church attended by many diplomats, someone painted obscenities directed at Joe. It drew considerable attention before a friend hurriedly arranged for its removal. Also during this time Susan Mary found notes on her car windshield attacking Joe as a "faggot" and other such names.

Worse, it appeared that someone in the Kremlin had targeted Joe for an intimidation campaign. Columnist Charles Bartlett opened his mail one day to find a collection of photographs of Joe, engaged in a sexual encounter with a young man. They were the photographs surreptitiously taken by Soviet intelligence during Joe's 1957 Moscow trip. Bartlett was horrified. Joe was not a close friend, but the two journalists were friendly acquaintances, and Bartlett didn't want to do anything that might harm him.

Bartlett called his friend Cord Meyer at the CIA. What should he do? Meyer said he would check with Richard Helms and call back. He later suggested that Bartlett should send the photos to Joe, and Bartlett said he would. But he didn't. He attributed it to procrastination, but in reality he didn't want to inflict such embarrassment on Joe. He went off on a European reporting trip and left the photos locked in a drawer; when he returned he had a call from Helms. "I thought you were going to send those photos to Alsop," said Helms. Bartlett finally did, attaching a note of reassurance, saying Joe's friends detested such despicable actions and supported him. But he didn't sign the note. Later Joe called.

"Charlie, did you send these photographs over here?"

"Yes, Joe, it was me."

"Why didn't you identify yourself?"

"Well, Joe, I didn't want to embarrass you."

Bartlett didn't know it, but Joe needed to know where the photos had come from because he had heard that copies had been sent to others around town, including Art Buchwald, and he had to identify everyone who had received prints. Bartlett said years later that a coolness emerged in Joe's dealings with him afterward. Their friendship couldn't withstand the embarrassment Joe had suffered in the episode.

But the matter was kept relatively quiet, and life proceeded for Joe. In December 1970 Billy Patten married a young woman named Kate Bacon, from a prominent Massachusetts family. She was Billy's second cousin, "and so the wedding was one vast scene of Susan Mary's relations," as Joe wrote to Odette Pol-Roger in Paris. "They all have what pass for very old names in this country." He added that they were all families in which striking physical beauty was hereditary, and he had "never seen anything so marvelous as the line of bridesmaids." Of course his family also had been around a long time, said Joe, but the bridesmaids made him feel "rather short and fat and thick-ankled."

It was the kind of wedding the Alsops had been attending for generations, and it contrasted sharply with the wedding of Stewart's son Joe in January 1971 to a young woman named Candy Aydelotte, from Waco, Texas. Young Joe, a computer executive in Cambridge, Massachusetts, had met her on an airplane. He had been particularly amused by the fact that she had never heard of the Alsop family.

She was a "beautiful blonde," as Elizabeth Winthrop later described her, who had come from a "very middle-class" family in Waco. She had been a sorority girl at Southern Methodist University in Dallas, and then, alone among her sorority sisters, had left Texas in pursuit of wider horizons. She had ended up taking a job in Boston.

Everyone in the family liked her, but everyone also was aware of the fact that she came from that vast segment of America that Alsops and their friends had described delicately for generations as "not our class, dear." But these were the 1970s, and even if anyone had wanted to enforce the dictates of class—and nobody in the Alsop family did—it would have been impossible. The institutions that had been designed to ensure marital matches within the class—the coming-out parties, the class dominance of America's elite schools, the general class isolation—had all broken down. Airplanes and television and the academic meritocracy had equalized America, and had separated the postwar generation from many of its confining influences of old, including the preference for class marriages.

Of all the Joseph Wright Alsops stretching back 170 years, Joe VI was the first to marry outside his class. When his father and uncle arrived to check in at the local Ramada Inn in Waco, the big sign outside read, WELCOME TO JOE AND CANDY'S WEDDING. That, recalled Elizabeth Winthrop, "set Uncle Joe's teeth on edge." Joe couldn't help noting to himself that the Aydelottes' one-story suburban house constituted his "nightmare of the future."

But the Aydelottes turned out to be "extremely pleasant people," as Joe later wrote to Billy Patten, "and were particularly nice to all of us, and very likable in themselves." Everyone was aware of the cultural gulf that separated the two families, and everyone sought assiduously to bridge the gap as smoothly as possible without acknowledging it. Candy's parents seemed well briefed on the Alsops' peculiar habits. "Otherwise," wrote Joe to Billy, "I don't imagine they would have greeted us with martinis when we arrived at 12:30 last Monday."

After martinis they all went to a prewedding luncheon at a place called Nick the Greek's, where the meal was served in a "windowless cavern" known as "the banquet room." Joe found the food "very odd indeed," and the wine—"American, since no other was available"—was served in splits, a little smaller than soda bottles.

The Alsops were a bit taken aback by the local custom that required young Joe to be married in a dinner jacket, and Joe was amused by the motel setting for the postwedding supper, which was another windowless cavern "mainly decorated with a large stainless steel steam-table." Stewart muttered several times to Joe, "Very unlike the last wedding I went to." Still, as Joe wrote to Billy, the people they met were all "very amiable." He added:

> But I must say, the occasion can only be described as a deep plunge into the depths of middle America. Uncle Stewart stood it rather less well than I did, I think. The food was so awful that none of us could eat anything but salad, and I am afraid I should have found it all pretty depressing, if I had not known that Candy had left Waco for the precise reason that she wanted to get away from that sort of thing.
>
> Nothing about it changed my mind, in the smallest degree, about the marriage itself. I am just as delighted now as I was when I first heard that they were planning to get married. . . . In fact, I was particularly impressed by Candy during this day that must have been rather difficult for her. For she must surely have been aware of how odd much of it seemed to us, and I suspect she thought (and I fear rightly, although we really did our best) that we must seem very odd to some of the Waconians. She gave no sign of any of this, however. She was obviously much attached to her family, even although they are obviously part of the Waco in which she boldly decided she did not wish to spend the rest of her life. All in all, I thought she was quite wonderful. . . .

After the reception, when the rice had been thrown, Joe, Stewart, and Tish drove straight to Dallas in order to take an early flight back to Washington the next morning. At their airport hotel they went into the restaurant for club sandwiches and conversation about the day's events. After the men had each consumed two double Scotch and sodas, "to repair the damage of the American champagne, we began to be ourselves again," as Joe wrote to Billy. "But I repeat, I was overjoyed by the event, and I still am."

———

BACK IN WASHINGTON, Stewart fretted more and more about the gathering force of the counterculture. He felt the Vietnam war was tearing the country apart. Even the army was disintegrating. In December he had written a column entitled "Vietnam: Out Faster," in which he had argued that the army had been rendered useless by the drug culture and an epidemic of disaffection. Nobody wanted to be the last man killed in a lost cause. "So it is time to take those bitter draftees in our crumbling Army out of Vietnam—and the sooner the better," he had written.

Three months later on Springland Lane, as Stewart was about to put out his bedside lamp and go to sleep, the phone rang. Tish answered, listened briefly, then hung up.

"What do we do about crank calls?" she asked.

"What do you mean?"

"That man said this house was going to blow up in seven minutes."

"Jumping Joe DiMaggio," bellowed Stewart, jumping out of bed. "Just what did he say?"

"He said, 'Is this the Alsop residence?' and when I said 'Yes,' he said, 'You have seven minutes to vacate the premises. Your house is going to be blown to bits.' Then he hung up."

"What did he sound like?" asked Stewart. "Was he a drunk or a kook?"

"No. He sounded sober, and adult. He pronounced Alsop 'Al-sop.' "

Stewart phoned the police emergency number and reported the call; he was assured that a squad car would be out immediately.

"Should I get my family out of the house?" asked Stewart.

"Can't say," said the officer. "That's up to you."

Stewart reasoned that if a bomb had been left it would have been left near the kitchen, which was nearest the road. He gathered the family at the other end of the house. By then it was twelve-fifteen a.m.—two minutes to go. They waited in silence. Nothing happened. Stewart put on a bathrobe and went downstairs to put on the outside light. Soon four policemen arrived. They asked questions, inspected the outside of the house with a flashlight, then promised to keep an eye on the house. "Back to bed, a sleeping pill, and that was that," wrote Stewart later.

But that wasn't really that. Stewart attributed the bomb threat to a sickness that had come over America. "The terrible strains of a long, hated war seem to have induced an epidemic irrationality . . . a certain hysteria," he wrote in his next column. It was not hard to believe that this epidemic was related to the bomb threat that had shattered the Alsops' domestic peace that early Monday morning. Less than an hour after that midnight call, and just a few miles from Springland Lane, a powerful explosion ripped through a portion of the U.S. Capitol. The war had indeed come home.

34

CANCER

"God Tempers the Wind
to the Shorn Lamb"

JULY 19, 1971, began for Stewart at Needwood Forest. His three-week vacation was over, and on this Monday he and Tish and the young boys had risen early so he could get to his *Newsweek* office by midmorning. By nine thirty, all they needed to do was toss the trash into the old wellhead that served as a family dump, and they would be on their way. Little Andrew, then four, threw two boxes of trash into the well, then scampered down the four-foot wellhead slope.

"Come on, Daddy!" he shouted. Stewart tossed in the rest of the weekend rubbish and turned toward the car.

Suddenly he couldn't move. His legs nearly gave way, and he gasped for breath like a trout out of water. His heart pounded ferociously. He struggled to stay on his feet, then slowly made his way to the car. Tish was at the wheel, as usual on their drives back from the country, and Stewart mentioned in passing that he felt a bit "lousy." Tish thought it was fortunate that he had scheduled a regular checkup with their family doctor for that afternoon. As they drove back into town, Stewart felt himself reviving, and he tried not to think about what had just happened.

During lunch at the Metropolitan Club with two old friends, Stewart ate a steak and drank a martini and felt as fit as ever. Then he set out on the four-block walk to the office of Dr. Richard Perry.

Halfway there, the breathlessness returned, and Stewart stood on the corner through two light changes waiting for it to subside. Then he proceeded to the doctor's office, where Dr. Perry put him through the standard examination. Afterward he sat in the waiting room and read old copies of *Country Life* as the doctor studied his test results. Finally a nurse summoned him to Perry's office. The doctor looked grave.

"You're anemic," he said. "You're *very* anemic. I want to get you into Georgetown University Hospital right away, this afternoon."

To Stewart it sounded serious, and a question emerged in his consciousness as if by instinct.

"Is it cancer?"

"That's not my first concern now," said the doctor.

At Georgetown Hospital, Stewart was placed in a comfortable room and subjected to an uncomfortable experience. In came platoons of young doctors who poked him, pricked him, drew blood, and asked questions. Then came his first bone-marrow test. A young doctor asked him to roll over on his stomach, then gave him shots of Novocain in the flat bony area at the bottom of the spine. The doctor poked a needle through the bone and extracted the marrow. Stewart's legs jerked involuntarily, like a frog's in a laboratory experiment.

The doctor gave the marrow to a technician, who smeared it on slides for inspection.

"Enough spicules?" asked the doctor. Yes, said the technician, and the doctor told Stewart that Dr. Perry would be in early the next morning to evaluate the results.

"Will it show whether I have cancer?" asked Stewart.

"Yes. Whether you have cancer, and what kind," replied the doctor with a matter-of-factness that was not reassuring.

When he was gone, Stewart reached out to Tish. Her hand was "warm and comforting and very much alive," as he wrote later. Tish spent the night on a cot beside Stewart's bed, and twice during the night he woke despite his sleeping pills and reached out for her hand. Each time she was awake.

The next morning another stream of doctors flowed in to poke and probe and ask questions. Then Stewart and Tish were left alone. Hours went by. No Dr. Perry.

Stewart and Tish began calling the family, beginning with Stewart's generation—Joe and Susan Mary; John up in Avon; Sis in New Jersey, where she also was in a hospital, recovering from a breast-cancer operation. Then the children. He reached young Joe in his Cambridge office.

"I thought you should know, Joe. I'm in the hospital down here."

"What's the matter?"

"My blood seems to have turned to water." Stewart attempted a laugh.

There was no responding laugh, instead a long pause. "I love you, man," said Joe. Suddenly feeling very emotional, Stewart hung up quickly.

He reached Fuff at Harper & Row, where she had landed a job as a book editor. When he used the line about his blood turning to water, she was taken aback.

"Daddy, what does that mean?"

"I don't know yet," replied Stewart. "I hope to find out soon."

Ian was in Katmandu, where he had gone after the Vietnam trip to sell Tibetan woodcut prints to tourists. Young Stewart was traveling through America with two friends in a van. Neither could be reached.

Soon Joe and Susan Mary arrived with fruit and words of reassurance. When they left, Tish left also, to fetch some magazines and the day's newspapers. Stewart was alone, and suddenly he felt more lonely than he had ever felt.

When Tish returned at about noon, she surreptitiously fixed Stewart a martini to help with the unappetizing hospital lunch and the suspense that had been building all morning. It tasted very good.

Finally Dr. Perry arrived with the verdict, and one look at his face made Stewart glad he had had the martini. There was a "sadly sympathetic air, a faint embarrassment . . . that smelled of bad news."

Acute myeloblastic leukemia.

The words rang with brutal force. From that moment forward Stewart knew he was in a struggle against death, and each new day was a gift.

Perry said he had arranged for Stewart to have treatment at the National Institutes of Health, "where they know more about leukemia than anywhere else in the world." The treatment, he said, would be chemotherapy—powerful chemicals to kill the malignant cells. Stewart asked how long the treatment would last. Difficult to say, said Perry; perhaps as short as two weeks, perhaps a month.

The next day Stewart returned home to get some clothes and books, and then Tish drove him out to NIH's Bethesda, Maryland, grounds. On the thirteenth floor of one of the big brick buildings he found the leukemia ward and met Dr. John Glick, a bright young specialist who spoke with a candor that was both refreshing and disturbing.

Glick told Stewart that NIH doctors had spent the previous morning arguing about his case. Everyone had agreed there were myeloblastic, or AML, cells in his marrow. But some of the cells looked like another kind of leukemia, and still others looked like a different marrow cancer, not a leukemia, called dysproteinemia. And even the AML cells didn't look exactly like AML cells. There were other curiosities, too. AML normally filled the marrow to overflowing with bad cells and led to a very high white-blood-cell count. Also, the bad cells normally made their way into the blood. But with Stewart there were few cells of any kind in his marrow, and no bad cells at all in his blood.

In any event, the diagnosis was officially AML, and the treatment was chemotherapy in a "laminar flow room." Glick explained that in a laminar flow room the air all flowed one way, pumped in from one side and then out the other. There was almost no chance of infection, which was the leading cause of death during chemotherapy, because the treatment killed off white blood cells and thus left the body vulnerable to infection. In the laminar flow room, doctors and nurses treated patients with rubber gloves through a transparent plastic wall, and everything was sterilized.

"Can you sterilize martinis?" asked Stewart.

Glick laughed and said yes, but not even martinis would make him feel good during chemo treatments.

What was the chance of a remission?

Better than 50 percent, replied the doctor. Clearly, thought Stewart, it wasn't just the air that left the laminar flow room through one way only.

And how long would a remission last, if there was one? Well, replied the doctor, he knew of one patient who had had a seven-year remission. About 50 percent of AML patients who go into remission last a year or more.

How many died before two years?

Glick's effort to put a cheerful note on the discussion collapsed. "About 95 percent," he said, and changed the subject.

That night there were more marrow tests, as Glick sought enough spicules—bits of marrow with fat in them, which give a representative sample of marrow cells—to assess the situation. Tish left for home at about ten o'clock, and again Stewart found himself very much alone. As he wrote later, "A sense of the reality of death crowded in on me—the end of a pleasant life, never to see Tish or Andrew or Nicky or the four older children again, never to go to Needwood again, or laugh with friends, or see the spring come. There came upon me a terrible sense of aloneness, of vulnerability, of nakedness, of helplessness." He got up to take a third sleeping pill and then dozed off.

The next day Stewart heard an assessment of his situation. His hemoglobin count was 6.8; his platelets, 18,000; his white blood count, 1,100 with 14 percent granulocytes. This meant Stewart was close to death. Hemoglobin supplies energy to the body, and a hemoglobin count of less than 10 means that the body lacks the energy required even for normal functions; congestive heart failure is a real danger as the heart races to supply energy to the body. Glick addressed the low hemoglobin with a series of blood transfusions.

Stewart also had been in the danger zone on platelets, the blood cells that control bleeding. A low normal level would be about 160,000; anything under 20,000 was ominous. Stewart's 18,000 was worse than ominous. He was lucky he hadn't died during his vacation when he gashed his leg while climbing over a fence. Stewart was given a platelet transfusion.

The problem with these transfusions was that they could bring hepatitis, and a leukemic with hepatitis was in mortal danger because leukemics normally lack sufficient white blood cells to fight infection. To present an effective vanguard against infection, the body needs 4,000 to 10,000 white cells, with at least 45 percent granulocytes. Stewart's white count of 1,100 with only 14 percent granulocytes, meant any serious infection could easily kill him.

Two days after Stewart's arrival at NIH, Glick decided against chemotherapy. He couldn't be sure this really was AML, he said, and he preferred to wait and see. Perhaps chemotherapy would bring on a remission, but it wasn't likely to last more than a year or so. And these strange cells might represent something that wouldn't require chemotherapy. Of course, there was a serious risk that Stewart would die of infection before the real medical answer could be found, but that seemed a better gamble than the chemical option. Glick said Stewart could go home the next day.

But he didn't go home. That night he contracted an infection. First came chills, then fever, and Stewart's temperature went up to 104 degrees Fahrenheit. Glick prescribed a large dose of powerful antibiotics, delivered intravenously. Though the fever subsided within a day, Stewart remained hooked up to the IV for another nine days. It was a time for reflection.

At the age of fifty-seven he knew he would die soon, perhaps even the next day, more likely within a few months, but surely within two to three years. He experienced periods of fear and depression. Once he went into the bathroom and sobbed for several minutes. But he also discovered that nobody could be afraid all the time. It was possible to forget about death for hours at a time, and he found that he longed for Tish's presence more powerfully than ever, or at least more than he had since those wild London days during the war. Slowly he found himself intrigued by this strange experience, by the routines of the hospital staff, the intensity of the human drama around him, the ebb and flow of emotions he had never before known. He jotted thoughts and impressions in his ever-ready notebooks. Stewart began thinking that, if he survived for a reasonable time, perhaps he could bundle up these new experiences into a book. A book about his own death.

Word of Stewart's illness got around town, and soon he was showered with expressions of support. President Nixon called to wish him well and say he would try to make it out to NIH for a visit. Stewart privately hoped it wouldn't happen; he had come under fire in a *New York Times Magazine* piece as a presidential toady, and he didn't want his critics to have any extra evidence of the charge. Cousin Alice sent a flower with a note: "Stew—what a nuisance—love from your aged coz." Lyndon Johnson also sent Stewart a note of encouragement.

Joe too heard from Johnson, who wrote that he and Lady Bird prayed "for the recovery and subsequent good health" of Stewart. Senator Edward Kennedy wrote to Joe, "The only thing worse than losing a brother is having one suffer. My prayers are with Stew and my thoughts with you."

Joe and Susan Mary visited Stewart nearly every day, bringing food and alcohol. Stewart wrote to Joe, "You have been as a strong right arm in a time of trouble, providing strong liquors when I needed strong liquors, cucumber soup when I needed cucumber soup, and cheerfulness when I needed cheerfulness."

Meanwhile, Dr. Glick continued to draw marrow and monitor Stewart's situation. His fears were that the abnormal cells would "fulminate" and threaten to take over the marrow, or that they would make their way into the blood. In either case, Stewart would be sent promptly into the laminar flow room for chemotherapy.

But neither happened. Instead, the monitoring revealed that the abnormal cells actually declined a bit—from 44 percent down to 40, then to 38. Glick decided to send Stewart home. He would be monitored, would get a blood test every week, a marrow test every other week. But he could be as active as his energy level would allow. On August 6, Tish picked him up at NIH and drove him to Springland Lane, and Stewart set about to resume his work.

His first column told of his NIH experience. For decades the Alsops had demonstrated a knack for writing about themselves—Joe's revelations about losing his fat, the brothers' reminiscence of Henderson House, Stewart's tales of John's run for governor and the transformation of his hometown. Certainly, reasoned Stewart, this was at least as interesting as those stories. Recounting the experience, he wrote that it had been a bit like a first taste of combat. There was that initial "naked sense of vulnerability, but then 'God tempers the wind to the shorn lamb.' " He explained: "The protective mechanism takes over, and the intolerable becomes tolerable, the fear less fearful, and death itself—'a necessary end, will come when it will come.' "

Upon finishing the piece, he had second thoughts about revealing his own medical problems to a national audience. He asked Mel Elfin what he thought.

"I think it's wonderful," said Elfin.

"But do you think anyone will care about my private life?" asked Stewart. Elfin assured him they would, and Stewart released the piece.

Throughout August, Stewart tried to carry on with life as of old. He spent weekends at Needwood or at Polly Wisner's Eastern Shore farm—and played lots of bridge but no tennis. He tapped out the column on his old typewriter. He tried to make contact with sources around town. But it was hard to keep going; he lacked both physical and psychological energy. Rowland Evans, the columnist, helped by arranging source lunches to which he nudged his old friend. Most were enjoyable and some highly valuable. But Stewart couldn't shake the lassitude.

On August 31, on his way to NIH for blood and marrow tests, he felt sure he would die soon. He and Tish drove past a rose garden and remarked upon the flowers' beauty. Suddenly Stewart knew he wouldn't see the roses the following summer. He was sure he would get the word that very day; John Glick would come in with the news after studying his blood. Glick would say the malignant cells had shot up, had taken over his marrow or invaded his blood. It was to be the laminar flow room, a short remission, then a relapse and death. He reached out his hand to Tish's.

"I have just now run out of my small store of courage," he said. She squeezed his hand without words.

The blood tests seemed to confirm his pessimism. His granulocyte count was near zero, and the hemoglobin was below 10.

"Not too good, John," said Stewart to Glick. He asked about the marrow, and Glick said they would have to wait for those results.

He went home and had a martini with lunch, then decided against going to the office. He had no zest for the reporter's trade that afternoon. Then Glick called.

"Now don't get excited about this; it may mean nothing," said Glick. But he was himself clearly excited. Glick explained that Stewart's abnormal cell count had dropped from 38 percent to 28 percent. He couldn't say yet what it meant, but it could be good news. Stewart fixed himself another martini, and it turned out to be one of the most enjoyable he had ever consumed.

Stewart was in high spirits as he and Tish began a lively Labor Day weekend at Needwood. Rowly and Kay Evans, Kay Graham, and Joe all stayed over Saturday night, before an onslaught of guests arrived the next day. Joe, getting into the spirit of things, actually slept on a mattress on the floor of the library. There were lots of martinis, aggressive bridge, and plenty of laughter. It was "the classic Labor Day country house party," as Stewart later recalled it.

But on Monday afternoon Stewart began feeling ill. His temperature was above normal. The weakness had returned. There followed nearly twenty days of high temperatures, night sweats, and fear. Glick said there was a one-in-three chance of an overwhelming infection that would kill Stewart. It was back to NIH for transfusions and potent antibiotics. His granulocyte count remained well below 10 percent. A vast indifference overcame Stewart. "I enjoyed nothing," he wrote later. He began to feel "a certain affection" for the being he had come to call "Uncle Thanatos."

Then on September 19 came evidence of a turnaround. His platelets were back up to 18,000, and they kept rising, hitting a new high every day. By September 27 they had reached 45,000, and Glick decided to send Stewart home. The hemoglobin was holding steady at 11.5, meaning the marrow was manufacturing red cells again. Then the white count began to rise, reaching 3,000, with the percentage of disease-fighting granulocytes at 16. As the medical record improved, so did Stewart's mood and outlook. He felt as though he wanted to feel life again very deeply, to "see it, and smell it, and taste it, and breathe it down deep inside myself." He began collecting his thoughts, impressions, and experiences into that book. The old zest returned.

"I really think I have escaped old Dr. Thanatos," Stewart wrote to Cy Sulzberger in Paris. He resumed the column and his radio broadcasts on the CBS network with renewed feistiness. He fulminated against a Senate amendment sponsored by Democratic senators John Sherman Cooper and Frank Church, which would have cut off all U.S. logistical support for South Vietnam—and ensured victory for the communists. It failed by a single vote, and Stewart considered it "an act of gross immorality . . . a terrible betrayal." It was hard to believe, he wrote, "that men of the stature of Edmund Muskie and Edward Kennedy and Hubert Humphrey and Walter Mondale could vote for such an act, however politically expedient . . ."

The column reflected the delicate reality of Vietnam. The U.S. Army had ceased to be a fighting army, as combat forces returned home and the impedimenta remained. But the situation in Vietnam continued to improve as Saigon's army improved, and under President Thieu the country had reached a greater level of stability than it had known for a decade. All this had bolstered the U.S. bargaining position with North Vietnam, and Hanoi was signaling a willingness to accept a reasonable agreement.

The sticking point had been the Thieu government. Hanoi wanted Washington to accept what amounted to an indirect overthrow of Thieu, and Nixon had refused to discuss the idea. Then in secret talks, Hanoi's negotiators offered a compromise: They would yield on the overthrow issue if the United States promised to withdraw all American troops and if the Thieu regime would stand aside during an agreed-upon presidential election in the South. As Kissinger told Stewart during one of their chats, the United States agreed to both points in late October, and on October 25 the communists sent a courteous message proposing a November 20 meeting to pursue the matter. Three days before the scheduled meeting, the communists canceled it.

What happened in the meantime? "The answer seems obvious," wrote Stewart in a column based on his chat with Kissinger. On October 28 the Senate had nearly passed the Cooper-Church amendment. The next day, in what Stewart considered "the most irresponsible vote in modern times," the Senate voted to cut off all foreign aid to South Vietnam. If the Senate was prepared to hand North Vietnam what Nixon had resolutely refused to discuss, wrote Stewart, then why should Hanoi negotiate further? Was America really prepared to force a communist-front government on this small ally by threatening to cut off that ally's means of defending itself?

"Perhaps we are," wrote Stewart. "But for this country to deny them the means, thus forcing a communist regime on them, would be an act of crass betrayal, the crowning tragedy of a tragic war, and a long farewell to all our greatness."

To Stewart the homefront war took on such new importance because the battlefield war might tilt either way. The North Vietnamese army, lavishly supported by the Soviet Union and China, maintained large elements in Laos and Cambodia, poised to pounce on the South at the earliest opportunity. It would be difficult to get Hanoi to accept a reasonable settlement even without Congress handing over the president's bargaining chips. With the domestic political mood what it was, Nixon's task was becoming nearly impossible.

Joe continued to be optimistic. In October he returned from three weeks in Southeast Asia buoyed by what he had seen. The Vietcong infrastructure was drying up, and the North Vietnamese main forces appeared at bay. But he was not optimistic generally, about the world or his own life.

In the world he saw an emboldened Soviet Union—continuing its influence in Egypt and the Middle East, threatening China with Manchurian border deployments, testing the United States at points of Western vulnerability. Marshal Grechko, the hard-line Soviet defense minister, was gaining influence, and the United States, preoccupied by Vietnam, was offering no counterforce. "This country seems to have lost its nerve," Joe wrote to Isaiah Berlin.

Joe was even more depressed about his personal life. Sis's breast cancer and Stewart's health problems were bad enough. But he also suffered lingering depression over the death of his mother, just a month before Stewart's leukemia diagnosis. She had been eighty-five, and her last two years had been uncomfortable and painful. Her time had come. But it was nearly impossible to get over the loss of such a woman as Corinne Alsop. Her death, Joe wrote to his friend Mrs. Milton Gendel in London, "was all too like having the roof fall in abruptly." She had been the center of their "extremely tribal family," and with her in Avon the Alsop children had always had a base. "And now . . . we have no base . . ."

It was more than that, of course. Corinne had represented the last link to the distant era of dominance for the kith and kin of the Alsops, Roosevelts, and Robinsons. She had bridged the decades that stretched back to the cult of TR, to wild family afternoons at Oyster Bay and summers at Henderson House, to the elite's easy grace as "owners . . . of the world," as Joe had put it in that wartime letter to Avon. Throughout her life she had personified the notion of "class" that had so beguiled people of that station and time—the flamboyance and force of personality, the ability to entertain others while swaying them with an iron will, the passion for things "amusing." Joe had inherited much of that, had cultivated and savored the traits associated with the cult of TR and the days of old. But those traits seemed more and more out of favor now in the new age wrought by America's cultural revolution.

Joe also felt he was getting too old for the kind of job he had carved out for himself in his youth. He spent his sixty-first birthday on an airplane flying from Hong Kong to Washington, typically buffeted by the requirements of the column. "As long as I want to do my job properly," he wrote to Isaiah Berlin, "I have to be able to do this sort of thing. And that depresses me a bit, too."

He sought surcease from these realities in a new project, a comprehensive study of aesthetic tastes in the major civilizations of history. Joe knew that art collecting and the contemplation of art could provide deep insights into culture and history, and he felt a book exploring this theme could be "a genuinely original contribution," as he wrote to Berlin. He devoted hours to his project each week, devouring books and papers on the subject and piecing together a comprehensive view of art collecting. Increasingly he found himself enjoying this work more than he did the column.

Even Joe's friends felt the column no longer reflected the care and thoughtfulness of his earlier work. They thought he often lacked a sense of proportion, devoted too many columns to too few issues, and engaged in hobby-horse journalism. Then there was Joe's tendency to eschew the arts of persuasion in favor of the bludgeon. Even Kay Graham was becoming concerned that her old friend was harming his reputation, and perhaps that of *The Washington Post*, with his approach. In early 1972, at a conference at Hot Springs, West Virginia, she expressed some mild criticism of Joe's work. Her remarks got back to Joe, and that led to a conversation between the two.

Kay gave vent to the standard criticisms, citing Joe's recent five-column series on forced busing to achieve racial balance in public schools. She had considered the series polemical overkill.

The columns had reflected Joe's view that forced busing was a social disaster for the country and a political disaster for the Democratic Party. The impetus behind busing was a bit of social science research called the Coleman Report, which posited that by mingling racial groups in the schools the performance of black children would rise dramatically, with no deleterious effect on white children. As Joe saw it, busing would destroy the concept of neighborhood schools, undermine parental influence, and unleash powerful political angers. The policy could not possibly work, suggested Joe, because parents would simply send their children to private schools or move farther out into suburban areas where race was not a factor. Joe viewed the Coleman Report as flawed, as it was based on a study of integrated schools where middle-class black children learned alongside white children of similar socioeconomic background. The latest evidence, said Joe, suggested that large-scale desegregation efforts that ignored class distinctions could not solve the problem of poor performance among black students. As before, he advocated a massive program to improve school quality in black areas.

The busing series represented an excellent research effort and a valuable contribution to public-policy discussion. But it lacked discipline. Joe repeated the same points endlessly, and his constant digs at "liberal educationists," whom he portrayed as hopelessly stupid, undermined his arguments. Phil Geyelin, the *Post*'s editorial-page editor, likened the series to a "stuck whistle," and although Kay Graham used more diplomatic language she sought to convey essentially the same message. Joe responded with a three-page letter defending the series as groundbreaking journalism, but he acknowledged the problem of style. The series, he said, "repeatedly fell into the cross, contentious tone you warned me about and which I now recognize as a great mistake."

As THE CAMPAIGN year heated up, Nixon struck Joe and Stewart as a politician of rare ability. Both brothers viewed the president's performance on the war as extremely adroit. Even with the Vietnam millstone around his neck, Nixon still managed to initiate imaginative new policies in both domestic and foreign affairs: a "revenue sharing" plan to forge a new relationship between the federal government and the states; a major crime bill to address a growing national concern; and a new directness with the Soviet Union that had led to an invitation for Nixon to visit Moscow in the spring.

But perhaps the most brilliant initiative had been Nixon's overture to China, which had been considered an outcast nation in the West for a generation. The result had been a triumphant election-year presidential visit to Beijing in February and March, with Nixon playing the role of preeminent world diplomat. Joe called the trip "grandiose" and a "glittering short-term success." The ultimate success wouldn't be known for some time, he added, because the real aim had been to deter the Soviet Union from a preemptive attack on China's emerging nuclear weapons facilities, and only time would tell if that aim had been fulfilled.

Joe saw the China initiative, as he did just about everything, through the prism of U.S.-Soviet relations. He noted in the column that the Soviets had increased their troop strength on the Soviet-Chinese border to at least twenty-two divisions, from just thirteen in 1965. Shortly after Nixon had taken office, the Soviets had sent out feelers inquiring about the likely U.S. reaction to a Soviet strike aimed at deterring China's nuclear weapons capability. When Joe had reported those feelers in his column, the Soviet newspaper *Pravda* had savaged him in a front-page article. Joe called the attack "a great honor."

Joe now viewed Nixon's Beijing initiative as a brilliant effort to hem in the Soviet Union, to exploit Soviet fears of China and soften the Kremlin's bargaining stance with the West. For many Americans who had supported Chiang Kai-shek over the years and despised the Mao communists, Nixon's action was an outrage. Joe welcomed it. To him, the primary enemy was the Soviet Union.

Richard Nixon's primary enemy remained Hanoi, which on March

30 launched a series of attacks throughout South Vietnam, committing 120,000 North Vietnamese regulars and thousands of Vietcong guerrillas to the fray. They captured vast territory in the northern provinces, including the provincial capital of Quangtri. They swept across the central highlands to the coast and hit the area north of Saigon, threatening Anloc, capital of Binh Long Province. As Thieu redeployed troops from the Mekong Delta to the northern battles, Vietcong guerrillas moved in, capturing or overrunning more than a hundred abandoned government posts. Pacification programs collapsed throughout vast areas.

By this time only six thousand of the seventy thousand U.S. ground troops in Vietnam were combat troops. The South Vietnamese army responded to the challenge with mixed success. In some areas they displayed courage and efficiency, in others a stunning lack of resolve. It was clear that the South would have collapsed without American air power and advisers providing backbone. Even with that backbone, Thieu's army—and Nixon's political standing—appeared tenuous.

Joe was in Vietnam as the offensive unfolded, and even he could see that this battle might be decisive. He applauded the success of Thieu's troops in defending Quangtri (before its eventual fall) and Anloc, and he emphasized the huge losses sustained by the communist troops. But he suggested this could turn out to be like 1968's Tet onslaught, which had proved a military defeat but a psychological victory. "It had better be faced," he wrote, "that a final U.S. defeat in Vietnam is entirely possible." With Saigon's extreme shortage of reserves and Hanoi's ruthless way of expending manpower, "the odds today have to be quoted as about even." For Joe writing about Vietnam, this was a rare specimen of pessimism—and realism.

But Nixon had no intention of allowing the offensive to continue without reply, for every day it diminished his bargaining position with Hanoi. On May 8, 1972, he ordered the expanded bombing of North Vietnam and the mining of Haiphong harbor. His critics deplored the moves, arguing they wouldn't impede communist activity in the South and would stir the Soviets to cancel the forthcoming summit meeting in Moscow. But the Soviets didn't react, and Nixon's show of resolve proved popular with the public. His approval rating moved up to 60 percent. Moreover, his actions blunted the psychological impact of the communist offensive, which had begun to lose force militarily.

Joe applauded Nixon's "bold decision," arguing that it would thwart Hanoi's effort to sustain a great offensive over a prolonged period. The bombing and mining, Joe wrote, would constrict the communists' ability to move precious petroleum products and weaponry into the South, and would require Hanoi to assign up to 200,000 men to the task of repairing roads and bridges and manning antiaircraft weapons.

Stewart took a more pessimistic view. The stated purposes of the president's decision—to protect American troops and give the South Vietnamese army a chance to defend itself in the current offensive—

didn't make sense, he wrote, because the president's actions wouldn't have any military effect for at least two months. The privately stated reason—to pressure Moscow to rein in Hanoi—also didn't make sense, because it wasn't clear that Moscow had that kind of influence in Hanoi. Hence there was a missing element.

The missing element, wrote Stewart, was Nixon's desperate need to convince Hanoi and Moscow that he would do almost anything to protect the vulnerable American troops remaining in Vietnam. He knew his actions couldn't in themselves prevent a South Vietnamese defeat or an American Dunkirk, but he wanted to signal that nobody could predict just what dire actions he might take. When Moscow declined to sabotage the forthcoming summit and the North Vietnamese signaled an eagerness to renew negotiations, Stewart speculated that the message was getting through.

By this time it seemed clear that the Democratic presidential nomination would go to South Dakota's Senator George McGovern, probably the Senate's leading dove. To the brothers, he represented the return of Midwestern isolationism in liberal guise; they could hardly stand the thought of such forces capturing the Democratic Party. In June Stewart wrote a column exploring some of McGovern's liberal promises uttered when he was staking out his territory in the early primary season, and he concluded that the senator would have to become an accomplished word-eater. "The words he is going to have to eat are right there, in black and white, dating from the days when nobody—but nobody—was going to get to the left of George McGovern."

Joe disliked McGovern so much that he wouldn't interview him or most of his people. Even when the senator's staff invited Joe in for a chat with McGovern in late June, he declined. His rather contorted reasoning was that he considered most of McGovern's positions "dangerous," and hence the senator would be wasting his time if he sought to enlighten Joe on his politics. Joe did speak occasionally with McGovern aides Pierre Salinger and Frank Mankiewicz, whom he considered friends, but otherwise he made no effort to gain a firsthand understanding of McGovernism.

At the Democratic convention in Miami Beach, Stewart summed up McGovern's political dilemma succinctly. "How," he asked, "is he to persuade a majority of the people to elect him in November, without infuriating the people who nominated him in July?" McGovern, he wrote, was a product of a new set of party nominating rules that he himself had devised, and through these rules he had become his party's leader without ever having to demonstrate any broad-based acceptability in the country. The people who gave McGovern to the Democratic Party represented, said Stewart, "a minority of a minority nationally." Going into the convention, McGovern trailed Nixon in the major opinion surveys by as much as 19 percentage points, and that gap was to grow.

A month later, Stewart was invited aboard Air Force One to accompany President Nixon to the Republicans' Miami Beach convention. The trip yielded a half-hour interview and a long column on Nixon's view of a second term.

"I'm sure of one thing," declared Nixon. "The war . . . won't be hanging over us in a second term."

The president seemed ebullient about what he could accomplish after his reelection, without the war dragging him down. He said he anticipated major developments in the international economy as his diplomatic overtures to China and the Soviets paid off in expanded trade. And with the war out of the way he could concentrate on the welfare mess, on education, health, a government reorganization plan. "And tax reform—that's another point, very important."

Nixon clearly anticipated a victory margin that would make him a strong majority president for the first time. George Wallace no longer was a factor; he had been paralyzed by an assassin's bullet during the spring Democratic primary campaign in Maryland. With a weak opponent in McGovern, Nixon expected a serious mandate from the voters, big enough for him to sway Congress as he never had been able to do in his first term. He would "strike fast," said Nixon, would "go to Congress and say, 'Let's get off our bottoms and get to work.' "

The interview contained no major revelations, but it offered a lively portrait of a man savoring the prospect of his greatest political triumph. Unlike the chaotic Democratic gathering, the Republican convention unfolded as a ritual political coronation, and the president cruised through the fall campaign. When the votes were counted, he had 60.7 percent. And yet something was missing for Republicans who had hoped Nixon might forge a new coalition of lasting significance. The party had picked up only thirteen seats in the House, and actually lost two in the Senate. It was more a personal triumph than a political one.

But for the Alsops, it was a good outcome. Even during Nixon's days as vice president, Stewart had been an admirer, and the president's deft handling of the treacherous Vietnam issue had impressed him immeasurably. Joe, placing aside his long-held misgivings about Nixon, now considered him the right man for the times. Besides, the president had been going out of his way to befriend Joe. He had invited him to an Oval Office ceremony to honor the longtime Vietnam warrior John Paul Vann, who had died in a helicopter crash in the spring, and in October he had written a letter wishing Joe a happy sixty-second birthday. Joe's regard for Nixon had led him to an action that was unprecedented in his long career: He had contributed $49 to the Nixon campaign, a dollar less than the level that would have triggered disclosure.

With the election over, Joe embarked on an odyssey of nostalgia; he and Susan Mary headed to China for a monthlong visit. Nixon's diplomatic initiative had opened up the country to foreign visitors, including foreign reporters, and a Chinese-American friend had returned from

Beijing with word that officials wondered why Joe hadn't sought a visa. He promptly had applied.

When the Alsops arrived in Beijing, Chinese officialdom was waiting. Four high information officers escorted them through the normal round of sightseeing—the Great Hall of the People, the palaces of the Forbidden City, the busy commercial street of Ta Sha La, the Great Wall. Joe's guides told of the turbulent Cultural Revolution that Mao had visited upon his people. Three of the guides had spent two years in camps aimed at "thought reform." It had been an unpleasant experience "at first," they said, but they had come to appreciate it. Now they understood their country much better, and themselves, too. Casting aside his years-long revulsion for Chinese communism and revealing the seduction he was undergoing, Joe wrote that the Cultural Revolution could be viewed as a "China-size omelette, for which numberless eggs were broken."

During the daylong Great Wall trip, Joe had a long conversation with Ma Yu-chen, vice director of the Foreign Ministry's information department. Ma seemed obsessed with the Soviet Union and the huge Soviet troop buildup on China's northern border. In a later session with top editors of the *People's Daily* and Hsin Hua News Agency, Joe found his hosts similarly preoccupied with the Soviet Union. He spent an evening with Chiao Kuan-hua, vice minister of foreign affairs, and again the primary topic was China's western neighbor. Joe wondered if he was being sized up to determine if he was the right man to carry an important message back to the United States. A Chinese official told him to hold himself in readiness for a "special appointment."

He and Susan Mary planted themselves in their hotel room and waited. At nine thirty one evening word arrived. "Please come right away. Prime Minister Chou En-lai is waiting for you outside the Great Hall of the People." There was no time to change. Susan Mary felt uncomfortable meeting the prime minister in slacks and a sweater, but she grabbed a coat, and they were whisked away in a limousine to the Great Hall. There, in a grandiose vestibule, smiling warmly, was Chou.

"We have met before, Mr. Alsop," said Chou, referring to a chance encounter during Joe's China days. "I know your views are very different, but after hearing you were in Beijing, I could not forestall my curiosity."

They went into an immense reception room and sat down, surrounded by Chinese officials. A young girl served as interpreter, and Susan Mary took notes for Joe, who felt it would be disrespectful to play the reporter so overtly with such a high official. "Well," said the prime minister, "would you like a boring formal interview? Or would you like to know what I really think?" Joe replied that an off-the-record interview would be preferred, and they set off on a three-hour exchange. "They got on like a house afire," recalled Susan Mary.

Chou talked of China's internal problems and opportunities, of agricultural output and the country's efforts at population control. More than an hour of the conversation was devoted to Chou's view of the Soviet government under Leonid Brezhnev, who had emerged as the top Kremlin leader after Khrushchev's ouster in 1964.

"Worse than Khrushchev," said Chou, which struck Joe as significant, since it had been Khrushchev who had terminated the Soviet Union's cooperative approach to China and had even helped foster an attempted coup against Mao Tse-tung a decade before. The Chinese fears of Soviet belligerence Joe had been hearing about were being felt at the top.

It was nearly one a.m. before the interview began to wind down.

"Is there anything I can do for you during your visit, Mr. Alsop?" asked Chou.

"There is, sir. I would like to take my wife traveling into the interior."

"Where?"

"To Yunnan and Szechwan," said Joe, noting that he had spent most of his wartime years in those two provinces. "Would that be impossible?"

"Not at all," said the prime minister. "When would you like to go? Would three hours suit you?"

And Joe and Susan Mary found themselves aboard a military plane, on what for Joe was a sentimental journey to Chongqing and Kunming, where so many ghosts of his past still roamed.

He found Kunming, Chennault's old headquarters, a city transformed. Once a remote retreat for exiled princes, now it was a thriving provincial capital and industrial center, with ample rail connections and huge factories. Yunnan steel production had reached 240,000 tons a year, from just 356 at the end of Chiang Kai-shek's reign. The total value of industrial production had climbed in the same period to 3.5 billion Chinese dollars from 180 million. In a column Joe compared Kunming to a burgeoning American industrial city of around 1900, except that Kunming lacked the wealthy industrialists who had sprung up in that heady American era.

The once-haunting gorge city of Chongqing was no less haunting now. But the ghostly defense plants that had been buried away in caves had been replaced by modern factories. The squalid wartime shanty-towns had given way to rows of bleak but reasonably comfortable workers' flats. Joe was in high spirits throughout the Chongqing visit, and Susan Mary could see that he was enjoying this flight of nostalgia.

Joe realized it was easy to exaggerate the industrial progress of China, whose economy was still 80 percent agricultural. But he felt certain that the new China, emerging from its isolation and from the chaos of Mao's Cultural Revolution, would eventually become the colossus of the East. With his old love of the country, he welcomed its awakening.

Upon his return to Washington, he recounted his China experiences in a two-part series for *The New York Times Magazine,* warning of the Soviet threat to China and praising the country's many virtues. Gone now was the anger about the loss of China and the moral outrage over the brutal zealotry of the communist overlords. As so often, Joe's emotions had got the best of him. He had been roundly seduced.

AT YEAR'S END, during Joe's China journey, Henry Kissinger had finally succeeded in negotiating a settlement with North Vietnam. It called for a cease-fire, withdrawal of all U.S. troops from South Vietnam, withdrawal of North Vietnamese troops from Laos and Cambodia, and a prisoner exchange. The political problems would fall to the jurisdiction of the opposing sides in the South—the Thieu regime and the communist National Liberation Front, which jointly would form a "council of national reconciliation" to oversee eventual elections. The military situation in the South would remain in place, with Thieu's army and the Vietcong controlling whatever territory they held at the signing.

Stewart called the truce "a simple trade-off—what they wanted for what we wanted." North Vietnam wanted an end to U.S. bombing and an end of air support for Thieu's army. Nixon wanted out of Vietnam on a reasonably respectable basis and the return of all U.S. prisoners of war. It was, Stewart said, "the best deal we could get." But he added that there shouldn't be any illusions about this truce actually bringing peace to Vietnam. He noted that the 1954 and 1962 Geneva settlements of the French Indochina war and the Laos war had come apart almost before the signatures had dried on the parchment. "It is hard to believe that something of the same sort will not happen again," wrote Stewart.

Stewart continued to follow political events closely during this time, but the specter of a cancer relapse was never far from his thoughts. Back in the fall of 1971, when his remission had begun, the abnormal cells in his marrow had declined to 6 percent from a high of 40 percent. A complete remission had seemed entirely possible.

But then the bad cells began coming back—16 percent in February 1972, 23 percent in March, 40 percent again in April. The marrow's platelet production declined to dangerous levels, and Stewart needed regular transfusions. The problem was that platelets are difficult to match, and Glick could find only three people whose platelets Stewart could take. One was Joe, who went through the uncomfortable process of donating platelets as often as Glick would allow. But Joe's age and evidence of heart irregularity made Glick reluctant to rely on him routinely. The others were Stewart Jr. and an NIH technician named Bob Park. Stewart Sr. could keep going with these transfusions, but it gave him a queasy feeling to live from week to week on the blood of others.

Glick theorized that Stewart's flu of the previous autumn had induced his temporary remission by stimulating the body's resistance to bad cells. He decided to inject a drug called Poly I-C, which causes a kind of artificial flu. It was highly experimental, said Glick. Stewart likened the treatment to coaxing an old bird dog, who wanted only to lie by the fire and doze, out into the field to hunt birds again.

The Poly I-C induced terrible sweats and chills and a fever of 104; but Stewart's temperature soon returned to normal, and the bad cells in the marrow declined to 25 percent. Stewart got the Poly I-C treatment three times a week for three weeks, and for a time it appeared to be working. The marrow resumed making good blood. The old bird dog bestirred himself. But then the bad cells multiplied again, and by summer another three-week treatment was necessary. Again there was a temporary response, and then the bad cells returned.

Propelled by resolve and grit, Stewart made it through the year, knocking out the column nearly every week, working away on his book, heading back to NIH for the regular blood and marrow tests that induced the regular bouts of fear. One Friday afternoon in the fall, as he played tennis, he began feeling a rawness in his chest. It wasn't enough to keep him from a small dinner party at Kay Graham's house that evening, but by ten o'clock he knew something was seriously wrong. Sure enough, he had lobar pneumonia, which meant another stay on the hated thirteenth floor of the NIH cancer ward, another ten-day hookup to potent antibiotics, another effort to fend off not just the specter of death but the weariness of life that crept over him now with growing frequency. For Stewart, a significant part of living was now devoted to the challenge of not dying.

WATERGATE

Witness to a Political Tragedy

RICHARD NIXON SAVORED his triumph of 1972 by boldly declaring a mandate to build a new reigning coalition for the nation. In truth, however, he sat precariously atop the pinnacle of his career. A dark scandal threatened his presidency. Back in June a team of burglars had been arrested inside the Democratic Party's national headquarters at the Watergate office complex. They had been linked to the White House, and investigators soon had traced the burglars' banknotes directly to Nixon's campaign apparatus. As the FBI's investigative machinery lurched into action, a scheme was hatched in the White House to cover up the involvement of top Nixon aides. The president himself had become entangled in a web of conspiracy and misfeasance.

By the time of Nixon's second inauguration on January 20, 1973, the burglars and two accomplices—Howard Hunt, a shadowy White House official with a CIA background, and a furtive former FBI agent named G. Gordon Liddy—had been convicted, and the scandal appeared contained. The president pressed on, as if to suggest that the lingering scandal was too trifling to bother with, beneath the grandeur of his vision for the nation. But the gathering clouds of Watergate darkened his administration and his plans.

The Alsop brothers didn't pay much attention to Watergate in the new year's early weeks. They were more interested in Nixon's grand strategy for changing the nation's political landscape. In early January they rushed to his defense when Hanoi's intransigence threatened the

Vietnam cease-fire and Nixon responded with a rain of bombs on North Vietnam.

Stewart, still fighting leukemia but feeling feisty on matters of public affairs, opened a *Newsweek* column with a bit of sarcasm directed at Nixon's critics:

> What is Mr. Nixon going to do now? Nuke Hanoi? Hit the dikes? Or just go on bombing North Vietnam till hell freezes over?
> These questions are being asked rather gloatingly, in a tone implying: little man, what now? They are being asked as though they were questions without an answer.

But there was an answer, and Nixon already had given it, said Stewart. The answer was that the president was going to turn the defense of South Vietnam over to South Vietnam itself. Even President Thieu welcomed that policy because it enabled him to thumb his nose at the United States and thus appeal to the nationalism of his people. But the policy did not include ending economic support for South Vietnam, cutting her off at the knees and ensuring a communist takeover. Most of the Democratic Party would make that deal, wrote Stewart, but Nixon had denounced it repeatedly as a betrayal. "He cannot now make such a deal, even if he wanted to, which he doesn't."

On the other hand, wrote Stewart, Nixon couldn't go on "bombing the bejesus out of North Vietnam forever." That not only would make the United States look like a brute but would also incite Congress to cut off all aid to Saigon. Thus, it was best merely to walk away from the settlement talks and support Thieu's effort to defend his country. The United States might not get its prisoners out of North Vietnamese jails, but the nation would have its honor.

In the end, Nixon's bombing reinforced the cease-fire and preserved the settlement. But in the meantime Stewart's column enraged Anthony Lewis, *The New York Times*'s New Left columnist, who wrote Stewart an angry letter. Why, asked Lewis, should anyone assume the president wouldn't just do what he wanted? "Do you sense some inner moral limitation that has escaped the notice of the rest of us?" Lewis denounced "the most powerful country in world history, pouring the greatest volume of destruction ever on a small country with no power to retaliate against us." He added:

> I happen to believe that the sanity of our country, and the last chance to save it from the eternal damnation that the Nazis earned Germany, rest with conservatives like yourself. If you cannot see that the mass bombing of one of the most densely populated areas on the face of the earth is a crime, then nothing can save us and we shall deserve the reputation we have earned.

The letter offended Stewart's sense of patriotism. In a subsequent column he presented the Lewis letter and then ripped into it. Lewis, said Stewart, seemed to think that Nixon's B-52 bombing of the Hanoi area was to be equated with the bombing of civilians in, say, Hamburg and Dresden in World War II, which had killed nearly 200,000 in two nights. Nixon's bombing had killed 1,318 (according to Hanoi) over twelve days. "That is a lot of dead people. But the fact remains that the bombing was not 'mass bombing' in the sense you employ." Stewart wrote that Lewis had been silent when the Israelis had employed "deep penetration bombing" to establish conquered territory as within Israel's de facto borders. "I do not recall that you denounced [that] as a crime worthy of the Nazis." He added:

> You refer to me as a conservative. I certainly did not vote for George McGovern. Maybe that makes me a conservative, although I voted for every previous Democratic Presidential candidate since I came of voting age. I have also pointed out such inconvenient facts as that children of working-class people, not of prosperous persons like you and me and Senator McGovern, are chiefly affected by racial busing. I have failed to grasp the shining morality of betraying the South Vietnamese by denying them the means to defend themselves. . . .
>
> Does all this make me a conservative? Perhaps, by the standards of your kind of liberalism. But consider the results of your kind of liberalism. The old liberalism identified itself with the interests of ordinary people, people who work for a living, enjoy "I Love Lucy," and wear American flags in their buttonholes. Your kind of liberalism excludes such people. . . .
>
> One result was last November's liberal disaster, which saw an unloved president, burdened with a smelly scandal, score a historic landslide. The reason was not that your kind of liberalism was against Mr. Nixon, whom hardly anybody likes very much, or against the war, which nobody likes at all.
>
> The reason was that a great many ordinary Americans perceived your kind of liberalism as against *them*—and worse, against the United States. To see why, it is only necessary to read the last paragraph of your letter.

The column—entitled "Eternal Damnation?"—touched a nerve. Pennsylvania's Republican senator Hugh Scott read it into the *Congressional Record*, and letters poured in from points around the world. Joe Fromm of *U.S. News & World Report* wrote from London to say Stewart was "one of the few commentators . . . who [seem] to have a real grasp of contemporary America beyond the East Coast." *Newsweek*'s roving international affairs writer, Arnaud de Borchgrave, wrote, "You really socked it to him. . . . Your column was the talk of the closing stages of the Paris conference." Judging by his mail, Stewart concluded, Lewis "must have been irritating a lot of people for a long time."

His leukemia had slowed Stewart down, and he needed regular blood transfusions in order to maintain a moderate professional schedule, a little tennis and, of course, his regular evening martinis. But he could still keep the columns coming, and he still enjoyed a good controversy.

The Alsop-Lewis controversy reflected a new reality: The center of political gravity in America had shifted, and the spectrum of discourse had widened. A few years before, it would have been unthinkable for a mainstream columnist to compare U.S. actions to those of Nazi Germany, but now such rhetorical flights could be seen routinely in *The New York Times*. A few years before, the political outlook of the major networks had been mildly liberal, like that of the Alsops—moderately interventionist on market issues, compassionate on social issues, internationalist on foreign issues. Now younger network reporters and producers were likely to inject into their work traces of antiwar fervor or the antiestablishment views of the counterculture. The moderation of outlook that had always been an Alsop hallmark now seemed threatened as much from the left as from the right—perhaps more from the left. Thus, Stewart directed his broadsides more often toward the left.

He also seemed genuinely taken by Nixon's bold resolve to remake the federal government and forge a new political era. Nixon, wrote Stewart, was what the French called *un homme serieux*—a man to be taken seriously. He had reached down into the depths of the government to rip out appointees who weren't devoted to his vision. He had shown his toughness by ordering those bombing raids on the Hanoi area. "He interprets his re-election," wrote Stewart, "as a mandate to act the 'homme serieux' abroad, and at home to strip away big hunks of the Great Society and to get the budget and the Federal bureaucracy under control." Nixon seemed poised to fashion a new conservative agenda for his second term.

Joe also felt increasingly comfortable with Nixon, and the president continued to cultivate his support. When Joe wrote that Nixon's bombing had worked in bringing Hanoi back to serious bargaining, the president expressed appreciation. "The decision to bomb military targets near Hanoi was difficult to make," he wrote, "and I am glad to know you share my feeling that it was in fact a step toward a peace agreement." Joe wrote back to say it was "a great honor to receive such a letter from anyone who leads our country." He added that it was "a special honor on this occasion, since your foresight and courage have carried us so far toward a good result in Asia, despite the most terrible, often needless difficulties along the way."

But the peace created by the Vietnam agreement, as Stewart had so often noted, was a fragile thing. It could survive only so long as Nixon was strong; and by early spring the Watergate scandal was sapping his political strength. The Senate had created a special committee headed by Senator Sam Ervin of North Carolina, and Stewart suspected that its hearings would make more trouble for Nixon than any Senate investigation had made for any modern president.

He described Ervin as "far and away the best of the Senate's . . . character actors"—master of the pregnant pause, the eyebrow lifted in surprise, the jowls shaken in indignation, the droll interjection, the deft historical reference. And the other six committee members, Republican and Democrat alike, would be of no help to the president. "They are shrewd political professionals," wrote Stewart, "who have to worry about their own skins, and who do not at all like the smell of the whole smelly business."

A month later, Stewart speculated on how Nixon might escape this "super-crisis." Most Americans, even most Americans who didn't like Nixon, hoped for his innocence. Their sentiment had less to do with Nixon than with the American political system, which would be seriously jolted by revelations that the president had been involved in crass illegality. The president's best approach would be to take charge, confront the crisis, and lead the cleansing process. Some of his most trusted lieutenants might have to go, wrote Stewart, but that was the price of a clean stable. Nixon already had suggested he would take such an approach. At a March 21 news conference he had announced "intensive new inquiries" that he himself was heading.

"One can imagine," Stewart wrote, "an aging president, all political ambition behind him now, telling more in sorrow than in anger the sad story of how he was betrayed, not so much by the wickedness as by the zeal of those who wished to preserve certain American values."

Joe took a less detached view of Watergate. He wanted it to go away, to stop threatening Nixon's global plans. For weeks he declined to write about the scandal, and when he finally did on April 4 it was to suggest that the morality of the matter weighed less heavily than the nation's need for a strong executive. "The American system does not work very well when the occupant of the White House is a political cripple," he wrote.

In Joe's world, it seemed inevitable that the Soviet Union would turn more adventuresome as it saw America hobbled by Watergate. He was convinced that the Soviets were contemplating a massive air strike against China to destroy her emergent nuclear capacity. The odds of such a strike would increase, Joe thought, if the United States allowed North Vietnam to renege on the peace accord, or if Congress managed to cut deeply into the U.S. defense budget. On the other hand, the odds would decline if the defense appropriation were increased by, say, $5 billion.

After all, Joe wrote to Meg Greenfield, a rising editorial writer at *The Washington Post*, Louis Johnson's disarmament had led directly to the

Korean War. Then the belt-tightening policies of Eisenhower's defense secretary, Charles Wilson, had brought on the Soviet intervention in the Middle East, plus the second Berlin crisis, "only licked after President Kennedy had mobilized and then come through the fairly hair-raising confrontation over the missiles in Cuba." Watergate, he said, could bring on a repeat of those difficult episodes.

IN APRIL, STEWART, who had been writing vigorously about matters of state, suffered another physical setback. His platelet counts collapsed, and John Glick said regular transfusions would be needed from Joe. "He hasn't a notion, of course, of the sort of sacrifice he is asking you to make," Stewart wrote to Joe. "I do." For one thing, it would be necessary for Joe to give up drinking intermittently, and Stewart jocularly suggested that a paraphrase of the Bible was in order: "Greater love hath no man than this, that he go on the wagon for his brother." He added: "We Alsops are lousy about expressing such things. But I really do appreciate what you have done and are doing."

Stewart's spirits declined along with his platelet count. "I am low," he wrote to Joe. "There is a feeling of doors closing." The family pulled together. John Alsop conducted a springtime search of his meadow and found a four-leaf clover. He sent it to Stewart. "I feel that we all could use a bit of luck," he wrote.

Joe was there to fill whatever of Stewart's needs he could. But he too was low. "I never have my new lesson very far from my mind," he wrote to a Vermont friend, Mrs. Richard Derby. "The lesson is that you never know what it will really be like to have great holes torn in the fabric of your life, until it begins to happen to you."

Stewart carried on with the column as best he could, but some weeks he just wasn't up to it. He wrote to Oz Elliott at *Newsweek* to say the proportion of abnormal cells in his marrow had declined to less than 30 percent, so whatever it was in his system that was combating the malignant cells was "still in there fighting." But the low platelet count was worrisome. "Don't count me out," he wrote. "But I'm tired, and running short, so I may stop writing for a couple of weeks." He said he wanted *Newsweek* to withhold payment for any columns not produced. For Elliott this was a unique experience—a writer actually demanding that he not be paid. He ignored the request.

No longer was Stewart the reporter of old. When he did file columns, they were more pure analysis than reporting. Unable to pursue inside information, he stepped back and provided insight into the big events of the day. The news now seemed to focus mostly on Watergate.

Stewart had become ambivalent about the scandal. As more information spilled out, he became appalled by the idea that high-level politicians would employ techniques of espionage against their domestic adversaries. "They were not practicing politics," he wrote. "They were making war." Those who employed such techniques—electronic eaves-dropping, political sabotage, information theft—should be not only punished by law but banned from the political process.

But he was disturbed by the "get Nixon" mentality so prevalent in parts of the government and the liberal community. The Justice Department and the FBI had become information sieves, leaking what they wanted to leak and withholding what they wanted to withhold. The concept of grand jury secrecy, designed to protect innocents from the flow of raw, unprocessed revelations, had been seriously violated. These developments should have offended the sensibilities of liberals, wrote Stewart, but most seemed gleeful. And they avidly cheered as the president's former counsel, John Dean III, sought to implicate his old boss in the scandal.

To Stewart, Dean was "a specimen of an unlovely breed—the turn-coat, squealer or fingerman." Yet, in the frenzied Watergate atmosphere, he wrote, to suggest that a turncoat's testimony is always suspect was to risk the most damning of liberal labels—that of apologist for the White House.

"The time may come," wrote Stewart, "when the ox to be gored is not the detested Mr. Nixon's, but a fine liberal ox. The wholesale leaking by the secret police and the grand jury, and the eager acceptance of turn-coat testimony, may then appear to liberals in a rather different light."

Aside from these crosscurrents of moral outrage, there was the question of whether the government of Richard Nixon could function. The president's legitimacy was under question, his political support seeping away. By summer, Nixon had been on the defensive for weeks, and every action he took in response to the building crisis seemed to render him more vulnerable. On April 30, he had forced out of the government some of his most trusted lieutenants—the White House "palace guard," H. R. Haldeman and John Ehrlichman, and Attorney General Richard Kleindienst. The new attorney general, Elliot Richardson, had been given authority to appoint a special prosecutor to pursue the case. On May 17, the "Sam Ervin Show" had opened on Capitol Hill and had moved inexorably to the damning testimony of John Dean. The president had lost control of the government and of his fate.

For Stewart, writing on July 9, there seemed to be only three possibilities. The president could tough it out for the remainder of his term, a "paraplegic president" who held the office but couldn't lead the nation; there could be impeachment proceedings in the House and a trial in the Senate, which likely would "tear the country apart like no event since the Civil War"; or the president could resign. "The president's resignation," wrote Stewart, "is the only tolerable way out of the tragic mess in which this country finds itself." But he didn't expect Nixon to resign.

Joe agreed. "I see no likelihood," he wrote to Marilyn Chandler, wife of Los Angeles Times publisher Otis Chandler, "that Mr. Nixon is going to cease to be president until his term expires." Others saw the forces of Watergate suffocating the presidency, but Joe felt Nixon could ride out the scandal. A week after John Dean testified before the Ervin committee, Joe warned of the impact of Watergate on the country's world standing. The dollar was sinking dangerously on foreign currency markets, Joe said, because of "the self-serving allegations of a bottom-dwelling slug like Dean."

Joe still knew how to turn a phrase for maximum impact. His description of Dean quickly became a conversation topic around town, and would be recalled decades later when old Washington hands congregated to trade Watergate stories. Dean's lawyers, fearful that Joe's column would undermine their client's credibility, launched a campaign to warn important Washington opinion shapers against jumping upon the Alsop bandwagon. Dean's testimony implicating the president, they predicted, would prove truthful in the end.

Joe didn't buy that. Ultimately, it would be Dean's word against the president's, and that wouldn't be enough to cut short the Nixon presidency. In a June 11 column, he reported the president was "unshakeably determined to ride out the horror," and that "no one with any knowledge of the House and Senate thinks there is any likelihood that the president will be impeached."

Joe was wrong. But he couldn't have known, as Watergate investigators were about to find out from presidential aide Alexander Butterfield, that for years Nixon had maintained a voice-activated recording device in the Oval Office. Now it was no longer a question of Dean's word against Nixon's. It was a matter of what was on those tapes.

The revelation plunged Nixon into a grave political crisis—and the nation into a grave constitutional crisis. Claiming executive privilege, Nixon sought to protect the tapes from inspection. Elliot Richardson's special prosecutor, Archibald Cox, went to court to get them. The battle shifted from a matter of wispy recollection and unsubstantiated allegation to the far graver question of why the nation couldn't get to the bottom of the mess once and for all. It was a game no president could win.

As Nixon foundered and the nation suffered, Joe's personal life came unstuck. Events in the country were making him more cantankerous than ever, and that in turn was causing an erosion in Susan Mary's emotional state. She found herself slipping into long moods of despondency. Finally, the only answer seemed to be a permanent escape from Joe. The culmination came when one of her favorite nephews visited the Alsops for a few days. Joe didn't like the young man, and sought to intimidate him with his worst bullying tactics. For Susan Mary it was a terrible humiliation, and the day after her nephew departed she moved out of the Dumbarton house.

A short item in the *Washington Star* of September 26 reported the separation. Susan Mary was quoted as saying it was a "very amicable separation" and that she expected to settle into permanent quarters sometime in October. "I am grateful for the twelve years I have had with him," she told the newspaper, "and I hope to see a great deal of him. Joe is a wonderful bachelor and a wonderful stepfather."

She moved into the fashionable Watergate apartment complex and sought to build a new life; but she was not happy. She suffered from long periods of depression, and her children and friends worried about her. For nearly a year she saw very little of Joe.

Joe too was depressed. He continued to speak of Susan Mary in the most admiring terms, referring to her as his "beautiful wife," his "extraordinary wife." He extolled her "high moral principles." He lamented her departure deeply, and he blamed himself. But there was nothing he could do. Susan Mary would never come back.

It seemed to Joe that the Alsop luck, so abundant all the way back to the day when Pa had bought the Avon farm, had run out with Ma's death in summer 1971. Everything and everyone he had known and loved seemed to be coming to an end, and he felt like a member of the Usher family in Poe's dark tale. The sense of gloom that had always hovered over Joe had struck friends and family as a bit of a pose, but now it seemed genuine. "As far as I could see," his stepdaughter, Anne Crile, wrote to Joe, "you couldn't have been any further 'down' than you've been the last couple of months."

Anne loved Joe, and she hated to see him slip into the dejection that gripped him now. She sat down to write him a tough but affectionate letter:

> You've mentioned the House of Usher feeling so many times lately . . . things have been rough I know: your brother, your marriage, your work—the general state of affairs has at times looked very very gloomy, personally & politically things haven't turned out the way one wished. . . .
>
> [But] you're not THAT old. People your age become president, join the peace corps, start families, write, compose. If you feel like a fossil, you'll behave like one and that's self indulgent . . . everyone knows you're the hardest working reporter and god knows your trade is demanding, plus the book.
>
> Now is the time for you to take care of yourself, with a bit of help from friends and family, especially from me who loves you more than anyone else. So Joseph if you can stand a bit of unasked for advice: physically work out at the Watergate, or some health place; be super conscious of the amount you drink, especially after dinner. When you drink you filibuster—sometimes it's fascinating but sometimes it ain't. And more often than not you feel awful the next day, and right now when things are difficult you've got to be reasonable about the effect of alcohol. . . .

Joe, things aren't just that terrible. Uncle Stewart slaughtered John and me in tennis, he's writing some very good pieces, he's living a goddamn full life in a lot of ways, in spite of being on the brink. Mummy is complicated, neurotic but she's putting together a very nice apartment and she often talks about the good times you had together. . . . You were not a complete failure as a husband, it just isn't that simple. . . . I ask you to be balanced when you start judging yourself on that score—hell I didn't live with you for eight years blindfolded. Now as for your two children, as far as I'm concerned they've never been in better shape and stronger and knowing what's best for them.

The point . . . is to show you that it's YOU and not the rest of us you should worry about . . . I just won't let you house of usher yourself out of existence—if there's going to be a third world war, keep on fighting against it in your columns—but be an open man, listen, remain open to opposing views. You talked to me the other day about how in the old days people just didn't take it so personally when they disagreed. Joe in some of your columns you've been so shrill and vicious against individuals that I feel your point is lost . . . and then you're surprised that they in return become equally nasty. . . . You are not unique in your views, you are not the lonely voice in the wilderness. . . . My friends who read you, consistently, have at one time or another mentioned that yours is the column with the most news, facts, they respect your work . . . they may not always agree with the conclusion. Please don't give in to being "unfashionable"; don't panic about the coming years—. . . it's rough sailing but stop thinking so much about sinking otherwise you just won't be able to sail period.

It was both sound and loving advice—and a good summation of Joe's mood. Yet there was another reason for his depression. It wasn't clear he would be able to continue the column on the generous terms Phil Graham had extended to him more than a decade before. Although Joe had been under contract to *The Washington Post*, the column had been distributed by the *Los Angeles Times* Syndicate. The *Post* contract was due to expire on January 1, 1975, and the *Post* now was contemplating its own syndication service. Thus, Joe faced the question of whether he should switch over to a full contract with the LA *Times* or sever the *Times* tie and enter into an expanded relationship with the new *Post* syndicate.

Joe asked John McCone, now a California industrialist, to assess Otis Chandler's thoughts on the subject, and McCone's report wasn't encouraging. Chandler appreciated Joe's column and wanted it as a full-fledged *Times* Syndicate offering. But he considered Joe's *Post* contract "overly generous." Any arrangement with the *Times* would have to be leaner, Chandler said; but he would be pleased to continue the current arrangement if the *Post* continued to back Joe as in the past.

It might be difficult for Kay Graham to continue the special arrangement with Joe, however, if the *Post* embarked on its own syndication service. And it would be difficult for Joe to accept any large loss of income. His taxable income already had dropped to somewhat above $30,000 a year, from a high of $50,000. The column now appeared in 175 U. S. newspapers, a drop of nearly twenty-five from his pre-Vietnam high. As always, Joe had insisted on maintaining his expenses at $36,000 a year, so he had little flexibility for negotiating.

Then there was Joe's feeling that Kay Graham didn't appreciate the column as she once did. To her previous complaints she had added a suggestion that perhaps Joe was too preoccupied with China, and his constantly aired fear that the Soviet Union would launch a preemptive nuclear strike against the Mao Tse-tung regime. Behind her mild critique was a fear that Joe's reputation would continue to suffer if he didn't change course. "I was worried for him," she recalled years later.

Joe had told Kay that Henry Kissinger himself had put the odds of such a strike within two years at fifty-fifty; so had Richard Helms, when he had lunched with Joe before leaving for his new job as ambassador to Iran. "If you give weight to Henry's assessment—and you can show him all this if you choose—it is unwise to assume that my perception of the present and probably future is sure to be proved dead wrong," he had written.

He added that he had lost papers in the past because of unpopular crusades, but he had always rebounded when later proved right. The number of papers gained during the Korean War, for example, had been three times greater than the losses he and Stewart had suffered during their previous attacks on Louis Johnson. As for China, if he should be proved right, "it should then be useful to the *Post* to have kept me around, so to say."

After Susan Mary left Joe, he found himself spending more time than ever with Kay Graham, seeing her at least once nearly every weekend. Often he would spend casual evenings at Kay's big Georgetown house on R Street, talking politics, gossiping, eating off of trays in the library. "He was so life-enhancing, so much fun," she recalled. And as always he drank plenty of alcohol. After he had consumed nearly an entire bottle of white wine before dinner, Kay would inquire about what he wanted with his meal.

"Joe, do you now want red wine too?"

"Of course, darling."

On the matter of the column, Kay wondered why Joe insisted on settling these things so early, since his contract wasn't up for more than a year. Joe felt he needed to get his future dealt with. "I am not poor," he wrote to her, "but I am not rich either." His house and its contents constituted a large share of his total assets; when he dropped the column, he would have to sell the house and much of his valuable furniture in order to live. To maximize the value, he would need time for "planning and deciding." Kay promised a *Post* decision as soon as possible.

Joe felt ambivalent about the column. He had pretty much decided to give it up in any event by January 1976, so why bother for an extra year? It was getting harder and harder to care about what was going on, because the news was so dreadful and nobody paid much attention to his increasingly dark musings. However stentorian his voice, it seemed to strike most people in Washington as a mere cry in the wilderness. Besides, his brother's ordeal was sapping his remaining enthusiasm for the work.

Stewart, meanwhile, had pushed forward despite the growing attrition of physical and psychological energy wrought by his persistent disease. In the fall of 1973 J. B. Lippincott brought out his book on dying. *Stay of Execution: A Sort of Memoir* numbered 312 pages and guided readers through some of the more memorable chapters of Stewart's life, including his desperate fight against leukemia. "This is," he wrote in the preface, "a mixed-up sort of book. But I have led a mixed-up sort of life, and no experience of that life . . . has been more mixed up than the peculiar hell-to-heaven-to-purgatory existence I have had since I was first diagnosed as an acute leukemic."

Stewart interspersed the story of his life-and-death battle with tales of his past—of meeting Tish, Miss Moonlight and Roses, on that magical wartime evening at Allerton Castle; of his parachute adventure behind enemy lines in France; of his door-to-door canvassing with Joe in the depths of a Wisconsin political winter; of his life as a leading Washington newsman for nearly three heady decades.

He rendered loving portraits of his six children, which struck some who knew of his aloofness in the family as a kind of settling up. But it wasn't easy for Stewart to write about something as intimate as his relationship with his children. His Lippincott editor had had difficulty coaxing personal material out of Stewart, and at one point she had called Elizabeth to complain: "This guy has six kids, and they aren't mentioned in his book." The editor had persisted until at Christmastime 1972 Stewart buried himself in his study and tapped out on his typewriter mini-profiles of each of the children. He emerged and gave each a copy of his or her individual profile. "He had us nailed," recalled Elizabeth. "It wasn't that he didn't know us."

Stay of Execution was a chatty, rambling, anecdotal book, full of the kind of pungent observation for which Stewart's column had become famous. It was also a courageous book, the product of a man who had become well known for his analytical detachment and dispassionate curiosity. Now he was applying those very traits to the subject of his own death.

"A dying man needs to die," wrote Stewart, "as a sleepy man needs to sleep, and there comes a time when it is wrong, as well as useless, to resist." In typical Alsop fashion he had captured a profound insight inside a capsule of eloquence. It was a sentence guaranteed to be quoted in every review of his book, as well as in every obituary written about him after he was gone.

36

END OF THE LINE

All Trains Stop in Baltimore

THE YEAR 1974 began ominously for the Alsops. Stewart was back at NIH. He shared his room with no one, which was ominous in itself. Just about everyone in his ward had a roommate, unless the doctors felt death was at hand.

Stewart had entered NIH with pneumonia before Christmas. Then he had developed an infection of the intestines. Then he had suffered a lung clot, then an edema of the lungs. He looked terrible. During a visit from Fuff, as Stewart sat up in bed, his bathrobe fell open. He looked down at his emaciated body, then looked back at Fuff.

"Auschwitz," he said with a wan smile.

But he wouldn't give up. Dr. John Glick, who had moved to California but stayed in touch by phone, marveled at his will to live. "Well," he said to Tish after one conversation, "at least he's still got all his fight. That's half the battle."

Stewart told Tish he didn't want visitors this time—except for her, the kids, and Joe. Joe would arrive every evening, bringing Scotch or martinis. Stewart would leave his bed and sit in an armchair, sometimes coming "half-way back to life," as Joe put it to a friend. Stewart didn't have much to say, so Joe would ramble on—"and then go home quite shattered." But Tish had noticed that when Joe arrived in a buoyant mood, Stewart's spirits would rise. One time Joe's mood was so cheery that it had affected Stewart, as Tish put it, "almost like taking oxygen." Joe considered this "the highest compliment she could have paid me."

By mid-January the doctors were beginning to sound hopeful. The pneumonia and infections were gone, and it appeared that Stewart would go home as soon as his latest antibiotic treatment was completed. Joe decided that Stewart needed a vacation, and he made arrangements for Tish, Stew, and himself (along with his crucial blood supply) to travel to Castle Hot Springs, an old-fashioned oasis resort outside Phoenix. It wasn't far from a highly regarded hospital; it would be convenient to drive there for blood transfusions. "I fervently believe," Joe wrote to Betsy Whitney, Jock Whitney's wife, "that if we can only get away in the end, a change of air and the resulting lift of spirit will put Stew on the right road again."

But before the antibiotic treatment was completed, Stewart contracted a second pneumonia, a persistent strain that doctors couldn't immediately identify. They had to open Stewart's chest and snip off a bit of lung for their diagnosis. It was a major operation—and a serious risk for a patient in such a weakened state. Joe's spirits collapsed. "I have begun to think," he wrote to Evangeline Bruce, "that the '70s are the very worst vintage years since the history of life began on earth—with the possible exception of such intervals as the wanderings of Attila in Europe."

Joe had other reasons for depression. He remained in a "sad state of uncertainty" about his own future, as he put it to Kay Graham. Kay had written to say that she would talk to Otis Chandler about continuing the current column arrangement, with Joe on contract with the *Post* and the *Times* Syndicate distributing the column. "Don't worry about your situation," she had written. "I'm sure it will work out." But Joe wasn't sure he wanted to continue, and the uncertainty about Stewart undermined his interest in the matter. "It really is beginning to loom as a major decision," he wrote to Kay, "now that I must really worry about whether Stew will still be here and will still need me. I believe he will be. I pray he will be. But there is always the dark shadow of doubt."

Joe also continued to mourn the end of his marriage. It was all the more depressing because Susan Mary still loved him, and he still loved her. In February she wrote to observe their wedding anniversary, "because it was such a good show—it lasted a long time—and gave great pleasure to many people—above all to me." They had begun to see each other again, and Joe had enlisted Susan Mary to be the hostess at a recent Dumbarton dinner. On that occasion, she wrote, she had found herself thinking about how fortunate she was to have had those years with Joe. "Circumstances did not aid us," she wrote. "Stars were crossed, but my marriage vows of Feb. 16th hold."

On January 1, Chip Bohlen died in his sleep after a months-long battle with stomach cancer. He had been in such pain that Joe had prayed each night that it would be Chip's last. "But somehow," he wrote to Evangeline Bruce, "that doesn't make it any less of a wrench when it really turns out to be the night." Joe played a large role in helping Avis

526 / PARALLEL CAREERS

Bohlen with funeral arrangements. "One begins to have the feeling of great chunks being torn out of one's own life," Joe had written to a friend, "with the loss . . . of close friends of many years like Chip."

Then in February Stewart developed another infection, and a lethal "infiltrate" spread relentlessly across his lungs. The prognosis was "grim."

One night Stewart woke suddenly and sat upright in bed. He felt wide awake as he pulled the bedside light cord.

"We'll be stopping in Baltimore," he announced in a strong, authoritative voice.

He looked around and discovered he was in a private railroad car filled with baskets of fruits and flowers. Nice of the railroad people to supply those, he thought. He noticed that the furniture looked a bit shabby, but what could he expect in 1974?

He got up to find Tish, who he assumed was in the connecting car. But the train was swaying heavily, and he almost fell before he managed to steady himself on a table, then a desk. As he sought to make his way across the floor the train gave a lurch, and he fell down. He sat on the floor in a daze, then scrambled to his feet and resumed the search for Tish. He opened a small door—a locker with his clothes. He opened another door—a small bathroom. Then he opened a large double door and leaned against the jamb. The swaying had stopped; the train was sitting in the Baltimore station. He looked out—wide platform, dim lights, green tile. No one in sight. It looked "hellishly grim."

"We won't be stopping in Baltimore!" Stewart announced in a stern voice. "Start up the train, and carry on."

He turned back toward his bed, and twice on the way back he fell as the train crew poured on the power. He got into bed, turned off the light, and fell instantly to sleep.

This small episode did not take place on a train, and the Baltimore station was no more than the hallway outside Stewart's room on the twelfth floor of NIH. But the falling down was real enough—he had the bruises to prove it. And Stewart came to believe that the dream sequence represented more than a wild hallucination born of his grim eight-week stay in the cancer ward. He became all the more convinced when almost immediately the X-rays of his lungs began looking much better. A day later, it was clear that the infiltrates were receding quickly. Within a week, his lungs were as close to normal as they would ever get.

"My guess," wrote Stewart in recounting the episode for his *Newsweek* readers, "is that my decision not to stop at Baltimore had something to do with it. In a kind of fuzzy, hallucinated way, I knew when I announced the decision that it was a decision not to die."

By late February Stewart again prepared to leave NIH for home and yet another effort to resume his life. Joe revived the plan for Castle Hot Springs. But Stewart developed a bedsore that required another delay of the vacation. "It's been very obstinate," Joe wrote to Betsy Whitney. "It makes him feel and sometimes almost talk like Job."

When the bedsore healed, Stewart tried to resume writing the column. He produced the piece about his "Baltimore episode," then explored a fundamental question about America: Was the country experiencing a process of *dégringolade?* That, explained Stewart, was a French word meaning "a kind of slithery, sudden coming apart." And it did indeed seem possible that such a collapse was occurring in America as the country struggled with Watergate and the fate of a president who had broken faith with the American people. The Watergate mess was becoming a genuine "crisis of the regime" as Americans' faith in their government seeped away.

But Stewart wasn't prepared to declare a state of dégringolade. He recalled the "Collapse of Civilization Party" he and John and two friends had put on in New York a month before Pearl Harbor. It called to mind the mood of that time, both national and personal, which in turn inspired Stewart to place a question mark after the word dégringolade in the title of his column. The feeling was widespread back then, he wrote, that Hitler's war would bring about a collapse of civilization. And yet civilization did not collapse.

"So perhaps all the evidence of the degringolade of the United States will prove deceptive, too," he wrote. The country had lived through a lot since that raucous party of young colts back on November 3, 1941—depression, a great war, the Cold War, near nuclear war, crisis after crisis. "And in its own rickety way, our free government survives," wrote Stewart. "It even survived that party, and it was one helluva party. So that cowardly question mark is no doubt needed."

A week later, on April 8, Stewart wrote of Lincoln's famous comments about a politician's ability to fool some of the people all of the time and all of the people some of the time. Lincoln had introduced his famous dictum, noted Stewart, with a sentence that was too often ignored: "If you once forfeit the confidence of your fellow citizens, you can never regain their respect and esteem."

Richard Nixon, wrote Stewart, had lost the respect and esteem of his fellow citizens; he had tried to fool too many people too many times. Since there was no good way out, "it may be that he should and will be impeached, convicted and evicted from the White House, and that it is right and just that these things should happen." But Stewart issued a warning also about Watergate.

The assault on Nixon, as necessary as it was, he wrote, should not also upset the balance of powers instituted by the Constitution or undermine presidential authority. This president no longer was master in his own house, no longer could hire and fire whomever he chose. "Until Mr. Nixon," wrote Stewart, "no president, back to George Washington, has abandoned that power."

The broad subpoena demands of the House Judiciary Committee, which claimed the right to any and all information on White House internal workings, constituted, Stewart said, a threat not just to Nixon but to the presidency itself. Stewart found troublesome the idea, expressed by some anti-Nixon lawmakers, that it wasn't necessary to prove actual crimes in order to throw the president out of office. For some, the vague allegation of "abuse of office" was enough. To Stewart, this was a terrible precedent that would have posed a mortal political threat to any White House occupant who became unpopular and had to contend with an opposition Congress.

Stewart was finding it more and more difficult to write his column, and once again he wrote to Oz Elliott to insist that he not be paid when he just couldn't produce:

> According to our contract, you pay me $800 per column (well worth the price when I'm in the groove) and nothing for no column, which is fair enough. . . . You can't (or I can't) produce consistently a respectable column if you're really sick. . . . But you've also paid me in the past when I was not really sick, and on those occasions, my New England conscience gave me a sharp twinge. . . .
>
> All this is to try to explain why I want to be in a position to say from time to time: "The hell with it. I haven't got a good enough column this week, so I'll skip it." I want to be able to say this even when I'm not hospitalized and wholly operational. But I can only do so in good conscience if it's understood between us that when I skip a column under such circumstances, there will be no check for $800 for S. Alsop.

Elliott had no desire to "prick the conscience of a good Puritan," so he would discontinue payment for "goof-off weeks." But he added that the magazine would continue to pay "whenever you are in the hospital or flat on your back—and, of course, whenever you are goofing *on!*"

But the April 8 column would be Stewart's last. His life was nearly spent.

On May 17 he turned sixty. There was a party at Joe's house, with family and a few friends—Stewart's leukemia specialist, John Macdonald (who had replaced Glick); Rowland Evans and his wife, Kay; Katharine Graham; and Susan Mary. When Fuff saw her father sitting alone on a couch in the sunroom, she walked over and sat down alongside him.

"Everybody's really pulling for you, Daddy," she said.

Stewart looked at her askance. "Tell them to stop," he said, without emotion.

"What do you mean?"

"I'm ready to go."

Nine days later he died.

HIS BEAT WAS THE WORLD, said the *New York Times* headline the next day, over a story recounting Stewart's life and three-year fight against cancer. The *Los Angeles Times*, in an editorial, opined that Stewart had covered the news "with honesty, fairness and intelligence," and had analyzed it "with thoughtfulness, concern and lucidity." *Newsweek* devoted Stewart's old back-page domain to a piece by Mel Elfin. Stewart had not gone gently into the night, Elfin wrote. "The way he died kept faith with the way he had lived—proudly, fully, wisely, lovingly." *Time* carried a full-page obituary that recounted a recent visit correspondent Art White had had with Stewart in the hospital. Stewart had talked of his career; of his love for Joe, who had given him forty blood transfusions, each one requiring three hours of physical discomfort (not to mention the temporary proscription on alcohol); and of his proudest accomplishment—that his column writing had been "not brilliant but sensible and fair." At the end of the interview, recalled White, Stewart had climbed out of bed, hitched up his blue pajamas, and shaken hands. "Always the gentleman."

William Buckley's *National Review*, the country's leading conservative journal, noted that as a self-described New Deal liberal Stewart had taken his positions cautiously and sensitively, and never got drawn into partisan or ideological wars. "If he usually wound up defending the status quo," said the magazine, "it was because he knew how necessary to social harmony a status quo is, and because he never descried a more humane one on the horizon. Nobody spoke better for the liberal establishment, or better embodied what virtues it has." Even in far-off London, *The Times* printed a lengthy obituary, calling Stewart "one of the last members of the eastern, Anglophile establishments which led the United States into its Atlantic role after the Second World War." *The Times* called *Stay of Execution* "a remarkable book" and said Stewart had "faced his own death without flinching and, writing about it, showed that he was a reporter to the end."

Joe encapsulated his own mournful musings in a column in which he called Stewart a "brave and stoical man." He had his eccentricities, as did most of those from the old stock, said Joe, but they were combined with "the best kind of conventionality." The values Stewart had cherished most, said Joe, were "warm affection for friends, deep love of family and, one must add, strong love of country, hearty dislike for what was cheap or mean, and positive detestation for anything phony."

Joe recounted a comment Stewart had made toward the end of his life. "You know," he had said, "I sometimes thank God you and I were born Americans so long ago—for although I don't enjoy getting older, I begin to suspect we have seen the best time in this country." Said Joe: "I look at the next generation, whom he cared for so intensely, and I hope against hope he was wrong."

The memorial service was at St. John's Episcopal Church, a yellow stucco structure across Lafayette Square from the White House. More than seven hundred people came for what *The Washington Post* called "a simple, dignified funeral service." It included no eulogy, but there were psalms and scripture readings from the King James Bible, and the hymns were the same that had been sung at the funeral of Corinne three years earlier: "Abide with Me," "The Strife Is O'er," and "God Be with You 'Til We Meet Again."

Attendees included Lady Bird Johnson, Alice Roosevelt Longworth, Alice Acheson, Ethel Kennedy, and top officials from White House administrations stretching back to Franklin D. Roosevelt—James Rowe, Robert McNamara, William Bundy, Arthur Schlesinger, Walt Rostow. Former Nixon hands George Shultz, Richard Kleindienst, and Bryce Harlow were there, as well as the aristocracy of the national press—Kay Graham and Ben Bradlee of *The Washington Post*, Clifton Daniel of *The New York Times*, Osborn Elliott of *Newsweek*, Crosby and Newbold Noyes of the *Washington Star*. Senators Henry Jackson and John Sherman Cooper also attended.

A buffet luncheon followed at Dumbarton, after which the family and close friends flew to Connecticut, where Stewart was buried with five generations of forebears in a family plot in Middletown.

Letters of condolence poured in to Joe, from old friends, heads of state, senators, governors, Supreme Court justices, famous newsmen. Richard Nixon wrote to say he and Mrs. Nixon were keeping Joe in their "thoughts and prayers." Nelson Rockefeller called Stewart "a great man," while Hubert Humphrey called him "a remarkable and admirable man." Supreme Court Justice Lewis Powell noted that he had met Stewart only once but had "long admired him as a columnist of distinction, perception and independence."

Tish, who had demonstrated unusual courage throughout Stewart's three-year fight, now fell apart. She fled into one of the deepest drinking binges of her life, and came close to what her friends feared would be an emotional breakdown. But she emerged from it with a new resolve. It took some time, but eventually she entered a program for alcoholics and never again succumbed to the lure of alcohol. She sold Needwood Forest, took a job at the National Institutes of Health as a medical research technologist, and built a stable life for herself and her young boys.

For Joe, his brother's death was "just like an amputation," as he wrote to Isaiah Berlin. The Alsops had always been a close clan, he wrote to another friend, and he had been "closer to no member of the family than to Stew, who was both a great man and a great life-enhancer." Joe sought solace in Susan Mary's children, whom he thanked lovingly for the help and comfort they had extended during the agonizing days after Stewart's death. "It meant more to me than I can say," he wrote to Anne Crile. "Indeed, it means more to me than I can say to have you in my life." He wrote a similar letter to Billy Patten.

With Stewart gone, Joe's lingering interest in his column quickly dissipated. "I really hate this city. . . . I find the column a dreadful chore," Joe wrote to Berlin in June. Meanwhile, he found himself increasingly excited by his study of art collecting, and he liked the idea of freeing himself for the project. "I am more and more confident," he wrote to Berlin, "that if I can just get my damn book right, it will be regarded as a major contribution."

He added that the recent period had been "the most disconcerting and distressing" of his life. "Mine has been a straight-line career and life, marked by really golden luck until about three years ago, just as Stew's career was marked by golden luck, and our whole family's life was marked by golden luck." The Alsop luck, he suggested, had run out with Corinne's death. "But I suppose that's superstition. And one must not give way to whining or gloom." His new aim, he said, was to "find a new way of pegging away, and thereby to create a reasonably satisfactory fin de carriere."

Watergate presented another reason for Joe's declining interest in the column. He had seen the issue primarily as a congressional assault on the executive branch, as a dangerous tilt in the nation's balance of power. As a lifelong believer in the power of presidents to chart the national course and address national problems, he had found himself defending Nixon against his Watergate enemies. This had put him at odds with The Washington Post and Kay Graham, as well as many other old friends. As the magnitude of Nixon's involvement in the scandal tumbled out, Joe's position became increasingly untenable. As in the Vietnam debates, events were rendering him vulnerable to attack and ridicule.

In the spring, when Kay Graham's newspaper had published a startling story on the Nixon team's threats of retaliation against the Post, Joe felt compelled to write Kay a letter of apology:

> I cannot tell you how much I admire the enormous courage that you have all shown, particularly you and Ben. Whether the final outcome will be happy, I cannot possibly say, and I sometimes have my doubts. But the fact is that a very dangerous system had grown up in the White House, which would have threatened this country if it had continued. It was destroyed by you and the other leaders of the Post and the Post reporters almost single-handed. . . .
>
> So I send you all my warmest congratulations, and also my apologies for giving our miserable president the benefit of the doubt—which now turns out to be a completely wrong thing to do.

The same week Joe wrote a column entitled "The Case for Presidential Resignation," and a week later he wrote that it had become clear that Nixon could not escape impeachment and conviction. The president, wrote Joe, "must eventually resign or expect the worst."

When Nixon did resign on August 9, Joe was on leave, and therefore he offered his readers no thoughts on the events of that tumultuous week, when the reins of presidential power passed peaceably from the disgraced Nixon to Gerald Ford, the longtime Michigan congressman whom Nixon had appointed to the vice presidency a year earlier upon the resignation of Spiro Agnew. But Joe remained near the center of the political world, where he had been for decades. When Nixon had wanted to track down Henry Kissinger, now secretary of state, on the evening of August 7 to reveal his resignation plans, he had had him called at Joe's, where Kissinger was having dinner. But for the first time in nearly four decades (with the exception of the war years), Joe had nothing to say on the biggest story of the day. He was in the process of "pulling down the shade," as he liked to put it.

He devoted much of August to a study of retirement finances. Young Joe Alsop, Stewart's son, worked on a cash-flow projection that showed Joe could count on at least $100,000 in annual pretax income if he sold the Dumbarton house and many of the valuables it contained. The question now was: Where did he wish to live?

He considered moving to London, then pondered Boston. Billy Patten, then working in a Boston bank, discussed it with his family and wrote to Joe, "There is almost nothing we can think of that would give us—all four of us—more pleasure." Joe discussed with friends the idea of moving to New York City. He even contemplated moving to Avon, and asked John about buying "life-use" of some of the old Alsop farmland in order to build a house, which would revert back to John and his heirs upon Joe's death. And he asked Tish if she would consider selling him the property below the Springland Lane house, where the tennis court was, so he could build a house there. Tish demurred, saying that with Needwood gone it was important that Springland remain a "family center" for visits from children and grandchildren. Privately, Tish felt she would love Joe more if she didn't have him living next door and interfering within her family, for which he was famous.

In the end, Joe made arrangements to move just a block or so away from his Dumbarton home, into an old Georgetown house at 2806 N Street owned by his old friend Johnny Walker. He secured favorable rental terms and made plans to move in early in the new year. He put the Dumbarton house on the market and promptly sold it.

And now it was time to announce his retirement. His column of September 25 broke the news: "Rather soon—next New Year's Day to be precise—the series of reports that have been appearing in this space will come to an end at long last." He noted that he had begun his career as reporter in July 1932, and his career as columnist in November 1937. "When you are not awfully far off half a century in the same job, it is time to stop," he wrote. The reporter's trade was for young men, whose legs could carry them to the endless parade of sources and adventures that were the raw material of column writing.

But in typical fashion Joe also provided a glimpse into areas of his private life that most writers considered their own business and of little interest to readers. Like anyone, said Joe, he would have to cash in his savings in order to live in retirement. "My savings, rather eccentrically, have gone into a much-loved house and garden and the house's endlessly pleasurable contents." Hence, he announced to his readers, he would sell his house. "Leaving a house I designed myself, built myself and have enjoyed since the Truman times," he wrote, "has turned out to be a bit like a hermit crab abandoning its shell." The *Post* accompanied the column with a photograph of Joe's house and garden.

Joe's announcement was big news in Washington and throughout the country's literary circles. The *New York Times* Washington bureau chief, Clifton Daniel, wrote a story saying Joe's retirement would end "what appears to be the oldest surviving example of . . . the nationally syndicated political column." Daniel stopped by Dumbarton to let Joe vent his thoughts and angers for the story, and then rendered a portrait of Joe the Curmudgeon. "The real villains these days," Joe told Daniel, "are not villainous people. They are a lot of virtuous asses." He called the exposure of Watergate a great achievement but a costly one, because it had tied up the country for nearly two years during a time of global dangers. "Now we ought to turn to what matters." As for the course of events at home and abroad, he said, "The front pages today almost make me sick."

James Reston wrote to lament Joe's departure from the editorial pages. "I have always felt you had the brightest intelligence of our newspaper generation," he wrote. "Some of us didn't see the problems of our time in quite the same way, and my regret is that we loitered into personal differences in the process." He regretted this, said Reston, because if Joe was right that most things had gone awry in their lifetimes, "then personal friendship is about all we have left."

President Ford wrote to say he had received the news of Joe's retirement "with a bit of sadness." He asked that Joe come by for a chat before he gave up the column. Joe replied, "I am most eager to crown my long reportorial career with a real talk with the eighth president of the United States whom I have known."

After the announcement, Joe headed to Europe for his last overseas reporting tour. His old friends in London and Paris turned his visits there into two continuous parties—"thereby," he wrote to Charles Whitehouse, "causing me to eat and drink far too much and to become even more dilapidated than my years deserve." He added that in the intervals, when he was working, he found himself thanking God that he was retiring, "for the news is so dreadful and the prospects are so ghastly that they hardly bear thinking about, much less writing about."

In London he found a Parliament that could not rule the nation. The trade unions had taken over the governing Labor Party, which meant the trade unions exercised final authority over the country, with alarming effects. For one thing, annual inflation was close to 20 percent. The British suffered from a terrible loss of will as hopes waned that the country could actually pull itself together. "It is sad to be in London now," wrote Joe.

Meanwhile, Europe seemed increasingly threatened by Persian Gulf sheikhs who had imposed an oil embargo on the West in 1973 and then fashioned a cartel of oil-producing countries that had quadrupled the price of oil. A vast transfer of wealth was taking place that in turn was fostering a significant shift of power from the West toward the Persian Gulf.

In Paris Joe found French officials struggling with a 15 percent inflation rate and rising unemployment. French President Valéry Giscard d'Estaing was so sure war would soon break out in the Middle East that he already was carrying on a flirtation with the Palestine Liberation Organization, headed by a man Joe called "the toad-like Yasser Arafat." Joe foresaw the Arab nations, emboldened by their growing wealth and power, launching yet another drive to destroy Israel or to cripple her by retaking lands lost in previous wars. He was sure that such a prospect would give rise to a flood of poisonous recriminations in the West.

All in all, it looked bleak. "The really thoughtful men in key positions in France and Britain," wrote Joe, "are no longer at all confident of the survival of the West."

Returning home, he found official Washington ignoring these signs of Western collapse in favor of titillating revelations about Nelson Rockefeller, who over the years had given large amounts of money to many of his friends, including Tom Braden. These tidbits of gossip had spilled out during House confirmation hearings on Ford's nomination of Rockefeller as vice president. Joe could hardly stand it, and he poured into the column a surge of Alsopian rage:

> In this former capital of the Western world, the pygmies now seem to reign supreme. Pygmy views on every subject are almost the only ones that are publicly heard. While the roof of our world visibly threatens to fall in, you only hear discussion of the wicked generosity of one of the finest public servants of this generation. . . .
>
> It is just a mite frivolous . . . to continue to think about trifles when another Mideast war is a better than even bet; and when the destruction of Israel is quite imaginable; and when a world war has begun to be remotely conceivable. . . .

Given such feelings, thought Joe, it was best to turn inward. "I always suspect, nowadays," he wrote to Sir Thomas Brimelow in London, "that I am wholly out-of-date, and ought to be removed from circulation, like those cans of this or that at a grocer's that have exceeded their 'shelf life.' " He told Scotty Reston that one reason he had decided to retire was that he had found himself becoming increasingly testy and contentious over political disagreements. "Nothing could be more foolish and I am deeply regretful," he wrote. He had made a new rule: "I don't care what anyone's political views are, and I am never even going to ask about them. In fact, after January 1, I hope never to talk about politics again."

Joe's new rule lasted about a week into 1975. But he did take himself off the shelf, and he showed little public interest in events of the day. Before Joe's retirement, Phil Geyelin had worked out an arrangement for him to produce a monthly commentary on the state of the world. After a few months, Joe quietly abandoned the enterprise.

He moved into the N Street house, which was to be his residence until his death, and continued to hold dinner parties as before. Washington's high and mighty still jumped at the chance to join his table company, and Joe continued to play the provocative host, throwing his opinions into the air like knives and forcing others to get into the fight or duck out of the way. In the late 1970s, shortly after Jimmy Carter of Georgia had become president, Joe invited to his table a young Carter official named Jack Watson.

"Tell me, Jack," Joe demanded at one point in the conversation. "Which does the Carter administration think is going to be the more serious problem in your term, unemployment or inflation?"

Watson, new to Washington and a bit intimidated by the prestigious pundit of Georgetown, replied that both obviously would be serious problems but that, if the administration had to choose one, it would probably be unemployment.

"Balls!" roared Joe, pounding a spoon on the table as he spoke. "Balls, balls, balls, balls, balls." The etiquette was questionable, but the analysis sound. Inflation was to play a major role in ending the Carter presidency at the next election.

On another occasion during the Carter years, Joe found himself at Kay Graham's seated next to the wife of Treasury Secretary G. William Miller. When Joe got into a heated exchange with a young Carter aide named Gerald Rafshoon, Mrs. Miller became uncomfortable. Finally she said, "Let's not get so agitated. I think we should all join hands and say a prayer for the president." She sought to take the hands of the two people next to her, one of whom was Joe.

"Madam, please!" exclaimed Joe, pushing away her hand with a look of horror. "I beg you to desist. I am an Episcopalian. Episcopalians pray only in church!"

Joe settled into a new routine, spending long hours on his book on art, socializing with friends at lunch and dinner, taking walks through town. At one point he asked Avis Bohlen to marry him. She declined, but they remained close friends. After David Bruce died, Joe dined frequently with Evangeline, exchanging gossip about their many mutual friends and reminiscing about the grand old days when America sat atop the world and David practically ran France. Through those conversations it became clear to Evangeline just what a watershed Stewart's death had been to Joe. "He basically gave up his Washington life," she recalled later.

In his later years, Joe could be seen trudging along Washington streets on his long walks, to a lunch with a friend, to the Library of Congress—where he planned to donate his voluminous papers—or just for exercise. To most of the new generation crowding into his trade, preoccupied with the fame that comes with television, this antique figure would be unknown. But to old hands he would be recognizable, rather like a twentieth-century version of Dr. Johnson himself, deep in thought, touching the lampposts as he passed.

Joe felt gratified throughout the Carter years that he didn't have to cover the moralistic Georgia Democrat. The Carter people struck him as lacking any understanding of the real world. "I remember hearing at a dinner," he recalled years later, "one of the Carter people asking another, that silly-ass man Rafshoon, who spends about $70 every time he has his hair arranged . . . one of them turning to Rafshoon and saying, 'Jerry, tell me if I'm wrong, but I have a feeling that the inflation at home and the fall of the dollar abroad haven't made any difference to the president's image.' To which Rafshoon replied, 'I'm glad you asked me that, Fred. We've made careful soundings, and neither has made any difference at all.' " This, recalled Joe, was four days before the dollar's decline drove Carter to a flurry of activity designed to arrest it. "This is childish stuff," said Joe. "Serious presidents aren't like that."

Joe felt more comfortable with Carter's successor, Ronald Reagan, even though Reagan's rigid conservatism had never appealed to him. Reagan, Joe told an interviewer during the Californian's second term, "is obviously a very much more formidable president than I would have expected or certainly than my Democratic friends would have expected." He particularly liked Reagan's tough stance toward the Soviets and his resolve to build up the U.S. military. Joe also respected most of the president's top men, particularly Secretary of State George Shultz and Treasury Secretary James Baker; but he didn't have much use for second-term White House chief of staff Donald Regan, the former chairman of Merrill Lynch, who reminded Joe of "the worst of Eisenhower's businessmen, and goodness knows they were a dreadful lot."

But politics no longer fueled Joe's passions. His passions in retirement were art and art collecting and his book on those grand themes. The more he got into it the more he realized what a massive subject it was. Determined to break new ground and keenly aware of his lack of a scholarly background in the field, Joe pushed further and further into his subject. By 1978 he had been working on the book for some fourteen years, and he still wasn't ready to submit a manuscript. But he had plenty of material for a lecture series that captivated the capital that summer.

He bundled up his knowledge into six Monday-evening lectures presented at the new East Wing of the National Gallery of Art. Each week the hall filled to overflowing with a reserved-seating audience that included some of the city's leading lights—Mrs. Hugh D. Auchincloss, the John Sherman Coopers, Health and Human Services Secretary Joseph Califano, the Clayton Fritcheys. At the third lecture, nearly six hundred people crowded into the 450-seat hall, spilling onto the carpeted auditorium stairs. Postlecture dinner parties became a popular feature of the city's social elite.

The lectures, as *Newsweek* described them, were a "lively amalgam of familiar lore, obscure history, and gossipy anecdotes." In one lecture he guided his audience from the tale of the first artist known to have signed his work (the ancient Egyptian Imhotep) to "one contemporary anti-artist masturbating in public and solemnly calling it an 'art act.' " He described art collecting as "a highly complex and specialized human behavioral system, almost as unlikely as the courtship behavior of bower birds."

Joe's basic thesis was that only five cultures in history had collected art strictly for art's sake—classical Greece, the West (beginning with the Renaissance), Japan, China, and the later Islamic civilization. This tradition of art collecting generated in turn certain habits and practices, such as the tendency to separate art objects from their practical uses. Joe cited the example of a Frenchman who exhibited as art a collection of eighteenth-century chamber pots. The five cultures, said Joe, also were unique in their passion for innovation in artistic expression and their tradition of signing art objects.

Joe told a *Newsweek* reporter that his art-history education had begun after he discovered there were no "authorities" on art collecting. The only books on the subject had been either "fashionably anecdotal or coffee-table, inaccurate and unreliable." So he had decided to become the authority himself.

One difficulty over the years had been his lack of language fluency, particularly in German. His French was entirely serviceable, but his Italian and Latin were barely sufficient to allow him to wade through a text and spot something he needed translated. His Chinese, learned during his World War II imprisonment in Hong Kong and later in East China, came in handy, but he knew only four thousand characters, about six thousand fewer than what was considered necessary to claim literacy. For Joe these were merely barriers to be surmounted, factors that affected not the project so much as the completion date.

Another timing factor was Joe's decision to interrupt his art studies to produce a short biography of Franklin Roosevelt, published by The Viking Press to celebrate the hundredth anniversary of FDR's birth. *FDR: A Centenary Remembrance* came out in 1982, with 256 large-size pages and numerous photographs. It was a Book-of-the-Month Club main selection, and sold well. *The New York Times* called it "superlative." Written in a breezy style and filled with anecdote and insight, the book had charm. Joe sought to explain Roosevelt both as man at rest and man of action, and he clearly found both inspiring.

Joe viewed the man of action as "singularly longheaded, singularly patient, singularly realistic, and singularly bold." His plans and aims matured invisibly, "seemingly like organic growths in the back of his mind," and he possessed an incomparable sense of timing. Roosevelt, wrote Joe, was "certainly no plaster saint," but he was a good man. "He loved the light and loathed the darkness, and in hard and testing times he was also inspired and sustained—a point no longer fashionable to make but a true point none the less—by a simple, rather old-fashioned, but deep and unshakable Christian faith."

A few months after the Roosevelt book appeared, Harper & Row brought out Joe's magnum opus, *The Rare Art Traditions*. It had everything his lecture series had had—and more. A historical summary of the fashions, styles, traditions, and eccentricities of art collecting, it portrayed collecting as a historical process that exerted a powerful influence on how society viewed art—and itself. The West particularly, said Joe, had tended to study itself in its art, and it was because of collecting that the West had so much art history and so many museums, art markets, forgeries, antiques, and ever-rising prices for art objects.

J. Carter Brown, director of the National Gallery of Art, called the book "a landmark." The *Economist* called it "agreeably sensational," a book that could change the way anyone looked at art. Dillon Ripley, secretary of the Smithsonian Institution, wrote in *Smithsonian* magazine that Joe's book combined "a rich anecdotal style with a synthesis of what art collecting is all about."

With his major work out of the way, Joe turned his attention to his memoirs. He would go to his study and pound away on his 1938 Underwood, but the task left him curiously unmoved. He knew his had been a life worthy of a meaningful autobiography, but he didn't feel like writing it. He preferred writing on the meaning of art.

Then in 1987 a young man named Adam Platt came by to interview Joe for a Washington-based magazine called *Insight*. Joe liked the article, and he liked Platt, whose parents had been part of the old establishment and had been friends for years. Joe suggested that Platt help him with his memoirs, and the two set about the task.

The book came out five years later, to respectful notices. It was the ninth book written or co-written by Joe. Its title, taken from Stewart's comment about America's decline, was *I've Seen the Best of It*. Running to 495 pages, it was a breezy, anecdotal volume filled with the sounds, smells, tastes, comical episodes, and dramatic moments of Joe's remarkable life. But he ended the story with the death of John Kennedy. He couldn't bring himself to engage the painful Vietnam issue again, even fifteen years after those tumultuous times.

JOE NEVER SAW the book in print. In 1987 he developed lung cancer, complicated by emphysema. He put up a grand fight, in the spirit of his brother, but on August 28, 1989, at the age of seventy-eight, he died quietly in bed at home.

The memorial service, like Stewart's, was at St. John's Episcopal Church, across the street from Lafayette Park. As at Stewart's service, there were no eulogies. The same hymns that had been sung at Corinne's memorial, and then at Stewart's, were sung for Joe. The large church was filled to overflowing with friends, acquaintances and admirers. Afterward, family and close friends flew to Connecticut, lunched at John Alsop's Avon house, then drove to Middletown for Joe's burial in the family crypt. Kay Graham was there, and Polly Fritchey, and Tish and Susan Mary, as well as John and Gussie. Also present, as Joe would have wanted, was Ginnana Pozza, known to the family as Gemma, who had served Joe as cook, receptionist, seamstress, laundress, and household ally for twenty-nine years. Her presence was a testament to Joe's ability to command the loyalty and affection of those he loved.

Although Joe had been out of the limelight for fifteen years, his death brought forth a torrent of obituaries and reminiscences. *The Washington Post* devoted nearly half a page to Joe, attributing to him "an encyclopedic memory, a quick pen, a quicker tongue and a demeanor that was sometimes imperious." Writing in *The New Republic,* Henry Fairlie said Joe's eminence was shared with no other newsman. This, he said, was not only because of his skills as a reporter, the quality of his writing, and his lustiness in controversy; more important were his "standards of independence and courage."

George Will, the columnist and pundit who rose to prominence about the time of Joe's retirement, picked out a distinctive Alsopian sentence for dissection: "The U.S. Army of the late 1920s and most of the 1930s was not only tiny and almost wholly without modern equipment, it was also almost completely dominated by an antiquated elite of cavalrymen, whose boots (always from Peel in London) shone splendidly, in contrast to their intellects, which did not." Wrote Will: "There, in one sentence, you have him—syntactically complex yet elegant, with an eye for the telling detail, and the sting of dry wit."

Joe's close friend Meg Greenfield, who had succeeded Phil Geyelin as editor of *The Washington Post*'s editorial page, protested against any tendencies to re-create Joe as some kind of lovable old curmudgeon, the blustery crank who doesn't really mean it when he scourges friends with the hot angers of old age. "Joe meant every damn word of it," wrote Greenfield. "His wrath was as genuine as his affection."

Perhaps the most telling reminiscence came from Edwin M. Yoder, Jr., columnist and editorial-page editor of the *Washington Star* before its 1981 demise. Writing in *National Review*, Yoder recalled a lecture Joe had delivered at the National Portrait Gallery in 1982. The subject was Franklin Roosevelt, and Joe's friends crowded into the front-row seats for what they presumed would be a stellar Alsopian performance.

But Joe had difficulty getting the lecture to take flight. He struggled with the manuscript, adjusted and readjusted his huge reading glasses. His friends held their breath, fearing that perhaps Joe had indulged a bit too liberally in the dinner wines earlier in the evening. Then he came to the famous cable Roosevelt had sent Winston Churchill during the dark days of the Battle of Britain, when the motherland faced its greatest threat and Joe was fighting to get America into the war. In his cable, said Joe, Roosevelt had quoted from Longfellow: "Sail on, O ship of state / Sail on, O Union, strong and great . . ."

Joe stopped in midpoem, then tried to continue. He couldn't. The audience realized he had been overcome with emotion at the power of that dramatic glance into American history. Then he broke down and wept unabashedly. He pulled out his big polka-dotted handkerchief, wiped his eyes and blew his nose, then continued his lecture. "Behind the facade of pomp, bluster, and epithet," wrote Yoder, "was a generous, kindly, vulnerable, deeply feeling, almost sentimental heart." And nothing stirred that heart more powerfully than the spirit of Thermopylae, particularly when it lent mettle, mission, and meaning to the United States of America.

EPILOGUE

"NOTHING ENDURES"

The Old Elite
and the American Century

A GENERATION BEFORE the Alsop brothers' births, near the turn of this century, their great-uncle Theodore Roosevelt expressed himself on the waves of immigrants then making their way to America. The prevailing culture accepted them and welcomed them, said the twenty-sixth president of the United States, but not without condition:

> We have no room for any people who do not act and vote simply as Americans, and as nothing else. . . . An immense number [of immigrants] have become completely Americanized, and these stand on exactly the same plane as the descendents of any Puritan, Cavalier, or Knickerbocker among us, and do their full and honorable share of the nation's work. But where immigrants, or the sons of immigrants, do not heartily and in good faith throw in their lot with us, but cling to the speech, the customs, the ways of life, and the habits of thought of the Old World which they have left, they hereby harm both themselves and us. If they remain alien elements, unassimilated, and with interests separate from ours, they are mere obstructions to the current of our national life, and, moreover, can get no good from it themselves. In fact, though we ourselves also suffer from their perversity, it is they who really suffer most. . . . We freely extend the hand of welcome and of good fellowship to every man, no matter what his creed and birthplace, who comes here honestly intent on becoming a good United States citizen like

the rest of us; but we have a right, and it is our duty, to demand that he shall indeed become so, and shall not confuse the issues with which we are struggling by introducing among us Old-World quarrels and prejudices.

Roosevelt's cultural manifesto rang as a powerful defense of the folkways, legends, and habits of mind of the old elite, and of the America it had created and guided through the generations. The nation's door was open to newcomers—so long as they accepted the country as they found it, so long as they deferred to the prevailing view of America as handed down by the Anglo-Saxon founders. Such words bespoke the immense confidence that fueled Roosevelt's class, along with the nation, in those earlier days. Hardly a voice was raised in the land to challenge the ethos of his manifesto.

But a day would come when the old elite could no longer speak with such confidence and authority, when the definition of the country and its direction no longer would be the prerogative of those classes and institutions that had guided it since birth. The very idea that an American majority should seek to impose arbitrarily its own mores and manners upon minority groups within the society would become so controversial as to deter any politician from even thinking the thoughts Theodore Roosevelt had so proudly proclaimed.

Though it remains little remarked upon, this transformation represents perhaps the most profound development in American society in the past century. Within the lifetimes of the Alsop brothers the country was remade, and its remaking during the period of their journalistic watch illuminates their careers, just as their careers illuminate the country's remaking.

The Alsops were acutely conscious of the disintegration of the old order and the ramifications of the sea change. In a speech after his retirement, Joe called the decline a "revolution" and added, "The after effects have been revolutionary, too, in the simple sense that American political and social patterns have been radically and all but universally transformed." In June 1970, Stewart wrote in *Newsweek* that "the old WASP elite . . . is dying and it may be dead."

Stewart's column, entitled "The Disintegration of the Elite," noted that the WASPs weren't the only American elite in decline as the nation grappled with the political and cultural discords of the turbulent Vietnam era. The church-centered, Irish-dominated Catholic elite, which once held sway over politicians and Hollywood producers, was fading. The authority of "Our Crowd," the Zionist-oriented Jewish elite, was "much reduced." The Negro elite, once a racial bridge to amity, was enfeebled as its three pillars—the church, the NAACP, and the Urban League—were attacked by young blacks as "havens for Uncle Toms." Clearly, the foundations of American society were shifting and the structure breaking up.

The most significant element of all this, in Stewart's view, was the decline of "the central elite," the Anglo-Saxons. This establishment, said Stewart, had been a long time a-dying.

It began in the Depression, when the country had lost faith in the "system" and those running its faltering factories and financial institutions. But even then, foreign policy had remained securely in the hands of the elite. After the war, under that "distinctly non–Ivy League WASP, Harry Truman," the old elite had enjoyed a kind of Indian summer, when a new era of American dominance was shaped by—and here Stewart ticked off the usual litany of the Alsops' well-born friends—Acheson, Harriman, Forrestal, Lovett, Bohlen, Kennan, Nitze.

If the first blow had been the Depression, the second was McCarthyism—"basically an assault on the WASP elite," according to Stewart. It was no accident, he wrote, that McCarthy chose as his principal target Dean Acheson, "whose mustache provided the perfect symbol of Eastern elitism." After McCarthy, the elite never fully regained its dominance of foreign policy.

Then came Suez. The humiliation of Britain, said Stewart, undermined the self-confidence of establishment Anglo-Saxons in America. "It wrecked their whole system of thinking about the world, and even about themselves." It destroyed the intellectual foundations of Groton and other preparatory schools of its stripe, and of the three Ivy League universities—Harvard, Yale, and Princeton—that had served as havens for the sons of the elite. There was always a strain in these institutions of what Stewart called "a rather naive anticolonialism," which contributed to irritations within the American establishment over what was viewed as Britain's arrogance of power. But nearly everyone in the establishment agreed that Britain's strength represented a force for good in the world, and nearly everyone shared a "profound and instinctive Anglophilia."

Now, instead of ruling the seas and roaming the world like the lion of the veld, Britain was producing the Beatles and Carnaby Street. "It was as though an irritating but powerful parent had turned quite suddenly into a lean and slippered pantaloon," wrote Stewart.

Later, in Stay of Execution, Stewart identified a fourth blow to the old elite. "Vietnam," he wrote, "completed the process of undermining the self-confidence of the WASP establishment." Without self-confidence, the elite couldn't exist, and soon it was not much more than a memory.

Of course there were other factors in all of this. Two gigantic wars had devastated the lands of the West and rearranged the world. Meanwhile, American politics reflected not only the election returns but also the census returns, and the census was confirming ethnic transformation throughout the country. America was becoming less and less an Anglo-Saxon country, and less and less did it look to its old elite for guidance and governance. New impulses, attitudes, and agendas—precisely what

Theodore Roosevelt had warned against—were making their way into the American consciousness with expanding and more diverse waves of immigration, and these had a profound effect upon the nation. Aside from the Depression, McCarthyism, Suez, and Vietnam, demographic realities rendered inevitable the decline of the central elite.

What did the Alsop brothers think of all this in their reflective moments?

Joe was deeply ambivalent. When he entitled his last book *I've Seen the Best of It*, he was saying implicitly that the country's best days were those when the old elite flourished. The first chapter, "My World," was a loving yet mildly sardonic memoir of life in what Joe called "the WASP Ascendancy." "It was delightful to live as I lived when I was a young man," he wrote. "The delights were many-sided. . . . The WASP Ascendancy had its own peculiar culture, its own peculiar cookery . . . , its own peculiar certainties, and its own particular advantages."

Susan Mary once described Joe as "an old-fashioned New Englander who regrets the passing of the WASP." Brendan Gill, prominent writer, scion of another Connecticut blue-blood family, and Yale classmate of Stewart's, recalled in a memoir an evening he had shared with Joe in New York after they had both returned from Europe by plane. Joe took Gill to his club, the Knickerbocker, for a nightcap, only to discover the bar closed and the night porter inhospitable. No matter; Joe retrieved a bottle of Scotch from his basement locker, and he and Gill spent half the night pondering the passing of the Anglo-Saxon: "Why had the WASP Ascendancy lost its grip? What had become of that sense of continuity by means of which, in the Connecticut in which we had both grown up, a certain class had maintained its firm hold on the reins of governance, both financial and political?"

As they talked they became increasingly sorrowful. "We groaned and growled and griped and drank our Scotch," wrote Gill, "feeling all the better for having made ourselves feel worse. . . ."

Sir Isaiah Berlin, probably Joe's closest friend, knew the extent of Joe's melancholy over the decline. Joe, recalled Berlin, "believed in an earlier America, a kind of old-fashioned WASP America." He preferred the gentler nation of his youth, "and that's what he wanted to defend from the barbarians." Joe's views, according to Berlin, weren't far different from those of his great-uncle Teddy Roosevelt.

Yet Joe never gave expression, publicly or privately, to any nativist impulses, or harbored animosity toward the newcomers who were dislodging the old elite. As author and critic Gore Vidal, who knew Joe from childhood, put it, "Joe was no mere nativist— Educated worldly gentlemen are not (TR was *not* a gentleman!)." Joe would never oppose the changes washing over America, however much he may have lamented them. As Berlin put it, "It was gradually ceasing to be the country he knew, and, while he may have hated the changes, he never admitted that, even to himself."

To Joe, being a patriotic American meant accepting America on America's terms, which meant in turn accepting the changes that were the country's democratic expression. In *I've Seen the Best of It*, he went so far as to say he was "glad every day" that the old elite had given way to make possible what he called the country's "greatest single feat in the twentieth century"—the inclusion of ethnic and racial minorities into mainstream America. "It is certainly an achievement no other major modern country can match," he wrote, "and one that makes me proud to be an American."

In sum, as Joe viewed it, the central elite had created and nurtured the nation based on its Anglo-Saxon culture and view of history, then bequeathed it to succeeding generations. "So we must somewhere along the line find a new American culture and a new American view of history," Joe wrote, "before we produce new 'wise men' more representative of the mixed America that gives me such pride. Thank God I am confident that this will happen."

Stewart was less confident. He chafed at the growing anti-WASP expression in the popular culture and in certain literary circles. In his NIH hospital room he found himself watching a number of television situation comedies, and he was struck by the prevailing rules of the air: " 'ethnics' are okay, Jews are okay, blacks are very okay, white Anglo-Saxon Protestants are a bunch of bigoted boobies," as he put it in an angry column. He attacked a harsh little book by Peter Schrag called *The Decline of the WASP*, which held the old elite responsible for most of the ills of the country and the world. And he called David Halberstam's best-selling *The Best and the Brightest* "a readable, inaccurate, grossly unfair exercise in ideological hindsight about the Vietnam war." It seemed to Stewart that "the very Waspishness" of Dean Acheson and the Bundy brothers was "clearly a main count in Halberstam's indictment."

Viewing developments from the vantage point of early-1970s turbulence, Stewart feared the result of the elite's passing would be social and political chaos. Perhaps, he wrote in *Stay of Execution*, America was better off without an establishment. "But I suspect not. I suspect that a great power needs an establishment, an elite, a class of self-confident and more or less disinterested people who are accustomed to running things."

In fact, he added, it was likely that much of the "sleaziness, the small-minded grubbiness" that had become such a part of the Washington scene owed its existence to the passing of the elite. For all their faults and stuffiness, most of the men of the old elite at least had been above the kind of behavior seen, for example, in Watergate. Their early years of tradition, training, and education had imbued them with a sense of duty and honor and conditioned them for national service.

The problem, as Stewart saw it, was that a society without a self-respecting and respect-commanding elite was a society without authority. "And a society without authority is one short step away from becoming an authoritarian society."

America was not to become an authoritarian society soon after the Alsops' days of influence. But the erosion of authority throughout American life would become a topic of increasing concern in public discussion, and the impulses of rigid conformity—often a precursor of authoritarianism—would grow, particularly on campuses, including those of some of the country's most prestigious institutions. Moreover, the intervening years would bring upon the land growing forces of ethnic and racial separatism that could foreshadow the kind of chaos Stewart feared. The very definition of the nation would become a divisive issue as the country's heritage and folk traditions—even some of its folk heroes—would come under attack. The need for some kind of new general consensus to supplant the old, as Joe had wished for, would become a matter of considerable national urgency, and yet nothing resembling such a development could be discerned.

The last great thrust of the old elite was the creation of the American Century to replace the Pax Britannica of the previous two centuries. The elite had brought to that task the vision, force, and self-confidence that had propelled America through its many stages of manifest destiny, from the westward migration to the advent of empire to the command over the breathtaking technologies of the new century. Indeed, for the elite, the American Century was merely the inevitable extension of this irrepressible national energy and talent.

It was at this moment in history, when America's Anglo-Saxon elite emerged as the custodian of world peace and stability, that the Alsop brothers thrived. As men of words, they joined the era's men of deeds who struggled with the profound geopolitical forces unleashed by the greatest war of all time. At every crisis and critical juncture, they were there to give expression to the principles and impulses that guided the nation's foreign-policy leaders and shaped America's role in the world. They operated at the margin of big events, and at the margin they often wielded crucial influence, leading the way toward what they considered the proper outlook on unfolding developments.

They broke stories, thus placing new facts into the public consciousness—on the accelerating crises in Greece and Turkey, on the country's quest for nuclear superiority, on the political chicanery of the Robert Taft forces in Texas, on the impending crisis in French Indochina. They pounded away on unpopular ideas that later became prevailing opinion—on the postwar threat of communism, on the follies of Louis Johnson's defense policies, on the meaning of McCarthyism, on the unfortunate consequences of forced busing for racial balance in the public schools. And through millions of words, they helped define an era, the era of the American Century.

Some have argued that the fundamental assumptions of this American Century were flawed from the beginning. World peace, according to this view, did not depend on American intrusion into the affairs of struggling nations, did not require the global competition with Soviet Russia that left America so overextended and despised throughout the world. Perhaps not. But this misses the essential point about the nation and its elite—that they were only fulfilling their destiny as determined by generations of training and influence. One might just as well argue that it was unnecessary for the Romans to build their empire. They built it precisely *because* they were Romans. The American nation, in creating the American Century, was propelled by similar mysterious impulses.

Postwar history is replete with lessons suggesting that the Alsop brothers and their friends in foreign-policy circles were correct in believing peace required a balance of power throughout the world. It was mainly at times and places of Western weakness, or perceived weakness, that Soviet expansionism threatened and challenged. It was indeed a *global* competition the West faced with Kremlin leaders after 1945. World stability was by its nature precarious, instability contagious. Even after Kremlin leadership passed from the bold, imaginative Khruschchev to the stolid, gray bureaucrats who followed, Soviet adventurism waxed and waned according to perceptions of Western strength and resolve.

More to the point, perhaps, is the question of whether the elite erred in thinking world stability could be maintained by a kind of benign, postcolonial imperialism. The idea was that lesser nations might keep their sovereignty but that they nonetheless could be swayed by their desire for American aid or protection, or, barring that, by the manueverings of U.S. intelligence agents. Military force was to be introduced only in extremis, when bribery and intrigue had failed.

This approach contained internal contradictions as it applied to the world at large and to America itself. For many nations around the world, sovereignty brought a level of self-respect that dictated resistance to U.S. efforts at influence, by money or by stealthy agents. And at home, many Americans lost their stomach for a policy that was billed as benign imperialism but suddenly turned nasty and bloody in the jungles and rice paddies of Vietnam.

In any event, the so-called American Century lasted a mere thirty years—from the fall of Germany and Japan in 1945 to the fall of Saigon in 1975. The era ended a year after Stewart's death and less than six months after Joe's retirement.

After that, America was never quite the same in its world role. It was still a great power, but it now lacked its earlier confidence, imagination, and boldness. Liberal isolationism had become an entrenched political force, ready to undercut and perhaps destroy any president who took the country too far into the thickets of global interventionism. And the bitter memory of Vietnam restrained the national will.

All this found political expression in the White House tenure of Jimmy Carter, the president Joe Alsop respected least. The gray bureaucrats of the Kremlin responded to Carter's soft, idealistic foreign policy with a new round of adventurism—in Afghanistan, Cuba, and Central America, as well as in nuclear arms development. The concerns engendered in the country led to Carter's defeat and to the election of Ronald Reagan in 1980.

Employing pugnacious rhetoric and adopting the Forrestal approach of massive defense spending, Reagan induced the collapse of the corrupt, internally rotting Soviet system. Its Eastern European empire crumbled in 1989, and its own communist regime followed into oblivion three years later.

And there stood America—the victor of the Cold War, and the lone superpower upon the globe. It was a moment of triumph to be savored.

Yet it differed markedly from that previous moment of triumph in 1945. Missing now was any sense of what kind of world the lone superpower wanted to help fashion, what kind of peace it envisioned. The nation and its leaders seemed bewildered by their own good fortune, unable to provide policy or direction. President George Bush sent a U.S. expeditionary force to the Middle East to protect the West's oil access from the latest wave of Arab nationalism, and when he succeeded he declared a New World Order. But nobody quite knew what this new order was, and the president couldn't explain it. He halted his troops before they had a chance to take enemy headquarters, lest America find itself attempting to enforce the peace, with all the challenges of diplomacy and military resolve that would follow. All this merely added to the confusion—at home and abroad—wrought by a lack of any coherent vision of world stability emanating from Washington.

That was the difference between the 1990s and the 1940s. At the end of World War II, the country was still guided by an elite with a strong sense of itself and a strong sense of the nation, with boldness and vision and zest for the challenges of world leadership. It was an elite that had been conditioned for precisely that moment by old habits of thought and by tested institutions steeped in the traditions and triumphs of the English-speaking peoples.

Few could imagine then that it was an elite at the twilight of its existence, that it soon would be consumed in fires of controversy ignited to some extent by its own principles. Few could foresee that the country and the world would soon find themselves searching for some kind of successor force to bring stability and prevent the chaos always engendered by vacuums of power.

History moves forward with crushing force and does not stay for answers or explanations. Joseph Alsop understood this as well as anyone, as he demonstrated in a 1973 letter to a friend, David Satter, in Chicago. Satter had brooded over events of the day in a previous letter, and Joe found himself in the novel position of attempting to salve someone else's gloom. Satter must stop brooding over the violence and harshness of life, Joe counseled, because violence and harshness, after all, were history's main ingredients. Indeed, he added, if one could call a rule with no known exceptions a law, then there were in fact three laws of history, all of which could be put into a single sentence:

"Nothing endures, because there is always change, and there is always war."

NOTES

In referring to the subjects of this book and their mother in these notes, I have employed three abbreviations: JWA is Joseph Wright Alsop V. SA is Stewart Alsop. CRA is Corinne Robinson Alsop. In referring to the Alsop Papers at the Library of Congress, I use the designation JWA Papers to denote Joseph Alsop's pre–World War II papers. After the war, I refer to the JWA & SA Papers, meaning the collection that commenced in late 1945 when the brothers began their collaboration. Even after 1958, when the brothers' column partnership ended, I retain the JWA & SA Papers designation, as many of SA's papers continued to make their way into JWA's files. From that date forward, however, SA's official papers were collected separately and eventually made their way to the Mugar Library at Boston University, referred to here as Special Collections, Boston University Libraries.

INTRODUCTION

page

xv   clear skies: Weather report, *Washington Post*, March 15, 1961, p. 1.

xv   a simple plan: "The Guests Danced 'Til 2: Lester Lanin Plays for Gala White House Party," *Washington Evening Star*, March 17, 1961, p. C1.

xv   no toasts: Dorothy McCardle, "By Kennedys: Florida Easter Is Planned," *Washington Post*, March 17, 1961, p. F3.

xv   family entrance: "Guests Danced 'Til 2."

xvi   saumon mousseline: Menu, "The White House, Wednesday, March 15, 1961," John F. Kennedy Library, Sanford Fox File, box 7.

xvi   Lester Lanin: "Guests Danced 'Til 2."

xvi   frequent ritual: Elizabeth Winthrop, interview, November 17, 1990.

xvi   red Saab: Elizabeth Winthrop, interview, February 7, 1994.

xvi   "You know . . .": Patricia Alsop, interview, January 16, 1995.

xvi   FDR seemed totally deaf: SA, letter to Martin Sommers, March 15, 1961, JWA & SA Papers, Library of Congress, container 30.

xvii   "my good man": Elizabeth Winthrop, interview, November 17, 1994.

xviii   "friendly acquaintance": SA, interview with Dick Cavett, ABC TV, March 1974 (aired after SA's death), tape provided by Patricia Alsop.

xviii   "voluptuous": Jacqueline Kennedy, letter to JWA, undated, JWA & SA Papers, container 130.

xviii   intimate Sunday night dinner: JWA, interview with Elspeth Rostow, June 18, 1964, Kennedy Library Oral History Project, JWA & SA Papers, container 82.

xviii   ". . . door to Mamie's room": Ibid.

xviii   "Dear Mr. President": Ibid.

xviii   Schlesingers and Evanses: Rowland Evans, memo to his file, March 16, 1961, Rowland Evans files.

xix   strong cocktails, caviar: Ibid.

xix   near the large windows: Ibid.

xix   "dramatic white sheath": McCardle.

xix   "divine": "Guests Danced 'Til 2."

xix   Joe moved quickly: Patricia Alsop, interview, February 23, 1994.

xix   tanned but fleshy: Evans memo.
xix   women's style and beauty: SA, letter to Martin Sommers, March 28, 1961, JWA & SA Papers, container 30.
xix   "dining-out" senators: Ibid.
xix   "Kennedy's private senator": Ibid.
xix   ". . . laudable taste": Ibid.
xix   guests: Guest List, "Dinner at the White House, Wednesday, March 15, 1961, at eight o'clock," John F. Kennedy Library, Sanford Fox File, box 7.
xxi   after nine: Evans memo.
xxi   tables for eight: McCardle.
xxi   candelabra and flowers: "Guests Danced 'Til 2."
xxi   Strolling musicians: Ibid.
xxi   Lyndon Johnson's table: Patricia Alsop, interview, February 23, 1994.
xxii   "so bad he can taste it": SA, letter to JWA, March 21, 1957, JWA & SA Papers, container 14.
xxii   "a bit sad": SA, letter to Martin Sommers, March 28, 1961.
xxii   Pinchot sisters: "Guests Danced 'Til 2."
xxii   clandestine visitor: Thomas C. Reeves, A Question of Character: A Life of John F. Kennedy (New York: The Free Press, 1991), pp. 240–41.
xxii   Evans's exchange with Helen Chavchavadze: Evans memo.
xxii   Joe's dance for Hussein: Katherine Evans, interview, February 16, 1995.
xxiii carpets taken up: McCardle.
xxiii Joe's large cigar: Letitia Baldrige, interview, February 11, 1994.
xxiii JFK by the fireplace: Evans memo.
xxiv   ". . . lunatic cathedral": Katharine Graham, interview, January 10, 1995.
xxiv   butler's whisper: Evans memo.
xxiv   the twist: Tony Bradlee, interview, February 11, 1994.
xxiv   People milling about: Evans memo.
xxiv   Lyndon and Bobby: SA, March 28, 1961.
xxiv   Johnson slipped: Katherine Evans, interview.
xxiv   "Good night, Mr. President": SA, March 28, 1961.
xxv   still smiling: Patricia Alsop, February 23, 1994.

CHAPTER ONE

page

4   "the self-same Saxon current . . .": Edgar Allan Poe, The Complete Works of Edgar Allan Poe, ed. James A. Harrison, 17 vols., vol. 11, Literary Criticism (New York: George D. Sproul, 1902), p. 148.
4   "Our past is theirs . . ." Robert K. Massie, Dreadnought: Britain, Germany, and the Coming of the Great War. (New York: Random House, 1991), p. 239.
5   Richard Alsop and descendants: The complete Alsop family tree is detailed in a loose-leaf book in the possession of Corinne Alsop Chubb.
5   Richard Alsop's shrewd insight: Stephen Birmingham, America's Secret Aristocracy (Boston: Little, Brown, 1987), p. 64.
5   "a soft, sweet man": Catherine Drinker Bowen, John Adams and the American Revolution (Boston: Little, Brown, 1950), p. 462. (Bowen doesn't note Alsop's given name in her text, but the index erroneously identifies him as "Joseph".)
5   "John the Non-Signer": SA, Stay of Execution: A Sort of Memoir (Philadelphia and New York: J. B. Lippincott, 1973), p. 89–90.
6   Rufus King: SA, "It Wasn't Born Yesterday," Saturday Evening Post, July 27, 1968, p. 30.
6   Richard Alsop's son: Ibid.
6   "remarkable aptitude for business": Obituary, Sentinel and Witness, March 1, 1878, JWA Papers, Library of Congress, container 1.
6   Joseph Wright Alsop II's business career: SA, "It Wasn't Born Yesterday."
6   images in the Vatican: brochure, Davison Art Center, Wesleyan University, Middletown, Conn.
6   country gentleman: Testimonial, undated and unsigned, delivered to Connecticut legislature, JWA Papers, container 1.
6   running for lieutenant governor: SA, "It Wasn't Born Yesterday."
7   JWA IV's early years: CRA reminiscences, John Alsop files; Corinne Alsop Chubb, interview, November 3, 1990; John Alsop, interview, November 15, 1990.
7   "He looked distinguished . . .": CRA reminiscences.
7   Peter Corne's vigils: SA, Stay of Execution, p. 90.
7   "probably the richest . . .": SA, "It Wasn't Born Yesterday."

7 Aunt Harriett and Henderson House: Ibid.
8 "bullied or ignored": David McCullough, *Mornings on Horseback* (New York: Simon and Schuster, 1981), p. 234.
8 Conie's pony and reading: Ibid., pp. 31–32, 227.
8 "a little feminine Atlas . . .": Ibid., p. 35.
9 extolling TR: Ibid., pp. 234–36. *Mornings on Horseback* provides an excellent account of Douglas Robinson's courtship of Corinne and her difficulties with the idea of marriage.
9 "To My Brother": Corinne Roosevelt Robinson, *Poems* (New York: Charles Scribner's Sons, 1921), p. 187.
9 "brother" of his country: Corinne Roosevelt Robinson, *My Brother Theodore Roosevelt* (New York: Charles Scribner's Sons, 1921), pp. vii–viii.
10 the retreat at Orange: CRA reminiscences. The accounts of TR's "obstacle walks" and the rowing expedition also are found in her unpublished memoirs.
10 August at Henderson House: JWA and SA, "Lament for a Long-Gone Past," *Saturday Evening Post*, January 26, 1957, p. 17.
11 "weary, leftover love": CRA's reminiscences. These writings contain telling details and human insight on Eleanor Roosevelt's early years, including descriptions of her childhood circumstances, the episode with the out-of-fashion dress, and life at Allenswood.
11 Mlle. Souvestre: Jospeh P. Lash, *Love, Eleanor: Eleanor Roosevelt and Her Friends* (Garden City, N.Y.: Doubleday, 1982), pp. 18–36.
11 Eleanor and Mlle. Souvestre: CRA reminiscences.
11 *"Mais pas gaie . . .":* Ibid.
12 "my kind of fun": Ibid.
12 Joseph Wright Alsop IV: Described in interviews with Corinne Alsop Chubb, John Alsop, Dorothy Kidder, and Paul H. Nitze.
12 ". . . excruciatingly hideous": CRA reminiscences. The wedding, honeymoon, and automobile trip are recounted here.

CHAPTER TWO

page

13 turn-of-the-century Avon: SA, "Revolution on Main Street," *Saturday Evening Post*, June 20, 1959, p. 19.
14 "How do you do?" CRA, letter to SA, undated, John Alsop files.
14 "the fine unemotional faces . . .": Ibid.
14 at the town store: Ibid.
14 "a strong face": John Alsop, interview, June 18, 1991.
14 "torrential influx": CRA reminiscences, John Alsop files
14 "I felt like some queen . . .": Ibid.
15 ". . . like the waves of the sea": CRA, "About Childbirth," essay, John Alsop files.
15 "filled with joy . . .": Ibid.
15 Corinne's "pleasant ways": CRA reminiscences.
15 Joe's political career: John Alsop, "Our Town," speech, June 7, 1976, John Alsop files.
15 little Joseph displayed: CRA reminiscences. (This essay included the stories about Joe's interest in animals, the visit to the zoo, and the discussion about babies.)
16 ". . . rather wizened mummy": JWA, "A Brave and Stoical Man," *Washington Post*, May 31, 1974.
16 visit with New York doctor: Corinne Alsop Chubb, interview, November 3, 1990.
16 ". . . into the hay barn": Ibid.
16 Corinne's Model T: JWA, with Adam Platt, *I've Seen the Best of It* (New York: W. W. Norton, 1992), p. 49.
16 Stutz Bearcat: John Alsop, interview, June 18, 1991.
16 buying the adjacent farm: Willie Gold, interview with Elizabeth Winthrop, Elizabeth Winthrop files.
16 his income grew: John Alsop, interview, November 15, 1990.
16 Italian influx: CRA, letter to SA, undated; SA, "Revolution on Main Street"; JWA, *I've Seen the Best of It*, p. 45.
17 childhood activities: JWA, *I've Seen the Best of It*, pp. 50–51.
17 Aggie's domain: CRA reminiscences.
18 "Mother's 'budwar' ": Ibid.
18 farmhouse expansion: John Alsop, interview, June 18, 1991.
18 Corinne's civic activities: Elizabeth Winthrop, notes from newspaper clippings provided by Charlotte Craig, Elizabeth Winthrop files.
18 ". . . twitching at her overcoat": John Alsop, letter to SA, December 12, 1958, John Alsop files.

18   "Goddam it, Corinne": Anne Anderson, interview with Elizabeth Winthrop, Elizabeth Winthrop files.
18   January and February trips: John Alsop, interview with Elizabeth Winthrop, Elizabeth Winthrop files.
18   dining without children: Corinne Alsop Chubb, interview, November 3, 1990.
18   "Father made it clear": John Alsop, interview, November 15, 1990.
18   a "tough cookie": John Alsop, interview, June 18, 1991.
19   evenings at Avon: Charlotte Craig, letter to Elizabeth Winthrop, Elizabeth Winthrop files.
19   children paired off: Corinne Alsop Chubb, interview, November 3, 1990.
19   "We looked to Joe . . .": John Alsop, interview, November 15, 1990.
19   one-room schoolhouse: CRA reminiscences.
19   Stewart often ill: J. M. Beard, letter to Joseph Wright Alsop IV, June 15, 1923, Patricia Alsop files.
19   "faithful, conscientious . . .": Ibid.
20   Joe's "mental power": George R. H. Nicholson, letter to Endicott Peabody, Groton School archives.
20   Joe's lack of athletic ability: JWA, *I've Seen the Best of It*, p. 51.
20   Douglas Robinson's sneer: Ibid., p. 55.
20   Joe wouldn't be intimidated: Dorothy Robinson Kidder, interview, October 25, 1990.
20   ". . . horribly handicapped": Ibid.
20   ". . . perfectly delighted": Joseph Wright Alsop IV, letter to SA, July 19, 1923, Patricia Alsop files.
20   long ride brings hay fever: SA, letter to CRA, undated, Patricia Alsop files.
20   ". . . a more perfect time": SA, letter to Corinne Roosevelt Robinson, undated, Houghton Library, Harvard University, Robinson/Alsop Papers, Theodore Roosevelt Collection.
21   breakfast at Henderson: JWA and SA, "Lament for a Long-Gone Past," *Saturday Evening Post*, January 26, 1957, p. 17.
21   Henderson daily schedule: Ibid.
21   Eleanor Roosevelt's experience: Ibid.
22   Joe's preoccupation with money: JWA, *I've Seen the Best of It*, pp. 40–41.
22   "So give me please . . .": JWA, letter to Douglas Robinson, undated, Houghton Library, Harvard University, Robinson/Alsop Papers, Theodore Roosevelt Collection.
22   "very urgently": Dorothy Robinson Kidder, interview, October 25, 1990.

CHAPTER THREE

page

23   "I am free to say": Sherrard Billings, letter to Joseph W. Alsop IV, February 5, 1929, Patricia Alsop files.
23   "When I went to Groton": Joseph W. Alsop IV, letter to Sherrard Billings, February 12, 1929, Groton School archives.
24   Peabody's family heritage: Frank D. Ashburn, *Peabody of Groton* (New York: Coward McCann, 1944), p. 2.
24   of serious mien: Ibid., p. 20.
24   ". . . manly, Christian character": "By Laws of the Declaration of Trust, Groton School, 1884," preface, quoted in Ashburn, p. 68. The subsequent description of the Groton experience also comes from Ashburn.
25   Peabody's sermons: Ted Morgan, *FDR: A Biography* (New York: Simon and Schuster, 1985), p. 56.
25   "a bit of a bully": Ashburn, p. 86.
25   family values: Stephen Birmingham, *America's Secret Aristocracy* (Boston: Little, Brown, 1987), p. 241.
25   "the way of the non-athlete . . .": Ashburn, p. 101.
25   "physical largeness": Joseph W. Alsop IV, JWA's Groton application, Groton School archives.
25   "personal ambitions . . .": Ibid.
25   "That's all right . . .": JWA, with Adam Platt, *I've Seen the Best of It* (New York: W. W. Norton, 1992), p. 59.
25   "My weeklies were fairly good . . .": JWA, letter to Corinne Roosevelt Robinson, undated, Houghton Library, Harvard University, Robinson/Alsop Papers, Theodore Roosevelt Collection.
26   Erastus Corning's academic success: Groton School yearbook, 1928, Groton School library.
26   "I was overweight . . .": JWA, *I've Seen the Best of It*, p. 54.

26 "fire-arms, and spiritous liquors": JWA, letter to Corinne Roosevelt Robinson, undated, Houghton Library, Harvard University, Robinson/Alsop Papers, Theodore Roosevelt Collection.
26 Dickie Bissell's stink bomb: Richard M. Bissell, Jr., interview, June 17, 1991.
26 abandoning human company: JWA, *I've Seen the Best of It*, pp. 58, 60.
26 "butt of teasing": Bissell, interview.
26 thinking of taking his own life: JWA, *I've Seen the Best of It*.
26 "enormous lesson": Ibid., p. 60.
27 ". . . perfectly ridiculous": Joseph W. Alsop IV, letter to Endicott Peabody, April 13, 1925, Groton School archives.
27 ". . . and I won": JWA, letter to Grandmother Robinson, undated, Houghton Library, Robinson/Alsop Papers.
27 school's top debaters: Groton School yearbook, 1928, p. 85.
27 Civics Club assignment: Ibid., p. 87.
27 Mrs. Kent: Ibid., p. 69.
28 backpacking in the Rockies: *Grotonian*, May 1927.
28 ". . . we foxed that old Jew": Warren D. Robbins, "Even a Jew," *Grotonian*, Prize Day issue, 1928, p. 304.
28 death of Empress Elizabeth: JWA, "The Bells," *Grotonian*, October 1926.
28 ". . . charming modulations": JWA, "A Eulogy of Buttered Toast," *Grotonian*, May 1927, p. 227.
28 ". . . a strange figure disengaged": JWA, "Repentence," *Grotonian*, April 1927, p. 197.
29 Stewart's prospects: George R. H. Nicholson, letter to Groton School, Groton School archives.
29 ". . . lack of self confidence": Joseph W. Alsop IV, SA's Groton School application, 1927, Groton School archives.
29 suitcases on Stewart's lap: SA, letter to his parents, undated, Patricia Alsop files.
29 "Joe . . . has been very nice": SA, letter to his parents, undated, Patricia Alsop files.
29 dim view of Stewart: Endicott Peabody, letter to Joseph W. Alsop IV, March 13, 1928, Patricia Alsop files.
30 ". . . on a bust": Joseph W. Alsop IV, letter to Endicott Peabody, March 22, 1928, Patricia Alsop files.
30 looking over another boy's paper: Endicott Peabody, letter to Joseph W. Alsop IV, October 30, 1928, Groton School archives.
30 "mediocre . . . carelessness": Endicott Peabody, letter to Joseph W. Alsop IV, December 21, 1928, Groton School archives.
30 February transgressions: Sherrard Billings, letter to Joseph W. Alsop IV, February 5, 1929, Patricia Alsop files.
30 ". . . slightly warped": JWA, letter to Joseph W. Alsop IV, undated, Groton School archives.
30 "I know the boy . . . intimately": Joseph W. Alsop IV, letter to Sherrard Billings, February 12, 1929, Patricia Alsop files.
30 "Fairly good . . .": Sherrard Billings, Groton School half term report, March 14, 1930, Patricia Alsop files.
30 "I had looked forward . . .": Joseph W. Alsop IV, letter to Endicott Peabody, March 25, 1991, Patricia Alsop files.
31 Stewart's letters of remorse: SA, undated letters home, Patricia Alsop files.
31 jocular letters: Ibid.
31 "grand old man of Wall Street": SA, "Defeat," *Grotonian*, Christmas 1930, p. 65.
31 "This one-sided portrayal": SA, *Grotonian*, April 1931, p. 166.
31 setting sights on Yale: Endicott Peabody, letter to Joseph W. Alsop IV, April 14, 1931, Patricia Alsop files.
32 during the Great War: Ashburn, p. 234.
32 Groton's political undercurrent: Ibid., p. 219.
32 nearly 90 percent from social register families: Ibid., p. 218.

CHAPTER FOUR

page

34 Stewart reading Boswell: SA, letter to Avon, undated, Patricia Alsop files.
34 Joe's transformation: Richard M. Bissell, Jr., interview, June 17, 1991.
35 dormitory, then "Gold Coast": JWA, with Adam Platt, *I've Seen the Best of It* (New York and London: W. W. Norton, 1992), p. 68; Bissell, interview.
35 $200-a-month allowance: JWA, *I've Seen the Best of It*, p. 68.
35 New London boat races: Bissell, interview.

35 Oliver, Wendell, and Holmes: Colin Campbell, "The Harvard Factor," *New York Times Magazine*, July 20, 1986, p. 17.
35 pro-British, partial to elites: Donald Fleming, quoted in Campbell.
35 proportion of preppies in 1920s: Hendrik Hertzberg, "Ivy Scoreboard," *New Republic*, August 8 and 15, 1988, p. 13.
35 proportion of preppies in 1880s: Campbell.
35 snobbery toward high school kids: Joseph L. Rauh, Jr., interview, June 14, 1991.
36 Groton's half-day holiday: JWA, *I've Seen the Best of It*, p. 61.
36 Joe's reading: Ibid., p. 61–62.
36 "Of course, I am delighted . . .": Ted Morgan, *FDR: A Biography* (New York: Simon and Schuster, 1985), p. 80.
37 FDR's disappointment: Ibid., p. 81.
37 Porcellian's honored guests: JWA, *I've Seen the Best of It*, pp. 63–64.
37 ". . . enormous breadth of knowledge": Paul Nitze, interview, October 25, 1990.
37 looking after Longworth: JWA, *I've Seen the Best of It*, p. 61.
37 Long Island dances: Ibid., pp. 26–27.
37 Personal finances: Bissell, interview.
38 family conference: JWA and SA, *The Reporter's Trade* (New York: Reynal & Co., 1958), pp. 1–2.
38 permission to attend Harvard: JWA, *I've Seen the Best of It*, p. 61.
39 father pleased about Yale: Joseph Alsop IV, letter to Tom Farnam, July 29, 1932, Patricia Alsop files.
39 Canby on Yale: Henry Seidel Canby, *Alma Mater* (New York: Farrar & Rinehart, 1936), p. 73.
39 do something to be someone: Owen Johnson, *Stover at Yale* (New York: Stokes, 1911).
39 percentage of prep school students: Hertzberg.
39 ". . . prestige and kudos": SA, letter to Avon, undated, Patricia Alsop files.
39 ". . . I really did my best . . .": SA, letter to Avon, undated, Patricia Alsop files.
40 ". . . talk on the whole situation": Joseph Alsop IV, letter to SA, November 8, 1932, Patricia Alsop files.
40 "Had you paid any attention . . .": Joseph Alsop IV, letter to SA, November 1, 1932, Patricia Alsop files.
40 "None of us really applied ourselves": Dillon Ripley, interview, November 1, 1990.
40 Stewart's freshman grades: Grade Report for S. J. O. Alsop, Yale University, September 30, 1932–June 10, 1933, Patricia Alsop files.
40 Russian skit: Described in fragmentary form by numerous persons interviewed; fullest description is from John Alsop, interview, November 15, 1990.
41 Stewart's interest in dramatics: *History of the Class of 1936*, Yale College, 1936.
41 Dottie Robinson's friends: Dorothy Robinson Kidder, interview, October 25, 1990.
41 probation: Notice, Office of the Registrar of Freshmen, Yale University, April 6, 1933, Patricia Alsop Files.
41 "college punks": SA, *Stay of Execution: A Sort of Memoir* (Philadelphia and New York: J. B. Lippincott, 1973), pp. 190–91.
41 autumn suspension: Clarence Mendell, letter to Joseph W. Alsop IV, November 26, 1935, Patricia Alsop files.
41 spring suspension: Clarence Mendell, letter to Joseph W. Alsop IV, May 22, 1936, Patricia Alsop files.
42 honors English, with third-place ranking: *History of the Class of 1936*.
42 Stewart's ambitions: Ibid.

CHAPTER FIVE

page

43 James Gordon Bennett's innovations: Robert A. Rutland, *The Newsmongers: Journalism in the Life of the Nation* (New York: Dial Press, 1973), pp. 156–57.
43 fast boats out to sea: "Mercy Killing," *Time*, August 26, 1966, p. 42.
43 Stanley and Custer: Richard Kluger, *The Paper: The Life and Death of the New York Herald Tribune* (New York: Alfred A. Knopf, 1986), p. 143.
43 Greeley's *Tribune*: Rutland, pp. 144–46.
44 sale of the *Herald* to the *Tribune*: Kluger, pp. 213–14.
44 *Herald Tribune* circulation: Ibid., p. 232.
44 "Republican inbreeding": Ibid., p. 252.
44 Walker inquired . . . : JWA, with Adam Platt, *I've Seen the Best of It* (New York: W. W. Norton, 1992), p. 71.
44 $18 a week: JWA and SA, *The Reporter's Trade* (New York: Reynal & Co., 1958), p. 2.

44 ". . . get me a pencil": Kluger, p. 253.

44 "he floundered": Stanley Walker, *City Editor* (New York: Blue Ribbon Books, 1934), p. 219.

45 obituary of Mrs. Benjamin Harrison: Anita Brewer Letters, Lessing Engelking File, Richard Kluger Papers, Manuscripts and Archives, Yale University Library.

45 "Suddenly, he found himself": Walker.

45 Sarah Greenspan's story: JWA, "Greenspan Tells Dice Players of Horatio Alger: Court, with Daughter, 10, 12 Guest Adviser, Sets Four on Path to Riches, Fame," New York *Herald Tribune*, September 17, 1934, p. 1.

46 Joe's assignments: JWA, *I've Seen the Best of It*, pp. 72–73.

47 Proust's writings: John Bogart, interview with Richard Kluger, Richard Kluger Papers, Joseph Alsop File, Manuscripts and Archives, Yale University Library.

47 professional yearnings: JWA, letter to Henry Cabot Lodge II, undated, Houghton Library, Harvard University, Robinson/Alsop Papers, Theodore Roosevelt Collection.

48 Joe's personal finances: JWA, *I've Seen the Best of It*, pp. 73–74.

48 "I need another brandy": Richard M. Bissell, Jr., interview, June 17, 1991. Bissell also described JWA's evening parties.

48 Bleeck's: "Hangouts: The Place Downstairs," *Time*, May 3, 1963, p. 65.

49 Joe's *Herald Tribune* friends: JWA, *I've Seen the Best of It*, pp. 74, 76.

49 "He was arrogant . . .": Homer Bigart, interview.

49 collapsed face-down into his soup: JWA, interview with Richard Kluger, Richard Kluger Papers, Joseph Alsop File, Manuscripts and Archives, Yale University Library.

49 description of Ogden Reid: Kluger, pp. 5, 280–81.

49 description of Helen Reid: Kluger, pp. 285–91.

50 arguing with his father: Corinne Alsop Chubb, interview, November 3, 1990.

50 Lindbergh trial: Stanley Walker, *Mrs. Astor's Horse* (New York: Blue Ribbon Books, 1935).

51 "A song-writing taxi driver": JWA, "Taxi Driving Actor, 'Star of Case,' Takes Top Billing in Day at Trial," New York *Herald Tribune*, February 9, 1935, p. 9.

51 Mrs. Anna Hauptmann: JWA, "Wife Is Brave in Ordeal for Hauptmann," New York *Herald Tribune*, January 31, 1935, p. 13.

51 Bruno Richard Hauptmann: JWA, "Enigma of Bronx, Cast as a Hamlet, Surprises by Playing Polonius, Calmly, Simply and Well," New York *Herald Tribune*, January 25, 1935, p. 1.

52 changing his "linens": Kluger, p. 254.

52 ancient country inn: JWA, *I've Seen the Best of It*, pp. 77–78.

CHAPTER SIX

page

54 Corinne's view of Eleanor and Franklin: John Alsop, interview, June 18, 1991.

54 Corinne and Franklin at social gatherings: Ibid.

54 "Dear Franklin": Joseph Wright Alsop IV, letter to Franklin Roosevelt, April 5, 1933, Franklin D. Roosevelt Library, Hyde Park, N.Y.

54 "If you show them this note . . .": Franklin D. Roosevelt, letter to Joseph Wright Alsop IV, April 20, 1933, Franklin D. Roosevelt Library.

54 glued to their chairs: John Alsop, interview, January 12, 1995.

54 New Year's Eve at the White House: JWA, with Adam Platt, *I've Seen the Best of It* (New York: W. W. Norton, 1992), p. 80.

54 "On the whole . . .": JWA, letter to Joseph Wright Alsop IV, undated, JWA Papers, Library of Congress, container 2.

54 the tutelage of Mrs. Dwight Davis: JWA, *I've Seen the Best of It*, p. 83.

55 JWA's first Washington party: Ibid.

55 dinner party customs: Ibid., pp. 84–85.

55 JWA and "Mrs. L": Patricia Alsop, interview, May 3, 1992.

55 Virginia Bacon's background: *Washington Star*, "Mrs. Robert Low Bacon, Grande Dame, Dies at 88," February 25, 1980.

55 Edith Eustis's background: *Washington Star*, "Mrs. William C. Eustis, Active in Charities, Dies," November 12, 1964.

56 ". . . a tiny little house . . .": JWA, letter to Charles Bohlen, March 8, 1938, JWA Papers, Library of Congress, container 2.

56 Roosevelt's trysts with Lucy Mercer: JWA, *FDR: A Centenary Remembrance* (New York: Viking Press, 1982), p. 69.

56 Mildred Bliss's background: "Blisses Are Honored on 50th Anniversary," *Washington Star*, April 13, 1958.

56   Joe's boarding house: Michael Straight, interview, December 14, 1990.

56   breakfast at 1718 H Street: Michael Straight, *After Long Silence* (New York: W. W. Norton, 1983), pp. 127–28.

56   Al Warner's ill-disguised skepticism: JWA, *I've Seen the Best of It*, p. 97.

57   Neutrality Act's requirements: Michael Barone, *Our Country: The Shaping of America from Roosevelt to Reagan* (New York: Free Press, 1990), p. 127.

57   "For God's sake, Joe . . .": JWA, letter to William Shawn, April 30, 1968, JWA & SA Papers, Library of Congress, container 146.

57   "On the subject of new writers . . .": "Keeping Posted," *Saturday Evening Post*, September 26, 1936, p. 120. The editors reported that they subsequently had lunch with JWA.

57   the *Post*'s journalistic lineage: Otto Friedrich, *Decline and Fall: The Struggle for Power at a Great American Magazine* (New York: Harper & Row, 1970), pp. 7–12.

58   the *Post* reached three million homes: John Tebbel, *George Horace Lorimer and the Saturday Evening Post* (Garden City, N.Y.: Doubleday, 1948), p. 218.

58   ". . . a parasite that sucks billions . . .": Editorial, *Saturday Evening Post*, October 31, 1936, p. 22.

58   Joe's fear of failure: Turner Catledge, interview with Richard Kluger, Richard Kluger Papers, Manuscripts and Archives, Yale University Library.

58   Catledge personality and background: "Keeping Posted," *Saturday Evening Post*, April 3, 1937, p. 120.

59   writing sessions: Turner Catledge, *My Life and the Times* (New York: Harper & Row, 1971), pp. 98–99.

59   "He is stout . . ." "Keeping Posted," *Saturday Evening Post*, September 26, 1936, p. 120.

59   $1,200: Catledge, *My Life and the Times*, p. 100.

59   "How will Corinne like that?" : JWA, *I've Seen the Best of It*, pp. 48–49.

60   opposition Republicans: Ted Morgan, *FDR: A Biography* (New York: Simon and Schuster, 1985), p. 441.

60   Roosevelt's 523-to-8 electoral vote victory: Ibid.

60   ". . . say him nay?" JWA and Turner Catledge, *The 168 Days* (Garden City, N.Y.: Doubleday, Doran, 1938), p. 2.

60   nine of eleven initiatives: Catledge, *My Life and The Times*, p. 90.

60   enough power to remake the court: Ibid.

61   "Suddenly the shabby comedy of national politics . . .": JWA and Catledge, *The 168 Days*, p. 10.

61   "His agreeably handsome face . . .": Ibid., p. 2.

61   "sore and vengeful": Ibid., p. 295.

61   "Nothing but praise . . .": Catledge, letter to JWA, October 29, 1937, JWA Papers, container 2.

61   Flat payment of $1,800: Catledge, *My Life and The Times*, p. 99.

61   ". . . shriek nepotism": Theodore Roosevelt, Jr., letter to JWA, November 5, 1937, JWA Papers, container 2.

61   another candidate: Catledge, *My Life and The Times*.

62   "one of the most brilliant accounts . . .": Rexford G. Tugwell, *The Democratic Roosevelt: A Biography of Franklin D. Roosevelt* (Garden City, N.Y.: Doubleday, 1957), p. 389n.

62   "random banging of a loose shutter": JWA, *I've Seen the Best of It*, p. 117.

62   diet prescribed by John Eager Howard: JWA, letter to Miss Rea, August 30, 1938, JWA Papers, container 2.

62   rigorous exercise program: JWA, *I've Seen the Best of It*, p. 118.

62   he had dropped sixty-five pounds: JWA, letter to Miss Rea.

62   "I'm not merely lighter on my feet": JWA, "How It Feels to Look Like Everybody Else," *Saturday Evening Post*, September 11, 1937, p. 16.

62   "I'm dying to have a look . . .": Maxine Davis, letter to JWA, October 30, JWA Papers, container 2.

63   Kintner background: Robert Kintner, promotional biography, JWA Papers, container 33.

63   the Reids' counteroffer: JWA, letter to Helen Reid, undated, JWA Papers, container 33.

63   "I cannot forebear from writing you . . .": Ibid.

63   NANA contract: Contract of JWA with North American Newspaper Alliance, October 20, 1937, JWA Papers, container 2.

63   sixty papers running the column: JWA, letter to Charles Bohlen, March 8, 1938.

63   heirloom furniture: JWA, letter to Corinne Alsop, October 24, 1938, JWA Papers, container 2.

64   "trot out the commissars": JWA, letter to Joseph W. Alsop IV, December 2, 1938, JWA Papers, container 2.

64 Noël Coward's reminiscence: Nöel Coward, *Autobiography* (London: Methuen, 1987), p. 368.

64 "admired Ben Cohen . . .": Isaiah Berlin, interview, November 27, 1991.

64 "I shan't soon forget": JWA, letter to Felix Frankfurter, September 7, 1938, JWA Papers, container 32.

64 Ruth Gordon episode: JWA, letter to Alexander Woollcott, February 26, 1940, JWA Papers, container 2.

65 *Life*'s circulation: Loudon Wainwright, *The Great American Magazine: An Inside History of* Life (New York: Alfred A. Knopf, 1938), p. 87.

65 but Luce worried . . . : Ibid., p. 101.

65 over lunch in New York . . . : JWA, letter to Henry R. Luce, July 25, 1938, JWA Papers, container 33.

65 "same kind of investigative job . . .": JWA, letter to Ralph D. Paine, Jr., August 29, 1938, JWA Papers, container 33.

65 Paine sent check for $1,500: Paine, Jr., letter to JWA, September 15, 1938, JWA Papers, container 33.

65 "a great deal more response . . .": JWA, letter to Paine, Jr., September 17, 1938, JWA Papers, container 33.

65 "light, cheerful sort of piece": JWA, letter to Eleanor Roosevelt, July 27, 1939, JWA Papers, container 2.

65 "delighted": Eleanor Roosevelt, letter to JWA, July 29, 1939, JWA Papers, container 2.

66 "struck out on his own course": JWA and Robert Kintner, "A Roosevelt Family Album," *Life*, September 9, 1940, p. 62.

66 Joe's new arrangement with the *Post*: JWA, letter to Martin Sommers, November 21, 1938, JWA Papers, container 34.

66 ". . . our *Post* connection": Ibid.

66 "If there is bias . . .": "Keeping Posted," *Saturday Evening Post*, September 18, 1937, p. 84.

66 "the man of wrath": JWA and Robert Kintner, "Ickes, the Man of Wrath," *Life*, November 21, 1938, p. 58.

66 "the pro-Roosevelt columns": Quincy Howe, *The News and How to Understand It* (New York: Simon & Schuster, 1940), p. 66.

67 "It is very rare . . .": JWA, letter to Arthur Vandenburg, February 24, 1939, JWA Papers, container 34.

67 "Being cautious, yet devoted . . .": JWA and Robert Kintner, " 'Henny Penny': Farmer at the Treasury," *Saturday Evening Post*, April 1, 1938, p. 8.

67 William Bullitt's counsel: Will Brownell and Richard N. Billings, *So Close to Greatness: A Biography of William C. Bullitt* (New York: Macmillan, 1987), p. 231.

67 ". . . best written . . .": Howe, p. 67.

67 "He is himself a Roosevelt": Ibid., p. 68.

67 incomes of $20,000 annually: This is based on an analysis of the *Herald Tribune* contract and the arrangements with *Life* and the *Post*.

67 Joe's working hours and concerns: JWA, letter to Roy Roberts, October 8, 1940, JWA Papers, container 33.

68 Stout demurred: Martin Sommers, letter to JWA, undated in 1939, JWA Papers, container 34.

68 Jack Wheeler's NANA offer: JWA, letter to Roy Roberts.

68 *Herald Tribune* offer: Outlined in various documents in JWA Papers, container 33.

68 "You have always been so generous . . .": JWA, letter to Wesley Winans Stout, October 3, 1940, JWA Papers, container 34.

68 "offered honest wedlock . . .": Wesley Winans Stout, letter to JWA, October 4, 1940, JWA Papers, container 34.

68 ". . . like coming home again": JWA, letter to Ogden Reid, October 3, 1940, JWA Papers, container 33.

68 "It is very wonderful to be back . . .": JWA, letter to Helen Reid, October 3, 1940, JWA Papers, container 33.

68 the Reids' gala dinner: Helen Reid, letter to JWA, October 5, 1940, JWA Papers, container 33.

CHAPTER SEVEN

page

69 Sis's wedding: Corinne Alsop Chubb, interview, December 19, 1994.

69 "well-trained western horse . . .": Endicott Peabody, letter to Joseph W. Alsop IV, April 4, 1931, Patricia Alsop files.

69 ". . . slightly inconsequential . . .": CRA, letter to SA, July 13, 1937, Patricia Alsop files.

70   $25 a week: SA, letter to Joseph W. Alsop IV, undated, Patricia Alsop files.
70   $100 monthly allowance: Ibid.
70   Uncle Ted's radio speech: "Col. Theodore Roosevelt Resigns as Governor General of Philippines," New York *Herald Tribune*, March 8, 1933.
70   "He was terribly bright . . .": Ken McCormick, interview, January 2, 1991.
70   "just the kind of thing I like . . .": SA, letter to his parents, undated, Patricia Alsop files.
70   "real erudition . . .": McCormick, interview.
70   not a motivating factor: John Alsop, interview, November 15, 1990.
70   Dottie Kidder's circle: Susan Mary Alsop, interview, December 14, 1990; Dorothy Robinson Kidder, interview, January 5, 1995.
70   evenings at LaRue: Ibid.
71   Young women's drinking and sexual habits: Ibid.
71   Stewart's social persona: Ibid.
71   Corinne shooting dice: Paul Nitze, interview, October 25, 1990.
71   special atmosphere: Susan Mary Alsop, interview, December 27, 1994.
72   trip to the barn: Susan Mary Alsop, interview, December 14, 1990.
72   Brooks Brothers excursion: SA, letter to Joseph W. Alsop IV, December 3, 1937.
72   new suit for SA's birthday: SA, letter to Joseph W. Alsop IV, undated, Patricia Alsop files.
72   ". . . turn to gold": SA, letter to Joseph W. Alsop IV, December 3, 1937, Patricia Alsop files.
72   Joe's Washington dinner parties: John Alsop, interview.
72   dinner at the White House: SA, letter to Joseph W. Alsop IV, undated, Patricia Alsop files.
73   At the "21" bar: John Alsop, interview.
73   Stewart as "Marxist liberal": SA, "Wanted: A Faith to Fight For," *Atlantic Monthly*, May 1941, p. 166.
73   ". . . go back to Russia . . .": SA, *Stay of Execution: A Sort of Memoir* (Philadelphia and New York: J. B. Lippincott Company, 1973), p. 91.
74   "crazy jack in the White House": Ibid.
74   absentee ballots: Corinne Alsop Chubb, interview, November 3, 1990.
74   Stewart's evolving political views: SA, "Wanted."
75   "complete disillusionment": "Topics of the Times," *New York Times*, May 7, 1941, p. 24.
75   "Collapse of Civilization Party": SA and John Alsop, invitation sent to their parents, October 1941, John Alsop files.

CHAPTER EIGHT

page

76   Poland on September 1: Richard M. Ketchum, *The Borrowed Years: America on the Way to War, 1938–1941* (New York: Random House, 1989), p. 202.
76   "This is Bill Bullitt . . .": JWA and Robert Kintner, *American White Paper: The Story of American Diplomacy and the Second World War* (New York: Simon & Schuster, 1940), p. 1.
77   "Our safety does not lie in fighting . . .": Ketchum, p. 216.
77   ". . . walking on eggs": Ibid., p. 227.
77   "very young Tory . . .": JWA, letter to Avon, January 17, 1939, JWA Papers, Library of Congress, container 2.
78   "deeply in accord . . .": JWA, letter to Eleanor Roosevelt, undated, JWA Papers, container 2.
78   arrangement with Morgenthau: JWA, letter to John W. Hanes, November 9, 1939, JWA Papers, container 32.
78   ". . . now very sorry . . .": JWA, letter to Henry Morgenthau, November 9, 1939, Henry Morgenthau Papers, FDR Library.
78   revised arrangement: Ibid.
78   Joe pressed for interview: Unsigned memorandum, "For The Secretary," December 1, 1939, Henry Morgenthau Papers.
79   "Now, Joe, don't get ugly . . .": Transcript of staff meeting, "Re Foreign Exchange Control," December 30, 1940, Henry Morgenthau Papers.
79   ". . . stacked the cards . . .": Wesley Winans Stout, letter to JWA, January 25, 1940, JWA Papers, container 34.
79   payment for unused article: JWA, letter to Alexander Woollcott, February 26, 1940, JWA Papers, container 2.
79   ". . . extremely generous to us . . .": JWA, letter to Martin Sommers, February 6, 1940, JWA Papers, container 34.

79   Henry Luce's reaction: JWA, letter to Martin Sommers, February 5, 1940, JWA Papers, container 34.

79   "which nobody reads": JWA, letter to Woollcott, February 26, 1940.

79   contract with Simon and Schuster: Contract signed March 19, 1940, JWA Papers, container 34.

79   *Ladies' Home Journal* buys serial rights: Leon Shimkin, letter to Morris Ernst, April 25, 1940, JWA Papers, container 34.

80   ". . . the poor Curtis Publishing Company . . .": JWA, letter to Woollcott, undated, JWA Papers, container 2.

80   "treble our Navy . . .": JWA and Kintner, *American White Paper*, p. 81.

80   ". . . a journalistic stunt . . .": Ralph Thompson, "Books of the Times," *New York Times*, April 22, 1940.

80   "reliable 'inside' information": "U. S. May Be Forced to Aid Allies Directly by '42, Two Columnists Predict in Daring Book," *Washington Star*, April 22, 1940, p. A2.

81   *American White Paper* sales: Maria Leiper, letters to JWA and Kintner, JWA Papers, container 34.

81   ". . . enjoyed reading the book": JWA, letter to Maria Leiper, April 30, 1940, JWA Papers, container 34.

81   ". . . some wise rooster . . .": JWA, undated letter to Woollcott, JWA Papers, container 2.

81   ". . . swept utterly away": JWA, undated letter to Woollcott, JWA Papers, container 2.

82   Vandenberg's views: Ketchum, p. 226.

82   talks with Morgenthau: JWA, undated typed notes, JWA Papers, container 32.

82   Reuther Plan: Joseph L. Rauh, Jr., interview, June 14, 1991.

82   "We leaked our socks off": Ibid.

82   "By nominating Wendell Willkie . . .": JWA and Kintner, "John L. Lewis and Wheeler," *Washington Star*, July 5, 1940.

82   joining the Century Group: Ketchum, pp. 474–80.

83   an unexpected visit: JWA and SA, *The Reporter's Trade* (New York: Reynal & Co., 1958), p. 8.

83   "All the things we hold most dear . . .": Ketchum, p. 476.

84   Joe's encounter with Admiral Stark: JWA and Harold Stark, correspondence, JWA Papers, container 32.

84   "specifically to contradict . . .": Arthur Krock, *New York Times*, August 6, 1940.

85   "I asked a question . . .": JWA, draft letter to *New York Times*, JWA Papers, container 32.

85   "nervous Nellie of a man . . .": JWA, letter to Helen Reid, August 12, 1940, JWA Papers, container 32.

85   ". . . to say nothing and write nothing . . .": JWA, draft letter to *New York Times*.

86   ". . . the thinnest available . . .": JWA, letter to E. Tautz and Sons, September 27, 1939, JWA Papers, container 2.

86   "I like my shirt fronts plain . . .": JWA, letter to E. & E. Hummel & Co. Ltd., May 29, 1940, JWA Papers, container 2.

86   cuffs too large: JWA, letter to Brooks Brothers, August 18, 1939, JWA Papers, container 2.

86   $9 a night: Voucher, July 24, 1940, JWA Papers, container 2. This voucher also noted the $64.80 plane fare, and the $4-a-night rate for the Hotel Stevens.

86   $25 bet with Guffey: Joseph F. Guffey, letter to JWA, April 11, 1939, JWA Papers, container 2.

86   wagers worth $200: JWA, letter to Joseph F. Guffey, November 25, 1940, JWA Papers, container 2.

87   Donovan's "glowing report": JWA and Kintner, "Donovan's Glowing Report on England's Chances Regarded as Officially Optimistic British View," *Washington Star*, August 10, 1940, p. A9.

87   ". . . at least an even chance . . .": JWA, letter to Felix Frankfurter, August 21, 1940, JWA Papers, container 2.

87   ". . . arrest you . . .": Arthur Krock, *The Consent of the Governed* (Boston: Little, Brown, 1971), p. 254.

87   Acheson-Alsop connection: JWA, with Adam Platt, *I've Seen the Best of It* (New York: W. W. Norton, 1992), p. 143.

87   Forrestal-Cowles connection: Ibid.

87   MacLeish-Alsop connection: Ibid., p. 143–44.

88   Lovett and McCloy background: Walter Isaacson and Evan Thomas, *The Wise Men: Six Men and the World They Made* (New York: Simon & Schuster, 1986), pp. 60–71.

88   just under $20,000: Mrs. Dewey Foster, letter to JWA, September 11, 1940, JWA Papers, container 2.

88   JWA's guest list: Sir Isaiah Berlin, interview, November 27, 1991.

88   "very much one of us": Ibid.
88   "I was taken aback": Katharine Graham, interview, February 12, 1991.
88   Alsop-Hopkins friendship: JWA, *I've Seen the Best of It*, p. 197.
89   description of Christmas at the White House and champagne later with Hopkins: JWA, letter to Avon, undated, JWA Papers, container 2.
89   inauguration day: JWA, letter to Marion Cristie, undated, JWA Papers, container 2. This letter also contains JWA's brief description of dinner at Alice Longworth's.
90   "offering their bodies to the flames": Ketchum, p. 582.

CHAPTER NINE

page

93   "This fat life . . .": JWA, letter to Eleanor Roosevelt, undated draft, JWA Papers, Library of Congress, container 2.
93   Kintner joined the army: Jean Pennybacker, formerly Jean Kintner, interview, May 16, 1992.
93   Roosevelt told friends: Ibid.
94   "A few weeks ago . . .": JWA, letter to Wesley Winans Stout, June 10, 1941, JWA Papers, container 2.
94   "I salute you both . . .": Hunt Clement, Jr., letter to JWA, June 11, 1941, JWA Papers, container 2.
94   "when and if it is resumed": Ben Reese, letter to JWA, June 9, 1941, JWA Papers, container 2.
94   " 'that zealous Anglophile' ": Helen Newman, letter to JWA, June 12, 1941, JWA Papers, container 2.
94   "Terribly sorry . . .": Paul Smith, telegram to JWA, June 12, 1941, JWA Papers, container 2.
94   ". . . done one on Adolf": J. D. Regan, letter to JWA, June 13, 1941, JWA Papers, container 2.
94   "My association with the *Post* . . .": JWA, letter to Wesley Winans Stout.
94   renting out Dumbarton house: JWA, letter to W. Hiles Pardoe, June 20, 1941, JWA Papers, container 2.
94   ceremonial naval uniform: JWA, with Adam Platt, *I've Seen the Best of It* (New York: W. W. Norton, 1992), p. 151.
94   "Those are battleships, sir": Ibid., p. 152.
94   "those wonderful British women . . .": JWA, letters to Avon, undated, John Alsop files. The saga of Joe's first Asian trip is contained in a series of undated letters culminating in a letter written immediately upon his release from Japanese prison camp.
95   ". . . total liquidation of their position": Ibid.
95   ". . . with an eye for the future . . .": Ibid.
95   trip to opium den: Ibid.
95   Chongqing in wartime: Theodore H. White and Annalee Jacoby, *Thunder Out of China* (New York: William Sloane Associates, 1946), pp. 3–19.
96   "The astonishing thing . . .": JWA, letters to Avon.
96   "perfect lunch": Ibid.
96   dinner with Clark-Kerr: JWA and SA, *The Reporter's Trade* (New York: Reynal & Co., 1958), p. 42.
96   "a very great man . . .": JWA, letters to Avon.
97   "gamecock of the wilderness": Ibid.
97   ". . . in the history of aerial warfare": White and Jacoby, p. 152. The description of Chennault's aerial exploits is from this work.
97   discussing AVG with Forrestal and Lovett: JWA, *I've Seen the Best of It*, p. 150.
97   "his aide and odd job man": JWA, letters to Avon. The description of Joe's work for Chennault, including his trip to the Philippines and Hong Kong, is taken from the Avon letters.
98   trip to Rangoon: JWA, *I've Seen the Best of It*, pp. 168–71.
99   Madame Kung's dog: John Alsop, interview, November 15, 1990. The incident, part of Alsop family lore, also is recounted in JWA's autobiography.
99   Joe cabled home: *Washington Star*, "Alsop Seen in Hong Kong About Two Weeks Ago," March 4, 1942.
99   JWA's plight in Hong Kong and incarceration at Stanley Prison: JWA, *I've Seen the Best of It*, chapter 9; JWA, "City in Prison," *Saturday Evening Post*, January 9, 1943, p. 12; and JWA, "Starvation Is Torture Too," *Saturday Evening Post*, January 16, 1943, p. 28.
103   Corinne's "little chat" with FDR: SA, *Stay of Execution: A Sort of Memoir* (Philadelphia and New York: J. B. Lippincott, 1973), p. 37.
103   the trip back home: JWA, *I've Seen the Best of It*, p. 192.

103 "I shall never be able to tell you . . .": JWA, letters to Avon.
104 dragged through a keyhole: John Alsop, interview, January 12, 1995.
104 Joe's feelings of good fortune: JWA, letters to Avon.
104 syphilis: Federal Bureau of Investigation, investigative report recapitulating JWA's military personnel file at the National Personnel Records Center, St. Louis, Mo., August 18, 1952. (There is no evidence of how JWA contracted the disease or from whom.)
104 JWA's new salary: Ibid.

CHAPTER TEN

page

105 flunking the draft physical: SA, *Stay of Execution: A Sort of Memoir* (Philadelphia and New York: J. B. Lippincott, 1973), p. 35; John Alsop, interview, November 15, 1990.
105 Joe's Washington contacts: Adolphus Andrews, letter to James Byrnes, May 20, 1941, JWA & SA Papers, Library of Congress, container 32.
105 "limited service": SA, *Stay of Execution*, p. 35.
105 "Eyes all right?": Ibid., pp. 35–36.
106 Hartford train station: John Alsop, interview, November 15, 1990.
106 six feet tall: Federal Bureau of Investigation, investigative report recapitulating SA's military personnel file at the National Personnel Records Center, St. Louis, Mo., August 18, 1952.
106 no sibling rivalry: John Alsop, interview, June 18, 1991.
106 Joe's avuncular lecture on drinking: Ibid.
106 ". . . very optimistic . . .": SA, letter to Avon, undated. A rich, detailed account of SA's wartime experience is recorded in his letters home and to his siblings and to Aggie Guthrie. Corinne Alsop had them typed, single-spaced, and they run to 275 pages. Some are dated, though many are not. The letters provide a complete chronology of SA's war experiences, the evolution of his thinking, his observations on England and the war, his evolving love for Tish Hankey, etc. Many of the details in this chapter come from the letters. Unless otherwise noted, details and quoted material from SA should be assumed to be from this record.
107 "very Brooks Brothers": Tom Braden, interview, October 27, 1990. Further details of the Alsop-Braden encounter are provided by SA, letters to Avon, and in *Stay of Execution*.
108 Cavendish Hotel: SA, *Stay of Execution*, pp. 69, 127, 288–89; SA, letters to Avon, also give the flavor of the Cavendish.
108 weekend with Baron Mowbray and Stourton: SA, *Stay of Execution*, pp. 56–60. Also, Patricia Alsop, interview, October 27, 1990; SA letters to Avon add details and flavor.
110 tea at the ambassador's: SA, *Stay of Execution*, pp. 36–37; also, Avon letters.
112 "Our dates were lunches . . .": Patricia Alsop, interview, October 27, 1990.
112 "We just about died from the heat": Braden, interview.
112 "mostly skirmishes . . .": Ibid.
114 ". . . he's found himself": Theodore Roosevelt, Jr., letter to CRA, included in bound volume of SA's letters to Avon.
114 "Jesus Christ, you two guys . . .": SA, *Stay of Execution*, p. 283.
115 "a Wall Street lawyer . . .": John Alsop, interview, June 18, 1991.
115 "Fifty-five . . .": SA, *Stay of Execution*, p. 287.
116 "a certain coolness": John Alsop, interview with the author, June 18, 1991.
116 Tish Hankey's background: Patricia Alsop, interview, October 27, 1990.
116 Tish's view of Stewart: Patricia Alsop, interview, December 28, 1992.
117 Prenuptial discussions: Details provided by Patricia Alsop, interview, October 27, 1990; John Alsop, interview, November 15, 1990; and SA, Avon letters.
118 "Because it's our honeymoon": Patricia Alsop, interview, October 27, 1990.
119 "Face it, Alsop . . .": SA, *Stay of Execution*, p. 294.
119 shot as a spy: John Alsop.
120 Patricia's voyage to America: Patricia Alsop, October 27, 1990.
120 Donovan's motivation: Braden, interview.
120 Croix de Guerre with Palm: SA, *Stay of Execution*, p. 295.
121 Interest in Foreign Service: Patricia Alsop, October 27, 1990.

CHAPTER ELEVEN

page

122 different route to China: JWA, letter to Avon, undated, John Alsop files (part of CWA's collection of JWA's wartime letters).

122   "A situation exists . . .": JWA, letter to Harry Hopkins, December 10, 1942, Hopkins Papers, Franklin Roosevelt Library, Hyde Park, N.Y.

123   Stilwell and *Dumbo*: Joseph W. Stilwell, *The Stilwell Papers*, ed. Theodore H. White (New York: William Sloane Associates, 1948), p. 12.

123   the AVG's stunning success: Claire Lee Chennault, *Way of a Fighter* (New York: G. P. Putnam's Sons, 1949), p. 174.

124   "probably a tactical genius": Harry Hopkins, memorandum, "CHINA—Generalissimo," July 15, 1943, Hopkins Papers.

124   generalissimo's Burma campaign performance: Charles F. Romanus and Riley Sunderland, *China-Burma-India Theater: Stilwell's Mission to China* (Washington, D.C.: Office of Military History, U.S. Dept. of the Army, 1953), pp. 118–48.

124   Stilwell's approach to Chiang: Brian Crozier, *The Man Who Lost China: The First Full Biography of Chiang Kai-shek* (New York: Charles Scribner's Sons, 1976), pp. 233–34.

124   Chiang's view of Stilwell's jungle trek: Chennault, p. 160.

124   ". . . startling exhibition . . .": Ibid.

125   ". . . endless petty persecution . . .": JWA, letter to Hopkins, December 10, 1942.

125   arrival in Chongqing: JWA, letter to Avon, December 19, 1942.

125   visit with Chennault: JWA, letter to Avon, undated; this letter recounted the episode of Chennault predicting Japanese plans and ordering an aerial ambush.

126   "I wouldn't give a damn . . .": JWA, letter to Hopkins, December 22, 1942, Hopkins Papers.

126   "so many thieves . . .": Ibid.

127   working at Twenty-second Street headquarters: JWA, letter to Hopkins, March 26, 1943, Hopkins Papers.

127   Chennault's promotion: JWA, with Adam Platt, *I've Seen the Best of It* (New York: W. W. Norton, 1992), p. 214.

127   Madame Chiang on Chennault and Stilwell: Robert E. Sherwood, *Roosevelt and Hopkins: An Intimate History* (New York: Harper & Brothers, 1948), p. 661.

127   "Hap" Arnold's views: Ibid., p. 681.

127   Joe briefed Hopkins and Roosevelt: JWA, *I've Seen the Best of It*, pp. 215–16.

127   Joe's twenty-one-page memo: JWA, letter to Hopkins, March 1, 1943, Hopkins Papers.

128   Chennault's social whirl in Washington: Chennault, p. 219.

129   Stilwell's Trident performance: Barbara W. Tuchman, *Stilwell and the American Experience in China* (New York: Macmillan, 1971), p. 367.

129   ". . . vacillating, tricky . . . scoundrel. . . .": Chennault, p. 226.

129   ". . . never broken a commitment . . .": Ibid.

129   Roosevelt's directive on Hump tonnage: Tuchman, p. 368. (Exact tonnage totals are recounted variously; totals cited are from Stilwell.)

129   "total misapprehension . . .": Tuchman, p. 369.

129   suckered by Chiang: Ibid.

129   ". . . ungrateful little rattlesnake": Stilwell, p. 207.

129   Marshall on Joe: Tuchman, p. 270.

129   Roosevelt's remarkable invitation: Chennault, p. 226.

129   "in view of the record . . .": JWA, letter to Hopkins, May 29, 1943, Hopkins Papers.

130   a retaliatory move: JWA, letter to Hopkins, April 26, 1943, Hopkins Papers.

130   promise from Roosevelt: JWA, letter to Hopkins, July 2, 1943, Hopkins Papers.

130   Soong's $10,000-a-year assistant: Federal Bureau of Investigation, report on JWA's military records, August 18, 1952.

130   "petty harassment": JWA, letter to Hopkins, July 2, 1943, Hopkins Papers.

130   farmers eating bark and leaves: Chennault, letter to Hopkins, July 2, 1943, Hopkins Papers.

130   "The effect of all these unexpected delays . . .": Chennault, letter to FDR, June 18, 1943, Hopkins Papers.

130   Chiang Kai-shek's request: Harry Hopkins, memorandum, "CHINA—Generalissimo," July 15, 1943, Hopkins Papers.

130   "an awful mess . . .": Ibid.

131   Roosevelt's bedroom session: Ibid.

131   "He is . . . a good soldier": Arnold, memo to Hopkins, July 23, 1943, Hopkins Papers.

131   ill-advised memo to Soong: JWA, letter to T. V. Soong, July 12, 1943, Marshall Papers, George C. Marshall Research Library, Lexington, Va., box 56.

131   Soong excised last paragraph: Altered copy of JWA letter, Hopkins Papers.

131   copy to Mountbatten: George C. Marshall, memorandum to the president, February 15, 1944, Marshall Papers, box 56.

131   life with Chennault: JWA, letter to Avon, July 28, 1943.

132   morning errand to Chiang Kai-shek: Ibid.

132   senators passed through: JWA, letter to Corinne Alsop Chubb, August 31, 1943, John Alsop files.
132   "I am more excited than I can say": JWA, letter to Avon, September 15, 1943.
132   Joe's brotherly pride: Ibid.
132   Joe's $10,000 life insurance policy: JWA, letter to Avon, April 14, 1944.
132   "If the promises made . . .": JWA, letter to Hopkins, September 1, 1943, Hopkins Papers.
132   "We have not had the tools . . .": Chennault, letter to FDR, September 5, 1943, Hopkins Papers.
133   "I am terribly disturbed . . .": FDR, letter to Marshall, September 27, 1943, Hopkins Papers.
133   "Almost everything seems to have gone wrong . . .": FDR, letter to Marshall, October 15, 1943, Hopkins Papers.
134   "China's Alexander Hamilton": "China: T.V.," *Time*, December 18, 1944.
134   money-loving banker: JWA, "Why We Lost China: The Feud Between Stilwell and Chiang," *Saturday Evening Post*, January 7, 1950, p. 16.
134   H. H. Kung known as "Daddy": "China: T.V."
134   the puppet of his wife: JWA, "Why We Lost China," January 7, 1950.
134   modernists' loss of prestige: Ibid.
134   Mei-ling and Ei-ling's subtle intrigue: Stilwell, p. 224.
134   "fellow co-conspirators": Ibid., p. 227.
134   "two intelligent dames": Ibid.
134   Madame Chiang argued strenuously: Tuchman, p. 394.
134   Madame Chiang uses Marshall threat of aid cutoff: JWA, "Why We Lost China," January 7, 1950.
134   Somervell and Mountbatten efforts: Tuchman, p. 394.
134   generalissimo wavered, sisters rallied: Stilwell, p. 232.
135   "put on the act": Ibid., pp. 232–33.
135   "Joe was so shook . . .": Annalee Fadiman (formerly Jacoby), interview, January 14, 1991.
135   T. V. Soong in tears: JWA, *I've Seen the Best of It*, p. 225.
135   threat of summary death sentence: JWA, "Why We Lost China," January 7, 1950.
135   "I cannot continue to do useful work . . .": JWA, letter to Hopkins, December 28, 1943, Hopkins Papers.
135   Chennault sent Joe to Stilwell: Chennault, letter to FDR, December 27, 1943, Hopkins Papers.
135   ". . . criminal waste . . .": Ibid.
135   "I hope you will approve": Chennault, letter to Henry H. Arnold, December 28, 1943, Marshall Papers, box 56.
135   "a civilian columnist . . .": Henry H. Arnold, letter to Chennault (annotated "not sent"), Marshall Papers, box 56.
136   ". . . seriously destructive force": Marshall, memorandum to FDR, February 15, 1944, Marshall Papers, box 56.
136   Roosevelt did not respond: Thomas Parrish, *Roosevelt and Marshall: Partners in Politics and War* (New York: William Morrow, 1989), p. 443.
136   "I am extremely cheerful": JWA, letter to Avon, March 17, 1944.
136   bourbon for Chennault: Ibid.
136   Joe's duties with Chennault: Seymour Janow, interview, November 10, 1990.
136   upgrading the officers' mess: JWA, letter to Avon, April 14.
137   "Let's take off anyway": Janow, interview.
137   "He was terribly arrogant . . .": Ibid.
137   ". . . this guy is Eleanor's cousin": Ibid.
137   "China is in mortal danger.": Chennault, *Way of a Fighter*, p. 281.
137   Chennault's Hump tonnage cut to a trickle: Romanus and Sunderland, *China-Burma-India Theater: Stilwell's Command Problems* (Washington, D.C.: Office of Military History, U. S. Department of the Army, 1956), p. 311.
137   ". . . operating on a shoe string": Chennault, *Way of a Fighter*, p. 281.
137   "Stopping anticipated Jap offensives . . .": Ibid., p. 282.
137   "No possibility . . .": Stilwell, letter to Chennault, quoted in Chennault, *Way of a Fighter*.
138   ". . . the decision rests . . .": Arnold to Chennault, quoted in Chennault, *Way of a Fighter*, p. 283.
138   "Japanese do not have offensive capabilities . . .": Ibid., p. 285.
138   only ninety planes operational: Ibid., p. 290.
138   Stilwell refused supplies: Romanus and Sunderland, p. 403.
138   "If this crisis were just sufficient . . .": Stilwell, p. 307.

138   "the only visible hope": Ibid, p. 317.

138   Henry Wallace arrives: Romanus and Sunderland, p. 374.

138   "full fig": JWA, letter to Avon, June 27, 1944.

138   Joe escorted Wallace: Ibid.

139   Wallace Recommends Stilwell recall: JWA, undated manuscript draft, JWA Papers, Library of Congress, container 65.

139   "surprisingly astute": JWA, letter to Avon, June 27, 1944.

139   Soong's secret consultant: JWA, *I've Seen the Best of It*, p. 238.

139   "If the G-mo gets distribution . . ." Stilwell, p. 331.

140   *The Care and Feeding of Infants:* JWA, letter to Avon, September 30, 1944.

140   ". . . a firecracker in every sentence": Stilwell, p. 333.

140   Hurley intervened: Russell D. Buhite, *Patrick J. Hurley and American Foreign Policy* (Ithaca, N. Y.: Cornell University Press, 1973), p. 155.

140   attacking Chiang's dignity: Romanus and Sunderland, p. 445.

140   generalissimo had broken down in tears: JWA, *I've Seen the Best of It*, p. 241.

140   helping Chinese officialdom: Ibid., p. 242.

140   "T. V. undoubtedly wrote the thing . . .": Stilwell, p. 336.

140   Roosevelt sought a compromise: Buhite, p. 158.

141   ". . . fundamentally incompatible . . ." Ibid., p. 159.

141   Joe pressed for Wedemeyer: JWA, *I've Seen the Best of It*, p. 255.

141   "F. D. R. proceeds to cut my throat . . .": Stilwell, p. 339.

141   "soundest and ablest . . .": JWA, letter to Avon, October 28, 1944.

141   gallantry medals piled up: Albert C. Wedemeyer, *Wedemeyer Reports!* (New York: Henry Holt, 1958), p. 288.

141   Ledo Road campaign ends: Ibid., p. 293.

141   "using honey instead of vinegar": F. F. Liu, quoted in Wedemeyer, p. 301.

142   "It is most gratifying to me . . .": Wedemeyer, memo to Marshall, April 13, 1945, reproduced in Albert C. Wedemeyer, *Wedemeyer on War and Peace*, ed. Keith E. Eiler (Stanford, Calif.: Hoover Institution Press, 1987), p. 104.

142   Chennault's pilots savaged the Japanese: Chennault, p. 328.

142   Marshall stymies Chennault's career: Ibid., p. 346.

142   John Alsop arrived: JWA, letter to Avon, January 30, 1944.

142   getting Joe the Legion of Merit: Janow, interview, November 10, 1990.

143   "exceptionally meritorious conduct . . ." FBI report on JWA's military records, August 18, 1952.

143   acknowledged questions of propriety: JWA, *I've Seen the Best of It*, p. 242.

143   a form of "subversion": John Alsop, interview, November 15, 1990.

144   ". . . extension of Russian influence . . .": JWA, letter to Avon, July 31, 1944.

144   "The British . . . are already quite drained": JWA, letter to Avon, undated (from Africa).

144   reminiscences of days past: JWA, letter to Avon, October 26, 1943.

145   back to civilian life on October 18, 1945: FBI report on JWA's military records, August 18, 1952.

CHAPTER TWELVE

page

150   Joe's return to Washington: Patricia Alsop, interview, May 3, 1992.

150   Stewart's reaction to column idea: Ibid.

151   foreign service exam: SA, *Stay of Execution: A Sort of Memoir* (Philadelphia and New York: J. B. Lippincott, 1973), p. 96.

151   "ridiculous": Patricia Alsop, interview.

151   going to Hollywood: Ibid.

151   The idea of a book: Tom Braden, interview, October 27, 1990.

151   audience with Bill Donovan: SA and Braden, *Sub Rosa: The OSS and American Espionage* 2nd ed. (New York: Harcourt, Brace & World, 1964), p. 2.

151   best-seller list: Braden, interview.

151   "reveal enough to fascinate . . .": Brigadier General Donald Armstrong, "Deeds of Derring-Do," *Saturday Review*, March 16, 1946.

152   sixty-forty split: Patricia Alsop, interview.

152   ". . . a column of information . . .": JWA, telegram to Harry Staton, undated, JWA & SA Papers, Library of Congress, container 144.

152   vexing name problem: Harry Staton, letter to JWA, December 4, 1945, JWA & SA Papers, container 144.

152   Joe's view of the column: Patricia Alsop, interview.

152   contract with the *Herald Tribune*: Agreement, September 27, 1945, JWA & SA Papers, container 146.

152   "I cannot adequately express . . .": JWA, letter to William E. Robinson, September 27, 1945, JWA & SA Papers, container 144.

152   goods from the Orient: Patricia Alsop, interview.

153   maid and butler: Katharine Graham, interview, February 12, 1991.

153   Stew and Tish get settled: Patricia Alsop, interview.

153   ". . . average man in a neat gray suit": JWA and SA, "An Average Man as President: The Task Before Harry Truman," New York *Herald Tribune*, December 31, 1945.

153   "not far from coming apart . . .": JWA and SA, "Critical Strains Are Reported Inside Truman Administration," New York *Herald Tribune*, January 16, 1946.

153   "uncertain attitude": JWA and SA, "Truman Seen in Grip of Doubts as He Seeks for a Labor Policy," New York *Herald Tribune*, January 6, 1946.

154   setback for Truman cronies: JWA and SA, "First Administration Crisis Seen as Strengthening New Dealers," New York *Herald Tribune*, February 13, 1956.

154   "the new Soviet imperialism . . .": JWA and SA, "Moscow Talks Emphasize Lack of American Policy on Russia," New York *Herald Tribune*, January 4, 1946.

154   Joe's first postwar dinner party: Patricia Alsop, interview.

154   assessing people's social finesse: Ibid.

154   ". . . extraordinary sense . . .": Warren Zimmermann, interview, December 27, 1990.

154   Joe's leek pie: Marie Ridder, interview, November 29, 1990.

155   ". . . a lion or two": JWA and SA, *The Reporter's Trade* (New York: Reynal & Co., 1958), p. 17.

155   twenty-one dinner parties: JWA, Business Entertainment Expense Account, JWA & SA Papers, container 197.

155   Chip Bohlen on a stool: Charles Whitehouse, interview, July 1, 1992.

155   Stewart's Washington friends: Patricia Alsop, interview.

155   " . . . we all had small kids . . .": Ibid.

156   Joe's effort to elicit information: Walter Isaacson and Evan Thomas, *The Wise Men* (New York: Simon & Schuster, 1986), p. 431.

156   Joe would get carried away: Polly Fritchey, interview, February 5, 1992.

156   Kidders' single invitation: Dottie Kidder, interview, October 31, 1990.

156   the Cooking Class: Patricia Alsop and Polly Fritchey, interview.

156   the Dancing Class: Patricia Alsop, interview.

157   interviewing Harold Stassen: Tom Lambert, interview, May 8, 1992.

157   "I hope . . . I wrote helpfully . . .": JWA, letter to Dwight Eisenhower, March 1946, JWA & SA Papers, container 2.

157   ". . . I feel affection and admiration": JWA, letter to Jimmy Byrnes, December 27, 1945, JWA & SA Papers, container 2.

157   ". . . nothing less than a tragedy": JWA, letter to James Forrestal, June 7, 1946, JWA & SA Papers, container 2.

157   "I feel I must apologize": JWA, letter to Carroll Wilson, May 8, 1946, JWA & SA Papers, container 2.

158   ". . . found his feet": JWA, letter to George Cornish, May 10, 1946, JWA & SA Papers, container 144.

158   ". . . that older brother of yours": George Cornish, letter to SA, September 21, 1946, JWA & SA Papers, container 144.

158   Stewart's column on Philip Murray: JWA and SA, "Murray Walks Shaky Tightrope as C.I.O. Splits on Communists," New York *Herald Tribune*, September 29, 1946.

158   "no damn use for American communists": JWA and SA, "Chicago Parley of Progressives Turned Liberals Against Reds," New York *Herald Tribune*, October 7, 1946.

159   ". . . muzzy sincerity . . .": Ibid.

159   "a shocking combination . . .": Jack Kroll, Hannah Dorner, and C. B. Baldwin, letter to New York *Herald Tribune* and *Washington Post*, October 7, 1946.

159   the brothers' reply: JWA and SA, letter to New York *Herald Tribune* and *Washington Post*, October 11, 1946.

159   probing motives and strategies: SA, letters to Martin Sommers, October 1 and November 15, 1946, JWA & SA Papers, container 26.

159   approaching Averell Harriman: JWA, letter to Averell Harriman, November 15, 1946, JWA & SA papers, container 2.

159   attending a UDA meeting: Alonzo L. Hamby, *Beyond the New Deal: Harry S. Truman and American Liberalism* (New York: Columbia University Press, 1973), pp. 161–62.

159   "a declaration of liberal independence . . .": Ibid.

160   Stout's departure from the *Post*: Otto Friedrich, *Decline and Fall: The Struggle for Power at a Great American Magazine* (New York: Harper & Row, 1970), p. 11.

160   ". . . iron in his soul": Ibid., p. 12.

160   *Post*'s circulation and revenue gains: Ibid.

160   Sommers offered $2,000 an article: Marty Sommers, letter to JWA, April 12, 1946, JWA & SA Papers, container 26.

160 "our oceanic moats . . .": JWA and SA, "Your Flesh Should Creep," *Saturday Evening Post*, July 13, 1946, p. 9.

160 *Reader's Digest* snapped it up: JWA and SA, Statement of Income and Expenses, December 31, 1946, JWA & SA Papers, container 117.

160 four magazine articles in 1947: JWA, letter to Sommers, October 26, 1946, JWA & SA Papers, container 26.

161 Joe suggests a consulting arrangement: JWA, letter to Sommers, December 18, 1946, JWA & SA Papers, container 26.

161 "We like the idea": Sommers, letter to JWA, December 27, 1946, JWA & SA Papers, container 26.

161 fee goes to $4,000: JWA, letter to Sommers, December 31, 1946, JWA & SA Papers, container 26.

161 fastest-growing column: Buel F. Weare, letter to JWA, October 24, 1946, JWA & SA Papers, container 144.

161 Alsop column firsts: SA, letter to Weare, December 23, 1946, JWA & SA Papers, container 144.

161 Alsops' first-year finances: JWA & SA, Statement of Income and Expenses.

162 Ogden Reid's legacy: Richard Kluger, *The Paper: The Life and Death of the New York Herald Tribune* (New York: Alfred A. Knopf, 1986), pp. 390–91.

162 Joe as honorary pallbearer: JWA, telegram to Whitie Reid, January 6, 1947, JWA & SA Papers, container 144.

162 "In a sense I am not sorry . . .": JWA, letter to Helen Reid, January 7, 1947, Richard Kluger Papers, Yale University Library.

162 ". . . being a Tribune man myself": Ibid.

CHAPTER THIRTEEN

page

163 Joe's trip to Paris and foreign ministers column: JWA and SA, *The Reporter's Trade* (New York: Reynal & Company, 1958), pp. 103–106.

164 "It is these realities . . .": JWA, "Peace Parley Is Called 'Episode' in Contest Between 2 Systems," New York *Herald Tribune*, July 31, 1946.

164 Theodore White's experiences: Theodore H. White, *In Search of History* (New York: Harper & Row, 1978), pp. 265–66.

164 to Berlin from Paris: JWA, expense voucher, December 30, 1946, JWA & SA Papers, container 144.

165 "stylish, intelligent . . .": Marietta Tree (formerly FitzGerald), foreword to Susan Mary Alsop, *To Marietta from Paris, 1945–1960* (Garden City, N.Y.: Doubleday, 1974) p. xi.

165 $75-an-hour model: Susan Mary Alsop, *To Marietta from Paris*, p. 83.

165 Susan Mary's charity ball: Ibid., p. 83.

165 "Paris is full of English": Susan Mary Patten, letter to JWA, undated, JWA & SA Papers, container 5.

165 "Twenty-five friends . . .": Ibid.

166 ". . . wish you the very best . . .": JWA, letter to Lucius Clay, January 7, 1947, JWA & SA Papers, container 2.

166 a day outside de Gaulle's office: Susan Mary Alsop, interview, December 14, 1990.

166 ". . . famous and distinguished . . .": Ibid.

166 "I . . . look forward . . .": C. L. Sulzberger, letter to JWA, March 26, 1948, JWA & SA Papers, container 3.

166 Joe's Nieman speech: JWA, speech, Harvard University, 1947, JWA & SA Papers, container 56.

167 Helen Reid's concerns: JWA, letter to Helen Reid, February 13, 1946, JWA & SA Papers, container 144.

168 "The first job . . .": Ibid.

168 Casting propriety aside: JWA, letter to Helen Reid, February 14, 1946, JWA & SA Papers, container 144.

168 Joe's raucous dinner party: Henry A. Wallace, *The Price of Vision: The Diary of Henry A. Wallace, 1942–1946*, ed. John Morton Blum (Boston: Houghton Mifflin, 1973), pp. 536–39.

169 copies sent to fifty newspapers: Buel F. Weare, letter to JWA, undated, JWA & SA Papers, container 144.

169 ". . . parlor politicians . . .": Elwood A. Rickless, letter to *Life*, undated clipping in scrapbook kept by Aggie Guthrie, Patricia Alsop files.

169 mouthpiece for hard-liners: Wallace, p. 573.

170 *New Republic* debate: "The Liberals and Russia," *The New Republic*, September 16, 1946, p. 321.

170   "nonimperialistic internationalism": JWA, letter to Geoffrey Crowther, May 27, 1947, JWA & SA Papers, container 3.

170   "We have assumed world leadership . . .": SA, letter to Mr. Nettels, October 8, 1947, JWA & SA Papers, container 23.

170   "very much disturbed": Wallace, p. 567.

171   Stewart's big story in Athens: JWA and SA, *The Reporter's Trade* (New York: Reynal & Co., 1958) pp. 109–11.

171   ". . . very close to panic": JWA, "Panic and Paralysis in the Face of World Crisis," New York *Herald Tribune*, February 26, 1947.

172   marshal at Harvard commencement: JWA, with Adam Platt, *I've Seen the Best of It* (New York: W. W. Norton, 1992), p. 281.

172   "beyond belief admirable . . .": Geoffrey Parsons, letter to JWA, April 2, 1947, JWA & SA Papers, container 144.

172   ". . . disproportionate return": JWA, letter to Parsons, April 8, 1947, JWA & SA Papers, container 144.

172   a kind of domino effect: JWA and SA, "If Russia Grabs Europe—" *Saturday Evening Post*, December 20, 1947, p. 15.

173   strange episode: JWA, letter to Martin Sommers, January 30, 1948, JWA & SA Papers, container 26.

173   Molotov's policy "faltering": JWA and SA, "The Cloud like a Hand," New York *Herald Tribune*, January 28, 1948.

173   details on Czech coup: SA, letter to Sommers, April 2, 1948, JWA & SA Papers, container 26.

173   Chip Bohlen's "guess": JWA, letter to Sommers, April 18, 1948, JWA & SA Papers, container 26.

173   in Kennan's office: JWA, letter to Sommers, June 29, 1948, JWA & SA Papers, container 26.

173   Kennan's policy advice: Dean Acheson, *Present at the Creation: My Years in the State Department* (New York: W. W. Norton, 1969), p. 332.

173   column echoes Kennan: JWA and SA, "The Tito Trouble," New York *Herald Tribune*, July 2, 1948.

174   ". . . a prewar atmosphere": JWA and SA, "How War Might Come," New York *Herald Tribune*, March 17, 1948.

174   "most dangerous development . . .": JWA and SA, "Berlin Story," New York *Herald Tribune*, April 5, 1948.

174   Bohlen's theory of Soviet bluff: SA, letter to Sommers, April 2, 1948, JWA & SA Papers, container 26.

174   "Kremlin's overall plans": JWA and SA, "Berlin Is a Wedge," New York *Herald Tribune*, September 17, 1948.

174   ". . . situation . . . extremely dark": JWA, letter to Sommers, April 2, 1948, JWA & SA Papers, container 26.

174   Disastrous implications: JWA and SA, "The Bomb and the Budget," New York *Herald Tribune*, December 1, 1948.

174   ". . . shock of disappointment . . .": JWA, letter to Clark Clifford, December 1, 1948, JWA & SA Papers, container 4.

175   "He has got into the picture . . .": JWA, letter to Sommers, December 7, 1948, JWA & SA Papers, container 26.

175   "fond farewells to the family": SA, letter to Sommers, December 14, 1948.

175   "We're ready to roll": JWA, "Big Easy 103," New York *Herald Tribune*, December 27, 1948.

175   Joe heartened in Rome: JWA, "The Plumper Cheek," New York *Herald Tribune*, January 24, 1949.

175   "miracle" of economic renewal: JWA, "The London Miracle," New York *Herald Tribune*, February 11, 1949.

175   ". . . a stalemate has been reached . . .": JWA, "Europe 1949: The Stalemate," New York *Herald Tribune*, March 2, 1949.

176   "Though I have 14 godchildren . . .": JWA, letter to Thomas Armstrong, December 3, 1948, JWA & SA Papers, container 3.

176   arriving on Christmas Eve: Susan Mary Alsop, *To Marietta from Paris*, p. 137.

176   two eye-catching pagan statues: Susan Mary Patten, letter to JWA, February 1, 1949, JWA & SA Papers, container 4.

176   "Joe had so many friends . . .": Evangeline Bruce, interview, May 4, 1992.

176   silk shirts in a diplomatic pouch: JWA, letter to Susan Mary Patten, February 13, 1949, JWA & SA Papers, container 4.

176   "the excitement of the hour": Susan Mary Patten, letter to JWA, February 1, 1949.

176   "superb job": JWA, letter to Sir Stafford Cripps, February 13, 1949, JWA & SA Papers, container 4.

176   Lady Colefax: Susan Mary Patten, letter to JWA, February 1, 1949.
176   "wonderfully good fun . . .": JWA, letter to Susan Mary Patten.
176   As house guest of Liz Cavendish: Ibid.

CHAPTER FOURTEEN

page

178   "There is only one question . . .": "Alsop Brothers Prefer Crow Be Fricasseed," *Watertown Daily Times*, November 3, 1948.
179   "warmest admirers . . .": "The Capital: Widow from Oklahoma," *Time*, March 14, 1949, p. 24.
179   ". . . article about the governor . . .": JWA, letter to Paul Lockwood, JWA & SA Papers, Library of Congress, container 3.
179   Dewey's hard choices: JWA, letter to Henry Cabot Lodge, undated copy, JWA & SA Papers, container 3.
180   "cockiness fairly oozes . . .": SA, letter to Martin Sommers, March 1, 1949, JWA & SA Papers, container 26.
180   "big, beefy Louis Johnson," "The Administration: Paid in Full," *Time*, March 14, 1949, p. 21.
180   ". . . That stinker Forrestal . . .": "The Capital: Widow From Oklahoma," p. 24.
180   "hideously tragic event": JWA, letter to Sommers, May 23, 1949, JWA & SA Papers, container 26.
180   ". . . to march into Truman's office . . .": JWA, letter to Sommers, March 23, 1949, JWA & SA Papers, container 26.
180   Symington's "shouting": Ibid.
180   "hair's breadth" victory: JWA, letter to Sommers, March 13, 1949, JWA & SA Papers, container 26.
181   "never seen another public servant . . .": JWA, letter to Robert Lovett, March 29, 1949, JWA & SA Papers, container 4.
181   ". . . served this country . . .": JWA, letter to George Kennan, December 31, 1949, JWA & SA Papers, container 5.
181   THE DUBIOUS FUTURE . . . : JWA, cablegram to Dean Acheson, January 7, 1949, Dean Gooderham Acheson Papers, Manuscripts and Archives, Yale University.
181   suggesting they get together: Acheson, letter to JWA, January 25, 1949, Acheson Papers.
181   sizing up Louis Johnson: JWA, letter to Sommers, May 23, 1949, JWA and SA Papers, container 26.
181   "You will be judged . . .": JWA, letter to Louis Johnson, May 19, 1949, JWA & SA Papers, container 4.
181   Johnson's austerity program and bluster: David McCullough, *Truman* (New York: Simon & Schuster, 1992), p. 741.
181   Johnson's feud with State: JWA, letter to Sommers, June 6, 1949, JWA & SA Papers, container 27.
182   Snyder protests to Truman: SA, letter to Sommers, August 26, 1949, JWA & SA Papers, container 27.
182   "scolding," "purse-lipped": SA, "Weary Men, Timid Men," New York *Herald Tribune*, August 15, 1949.
182   acute danger of war: SA, letter to Sommers, August 26, 1949.
182   "an Anglo-American partnership . . .": SA, letter to Ben Hibbs, September 10, 1949, JWA & SA Papers, container 27.
182   "wiser Americans": JWA & SA, "Matter of Fact," untitled column, New York *Herald Tribune*, September 14, 1949.
182   precursor of another war: SA, letter to Westmore Willcox, August 3, 1949, JWA and SA Papers, container 23.
182   "hair-raising": JWA, letter to Sommers, October 16, 1949, JWA & SA Papers, container 27. This letter includes the numbers on air groups.
183   ". . . year of the Beria bomb": JWA and SA, "Our Fake Defense," New York *Herald Tribune*, October 21, 1949.
183   disagreements on Soviet threat: JWA and SA, "Leadership in a Democracy," New York *Herald Tribune*, October 24, 1949.
183   probing for weaknesses: JWA and SA, "A Few Facts to Face," New York *Herald Tribune*, November 2, 1949.
183   ". . . stood there, saying nothing . . .": JWA and SA, *The Reporter's Trade* (New York: Reynal & Co., 1958), pp. 73–74.
183   ". . . a very long time . . .": JWA, letter to Acheson, October 25, 1949, JWA & SA Papers, container 5.

184 "I have missed seeing you": Acheson, letter to JWA, November 1, 1949, JWA & SA Papers, container 5.

184 "greatly troubled . . .": JWA, letter to Acheson, November 30, 1949, JWA & SA Papers, container 5.

184 ". . . cut me dead": JWA, letter to Felix Frankfurter, January 6, 1950, JWA & SA papers, container 5.

184 Joe's row with Frankfurter: Ibid.

184 ill-informed but shrewd voters: JWA and SA, *The Reporter's Trade*, p. 38.

185 ". . . a direct attack . . .": JWA, letter to Frankfurter, January 6, 1950, JWA & SA Papers, container 5.

185 "Joe suspects. . . .": SA, letter to Sommers, November 19, 1949, JWA & SA Papers, container 27.

185 "to pursue the shadow . . .": SA, "Two Steps Back," New York *Herald Tribune*, December 7, 1949.

185 Bohlen's anger at Joe: Demaree Bess, memo to *Saturday Evening Post* editors, undated, JWA & SA Papers, container 27.

186 breaking H-bomb news: JWA & SA, "It's Not So Funny, Really," New York *Herald Tribune*, December 2, 1949.

186 ". . . remarkable journalistic performances . . .": Richard Rovere, quoted in JWA and SA, *The Reporter's Trade*, p. 69.

186 Acheson review: SA, letter to Sommers, February 6, 1950, JWA & SA Papers, container 27.

186 "fight the Cold War . . .": SA, letter to Sommers, undated, JWA & SA Papers, container 27.

186 "the only sober man . . .": JWA & SA, "Acheson's First Year," New York *Herald Tribune*, January 20, 1950.

186 Overseas Press Club award: SA, telegram to Leo Branham, undated, JWA & SA Papers, container 20.

186 sale price of $47,000: JWA, telegram to D. A. Hanes Co., September 28, 1948, JWA & SA Papers, container 60.

186 double lot for $17,425: JWA, telegram to Olin Dows, September 28, 1948, JWA & SA Papers, container 60.

186 construction price of $50,000: Various documents, JWA & SA Papers, container 60.

186 ". . . outrage against Georgetown charm": JWA, "I'm Guilty! I Built a Modern House," *Saturday Evening Post*, May 20, 1950.

187 "Now, Stooooo . . .": Tom Braden, interview, October 27, 1990.

187 Joe's behavior would become unbearable: Patricia Alsop, interview, May 3, 1992.

187 "He probably just shoved it . . .": Elizabeth Winthrop, November 17, 1990.

187 brothers' heated arguments: Patricia Alsop, interview, January 16, 1995; Elizabeth Winthrop, interview, November 17, 1990.

188 "The basic familial relationship . . .": Patricia Alsop, interview, January 16, 1995.

188 "badgered her": SA, letter to Arthur Schlesinger, December 31, 1947, JWA & SA Papers, container 2.

188 ". . . he admired me . . .": Patricia Alsop, interview, January 16, 1995.

188 "wretched little white suits": Ibid.

188 Polecat Park: SA, *Stay of Execution: A Sort of Memoir* (New York: J. B. Lippincott, 1973), pp. 95–96.

189 social life at Polecat Park: Patricia Alsop, interview, May 3, 1992.

189 little familial affection: Elizabeth Winthrop, interview, May 6, 1992.

189 SA lost interest in his children: John Alsop, interview, November 15, 1990.

189 crawl over him: Elizabeth Winthrop, interview, December 22, 1994.

189 no "good night" ritual: Ibid.

189 marital aloofness: Marie Ridder, interview, November 29, 1990 (confirmed by various family members).

189 displays of affection rare: Stewart Alsop, interview with the author, November 21, 1990; Elizabeth Winthrop, December 22, 1994.

189 left Tish in West Virginia: Marie Ridder, interview.

190 evening in Philadelphia: Ibid.

190 Tish's occasional excessive drinking: Patricia Alsop, interview, November 4, 1993.

190 indifference: Elizabeth Winthrop, interview, December 22, 1994.

190 ". . . my palms visibly sweating": SA, letter to Sommers, February 6, 1950, JWA & SA Papers, container 27.

190 "not very far": Ibid.

190 "It is a grave act . . .": JWA and SA, "Mr. Johnson's Untruths," New York *Herald Tribune*, February 13, 1950.

191 "confidence trick": JWA and SA, "Mr. Johnson's Untruths," New York *Herald Tribune*, February 15, 1950.

191 undermined U.S. leadership: JWA and SA, "The Cost of Mr. Johnson," New York *Herald Tribune*, February 17, 1950.

191 "favoritism and intimidation": JWA and SA, "Johnson and the Generals," New York *Herald Tribune*, February 20, 1950.

191 "impugned his motives": *Washington Post* editorial, February 16, 1950.

191 the brothers' defense: JWA and SA, draft letter to the editor, February 16, 1950, JWA & SA Papers, container 25.

191 "nailed Mr. Johnson to the mast": "War Can Come; Will We Be Ready?" *Life*, February 27, 1950, p. 19.

192 "I am leaving out a column . . .": William R. Matthews, letter to JWA and SA, February 20, 1950, JWA & SA Papers, container 24.

192 "a gross abuse . . .": Editorial entitled "Secretary Johnson and His Critics," *Arizona Daily Star*, February 20, 1950.

CHAPTER FIFTEEN

page

193 night of June 24, 1950: JWA, with Adam Platt, *I've Seen the Best of It* (New York: W. W. Norton, 1992), pp. 307–308; JWA and SA, *The Reporter's Trade* (New York: Reynal & Co., 1958), p. 147; SA, *The Center: The Anatomy of Power in Washington* (New York: Harper & Row, 1968), pp. 7–8; JWA, business entertainment expenses for June 1950, JWA & SA Papers, Library of Congress, container 197; Dean Rusk, interview with the author, July 1, 1991.

194 events in Korea: Cabell Phillips, *The Truman Presidency: The History of a Triumphant Succession* (New York: Macmillan, 1966), pp. 289–304.

194 "at whatever cost . . .": JWA and SA, "Staying the Course in Korea," New York *Herald Tribune*, June 30, 1950.

195 praise for George Kennan: JWA and SA, "An Unsung Hero's Exodus," New York *Herald Tribune*, July 2, 1950.

195 attacking those who fostered weakness: JWA and SA, "The Republican Party-Liners," New York *Herald Tribune*, July 7, 1950.

195 "process of crumbling . . .": JWA and SA, "What Would Have Happened," New York *Herald Tribune*, July 3, 1950.

195 "full-dress strategic review": JWA, letter to Martin Sommers, June 12, 1950, JWA & SA Papers, container 27.

195 "He came in for a drink . . .": JWA, letter to Sommers, June 29, 1950, JWA & SA Papers, container 27.

195 ". . . cheap and sordid . . .": JWA and SA, "The Lesson of Korea," *Saturday Evening Post*, September 2, 1950, p. 17.

196 July 31 departure: JWA, letter to CRA, July 14, 1950, JWA & SA Papers, container 5.

196 Joe's adventure as combat reporter: JWA, *I've Seen the Best of It*, pp. 310–25. (All of the descriptive narrative on Joe's Korean war experiences comes from this work, unless otherwise noted.)

196 Tokyo Press Club: Joseph Fromm, interview, October 3, 1990.

196 "Joe, you have five minutes . . .": Ibid.

197 "He was immensely curious": Carl Mydans, interview, November 29, 1992.

197 "Hand grenades": Ibid.

198 fearless battlefield reporter: Ibid.

199 "What the hell are you doing up there?": Tom Lambert, interview, May 8, 1992.

199 with Chambers and Bernard Kaplan: George G. Chambers, Jr., letter to JWA, December 13, 1951, JWA & SA Papers, container 7.

199 assault by six T-34 tanks: JWA, "How They Took Kimpo: I," New York *Herald Tribune*, September 20, 1950.

200 battle at Bupyong: Ibid.

200 predawn attack: JWA, "How They Took Kimpo: II," New York *Herald Tribune*, September 22, 1950.

201 Joe broke his glasses: Joseph Fromm, interview.

201 ". . . the real feel of battle . . .": Cass Canfield, letter to JWA, August 31, 1950, JWA & SA Papers, container 5.

201 ". . . where Ernie Pyle left off": Desmond FitzGerald, letter to JWA, October 17, 1950, JWA & SA Papers, container 5.

201 ". . . like Tolstoy's passages . . .": George Kennan, letter to JWA, October 20, 1950, JWA & SA Papers, container 5.

201 ". . . work of the Alsop[s] stands out": Editorial, *Mobile Press*, September 9, 1950.

201 Check's letter to *Post*: G. J. Check, letter to *Washington Post*, October 3, 1950.

201 "a fairly lively jig": SA, letter to Sommers, September 15, 1950, JWA & SA Papers, container 27.

202 Joe and Omar Bradley: JWA, letter to Sommers, November 14, 1950, JWA & SA Papers, container 27.

202 "... horrible hopelessness ...": JWA, letter to Sir John Slessor, December 11, 1950, JWA & SA Papers, container 6.

202 "... like attending a drunken picnic...": JWA, letter to Bernard Baruch, December 28, 1950, JWA & SA Papers, container 6.

202 "... feeling pretty low in mind ...": SA, letter to Sommers, April 24, 1951, JWA & SA Papers, container 27.

204 persuading Heidrich on direct quotes: SA, letter to Sommers, March 27, 1951, JWA & SA Papers, container 27.

204 MacArthur's complaints about "privileged sanctuary": Phillips, p. 327.

204 "Either President Truman ...": SA, "Truman and MacArthur; The Battle Is Joined," New York *Herald Tribune,* April 13, 1951.

204 pride in conquering fear: JWA, *I've Seen the Best of It,* pp. 315–16.

204 proud of his fellow countrymen: Carl Mydans, interview.

205 "Far from ... sarcastic or self-pitying ...": JWA, "The Conquerors," New York *Herald Tribune,* September 27, 1950.

205 "I hardly know how to reply ...": JWA, letter to Mrs. J. J. Brower, January 16, 1951, JWA & SA Papers, container 22.

205 "We were dead wrong once ...": SA, letter to Chip Bohlen, November 9, 1951, JWA & SA Papers, container 7.

206 Overseas Press Club award: John Daly, letter to JWA and SA, April 17, 1952, JWA & SA Papers, container 7.

CHAPTER SIXTEEN

page

207 Stewart's China-coverage plans: SA, telegram to New York *Herald Tribune* Syndicate, April 26, 1949, JWA & SA Papers, Library of Congress, container 57; Patricia Alsop, interview, December 28, 1992.

207 DEPRESSED BAFFLED ... : SA, telegram to NYHT Syndicate, May 5, 1949, JWA & SA Papers, container 57.

208 "Trust last three China columns ...": JWA, telegram to SA, May 24, 1949, JWA & SA Papers, container 57.

208 "Know you will wish to be told ...": JWA, telegram to SA, May 31, 1949, JWA & SA Papers, container 57.

208 "Agree your strictures ...": SA, telegram to JWA, June 2, 1949, JWA & SA Papers, container 57.

208 "... too light for summing up ...": JWA, telegram to SA, June 4, 1949, JWA & SA Papers, container 57.

208 "... uncomfortable feeling ...": SA, telegram to JWA, undated, JWA & SA Papers, container 57.

209 white paper's 1,054 pages: JWA, "Why We Lost China: The Feud Between Stilwell and Chiang," *Saturday Evening Post,* January 7, 1950, p. 16.

209 "not ... lacking in foresight": JWA, letter to Martin Sommers, April 22, 1949, JWA & SA Papers, container 26.

209 Joe's reporting for China series: JWA, letter to Sommers, April 30, 1949, JWA & SA Papers, container 26.

209 "... retired prostitutes ...": JWA, letter to Sommers, June 4, 1949, JWA & SA Papers, container 26.

209 "Poor fellow ...": Ibid.

209 exchange with Kennan: JWA, letter to George Kennan, June 6, 1949, JWA & SA Papers, container 4.

210 violating *Post* strictures: JWA, letter to Kennan, September 21, 1949, JWA & SA Papers, container 5.

210 "happy to let the past ...": Kennan, letter to JWA, September 27, 1949, JWA & SA Papers, container 5.

210 "Throughout the fateful years ...": JWA, "Why We Lost China: The Feud Between Stilwell and Chiang."

211 "chillingly impressive": Anne McCormick, letter to JWA, October 7, 1949, JWA & SA Papers, container 5.

211 "I'm glad ...": Stanley Hornbeck, quoted in Sommers, letter to JWA, January 13, 1950, JWA & SA Papers, container 27.

211   "outraged": JWA, letter to Claire Chennault, June 26, 1950, JWA & SA Papers, container 5.

211   "enraged": JWA, letter to Sommers, January 19, 1950, JWA & SA Papers, container 27.

211   JWA dismisses Mesdames Chiang and Kung: JWA, letter to Chennault.

211   ". . . advanced state of neurosis . . .": JWA, letter to Sommers, January 19, 1950.

211   Joe's friends at State: Ibid.

211   the China Lobby: Thomas C. Reeves, *The Life and Times of Joe McCarthy: A Biography* (New York: Stein and Day, 1982), pp. 219–21.

212   Alger Hiss and Klaus Fuchs: Ibid., pp. 221–22.

212   "I have here in my hand . . .": Ibid., p. 224.

212   Tydings committee: Ibid., p. 249.

212   ". . . big, raw-boned pride and joy . . .": SA, "Senator McCarthy and his 'Big Three,' " New York *Herald Tribune*, March 5, 1950.

213   ". . . capacity for self-delusion": SA, "Three 'Insiders' Cited as Pulling 'Strings' for Wallace's 'Dance,' " New York *Herald Tribune*, July 25, 1948.

213   "I am sure you are sincere . . .": SA, letter to Mr. Marshall, August 25, 1948, JWA & SA Papers, container 23.

213   "This whole McCarthy thing . . .": SA, letter to Sommers, March 23, 1950, JWA & SA Papers, container 27.

213   ". . . the new postwar isolationism . . .": Ibid.

214   Stewart delivers Joe's letter: SA, letter to Herbert Elliston, May 5, 1950, JWA & SA Papers, container 5.

214   "I think it my duty . . .": JWA, letter to Millard Tydings, New York *Herald Tribune*, May 8, 1950.

214   "I admire your courage . . .": Robert Kintner, letter to JWA, May 31, 1950, JWA & SA Papers, container 5.

214   "one of the more cogent . . .": James K. Penfield, letter to JWA, June 14, 1950, JWA & SA Papers, container 5.

215   Tydings committee report: Reeves, pp. 304–306.

215   "miasma of neurotic fear . . .": JWA and SA, "Has Washington Gone Crazy?" *Saturday Evening Post*, July 29, 1950, p. 20.

216   "extremely disturbing": Joseph McCarthy, letter to the editor, *Saturday Evening Post*, August 8, 1950; *Congressional Record*, August 8, 1950.

216   "a particularly slimy business": SA, letter to Ben Hibbs, August 11, 1950, JWA & SA Papers, container 27.

216   speculation about Joe's sexuality: Warren Zimmermann, interview, January 20, 1995.

216   "cheap pleasures of spy hunting": SA, "We Might as Well Confess," New York *Herald Tribune*, August 11, 1950.

217   "wild, unsupported charges": Hibbs, letter to Joseph McCarthy, August 10, 1950, JWA & SA Papers, container 27.

217   30 percent of *Post* readers: Edwin R. Bayley, *Joe McCarthy and the Press* (New York: Pantheon, 1981), p. 163.

217   article suggestions turned down: Ibid.

217   "a victim of palsy": Joseph McCarthy, letter to Hibbs, August 24, 1950, JWA & SA Papers, container 27.

217   "no special majesty": JWA, "Before the Loyalty Board," New York *Herald Tribune*, July 25, 1951.

218   "played footsie with communists": David McCullough, *Truman* (New York: Simon & Schuster, 1992), p. 813.

218   electoral results of 1950: Ibid., p. 814.

218   "immense new power and authority . . .": JWA and SA, "Post-Mortem," New York *Herald Tribune*, November 10, 1950.

218   "Communist Party headquarters": John Alsop, interview, January 12, 1995.

218   "wonderful gaiety of spirit": Patricia Alsop, interview, January 16, 1995.

218   Sheffield Cowles often present: Ibid.

218   Joe Sr. baited the brothers: Ibid.

218   Christmas morning at Avon: Elizabeth Winthrop, interview, December 22, 1994.

219   ". . . much better with a little cream . . .": Ibid.

219   paper-plate compromise: Ibid.

219   the career of Louis Budenz: JWA, "The Strange Case of Louis Budenz," *Atlantic Monthly*, April 1952.

220   ". . . astonishingly belated . . .": JWA, draft article, JWA & SA Papers, container 65.

220   JWA's view of Vincent: Ibid.

220   "a profoundly anticommunist document . . .": JWA, "Investigate Everybody," New York *Herald Tribune*, September 5, 1951.

220   quoting from classified documents: JWA, "Wallace's Report on China," New York *Herald Tribune*, September 10, 1951.

220 "justify McCarthy": JWA, "Is It Accurate?" New York *Herald Tribune*, September 12, 1951.

220 attacking Robert Morris: JWA, "Budenz and Morris," New York *Herald Tribune*, September 14, 1951.

221 "distinguished lawyers": *Herald Tribune* editorial, quoted by Arthur Schlesinger, letter to August Hockscher, September 18, 1951, JWA & SA Papers, container 6.

221 "legal difficulties": JWA, letter to Whitelaw Reid, undated draft, JWA & SA Papers, container 7.

221 ". . . empire builders": JWA, "The Empire Builder," October 31, 1951. (Other revelations involving Pan Am were contained in "You Can't Beat Pan Am," and "It Took Ace to Win for Pan Am," New York *Herald Tribune*, November 2 and 4, 1951.)

221 ". . . the accuracy of your information": T. E. Braniff, letter to JWA, November 8, 1951, JWA & SA Papers, container 7.

222 "They stripped the mask off": JWA, letter to SA, November 9, 1951, JWA & SA Papers, container 7. (JWA's rendition of the controversy with the *Herald Tribune* is contained in this letter and in JWA, letter to Whitelaw Reid, October 30, 1951, JWA & SA Papers, container 7.)

222 ". . . very wrong somewhere . . .": Arthur Schlesinger, letter to Helen Reid, October 10, 1951, JWA & SA Papers, container 7.

222 ". . . reflect on this body": *Congressional Record*, September 14, 1951.

223 Lehman-McCarran exchange: Associated Press, "Lehman Is Undecided on Pressing Writer's Charges of Perjury," *Washington Star*, September 15, 1951.

223 Truman's release of cables: Murrey Marder, "Henry Wallace Cables Made Public to Show He Supported Chiang in '44, Urged More Aid," *Washington Post*, September 24, 1951.

223 Lehman's Senate floor battle: *Congressional Record*, September 24, 1951.

223 Joe asks to testify: "Alsop Asks McCarran for Chance to Refute Testimony by Budenz," New York *Herald Tribune*, October 7, 1951.

223 Wallace's casual plans: Henry Wallace, letter to JWA, August 18, 1952, JWA & SA Papers, container 6.

224 "for the wretched Henry Wallace": JWA, letter to Sommers, October 5, 1951.

224 "with great orotundity . . .": Ibid.

224 thirty lawyers: JWA, letter to Hibbs, October 10, 1951, JWA & SA Papers, container 80.

224 Rauh's recommendation: Joseph Rauh, interview, June 14, 1991.

224 "touched with so much folly": George W. Ball, *The Past Has Another Pattern* (New York: W. W. Norton, 1982), p. 108.

224 "obstinance of his idealism": Ibid. (The description of Wallace's initial statement and plans also comes from Ball.)

224 Wallace's broadcast commitment: JWA, letter to Hibbs, October 10, 1951. (This letter also contains the subsequent description of Joe's effort to get Wallace to relent on the broadcast while Ball threatened to leave the case.)

225 "misleading and untruthful": JWA, testimony before McCarran committee, JWA & SA Papers, container 64.

225 "with courage and bravura": Ball, p. 109.

225 "stumbling through his testimony . . .": Ball, p. 109.

225 refusing to shake hands: JWA, with Adam Platt, *I've Seen the Best of It* (New York: W. W. Norton, 1992), p. 333.

225 altering the story: Whitelaw Reid, précis of Morris's complaints against JWA, undated, JWA & SA Papers, container 7.

226 "He did not play": SA, *The Center: The Anatomy of Power in Washington* (New York: Harper & Row, 1968), p. 12.

CHAPTER SEVENTEEN

page

227 "paralyzed" and "suicidal": JWA and SA, "The Isolated President," New York *Herald Tribune*, January 20, 1952.

227 "shortage of inspiring . . . leaders . . .": JWA and SA, "Truman's Deadline," New York *Herald Tribune*, January 11, 1952.

227 "de-brain-washing": JWA and SA, *The Reporter's Trade* (New York: Reynal & Co., 1958), p. 136.

228 "directly or indirectly opposed . . .": JWA, letter to Basil Brewer, October 14, 1949, JWA & SA Papers, container 25.

228 Taft's harsh politics: Robert W. Merry, "Robert A. Taft: A Study in the Accumulation of Legislative Power," in Richard A. Baker and Roger H. Davidson, eds., *First Among*

Equals: Outstanding Senate Leaders of the Twentieth Century (Washington, D.C.: Congressional Quarterly, Inc., 1991), pp. 187–89.

228 ". . . great mass of voters,": JWA, "The Eisenhower Unveiling," New York *Herald Tribune*, November 19, 1951.

228 wager with Clark Clifford: Clifford, letter to JWA, August 1, 1952, JWA & SA Papers, container 8.

228 ". . . break the Solid South . . .": JWA and SA, "Can Taft Win?" New York *Herald Tribune*, February 8, 1952.

228 ". . . pro-Eisenhower propaganda . . .": Jack Craemer, letter to Keith Spalding, April 3, 1952, JWA & SA Papers, container 25.

229 "a startling ignorance . . .": John Hollister, letter to JWA, February 14, 1952, JWA & SA Papers, container 25.

229 "no bill of goods . . .": JWA, letter to Craemer, April 23, 1952, JWA & SA papers, container 25.

229 ". . . entirely honest . . .": JWA, letter to Hollister, February 15, 1952, JWA & SA Papers, container 25.

229 New Hampshire results: James T. Patterson, *Mr. Republican: A Biography of Robert A. Taft* (Boston: Houghton Mifflin, 1972), p. 523.

229 ". . . political magic . . ." Robert W. Elson, "A Question for Democrats: If Not Truman, Who?" *Life*, March 24, 1952, p. 118.

229 ". . . do not challenge . . .": SA, "A Lesson for Kefauver," New York *Herald Tribune*, March 9, 1952.

229 *Time* had fun: "Fried Crow, à la Mode," *Time*, March 24, 1952.

229 Kefauver interview: Ibid.

230 "Even Taft-minded people . . .": SA, letter to Martin Sommers, March 29, 1952, JWA & SA Papers, container 27.

230 "disgraceful un-American tactics": John Minor Wisdom, telegram to JWA, undated, JWA & SA Papers, container 8.

230 Lodge's urging: JWA, with Adam Platt, *I've Seen the Best of It* (New York: W. W. Norton, 1992), p. 339.

230 ". . . on-the-spot approval . . .": JWA, "Theft in Texas," New York *Herald Tribune*, May 30, 1952.

230 Harris County episode: Ibid.

231 "If Taft gets away with . . .": Frederic Winthrop, letter to JWA, July 5, 1952, JWA & SA Papers, container 8.

231 ". . . for Eisenhower now": John H. Blaffer, letter to JWA, May 30, 1952, JWA & SA Papers, container 8.

231 "an amiable old gentleman": JWA, "Skulduggery in Texas," New York *Herald Tribune*, June 1, 1952.

232 ". . . a common liar . . .": Orville Bullington, letter to JWA, June 7, 1952, JWA & SA Papers, container 8.

232 ". . . emotion of the moment": JWA, letter to Bullington, June 17, 1952, JWA and SA Papers, container 8.

232 "insanely expensive" Chicago suite: JWA, letter to Judy Montagu, June 25, 1952, JWA & SA Papers, container 8.

232 "He will be governor someday . . .": Ibid.

232 Frank Kent's compliment: JWA, letter to William White, October 21, 1952, JWA & SA Papers, container 25.

232 "You made the . . . issue": JWA, *I've Seen the Best of It*, p. 339.

232 ". . . a good man to bet with . . .": JWA, letter to Clark Clifford, August 4, 1952, JWA & SA Papers, container 8.

233 Truman on Stevenson: Elson.

233 ". . . kindness and hospitality": JWA, letter to Adlai Stevenson, February 27, 1952, JWA & SA Papers, container 7.

233 ". . . horrid women . . .": JWA, letter to Montagu.

233 Joe's romanticism on women: Patricia Alsop, interview, January 16, 1995.

233 slapped a friend's hand: Nathan Kingsley, interview, May 14, 1992.

234 ". . . separate relationships . . .": Katharine Graham, interview, February 12, 1991.

234 "It does seem ridiculous . . .": JWA, letter to Montagu.

234 "He lacks the majesty . . .": JWA, "He'd Rather Not Be President," *Saturday Evening Post*, June 28, 1952, p. 26.

234 "literally to drink": JWA, *I've Seen the Best of It*, p. 340.

234 heirloom silver flask: Ibid.

235 "If both sides . . .": JWA, letter to William White.

235 "silent treatment": JWA, "Eisenhower and McCarthy," New York *Herald Tribune*, August 4, 1952.

235   retreat on Indiana: JWA, "Eisenhower, McCarthy and Jenner," New York *Herald Tribune*, August 18, 1952.

235   "It is . . . significant . . .": JWA, "The Terrible Day," New York *Herald Tribune*, October 13, 1952.

236   ". . . intellectual and literate . . .": SA, "The Springfield Amateurs," New York *Herald Tribune*, September 29, 1952.

236   "egghead": SA, "How Many Egg-Heads Are There?" New York *Herald Tribune*, September 26, 1952.

236   ". . . and mush inside": SA, letter to Eric F. Goldman, March 18, 1955, JWA & SA Papers, container 26.

236   big issues ignored: JWA and SA, "The Biggest Skeleton," New York *Herald Tribune*, August 8, 1952.

236   ". . . the Paris sewers": JWA, letter to Isaiah Berlin, October 20, 1952, JWA & SA Papers, container 8.

236   ". . . the splendor . . .": JWA, letter to Susan Mary Patten, October 21, 1952, JWA & SA Papers, container 8.

237   election results: Stephen E. Ambrose, *Eisenhower: Soldier and President* (New York: Simon and Schuster, 1990), p. 286.

237   Congressional results: Ibid.

237   Joe voted for Eisenhower: JWA, letter to John Hay (Jock) Whitney, October 10, 1958, JWA & SA Papers, container 14.

237   Stewart couldn't vote for Ike: SA, "Eternal Damnation," *Newsweek*, January 29, 1973, p. 78.

237   contract request: JWA, letter to Whitelaw Reid, May 19, 1952, JWA & SA Papers, container 145.

237   Nearly $35,000: JWA, tax return form, 1951 and 1953, JWA & SA Papers, container 111.

238   "I just laughed . . .": Robert Donovan, interview, June 11, 1993.

238   "Oh, no, no, no . . .": Ibid.

238   ". . . end of civilization . . .": Kingsley, interview.

238   ". . . historic moment . . .": Ibid.

238   Joe didn't notice: Joseph Fromm, interview, October 3, 1990.

239   ". . . unemotional and detached": Ibid.

239   ". . . God's gentlemen": Kingsley, interview.

239   Springland Lane: SA, *Stay of Execution: A Sort of Memoir* (Philadelphia and New York: J. B. Lippincott, 1973), pp. 87–88.

239   large family portraits: Patricia Alsop, interview, January 16, 1995.

239   Spanish nannies: Elizabeth Winthrop, interview, December 23, 1994.

239   Shakespeare in the shower: Ibid.

239   Stewart got a call: Patricia Alsop, interview, December 28, 1990.

240   John and Gussie there: John Alsop, interview, January 12, 1995.

240   "Oh . . . my Joseph": Gussie Alsop, interview, January 12, 1995.

240   Corinne very loving: Ibid.

240   Corinne wept: Patricia Alsop, interview, January 16, 1995.

240   dinner at the Roosevelts': Ibid.

241   "Goddam it": John Alsop, interview, January 12, 1995.

241   Joe Sr.'s private sanctum: Patricia Alsop, interview.

241   tears in John's eyes: Gussie Alsop, interview.

241   ". . . one last look. . . .": John Alsop, interview.

241   "I don't believe in it": Patricia Alsop, interview, January 16, 1995.

241   The funeral: John Alsop, interview.

241   obituaries: "Joseph Wright Alsop Dies at 76; Leading Eastern Cattle Breeder," New York *Herald Tribune*, March 18, 1953.

241   more than 120 letters and telegrams: JWA, list, JWA & SA Papers, container 9.

241   ". . . special New England breed . . .": SA, letter to Sommers, March 26, 1953, JWA & SA Papers, container 28.

CHAPTER EIGHTEEN

page

242   "an amusing, malicious piece": SA, letter to Martin Sommers, April 21, 1953, JWA & SA Papers, Library of Congress, container 28.

242   the president himself: Patricia Alsop, interview, December 28, 1992.

242   ". . . dull fellows . . .": SA, letter to Sommers, April 21, 1953.

242   "eight millionaires and a plumber": Editorial, *New Republic*, December 15, 1952.

243   gravitating to Spring Valley: Patricia Alsop, interview.

243   "Eisenhower's Washington . . .": JWA, letter to Diana Cooper, January 5, 1953, JWA & SA Papers, container 8.

243   "Taking this job . . .": JWA & SA, "The Man Ike Trusts With the Cash," *Saturday Evening Post*, May 23, 1953.

243   "the best test case . . .": Ibid.

243   ". . . too complimentary . . .": George Humphrey, note to SA, undated, JWA & SA Papers, container 41.

243   ". . . shield and spear . . .": JWA, letter to Humphrey, May 8, 1953, JWA & SA Papers, container 41.

243   Alsops' view of Dulles: JWA, interview, March 4, 1966, Oral History Project, Papers of John Foster Dulles, Princeton University Library.

243   "good beginning": JWA, letter to John Foster Dulles, February 11, 1953, JWA & SA Papers, container 8.

244   ". . . bottom of my heart . . .": JWA, letter to John Foster Dulles, March 5, 1953, JWA & SA Papers, container 8.

244   Project Lincoln report: SA and Ralph Lapp, "We Can Smash the Red A-Bombers," *Saturday Evening Post*, March 21, 1953.

244   "few if any graver choices . . .": JWA and SA, untitled column file, sent to New York *Herald Tribune*, March 16, 1953, JWA & SA Papers, container 8.

245   ". . . a defensive vacuum": JWA and SA, "Soviet Eyes Over Alaska," New York *Herald Tribune*, March 17, 1953.

245   ". . . a pricked balloon": "Maginot Line of the Air," *Time*, March 30, 1953.

245   "lousy reporting": SA, letter to Sommers, April 3, 1953, JWA & SA Papers, container 28.

245   Joe called Luce: JWA, letter to Henry Luce, March 26, 1953, JWA & SA Papers, container 8.

245   "whose verdict . . .": JWA and SA, "Alsops & Project Lincoln" (letter to the editor), *Time*, April 13, 1953.

245   "Great éclat . . .": Blair Clark, letter to JWA, March 30, 1953, JWA & SA Papers, container 8.

245   ". . . the end of the world . . .": William Block, letter to SA, April 2, 1953, JWA & SA Papers, container 25.

246   ". . . half-witted babe . . .": M. A. Fulton, letter to Willet Weeks, February 2, 1953, JWA & SA Papers, container 24.

246   ". . . unusual unanimity . . .": Willet Weeks, letter to JWA, March 4, 1953, JWA & SA Papers, container 145.

246   ". . . gloom merchants . . .": JWA, draft letter to Willet Weeks, undated and annotated "unsent," JWA & SA Papers, container 145.

247   "I simply *caaaan't* work . . .": Tom Braden, interview, October 27, 1990.

247   "That son of a bitch . . .": Ibid.

247   "Goddam it, Stew. . . .": Patricia Alsop, interview, May 3, 1992.

247   "I just don't know . . .": Ibid.

247   J. B. Matthews on the clergy: Thomas C. Reeves, *The Life and Times of Joe McCarthy* (New York: Stein and Day, 1982), pp. 499–502.

248   "wild falsification": Eugene Lyons, letter to New York *Herald Tribune*, July 13, 1953, JWA & SA Papers, container 145.

248   "great regret": Helen Reid, letter to Lyons, July 15, 1953, JWA & SA Papers, container 145.

248   "unfortunate": Helen Reid, letter to JWA, July 16, 1953, JWA & SA Papers, container 145.

248   "I feel great regret": JWA, letter to Helen Reid, July 20, 1953, JWA & SA Papers, container 145.

248   "I do not feel obliged . . .": JWA, letter to Lyons, July 20, 1953, JWA & SA Papers, container 145.

248   ". . . self-righteous smugness": Lyons, letter to Helen Reid, July 30, 1953, JWA & SA Papers, container 145.

248   "a dangerous fool": JWA, letter to Lyons, August 4, 1953, JWA & SA Papers, container 145.

248   ". . . loss of balance . . .": Helen Reid, letter to JWA, August 10, 1953, JWA & SA Papers, container 145.

248   ". . . enemies of this republic": JWA, letter to Helen Reid, August 13, 1953, JWA & SA Papers, container 145.

248   "Regret for an inaccuracy . . .": Helen Reid, letter to JWA, August 24, 1953, JWA & SA Papers, container 145.

248   Joe's concession: JWA, letter to Helen Reid, September 1, 1953, JWA & SA Papers, container 145.

249 Operation Candor: JWA and SA, "Candor Is Not Enough," New York *Herald Tribune*, September 18, 1953.

249 "mush of platitudes": JWA and SA, *The Reporter's Trade* (New York: Reynal & Co., 1958), p. 162.

249 "new look": SA, "Old Loyalties Cloud 'New Look' at Defense," New York *Herald Tribune*, November 1, 1953.

249 ". . . informed officials and officers": SA, "The Bang and the Buck," New York *Herald Tribune*, December 21, 1953.

249 "chain reaction of disasters": JWA, letter to Willet Weeks, August 19, 1953, JWA & SA Papers, container 145.

249 enchanting city: JWA, with Adam Platt, *I've Seen the Best of It* (New York: W. W. Norton, 1992), p. 366.

250 under the placid surface: Ibid.

250 firefight in Tonkin: JWA, "Taking Phu Nho Quan," New York *Herald Tribune*, November 11, 1953.

250 with the Foreign Legion: JWA, "Salute to French Army for Indochina Fight," New York *Herald Tribune*, November 15, 1953.

251 ". . . omnipresence of the enemy . . .": JWA, "The Enemy," New York *Herald Tribune*, November 16, 1953.

251 interviews with Jacquet and Bidault: JWA and SA, *The Reporter's Trade*, p. 49.

251 ". . . thoroughly infiltrated . . .": JWA, "Troops for Indochina?" New York *Herald Tribune*, January 4, 1954.

251 ". . . major news developments . . .": George Cornish, letter to JWA, January 8, 1954, JWA & SA Papers, container 145.

251 Bidault's explanation: JWA and SA, *The Reporter's Trade*, p. 49.

252 four hundred mechanics: JWA and SA, "Where Is Dienbienphu?" New York *Herald Tribune*, January 27, 1954.

252 ". . . onto the front pages . . .": JWA, letter to Willet Weeks, February 10, 1954, JWA & SA Papers, container 145.

252 "You were right": C. L. Sulzberger, letter to JWA, April 15, 1954, JWA & SA Papers, container 10.

252 tentative decision to send troops: JWA and SA, "U.S. Was Near Intervention in Indochina," New York *Herald Tribune*, May 2, 1954.

252 "The whole countryside . . .": JWA, letter to Sommers, October 30, 1954, JWA & SA Papers, container 28.

252 "false peace": JWA and SA, *The Reporter's Trade*, p. 206.

253 brothers had disagreed on Korea: Ibid.

253 ". . . nothing I can see we can do. . . .": John Foster Dulles, quoted in SA, letter to Sommers, undated, JWA & SA Papers, container 28. (The document recounts the JWA-Dulles interview.)

253 ". . . succession of false slogans. . . .": JWA, letter to Sommers, June 25, 1954, JWA & SA Papers, container 28.

CHAPTER NINETEEN

page

254 drama in Temporary Building III: "The Atom: A Matter of Character," *Time*, June 14, 1954, p. 23.

254 "I really do miss talking to you . . .": JWA, letter to J. Robert Oppenheimer, July 29, 1948, JWA & SA Papers, container 3.

254 "a very great American . . .": JWA, letter to Irving Billiard, November 5, 1951, JWA & SA Papers, container 25.

254 Oppenheimer's early background: Oppenheimer, response to charges, addressed to General Kenneth Nichols, March 4, 1954; reprinted in Charles P. Curtis, *The Oppenheimer Case: The Trial of a Security System* (New York: Simon and Schuster, 1954), pp. 25–39.

256 Oppenheimer's government experience: JWA & SA, "We Accuse!" *Harper's*, October 1954, p. 25.

256 "the only American physicist . . .": Ibid.

256 Lewis Strauss background and personality: Ibid.

257 "It's certainly true . . .": SA, letter to Martin Sommers, May 21, 1954, JWA & SA Papers, container 28.

257 advocate of government secrecy: SA, letter to Sommers, April 19, 1954, JWA & SA Papers, container 28.

257 ". . . just wasted half an hour . . .": JWA and SA, *The Reporter's Trade* (New York: Reynal & Co., 1958), pp. 12–13.

257 how the affair began: JWA and SA, "We Accuse!"

258 ". . . incense-swinger": JWA and SA, "We Accuse!"

258 on April 13: JWA and SA, "Security Risk Hearing on Dr. Oppenheimer Begun by U.S. Board," New York *Herald Tribune*, April 13, 1954.

258 ". . . into outer darkness . . .": JWA and SA, "The Oppenheimer Case," New York *Herald Tribune*, April 14, 1954.

258 ". . . no evidence of disloyalty": Gray Board report, Curtis, p. 182.

258 ". . . a high degree of discretion . . .": Ibid., p. 183.

259 ". . . arrogance of his own judgment . . .": "The Atom: A Matter of Character."

259 "a black mark . . .": "The Atom: A Matter of Character."

259 ". . . 'enthusiastic support' . . .": Ernest Angell, public statement for American Civil Liberties Union, June 8, 1954, JWA & SA Papers, container 158.

259 ". . . personal spite . . .": JWA and SA, "What Is Security?" New York *Herald Tribune*, June 4, 1954.

260 ". . . ignoble act . . .": JWA, letter to Gordon Gray, June 2, 1954, JWA & SA Papers, container 10.

260 "In all candor . . .": Gray, letter to JWA, June 4, 1954, JWA & SA Papers, container 10.

260 "You are entirely right . . .": JWA, letter to Gray, June 19, 1954, JWA & SA Papers, container 10.

261 Arthur Krock and the gossip mill: Krock, letter to JWA, June 11, 1954, JWA & SA Papers, container 10.

261 ". . . intemperate and unfair . . .": Ibid.

261 "a dishonor and disgrace . . .": JWA, letter to Krock, June 14, 1954, JWA & SA Papers, container 10.

261 "substantial defects of character": JWA and SA, "We Accuse!"

262 the Chevalier affair: Ibid.

262 ". . . schoolboy attitude . . .": Curtis, p. 89.

262 Joe called Jack Fischer: JWA, letter to Russell Lynes, August 5, 1954, JWA & SA Papers, container 158.

263 "the most readable serious piece": Ibid.

263 "The title of this report . . .": JWA and SA, "We Accuse!"

264 Lynes taken aback: Lynes, letter to JWA, August 12, 1954, JWA & SA Papers, container 158.

265 ". . . too much for tender stomachs": Felix Frankfurter, letter to JWA, August 13, 1954, JWA & SA Papers, container 158.

265 "You would have squirmed . . .": Archibald MacLeish, letter to JWA, undated, JWA & SA Papers, container 158.

265 rejecting eighteen of forty changes: Eric Larrabee, memo to JWA, annotated by JWA, August 16, 1954, JWA & SA Papers, container 158.

265 problem of libel: Morris L. Ernst, letter to JWA, August 24, 1954, JWA & SA Papers, container 158.

265 ". . . this isn't a large sum . . .": Lynes, letter to JWA, September 10, 1954, JWA & SA Papers, container 158.

265 "enormously heavy sacrifices . . .": JWA, letter to Lynes, September 14, 1954, JWA & SA Papers, container 158.

265 "If I were in your position . . .": *Harper*'s editors, nonverbatim transcript of conversation with John Cahill, September 15, 1954, JWA & SA Papers, container 158.

266 ". . . you felt strongly . . .": Lynes, letter to JWA, September 16, 1954, JWA & SA Papers, container 158.

266 "I enclose our check . . .": Lynes, letter to JWA, September 21, 1954, JWA & SA Papers, container 158.

266 Simon and Schuster's interest: Storer B. Lunt, letter to JWA & SA, October 8, 1954, JWA & SA Papers, container 158; Morton Puner, letter to JWA and SA, October 18, 1954, JWA & SA Papers, container 158.

267 ". . . remaining relics . . .": Groucho Marx, letter to JWA and SA, October 14, 1954, JWA & SA Papers, container 158.

267 "one of the most moving . . .": Thurman Arnold, letter to JWA, September 30, 1954, JWA & SA Papers, container 158.

267 ". . . shrill tone . . .": Peter Drucker, letter to the editor, *Harper*'s, November 1954.

267 first time in recent memory: *New York Times*, editorial, December 20, 1954, p. 26.

267 Alsops' rebuttal: "New Debate on the Oppenheimer Case," *U.S. News & World Report*, December 24, 1954, p. 86.

267 "sin of Alamogordo": James Shepley and Clay Blair, Jr., *The Hydrogen Bomb: The Men, the Menace, the Mechanism* (New York: David McKay, 1954); quoted in "The Atom: The H-Bomb Delay," *Time*, November 8, 1954, p. 25. (References from the book come from the extensive *Time* piece, which ran over two pages in the magazine.)

268   full of distortions: JWA and SA, "Do We Need Scientists?" New York *Herald Tribune*, October 1, 1954.

268   "a major mistake of our time . . .": Philip L. Graham, "Popularized and Opinionated," *Washington Post*, October 3, 1954.

268   "The Alsopian myth . . .": "The Atom: The H-Bomb Delay."

269   syndicate's response: Willet Weeks, "Presenting a Reply," letter to editors of subscribing newspapers, November 18, 1954, JWA & SA Papers, container 82.

269   "There is no dirtier thing . . .": "The Atom: The H-Bomb Delay."

CHAPTER TWENTY

page

271   fifteen-thousand-word document: JWA, letter to E. Douglas Hamilton, March 21, 1954, JWA & SA Papers, container 156. (A complete account of Joe's dealings with John G. Adams and the Adams memorandum is contained in this letter.)

271   Joe pleaded with Adams . . . : JWA, testimony before Senate Permanent Subcommittee on Investigations of the Government Operations Committee, May 7, 1954.

272   the McCarthy-Eisenhower endgame: Thomas C. Reeves, *The Life and Times of Joe McCarthy: A Biography* (New York: Stein and Day, 1982), pp. 513–25.

272   Herbert Brownell's actions: Ibid., p. 526–27.

272   "fighting fire with fire": SA, "The McCarthy Challenge," New York *Herald Tribune*, November 27, 1953.

272   ". . . perfectly obvious . . .": SA, letter to Martin Sommers, February 22, 1954, JWA & SA Papers, container 28.

272   ". . . serious infiltration . . .": Ibid.

273   Nabokov's information: JWA, with Adam Platt, *I've Seen the Best of It* (New York: W. W. Norton, 1992), pp. 292–93.

273   ". . . his big stick . . .": SA, letter to Sommers.

273   visit with Sherman Adams: JWA, *I've Seen the Best of It*, pp. 358–59.

274   "The worst of the damage . . .": JWA and SA, "McCarthy-Stevens: Step-by-Step Account," New York *Herald Tribune*, February 28, 1954.

274   "tin-horn politicians": JWA and SA, "After Munich What?" New York *Herald Tribune*, March 3, 1954.

274   "Why, the yellow son of a bitch!": Reeves, p. 558.

274   Cohn background: Ibid., p. 463–65.

274   "contempt for all . . .": Ibid., p. 464.

274   Schine background: Ibid., p. 465.

275   Wilson's ultimatum: Ibid., p. 566.

275   ARMY CHARGES McCARTHY . . . : Ibid., p. 569.

275   "sensational": Ibid.

275   "disgusting obscenities": JWA and SA, "The Tale Half Told," New York *Herald Tribune*, March 15, 1954.

275   McCarthy accuses Joe: News dispatch of unidentified wire service, JWA & SA Papers, container 156.

276   "As a newsman . . .": JWA, testimony before Permanent Subcommittee on Investigations.

276   urging of Douglas Hamilton: Hamilton, letter to JWA, March 24, 1954, JWA & SA Papers, container 156.

276   "extremely foggy": JWA, letter to Thomas R. Prewitt, May 26, 1954, JWA & SA Papers, container 156.

277   Cohn threatened a lawsuit: Hamilton, letter to JWA.

CHAPTER TWENTY-ONE

page

278   nearly 190 newspapers: JWA, testimony before Senate Permanent Subcommittee on Investigations of the Government Operations Committee, May 7, 1954.

278   "I see no reason . . .": Willet Weeks, letter to JWA, August 10, 1955, JWA & SA Papers, Library of Congress, container 145.

278   six-letter word in 32 across: *New York Times*, March 27, 1953.

278   *New Yorker* cartoon: Tear sheet, John Alsop files.

278   Benjamin Franklin award: Norman Cousins, letter to SA, May 20, 1955, JWA & SA Papers, container 20.

278   Civil Liberties Award: JWA, letter to Joseph P. Murphy, May 4, 1955, JWA & SA Papers, container 20.

278 Overseas Press Club Award: Robert A. Lovett, letter to JWA, March 8, 1954, JWA & SA Papers, container 10.

279 basement hobby shop: Joseph Wright Alsop VI, interview, December 23, 1994.

279 private telephone line: Elizabeth Winthrop, interview, December 22, 1994.

279 bugging his sister's room: Ibid.

279 "double-bucket system": Joseph Wright Alsop VI, interview.

279 "Lord of the Flies" manner: Elizabeth Winthrop, interview, December 22, 1994.

279 a deal with Jessie Mae: Ibid.

279 selective interest in grades: Ibid.

279 weekends at Polecat Park: Interviews with Patricia Alsop, January 16, 1995; Elizabeth Winthrop, December 22, 1994; Joseph Wright Alsop VI; Stewart Alsop, Jr., November 21, 1990.

280 ". . . too, too solid flesh . . .": Elizabeth Winthrop, interview, December 22, 1994.

280 Tish's drinking habits: Elizabeth Winthrop, interview with the author, May 6, 1992.

280 One kiss seen: Stewart Alsop, Jr., interview.

280 "upstairs": Elizabeth Winthrop, interview, May 6, 1992.

280 "I'm sorry . . .": Ibid.

280 children kept in the dark: Elizabeth Winthrop, interview, December 22, 1994.

281 ". . . like little savages": Ibid.

281 ". . . the dollar man . . .": Ibid.

281 $10 for every A: Ibid.

281 "I don't pay . . .": Ibid.

281 Francis Scott Key bookstore: Elizabeth Winthrop, interview, November 17, 1990.

281 dinner at Uncle Joe's: Ibid.; Joseph Wright Alsop VI, interview.

282 Geneva Indochina settlement: Stanley Karnow, *Vietnam: A History* (New York: Viking Press, 1983), pp. 203–204.

282 ". . . inherent weakness . . .": JWA, "Underground Government in Vietnam," New York *Herald Tribune*, December 13, 1954.

282 visit to Camau peninsula: JWA (with Adam Platt), *I've Seen the Best of It* (New York: W. W. Norton, 1992), pp. 381–85.

284 "How did the communists do it?": JWA, "Thoughts Under Guard," New York *Herald Tribune*, December 22, 1954.

284 Stewart's missile reporting: SA, letter to Martin Sommers, January 1, 1955, JWA & SA Papers, container 28.

285 concerns about Gardner: SA, letter to Sommers, January 17, 1955, JWA & SA Papers, container 28.

285 "It can be fired . . .": SA, "The Race We've Got to Win," New York *Herald Tribune*, January 21, 1955.

285 Strauss announcement: SA, "Can We Rely on the H-Bomb?" New York *Herald Tribune*, February 18, 1955.

286 "bandits of the pen": *Pravda*, characterizations recounted in JWA and SA, *The Reporter's Trade* (New York: Reynal & Co., 1958), p. 138.

286 seeking Bohlen's help: SA, letter to Charles E. Bohlen, February 18, 1955, JWA & SA Papers, container 20.

286 ". . . harsh criticism . . .": SA, letter to Nikita Khrushchev, April 25, 1955, JWA & SA Papers, container 57.

286 "The general bleakness . . .": SA, "Those Smug, Smug Russians," *Saturday Evening Post*, January 1, 1956.

286 smugness: Ibid.

286 Dnieper River encounter: Ibid.

287 meeting Khrushchev: SA, "Behind Khrushchev's Smile," *Saturday Evening Post*, February 1, 1958.

287 "strangely compelling man": Ibid.

287 "a somber old firetrap": SA, "Communism Is Their Religion," *Saturday Evening Post*, January 7, 1956.

287 Red Square parties: Ibid.

288 ". . . change will not . . .": SA, "The Change," New York *Herald Tribune*, July 3, 1955.

288 ". . . remarkable aircraft . . .": SA, "In the Moscow Skies," New York *Herald Tribune*, June 27, 1955.

288 "breathing spell": SA, "The Tacit Agreement," New York *Herald Tribune*, July 22, 1955.

288 Eisenhower's diplomacy: SA, "Eisenhower's Performance," New York *Herald Tribune*, July 24, 1955.

288 Jedburgh reunion stories: Thomas Braden, interview, February 5, 1993.

289 "the smell of sickness . . .": SA, "A Sick City," New York *Herald Tribune*, August 22, 1955.

289 visit to Oued Zem: SA, "Horror in the Bled," New York *Herald Tribune*, August 24, 1955.
289 "a wolfish hatred . . .": Ibid.
290 ". . . free all your colonies": SA, "The War for North Africa," New York *Herald Tribune*, September 5, 1955.
290 "France . . . would cease . . .": Ibid.
290 "could fatally weaken . . .": Ibid.

CHAPTER TWENTY-TWO

page

291 "The vast majority . . .": JWA, letter to W. A. Smart, July 5, 1956, JWA & SA Papers, Library of Congress, container 23.
291 Ritz Hotel: JWA, letter to Barbie and Herbert [last name unidentified], March 9, 1956, JWA & SA Papers, container 216.
291 dinner at Connaught Square: Sir Isaiah Berlin, letter to JWA, July 27, 1956, JWA & SA Papers, container 13.
292 confirming the story: SA, cable to JWA, undated, JWA & SA Papers, container 216.
292 ". . . chilly and discourteous . . .": Berlin, letter to JWA.
292 "The hard-driven Eden . . .": JWA, "The Hidden Crisis," New York *Herald Tribune*, April 2, 1956.
292 THE FOREGOING . . . : JWA, cable to George Cornish and SA, March 30, 1956, JWA & SA Papers, container 216.
292 " . . . no recent thing . . .": SA, "The President and the Eden Message," April 9, 1956.
292 ". . . cotton batting": Ibid.
293 "hysterical": SA, cable to JWA, April 2, 1956, JWA & SA Papers, container 216.
293 Dulles's anticolonialism: "Foreign Relations: The Peacemaker," *Time*, August 13, 1951, p. 18.
293 Dulles on Soviet Mideast presence: Donald Neff, *Warriors at Suez: Eisenhower Takes America into the Middle East* (New York: Linden Press/Simon & Schuster, 1981), pp. 83–84.
293 Eden's medical problem: Neff, pp. 182–83.
294 Eden's driving force: Ibid., p. 75.
294 "the embodied symbol": JWA, "Gamal Abdel Nasser," New York *Herald Tribune*, April 20, 1956.
294 Nasser's fears: Neff, pp. 82–83.
294 Khrushchev and Nasser: Ibid., pp. 78–79.
294 Israel's population expansion: Ibid., p. 45.
295 Eisenhower outlook: Ibid., pp. 46–47.
295 the story of Glubb: JWA, "They Mean to Fight," New York *Herald Tribune*, April 4, 1956.
295 "What is chiefly feared. . . .": Ibid.
297 ". . . jugular vein . . .": JWA, "The Hidden Crisis," New York *Herald Tribune*, April 2, 1956.
297 "fighting Arab nationalism . . .": JWA, "Price of Drift," New York *Herald Tribune*, April 16, 1956.
297 ". . . over their depth . . .": Ibid.
297 Bloody April: Neff, pp. 219–23.
297 ". . . a grimmer mood . . .": JWA, "Where We're Drifting," New York *Herald Tribune*, April 18, 1956.
297 second Nasser interview: JWA, "Gamal Abdel Nasser."
298 "Western statesmanship . . .": Ibid.
298 "Take the oil . . .": JWA, "Moment of Choice," New York *Herald Tribune*, April 23, 1956.
298 dinner with King Saud: JWA, "The House Aramco Built," New York *Herald Tribune*, April 27, 1956.
298 "rather monstrous country": JWA, letter to Martin Sommers, July 11, 1956, JWA & SA Papers, container 28. (Most of JWA's description of Saudi Arabia comes from this letter.)
299 slave prices: JWA, "Arabian Ferment," New York *Herald Tribune*, April 30, 1956.
299 "Saudi Arabia must now be regarded . . .": Ibid.
299 ". . . a vast oil well . . .": JWA, "Hole Card," New York *Herald Tribune*, May 11, 1956.
299 "imperial kousy": JWA, letter to Sommers, July 11, 1956.
299 "All the nationalist emotions . . .": JWA, "The Strong Man," New York *Herald Tribune*, May 21, 1956.

299 "... touching off a war ...": JWA, "The Young Men," New York *Herald Tribune*, June 3, 1956.
299 "... dangers are commensurate": Ibid.
299 legendary age: JWA, "Why Israel Will Survive," *Saturday Evening Post*, September 8, 1956, p. 38.
299 "The picture there is ominous ...": JWA, "Threat to the Alliance," New York *Herald Tribune*, June 25, 1956.
299 "... pretty terrifying ...": Ibid.
299 "... coffee-colored politicians ...": JWA, letter to Lady Elizabeth von Hoffmansthal, July 12, 1956, JWA & SA Papers, container 13.
300 "Alsop's dramatic flair ...": "Alsop's Fables," *Time*, June 18, 1956.
300 "I was delighted ...": Henry Luce, letter to JWA, July 2, 1956, JWA & SA Papers, container 13.
300 "You call Nasser 'wise' ...": Isaiah Berlin, letter to JWA, June 29, 1956, JWA and SA Papers, container 12.
300 "... covert operations ...": JWA, letter to M. L. Burstein, July 13, 1956, JWA & SA Papers, container 13.
301 the marvel of the Suez Canal: Theodore H. White, *America in Search of Itself: The Making of the President 1956–1980* (New York: Harper & Row, 1982), pp. 87–88.
301 "all hideously unattractive": JWA and SA, "To Waffle or Not to Waffle," New York *Herald Tribune*, July 30, 1956.
301 Joe's health spa: JWA, letter to Sommers, September 25, 1956, JWA & SA Papers, container 28.
301 "glowing personality": Ibid.
302 "... a taxidermist first": JWA, letter to Berlin, July 12, 1956, JWA & SA Papers, container 13.
302 October 30 ultimatum: White, p. 91.
302 November 5 invasion: Kenneth O. Morgan, *The People's Peace: British History 1945–1989* (Oxford: Oxford University Press, 1990), p. 155.
302 "... another for our friends": White, pp. 91–92.
303 November 8 cease-fire: Morgan, p. 156.
303 "... for good or ill ...": JWA and SA, "Why a Silver Platter," New York *Herald Tribune*, November 16, 1956.
303 "... on a silver platter ...": Ibid.
303 "swung even more wildly": "Foxes and Lions," *Time*, November 26, 1956.
304 "pretty surprised": Hugh Gaitskell, letter to JWA, December 5, 1956, JWA & SA Papers, container 13.
304 "I can foresee a day ...": JWA, letter to Gaitskell, December 12, 1956, JWA & SA Papers, container 13.
304 OVER TO YOU: Harold Macmillan, quoted in SA, *Stay of Execution: A Sort of Memoir* (Philadelphia and New York: J. B. Lippincott, 1973), p. 171.
305 "matricidal role": Ibid., p. 170.

CHAPTER TWENTY-THREE

page

306 JWA's two wardrobes: Katharine Graham, interview, February 12, 1991.
306 income of $36,000: SA, letter to JWA, December 27, 1957, JWA & SA Papers, container 14.
306 "It is a little depressing ...": JWA, letter to Selma Janow, July 5, 1955, JWA & SA Papers, container 11.
306 "... something rancid ...": JWA, letter to Charles E. Bohlen, August 8, 1956, JWA & SA Papers, container 13.
306 "a boatload of happy people ...": JWA, letter to Martin Sommers, March 8, 1956, JWA & SA Papers, container 28.
307 "The tempo of events ...": JWA, letter to Brown Reid, December 11, 1956, Richard Kluger Papers, Manuscripts and Archives, Yale University Library.
307 additional $4,000: JWA, letter to SA, December 28, 1956, JWA and SA Papers, container 111.
307 arrangement with Ben Hibbs: Hibbs, letter to JWA, December 10, 1956, JWA & SA Papers, container 111.
307 SA frequently moaned: Patricia Alsop, interview, January 16, 1995.
307 he enjoyed life: Ibid.
307 partnership shares: SA, letter to JWA, December 9, 1956, JWA & SA Papers, container 14.

307 "Stooo, you have to remember . . .": Joseph Wright Alsop VI, interview, December 13, 1994.

307 "deeply unhappy": Patricia Alsop, interview, January 16, 1995.

307 SA's concern about expenses: JWA, letter to SA, December 28, 1956.

307 SA's other concerns: Patricia Alsop, interview, December 28, 1992.

308 professional alternatives: SA, letter to JWA, October 25, 1957, JWA & SA Papers, container 14.

308 a bluff: JWA, letter to SA, November 19, 1957, SA Collection, Special Collections, Boston University Libraries.

308 $300 a month: JWA, letter to Oatsey Leiter, December 12, 1956, JWA & SA Papers, container 13.

308 "Love is the great secret . . .": JWA, letter to Oatsey Leiter, December 21, 1956, JWA & SA Papers, container 13.

308 Joe's Paris quarters: JWA, letter to SA, February 28, 1957, SA Collection.

308 Christmas with the Pattens: JWA, letter to John Alsop, January 7, 1957, John Alsop files.

308 dinner at the embassy: Susan Mary Patten, letter to JWA, December 19, 1956, JWA & SA Papers, container 13.

308 "all but bathed": JWA, letter to John Alsop, January 7, 1957, John Alsop files.

309 advice of CIA friends: JWA, letter to Bohlen, December 28, 1956, JWA & SA Papers, container 13.

309 ". . . worst possible light": Bohlen, letter to JWA, December 19, 1956, JWA & SA Papers, container 13.

309 strange-sounding names: JWA, letter to CRA, February 9, 1956, John Alsop files.

309 ". . . best reporting days . . .": JWA, letter to Sommers, February 28, 1957, JWA & SA Papers, container 28.

309 "a human phenomenon . . .": JWA, "Aleksandr Nikolaievich," New York *Herald Tribune*, February 6, 1957.

309 ". . . remarkable experience": JWA, letter to CRA.

309 vodka and smorgasbord feast: Ibid.

309 an evening in Moscow: Ibid.

310 ". . . feel the longing . . .": Ibid.

310 impressions of Khrushchev: JWA, letter to Sommers, February 28, 1957.

310 propaganda ploy: JWA, "Khrushchev Talks to Alsop; His Proposal: End All Bases on Foreign Soil, Hold East-West Summit Talks, Start 'Normal' Relations." New York *Herald Tribune*, February 20, 1957.

311 ". . . inherent conflict": JWA, letter to Sommers, January 23, 1957, JWA & SA Papers, container 28.

311 "How was Djakarta?": JWA, letter to Katharine Graham, July 31, 1957, JWA & SA Papers, container 129.

311 ". . . tricky sort of policy . . .": JWA, letter to Martin Sommers, May 16, 1957, JWA & SA Papers, container 29.

311 King Saud's change of heart: Ibid.

311 "like a rotten tooth . . .": Ibid.

311 plot against the king: JWA, "How the Boy King Foiled the Plotters," *Saturday Evening Post*, November 23, 1957, p. 31.

312 ". . . wonderfully corrupt . . .": Ibid.

312 "You're full of shit!": Phil Geyelin, interview, April 27, 1993.

312 "Joe was always the guy . . .": Ibid.

313 "I must see the foreign minister . . .": Ibid.

313 Joe's uncensored copy: Ibid.

313 Joe's optimism: JWA, "U.S. Guards Interests of West in Arab Lands," New York *Herald Tribune*, June 21, 1957.

313 "Oh, Joe . . .": Phil Geyelin, interview.

313 "a tough little egg . . .": Susan Mary Alsop, interview, May 21, 1992.

313 "Now Mr. Alsop . . .": Isaiah Berlin, interview, November 27, 1991.

314 lunch and drinks with Lyndon Johnson: SA, letter to JWA, March 21, 1957, JWA & SA Papers, container 14.

314 at the LBJ Ranch: Patricia Alsop, interview, November 4, 1993; SA, letter to JWA, November 25, 1957, JWA & SA Papers, container 14.

315 ". . . first rate intelligence . . .": SA, letter to Sommers, November 14, 1957, JWA & SA Papers, container 29.

315 ". . . one great central asset . . .": SA, letter to Sommers, October 31, 1957, JWA & SA Papers, container 29.

315 ". . . feel grateful": SA, letter to JWA, July 29, 1957, JWA & SA Papers, container 14.

315 scoop for Stewart: SA, letter to Sommers, October 31, 1957.

315   dinner for 26: SA, letter to JWA, March 8, 1957, JWA & SA Papers, container 14.
315   "enchantress": Polly Fritchey, interview, February 5, 1992.
315   the Alsop ball: Guest list, October 25, 1957, JWA & SA Papers, container 129.
315   ". . . grave international significance": SA, "Successful Soviet Test of ICBM Is Reported," New York *Herald Tribune*, July 5, 1957.
315   officials pooh-poohed the story: "Mr. Alsop Knows His Missiles," editorial sidebar, *Saturday Evening Post*, December 14, 1957, p. 26.
315   Charles Wilson's proposal: SA, "Soothing Syrup," New York *Herald Tribune*, July 17, 1957.
316   Eisenhower "blew his stack": SA, letter to JWA, July 29, 1957, JWA & SA Papers, container 14.
316   "It is nobody's business. . . .": Ibid.
316   ". . . entirely earned by you . . .": JWA, letter to SA, September 24, 1957, JWA & SA Papers, container 14.
316   Little Rock events: Stephen E. Ambrose, *Eisenhower: Soldier and President* (New York: Simon & Schuster, 1990), pp. 446–448.
316   ". . . stranger in a foreign land": SA, letter to Sommers, September 27, 1957, JWA & SA Papers, container 29.
317   Monday scene in Little Rock: SA, "Tragedy in the Sunshine," New York *Herald Tribune*, September 25, 1957.
318   "magnificent reporting": SA, letter to JWA, September 30, 1957, JWA & SA Papers, container 14.
318   "really brilliant": JWA, letter to SA, November 1, 1957, SA Collection.
318   two cancellations: SA, letter to JWA, September 30, 1957.
318   ". . . a Yankee nigger-lover": Ibid.
318   "It helps me . . .": JWA, letter to SA, September 8, 1957, JWA & SA Papers, container 14.
318   "It is impossible . . .": SA, letter to JWA, September 30, 1957.
318   "Goddam it, Stew . . .": JWA, letter to SA, December 11, 1957, JWA & SA Papers, container 14.
318   "irritable and irritating": SA, letter to JWA, September 30, 1957.
319   ". . . grossly misled . . .": JWA, letter to SA, December 21, 1957, JWA & SA Papers, container 14.
319   dinner with Sommers: Sommers, letter to SA, February 8, 1957, JWA & SA Papers, container 28.
319   ". . . I am grateful . . .": SA, letter to JWA, October 25, 1957, JWA & SA Papers, container 14.
319   "reasonable": JWA, letter to SA, November 1, 1957, SA Collection.
320   "too shrilly . . .": SA, letter to JWA, November 29, 1957, JWA & SA Papers, container 14.
320   Stewart informed Joe: SA, letter to JWA, November 25, 1957, JWA & SA Papers, container 14.
320   chat with Ben Hibbs: SA, letter to Hibbs, December 20, 1957, JWA & SA Papers, container 29.
320   "I am really delighted . . .": Ibid.
320   financial implications: SA, letter to JWA, December 27, 1957, JWA & SA Papers, container 14.
320   Reid accepts the idea: Ibid.
320   ". . . oddly sentimental . . .": Ibid.
321   "For God's sake . . .": JWA, letter to SA, January 3, 1958, JWA & SA Papers, container 14.
321   "Perhaps I have been very foolish . . .": SA, letter to JWA, February 8, 1958, JWA & SA Papers, container 14.
321   March 10 announcement: Hibbs, memo "To All Editors," March 10, 1958, JWA & SA Papers, container 29.
321   ". . . sentimental business": JWA and SA, "Hail and Farewell," New York *Herald Tribune*, March 12, 1958.
321   "painful to see . . .": Walter Lippmann, letter to JWA and SA, April 3, 1958, JWA & SA Papers, container 14.
321   "with astonishment": C. L. Sulzberger, letter to JWA and SA, March 10, 1958, JWA & SA Papers, container 14.
321   "the voice of doom . . .": Edward W. Barnett, letter to JWA and SA, March 17, 1958, JWA & SA Papers, container 14.
321   ". . . minor Greek chorus . . .": JWA, quoted in *Time*, March 17, 1958.
321   ". . . most influential and provocative . . .": "Brothers in Arms," *Newsweek*, November 11, 1957, p. 81.

321   Doris Fleeson's comment: Rowland Evans, interview, September 27, 1991.
322   Stewart as "balance wheel": Robert Donovan, interview, June 11, 1993.

CHAPTER TWENTY-FOUR

page

325   no longer invited: Patricia Alsop, interview, November 4, 1993.
325   "He was angry . . .": Ibid.
326   "In my middle aged way . . .": JWA, letter to Isaiah Berlin, April 30, 1958, JWA & SA Papers, Library of Congress, container 14.
326   "Excuse me": Rowland Evans, interview, September 27, 1991.
326   "Young Rogers": Warren Rogers, interview, October 6, 1993.
326   "Now, Dr. Rubell . . .": Ibid.
326   Stewart's concentration: Patricia Alsop, interview, November 4, 1993.
327   "guinea pig": Patricia Alsop, interview with Edward R. Murrow, "Person to Person," CBS-TV, date unknown, videotape in Patricia Alsop files.
327   25 million readers: A. J. Liebling, "A View with Alarm," *New Yorker*, December 20, 1958, p. 113.
327   6 million subscribers: SA, draft letter to secretary of British prime minister, undated, JWA & SA Papers, container 29.
328   "Number One national magazine . . .": SA, letter to Martin Sommers, June 10, 1959, JWA & SA Papers, container 29.
328   ". . . second most important political figure . . .": SA, letter to Sommers, January 15, 1958, JWA & SA Papers, container 29.
328   SA's Nixon reporting: SA, letter to Ralph Knight, June 9, 1958, SA Collection, Special Collections, Boston University Libraries.
328   preparing for Nixon interview: SA, letter to Sommers, April 25, 1958, JWA & SA Papers, container 29.
328   exchanging chitchat: SA, transcript of Nixon interview, undated, JWA & SA Papers, container 47.
329   "a publicity blurb": *Louisville Courier Journal*, quoted in SA, letter to the editor, *Courier Journal*, July 31, 1958, JWA & SA Papers, container 47.
329   ". . . hermetically sealed . . .": SA, letter to *Courier Journal*.
329   "perceptive . . .": William S. White, letter to SA, July 3, 1959, JWA & SA Papers, container 47.
329   "one of the most searching studies . . .": "The Nixon Underneath," *Newsweek*, July 14, 1958, p. 62.
329   *Reader's Digest* snapped it up: "Richard Nixon: The Mystery and the Man," *Reader's Digest*, undated page proofs, JWA & SA Papers, container 47.
329   "everyone . . . read it": SA, letter to Sommers, July 25, 1958, JWA & SA Papers, container 29.
329   concerns at *Herald Trib*: George Cornish, letter to JWA, March 21, 1958, Kluger Papers, Manuscripts and Archives, Yale University Library.
329   "But it's hard . . .": JWA, letter to George Cornish, March 24, 1958, Kluger Papers.
329   ". . . stinks of defeat": JWA, "London: Facade and Reality," New York *Herald Tribune*, February 24, 1958.
329   *Daily Express* attack: JWA, letter to Donald Tyerman, March 14, 1958, JWA & SA Papers, container 14.
330   *Economist* treatment: JWA, letter to the editor, *Economist*, March 6, 1958, JWA & SA Papers, container 14.
330   Tyerman's wrath: JWA, letter to Isaiah Berlin, March 20, 1958, JWA & SA Papers, container 14.
330   high-level lunch and dinner: Ibid.
330   ". . . your Tory friends . . .": Dora Gaitskell, letter to JWA, February 26, 1958, JWA & SA Papers, container 14.
330   "unduly gloomy": Hugh Gaitskell, letter to JWA, March 12, 1958, JWA & SA Papers, container 14.
330   events in Algiers: Brian Crozier, *De Gaulle* (New York: Charles Scribner's Sons, 1973), pp. 453–78.
330   "It's Joe . . .": Susan Mary Alsop, interview, January 10, 1995.
331   Joe's Paris adventure: Susan Mary Alsop, *To Marietta from Paris, 1945–1960* (New York: Doubleday, 1974), pp. 316–23.
332   ". . . a very great pleasure . . .": JWA, letter to Richard Nixon, April 2, 1958, JWA & SA Papers, container 14.

332 ". . . without qualification": JWA, letter to Lyndon Johnson, March 18, 1958, JWA & SA Papers, container 14.

332 ". . . the door is always open . . .": Lyndon Johnson, letter to JWA, March 21, 1958, JWA & SA Papers, container 14.

332 "Is there anything I can do . . .": JWA, letter to Claire Chennault, March 11, 1958, JWA & SA Papers, container 14.

332 ". . . I must fight alone": Chennault, letter to JWA, March 14, 1958, JWA & SA Papers, container 14.

332 Aggie's death: SA, letter to JWA, May 29, 1958, JWA & SA Papers, container 14; Patricia Alsop, interview, January 16, 1995.

332 ". . . the most successful man . . .": JWA, letter to Berlin, March 20, 1958.

332 "an energetic charmer . . .": "Guest at Breakfast," *Time*, April 16, 1956, p. 64.

333 ". . . dust and ashes . . .": JWA, letter to Berlin, March 20, 1958.

333 Frank Wisner's calamity: Burton Hersh, *The Old Boys: The American Elite and the Origins of the CIA* (New York: Charles Scribner's Sons, 1992), pp. 421–23.

333 John's business enterprises: John Alsop, letter to JWA, March 11, 1957, John Alsop files.

333 "The pros slit his throat . . .": SA, letter to Sommers, June 24, 1958, JWA & SA Papers, container 29.

333 ". . . amateur repairs": JWA, "A Brave and Stoical Man," *Washington Post*, May 31, 1974.

333 glue on Aubusson carpet: Elizabeth Winthrop, interview, November 17, 1990.

333 Richard Nicholas's godfather: Patricia Alsop, interview, December 28, 1992.

334 ideal American family: "Person to Person," CBS-TV, unknown date in 1957, videotape in Patricia Alsop files.

334 "the hit of the evening": John Alsop, letter to JWA.

334 SWA's new office: Trevor Armbrister, interview, September 9, 1990.

334 Arthur Godfrey and "I Call On" series: Otto Friedrich, *Decline and Fall: The Struggle for Power at a Great American Magazine* (New York: Harper & Row, 1969), pp. 12–13.

334 embarrassing rejections: SA, letter to Dean Acheson, August 23, 1958, JWA & SA Papers, container 29; Corinne Alsop Cole, annotated manuscript, John Alsop files.

335 a matter of $270: SA, letter to JWA, April 12, 1958, JWA & SA Papers, container 14.

335 "Sometimes I wonder . . .": JWA, letter to SA, April 10, 1958, JWA & SA Papers, container 14.

335 ". . . any fair minded man . . .": SA, letter to JWA, April 12, 1958.

335 "I dislike intensely . . .": JWA, letter to SA, October 9, 1958, JWA & SA Papers, container 14.

335 "I return your check . . .": SA, letter to JWA, October 11, 1958, JWA & SA Papers, container 14.

336 Reynal's book proposal: Eugene Reynal, letter to SA, April 3, 1958, JWA & SA Papers, container 14.

336 $6,000 advance: Contract between Alsop brothers and Reynal & Co., July 22, 1958, JWA & SA Papers, container 98.

336 agreement with Ben Hibbs: JWA, letter to Hibbs, May 7, 1958, JWA & SA Papers, container 14.

336 "the rest to be my gamble . . .": JWA, letter to SA, June 24, 1958, JWA & SA Papers, container 14.

336 new agreement: SA, letter to JWA, July 30, 1958, JWA & SA Papers, container 14.

336 "But why in Hell . . .": SA, letter to JWA, August 1, 1958, JWA & SA Papers, container 14.

336 changing "junior" to "younger": SA, letter to JWA, August 6, 1958, JWA & SA Papers, container 14.

336 brothers simmered down: JWA, letter to SA, August 14, 1958, JWA & SA Papers, container 14.

336 Republicans: JWA, letter to SA, September 3, 1958, JWA & SA Papers, container 14.

337 "must book . . .": Virginia Kirkus Service, November 19, 1958.

337 "monument": "The Alsops: Veracity in News Coverage," *Washington Star*, November 23, 1958.

337 "Alsop Major": A. J. Liebling, "A View with Alarm."

337 "overly pessimistic": *Time*, quoted in Eugene Reynal, letter to James Linen, October 22, 1958, JWA & SA Papers, container 14.

337 book sales: Eugene Reynal, letter to JWA, August 27, 1959, JWA & SA Papers, container 14.

337 "I cannot understand . . .": Ibid.

337 *Herald Tribune*'s downward spiral: Richard Kluger, *The Paper: The Life and Death of the New York* Herald Tribune (New York: Alfred A. Knopf, 1986), p. 521.

337 Jock Whitney's background: Ibid., pp. 522–527.
338 "... immense responsibility ...": JWA, letter to Jock Whitney, undated, JWA & SA Papers, container 14.
338 blow for "our side": Whitney, letter to JWA, October 21, 1958, JWA & SA Papers, container 14.
338 Nitze's garbled translation: JWA, letter to Whitney, October 10, 1958, JWA & SA Papers, container 14.
338 "I am ... a Republican ...": Ibid.
338 "In absolutely no way ...": Whitney, letter to JWA, October 21, 1958.
338 "great relief": JWA, letter to Whitney, October 27, 1958, JWA & SA Papers, container 14.
338 Joe wants contract changes: JWA, letter to Robert M. White, September 25, 1959, JWA & SA Papers, container 145.
338 Joe's income below $40,000: JWA, Income and Expense Statement for Year Ended December 31, 1959, JWA & SA Papers, container 203.
339 Ken McCormick's proposal: SA, letter to Sommers, November 18, 1958, JWA & SA Papers, container 29.
339 "one book ...": Tom Braden, "Candidates Nixon, Rockefeller and Our U.S. Political Animal," *Oceanside Blade-Tribune*, February 28, 1960.
339 two-month, three-thousand-mile trip: SA, letter to Gladys Muller, November 16, 1959, JWA & SA Papers, container 57.
339 "... tired old word": SA, "I Saw What Makes Communism Work," *Saturday Evening Post*, January 30, 1960, p. 24; February 6, 1960, p. 40; February 13, 1960, p. 40.

CHAPTER TWENTY-FIVE

page

340 GNP plunged 2.8 percent: Allan J. Lichtman and Ken DeCell, *The 13 Keys to the Presidency* (New York: Madison Books, 1990), p. 311.
340 unemployment 7 percent: Ibid.
340 "... deeper meaning ...": JWA, "The Year of Decision," New York *Herald Tribune*, January 1, 1960.
340 "... former view of him ...": JWA, letter to Mrs. Andrew Gagarin, July 20, 1959, JWA & SA Papers, Library of Congress, container 15.
341 $100 bet: JWA, letter to Philip H. Watts, April 6, 1959, JWA & SA Papers, container 16.
341 Joe's bet with senators: JWA, letters to Kenneth Keating and Hugh Scott, January 21, 1960, JWA & SA Papers, container 16.
341 Joe and Kick Kennedy: JWA, with Adam Platt, *I've Seen the Best of It* (New York: W. W. Norton, 1992), pp. 407–409.
341 "and one by one ...": Ibid., p. 410.
341 "... the damn disease ...": JWA, quoted in *Newsweek*, November 28, 1983, p. 83.
341 dearth of women: JWA, *I've Seen the Best of It*, p. 411.
342 "The inward seriousness ...": Ibid.
342 "The balance of power ...": Ibid.
342 "authentic voice of America ...": Ibid.
342 "... your original suggestion": John F. Kennedy, letter to JWA, August 23, 1958, JWA & SA Papers, container 14.
342 "startling news": JWA, "Startling News from Queens," New York *Herald Tribune*, August 3, 1959.
342 Rowe questioned methodology: Rowe, letter to JWA, August 10, 1959.
343 "... loyalty to the facts": JWA, "Letter to a Humphreyite," New York *Herald Tribune*, August 10, 1959.
343 phony argument: Rowe, letter to JWA, August 10, 1959.
343 Kennedy's campaign liabilities: SA, letter to Martin Sommers, December 5, 1958, JWA & SA Papers, container 29.
343 brutal brevity: Ibid.
343 "... people's choice ...": SA, "Who Will Be the Democrats' Candidate?" *Saturday Evening Post*, March 28, 1959.
343 "buck-and-wing": SA, letter to Sommers, December 15, 1959, JWA & SA Papers, container 30.
344 Marietta's party: Ibid.
344 and sometime lover: Marie Brenner, "Serious Money," *Vanity Fair*, December 1991, p. 210.
344 canvassing in Wisconsin: SA, *Stay of Execution* (Philadelphia and New York: J. B. Lippincott, 1973), pp. 108–10.

345   "... being a Catholic ...": JWA, "In Aniwa and Edgar," New York *Herald Tribune*, February 12, 1960.

345   "... self-conscious and diffident ...": SA, "Kennedy vs. Humphrey," *Saturday Evening Post*, April 2, 1960, p. 34.

346   "Spontaneity": Ibid.

346   photo of SA and Kennedy: SA, letter to Douglas Borgstedt, August 3, 1960, JWA & SA Papers, container 30.

346   among his closest friends: Jacqueline Onassis, reminiscence of Joe Alsop, conveyed to the author by her secretary, March 22, 1993. Also, the nature of the Kennedy-Alsop relationship was explored by Benjamin Bradlee in an interview with the author, February 10, 1993.

346   "... that much more magical ...": Jacqueline Kennedy, letter to JWA, undated, JWA & SA Papers, container 130.

347   Wisconsin results: Theodore H. White, *The Making of the President 1960* (New York: Atheneum, 1961), p. 113.

347   Slab Fork: JWA, "The Folks of Slab Fork," New York *Herald Tribune*, April 15, 1960.

347   "... disgusting performance ...": Rowe, letter to JWA, April 16, 1960, JWA & SA Papers, container 16.

347   temperate reply: JWA, letter to Rowe, April 18, 1960, JWA & SA Papers, container 16.

347   West Virginia results: JWA, "Anatomy of a Victory," New York *Herald Tribune*, May 13, 1960.

347   "... formidable": Ibid.

348   "... bumblingly": SA, letter to Sommers, May 9, 1960, JWA & SA Papers, container 30.

348   no missile gap: Michael R. Beschloss, *May-Day: Eisenhower, Khrushchev and the U-2 Affair* (New York: Harper & Row, 1986), p. 5.

348   "... form of animal life ...": Dwight Eisenhower, paraphrased in George B. Kistiakowsky, *A Scientist at the White House* (Cambridge, Mass.: Harvard University Press, 1976), p. 250.

348   "... Chase Bank will miss you ...": JWA, letter to John McCloy, January 29, 1960, JWA & SA Papers, container 16.

348   George Cornish retires: JWA, letter to Sol Sanders, February 5, 1960, JWA & SA Papers, container 16.

349   "sweet, affectionate letter": Susan Mary Patten, letter to JWA, May 2, 1960, JWA & SA Papers, container 16.

349   Susan Mary "delighted": C. L. Sulzberger, telegram to JWA, April 13, 1960, JWA & SA Papers, container 16.

349   "Bill would have been furious ...": Susan Mary Patten, letter to JWA.

349   Daley's support: JWA, *I've Seen the Best of It*, p. 424.

349   dinner for the Kennedys: JWA, letter to Llewellyn Thompson, June 9, 1960, JWA & SA Papers, container 16.

349   fourteen bottles of wine: JWA, "Wines and spirits used for business entertainment for June, 1960," JWA & SA Papers, container 197.

349   Stewart's Los Angeles arrival: SA, letter to Sommers, June 28, 1960, JWA & SA Papers, container 30.

349   "... I'll make you an offer ...": SA, letter to Dan Knapp, July 1, 1960, JWA & SA Papers, container 30.

350   "How in hell did he do it?": SA, "Kennedy's Magic Formula," *Saturday Evening Post*, August 13, 1960, p. 26.

350   Kennedy's LBJ decision: JWA, *I've Seen the Best of It*, 425–428.

351   Joe's column on LBJ episode: JWA, "What Really Happened," New York *Herald Tribune*, July 18, 1960.

351   Alsops' Los Angeles bash: SA, letter to Ben Hibbs, August 8, 1960, SA Collection, Special Collections, Boston University Libraries.

351   "... most lavish host": Richard Dilworth, letter to JWA, July 19, 1960, JWA & SA Papers, container 16.

351   dinner at Perino's: SA, letter to Hibbs, August 8, 1960.

351   "Please think of me ...": Jacqueline Kennedy, letter to JWA, undated, JWA & SA Papers, container 130.

351   "Fifth Avenue compact": Described in JWA, "Into the '60s By Force!" and "Off the Eisenhower Road onto Nixon-Rockefeller," New York *Herald Tribune*, July 25 and 26, 1960.

352   "... Republican fogies ...": JWA, "Off the Eisenhower Road onto Nixon-Rockefeller."

352   "... bravest behavior by a child ...": JWA, letter to Ethel Kennedy, August 4, 1960, JWA & SA Papers, container 16.

352 "ghastly little Shirley Temple . . .": Jacqueline Kennedy, letter to JWA, undated, JWA & SA Papers, container 130.

352 ". . . worth the candle . . .": Ibid.

352 "If Mummy . . .": Ibid.

353 "oddly humorous . . .": JWA, letter to Jacqueline Kennedy, August 4, 1960, JWA & SA Papers, container 130.

353 "most touched": Jacqueline Kennedy, letter to JWA, undated.

354 ". . . a joyous moment . . .": Jacqueline Kennedy, letter to JWA, undated, JWA & SA Papers, container 130.

354 ". . . rather moving . . .": JWA, letter to Jacqueline Kennedy, August 4, 1960.

354 "brilliantly organized": SA, letter to Robert Fuoss, September 26, 1960, JWA & SA Papers, container 30.

354 Kennedy-Nixon debate: JWA, I've Seen the Best of It, p. 430.

354 ". . . statutory rape case": Sommers, letter to JWA, September 27, 1960, JWA & SA Papers, container 16.

355 "enormously impressive . . .": JWA, "Disappointment for Ghouls," New York Herald Tribune, September 28, 1960.

355 ". . . my man's finished": JWA, I've Seen the Best of It, p. 430.

355 ". . . poor tired Jack . . .": Jacqueline Kennedy, letter to JWA, undated, JWA & SA Papers, container 130.

355 nearly 90 guests: Guest List, Dinner for Mr. Joseph Alsop, JWA & SA Papers, container 212.

355 ". . . become tearful . . .": Jacqueline Kennedy, letter to JWA, undated, JWA & SA Papers, container 130.

355 "What I remember of that morning . . .": Philip Graham, "Joe's 50th Birthday," typewritten remarks, JWA & SA Papers, container 212.

356 rising early to join Johnson: JWA, letter to Sommers, October 15, 1960, JWA & SA Papers, container 16.

356 "Oh, dear boy . . .": Robert Novak, interview, May 18, 1994.

356 "Mr. Facing-Both-Ways": SA, letter to Hibbs, August 16, 1960, SA Collection.

356 election night at Dumbarton: JWA, I've Seen the Best of It, pp. 430–31.

357 "shining shibboleths . . .": JWA, "Kennedy and the Liberals," New York Herald Tribune, November 14, 1960.

357 Joe's view of Fulbright: JWA, I've Seen the Best of It, p. 431.

357 David Bruce for State: Thomas C. Reeves, A Question of Character (New York: Free Press, 1991), p. 224.

357 influencing Treasury choice: JWA, I've Seen the Best of It, p. 432.

357 Kennan and Harriman: Ibid, p. 433.

358 inauguration dinner: Katharine Graham, interview, February 12, 1991.

358 champagne along the way: JWA, I've Seen the Best of It, p. 434.

358 Joe invites Graham for drinks: Katharine Graham, interview.

358 ". . . close to hysterical": Phil Geyelin, interview, April 27, 1993

358 bevy of starlets: C. David Heymann, A Woman Named Jackie (New York: New American Library, 1989), p. 265. (Much has been made of this occasion as a prearranged opportunity for Kennedy to have a sexual encounter with Hollywood starlets. Longtime Washington society writer Betty Beale has said that Joe played the role of a "beard" on this occasion, and several books have stated flatly that the new president engaged in sex at Joe's house. However, no one at the party has given a credible account supporting this hypothesis, and it would seem unlikely that even Kennedy, with his now-known passion for the sexual chase, would be so indiscreet as to enter a home filled with strangers and casual acquaintances on his inauguration night and then disappear into a bedroom for a tryst that would be apparent to all. If he did, it seems doubtful that Joe, with his sense of loyalty and his affection for Jackie, would have been party to it.)

358 Kennedy leaves Statler-Hilton: Garnett Horner, "Presidential Day Ends At Early A.M. Party," Washington Star, January 21, 1961.

358 The scene at Dumbarton: Ibid.; JWA, I've Seen the Best of It, p. 434–35.

358 "the ultimate nightmare . . .": Geyelin, interview.

CHAPTER TWENTY-SIX

page

360 "There's . . . uh . . .": Sir Isaiah Berlin, interview, November 27, 1991.

361 Moscow episode: Lewis Ferguson, interview, March 12, 1993; Adam Platt, interview, March 1, 1993; Federal Bureau of Investigation, Joseph Alsop File, obtained under Freedom of Information Act request.

361 Stewart worried: Tom Braden, interview, February 5, 1993.
362 San Francisco incident: Ibid.
362 Corinne never suspected: John Alsop, interview, January 12, 1995.
362 "shocked": Ibid.
362 Stewart didn't discuss it: Ibid; Patricia Alsop, interview, January 16, 1995.
362 Joe's friends thought him asexual: Seymour Janow, interview, November 10, 1990.
362 speculation: Warren Zimmermann, interview, January 20, 1995.
362 Frank Merlo affair: Gore Vidal, letter to the author, undated, response to author's letter dated February 26, 1992.
362 "warm, decent man . . .": Donald Spoto, *The Kindness of Strangers: The Life of Tennessee Williams* (Boston: Little, Brown, 1985), pp. 167–70.
362 Vidal twitted Joe: Vidal, letter to author.
362 "pansy," "fairy": Elizabeth Winthrop, interview, December 22, 1994.
362 "He's one of *those* . . .": Evangeline Bruce, interview, May 19, 1993.
362 "queer . . . faggot": Janow, interview.
362 McCarthy hinted darkly: Joseph McCarthy, letter to the editor of the *Saturday Evening Post*, August 8, 1950; *Congressional Record*, August 8, 1950.
362 Jenner episode: Recounted by William Schultz in conversation with author, fall 1993.
362 a "warmer": FBI internal memo, quoted in Athan Theoharis (editor), *From the Secret Files of J. Edgar Hoover* (Chicago: Ivan R. Dee, 1991).
363 ". . . Adams expressed his appreciation . . .": J. Edgar Hoover, internal memo, April 17, 1957, obtained through Freedom of Information Act request.
363 Jim Hagerty's outburst: Robert Donovan, interview, June 11, 1993.
363 Joe's greatest regret: Platt, interview.
363 Lily Emmett's charms: Bruce, interview.
363 "Joe absolutely loved her . . .": Ibid.
364 marriage without sex: Arthur Schlesinger, interview, May 7, 1992.
364 proposal to Judy Montagu: Vidal, letter to author.
364 "She knew more . . .": Benjamin Bradlee, interview, February 10, 1993.
364 Duff Cooper a rake: Philip Zeigler, *Diana Cooper: A Biography* (New York: Alfred A. Knopf, 1982), p. 234.
364 Diana's view of Susan Mary: Ibid., p. 239.
365 Susan Mary's affair: Ibid., pp. 239–40. (Zeigler's book was written with extensive cooperation from Lady Diana Cooper, with whom Zeigler had a close friendship.)
365 Joe's initial proposal: Susan Mary Alsop, interview, February 23, 1994.
365 Susan Mary accepts: Ibid.
365 "What wonderful news . . .": Harriet Aldrich, letter to JWA, January 11, 1961, JWA & SA Papers, container 17.
365 "in Scotch . . .": Martin Sommers, letter to JWA, January 15, 1961, JWA & SA Papers, container 17.
365 ". . . beautiful, intelligent . . .": Mary Whitehouse, letter to JWA, January 11, 1961, JWA & SA Papers, container 17.
365 ". . . luckiest man . . .": JWA, letter to Harriet Aldrich, January 16, 1961, JWA & SA Papers, container 17.
365 Susan Mary's arrival: JWA, letter to Mrs. Peter Jay, January 31, 1961, JWA & SA Papers, container 17.
366 Social whirl: Susan Mary Alsop, interview, February 23, 1994.
366 "I was married to Joe . . .": Patricia Alsop, interview.
366 Susan Mary's story about Macmillan: JWA, interview with Elspeth Rostow, June 18, 1964, Kennedy Library Oral History Project.
366 Small wedding: Ibid.
366 "Come on, Joe . . .": Philip Geyelin, interview, April 27, 1993.
367 ". . . intellectual interest": Ibid.
367 the new regulars: JWA, "Reimbursement for wines and liquors used for business entertainment," 1961, JWA and SA Papers, container 197.
367 changes at Dumbarton: Susan Mary Alsop, interview, February 23, 1994.
367 "I never saw . . .": Ibid.
367 ". . . never really been happy . . .": Susan Mary Alsop, interview, December 27, 1994.
368 "born in this century . . .": John F. Kennedy, inaugural address, quoted in Arthur M. Schlesinger, Jr., *A Thousand Days: John F. Kennedy in the White House* (New York: Houghton Mifflin, 1965), p. 13.
368 "I wake up . . .": JWA, letter to Sir John Slessor, December 21, 1960, JWA & SA Papers, container 17.
368 "It cheers me up . . .": JWA, letter to George Kennan, February 10, 1961, JWA & SA Papers, container 17.
368 "it hardly reeks of 'nepotism' . . .": JWA, "The Story of Two Brothers," New York *Herald Tribune*, December 23, 1960.

368   "The defense effort . . .": JWA, "Arming and Parleying," New York *Herald Tribune*, December 30, 1960.

368   trouble in Laos: Herbert S. Parmet, *JFK: The Presidency of John F. Kennedy* (New York: Dial Press, 1983), pp. 132–155.

368   alerted by Dick Bissell: JWA, quoted in Montague Kern, Patricia W. Levering, and Ralph B. Levering, *The Kennedy Crises: The Press, the Presidency, and Foreign Policy* (Chapel Hill: University of North Carolina Press, 1983), p. 28.

368   "Dear Jack" letter: Ibid.

369   "naked choice": JWA, "The Crunch," New York *Herald Tribune*, March 6, 1961.

369   ". . . hard meaning . . .": JWA, "If If If," New York *Herald Tribune*, March 29, 1961.

370   "the first bad bobble . . .": JWA, "Tiddlywinks with the Estimates," New York *Herald Tribune*, February 10, 1961.

370   reconnaissance satellite: JWA, with Adam Platt, *I've Seen the Best of It* (New York: W. W. Norton, 1992), pp. 413–15.

370   only fifty ICBMs: JWA, "Facts About the Missile Balance," New York *Herald Tribune*, September 25, 1961.

370   Khrushchev's "hostages": Ibid.

370   Vienna summit: Schlesinger, 333–48.

370   "amiable" discussion: Kern et al., p. 64.

370   Joe missed the mark: JWA, "After Vienna," New York *Herald Tribune*, June 7, 1961.

371   "a little chilling . . .": JWA, interview with Elspeth Rostow; also quoted in Kern et al.

371   "chilling": JWA, "Chilling—Yet Invigorating," New York *Herald Tribune*, June 12, 1961.

371   ". . . melancholy situation": JWA, "Somber Was the Word," New York *Herald Tribune*, June 9, 1961.

371   "the new doctrine . . .": JWA, "Getting Back to the Fighting Soldier," New York *Herald Tribune*, July 28, 1961.

371   turmoil at the *Herald Tribune*: Richard Kluger, *The Paper: The Life and Death of the New York Herald Tribune* (New York: Alfred A. Knopf, 1986), pp. 608–15.

371   *Times* market position: Ibid., p. 662.

371   Joe's talk with Denson: JWA, letter to Jock Whitney, October 4, 1961, JWA & SA Papers, container 145.

372   copy to Ernest Cuneo: JWA, letter to Ernest Cuneo, October 5, 1961, JWA & SA Papers, container 145.

372   Joe's lament: JWA, letter to Whitney.

372   Whitney's formula: Whitney, letter to JWA, October 7, 1961, Kluger Papers, Manuscripts and Archives, Yale University Library.

372   troubling new issues: Ibid.

372   Joe signs contract: Walter N. Thayer, letter to JWA, December 13, 1961, Kluger Papers, Manuscripts and Archives, Yale University Library.

372   Kennedys for dinner: JWA, "Reimbursement for wines and liquors"

372   ". . . herds and droves": JWA, letter to Billy Patten, January 30, 1962, JWA & SA Papers, container 17.

373   "gossiped agreeably": JWA, letter to Billy Patten, January 16, 1961, JWA & SA Papers, container 17.

373   ". . . one man sings . . .": JWA, letter to Billy Patten, January 16, 1961.

373   Phil Graham's proposal: JWA, letter to Whitney, October 10, 1962, Kluger Papers, Manuscripts and Archives, Yale University Library.

CHAPTER TWENTY-SEVEN

page

374   tennis afternoons: Trevor Armbrister, interview, September 9, 1990.

374   "incredible candor": SA, letter to Martin Sommers, March 26, 1961, JWA & SA Papers, Library of Congress, container 30.

374   ". . . likable chap": SA, letter to Sommers, April 18, 1961, JWA & SA Papers, container 30.

375   Stewart gingerly raised the question: Patricia Alsop, interview, May 3, 1992.

375   Christmas at Springland Lane: Patricia Alsop, interview, January 16, 1995; Elizabeth Winthrop, interview, December 22, 1994.

375   Christmas lunch at Joe's: Ibid.

375   young Joe expelled from Groton: SA, *Stay of Execution: A Sort of Memoir* (Philadelphia and New York: J. B. Lippincott, 1973), p. 21.

375   Stewart showed understanding: Joseph Wright Alsop VI, interview, December 23, 1994.

375   Hill School incident: Patricia Alsop, January 16, 1995.

375 "... you can take your son": Ibid.
375 Suffield enrollment: Ibid.
376 "He just survived ...": SA, *Stay of Execution*, p. 21.
376 African itinerary: SA, itinerary, undated, JWA & SA Papers, container 57.
376 visit with Mobutu: SA, undated and untitled manuscript, SA Collection, Special Collections, Boston University Libraries.
376 "... a sad and harried man ...": Ibid.
377 visit with Dayal: Ibid.
377 Cold War prism: SA, "Khrushchev's Saucepan," *Washington Post*, February 20, 1961.
377 Allen Dulles an old friend: Patricia Alsop, interview, May 3, 1992.
377 how Dulles met Bissell: Richard Bissell, interview, June 17, 1991.
377 "at the going rate ...": SA, undated and untitled manuscript, SA collection.
378 "... prehistoric past ...": Ibid.
378 "Patches of blue ...": *National Review*, March 11, 1961, p. 135.
378 "much admiring comment": Dean Acheson, letter to SA, May 4, 1961, SA Collection.
378 "a breath of fresh air": Thomas Dodd, letter to SA, February 4, 1961, SA Collection.
378 "... our new rulers ...": SA, letter to Sommers, March 15, 1961, SA Collection.
378 Lansdale report: SA, letter to Sommers, February 21, 1961, SA Collection.
378 "This is a wonderful story ...": Ibid.
378 "Behind the official language ...": SA, draft of sidebar to go with article, JWA & SA Papers, container 30.
378 Bay of Pigs fiasco: Herbert S. Parmet, *JFK: The Presidency of John F. Kennedy* (New York: Dial Press, 1983), pp. 157–179.
379 "... astonishing errors ...": SA, "The Lessons of the Cuban Disaster," *Saturday Evening Post*, June 24, 1961, p. 26.
380 Schlesinger's party: SA, letter to Robert Kennedy, June 28, 1961, SA Collection.
380 "... widely quoted": Robert Kennedy, letter to SA, July 12, 1961, SA Collection.
380 "... you are quite right.": SA, letter to Robert Kennedy, July 17, 1961, SA Collection.
380 "... have the matter dropped": Robert Kennedy, letter to SA, undated, SA Collection.
381 "terribly distressed": SA, letter to Sommers, July 5, 1961, JWA & SA Papers, container 30.
381 "... downright astonishing ...": SA, "How's Kennedy Doing?" *Saturday Evening Post*, September 16, 1961.
381 redesign at the *Post*: Otto Friedrich, *Decline and Fall: The Struggle for Power at a Great American Magazine* (New York: Harper & Row, 1969), pp. 16–18.
382 emergence of Amman Erpf: SA, letter to Sommers, December 29, 1961, JWA & SA Papers, container 30.
382 Erpf as the villain: Ibid.
382 folly at Curtis: Friedrich, pp. 14–15.
382 "... the turbulence ...": Sommers, letter to SA, August 18, 1961, JWA & SA Papers, container 30.
382 call from John Wheeler: John N. Wheeler, letter to SA, January 11, 1962, SA Collection.
382 "I cannot emphasize too much ...": JWA, letter to John Alsop, undated, John Alsop files.
382 Stewart calms situation: SA, letter to John Alsop, February 1, 1962, John Alsop files.
382 Stewart's visibility concern: Ibid.
383 Joe's multiyear contract idea: JWA, letter to John Alsop, undated.
383 Stewart's multiyear contract: SA, letter to Robert Fuoss, March 16, 1962, SA Collection.
383 Stewart's new title: Ben Hibbs, letter to SA, May 2, 1962, SA Collection.
383 "... performed magnificently ...": Ibid.
383 Phil Graham's offer: SA, memorandum for files, October 9, 1962, SA Collection.
383 Tish "emphatic": Patricia Alsop, interview, May 3, 1992.
383 "... frankly, tempting ...": SA, letter to Robert Fuoss, October 11, 1962, SA Collection.
383 "truly on the way up": Matthew J. Culligan, letter to SA, October 10, 1962, SA Collection.
383 June nominating convention: SA, "My Brother Runs for Governor," September 1, 1962.
384 "Don't expect me ...": Ibid.
384 "... us Yankees ...": SA, letter to Igor I. Sikorsky, Jr., June 20, 1963, SA Collection.

CHAPTER TWENTY-EIGHT

page

385   guest list and menu: JWA, "Reimbursement for wines and liquors used for business entertainment," JWA & SA Papers, container 197.

385   farewell to the Bohlens: Susan Mary Alsop, *To Marietta from Paris, 1945–1960* (Garden City, N.Y.: Doubleday, 1974), pp. 42–43.

385   Kennedy-Bohlen chat: Ibid.: JWA, with Adam Platt, *I've Seen the Best of It* (New York: W. W. Norton, 1992), p. 447.

386   Alphand visibly nervous: JWA, *I've Seen the Best of It.*

386   Susan Mary's concerns: Susan Mary Alsop, *To Marietta from Paris.*

386   Kennedy wanted Bohlen to remain: Ibid.

386   JFK's questions for Bohlen: Ibid.

386   "chilling": JWA, quoted in Montague Kern, Patricia W. Levering, and Ralph B. Levering, *The Kennedy Crises: The Press, the Presidency, and Foreign Policy* (Chapel Hill, N.C.: University of North Carolina Press, 1983), p. 126.

386   five hours in Connecticut: Dino A. Brugioni, *Eyeball to Eyeball: The Cuban Missile Crisis* (New York: Random House, 1990), p. 272.

387   Stewart's call from Bartlett: Charles Bartlett, interview, October 8, 1992.

387   Forrestal's cooperation: Ibid.

388   ". . . this amazing story . . .": Ibid.

388   ". . . madder than a jack . . .": Ibid.

388   Kennedy's handwriting: Ibid.

388   "certain untold episodes . . .": SA and Charles Bartlett, "The White House in the Cuban Crisis," *Saturday Evening Post*, December 8, 1962, p. 15.

390   Bartlett's ties to the Kennedys: "The Administration: The Stranger on the Squad," *Time*, December 14, 1962, p. 15.

391   "inaccurate and untrue": "Charge That Stevenson Differed with Kennedy at Time of the Cuban Crisis Is Flatly Denied," *Washington Post*, December 3, 1962.

391   "Nobody in the White House . . .": Ibid.

391   Stewart unhappy with Bartlett: Bartlett, interview.

391   Bartlett went underground: Ibid.

391   "Charlie, where are you?": Ibid.

392   "a grave crime": Roscoe Drummond, "Secrets and Tactics," *Washington Post*, undated, Charles Bartlett files.

392   ". . . it came from above": Mauldin, cartoon, *Chicago Sun Times*, undated, Charles Bartlett files.

392   ". . . irresponsible journalism": "The Big Flap—Doves, Hawks, 'Dawks,' 'Hoves,' " *Newsweek*, December 17, 1962, p. 17.

392   "I couldn't figure out their motives . . .": Ibid.

392   "demonstrable inaccuracies": "The Administration: The Stranger on the Squad."

392   chat with the president: Chalmers M. Roberts, "President and Adlai Hold Chat," *Washington Post*, December 7, 1962.

392   "strongly supported . . .": Ibid.

392   "grateful to the president . . .": Ibid.

393   ". . . print a retraction": "The Administration: The Stranger on the Squad."

393   ". . . no attempt to show warmth . . .": Ibid.

393   "a pat on the back": "Kennedy Remands Real Story on Stevenson to Historians," *Washington Star*, December 13, 1962.

393   *Life*'s report: Laurence Stern, "Adlai Affair Develops New Twist," *Washington Post*, December 10, 1962.

393   press focus shifts: Associated Press, "Adlai Affair Focus Shifts to Sources," undated clip, Charles Bartlett files.

393   "On contrary . . .": SA, draft wire to Clay Blair, undated, SA Collection, Special Collections, Boston University Libraries.

393   talks with Fritchey: SA, "Footnote for the Historians," *Saturday Evening Post*, January 22, 1963.

394   incomplete: Arthur M. Schlesinger, *Robert Kennedy and His Times* (New York: Houghton Mifflin, 1978), p. 555.

395   ". . . supreme dove": Ibid.

395   ". . . a weak man . . .": Ibid.

395   "We're counting on you . . .": Ibid., p. 556.

395   "delighted": Otto Friedrich, *Decline and Fall: The Struggle for Power at a Great American Magazine* (New York: Harper & Row, 1969), p. 39.

CHAPTER TWENTY-NINE

page

396 February 6 dinner guests: JWA, "Business Entertainment for February 1963," JWA & SA Papers, Library of Congress, container 197.
396 February 6 menu: Ibid.
396 "politics, politics . . .": Philip Zeigler, *Diana Cooper: A Biography* (New York: Alfred A. Knopf, 1982), p. 307.
396 "frustrated force of nature": Ibid, pp. 307–308.
396 "looks like him . . .": Ibid, p. 308.
397 February 14 dinner guests: JWA, "Business Entertainment for February 1963."
397 February 14 menu: Ibid.
397 "Nice to see you again": Zeigler, p. 308.
397 "What Diana means is . . .": Evangeline Bruce, interview, May 19, 1993.
397 Diana and Jackie: Zeigler, p. 308.
397 "What a woman!": Ibid.
397 "grand review": JWA, "Kennedy and the Ambassadors," *Washington Post*, February 20, 1963.
398 "In New Deal terms . . .": SA, letter to Bill Emerson, May 6, 1963, JWA & SA Papers, container 31.
398 "Collapse of Kennedy's Grand Design": SA, reference to 1963 article, "Sorenson on Kennedy—a Footnote," *Saturday Evening Post*, October 9, 1965.
398 "Kennedy's Grand Strategy": SA, reference to 1962 article, Ibid.
398 ". . . my stock is not high . . .": SA, letter to Emerson, May 6, 1963.
398 "I rewrite every sentence . . .": SA, letter to Robert Johnson, SA Collection, Special Collections, Boston University Libraries.
398 Stewart had loved Marty: Patricia Alsop, interview, November 4, 1993.
399 column concept: Don Schanche, letter to SA, September 1, 1963, SA Collection.
399 fourteen hundred words: SA, letter to Otto Friedrich, August 29, 1963, SA Collection.
399 ". . . sonofabitch . . .": SA, letter to Friedrich.
399 Stewart's new contract: Don Schanche, letter to SA.
399 Culligan's ad campaign: Clay Blair, letter to SA, September 17, 1963, JWA & SA Papers, container 31.
399 visit to Rome, Georgia: SA, "They Hate Kennedy," *Saturday Evening Post*, October 5, 1963, p. 18.
400 ". . . just another American city . . .": SA, "A Tale of Two Cities," *Saturday Evening Post*, November 16, 1963, p. 20.
400 reissue of *Sub Rosa*: SA, letter to Constantin Melnik, November 1963, SA Collection.
400 "low, but what the hell": SA, letter to Tom Braden, January 7, 1964, SA Collection.
401 missile-crisis fallout: SA, letter to Robert Johnson, October 21, 1963, SA Collection.
401 Joe and Lippmann: McGeorge Bundy, interview, November 11, 1993.
401 positing a theory: Ibid.
401 "hand grenade technique": Dean Rusk (as told to Richard Rusk), *As I Saw It* (New York: W. W. Norton, 1990), p. 567.
401 frequent chats with the president: Bundy, interview.
402 intimate White House dinners: Susan Mary Alsop, interview, December 27, 1994.
402 "with comic emphasis": JWA, with Adam Platt, *I've Seen the Best of It* (New York: W. W. Norton, 1992), p. 449.
402 "Our people believe him": Susan Mary Alsop, interview.
403 ". . . Mr. Bang": Evelyn Puffenberger, interview, March 1, 1993.
403 "Let's get cracking": Ibid.
403 Joe's temperament: Ibid.
403 Joe began to express displeasure: Susan Mary Alsop, interview.
403 ". . . trapped by marriage": Ibid.
404 ". . . barely detectable smell": JWA, "The War We May Be Winning," New York *Herald Tribune*, September 28, 1962.
404 Lodge arrives in Vietnam: Stanley Karnow, *Vietnam: A History* (New York: Viking Press, 1983), p. 286.
405 Joe visits Nhu and Diem: JWA, "In the Gia Long Palace," *Washington Post*, September 20, 1963.
405 ". . . stark, raving mad": Montague Kern, Patricia W. Levering, and Ralph B. Levering, *The Kennedy Crises: The Press, the Presidency, and Foreign Policy* (Chapel Hill, N.C.: University of North Carolina Press, 1983), p. 174.
405 "The constant pressure . . .": JWA, "The Crusaders," *Washington Post*, September 23, 1963.
406 ". . . call off Alsop": Kern et al., p. 175.
406 "Don't you believe in freedom of the press?": Ibid.

406 "right around the bend": JWA, "The Crusaders."

406 "I don't think this is viable": Kern et al., p. 175.

406 word of coup reaches Washington: Richard Reeves, *President Kennedy: Profile of Power* (New York: Simon & Schuster, 1993), p. 649.

406 Joe felt some guilt: JWA, *I've Seen the Best of It*, p. 462.

406 sitting in garden room: Ibid., p. 463.

406 sobbing uncontrollably: Evelyn Puffenberger, interview.

407 ". . . forbidden to have the flu . . .": Otto Friedrich, *Decline and Fall: The Struggle for Power at a Great American Magazine* (New York: Harper & Row, 1969), p. 53.

407 "An extraordinarily complex man . . .": SA, "The New President," *Saturday Evening Post*, November 23, 1963, p. 20.

407 dinner with Cousin Alice: SA, letter to Friedrich, November 24, 1963, SA Collection.

407 "Goddam it, I'm depressed . . .": SA, letter to Friedrich, November 25, 1963, JWA & SA Papers, container 31.

407 Joe and Susan Mary at funeral: JWA, *I've Seen the Best of It*, p. 464.

407 ". . . a nation great and free . . .": JWA, "Go, Stranger!" New York *Herald Tribune*, November 25, 1963.

407 Helping Jackie with correspondence: JWA, letter to Philippe de Rothschild, January 9, 1964, JWA & SA Papers, container 70; SA, letter to Jacqueline Kennedy, March 23, 1964, SA Collection.

407 "It all but broke my heart . . .": JWA, letter to Jacqueline Kennedy, August 28, 1964, JWA & SA Papers, container 70.

407 "People always say . . .": Jacqueline Kennedy, letter to JWA, August 31, 1964, JWA & SA Papers, container 70.

407 "So thank you . . .": Jacqueline Kennedy, letter to JWA, January 14 (year unspecified), JWA & SA Papers, container 130.

408 "I appreciate . . . your calling": Transcript of LBJ-JWA phone conversation, November 25, 1963, LBJ Library and U.S. National Archives.

409 "common sense, courage . . .": JWA, "President Johnson," New York *Herald Tribune*, November 27, 1963.

409 Joe and Kay Graham shed tears: Transcript of LBJ-JWA conversation, November 27, 1963, LBJ Library and U.S. National Archives.

409 ". . . how grateful I am . . .": Ibid.

409 Johnson as 1930s source: Robert Kintner, letter to Harry Stanton, May 2, 1941, JWA & SA Papers, container 33.

409 "That's just fine, sir . . .": Transcript of LBJ-JWA phone conversation, November 29, 1963, LBJ Library and U.S. National Archives.

409 "Politics in this city . . .": JWA, letter to M. and Mme. Philippe de Rothschild, January 9, 1964, JWA & SA Papers, container 70.

410 thinking of giving up the column: JWA, letter to Mrs. Milton Gendel, February 4, 1964, JWA & SA Papers, container 69.

410 "This resurrected Pylos . . .": JWA, *From the Silent Earth: A Report on the Greek Bronze Age* (New York: Harper & Row, 1964), p. 2.

410 ". . . near professional learning": Orville Prescott, "The Bureaucracies of the Bronze Age," *New York Times*, March 2, 1964, p. 25.

410 ". . . very respectful . . .": Alfred R. Bellinger, "Archeological Novice Abop Shows Courage-cum-Modesty," *Washington Post*, March 3, 1964, p. A4.

410 "How-oh-how . . .": Lady Bird Johnson, letter to JWA, February 19, 1964, JWA & SA Papers, container 69.

410 "My countrymen are indebted . . .": George A. Mylonas, letter to JWA, March 28, 1964, JWA & SA Papers, container 70.

411 more than ten thousand copies: Genevieve Young, letter to JWA, September 11, 1964, JWA & SA Papers, container 178.

411 ". . . the damned book . . .": JWA, letter to Mrs. Milton Gendel.

411 "downright dazzling": SA, radio script, undated, SA Collection.

411 man of force and intellect: SA, "Johnson Takes Over: The Untold Story," *Saturday Evening Post*, February 15, 1964, p. 17.

411 "a born conciliator . . .": SA, "A Second Era of Good Feeling?" *Saturday Evening Post*, May 9, 1964.

411 "perfect success": JWA, letter to Lyndon Johnson, April 7, 1964, JWA & SA Papers, container 69.

411 ". . . lunch with you . . .": Lyndon Johnson, letter to JWA, April 8, 1964, JWA & SA Papers, container 69.

411 civil rights bill: Theodore H. White, *The Making of the President 1964* (New York: Atheneum, 1965), p. 211.

411 ". . . a moral duty . . .": JWA, letter to J. Hubert Farmer, June 22, 1964, JWA & SA Papers, container 69.

411   Joe applauds cloture: JWA, "The Last, Best Chance," *Washington Post*, March 30, 1964.

411   ". . . rarely . . . better served": JWA, "Poor Everett Dirksen," *Washington Post*, June 12, 1964.

412   ". . . ulcerous . . . dilemma . . .": SA, "The X Factor Is Race," *Saturday Evening Post*, February 8, 1964, p. 10.

412   "an empty gesture . . .": SA, "The Doomed Ones," *Saturday Evening Post*, April 4, 1964, p. 16.

412   episode in Cambridge: SA, "People in a Trap," *Saturday Evening Post*, June 6, 1964, p. 12.

413   economy growing at 4 percent: Allen J. Lichtman and Ken DeCell, *The 13 Keys to the Presidency* (New York: Madison Books, 1990), p. 328.

413   race an issue: SA, "Can Goldwater Win?" *Saturday Evening Post*, August 8, 1964, p. 13.

414   61 percent to 39 percent: Theodore H. White, p. 480.

414   Joe's bet with LBJ: JWA, letter to Lady Bird Johnson, undated, JWA & SA Papers, container 69.

414   ". . . a happier debtor": Lady Bird Johnson, letter to JWA, November 14, 1964, JWA & SA Papers, container 69.

414   warning against hubris: JWA, "Johnson Triumphant," *Washington Post*, November 6, 1964.

414   ". . . professional country-runner . . .": SA, "The President," *Saturday Evening Post*, November 7, 1964, p. 12.

414   ". . . alternative to defeat . . .": SA, "Vietnam: Go North?" *Saturday Evening Post*, p. 10.

414   ". . . ghastly . . .": JWA, letter to Sol Sanders, May 18, 1964, JWA & SA Papers, container 70.

415   ". . . nothing fails like failure": JWA, "President Johnson's Choice," *Washington Post*, May 22, 1964.

415   "failed . . . irrevocably": JWA, "Harsh Test for Johnson," *Washington Post*, September 2, 1964.

415   "As President Truman did . . .": JWA, "The World He Never Made," *Washington Post*, November 30, 1964.

415   ". . . catastrophe now being invited": JWA, "Johnson's Cuba II," *Washington Post*, December 30, 1964.

415   ". . . alarm and urgency . . .": Jack Valenti, *A Very Human President* (New York: W. W. Norton, 1975), pp. 300–301.

416   ". . . hated to be hedged in": Jack Valenti, interview, November 5, 1993.

416   "You call McNamara . . .": Ibid.

416   ". . . rather bitter offense . . .": JWA, letter to McGeorge Bundy, January 5, 1965, JWA & SA Papers, container 71.

416   ". . . time to retire . . .": Ibid.

CHAPTER THIRTY

417   "My sword . . .": Leonard Baker, *Brandeis and Frankfurter: A Dual Biography* (New York: New York University Press, 1986), p. 491.

417   "a quite astonishing assemblage": JWA, letter to Mr. and Mrs. Jean Monnet, February 26, 1965, JWA & SA Papers, Library of Congress, container 72.

418   ". . . still very painful . . .": Ibid.

418   Dumbarton routine: Susan Mary Alsop, interview, December 27, 1994.

418   outbursts and bullying: Ibid.

419   domino theory: JWA, "The Domino Theory," *Washington Post*, January 29, 1965.

419   "poison our national life . . .": JWA, letter to Richard Rovere, January 15, 1965, JWA & SA Papers, container 72.

419   "a presidential weakness so grave . . .": JWA, "Johnson's Achilles Heel," *Washington Post*, February 17, 1965.

419   "Then a time will come . . .": JWA, letter to McGeorge Bundy, JWA & SA Papers, container 71.

419   night of February 7: Stanley Karnow, *Vietnam: A History* (New York: Viking, 1983), pp. 411–12.

419   "assume no limitations . . .": Ibid., p. 417.

419   Johnson's Johns Hopkins address: Ibid, pp. 418–19.

420   "full of lies and deceptions": Ibid.

420   "subside by degrees . . ."; JWA, "The Art of War," *Washington Post*, March 5, 1965.

420   "a great speech": JWA, "A Great Speech," *Washington Post*, April 9, 1965.

420   ". . . love and sorrow . . .": JWA, letter to Jacqueline Kennedy, August 28, 1964, JWA & SA Papers, container 70.

420   ". . . broke my life in half . . .": JWA, letter to Jacqueline Kennedy, September 9, 1964, JWA & SA Papers, container 70.

420   "This November . . .": Jacqueline Kennedy, letter to JWA, November 24, 1964, JWA & SA Papers, container 70.

420   "perfect heaven . . .": JWA, letter to Jacqueline Kennedy, February 4, 1965, JWA & SA Papers, container 72.

420   a ticklish subject: JWA, letter to Jacqueline Kennedy, February 26, 1965, JWA & SA Papers, container 72.

420   Joe's advice to Robert Kennedy: JWA, letter to Robert Kennedy, November 1964, JWA & SA Papers, container 70.

421   "On advice of counsel . . .": JWA, letter to Harry Truman, March 12, 1965, JWA & SA Papers, container 73.

422   ". . . welcome your reassessment . . .": Harry Truman, letter to JWA, March 19, 1965, JWA & SA Papers, container 73.

422   communist attacks: Karnow, pp. 421–22.

422   the Mao-Giap rulebook: JWA, "Charting Terra Incognita," *New Yorker*, January 28, 1967, p. 112.

422   Westmoreland troop requests: Karnow, p. 422.

422   Joe's assessment of bombing: "On Losing Momentum," *Washington Post*, May 21, 1965.

423   ". . . more ominous . . .": JWA, "Civil War, Hell!" *Washington Post*, May 26, 1965.

423   situation at Pleiku: JWA, "End of the Line," *Washington Post*, May 31, 1965.

423   Joe's Saigon schedule: JWA, "Expenses in Connection with Recent Round-the-World Reporting Trip—April 26–May 29," JWA & SA Papers, container 84.

423   Keyes Beech: Ray Coffey, interview, October 14, 1993.

423   Majestic Hotel: Frank Wisner, Jr., interview, September 29, 1993.

424   "Take him off my hands . . .": Barry Zorthian, interview, December 2, 1993.

424   "some kind of history": Ibid.

424   Joe's special treatment: Ibid.

424   ". . . stomp them to death": Neil Sheehan, *A Bright Shining Lie: John Paul Vann and America in Vietnam* (New York: Random House), p. 568.

424   meetings with DePuy: JWA, "Expenses in Connection with Recent Round the World Reporting Trip—August 27–October 8," JWA & SA Papers, container 84.

425   ". . . Yankee ingenuity": JWA, "Power's Long Arm," *Washington Post*, September 17, 1965.

425   defector at My Tho: JWA, "The Enemy's Lost Bet," *Washington Post*, September 24, 1965.

425   "every form of pollution . . .": Frank Wisner, Jr., interview.

425   "Oh, my word . . .": Warren Rogers, interview, October 6, 1993.

426   generational rift: R. W. Apple, Jr., interview, November 15, 1993.

426   views of John Vann: Sheehan, pp. 537–542.

426   "He gets everything wrong": Robert Novak, interview, May 18, 1994.

426   ". . . patron saint . . .": Ray Coffey, interview.

426   ". . . always leaking . . .": Ibid.

426   reporters' view of Joe: R. W. Apple, Jr., interview.

427   Ia Drang battle: Lieutenant General Harold G. Moore (Ret.) and Joseph L. Galloway, *We Were Soldiers Once . . . and Young* (New York: Random House, 1992), pp. xviii–xxi.

427   encouraging news to Westmoreland: Karnow, p. 480.

427   ". . . something to wonder at . . .": JWA, "No Bull Run This Time," *Washington Post*, November 22, 1965.

427   rules of engagement: Moore and Galloway, p. 402.

427   tactics vs. strategy: Ibid., p. 399.

428   ". . . a bleak winter . . .": James Reston, letter to JWA, undated, JWA & SA Papers, container 72.

428   "disgraceful": JWA, letter to Reston, November 24, 1965, JWA & SA Papers, container 72.

428   "You are dogmatic . . .": Reston, letter to JWA, November 27, 1965, JWA & SA Papers, container 72.

428   "like a very old dog . . .": JWA, letter to Philippe de Rothschild, January 17, 1966, JWA & SA Papers, container 75.

428   well-established routine: JWA, "VIETNAM—Daily Schedule—January 23–February 14," JWA & SA Papers, container 84.

429   ". . . his mind was made up": Frank Wisner, Jr., interview.

429 "... all wrong, Bill ...": Barry Zorthian, interview.
429 "... dreadful shape": JWA, "The Ever Victorious," *Washington Post*, February 18, 1966.
429 "... out of the ring": JWA, "If We Were They," *Washington Post*, February 21, 1966.
429 more manpower: JWA, "Again, a New War," *Washington Post*, February 4, 1966.
429 Joe favored the call-up: JWA, "Why the Reserves?" *Washington Post*, February 2, 1966.
430 the homefront: Karnow, pp. 486–88.
430 structure would crumble: JWA, "The Untold Story: Victory?" *Washington Post*, March 2, 1966.
430 "... successive stories": JWA, "The Untold Story: Reporting," *Washington Post*, March 4, 1966.
431 shortcomings in critique: Neil Sheehan, letter to Sydney Gruson, May 5, 1966, JWA & SA Papers, container 74.
431 "not to get into an argument ...": Gruson, letter to JWA, June 20, 1966, JWA & SA Papers, container 74.
431 "Nonsense": JWA, letter to Gruson, June 24, 1966, JWA & SA Papers, container 74.
431 "fluttered the dovecotes": JWA, letter to Isaiah Berlin, March 18, 1966, JWA & SA Papers, container 73.
431 "... more optimistic ...": Robert Shaplen, letter to JWA, March 22, 1966, JWA & SA Papers, container 75.
432 Democrats lose forty-seven House seats: *Congressional Quarterly Weekly Report*, November 12, 1994, p. 3209.
432 "THE turning point ...": William DePuy, letter to JWA, January 24, 1967, JWA & SA Papers, container 76.
432 "silly": JWA, "Schlesinger's Silly Book," *Washington Post*, January 16, 1967.
432 blunt exchange: JWA, letter to Arthur Schlesinger, February 10, 1967, JWA & SA Papers, container 77; Schlesinger, letter to JWA, February 8, 1967, JWA & SA Papers, container 77.
433 "... cult hero ...": JWA, "Robert Kennedy's Dilemma," *Washington Post*, February 13, 1966.
433 "... no pleasure at all ...": JWA, letter to Robert Kennedy, undated, JWA & SA Papers, container 77.
433 polls on the war: Karnow, p. 488.
433 "Balls, madame ...": Stanley Karnow, interview, December 2, 1993.
434 "... insufferable?": Ibid.
434 "... old codger ...": JWA, letter to Isaiah Berlin, June 16, 1967, JWA & SA Papers, container 130.
434 Alsop-Rostow collaboration: JWA, letter to Lyndon Johnson, November 3, 1967, JWA & SA Papers, container 130.
434 Alsop-Johnson outlook: JWA, draft statement, November 8, 1967, JWA & SA Papers, container 130.
435 "... just about worthless": JWA, letter to Lyndon Johnson, November 3, 1967.
435 "The enemy ...": JWA, "Hanoi Plans Coalition Ploy as Easy Way Out of Its Bind," *Washington Post*, December 18, 1967.
435 Hanoi's induction statistics: Don Oberdorfer, *Tet!* (Garden City, N.Y.: Doubleday, 1971), p. 53.
436 600,000 U.S. troops: Ibid., p. 79.
436 "... it isn't working": Ibid., p. 85.
436 Keyes Beech's perceptions: Ray Coffey, interview.

CHAPTER THIRTY-ONE

page

437 "So, why are you down here?": Elizabeth Winthrop, interview, December 22, 1994.
438 "... secret documents": Ibid.
438 sluggish and flabby: SA, "What's Wrong with Our Army?" *Saturday Evening Post*, February 13, 1965, p. 18.
439 "He don't know enough ...": SA, letter to Robert Johnson, June 21, 1965, SA Collection, Special Collections, Boston University Libraries. (Other observations on Lyndon Johnson in this passage come from the same letter.)
439 "listening too much ...": SA, "The Inner-Directed Mood," *Saturday Evening Post*, March 13, 1965, p. 18.
440 "least global-minded": Ibid.
440 "... our southern brothers": SA, "We Can't Let Them Down," *Saturday Evening*

Post, March 27, 1965, p. 18. Stewart's portrait of Robert Alhouse comes from the same column.

442   "If the price is high enough . . .": SA, "The Meaning of the Dead," *Saturday Evening Post*, April 24, 1965, p. 18.

442   talking to sources: SA, radio commentary transcript, April 28, 1965, SA Collection.

442   "fuzzy in the extreme": Ibid.

442   ". . . at least as nasty . . .": SA, radio commentary transcript, week of July 19, 1965, SA Collection.

442   the general's map: SA, "War's Awful Logic," *Saturday Evening Post*, September 11, 1965, p. 14.

443   ". . . bloodily, on the ground . . .": SA, "The Twin Illusions," *Saturday Evening Post*, October 23, 1965, p. 18.

443   Watts riots: Theodore H. White, *The Making of the President 1968* (New York: Atheneum, 1969), p. 26.

443   "You damn right . . .": SA, "Watts: The Fire Next Time," *Saturday Evening Post*, November 6, 1965, p. 20.

444   6.5 million: John B. Bettew, memorandum to Maurice W. Poppei, April 25, 1966, SA Collection.

444   new biweekly schedule: SA, letter to J. M. Clifford, August 11, 1965, SA Collection.

444    $6,000 pay cut: J. M. Clifford, contract letter to SA, August 5, 1965, SA Collection.

444   New York weekend: Otto Friedrich, *Decline and Fall: The Struggle for Power at a Great American Magazine* (New York: Harper & Row, 1969), pp. 140–46.

446   Culligan's fate: Ibid., p. 148.

446   "wholly alienated . . .": SA, "Portrait of a Klansman," *Saturday Evening Post*, April 9, 1966, p. 23.

446   "You speared this guy . . .": Harold H. Martin, letter to SA, March 31, 1966, SA Collection.

447   ". . . 'a public trust' ": SA, "The Johnsonization of Washington," *Saturday Evening Post*, February 26, 1966, p. 20.

447   ". . . totally unwilling . . .": SA, "Vietnam: How Wrong Was McNamara?" *Saturday Evening Post*, March 12, 1966, p. 14.

447   ". . . an Asian Churchill": SA, "Vietnam: Great Miscalculation?" *Saturday Evening Post*, September 10, 1966, p. 18.

448   evening with students: SA, "Vietnam: Whose War?" *Saturday Evening Post*, January 28, 1967, p. 10.

448   Mekong Delta challenge: SA, "Love and Hate in the Mekong Delta," *Saturday Evening Post*, December 31, 1966, p. 12.

450   ". . . my brother Joe . . .": Tom Braden, interview, October 27, 1990.

450   ". . . most professional . . .": SA, "The Amazing Americans," *Saturday Evening Post*, January 14, 1967, p. 12.

451   ". . . faces . . . blown off": Philip Geyelin, interview, April 27, 1993.

451   "Like a tethered goat . . .": Ibid.

451   "I'm not looking forward . . .": Ibid.

451   the brothers pulled back: Patricia Alsop, interview, January 16, 1995.

451   visit with McNamara: SA, typed notes, May 13, 1967, SA Collection.

452   ". . . erosion of confidence . . .": SA, "The Jam We Are In," *Saturday Evening Post*, July 29, 1967, p. 4.

452   visit with LBJ: SA, letter to Otto Friedrich, August 3, 1967, SA Collection.

454   ". . . his light has failed . . .": SA, "McNamara: The Light That Failed," *Saturday Evening Post*, November 18, 1967, p. 16.

CHAPTER THIRTY-TWO

page

457   Tet offensive: Stanley Karnow, *Vietnam: A History* (New York: Viking Press, 1983), pp. 523–30.

457   kamikaze raids: JWA, "Red Raids on Cities Are Sign of Weakness, Not Strength," *Washington Post*, February 2, 1968.

457   Tet death toll: Peter Braestrup, *Big Story* (New Haven: Yale University Press, 1977), p. 127.

457   ". . . a great enemy victory?": Ibid.

457   disgust with news coverage: JWA, "Brooding on Viet Setback Ignores Fearful Cost to Enemy," *Washington Post*, February 7, 1968.

458   nearly thirty thousand: JWA, "Major Failure in City Battles Was Enemy's, Not the Allies'," *Washington Post*, February 19, 1968.

458   "breathless moment": JWA, "Hanoi Places Heavy Stakes on Two Throws of the Dice," *Washington Post*, February 9, 1968.

458   dismissive of McCarthy: JWA, "McCarthy's Campaign Debut Is Bad News for Johnson Foes," *Washington Post*, December 20, 1967.

458   "hedge, waffle and straddle": SA, "Hedging, Waffling and Straddling," *Saturday Evening Post*, January 27, 1968, p. 14.

458   New Hampshire results: Theodore H. White, *The Making of the President 1968* (New York: Atheneum, 1969), appendix C.

458   "reassessing": Ibid., p. 90.

458   "shameful, humiliating . . .": JWA, "Kennedy's Viet Defeatism Contradicts Facts of War," *Washington Post*, March 27, 1968.

459   "Accordingly . . .": Theodore H. White, p. 124.

459   "gloom, bitterness . . .": JWA, " 'By God, There's a Man . . . His Hands Are Free Now,' " *Washington Post*, April 3, 1968.

459   ". . . whines of the muddleheaded . . .": Ibid.

459   ". . . perhaps even probable . . .": SA, "Defeat?" *Saturday Evening Post*, April 20, 1968, p. 20.

459   "Canada, Chippewa, and Lundy's Lane . . .": JWA, "Honors Rites in Vietnam Raise a Question for Bobby," *Washington Post*, April 15, 1968.

460   Wisconsin results: Theodore H. White, Appendix C.

461   ". . . since Theodore Roosevelt": JWA, "Two Wallace Triumphs Insure Great Impact on '68 Election," *Washington Post*, January 10, 1968.

461   ". . . bad political novels . . .": SA, "The Little Man in the Catbird Seat," *Saturday Evening Post*, March 23, 1968, p. 20.

461   "that presidential smell": SA, "Hubert Humphrey and the Presidential Smell," *Saturday Evening Post*, May 18, 1968, p. 18.

461   Stewart's view of Kennedy: SA, "Bobby's Red Guards," *Saturday Evening Post*, May 4, 1968, p. 18.

462   "youth-in-revolt": JWA, "Kennedy Won but Indiana Raises Questions for Senator," *Washington Post*, May 10, 1968.

462   Nebraska and Kennedy: JWA, "Kennedy Camp is Troubled Despite Nebraska Victory," *Washington Post*, May 17, 1968.

462   "These wicked 'bosses' . . .": Ibid.

462   "downright alarming": JWA, "Democrats Lucky in Men Like Kennedy and Humphrey," *Washington Post*, May 31, 1968.

462   Joe would vote for Kennedy: JWA, letter to Robert Kintner, June 13, 1968, JWA & SA Papers, container 130.

462   "At this dark moment . . .": JWA, telegram to Ethel Kennedy, June 5, 1968, JWA & SA Papers, container 130.

462   invitation to Kennedy Mass: Kennedy Family, telegram to JWA and Susan Mary, June 7, 1968, JWA & SA Papers, container 130.

463   "so stricken . . .": Daniel P. Moynihan, letter to JWA, undated, JWA & SA Papers, container 131.

463   "beyond belief pleasurable . . .": JWA, letter to Ethel Kennedy, undated, JWA & SA Papers, container 131.

463   "The depth of your affection . . .": Ethel Kennedy, letter to JWA, undated, JWA & SA Papers, container 130.

463   "despite the block of Vietnam . . .": JWA, letter to Allen Whiting, June 18, 1968, JWA & SA Papers, container 162.

463   "the super-hawk . . .": Zalin B. Grant, "Alsop Lets His Friends Down," *New Republic*, May 18, 1968, p. 9.

463   inadvertent indiscretion: JWA, letter to the editor, *New Republic*, May 15, 1968, JWA & SA Papers, container 131.

464   ". . . washed him with Top Secrets . . .": Grant.

464   "comparable seniority": JWA, letter to the editor, *New Republic*.

464   "imperial" . . . "arrogant": Merle Miller, "Washington, the World, and Joseph Alsop," *Harper's*, June 1968.

465   "such a gift for inaccuracy": JWA, letter to the editor, *Harper's*, June 5, 1968, JWA & SA Papers, container 130.

465   "If I have the facts right . . .": JWA, letter to Winant Sidle, June 6, 1968, JWA & SA Papers, container 162.

465   "If you are guilty . . .": Sidle, letter to JWA, June 16, 1968, JWA & SA Papers, container 162.

465   "took more risks . . .": Ward Just, letter to the editor, *Harper's*, July 1968.

465   "grubby operation": John O'Hara, letter to JWA, May 31, 1968, JWA & SA Papers, container 131.

465 ". . . unpleasantly noticed . . .": JWA, letter to O'Hara, June 17, 1968, JWA & SA Papers, container 130.

466 "intellectual bankruptcy": Quoted by John Kenneth Galbraith, statement for the press, September 22, 1968, JWA & SA Papers, container 130.

466 "the leading non-combatant casualty . . .": Ibid.

466 "torn the city apart": SA, *The Center: People and Power in Political Washington* (New York: Harper & Row, 1968), p. 351.

466 ". . . real feel and flavor . . .": Philip Geyelin, "Insider's Washington," *Washington Post*, May 2, 1968.

466 "special distinction": Arthur Schlesinger, "Washington in Perspective," *New Leader*, June 17, 1968, p. 26.

466 ". . . being invited back": William V. Shannon, "Stewart Alsop Dines with Imperial Washington," *Book World*, May 28, 1968.

466 $15 million purchase: Carol Felsenthal, *Power, Privilege and the Post* (New York: G. P. Putnam's Sons, 1993), p. 180.

466 "one of the great steals . . .": David Halberstam, quoted in Ibid.

466 Graham invested in *Newsweek*: Osborn Elliott, *The World of Oz* (New York: Viking Press, 1980), p. 14.

466 circulation of 1.4 million: Felsenthal, p. 180.

466 circulation topped 2 million: Elliot, p. 51.

467 $800 a column: Ibid.

467 bringing along Amanda Zimmerman: Amanda Zimmerman, interview, September 26, 1990.

467 little regret: Patricia Alsop, interview, November 4, 1993.

467 a bit lost: SA, letter to Robert Johnson, July 23, 1968, SA Collection.

467 instantly to his liking: Patricia Alsop, interview.

467 a gray eminence: Mel Elfin, interview, October 29, 1990.

467 ". . . the end of an era . . .": SA, "No Pax Americana," *Newsweek*, August 12, 1968, p. 88.

468 political reality facing Nixon: JWA, "Nixon Eyes Rightward Jump as Way Out of Election Plight," *Washington Post*, August 5, 1968.

468 "politically well contrived": JWA, "Southern Strategy of Nixon Is Seen Likely to Succeed," August 12, 1968.

468 "The words and acts . . .": Ibid.

468 privately more outspoken: JWA, letter to Kenneth Crawford, August 13, 1968, JWA & SA Papers, container 131.

468 ". . . public issue with you . . .": John Alsop, letter to JWA, September 4, 1968, JWA & SA Papers, container 131.

468 "certain automatic effects . . .": JWA, letter to John Alsop, September 6, 1968, JWA & SA Papers, container 131.

468 the Wallace voter: SA, "The Wallace Man," *Newsweek*, October 21, 1968, p. 116.

469 "The place is crawling . . .": JWA, "Complete Falsehood of McCarthy's Views Spotlighted by Invasion," *Washington Post*, August 26, 1968.

469 "academic-intellectual liberalism": JWA, "Ghastly Convention Suggests Bankruptcy for Liberalism," *Washington Post*, September 2, 1968.

469 "a four-letter transitive verb . . .": SA, "Virus X and the Body Politic," *Newsweek*, September 16, 1968, p. 108.

470 "more like an execution": SA, "Can Humphrey Win?" *Newsweek*, September 9, 1968, p. 104.

471 Electoral margin: Theodore H. White, Appendix A.

471 Wallace got 13.5 percent: Ibid.

CHAPTER THIRTY-THREE

page

473 Joe's 1968 vote: JWA, letter to Phillip B. Davidson, Jr., February 27, 1969, JWA & SA Papers, Library of Congress, container 162.

473 "I must say . . .": Ibid.

473 "much encouraged": JWA, letter to Ellsworth Bunker, February 18, 1969, JWA & SA Papers, container 132.

473 "The *proletariat* . . .": SA, "Nixon and the New Bourgeoisie," *Newsweek*, January 27, 1969, p. 96.

474 "the quintessential square": SA, "The Quintessential Square," *Newsweek*, October 7, 1968, p. 118.

474 "... so well arranged ...": JWA, letter to Henry Kissinger, February 27, 1969, JWA & SA Papers, container 132.

475 "... call the hostess yourself": William Safire, *Before the Fall* (Garden City, N.Y.: Doubleday, 1975), p. 158.

475 Helms's discussion with SA: SA, typed notes from interview, source identified as RH, undated, SA Collection, Special Collections, Boston University Libraries.

475 Stewart's question to Rogers: SA, typed notes from interview, source identified as WRogers, undated, SA Collection.

476 "in flexible form ...": SA, typed notes from interview, source identified as WRogers, undated, SA Collection. (This is a separate document from citation immediately above.)

476 "A great nation ...": SA, "No 'Disguised Defeat'?" *Newsweek*, June 9, 1969, p. 124.

476 "... booze was spilling ...": Benjamin Bradlee, interview, February 10, 1993.

477 "He got tiresome ...": Evangeline Bruce, interview, May 19, 1993.

477 Walter Ridder and Joe: Marie Ridder, interview, November 29, 1990.

477 "He was wonderful ...": Katharine Graham, interview, January 10, 1995. (The subsequent anecdotes involving Joe and Kay Graham are from this interview.)

478 "... petty nonsense": Charles Whitehouse, interview, July 1, 1992.

478 Susan Mary's silence: Evangeline Bruce, interview.

478 sometimes she would rebel: Katharine Graham, interview.

478 "ghastly, long and tense": Elizabeth Winthrop, interview, October 29, 1993.

478 "Goddam it, Susan Mary": Elizabeth Winthrop, interview, May 6, 1992.

478 "by order of the management": Ibid.

479 Susan Mary berated: Charles Whitehouse, interview.

479 he spoke of her glowingly: Evangeline Bruce, interview.

479 "Yes, I did try to reform you ...": Susan Mary Alsop, letter to JWA, Sept. 22 (year not noted), JWA & SA Papers, container 128.

479 "I have no one else ...": Susan Mary Alsop, letter to JWA, Aug. 30 (year not noted), JWA & SA Papers, container 128.

479 Joe and his stepchildren: Susan Mary Alsop, interview, November 6, 1992.

479 "... never do better": Elizabeth Winthrop, interview, October 29, 1993.

479 Stewart's children in 1969: SA, *Stay of Execution: A Sort of Memoir* (Philadelphia and New York: J. B. Lippincott, 1973), pp. 20–21.

480 Groton experiences: Ibid., p. 198.

480 "You're *supposed* to be miserable ...": Elizabeth Winthrop, interview, October 29, 1993.

480 "All three of my boys ...": SA, *Stay of Execution*, p. 199.

480 Polecat Park: Ibid., pp. 96–97.

480 Needwood Forest: Ibid., pp. 98–100.

481 "Aunt Gussie ...": Gussie Alsop, interview, January 12, 1995.

481 "... not the most loving ...": Stewart Alsop, Jr., interview, November 21, 1990.

481 "... death of an old friend": SA, "Requiem for the *Post*," *Newsweek*, January 20, 1969, p. 96.

481 "good-hearted nuttiness": SA, "Yale Revisited," *Newsweek*, May 19, 1969, p. 120.

482 nominal withdrawal: Henry Kissinger, *White House Years* (Boston: Little, Brown, 1979), p. 274.

482 "... bleeding heart ...": JWA, letter to Bunker, June 9, 1969, JWA & SA Papers, container 216.

482 to not lose the war: SA, "Vietnam: The Nixon Game Plan," *Newsweek*, September 15, 1969, p. 108.

482 "impedimenta": SA, "The Flaw in the Game Plan," *Newsweek*, September 29, 1969, p. 132.

482 "... irretrievable disaster ...": Ibid.

483 Firebase Rendezvous: JWA, "Battlefield Facts Cast Doubt on Wisdom of Hasty Pullout," *Washington Post*, September 19, 1969.

483 ten thousand deaths in 1969: Stanley Karnow, *Vietnam: A History* (New York: Viking Press, 1983), p. 601.

483 "The president would like to see you": SA, memorandum to Oz Elliott, October 2, 1969, SA Collection.

484 "Our Coming Defeat in Vietnam": Ibid.

484 column on Oval Office visit: SA, "The President on Vietnam," *Newsweek*, October 13, 1969, p. 33.

484 Ian in 1969: SA, *Stay of Execution*, p. 20.

485 in the Mekong Delta: William Colby, with James McCargar, *Lost Victory* (Chicago: Contemporary Books), pp. 272–73.

485 up in III Corps: Ibid.

485 "... chance to make it ...": SA, "They May Make It," *Newsweek*, December 29, 1969, p. 60.

485 "... political leadership ...": JWA, "Nixon Leadership Is Underestimated," *Washington Post*, December 29, 1969.

485 Art Buchwald episode: Barnard Law Collier, "The Joe Alsop Story," *New York Times Magazine*, May 23, 1971, p. 22.

486 "... one of those things": Robert Kintner, letter to JWA, February 2, 1970, JWA & SA Papers, container 134.

486 "... exceedingly nice letter ...": JWA, letter to Kintner, February 4, 1970, JWA & SA Papers, container 134.

486 "extremely cool ...": JWA, letter to Charles Whitehouse, December 4, 1969, JWA & SA Papers, container 162.

486 "a showy local disaster ...": JWA, letter to Richard Nixon, March 9, 1970, JWA & SA Papers, container 134.

486 Laos and Cambodia: Kissinger, p. 434.

486 pullout of 115,000 troops: Ibid., p. 475.

486 April 26 approval: Ibid., p. 499.

486 "incursion" announcement: Ibid., p. 504.

486 vast stores of materiel: Ibid., pp. 506–507.

487 sheets of yellow lined paper: SA, typed notes entitled "P. Yellow Pad," undated, SA Collection.

487 Kissinger interview: Ibid.

488 two myths dispelled: SA, "On the President's Yellow Pad," *Newsweek*, June 1, 1970, p. 106.

488 "The spasm of national hysteria ...": SA, "Mr. Nixon's Great Retreat," *Newsweek*, May 25, 1970, p. 120.

488 "it is fashionable ...": David Warsh, letter to SA, June 2, 1970, SA Collection.

488 object of ridicule: Mel Elfin, interview, October 29, 1990.

488 "Well, that's Joe ...": Warren Rogers, interview, October 6, 1993.

489 "Quite impossible, darling": Katharine Graham, interview.

489 "the most beautiful party ...": JWA, letter to Isaiah Berlin, October 14, 1970, JWA & SA Papers, container 215.

489 John, Stewart, and Kay Graham at Joe's party: John McCone, letter to Katharine Graham, October 21, 1970, JWA & SA Papers, container 212.

489 "... at peace with himself": Anne Patten Crile, letter to Katharine Graham, October 19, 1970, JWA & SA Papers, container 212.

489 an ugly incident: Susan Mary Alsop, letter to JWA, November 24, 1970, JWA & SA Papers, container 128.

489 notes on Susan Mary's car: Susan Mary Alsop, interview.

489 photographs in Bartlett's mail: Charles Bartlett, interview, October 8, 1992.

489 copies to Art Buchwald: Benjamin Bradlee, interview, February 10, 1993.

490 a coolness emerged: Bartlett, interview.

490 "... one vast scene ...": JWA, letter to Odette Pol-Roger, December 22, 1970, JWA & SA Papers, container 134.

490 never heard of the Alsops: Elizabeth Winthrop, interview, October 29, 1993.

490 "beautiful blonde": Ibid.

490 "Not our class, dear": Ibid.

490 "... Uncle Joe's teeth on edge": Ibid.

490 "nightmare of the future": JWA, letter to William Patten, Jr., January 8, 1971, JWA & SA Papers, container 129. (Other observations of the wedding, except as noted, come from JWA's January 8 letter.)

492 tearing the country apart: SA, "Vietnam: Out Faster," *Newsweek*, December 7, 1970, p. 104.

492 "What do we do about crank calls?": Patricia Alsop, interview, November 4, 1993.

492 "... in seven minutes": SA, "Madness Past Midnight," *Newsweek*, March 15, 1971, p. 116. (The account of the rest of the episode is based on the March 15 column.)

CHAPTER THIRTY-FOUR

page

493 morning of July 19, 1971: SA, *Stay of Execution: A Sort of Memoir* (Philadelphia and New York: J. B. Lippincott, 1973), p. 15. (Unless otherwise noted, the story of Stewart's leukemia is taken from *Stay of Execution*.)

494 "You're anemic": Ibid., p. 17.

494 "Enough spicules?" Ibid., p. 19.

494 "Will it show ...": Ibid.

494 "I thought you should know ...": Ibid., p. 21.

495 "Daddy, what does that mean?" Elizabeth Winthrop, interview, October 29, 1993.

495   "sadly sympathetic air": SA, *Stay of Execution*, p. 22.

496   "Can you sterilize martinis?": Ibid., p. 28.

496   ". . . the reality of death . . .": Ibid., pp. 30–31.

497   Stewart jotted down impressions: Ibid., p. 77.

497   "Stew—what a nuisance . . .": Ibid., p. 66.

497   ". . . subsequent good health": Lyndon Johnson, letter to JWA, August 18, 1971, JWA & SA Papers, container 135.

497   ". . . losing a brother . . .": Edward Kennedy, letter to JWA, July 31, 1971, JWA & SA Papers, container 135.

498   ". . . a strong right arm . . .": SA, letter to JWA, August 10, 1971, JWA & SA Papers, container 128.

498   "naked sense of vulnerability . . .": SA, "God Tempers the Wind," *Newsweek*, August 30, 1971, p. 84.

498   "I think it's wonderful": Mel Elfin, interview, January 11, 1995.

499   ". . . my small store of courage": SA, *Stay of Execution*, p. 113.

499   "Not too good, John": Ibid., p. 114.

499   "Now don't get excited . . .": Ibid., p. 115.

499   "the classic . . . house party": Ibid., p. 117.

499   "I enjoyed nothing": Ibid., p. 133.

499   "a certain affection": Ibid., p. 134.

500   to "see it, and smell it . . .": Ibid., p. 141.

500   ". . . I have escaped . . .": SA, letter to C. L. Sulzberger, December 10, 1971, SA Collection, Special Collections, Boston University Libraries.

500   ". . . a terrible betrayal": SA, "Gross Immorality," *Newsweek*, November 8, 1971, p. 122.

500   as Kissinger told Stewart: SA, typed notes entitled "HK," undated, SA Collection.

500   "The answer seems obvious": SA, "Vietnam: The Real Issue," *Newsweek*, February 14, 1972, p. 100.

501   Joe buoyed: JWA, letter to Isaiah Berlin, October 13, 1971, JWA & SA Papers, container 135.

501   "This country . . .": Ibid.

501   ". . . like having the roof fall in . . .": JWA, letter to Mrs. Milton Gendel, October 12, 1971, JWA & SA Papers, container 135.

502   birthday on an airplane: SA, letter to Isaiah Berlin.

502   ". . . depresses me a bit, too": Ibid.

502   ". . . original contribution": Ibid.

502   a social disaster: JWA, *Washington Post*: "How McGovern Switched," February 7, 1972; "The Facts on Busing," February 9, 1972; "Is It Really Worth It?" February 11, 1972; "White Flight to Suburbs," February 14, 1972; "Real Busing Balance," February 16, 1972.

503   "stuck whistle": JWA, letter to Katharine Graham, February 24, 1972, JWA & SA Papers, container 137.

503   ". . . cross, contentious tone . . .": Ibid.

503   "grandiose": JWA, "Nixon Feat Is Short-Term," *Washington Post*, February 28, 1972.

503   "a great honor": JWA, "Origins of the Trip," *Washington Post*, February 18, 1972.

504   Hanoi's 1972 offensive: Stanley Karnow, *Vietnam: A History* (New York: Viking Press, 1983), pp. 640–43.

504   "It had better be faced . . .": JWA, "Nixon's Grimmest Crisis," *Washington Post*, May 8, 1972.

504   Nixon's expanded bombing: Karnow, p. 646.

504   "bold decision": JWA, "Nixon's Viet Decision," *Washington Post*, May 12, 1972.

505   the missing element: SA, "The Non-Barking Dog," *Newsweek*, May 1, 1972, p. 124.

505   ". . . in black and white . . .": SA, "McGovern as Word-Eater," *Newsweek*, June 19, 1972, p. 104.

505   "dangerous": JWA, letter to Nick Kotz, July 5, 1972, JWA & SA Papers, container 135.

505   "a minority of a minority . . .": SA, "McGovern's Dilemma," *Newsweek*, July 24, 1972, p. 88.

506   "I'm sure of one thing . . .": SA, "With President Nixon Aboard Air Force One," *Newsweek*, September 4, 1972, p. 25.

506   60.7 percent: Theodore H. White, *The Making of the President 1972* (New York: Atheneum, 1973), p. 502.

506   Oval Office ceremony: Neil Sheehan, *A Bright Shining Lie: John Paul Vann and America in Vietnam* (New York: Random House, 1988), p. 31.

506   happy birthday: Richard Nixon, letter to JWA, October 18, 1972, JWA & SA Papers, container 212.

506    $49 contribution: Maurice H. Stans, letter to JWA, December 8, 1972, JWA & SA Papers, container 137.

506   odyssey of nostalgia: JWA, *New York Times Magazine*: "Thoughts Out of China I, Go Versus No-Go," March 11, 1973, p. 30; "Thoughts Out of China II, Doing It Yourself," March 18, 1973, p. 16. (Unless otherwise noted, the China trip story comes from this two-part series.)

507   "China-size omelette": JWA, "Partial Moment of Truth," *Washington Post*, November 27, 1972.

507   at nine thirty one evening: JWA, "The Honesty of Chou," *Washington Post*, December 4, 1972.

507   "Please come right away . . .": Susan Mary Alsop, interview, November 13, 1992.

507   "We have met before . . .": Ibid.

507   ". . . like a house afire": Ibid.

508   "Is there anything I can do . . .": Ibid.

508   Vietnam settlement: Karnow, p. 648.

509   "a simple trade-off . . .": SA, "The Best Deal We Could Get," *Newsweek*, December 11, 1972, p. 124.

509   bad cells down to 6 percent: SA, "All Will Be Well," *Newsweek*, July 31, 1972.

509   bad cells return: Ibid.

509   platelet donations: SA, *Stay of Execution*, p. 275.

509   a queasy feeling: Ibid.

510   Poly I-C: SA, "All Will Be Well."

510   one Friday afternoon: SA, *Stay of Execution*, p. 277.

CHAPTER THIRTY-FIVE

page

511   a dark scandal: Theodore H. White, *Breach of Faith: The Fall of Richard Nixon* (New York: Atheneum/Reader's Digest Press, 1975), pp. 139–68.

512   ". . . little man . . .": SA, "What Now?" *Newsweek*, January 1, 1973, p. 60.

512   ". . . inner moral limitation . . .": Anthony Lewis, letter to SA, December 28, 1972, SA Collection, Special Collections, Boston University Libraries.

513   ". . . a lot of dead people . . .": SA, "Eternal Damnation?" *Newsweek*, January 29, 1973, p. 78.

513   *Congressional Record*: SA, letter to Hugh Scott, February 7, 1973, SA Collection.

513   ". . . few commentators . . .": Joseph Fromm, letter to SA, January 29, 1973, SA Collection.

514   ". . . socked it to him . . .": Arnaud de Borchgrave, letter to SA, January 29, 1973, SA Collection.

514   ". . . irritating a lot of people . . .": SA, letter to Paul Johnson, February 7, 1973, SA Collection.

514   *un homme serieux*: SA, "The Serious Man," *Newsweek*, January 22, 1973, p. 96.

514   Nixon's bombing had worked: JWA, "President Nixon: Out of Seclusion," *Washington Post*, January 31, 1973.

514   "The decision to bomb . . .": Richard Nixon, letter to JWA, February 6, 1973, JWA & SA Papers, Library of Congress, container 212.

514   "a great honor . . .": JWA, letter to Nixon, February 8, 1973, JWA & SA Papers, container 212.

515   ". . . character actors": SA, "The Sam Ervin Show," *Newsweek*, April 2, 1973, p. 100.

515   "super-crisis": SA, "Mr. Nixon's Super-Crisis," *Newsweek*, April 30, 1973, p. 90.

515   ". . . a political cripple": JWA, "Watergate Warning," *Washington Post*, April 4, 1973.

515   Joe on Soviet Union and China: JWA, letter to Meg Greenfield, April 4, 1973, JWA & SA Papers, container 138.

516   "He hasn't a notion . . .": SA, letter to JWA, April 3, 1973, JWA & SA Papers, container 128.

516   "I am low . . .": Ibid.

516   ". . . a bit of luck": John Alsop, letter to SA, May 20, 1973, SA Collection.

516   ". . . my new lesson . . .": JWA, letter to Mrs. Richard Derby, June 26, 1973, JWA & SA Papers, container 138.

516   ". . . don't count me out . . .": SA, letter to Osborn Elliott, quoted in Elliott, *The World of Oz* (New York: Viking Press, 1980), p. 204.

516   a unique experience: Elliott, *World of Oz*, p. 204.

517   ". . . making war": SA, "War, Not Politics," *Newsweek*, May 14, 1973.

517   ". . . the ox to be gored . . .": SA, "Watergate and the Liberals," *Newsweek*, June 25, 1973.

517   Nixon's April 30 actions: Theodore H. White, pp. 220–21.

517   "paraplegic president": SA, "A Paraplegic Presidency," *Newsweek*, July 9, 1973.

517 "I see no likelihood . . .": JWA, letter to Marilyn Chandler, August 13, 1973, JWA & SA Papers, container 138.

518 ". . . bottom-dwelling slug . . .": JWA, "Dealing with Dean and the Dollar," *Washington Post*, June 6, 1973.

518 Dean's lawyers' campaign: Robert McCandless, conversation with the author, March 13, 1991.

518 "unshakeably determined . . .": JWA, "Why Wallow in Watergate?" *Washington Post*, June 11, 1973.

518 Butterfield's revelation: Theodore H. White, p. 188.

518 a favorite nephew: Dorothy Kidder, interview, October 31, 1990.

519 "very amicable separation": *Washington Evening Star*, untitled item, September 26, 1973.

519 periods of depression: Anne Crile, letter to JWA, undated, JWA & SA Papers, container 129.

519 "beautiful wife": Evangeline Bruce, interview, May 19, 1993.

519 ". . . the House of Usher feeling . . .": Anne Crile, letter to JWA.

520 problems with the column: JWA, letter to Katharine Graham, November 12, 1973, JWA & SA Papers, container 139.

520 "overly generous": John McCone, letter to JWA, May 17, 1973, JWA & SA Papers, container 139.

521 "I was worried for him": Katharine Graham, interview, January 10, 1995.

521 "If you give weight . . .": JWA, letter to Katharine Graham, November 12, 1973, JWA & SA Papers, container 129.

521 ". . . red wine too?": Katharine Graham, interview, January 10, 1995.

522 ". . . a mixed-up sort of book . . .": SA, *Stay of Execution: A Sort of Memoir* (Philadelphia and New York: J. B. Lippincott, 1973), p. 11.

522 "This guy has six kids . . .": Elizabeth Winthrop, interview, October 29, 1993.

522 "He had us nailed . . .": Ibid.

522 "A dying man needs to die . . .": SA, *Stay of Execution*, p. 299.

CHAPTER THIRTY-SIX

page

524 back at NIH: SA, "I Didn't Stop in Baltimore," *Newsweek*, March 11, 1974, p. 92.

524 "Auschwitz": Elizabeth Winthrop, interview, October 29, 1993.

524 ". . . half the battle": Elizabeth Winthrop, letter to JWA, January 3, 1974, JWA & SA Papers, Library of Congress, container 129.

524 didn't want visitors: Patricia Alsop, interview, November 4, 1993.

524 "half-way back to life": JWA, letter to Mrs. Poes Berling, January 9, 1974, JWA & SA Papers, container 140.

525 mid-January hopes: JWA, letter to unnamed recipient, January 16, 1974, JWA & SA Papers, container 128.

525 ". . . on the right road again": JWA, letter to Betsy Whitney, February 15, 1974, JWA & SA Papers, container 143.

525 a second pneumonia: SA, "I Didn't Stop in Baltimore."

525 ". . . very worst vintage years . . .": JWA, letter to Evangeline Bruce, January 3, 1974, JWA & SA Papers, container 140.

525 "sad state of uncertainty": JWA, letter to Katharine Graham, January 8, 1974, JWA & SA Papers, container 141.

525 "Don't worry . . .": Katharine Graham, letter to JWA, December 31, 1973, JWA & SA Papers, container 141.

525 ". . . a major decision": JWA, letter to Katharine Graham, January 8, 1974.

525 ". . . such a good show . . .": Susan Mary Alsop, letter to JWA, February 25, 1974, JWA & SA Papers, container 129.

525 Chip Bohlen died on January 1: Walter Isaacson and Evan Thomas, *The Wise Men: Six Friends and the World They Made* (New York: Simon & Schuster, 1986), p. 722.

525 ". . . a wrench . . .": JWA, letter to Evangeline Bruce.

526 ". . . great chunks being torn out . . .": JWA, letter to unnamed recipient, April 12, 1973, JWA & SA Papers, container 139. (The letter related to news of Chip Bohlen's cancer in 1973, and referred to "the loss, or even the threatened loss, of close friends of many years like Chip.")

526 prognosis "grim": SA, "I Didn't Stop in Baltimore."

526 "We'll be stopping in Baltimore": Ibid. (The entire episode comes from SA's March 11, 1974, column, except as noted.)

526 "We won't be stopping in Baltimore," interview with Dick Cavett, ABC TV, late March 1974 (aired after SA's death), tape provided by Patricia Alsop.

527   talking "like Job": JWA, letter to Betsy Whitney.

527   "slithery, sudden coming apart": SA, "Degringolade?" *Newsweek*, April 1, 1974, p. 88.

527   ". . . impeached, convicted and evicted . . .": SA, "Could He Be Right?" *Newsweek*, April 8, 1974, p. 96.

528   "According to our contract . . .": Osborn Elliott, *The World of Oz* (New York: Viking Press, 1980), p. 204.

528   ". . . a good Puritan": Ibid., p. 205.

528   "Everybody's really pulling for you . . .": Elizabeth Winthrop, interview, October 29, 1993.

529   "His Beat Was the World": John T. McQuiston, "Stewart Alsop, Columnist, Is Dead at 60; His Beat Was the World," *New York Times*, May 27, 1974.

529   "with honesty, fairness . . .": Editorial, "Stewart Alsop," *Los Angeles Times*, May 29, 1974.

529   ". . . the way he had lived . . .": Mel Elfin, "Stewart Alsop, 1914–1974," *Newsweek*, June 3, 1974, p. 88.

529   "Always the gentleman": "An Instinct for the Center," *Time*, June 10, 1974, p. 65.

529   ". . . defending the status quo": "Stewart Alsop, RIP," *National Review*, June 21, 1974, p. 689.

529   ". . . Anglophile establishments . . .": "Mr. Stewart Alsop, American Political Columnist," *The Times* of London, May 28, 1974.

529   "brave and stoical man": JWA, "A Brave and Stoical Man," *Washington Post*, May 31, 1974.

530   memorial service for Stewart: Barbara Bright-Sagnier, "Notables Mourn Stewart Alsop at St. John's," *Washington Post*, May 30, 1974.

530   "thoughts and prayers": Richard Nixon, letter to JWA, May 30, 1974, JWA & SA Papers, container 214.

530   "a great man": Nelson Rockefeller, letter to JWA, May 28, 1974, JWA & SA Papers, container 214.

530   "a remarkable and admirable man": Hubert H. Humphrey, letter to JWA, May 29, 1974, JWA & SA Papers, container 214.

530   "long admired him . . .": Lewis F. Powell, Jr., letter to JWA, June 3, 1974, JWA & SA Papers, container 214.

530   Tish fell apart: Patricia Alsop, interview with the author, November 4, 1993; interview with Elizabeth Winthrop, November 17, 1990.

530   ". . . like an amputation": JWA, letter to Isaiah Berlin, June 10, 1974, JWA & SA Papers, container 213.

530   ". . . a great life-enhancer": JWA, letter to Mrs. Rudolf Witthower, September 25, 1974, JWA & SA Papers, container 143.

531   ". . . to have you in my life": JWA, letter to Anne Crile, May 31, 1974, JWA & SA Papers, container 129.

531   similar letter to Billy: JWA, letter to William S. Patten, May 31, 1974, JWA & SA Papers, container 129.

531   ". . . hate this city . . .": JWA, letter to Isaiah Berlin, June 17, 1974, JWA & SA Papers, container 140.

531   ". . . enormous courage . . .": JWA, letter to Katharine Graham, May 17, 1974, JWA & SA Papers, container 141.

532   "Case for . . . Resignation": JWA, "The Case for Presidential Resignation," *Washington Post*, May 15, 1974.

532   ". . . resign or expect the worst": JWA, "The Growing Certainty of Impeachment," *Washington Post*, May 24, 1974.

532   Nixon finds Kissinger at Joe's: Henry Kissinger, *Years of Upheaval* (Boston: Little, Brown, 1982), p. 1207.

532   "pulling down the shade": JWA, letter to Katharine Graham, November 12, 1973, JWA & SA Papers, container 139.

532   Cash-flow projection: William S. Patten, letter to JWA, August 24, 1974, JWA & SA Papers, container 129.

532   contemplated London: JWA, letter to Isaiah Berlin, June 17, 1974.

532   ". . . nothing we can think of . . .": William S. Patten, letter to JWA, June 30, 1974, JWA & SA Papers, container 129.

532   discussed New York: Evangeline Bruce, interview, May 19, 1993.

532   contemplated Avon: JWA, letter to John Alsop, December 18, 1974, JWA & SA Papers, container 128.

532   a house on Tish's property: JWA, letters to Patricia Alsop, November 11 and December 10, 1974, JWA & SA Papers, container 128.

532   "family center": Patricia Alsop, letter to JWA, December 2, 1974, JWA & SA Papers, container 128.

532   she would love Joe more: Patricia Alsop, interview, December 28, 1992.

532   2806 N Street: JWA, letter to John Walker, December 23, 1974, JWA & SA Papers, container 143.

532   "Rather soon . . .": JWA, "After 42 Years, a Decision to Retire," *Washington Post*, September 25, 1974.

533   ". . . oldest surviving example . . .": Clifton Daniel, "Joseph Alsop, After 37 Years, Ready for Less Combat," *New York Times*, September 30, 1974.

533   ". . . the brightest intelligence . . .": James Reston, letter to JWA, September 27, 1974, JWA & SA Papers, container 142.

533   "with a bit of sadness": Gerald Ford, letter to JWA, October 3, 1974, JWA & SA Papers, container 141.

533   ". . . the eighth president . . .": JWA, letter to Ford, October 7, 1974, JWA & SA Papers, container 141.

533   ". . . even more dilapitated . . .": JWA, letter to Charles Whitehouse, November 4, 1974, JWA & SA Papers, container 143.

534   trade union rule: JWA, " 'Parliament Does Not Rule,' " *Washington Post*, October 14, 1974.

534   ". . . sad to be in London . . .": JWA, "Great Britain's Loss of National Will," *Washington Post*, October 16, 1974.

534   Persian Gulf shiekhs: JWA "The Power of Oil," *Washington Post*, October 21, 1974.

534   15 percent inflation: JWA, "Inflation and the Common Market," *Washington Post*, October 28, 1974.

534   "the toad-like Yasser Arafat": JWA, "The Decay of the West," *Washington Post*, October 30, 1974.

534   "The really thoughtful men . . .": JWA. "The Loss of Hope," *Washington Post*, November 1, 1974.

534   ". . . the pygmies . . .": JWA, "The Realities and the Chatter," *Washington Post*, November 4, 1974.

535   ". . . wholly out-of-date . . .": JWA, letter to Sir Thomas Brimelow, November 7, 1974, JWA & SA Papers, container 143.

535   "Nothing could be more foolish . . .": JWA, letter to Reston, October 4, 1974, JWA & SA Papers, container 142.

535   abandoned the enterprise: Philip Geyelin, interview, April 27, 1993.

535   "Tell me, Jack . . .": Meg Greenfield, "The Autocrat of the Dinner Table," *Washington Post*, August 31, 1989.

535   "Madam, please!": Mel Elfin, interview, October 29, 1990.

536   proposed to Avis Bohlen: Evangeline Bruce, interview, May 19, 1993.

536   dinners with Evangeline Bruce: Evangeline Bruce, interview, May 4, 1992.

536   ". . . gave up his Washington life": Ibid.

536   ". . . that silly-ass man . . .": Duncan Christy, "Columnist Joseph Alsop: The Antique Wasp," *M*, September 1985, p. 46.

536   ". . . much more formidable president . . .": Adam Platt, "A Curmudgeon in His Own Write," *Insight*, June 8, 1974, p. 50.

537   East Wing lecture series: David Gelman, with Jane Whitmore, "Alsopian Art Tour," *Newsweek*, July 3, 1978, p. 95.

538   "superlative": "Joe Alsop's Kith," *New York Times*, September 1, 1989.

538   "singularly longheaded . . .": JWA, *FDR: A Centenary Remembrance* (New York: Viking Press, 1982), p. 8.

538   "certainly no plaster saint": Ibid., p. 9.

538   "a landmark": Platt.

538   "agreeably sensational": "Ways of Seeing," *Economist*, July 9, 1983.

538   "a rich anecdotal style . . .": Dillon Ripley, "The View from the Castle," *Smithsonian*, Summer 1993, p. 8.

538   curiously unmoved: Platt.

539   495 pages: JWA, with Adam Platt, *I've Seen the Best of It* (New York: W. W. Norton, 1992).

539   he died quietly: Bart Barnes, "Columnist Joseph Alsop Dies at 78," *Washington Post*, August 29, 1989.

539   memorial service and burial: Patricia Alsop, interview, December 28, 1992.

539   "an encyclopedic memory . . .": Barnes.

539   ". . . courage": Henry Fairlie, "Joseph Alsop, R.I.P.," *New Republic*, September 18/25, 1989, p. 10.

539   ". . . you have him . . .": George Will, "Joseph Alsop, 1910–1989," *Newsweek*, September 11, 1989.

540   ". . . every damn word of it . . .": Meg Greenfield, "The Autocrat of the Dinner Table."

540   Joe's Roosevelt lecture: Edwin M. Yoder, Jr., "Remembering Joe Alsop," *National Review*, November 10, 1989, p. 48.

EPILOGUE

page

541 "We have no room . . .": Theodore Roosevelt, "True Americanism," *Forum*, April 1894; reprinted in *Theodore Roosevelt: An American Mind*, ed. Mario R. DiNunzio (New York: St. Martin's Press, 1994), p. 165.

542 "revolution": JWA, "America's Peaceful Revolution," speech draft, undated, SA Collection, Special Collections, Boston University Libraries.

542 ". . . may be dead": SA, "The Disintegration of the Elite," *Newsweek*, June 8, 1970, p. 108.

543 "Vietnam completed the process . . .": SA, *Stay of Execution: A Sort of Memoir* (Philadelphia and New York: J. B. Lippincott, 1973), p. 171.

544 "It was delightful . . .": JWA, with Adam Platt, *I've Seen the Best of It* (New York: W. W. Norton, 1992), pp. 35–36.

544 ". . . the passing of the WASP": Susan Mary Alsop, quoted in Adam Platt, "A Curmudgeon in His Own Write," *Insight*, June 8, 1987, p. 50.

544 "We groaned and growled . . .": Brendan Gill, *A New York Life: Of Friends and Others* (New York: Poseidon Press, 1990), pp. 19–20.

544 ". . . an earlier America . . .": Isaiah Berlin, interview, November 27, 1991.

544 ". . . no mere nativist . . .": Gore Vidal, letter to the author, undated, postmarked April 6, 1992.

545 "glad every day": JWA, *I've Seen the Best of It*, p. 36.

545 ". . . somewhere along the line . . .": Ibid., p. 39.

545 " 'ethnics' are okay . . .": SA, "Quick Looks," *Newsweek*, November 27, 1972, p. 112.

545 "But I suspect not . . .": SA, *Stay of Execution*, p. 171.

545 "sleaziness . . .": Ibid., p. 172.

546 ". . . authoritarian society": SA, "The Disintegration of the Elite."

549 "Nothing endures . . .": JWA, letter to David Satter, August 27, 1973, JWA & SA Papers, Library of Congress, container 140.

BIBLIOGRAPHY

INTERVIEWS

Alice Acheson; John Alsop; Gussie Alsop; Joseph Wright Alsop VI; Patricia Alsop; Stewart Alsop; Susan Mary Alsop; R. W. Apple, Jr.; Trevor Armbrister; Charles Bartlett; Sir Isaiah Berlin; Homer Bigart (telephone interview); Richard M. Bissell; Tom Braden; Joan Braden; Benjamin C. Bradlee; Peter Braestrup; Henry Brandon; Evangeline Bruce; McGeorge Bundy; Corinne Chubb; Ray Coffey; William Colby; Timothy Dickinson; Robert Donovan; Mel Elfin; Osborn Elliott; Rowland Evans; Katherine Evans; Annalee Fadiman (formerly Jacoby) (telephone interview); Polly Fritchey; Joseph Fromm; Lewis H. Ferguson III; Philip Geyelin; Katharine Graham; Donald Graham; Richard Helms; Seymour Janow; Ward Just; Robert Kaiser; Stanley Karnow; Dottie Kidder; Ken McCormick (telephone interview); Carl Mydans (telephone interview); Paul Nitze; Robert D. Novak; Adam Platt; Evelyn Puffenberger; Joseph S. Rauh, Jr.; Marie Ridder; Dillon Ripley; Warren Rogers; Lynn Rosellini; Dean Rusk; Arthur Schlesinger, Jr.; Michael Straight (telephone interview); Jack Valenti; Charles Whitehouse; Elizabeth Winthrop; Frank Wisner, Jr.; Amanda Zimmerman; Corinne Chubb Zimmermann; Warren Zimmermann; Barry Zorthian.

ARCHIVES

Joseph W. Alsop and Stewart Alsop Papers, Library of Congress, Washington, D.C.

Stewart Alsop Collection, Special Collections, Mugar Library, Boston University Libraries, Boston, Massachusetts.

Richard Kluger Papers, Manuscripts and Archives, Yale University Library, New Haven, Connecticut.

Chester Bowles Collection, Manuscripts and Archives, Yale University Library, New Haven, Connecticut.

Jerome Frank Collection, Manuscripts and Collections, Yale University Library, New Haven, Connecticut.

Dean Acheson Collection, Manuscripts and Collections, Yale University Library, New Haven, Connecticut.

Ogden Reid Collection, Manuscripts and Collections, Yale University Library, New Haven, Connecticut.

Walter Lippmann Collection, Manuscripts and Collections, Yale University Library, New Haven, Connecticut.

Robinson/Alsop Papers, Theodore Roosevelt Collection, Houghton Library, Harvard University, Cambridge Massachusetts.

Eleanor Roosevelt Collection, Franklin D. Roosevelt Library, Hyde Park, New York.

Henry Morgenthau Collection, Franklin D. Roosevelt Library, Hyde Park, New York.

Harry Hopkins Collection, Franklin D. Roosevelt Library, Hyde Park, New York.

Marshall Papers, George C. Marshall Research Library, Lexington, Virginia.

Sanford Fox File, John F. Kennedy Library, Cambridge, Massachusetts.

Joseph W. Alsop File, Justice Department Archives, Washington, D.C. (access obtained through Freedom of Information Act request).

Stewart J. O. Alsop File, Justice Department Archives, Washington, D.C. (access obtained through Freedom of Information Act request).

ORAL HISTORIES

Joseph W. Alsop interview, June 18, 1964, Kennedy Library Oral History Project, John F. Kennedy Library, Cambridge, Massachusetts.

Joseph W. Alsop interview, March 4, 1966, Papers of John Foster Dulles, Princeton University Library, Princeton, New Jersey.

BOOKS

Abel, Elie. *The Missile Crisis*. Philadelphia and New York: J. B. Lippincott, 1966.

Aldrich, Nelson W., Jr. *Old Money: The Mythology of America's Upper Class*. New York: Alfred A. Knopf, 1988.

Alsop, Joseph. *FDR: A Centenary Remembrance*. New York: The Viking Press, 1982.

———. *From the Silent Earth: A Report on the Greek Bronze Age*. New York: Harper & Row, 1964.

———. *The Rare Art Traditions*. New York: Harper & Row, 1982.

Alsop, Joseph, with Adam Platt. *I've Seen the Best of It*. New York: W. W. Norton, 1992.

Alsop, Joseph, and Stewart Alsop. *The Reporter's Trade*. New York: Reynal & Company, 1958.

Alsop, Joseph, and Turner Catledge. *The 168 Days*. Garden City, N.Y.: Doubleday, Doran, 1938.

Alsop, Joseph, and Robert Kintner, *Men Around the President*. Garden City, N.Y.: Doubleday, Doran, 1939.

Alsop, Stewart. *Nixon and Rockefeller: A Double Portrait*. Garden City, N.Y.: Doubleday, 1960.

———. *The Center: The Anatomy of Power in Washington*. New York: Harper & Row, 1968.

———. *Stay of Execution: A Sort of Memoir*. Philadelphia and New York: J. B. Lippincott, 1973.

Alsop, Stewart, and Tom Braden. *Sub Rosa: The OSS and American Espionage*. New York: Reynal & Hitchcock, 1946.

Alsop, Susan Mary. *To Marietta from Paris 1945–1960*. Garden City, N.Y.: Doubleday, 1974.

Ambrose, Stephen E. *Eisenhower: Soldier and President*. New York: Simon & Schuster, 1990.

Anderson, Jack, and Ronald W. May. *McCarthy: The Man, the Senator, the "Ism."* Boston: The Beacon Press, 1952.

Anonymous. *History of the Class of 1936*. New Haven: Yale College, 1936.

———. *Harvard Class of 1932: Fiftieth Anniversary Report*. Cambridge: Crimson Printing Company, 1982.

Ashburn, Frank D. *Peabody of Groton: A Portrait*. New York: Coward McCann, 1944.

Baker, Richard A., and Roger H. Davidson, eds. *First Among Equals: Outstanding Senate Leaders of the Twentieth Century*. Washington, D.C.: Congressional Quarterly Inc., 1991.

Ball, George W. *The Past Has Another Pattern: Memoirs*. New York: W. W. Norton, 1982.

Barone, Michael. *Our Country: The Shaping of America from Roosevelt to Reagan*. New York: The Free Press, 1990.

Bayley, Edwin R. *Joe McCarthy and the Press*. Madison: University of Wisconsin Press, 1981.

Beard, Charles A. *President Roosevelt and the Coming of the War 1941*. New Haven: Yale University Press, 1948.

Beschloss, Michael R. *May-Day: Eisenhower, Khrushchev and the U-2 Affair*. New York: Harper & Row, 1986.

Birmingham, Stephen. *America's Secret Aristocracy*. Boston: Little, Brown, 1987.

Bowen, Catherine Drinker. *John Adams and the American Revolution*. Boston: Little, Brown, 1950.

Brandon, Henry. *Special Relationships: A Foreign Correspondent's Memoirs from Roosevelt to Reagan*. New York: Atheneum, 1988.

Brendon, Piers. *Ike: His Life & Times*. New York, Harper & Row, 1986.

Brownell, Will, and Richard N. Billings. *So Close to Greatness: A Biography of William C. Bullitt.* New York: Macmillan, 1987.

Brugioni, Dino A. *Eyeball to Eyeball: The Inside Story of the Cuban Missile Crisis.* New York: Random House, 1990.

Buhite, Russell D. *Patrick J. Hurley and American Foreign Policy.* Ithaca: Cornell University Press, 1973.

Callahan, David. *Dangerous Capabilities: Paul Nitze and the Cold War.* New York: Harper-Collins, 1990.

Catledge, Turner. *My Life and* The Times. New York: Harper & Row, 1971.

Chambers, Whittaker. *Ghosts on the Roof: Selected Journalism of Whittaker Chambers 1931–1959.* Terry Teachout, ed. Washington, D.C.: Regnery Gateway, 1989.

Charmley, John. *Duff Cooper: The Authorized Biography.* London: Weidenfeld & Nicolson, 1986.

Chennault, Claire L. *Way of a Fighter.* New York: G. P. Putnam's Sons, 1949.

Chevalier, Haakon. *Oppenheimer: The Story of a Friendship.* London: Andre Deutsch, 1966.

Clubb, O. Edmund. *20th Century China.* New York: Columbia University Press, 1964.

Coffey, Thomas M. *Hap: The Story of the U.S. Air Force and the Man Who Built It.* New York: The Viking Press, 1982.

Colby, William, with James McCargar. *Lost Victory.* Chicago: Contemporary Books, 1989.

Cooper, Artemis, ed. *The Letters of Evelyn Waugh and Diana Cooper.* New York: Ticknor & Fields, 1992.

Costello, John. *The Pacific War 1941–1945.* New York: Quill, 1982.

Coward, Noël. *Autobiography.* London: Methuen London Ltd., 1987.

Crozier, Brian. *De Gaulle: The First Complete Biography.* New York: Charles Scribner's Sons, 1973.

Crozier, Brian, with Eric Chou. *The Man Who Lost China: The First Full Biography of Chiang Kai-shek.* New York: Charles Scribner's Sons, 1976.

Curtis, Charles P. *The Oppenheimer Case: The Trial of a Security System.* New York: Simon & Schuster, 1955.

Davis, Deborah. *Katharine the Great: Katharine Graham and Her Washington Post Empire.* New York: Sheridan Square Press, 1991.

Dayton, Eldorous L. *Walter Reuther: Autocrat of the Bargaining Table.* New York: Devin-Adair Company, 1958.

Drury, Allen. *A Senate Journal 1943–1945.* New York: McGraw-Hill, 1963.

Eiler, Keith E., ed. *Wedemeyer on War and Peace.* Stanford, Calif.: Hoover Institution Press, 1987.

Eldridge, Fred. *Wrath in Burma: The Uncensored Story of General Stilwell.* Garden City, N.Y.: Doubleday & Company, 1946.

Elliott, Osborn. *The World of Oz.* New York: The Viking Press, 1980.

Felsenthal, Carol. *Princess Alice: The Life and Times of Alice Roosevelt Longworth.* New York: St. Martin's Press, 1988.

———. *Power, Privilege and the* Post: *The Katharine Graham Story.* New York: G. P. Putnam's Sons, 1993.

Finer, Herman. *Dulles Over Suez: The Theory and Practice of His Diplomacy.* Chicago: Quadrangle Books, 1964.

Fite, Gilbert C. *Richard B. Russell, Jr.: Senator from Georgia.* Chapel Hill: The University of North Carolina Press, 1991.

Friedrich, Otto. *Decline and Fall: The Struggle for Power at a Great American Magazine.* New York: Harper & Row, 1970.

Goulden, Joseph C. *Korea: The Untold Story of the War.* New York: Times Books, 1982.

Graham, Robert. *Spain: A Nation Comes of Age.* New York: St. Martin's Press, 1984.

Halberstam, David. *The Best and the Brightest.* New York: Random House, 1972.

Hamby, Alonzo L. *Beyond the New Deal: Harry S. Truman and American Liberalism.* New York: Columbia University Press, 1973.

Heyman, C. David. *A Woman Named Jackie.* New York: Lyle Stuart, 1989.

Hoopes, Townsend. *The Devil and John Foster Dulles.* Boston: Little, Brown, 1973.

Howe, Quincy. *Ashes of Victory: World War II and Its Aftermath.* New York: Simon & Schuster, 1972.

———. *The News and How to Understand It.* New York: Simon & Schuster, 1940.

———. *The World Between the Wars.* New York, Simon & Schuster, 1953.

Humphrey, Hubert H. *The Education of a Public Man: My Life and Politics.* Garden City, N.Y.: Doubleday & Company, 1976.

Hurd, Charles. *Washington Cavalcade.* New York: E. P. Dutton, 1948.

Isaacson, Walter, and Evan Thomas. *The Wise Men: Six Friends and the World They Made.* New York: Simon & Schuster, 1986.

Johnson, Lyndon B. *The Vantage Point: Perspectives of the Presidency 1963–1969.* New York: Holt, Rinehart and Winston, 1971.

Kahn, E. J., Jr. *The China Hands: America's Foreign Service Officers and What Befell Them.* New York: Viking Press, 1975.

Karnow, Stanley. *Vietnam: A History.* New York: Viking Press, 1983.

Kennedy, Robert F. *Thirteen Days: A Memoir of the Cuban Missile Crisis.* New York: W. W. Norton, 1969.

Ketchum, Richard M. *The Borrowed Years: America on the Way to War 1938–1941.* New York: Random House, 1989.

Kistiakowsky, George B. *A Scientist at the White House.* Cambridge: Harvard University Press, 1976.

Kluger, Richard. *The Paper: The Life and Death of the New York Herald Tribune.* New York: Alfred A. Knopf, 1986.

Koskoff, David E. *Joseph P. Kennedy: A Life and Times.* Englewood Cliffs, N.J.: Prentice-Hall, 1974.

Larrabee, Eric. *Commander in Chief: Franklin Delano Roosevelt, His Lieutenants & Their War.* New York: Harper & Row, 1987.

Lash, Joseph P. *Love, Eleanor: Eleanor Roosevelt and Her Friends.* Garden City, N.Y.: Doubleday & Company, 1982.

Lichtman, Allan J., and Ken DeCell. *The 13 Keys to the Presidency: Prediction Without Polls.* Lanham, N.Y.: Madison Books, 1990.

McCarthy, Joseph R. *America's Retreat from Victory: The Story of George Catlett Marshall.* New York: The Devin-Adair Company, 1954.

McCullough, David. *Mornings on Horseback.* New York: Simon & Schuster, 1981.

———. *Truman.* New York: Simon & Schuster, 1992.

Manchester, William. *American Caesar: Douglas MacArthur, 1990–1964.* Boston: Little, Brown, 1978.

———. *The Glory and the Dream: A Narrative History of America 1932–1972.* Boston: Little, Brown, 1974.

Moore, Lieutenant General Harold G., and Joseph L. Galloway. *We Were Soldiers Once . . . And Young.* New York: Random House, 1992.

Morgan, Kenneth O. *The People's Peace: British History 1945–1989.* Oxford: Oxford University Press, 1990.

Morgan, Ted. *FDR: A Biography.* New York, Simon & Schuster, 1985.

Mosely, Leonard. *Dulles: A Biography of Eleanor, Allen, and John Foster Dulles and Their Family Network.* New York: The Dial Press/James Wade, 1978.

———. *Power Play: Oil in the Middle East.* New York: Random House, 1973.

Neal, Steve. *Dark Horse: A Biography of Wendell Willkie.* Garden City, N.Y.: Doubleday & Company, 1984.

Neff, Donald. *Warriors at Suez: Eisenhower Takes America into the Middle East.* New York: Linden Press/Simon & Schuster, 1981.

Newman, Robert P. *Owen Lattimore and the "Loss" of China.* Berkeley and Los Angeles: University of California Press, 1992.

Oberdorfer, Don. *Tet!* Garden City, N.Y.: Doubleday & Company, 1971.

Parmet, Herbert S. *JFK: The Presidency of John F. Kennedy.* New York: The Dial Press, 1963.

Parrish, Thomas. *Roosevelt and Marshall: Partners in Politics and War.* New York: William Morrow, 1989.

Patterson, James T. *Mr. Republican: A Biography of Robert A. Taft.* Boston: Houghton Mifflin, 1972.

Phillips, Cabel. *The 1940s: Decade of Triumph and Trouble.* New York: Macmillan, 1975.

———. *The Truman Presidency: The History of a Triumphant Succession.* New York: Macmillan, 1966.

Quennell, Peter. *A History of English Literature.* Springfield, Mass.: Merriam, 1973.

Reeves, Richard. *President Kennedy: Profile of Power.* New York: Simon & Schuster, 1993.

Reeves, Thomas C. *The Life and Times of Joe McCarthy: A Biography.* New York: Stein and Day, 1982.

———. *A Question of Character: A Life of John F. Kennedy.* New York: The Free Press, 1991.

Robinson, Corinne Roosevelt. *My Brother Theodore Roosevelt.* New York: Charles Scribner's Sons, 1921.

———. *The Poems of Corinne Roosevelt Robinson.* New York: Charles Scribner's Sons, 1921.

Romanus, Charles F. and Riley Sunderland. *China-Burma-India Theater: Stilwell's Command Problems.* Washington, D.C.: Office of Military History, U.S. Department of the Army, 1956.

———. *China-Burma-India Theater: Stilwell's Mission to China.* Washington, D.C.: Office of Military History, U.S. Department of the Army, 1953.

Rusk, Dean (as told to Richard Rusk). *As I Saw It.* New York: W. W. Norton, 1990.

Rutland, Robert A. *Newsmongers: Journalism in the Life of the Nation.* New York: The Dial Press, 1973.

Safire, William. *Before the Fall: An Inside View of the Pre-Watergate White House*. Garden City, N.Y.: Doubleday & Company, 1975.

Schlesinger, Arthur M., Jr. *The Crisis of the Old Order*. Boston: Houghton Mifflin, 1957.

———. *Robert F. Kennedy and His Times*. Boston: Houghton Mifflin, 1978.

———. *A Thousand Days: John F. Kennedy in the White House*. Boston: Houghton Mifflin, 1965.

Seagrave, Sterling. *The Soong Dynasty*. New York: Harper & Row, 1985.

Shaplen, Robert. *Time Out of Hand*. London: Andrew Deutsch, 1969.

Sheehan, Neil. *A Bright Shining Lie: John Paul Vann and America in Vietnam*. New York: Random House, 1988.

Sherwood, Robert E. *Roosevelt and Hopkins: An Intimate History*. New York: Harper & Brothers, 1948.

Smith, Jean Edward. *Lucius D. Clay: An American Life*. New York: Henry Holt, 1990.

Smith, R. Harris. *OSS: The Secret History of America's First Central Intelligence Agency*. Berkeley: University of California Press, 1972.

Smith, Richard Norton. *Thomas E. Dewey and His Times*. New York: Simon & Schuster, 1982.

Solberg, Carl. *Riding High: America in the Cold War*. New York: Mason & Lipscomb, 1973.

Spoto, Donald. *The Kindness of Strangers: The Life of Tennessee Williams*. Boston: Little, Brown, 1985.

Steel, Ronald. *Walter Lippmann and the American Century*. Boston: Atlantic-Little, Brown, 1980.

Stilwell, Joseph W. *The Stilwell Papers*. Theodore H. White, ed. New York: William Sloane Associates, 1948.

Sulzberger, C. L. *A Long Row of Candles: Memoirs & Diaries 1934–1954*. Toronto: Macmillan, 1969.

Swanberg, W. A. *Luce and His Empire*. New York: Charles Scribner's Sons, 1972.

Tansill, Charles Callan. *Back Door to War: Roosevelt Foreign Policy 1933–1941*. Chicago: Henry Regnery Company, 1952.

Tebbel, John. *George Horace Lorimer and* The Saturday Evening Post. Garden City, N.Y.: Doubleday & Company, 1948.

Teichmann, Howard. *Alice: The Life and Times of Alice Roosevelt Longworth*. Englewood Cliffs, N.J.: Prentice-Hall, 1979.

Tuchman, Barbara W. *Stilwell and the American Experience in China 1911–45*. New York: Macmillan, 1970.

Tugwell, Rexford G. *The Democratic Roosevelt*. Garden City, N.Y.: Doubleday & Company, 1957.

Unger, Sanford J. *FBI: An Uncensored Look Behind the Walls*. Boston: Atlantic-Little, Brown, 1976.

Wainwright, Loudon. *The Great American Magazine: An Inside History of* Life. New York: Alfred A. Knopf, 1986.

Valenti, Jack. *A Very Human President: A First-Hand Report*. New York: W. W. Norton, 1975.

Walker, Stanley. *City Editor*. New York: Blue Ribbon Books, 1934.

———. *Mrs. Astor's Horse*. New York: Blue Ribbon Books, 1935.

Wallace, Henry. *The Price of Vision (Diary: 1942–1946)*. John Morton Blum, ed. Boston: Houghton Mifflin, 1973.

Walton, Richard J. *Henry Wallace, Harry Truman and the Cold War*. New York: The Viking Press, 1978.

Watkins, T. H. *Righteous Pilgrim: The Life and Times of Harold L. Ickes, 1874–1952*. New York: Henry Holt, 1990.

Wedemeyer, Albert C. *Wedemeyer Reports!* New York: Henry Holt, 1958.

Weinstein, Allen. *Perjury: The Hiss-Chambers Case*. New York: Alfred A. Knopf, 1978.

Whalen, Richard J. *The Founding Father: The Story of Joseph P. Kennedy*. New York: New American Library, 1964.

White, Theodore H. *America in Search of Itself: The Making of the President 1956–1980*. New York: Harper & Row, 1982.

———. *Breach of Faith: The Fall of Richard Nixon*. New York: Atheneum/Reader's Digest Press, 1975.

———. *In Search of History: A Personal Adventure*. New York: Harper & Row, 1978.

———. *The Making of the President 1960*. New York: Atheneum, 1961.

———. *The Making of the President 1964*. New York: Atheneum, 1965.

White, Theodore H., and Annalee Jacoby. *Thunder Out of China*. New York: William Sloane Associates, 1946.

Winks, Robin W. *Cloak & Gown: Scholars in the Secret War, 1939–1961*. New York: William Morrow, 1987.

Winthrop, Elizabeth. *In My Mother's House*. Garden City, N.Y.: Doubleday, 1988.

Wyden, Peter. *Bay of Pigs: The Untold Story.* New York: Simon & Schuster, 1979.
Ziegler, Philip. *Diana Cooper: A Biography.* New York: Alfred A. Knopf, 1982.

ARTICLES

Alsop, Joseph. "The Bells." *Grotonian,* October 1926.
———. "Repentence." *Grotonian,* April 1927.
———. "A Eulogy of Buttered Toast." *Grotonian,* May 1927.
———. "How It Feels to Look Like Everybody Else." *Saturday Evening Post,* September 11, 1937.
———. "City in Prison." *Saturday Evening Post,* January 9, 1943.
———. "Starvation Is Torture Too." *Saturday Evening Post,* January 16, 1943.
———. "Why We Lost China: The Feud Between Stilwell and Chiang." *Saturday Evening Post,* January 7, 1950.
———. "Why We Lost China: We Opened the Door for the Communists." *Saturday Evening Post,* January 14, 1950.
———. "Why We Lost China: The Foredoomed Mission of General Marshall." *Saturday Evening Post,* January 21, 1950.
———. "I'm Guilty! I Built a Modern House." *Saturday Evening Post,* May 20, 1950.
———. "The Strange Case of Louis Budenz." *Atlantic Monthly,* April 1952.
———. "He'd Rather Not Be President." *Saturday Evening Post,* June 28, 1952.
———. "We Are Losing Asia Fast." *Saturday Evening Post,* March 13, 1954.
———. "Thinking Ahead: Businessmen and Government." *Harvard Business Review,* May–June 1954.
———. "Why Israel Will Survive." *Saturday Evening Post,* September 8, 1956.
———. "How They Meet Payrolls in Russia." *Saturday Evening Post,* June 15, 1957.
———. "Khrushchev Has His Troubles, Too." *Saturday Evening Post,* July 20, 1957.
———. "How the Boy King Foiled the Plotters." *Saturday Evening Post,* November 23, 1957.
———. "Charting Terra Incognita." *New Yorker,* January 28, 1967.
———. "Thoughts Out of China I: Go Versus No-Go." *New York Times Magazine,* March 11, 1973.
———. "Thoughts Out of China II: Doing It Yourself." *New York Times Magazine,* March 18, 1973.
Alsop, Joseph, and Stewart Alsop. "The Tragedy of Liberalism." *Life,* May 20, 1946.
———. "Your Flesh Should Creep." *Saturday Evening Post,* July 13, 1946.
———. "The Liberals and Russia: A Program for Progressives." *New Republic,* September 16, 1946.
———. "Are We Ready for a Push-Button War?" *Saturday Evening Post,* September 6, 1947.
———. "If Russia Grabs Europe—." *Saturday Evening Post,* December 20, 1947.
———. "How Foreign Policy Is Made." *Saturday Evening Post,* April 30, 1949.
———. "Why Has Washington Gone Crazy?" *Saturday Evening Post,* July 29, 1950.
———. "The Lesson of Korea." *Saturday Evening Post,* September 2, 1950.
———. "Our Trouble With the British." *Saturday Evening Post,* October 6, 1951.
———. "Must We Surrender the Middle East to Stalin?" *Saturday Evening Post,* April 12, 1952.
———. "What the G.O.P. Must Do to Win." *Saturday Evening Post,* Sept. 13, 1952.
———. "The Man Ike Trusts With the Cash." *Saturday Evening Post,* May 23, 1953.
———. "Is This Our Last Chance for Peace?" *Saturday Evening Post,* June 27, 1953.
———. "We Accuse!" *Harper's,* October 1954.
———. "Lament for a Long-Gone Past." *Saturday Evening Post,* January 26, 1957.
Alsop, Joseph, and Turner Catledge. "Joe Robinson, the New Deal's Old Reliable." *Saturday Evening Post,* September 26, 1936.
———. "Tom Jeff—He Loves the President, But—." *Saturday Evening Post,* January 9, 1937.
———. "The 168 Days." *Saturday Evening Post,* September 18, October 5, and October 16, 1937.
Alsop, Joseph, and Robert Kintner. "The Guffy: Biography of a Boss, New Style." *Saturday Evening Post,* March 26, 1938.
———. "The Battle of the Market Place." *Saturday Evening Post,* June 11 and June 25, 1938.
———. "Republican With a Bite." *Saturday Evening Post,* July 30, 1938.
———. " 'Henny Penny': Farmer at the Treasury." *Saturday Evening Post,* April 1, April 8, and April 15, 1939.
———. "Farley and the Future." *Life,* September 26, 1938.
———. "Ickes, The Man of Wrath." *Life,* November 21, 1938.
Alsop, Stewart. "Defeat." *Grotonian,* Christmas 1930.
———. "Book Reviews." *Grotonian,* April 1931.

————. "Wanted: A Faith to Die For." *Atlantic Monthly*, May 1941.
————. "Stalin's Plans for the U.S.A." *Saturday Evening Post*, July 14, 1951.
————. "Those Smug, Smug Russians." *Saturday Evening Post*, January 1, 1956.
————. "Communism Is Their Religion." *Saturday Evening Post*, January 7, 1956.
————. "I Found Out What Supersonic Means." *Saturday Evening Post*, November 16, 1957.
————. "How Can We Catch Up?" *Saturday Evening Post*, December 14, 1957.
————. "Behind Khrushchev's Smile." *Saturday Evening Post*, February 1, 1958.
————. "The Mystery of Richard Nixon." *Saturday Evening Post*, July 12, 1958.
————. "How We Drifted Close to War." *Saturday Evening Post*, December 13, 1958.
————. "Who Will Be the Democrats' Candidate?" *Saturday Evening Post*, March 28, 1959.
————. "Revolution on Main Street." *Saturday Evening Post*, June 20, 1959.
————. "The Rockefeller Nobody Knows." *Saturday Evening Post*, July 25, 1959.
————. "Is Herter Tough Enough?" *Saturday Evening Post*, September 12, 1959.
————. "I Saw What Makes Communism Work I." *Saturday Evening Post*, January 30, 1960.
————. "I Saw What Makes Communism Work II." *Saturday Evening Post*, February 6, 1960.
————. "What's In Store for the Captive Nations?" *Saturday Evening Post*, February 13, 1960.
————. "Kennedy vs. Humphrey." *Saturday Evening Post*, April 2, 1960.
————. "Kennedy's Magic Formula." *Saturday Evening Post*, August 13, 1960.
————. "Campaigning With Nixon." *Saturday Evening Post*, November 5, 1960.
————. "What Africa Is Really Like." *Saturday Evening Post*, March 25, 1961.
————. "What Chance Have We in Africa?" *Saturday Evening Post*, April 15, 1961.
————. "The Lessons of the Cuban Disaster." *Saturday Evening Post*, June 24, 1961.
————. "How's Kennedy Doing?" *Saturday Evening Post*, September 16, 1961.
————. "Washington Views Berlin." *Saturday Evening Post*, October 21, 1961.
————. "Khrushchev's Weakness." *Saturday Evening Post*, December 16, 1961.
————. "Khrushchev's Strength." *Saturday Evening Post*, December 23, 1961.
————. "My Brother Runs for Governor." *Saturday Evening Post*, September 1, 1962.
————. "A Communication: Footnote for the Historians." *Saturday Evening Post*, January 22, 1963.
————. "CIA: The Battle for Secret Power." *Saturday Evening Post*, July 27–August 3, 1963.
————. "The Real Meaning of the Test Ban." *Saturday Evening Post*, September 23, 1963.
————. "They Hate Kennedy." *Saturday Evening Post*, October 5, 1963.
————. "The Tiger Will Bite." *Saturday Evening Post*, October 19, 1963.
————. "A Tale of Two Cities." *Saturday Evening Post*, November 16, 1963.
————. "The New President." *Saturday Evening Post*, November 23, 1963.
————. "Johnson Takes Over: The Untold Story." *Saturday Evening Post*, February 15, 1964.
————. "The X Factor Is Race." *Saturday Evening Post*, February 8, 1964.
————. "The Doomed Ones." *Saturday Evening Post*, April 4, 1964.
————. "People in a Trap." *Saturday Evening Post*, June 6, 1964.
————. "Vietnam: Go North?" *Saturday Evening Post*, June 20, 1964.
————. "Can Goldwater Win?" *Saturday Evening Post*, August 8, 1964.
————. "The President." *Saturday Evening Post*, November 7, 1964.
————. "A Second Era of Good Feeling?" *Saturday Evening Post*, May 9, 1964.
————. "What's Wrong With Our Army?" *Saturday Evening Post*, February 13, 1965.
————. "The Inner-Directed Mood." *Saturday Evening Post*, March 13, 1965.
————. "We Can't Let Them Down." *Saturday Evening Post*, March 27, 1965.
————. "The Meaning of the Dead." *Saturday Evening Post*, April 24, 1965.
————. "America's New Big Rich." *Saturday Evening Post*, July 17, 1965.
————. "War's Awful Logic." *Saturday Evening Post*, September 11, 1965.
————. "Sorensen on Kennedy—A Footnote." *Saturday Evening Post*, October 9, 1965.
————. "The Twin Illusions." *Saturday Evening Post*, October 23, 1965.
————. "Watts: The Fire Next Time." *Saturday Evening Post*, November 6, 1965.
————. "The Johnsonization of Washington." *Saturday Evening Post*, February 26, 1966.
————. "Vietnam: How Wrong Was McNamara?" *Saturday Evening Post*, March 12, 1966.
————. "Portrait of a Klansman." *Saturday Evening Post*, April 9, 1966.
————. "The Loaded Pistol." *Saturday Evening Post*, April 23, 1966.
————. "Vietnam: Great Miscalculation?" *Saturday Evening Post*, September 10, 1966.
————. "Love and Hate in the Mekong Delta." *Saturday Evening Post*, December 31, 1966.
————. "The Amazing Americans." *Saturday Evening Post*, January 14, 1967.
————. "Vietnam: Whose War?" *Saturday Evening Post*, January 28, 1967.
————. "The Jam We Are In." *Saturday Evening Post*, July 29, 1967.
————. " 'Mr. Genocide.' " *Saturday Evening Post*, September 9, 1967.
————. "McNamara: The Light That Failed." *Saturday Evening Post*, November 18, 1967.
————. "Hedging, Waffling and Straddling." *Saturday Evening Post*, January 27, 1968.
————. "The Little Man in the Catbird Seat." *Saturday Evening Post*, March 23, 1968.
————. "DEFEAT?" *Saturday Evening Post*, April 20, 1968.

———. "Bobby's Red Guards." *Saturday Evening Post*, May 4, 1968.

———. "Hubert Humphrey and the Presidential Smell." *Saturday Evening Post*, May 18, 1968.

———. "It Wasn't Born Yesterday." *Saturday Evening Post*, July 27, 1968.

———. "No Pax Americana." *Newsweek*, August 12, 1968.

———. "Can Humphrey Win?" *Newsweek*, September 9, 1968.

———. "Virus X and the Body Politic." *Newsweek*, September 16, 1968.

———. "The Case for Nixon." *Newsweek*, September 30, 1968.

———. "The Quintessential Square." *Newsweek*, October 7, 1968.

———. "The Wallace Man." *Newsweek*, October 21, 1968.

———. "Requiem for the Post." *Newsweek*, January 20, 1969.

———. " 'The Coming Holocaust.' " *Newsweek*, March 3, 1969.

———. "Yale Revisited." *Newsweek*, May 19, 1969.

———. "No 'Disguised Defeat'?" *Newsweek*, June 9, 1969.

———. "The Powerful Dr. Kissinger." *Newsweek*, June 16, 1969.

———. "The New Snobbism." *Newsweek*, September 8, 1969.

———. "Vietnam: The Nixon Game Plan." *Newsweek*, September 15, 1969.

———. "The Flaw in the Game Plan." *Newsweek*, September 29, 1969.

———. "Mr. Nixon's Great Retreat." *Newsweek*, May 25, 1970.

———. "On the President's Yellow Pad." *Newsweek*, June 1, 1970.

———. "Vietnam: Out Faster." *Newsweek*, December 7, 1970.

———. "Madness Past Midnight." *Newsweek*, March 15, 1971.

———. "God Tempers the Wind." *Newsweek*, August 30, 1971.

———. "The Big, Ugly Sleeper." *Newsweek*, October 18, 1971.

———. "Gross Immorality." *Newsweek*, November 8, 1971.

———. "Vietnam: The Real Issue." *Newsweek*, February 14, 1971.

———. "The Non-Barking Dog." *Newsweek*, May 1, 1972.

———. "McGovern as Word-Eater." *Newsweek*, June 19, 1972.

———. "McGovern's Dilemma." *Newsweek*, July 24, 1972.

———. " 'All Will Be Well.' " *Newsweek*, July 31, 1972.

———. "With President Nixon Aboard Air Force One." *Newsweek*, September 4, 1972.

———. "The Best Deal We Could Get." *Newsweek*, December 11, 1972.

———. "What Now?" *Newsweek*, January 1, 1973.

———. "Smorgasbord." *Newsweek*, January 8, 1973.

———. "The Serious Man." *Newsweek*, January 22, 1973.

———. "Eternal Damnation?" *Newsweek*, January 29, 1973.

———. "The Sam Ervin Show." *Newsweek*, April 2, 1973.

———. "Mr. Nixon's Super-Crisis." *Newsweek*, April 30, 1973.

———. "War, Not Politics." *Newsweek*, May 14, 1973.

———. "Watergate and the Liberals." *Newsweek*, June 25, 1973.

———. "A Paraplegic Presidency." *Newsweek*, July 9, 1973.

Alsop, Stewart, and Charles Bartlett. "The White House in the Cuban Crisis." *Saturday Evening Post*, December 8, 1962.

Alsop, Stewart, and Col. Samuel B. Griffith. "We Can Be Guerrillas Too." *Saturday Evening Post*, December 2, 1950.

Alsop, Stewart, and Dr. Ralph Lapp. "The Inside Story of Our First Hydrogen Bomb." *Saturday Evening Post*, October 25, 1952.

———. "We Can Smash the Red A-Bombers." *Saturday Evening Post*, March 21, 1953.

———. "The Strange Death of Louis Slotin." *Saturday Evening Post*, March 6, 1954.

Bagdikian, Ben H. "The Five Different Washingtons." *New York Times Magazine*, December 26, 1965.

Brenner, Marie. "Marietta Tree: Serious Money." *Vanity Fair*, December 1991.

Campbell, Colin. "The Harvard Factor." *New York Times Magazine*, July 20, 1986.

Chennault, Claire L. "Last Call for China." *Saturday Evening Post*, July 11, 1949.

Chiang Kai-shek. "Chiang Versus Communism: His Personal Account." *Saturday Evening Post*, June 24, 1957.

Childs, Marquis W. "The President's Best Friend." *Saturday Evening Post*, April 19–April 26, 1941.

Collier, Barnard Law. "The Joseph Alsop Story." *New York Times Magazine*, May 23, 1971.

Elson, Robert T. "A Question for Democrats: If Not Truman, Who?" *Life*, March 24, 1952.

Flynn, John T. "How Whitney Went Broke." *New Republic*, July 13, 1938.

Grant, Zalin. "Alsop Lets His Friends Down." *New Republic*, May 18, 1968.

Hertzberg, Hendrick. "Ivy Scoreboard." *New Republic*, August 8 and 15, 1988.

Lerner, Max. "The Liberals and Russia: Who Can Build the New World?" *New Republic*, September 16, 1946.

Liebling, A. J. "A View With Alarm." *New Yorker*, December 20, 1958.

Life. "War Can Come: Will We Be Ready?" Editorial, February 27, 1950.

Miller, Merle. "Washington, the World, and Joseph Alsop." *Harper's*, June 1968.
National Review. "Charade Ending?" March 11, 1961.
Newsweek. "Brothers in Arms." November 11, 1957.
––––––. "To Their Taste." March 17, 1958.
––––––. "The Nixon Underneath?" July 14, 1958.
––––––. "The Big Flap—Doves, Hawks, 'Dawks,' 'Hoves.' " December 17, 1962.
––––––. "The Days of Good Cheer." November 28, 1983.
Robbins, Warren D. "Even a Jew." *Grotonian*, Prize Day 1928.
Schlesinger, Arthur, Jr. "Washington in Perspective." *New Leader*, June 17, 1968.
Time. "City Editor." September 7, 1931.
––––––. "City Room Prophet." October 22, 1934.
––––––. "China: T.V." December 18, 1944.
––––––. "Brother Act." October 15, 1945.
––––––. "The Trib's Mrs. Reid." November 12, 1945.
––––––. "The Administration: Paid in Full." March 14, 1949.
––––––. "The Capital: Widow from Oklahoma." March 14, 1949.
––––––. "Foreign Relations: The Peacemaker." August 13, 1951.
––––––. "Fried Crow, a la Mode." March 24, 1952.
––––––. "Maginot Line of the Air." March 30, 1953.
––––––. "Alsops & Project Lincoln." Published letter from Alsop brothers. April 13, 1954.
––––––. "The Atom: A Matter of Character." June 14, 1954.
––––––. "The Atom: The H-Bomb Delay." November 8, 1954.
––––––. "Guest at Breakfast." April 16, 1956.
––––––. "Alsop's Fables." June 18, 1956.
––––––. "Foxes and Lions." November 26, 1956.
––––––. "Alsop's Foible." October 27, 1958.
––––––. "Splitting the Alsops." March 17, 1958.
––––––. "The Administration: The Stranger on the Squad." December 14, 1962.
––––––. "The Place Downstairs." May 3, 1963.
––––––. "Mercy Killing." August 26, 1966.
U.S. News & World Report. "The New Debate on the Oppenheimer Case." December 24, 1954.

INDEX